2nd edition

COMPUTER-BASED INSTRUCTION
Methods and Development

STEPHEN M. ALESSI
University of Iowa

STANLEY R. TROLLIP
S.R. Trollip & Associates, Inc.
Mendota Heights, Minnesota

PRENTICE HALL, Englewood Cliffs, New Jersey 07632

Library of Congress Cataloging-in-Publication Data

Alessi, Stephen M.
    Computer-based instruction : methods and development / Stephen M.
Alessi, Stanley R. Trollip. -- 2nd ed.
        p.   cm.
    Includes bibliographical references and indexes.
    ISBN 0-13-168592-9
    1. Computer-assisted instruction. 2. Education--Data processing.
3. Interactive video. 4. Artificial intelligence--Educational
applications.   I. Trollip, Stanley R.   II. Title.
LB1028.5.A358 1991
371.3'34--dc20
                                                90-22106
                                                    CIP

Editorial/production supervision: Virginia L. McCarthy
Pre-press buyer: Debbie Kesar
Manufacturing buyer: Mary Ann Gloriande

 © 1991, 1985 by Prentice-Hall, Inc.
A Division of Simon & Schuster
Englewood Cliffs, New Jersey 07632

Printed in the United States of America
10   9   8

ISBN 0-13-168592-9

Prentice-Hall International (UK) Limited, *London*
Prentice-Hall of Australia Pty. Limited, *Sydney*
Prentice-Hall Canada Inc., *Toronto*
Prentice-Hall Hispanoamericana, S.A., *Mexico*
Prentice-Hall of India Private Limited, *New Delhi*
Prentice-Hall of Japan, Inc., *Tokyo*
Simon & Schuster Asia Pte. Ltd., *Singapore*
Editora Prentice-Hall do Brasil, Ltda., *Rio de Janeiro*

To our parents.

CONTENTS

PREFACE   **xi**

Part 1   COMPUTER-BASED INSTRUCTION METHODOLOGIES

1   INTRODUCTION   **1**

A Short History of Educational Computing   1
Current Educational Applications of Computers   3
Using the Computer for Instruction   5
The Process of Instruction   6
Instructional Methodologies   9
Cognitive Psychology and Computer-Based Instruction   11
References and Bibliography   14

2   TUTORIALS   **17**

Introduction of the Tutorial   18
Student Control of the Lesson   23
Motivation   31
Presentation of Information   33
Questions and Responses   49
Judgment of Responses   65
Feedback about Responses   70
Remediation   77
Sequencing Lesson Segments   77
Closing of the Tutorial   83
Conclusion   84
References and Bibliography   85
Summary of Tutorials   88

3   DRILLS   **91**

Introduction   91
Applications of Drills   92
Basic Drill Procedure   92
The Introduction of a Drill   93
Item Characteristics   94

Item Selection Procedures   97
Feedback   106
Item Grouping Procedures   108
Motivating the Student   112
Data Storage   114
Advantages of Computer-Based Drills   115
References and Bibliography   116
Summary of Drills   117

4   SIMULATIONS   **119**

Introduction   119
Physical Simulations   120
Process Simulations   123
Procedural Simulations   126
Situational Simulations   127
Advantages of Simulations   130
Fidelity in Simulations   135
Factors in Simulations   137
Introduction to the Simulation   138
The Body of the Simulation   140
Completion of the Simulation   153
A Taxonomy for Fidelity Analysis   154
Simulation Systems and Languages   157
Conclusion   159
References and Bibliography   159
Summary of Simulations   161

5   INSTRUCTIONAL GAMES   **162**

Definition   162
Major Characteristics of Games   170
Types of Games   172
The Purpose of Using Games in Instruction   182
The Structure of Games   183
Factors in the Introduction of a Game   183
Factors in the Body of a Game   186
Factors in the Conclusion of the Game   200
Art of Game Design   201
Conclusion   202
References and Bibliography   202
Summary of Games   203

6   TESTS   **205**

Computerized Test Construction   205
Computerized Test Administration   208
Factors in Tests   208
An Example of a Testing Program   223
Other Testing Approaches in the Computer Environment   232
Conclusion   241
References and Bibliography   241
Summary of Tests   242

Birmingham City University - Kenrick Library
Self Service Receipt for items borrowed

Title: age of information : the past development
and future significance of com
Item: 6130202744
Due: 05/Oct/2014

Title: Internet commerce development
Item: 6131915264
Due: 12/Oct/2014

Title: Computer-based instruction : methods
and development
Item: 6131494242
Due: 12/Oct/2014

Total items: 3
03/08/2014 20:03

Normal Loans are now for 4 weeks - please
check due dates

Part 2   DEVELOPMENT OF COMPUTER-BASED INSTRUCTION

7   PREPARATION   **244**

Introduction to Development of CBI   244
The Telephone Example   248
Computer Tools   249
Step 1—Determine Needs and Goals   251
Step 2—Collect Resource Materials   258
Step 3—Learn the Content   262
Step 4—Generate Ideas   265
Conclusion   271
References and Bibliography   271
Summary of the First Four Steps   272

8   DESIGN   **274**

Elimination of Ideas   274
Task and Concept Analysis   278
Preliminary Lesson Description   286
Evaluation and Revision of the Design   292
Conclusion   293
References and Bibliography   294
Summary of Design   294

9   FLOWCHARTING   **295**

Definitions and Issues   295
Procedures   297
Computer Tools   307
Telephone Example   311
Conclusion   314
References and Bibliography   318
Summary of Flowcharting   318

10   STORYBOARDING   **319**

Write and Revise Primary Text   319
Write and Revise Secondary Text   321
Produce Storyboards   321
Check the Fit of Overlaying Displays   324
Draw and Revise Graphic Displays and Plan Other Output   325
Check Graphics and Simultaneous Text for Fit   326
Review the Flowcharts and Storyboards   327
Telephone Example   329
Conclusion   339
References and Bibliography   339
Summary of Storyboarding   340

11   PROGRAMMING AND SUPPORT MATERIALS   **341**

Step 8—Programming   341
Step 9—Support Material Production   353
Conclusion   360

References and Bibliography 360
Summary of Programming 361
Summary of Support Materials 363

12 EVALUATION   364

Quality Review Phase 365
Pilot Testing 378
Validation 381
Computer Tools for Evaluation 383
Revision and Subsequent Evaluation 384
Conclusion 384
References and Bibliography 385
Summary of Evaluation 385

Part 3 ADVANCED TOPICS IN COMPUTER-BASED INSTRUCTION

13 COMPUTER-MANAGED INSTRUCTION   387

Introduction 387
Early CMI Systems 388
Functions of CMI Systems 389
Factors Inhibiting CMI in Schools 391
Recent Factors Encouraging CMI in Schools 392
CMI as a Basis for CBI Implementation 392
Incremental Implementation of CMI and CBI 394
A Prototype CMI System 396
Conclusion 408
References and Bibliography 408

14 INTERACTIVE VIDEO   410

What Is Interactive Video? 410
Background 411
Levels of Interactive Videodiscs 413
Visual Presentation Modes of Interactive Video 415
Advantages of Interactive Video and Videodiscs 417
Constraints of Interactive Video 420
Types of Instructional Interactive Video Programs 423
Factors in the Design of Interactive Video Programs 426
Development of Interactive Video Programs 438
The Future of Interactive Video 448
Conclusion 449
References and Bibliography 450

15 ARTIFICIAL INTELLIGENCE AND INSTRUCTION   452

What Is Artificial Intelligence? 452
Expert Systems 453
Instructional Modeling 461
Natural Language Understanding 471
Conclusion 474
References and Bibliography 475

APPENDIXES

A   SUMMARY OF INSTRUCTIONAL FACTORS   **477**

Factors in Tutorials   477
Factors in Drills   478
Factors in Simulations   479
Factors in Games   479
Factors in Tests   480

B   QUALITY REVIEW CHECKLIST   **482**

Part 1: Language and Grammar   483
Part 2: Surface Features   484
Part 3: Questions and Menus   485
Part 4: Other Issues of Pedagogy   486
Part 5: Invisible Functions   487
Part 6: Subject Matter   488
Part 7: Off-Line Materials   489

C   STORYBOARD FORMS   **490**

TRADEMARK NOTIFICATION   **498**

INDEX   **501**

Author   501
Subject   504

PREFACE

When we were completing the first edition of this book in 1983, microcomputers were still uncommon, and most students taking their first course on computer-based instruction (CBI) usually had little experience with a microcomputer.

The field has changed dramatically. Students taking a computer-based instruction course today often own a computer. Most have at least used a microcomputer for word processing, and many have used some instructional programs. Almost all know the difference between software and hardware, a keyboard and a mouse, a word processor and a CBI lesson.

These changes made this second edition of the book dramatically different from the first. We have dropped all the introductory chapters about the history of computers, hardware and software, and types of application software. Instead we have included a brief synopsis in the single introductory chapter.

In place of these chapters, we have added new ones and changed others in the light of new developments in the field, in such areas as artificial intelligence and interactive video.

Changes have also been necessitated by the increased power and flexibility of newer microcomputer hardware. The few short years since our first edition have seen the introduction of the Macintosh and IBM PS/2 computers, and more recently the NeXT computer. These new types of microcomputers are faster, more graphical in nature, and use pointing devices such as the mouse, giving them the capability for much better computer-based instruction than was possible on the older model computers such as the Apple II.

The production of these powerful, new-generation microcomputers have resulted in better sound capability, better operating systems, and for the first time authoring systems for creating CBI that are both easy to use and capable of producing high-quality, effective lessons.

Thus, we forsake the chapters on history, software, hardware, and the like for new chapters on artificial intelligence, computer-managed instruction, and interactive video—topics more pertinent to today's CBI development. Similarly, we have changed our model for developing lessons in response to the powerful new automated authoring tools.

The organization of this second edition is as follows.

Part 1 is a comprehensive analysis of the primary methods of computer-based instruction. We have two goals in Part 1. The first is to describe the variety of instructional techniques possible with computer-based instruction. Our second and more important goal is to help improve the characteristics that facilitate learning and enhance student satisfaction. When used as a text on CBI, Part 1 represents slightly more than one third of a college course, with two weeks devoted to the first two chapters and a week for each of the other four chapters. Chapter 2, on tutorial instruction, is a pivotal chapter, and the subsequent chapters depend on a thorough reading and understanding of it.

Many of the characteristics of good instruction are common to all instructional methodologies and we treat such commonalities only once, in Chapter 2. The methodologies are basically the same as the first edition, but have been updated in the light of current research on human learning and instruction, and the new capabilities of more modern microcomputers. In the last regard, we have recommendations to make concerning the relative value of modern computers, input devices such as the keyboard versus the mouse, and output devices such as computer display, video, and sound. It is still the sad state of affairs that education is a stepchild that gets the "low end" computers the market has to offer. But we see that changing as even the low end becomes better, and as the first generation of school microcomputers and software must inevitably be replaced.

In Part 2 we present a model for the design and development of computer-based instruction. An appreciation of Part 2 depends on a thorough familiarity with the content of Part 1, becasue the most important part of developing instruction is understanding the characteristics of instruction that most facilitate learning.

The model is practical in its orientation (rather than theoretical) and is designed for the novice instructional designer. We believe, however, that the model is flexible and that you can adapt it to your own style and needs as you gain experience. Part 2 also represents slightly more than one third of a college course, with a week devoted to each of its six chapters.

Part 2 has evolved considerably from what we presented in the first edition. The processes of flowcharting and storyboarding have changed both in response to the new authoring tools available and to evolution in our own experience and thinking. Most importantly, we place more emphasis on the cyclic nature of development, with more intermediate evaluations and revisions. We have also placed more emphasis on the development of supplementary print materials such as manuals.

A course on the development of computer-based instruction will necessarily include some programming, although with authoring systems the word *programming* may no longer accurately represent the process. Although we still do not teach programming, we strongly encourage the use of modern authoring systems that are iconic, graphical, and top-down in their approach. We still believe our treatment of development to be "language free" so that instructors can use this text in conjunction with any language or authoring system and an accompanying textbook that teaches it. But unlike the first edition, where we strictly avoided any examples of program languages, we now include illustrations showing the use of modern authoring systems and the ways they can facilitate CBI development. It is our recommendation that instructors use this book in conjunction with one of the modern systems, for that will allow students to spend their time on design and evaluation, rather than on figuring out how to make the computer run even a simple program.

Part 3 deals with three advanced topics. While many people in the field of instructional computing consider these topics—computer-managed instruction, interactive video, and artifical intelligence—to be methodologies in their own right, we do not agree. We believe that these topics cut across all the basic methodologies. Computer-managed instruction is a topic in curriculum theory and administration. Interactive video is a new hardware technology that is a marriage of computer and television technology. Artificial intelligence primarily provides new programming techniques that can improve all kinds of computer applications. The three chapters of Part 3 represent slightly less than one third of a college course.

The progress of instructional computing has been slow. Many educators love to remind us of the early promise and predictions for computers in education—predictions that have remained unfulfilled or barely fulfilled. However, progress has been made, and the future, though farther off than once thought, is still exciting. But we cannot wait for the future: We must make it. We can all contribute to that in our own ways. Computer companies must provide better and cheaper computers and software. School administrators must modernize their computer labs, provide inservice training to teachers, and encourage more experimentation and evaluation of using computers in instruction. Corporations must use their resources to push the limits of the various hardware and software technologies associated with CBI.

Our own purpose in writing and revising this book is to provide a sound foundation for future developers of computer-based instruction, in the hope that we can thereby help improve the quality of computer-based instruction in the schools and workplace.

In addition to those people we thanked for the first edition, we are also very grateful to the insights, comments, and suggestions of our colleagues in the field, and particularly of our students. We would like to thank Gertrude W. Abramson, City University of New York; Wallace Hannum, University of North Carolina; and Dr. Eugene F. Stafford, Iona College for reviewing the manuscript and making helpful suggestions.

S.M.A.
S.R.T.

1

INTRODUCTION

A SHORT HISTORY OF EDUCATIONAL COMPUTING

It has been about thirty years since educators and computer scientists began using computers for instructional purposes. In that time span incredible advances have been made in computer technology and its availability. In the 1960's and most of the 1970's instructional computing took place on large mainframe computers or occasionally on medium-sized computers. Educational computing existed only at large universities and was largely restricted to reading and typing text. To develop instructional materials required learning computer programming, often in a low-level language unsuitable for the purpose.

With the invention of the microcomputer near the end of the 1970's, we have seen the rapid spread of computing in businesses, schools, and homes. Microcomputers have evolved from machines dependent on typing and text printouts that were difficult to program, to machines that allow interaction via text, graphics, voice, and pointing. The most recent developments in microcomputer technology provide even greater power and ease of use through advanced visual and auditory devices. They also permit networking of many microcomputers to share information and resources. With all of these advances has been a steady decrease in cost.

Educational computing began with a few, large, government-funded projects on mainframe and minicomputers. The University of Illinois PLATO project began in 1960 (Alpert & Bitzer, 1970). The PLATO project eventually enabled computer-based instruction to integrate text and graphics, and provided instructors with one of the first programming environments for computer-based instruction. Beginning in 1972 the Mitre Corporation's TICCIT project (Merrill, Schneider, & Fletcher, 1980) introduced computer-based instruction on minicomputers. With it came the concept of *learner-controlled instruction* (Wydra, 1980), and a particular philosophy for the design of computer-based instruction, today known as *component design theory* (Merrill, 1983, 1987, 1988).

In 1978 the first widely available microcomputers were released. The Apple II microcomputer succeeded in becoming the most common microcom-

1

puter for use in schools. Most early microcomputer *courseware* was designed for the Apple II, thus increasing its popularity in the schools even more.

The release of the IBM Personal Computer in 1981 resulted in a sudden expansion of the microcomputer market into business and industry. But the Apple II's early lead, lower cost, availability of courseware, and better integration of text, graphics, and color prevented the IBM-PC from penetrating the elementary and secondary school market. In contrast, the IBM-PC has become the more popular microcomputer for higher education, and for training in business and industry.

The 1984 release of Apple's Macintosh computer instigated many changes in the field of microcomputing. This computer provided far better integration of text and graphics, better voice and music capability, and permitted not only typing for user input, but the *mouse* for pointing at and drawing on the screen. These and other features made the Macintosh much easier to use than previous computers. But its cost, lack of color, and lack of courseware prevented it from having much initial impact on education. Its impact, rather, has been on the improved design of subsequent microcomputers which have copied its graphical power (and its overall ease of use), and put the mouse on par with the keyboard.

In 1989 the NeXT computer was released. This, the latest generation of microcomputers, combines the graphical user interface of the Macintosh with far greater speed, storage, networking potential, multi-tasking, and flexibility. It is, however, an expensive microcomputer and currently viewed only as a machine for higher education. Clearly, computer hardware and software is evolving towards mouse-controlled graphical interfaces as on the NeXT computer and the Macintosh. New hardware and software from IBM and other computer companies use similar human interfaces. The quality of computer-based instruction and the ease of its development is enhanced considerably by these more natural and flexible systems.

The early days of instructional computing saw much excitement for its potential and many prophecies of great educational improvement through computer-based instruction. However, while there have been great strides in technology and availability, actual improvement of instruction is less dramatic. The current state of instructional computing is a confusing mixture of many types of computers. This, and the accompanying problems in software and hardware incompatibility, is a major factor hindering the success of computer-based instruction for improving education. Other factors hindering its success are a shortage of people skilled in developing quality courseware (which has resulted in much low quality courseware), and disagreement within the field on how computers *should* be used in education. Several surveys (Becker, 1983, 1985, 1986; Bruder, 1988) have substantiated this confusion. And many attempts to prove the effectiveness of CBI (Bangert-Drowns, Kulik, & Kulik, 1985; Kulik & Kulik, 1986; Kulik, Kulik, & Bangert-Drowns, 1985) have shown small effects that do not approach the early promise of the field.

Our position is that the field of instructional computing is still young and evolving. We have made progress in some ways, but much remains to be learned regarding the best ways to use computers. With further improvements in the technology, decrease in its cost, improvements in courseware development and quality, and teacher education about CBI, the computer has an important role in instruction *alongside* the teacher, the book, and other instructional media.

CURRENT EDUCATIONAL APPLICATIONS OF COMPUTERS

Taylor (1980) was one of the first authors to bring some organization to the plethora of instructional computing activities. He classified instructional computing into three categories: tool, tutor, and tutee. As tool, the computer is used by teachers and students to aid learning and facilitate academic work, such as with word processors. As tutor, the computer delivers instruction, as is the case with most CBI. As tutee, the student teaches the computer and in doing so must learn as well, as with the use of Logo for geometry instruction.

These distinctions have blurred somewhat as software for educational purposes evolves and improves. Many examples of current software do not fit into one of these categories. How a piece of software is used is often more important. Furthermore, the tool, tutor, tutee categorization does not deal with other important uses of the computer in education: administration (Bluhm, 1987), education about computers (Hunter, 1984), and peer learning which utilizes computers (Johnson & Johnson, 1985; Johnson, Johnson, & Stanne, 1985; Yueh & Alessi, 1988). Thus, at a more general level we divide computer applications into administration, teaching about the computer, and teaching with the computer. Administrative applications are primarily tools. But all three modes, tool, tutor, and tutee, are relevant for teaching about the computer (computer literacy and computer science instruction) and for teaching other subject areas *with* the computer.

The field of instructional computing contains many advocates of *one way* the computer should be used. Luehrman (1985) has claimed that computers should only be an object of instruction. Slesnick (1983) promotes the use of general computer tools, rather than instructional programs, by students. Papert (1980) advocates the tutee mode via Logo programming. Jonassen (1988) claims that artificial intelligence (expert systems and student modeling) should predominate in research and development.

We believe the field needs a more eclectic approach spanning administration, teaching, and learning. Teachers have a great deal of routine administrative work, such as grading, producing assignments and handouts, writing letters, and keeping track of resources and materials. When a computer can perform or speed up such tasks, the teacher has more time to work with students. Learning about computer technology and programming is appropriate for some students, although we would claim that basic computer literacy will be a natural byproduct of teaching with the computer and that specific courses aimed at computer literacy are often unnecessary and should not be required of all students. Within the category of teaching *with* computers (the emphasis of this text), many approaches should and will be used. Computer tools, traditional computer-based instruction, and artificial intelligence techniques all are beneficial. Instructional methods and techniques should be chosen based upon several criteria: student characteristics, content, instructor style and knowledge, equipment availability, and cost.

As demonstrated by the literature reviews of Kulik and his associates, there is much interest in the impact of computers in education. In addition to the many small studies looking at the impact of educational computing, there have been a few larger studies with a somewhat more futuristic aim. The IBM Secondary School Computer Education Program (Cline, Bennett, Kershaw, Schneiderman, Stecher, & Wilson, 1986) and the Apple Classroom of Tomorrow (ACOT) project (Baker, 1988; Kitabchi, 1987) have been investigating the effects when schools have an abundance of computer resources, as can be expected in the future. The ACOT project is particularly interesting. In selected classrooms every student is provided with a computer. In addition, a second computer is given to each student to take home and use there. The idea is for teachers in those classrooms to be able to depend on every student having a computer any time the teacher wants them to be used. Teachers can give homework which depends upon computer use and students can continue classwork at home. In most schools, teachers must plan far ahead to schedule centrally located school computers, and typically there are not enough computers for a large class of students.

The unfortunate aspect of both the IBM Secondary School Computer Education Program and the Apple Classroom of Tomorrow project is that the emphasis has been on providing schools with an abundance of hardware. Little funding or effort was provided for courseware. In the case of the ACOT project, it was the attitude of Apple Computer Corporation that courseware would be donated by companies producing it, just as Apple had donated the hardware. But it is unlikely that high quality software will come from donations. More likely courseware producers will donate material that they cannot sell or for which they need exposure.

While schools in the United States and other countries are rushing headlong into the purchase of computers (Alessi & Shih, 1989; Fakhro & Kahn, 1987; Kerr, 1990; Oberem, 1987; Okamota, 1987), several perplexing problems confront teachers who are expected to use them. The first problem is that once a school has a few computers, typically placed in a central laboratory, teachers are expected to use them in their teaching. That is extremely difficult when the computers are in a different room, must be scheduled far ahead of time, and often are too few in number to accommodate an entire class. When a teacher does have computers in the classroom it is typically only one or two. It is difficult to see what a teacher with thirty students and one computer can do.

A second problem facing the teacher is selection of courseware that meets classroom needs and is well designed. Most instructional materials such as textbooks are selected and purchased by school districts. However, procedures for courseware evaluation, selection, and purchase are not yet well developed. This has resulted in much wasted money in schools due to purchases of courseware which turned out to be useless.

A third problem facing the teacher is computer literacy. This is a two-fold problem. The teacher must become computer-literate to take advantage of the computer for instruction. And while schools see student computer literacy as a goal teachers should foster, few teachers know how to do it.

Perhaps the greatest problem is that computers are changing the need for traditional academic skills and hence are affecting the roles of teachers (Chaiklin & Lewis, 1988; Hannafin, Dalton, & Hooper, 1987). Just as a few years ago math teachers worried whether hand calculators would obviate the need to teach arithmetic, English teachers now wonder whether current word processing software, which incorporate spelling and grammar checkers, will eliminate the need for spelling and grammar instruction. Teachers are debating whether such software should be banned from the classroom, just as some teachers felt calculators should have been. Indeed, in the not too distant future we will have word processors into which you can speak. Computers which can read aloud from an ordinary book already exist. More and more, teachers will face the complicated and controversial issues of whether traditional skills such as reading and writing should be taught, or taught differently, because computers can do these things for us.

USING THE COMPUTER FOR INSTRUCTION

Hundreds of research studies have been performed attempting to prove that using a computer to teach something is better than using a book, a teacher, a film, or some other more traditional method. Overall, a very small effect in favor of computer-based instruction has been claimed from reviews of these studies (Kulik & Kulik, 1986). Some researchers have argued that small differences are either a research artifact or caused by some reason other than the use of computers (Clark, 1983). Researchers claiming the effect is true have argued that it really should be greater but has been artificially lowered because much of the CBI used was poorly designed. It is for another reason we maintain that little or no difference could be demonstrated by these many studies. Different media have different advantages. For teaching one topic (a particular aspect of reading comprehension, for example) with one set of students (sixth graders), a book may be better. For another topic (operating a drill press) and different students (factory workers) instructional video may be better.

If we were to chart out all the instructional topics, the wide variety of students, and the many instructional situations, we would sometimes find the advantage for books, sometimes teachers, sometimes film or video, sometimes peer-tutoring, sometimes hands-on field experience, sometimes listening to an audiotape, and sometimes computers. It should not be surprising that across these many studies which utilized a variety of topics, students, and situations, there was little or no overall effect.

To take advantage of the computer's particular capabilities and not to waste them, the first rule for correctly using or developing CBI is to do so in situations where the computer is *likely* to be beneficial (Trollip & Alessi, 1988). Those situations are where the cost of instruction by other methods is very high (for example in military training), safety is a concern (chemistry laboratories), the material is very hard to teach by other methods (graphing in calculus), extensive individual student practice is needed (foreign language grammar and vocabulary), student motivation is typically lacking (ancient world history), or where there are logistic difficulties in traditional instruction (science experiments that take a long time to complete).

While none of these situations guarantees that a computer will be beneficial, they increase the probability. High quality and creative instructional design coupled with careful evaluation and revision are also necessary.

THE PROCESS OF INSTRUCTION

Instructional computer programs, also known as *courseware*, are referred to by a variety of names. Some of these are:

CAI —computer-assisted instruction
CBE —computer-based education
CAL —computer-assisted learning
IAC —instructional applications of computers
CBI —computer-based instruction

We use the term *computer-based instruction* (CBI) because our emphasis is on instruction rather than education in general. In the next five chapters we discuss the characteristics of different types of CBI programs. Our discussion of these basic methodologies rests upon an expository model of instruction. According to that model, for instruction to be effective the following four phases should be present:

Presenting information
Guiding the student
Practicing by the student
Assessing student learning

In contrast to the expository model of instruction, discovery learning usually omits the first phase or changes the order of the first two phases. Research evidence in favor of discovery learning is usually limited to some students (usually higher ability students) and some kinds of learning (such as problem solving). Our opinion is that discovery learning activities are beneficial when placed within the context of an expository instruction model. That is, the "guiding the student" phase may often use discovery techniques. But as a complete model of instruction, discovery learning has not adequately been proven beneficial for most students and most subject areas.

Presenting Information

The first three phases are based upon research on classroom instruction (Rosenshine & Stevens, 1986). To teach something new, the instructor must first present information. This may take a number of forms. For verbal or pictorial information, an instructor may present rules and examples, show pictures, or provide other nonverbal information. To teach skills, such as operating a 35-mm camera or doing long division, the instructor will probably model the skills to be learned. That is, the instructor will perform the skills so that students can imitate them.

An important method of presenting information is through example. Thus, in addition to stating the physical rule "force equals mass times acceleration," the instructor will demonstrate applications of that physical rule, such as a truck accelerating more quickly when it is empty. The skill of long division would be modeled using a variety of numbers in the dividend and the divisor. Most students require more than one example before they are able to apply a rule or skill.

Guiding the Student

The first phase, *presenting information,* is instructor centered. The second phase, *guiding the student,* is more interactive and includes both the student and the instructor. Having observed the presentation, the student must now perform under instructor guidance. Again, this means different things depending on the nature of the material. The student may answer questions about factual information, may apply rules and principles in problem-solving activities, or practice procedural skills. In each case, the instructor observes the student, corrects errors, and gives suggestions or hints. If the student distorts factual information, the instructor should remind the student of the correct information, perhaps by repeating it. When the student performs a skill incorrectly, the instructor may model the procedure or part of it again. If the student demonstrates misunderstanding of concepts or principles, the instructor will try to understand the student's confusion and dispel it.

In the classroom, guidance often takes the form of the instructor asking questions that students must answer. When a question is answered incorrectly, the instructor may either tell the student the correct answer or may ask leading questions to help the student recall the correct information.

When the student learns from a book, questions or suggested activities are sometimes included as guidance. But unlike the classroom, if the student does not perform correctly, true guidance does not occur. The student may receive help only at some later time, when the instructor checks the student's work and provides feedback.

Guidance is important in instruction because no student learns all that is taught on a single exposure. Students will make errors and frequently be unaware that they have made them. It is necessary that the student be made aware of these and can correct them. The interactive process of the student attempting to apply new knowledge, the instructor correcting and guiding, and the student making further attempts is frequently omitted in instruction and yet is probably its most important component.

As previously stated, not all models of teaching begin with the presentation of information. Discovery learning is based on the assumption that students discover principles or develop skills through experimentation and practice. There is evidence that for some kinds of information, such as in the sciences and for the development of self-directed learning strategies, student inquiry and discovery are effective (Osborne & Freyberg, 1985; Wittrock, 1974). For the majority of regular school subjects and most procedural or physical skills, we regard a model that begins with the presentation of information as more efficient and demonstrably more successful (Klausmeier & Feldman, 1975; Koran, 1971; Merrill, 1974). In cases where a discovery approach is believed to have some advantage, we would stress that *guided* discovery (in contrast to undirected, free discovery) is more successful. The discovery activity should be a part of the guidance phase of instruction. It should follow some initial exposure to relevant material. And it usually should be followed by the other phases of instruction.

Practice

The instructional process is not complete when the student can do something once or can demonstrate that he or she currently understands the material. The student must usually be able to perform quickly or fluently, sometimes under conditions of distraction, with few or no errors. Furthermore, we usually want students to learn information permanently rather than for a short time. Practicing a skill once or answering a single question will not guarantee retention. Repeated practice is often required for a student to retain information and to become fluent with it.

The third phase, *practice,* is student centered. Although the instructor often observes the student and makes corrections when errors are observed, the emphasis is on the student practicing and the instructor making only short corrective statements.

Fluency and speed are related but slightly different aspects of well-learned information. To be fluent in a skill not only means doing it quickly, but doing it without thinking about it. To speak French fluently, for example, it is necessary that the correct words come automatically, without thinking. Reading, writing, spelling, arithmetic, driving a car, and countless other skills are almost worthless if not performed in this way.

On the other hand, some information does not require fluency. It does not matter whether one can perform a chemistry experiment or write a critical essay quickly. One need not be able to make decisions about starting a business without thinking about it. It is more important that such things be done carefully and correctly. However, the student should remember how to do these things. Practice not only enhances speed and fluency but also retention.

Many examples of practice in classroom instruction exist. In elementary school reading instruction, the instructor frequently asks students questions or requires them to read passages from primers. In arithmetic instruction, workbooks are the most common method of practice. They allow all students to practice simultaneously rather than having most students listen while one student at a time practices. Unfortunately, when a student makes an error practicing in a workbook, it might never be corrected.

In foreign-language instruction, a common type of practice is flashcards. The student produces a pile of cards, for example, with French words on one side and equivalent English words on the reverse. The student then goes through the deck of cards trying to translate the words correctly and receives immediate corrective feedback by looking at the other side of the card.

Assessing Student Learning

The first three phases just discussed are what most people consider to be instruction. However, we should not assume that instruction will be successful for all students. Rather, student learning should be *assessed,* usually with tests, which are an important part of the instructional process. Tests provide information about the level of learning, the quality of teaching, and future instructional needs. Instructors and students alike place undue emphasis on tests as a means of assigning grades. Our emphasis is on tests as a means of guiding instructional decisions—to determine what instruction is needed for which students.

INSTRUCTIONAL METHODOLOGIES

According to the model we have described, the process of instruction includes the instructor presenting information to students, then guiding the students' first interaction with the material, the student practicing the material to enhance fluency and retention, and finally, assessment of students to determine if they have learned the material and what they should do next.

This model, which we have related primarily to classroom instruction, can also be applied to computer-based instruction. That is not to say that the computer must fulfill *all* the phases of instruction. Computers are but one element in an instructional environment, along with teachers and other media. The computer may serve one or a combination of the four phases. It may present initial information after which the student receives guidance from an instructor and practices using a workbook. The student may learn initial information from a lecture, after which the computer is used to practice some parts of the material to fluency. The computer may be used for the first three phases, with testing being done in the traditional way. In all cases, the four phases of instruction should be present, possibly using a combination of media.

When the computer *is* responsible for total instruction, it is important that all four phases be included. This is not always done. It is common, for example, for computer programs intended for practice (drills) to be expected to carry the load of total instruction. When this is done, students may fail to learn what is desired.

The next five chapters deal with five major types of computer-based instruction programs. They are:

Tutorials

Drills

Simulations

Games

Tests

Tutorials are programs that generally engage in the first two phases of instruction. They take the role of the instructor by presenting information and guiding the learner in initial acquisition. Drills and games typically engage in the third phase, requiring the student to practice for fluency and retention. Tests almost always represent the last phase, assessing the level of learning.

Simulations are more complicated. A simulation may be used to present information and guide the learner, to guide and drill, to do all three, or to test the student's knowledge. However, it is rare for a single lesson of *any* methodology to provide all four phases of instruction. Most instructional computer programs must be used in conjunction with other programs or media to provide complete instruction. The four phases of instruction typically occur over days or weeks, not a single instructional session.

We devote a chapter to each of these five methodologies, and so it might be assumed that any CBI lesson must be classifiable as one of them. This is not the case. First, many lessons combine methodologies, such as a lesson that begins with a tutorial and then follows with a drill; or a drill that is done in the context of a game to make it more enjoyable.

Second, there are methodologies we do not discuss, such as problem solving and demonstration. Although we contend that most other methodologies are really variations of the five basic ones we discuss, other educators argue that they are different. For example, we regard the use of word processing for writing instruction as an activity in the practice phase of instruction which permits the student to get extensive writing practice more easily and enjoyably than with paper and pencil. Similarly, using Logo for teaching problem solving is an activity in the practice phase.

Others in the CBI field consider "artificial intelligence" to be an instructional methodology. We see artificial intelligence as a set of programming techniques that may improve any methodology, tutorial, drill, simulation, game, or test. So-called problem-solving environments and the use of tools, such as spreadsheets and databases, are more examples of the practice phase. Some of the programs being labeled "intelligent environments" (White & Horowitz, 1987) are little different than what we will describe as simulations. Like artificial intelligence, interactive video is not a methodology, but the coupling of another technology (television) with the computer to improve all of the basic methodologies we discuss.

The five methodologies that we discuss in this book provide the basic groundwork for understanding and developing good computer-based instruction.

COGNITIVE PSYCHOLOGY AND COMPUTER-BASED INSTRUCTION

As we discuss the major methodologies and later the design of CBI lessons, we are primarily guided by several issues in cognitive psychology (J. Anderson, 1980; R.C. Anderson, 1977; Berger, Pezdek, & Banks, 1986; Bower & Hilgard, 1981; E. Gagne, 1985; Kozma, 1987; Ragan, 1986; Wildman & Burton, 1981; Wilkinson, 1983). The areas of cognitive theory we believe are most important to CBI design are those relating to perception and attention, memory, comprehension, active learning, motivation, locus of control, transfer of learning, and individual differences. This short list of issues is also the best way to summarize what is important in the evaluation and the design of CBI.

Perception and Attention

All human learning is dependent on the learner attending to stimuli and correctly perceiving them. Perception is constantly strained by many competing stimuli. Attention may falter during instruction or be attracted to different stimuli than desired.

Effective instruction depends on presentations designed for easy and accurate perception. Perception may be facilitated by many presentation design factors: detail and realism, the use of sound versus visuals, color, characteristics of text such as its size and font, animation, and position of screen elements are but a few.

For perception of proper lesson elements to occur, the attention of the student must not only be initially attracted but maintained throughout the lesson. In addition to the factors just mentioned, attention is affected by many additional considerations including level of student involvement, personal interests and prior knowledge of the student, lesson difficulty, novelty and familiarity, pacing, and variety.

Throughout the chapters that follow, principles of display design, methods of interaction, and motivational considerations all are guided by the importance of perception and attention in learning.

Memory

Much of what we perceive we must store and be able to retrieve later. While the information storage and retrieval capacity of human intelligence is immense, assuring that the important things are not only perceived but properly stored is not trivial. Especially when faced with new and large bodies of information, such as the vocabulary of a new language, instructional techniques for efficient storage of information are essential.

Two principles underlie almost all methods of enhancing memory—the principle of organization and the principle of repetition (Fleming & Levie, 1978). In general, organization is easier and more powerful. Showing the student the organization of new information or imposing organization upon it aids recall. When the use of organization is inappropriate or impossible, the use of repetition is often used. This is the case when there is a large amount of information, when the information has no inherent organization, or for psychomotor skills.

Comprehension

What we perceive must be interpreted and integrated into our current knowledge of the world (R. Anderson, 1977). We must not only store and retrieve information but be able to classify it, apply it, evaluate it, manipulate it, and so on. Principles of concept acquisition and rule application, for example, guide much CBI design. These principles include the use of prior knowledge, defining and exemplifying concepts, rule application, and information paraphrasing. The type of learning desired must determine the type of presentations and activities of a lesson, such as whether to use multiple-choice versus short-answer questions.

Active Learning

We not only learn by observing but by doing. Interaction not only maintains attention but creates and stores new knowledge and skills. One of the essential features of CBI in contrast to some other media is its capacity to require and act upon student interactions. Although everyone stresses this important aspect of CBI, it is the characteristic on which much commercial courseware falls short. Designing interactions which are frequent, relevant, and increase learning is harder than even experienced developers believe.

Motivation

Proper motivation is essential to learning. Several theories of motivation suggest CBI techniques that will enhance motivation. Some unique aspects of CBI, which permit methodologies like simulation and gaming, are very valuable for motivation enhancement. Motivation theories particularly relevant to CBI are those of Lepper (Lepper & Chabay, 1985), Malone (Malone, 1981; Malone & Lepper, 1987), and Keller (Keller & Suzuki, 1988). Lepper maintains that motivators should be used which are intrinsic to the instruction rather than externally applied. Malone hypothesizes that four elements which foster motivation are challenge, curiosity, control, and fantasy. Keller also suggests four factors (some similar to Malone's) are essential to motivation: maintenance of attention, relevance of the material, student confidence, and student satisfaction.

Locus of Control

A crucial design variable in all CBI is instructional locus of control, which means whether control of sequence, content, methodology and other instructional factors is determined by the student, the lesson (actually the lesson author), or some combination of the two. While the potential for flexible student control is an often claimed advantage of CBI (Laurillard, 1987), its effects on motivation and learning are complex (Hannafin, 1984; Steinberg, 1989). In reality, all lessons have a mixture of student and lesson control. Whether the lesson is successful depends on which aspects of instruction are controlled by the student and which by the lesson.

Transfer of Learning

Learning in a CBI lesson is usually just a precursor to applying or using that knowledge in the real world. *Transfer* (Clark & Voogel, 1985; Cormier & Hagman, 1987) refers to the extent to which improved performance in the lesson is reflected in the real world as well. Transfer is affected by type, amount, and variety of interaction, by realism of the instruction, and by the methodologies used. In training situations, transfer is ultimately the most important instructional outcome.

Individual Differences

Students do not all learn alike or at the same rate. Some instructional methods are better for some students. Another often praised advantage of CBI is its capability to individualize. But just like interactivity, this supposed advantage is not often taken advantage of. Most commercial software works about the same for all students. Good software will adapt to the learner, capitalizing upon his or her talents, giving extra help where the student is weak, and providing motivators each student responds to. Because not every lesson will work for every student, matching students up with appropriate lessons and methodologies is important. That in turn depends on continual assessment of individual differences so that proper matching and other decision making can take place.

Conclusion

These eight issues will arise repeatedly as we discuss lesson methodology, design, and evaluation. They are the reasons for many of our recommendations on screen design, lesson sequence, interaction techniques, and evaluation. There is much for the CBT designer to learn from the field of cognitive psychology. For further study in the basic theoretical foundations underlying instructional design, the following references are recommended: J. Anderson (1980, 1981); Berger, Pezdek, & Banks (1986); Bower & Hilgard (1981); Fleming & Levie (1978); E. Gagne (1985); and R. Gagne (1985).

See the bibliography at the end of this chapter for additional readings on computers for administration, as classroom tools, and in specific subject areas. Also included are some of the classic books on the instructional uses of computers.

REFERENCES AND BIBLIOGRAPHY

ALESSI, S.M., & SHIH, Y.-F. (1989). The growth of computer-assisted instruction in Taiwan schools. *Computers & Education, 13*(4), 337–341.

ALPERT, D., & BITZER, D.L. (1970). Advances in computer-based education. *Science, 167,* 1582–1590.

ANDERSON, J.R. (1980). *Cognitive Psychology and Its Implications.* San Francisco: W.H. Freeman.

ANDERSON, J.R. (1981). *Cognitive Skills and Their Acquisition.* Hillsdale, NJ: Lawrence Erlbaum.

ANDERSON, R.C. (1977). The notion of schemata and the educational enterprise. In R.C. Anderson, R.J. Spiro, & W.E. Montague (Eds.), *Schooling and the Acquisition of Knowledge.* Hillsdale, NJ: Lawrence Erlbaum.

BAKER, E.L. (1988). *Sensitive Technology Assessment of ACOT.* Paper presented at the Annual Meeting of the American Educational Research Association, New Orleans. (ERIC Document Reproduction Service No. ED 303 156)

BALAJTHY, E. (1986). *Microcomputers in Reading & Language Arts.* Englewood Cliffs, NJ: Prentice-Hall.

BALAJTHY, E. (1989). *Computers and Reading.* Englewood Cliffs, NJ: Prentice-Hall.

BANGERT-DROWNS, R.L., KULIK, J.A., & KULIK, C-L.C. (1985). Effectiveness of computer-based education in secondary schools. *Journal of Computer-Based Instruction, 12*(3), 59–68.

BECKER, H. (1983). *School Uses of Microcomputers.* Baltimore, MD: Johns Hopkins University, Center for Social Organization of Schools.

BECKER, H.J. (1985). *The Second National Survey of Instructional Uses of School Computers: A Preliminary Report.* Paper presented at the World Conference on Computers in Education, Norfolk, VA. (ERIC Document Reproduction Service No. ED 274 307)

BECKER, H.J. (1986). *Instructional Uses of School Computers: Reports from the 1985 National Survey.* Baltimore, MD: Johns Hopkins University, Center for Social Organization of Schools.

BERGER, D.E., PEZDEK, K., & BANKS, W.P. (1986). *Applications of Cognitive Psychology.* Hillsdale, NJ: Lawrence Erlbaum.

BITTER, G.G., & CAMUSE, R.A. (1988). *Using a Microcomputer in the Classroom.* 2nd ed. Englewood Cliffs, NJ: Prentice-Hall.

BLUHM, H.P. (1987). *Administrative Uses of Computers in the Schools.* Englewood Cliffs, NJ: Prentice-Hall.

BORK, A. (1981). *Learning with Computers.* Bedford, MA: Digital Press.

BOWER, G.H., & HILGARD, E.R. (1981). *Theories of Learning.* Englewood Cliffs, NJ: Prentice-Hall.

BRUDER, I. (1988, October). Electronic Learning's 8th annual survey of the states, 1988. *Electronic Learning, 8*(2), 38–45.

CHAIKLIN, S., & LEWIS, M.W. (1988). Will there be teachers in the classroom of the future? . . . But we don't think about that. *Teachers College Record, 89*(3), 431–440.

CLARK, R.E. (1983). Reconsidering research on learning from media. *Review of Educational Research, 53*(4), 445–459

CLARK, R.E., & VOOGEL, A. (1985). Transfer of training principles for instructional design. *Educational Communication and Technology Journal, 33*(2), 113–123.

CLEMENTS, D.H. (1989). *Computers in Elementary Mathematics Education.* Englewood Cliffs, NJ: Prentice-Hall.

CLINE, H.F., BENNETT, R.E., KERSHAW, R.C., SCHNEIDERMAN, M.B., STECHER, B., & WILSON, S. (1986). *The Electronic Schoolhouse: The IBM Secondary School Computer Education Program.* Hillsdale, NJ: Lawrence Erlbaum.

CORMIER, S.M., & HAGMAN, J.D. (Eds.). (1987). *Transfer of Learning: Contemporary Research and Applications.* San Diego: Academic Press.

DAIUTE, C. (1985). *Writing and Computers.* Reading, MA: Addison-Wesley.

FAKHRO, S.Q., & KAHN, E.H. (1987). Computers in Bahrain's private schools. *Journal of Computer-Based Instruction, 14*(3), 98–103.

FLEMING, M., & LEVIE, W.H. (1978). *Instructional Message Design: Principles from the Behavioral Sciences.* Englewood Cliffs, NJ: Educational Technology Publications.

GAGNE, E.D. (1985). *The Cognitive Psychology of School Learning.* Boston: Little, Brown and Company.

GAGNE, R.M. (1985). *The Conditions of Learning and Theory of Instruction.* 4th ed. New York: Holt, Rinehart and Winston.

GEBHARDT-SEELE, P.G. (1985). *The Computer and the Child: A Montessori Approach.* Rockville, MD: Computer Science Press.

GOLDENBERG, E.P., RUSSEL, S.J., CARTER, C.J., STOKES, S., SYLVESTER, M.J., & KELMAN, P. (1984). *Computers, Education and Special Needs.* Reading, MA: Addison-Wesley.

HANNAFIN, M.J. (1984). Guidelines for using locus of instructional control in the design of computer-assisted instruction. *Journal of Instructional Development, 7*(3), 6–10.

HANNAFIN, M.J., DALTON, D.W., & HOOPER, S.R. (1987). Computers in education: Barriers and solutions. In E.E. Miller & M.L. Mosley (Eds.), *Educational Media and Technology Yearbook.* Littleton, CO: Libraries Unlimited.

HAWISHER, G.E., & SELFE, C.L. (Eds.). (1989). *Critical Perspectives on Computers and Composition Instruction.* New York: Teachers College Press.

HAWKINS, J. (1987). The interpretation of Logo in practice. In R.D. Pea & K. Sheingold (Eds.), *Mirrors of Minds: Patterns of Experience in Educational Computing.* Norwood, NJ: Ablex Publishing.

HUNTER, B. (1984). *My Students Use Computers: Learning Activities for Computer Literacy.* Reston, VA: Reston Publishing.

JOHNSON, D.W., & JOHNSON, R.T. (1985). Cooperative learning: One key to computer assisted learning. *The Computing Teacher, 13*(2), 11–15.

JOHNSON, R.T., JOHNSON, D.W., & STANNE, M.B. (1985). Effects of cooperative, competitive, and individualistic goal structures on computer-assisted instruction. *Journal of Educational Psychology, 77*, 668–677.

JONASSEN, D.H. (1988). Integrating learning strategies into courseware to facilitate deeper processing. In D.H. Jonassen (Ed.), *Instructional Designs for Microcomputer Courseware.* Hillsdale, NJ: Lawrence Erlbaum.

KELLER, J.M., & SUZUKI, K. (1988). Use of the ARCS motivation model in courseware design. In D.H. Jonassen (Ed.), *Instructional Designs for Microcomputer Courseware.* Hillsdale, NJ: Lawrence Erlbaum.

KERR, S.T. (1990). The Soviet "conception of the informatization of education." *Journal of Computer-Based Instruction, 17*(1), 1–7.

KITABCHI, G. (1987). *Evaluation of the Apple Classroom of Tomorrow.* Paper presented at the 16th Annual Meeting of the Mid-South Educational Research Association, Mobile, AL. (ERIC Document Reproduction Service No. ED 295 600)

KLAUSMEIER, H.J., & FELDMAN, K.V. (1975). Effects of a definition and a varying number of examples and nonexamples on concept attainment. *Journal of Educational Psychology, 67*, 174–178.

KORAN, M.L. (1971). Differential response to inductive and deductive instructional procedures. *Journal of Educational Design, 62*, 300–307.

KOZMA, R.B. (1987). The implication of cognitive psychology for computer-based learning tools. *Educational Technology, 27*(11), 20–25.

KULIK, C-L.C., & KULIK, J.A. (1986). Effectiveness of computer-based education in colleges. *AEDS Journal, 19*, 81–108.

KULIK, J.A., KULIK, C-L.C., & BANGERT-DROWNS, R.L. (1985). Effectiveness of computer-based education in elementary schools. *Computers in Human Behavior, 1*, 59–74.

LAURILLARD, D. (1987). Computers and the emancipation of students: Giving control to the learner. *Instructional Science, 16*, 3–18.

LEPPER, M.R., & CHABAY, R.W. (1985). Intrinsic motivation and instruction: Conflicting views on the role of motivational processes in computer-based education. *Educational Psychologist, 20*(4), 217–230.

LOCKARD, J., ABRAMS, P.D., & MANY, W.A. (1987). *Microcomputers for Educators.* Boston: Little, Brown and Company.

LUEHRMANN, A. (1985, January). A new trend: Ed-Teching the computer. *Electronic Learning,* 22.

MALONE, T.W. (1981). Towards a theory of intrinsically motivating instruction. *Cognitive Science, 5*, 333–369.

MALONE, T.W., & LEPPER, M.R. (1987). Making learning fun: A taxonomy of intrinsic motivations for learning. In R.E. Snow & M.J. Farr (Eds.), *Aptitude, Learning, and Instruction: III. Conative and Affective Process Analysis.* Hillsdale, NJ: Lawrence Erlbaum.

MERRILL, M.D. (1983). Component display theory. In C.M. Reigeluth (Ed.), *Instructional Design Theories and Models.* Hillsdale, NJ: Lawrence Erlbaum.

MERRILL, M.D. (1987). The new component design theory: Instructional design for courseware authoring. *Instructional Science, 16*, 19–34.

MERRILL, M.D. (1988). Applying component display theory to the design of courseware. In D.H. Jonassen (Ed.), *Instructional Designs for Microcomputer Courseware.* Hillsdale, NJ: Lawrence Erlbaum.

MERRILL, M.D., SCHNEIDER, E.W., & FLETCHER, K.A. (1980). *TICCIT.* Englewood Cliffs, NJ: Educational Technology Publications.

MERRILL, P.F. (1974). Effects of the availability of objectives and/or rules on the learning process. *Journal of Educational Psychology, 66*, 534–539.

O'NEIL, H.F. (Ed.). (1981). *Computer-Based Instruction: A State-of-the-Art Assessment.* New York: Academic Press.

O'SHEA, T., & SELF, J. (1983). *Learning and Teaching with Computers: Artificial Intelligence in Education.* Englewood Cliffs, NJ: Prentice-Hall.

OBEREM, G.E. (1987). Computer assisted instruction in South Africa: An overview. *Journal of Computer-Based Instruction, 14*(3), 111–113.

OKAMOTO, T. (1987). The trends of computer-based instruction in Japan. *Journal of Computer-Based Instruction, 14*(3), 114–118.

OSBORNE, R., & FRYEBERG, P. (1985). *Learning in Science: The Implications of Children's Science.* Auckland, New Zealand: Heinemann Publishers.

PAPERT, S. (1980). *Mindstorms: Children, Computers and Powerful Ideas.* New York: Basic Books.

RAGAN, T.J. (1986). *Instructional Strategies in CAI: Instructional Design Theory Needs.* Paper presented at the Annual Convention of the Association for Educational Communications and Technology, Las Vegas, NV. (ERIC Document Reproduction Service No. ED 267 786)

ROBERTS, N., FRIEL, S., & LADENBURG, T. (1988). *Computers and the Social Studies: Educating for the Future.* Menlo Park, CA: Addison-Wesley.

ROBLYER, M.D. (1985). *Measuring the Impact of Computers in Instruction: A Non-Technical Review of Research for Educators.* Washington, D.C.: Association for Educational Data Systems.

ROSENSHINE, B., & STEVENS, R. (1986). Teaching functions. In M.C. Wittrock (Ed.), *Handbook of Research on Teaching. 3rd ed.* New York: Macmillan.

SLESNICK, T. (1983). Hold it: You're using computers the wrong way. *Executive Educator, 5*(4), 29–30.

SLOAN, D. (Ed.). (1985). *The Computer in Education: A Critical Perspective.* New York: Teachers College Press.

SOLOMON, G. (1986). *Children, Writing, & Computers: An Activities Guide.* Englewood Cliffs, NJ: Prentice-Hall.

STEINBERG, E.R. (1977). Review of student control in computer-assisted instruction. *Journal of Computer-Based Instruction, 3*, 84–90.

STEINBERG, E.R. (1984). *Teaching Computers to Teach.* Hillsdale, NJ: Lawrence Erlbaum.

STEINBERG, E.R. (1989). Cognition and learner control: A literature review, 1977–1988. *Journal of Computer-Based Instruction, 16*(4), 117–121.

STRICKLAND, D.S., FEELEY, J.T., & WEPNER, S.B. (1987). *Using Computers in the Teaching of Reading.* New York: Teachers College Press.

TAYLOR, R. (Ed.). (1980). *The Computer in the School: Tutor, Tool, Tutee.* New York: Teachers College Press.

TROLLIP, S.R., & ALESSI, S.M. (1988). Incorporating computers effectively into classrooms. *Journal of Research on Computing in Education, 21*(1), 70–81.

WALKER, D.F, & HESS R.D. (Eds.) (1984). *Instructional Software: Principles and Perspectives for Design and Use.* Belmont, CA: Wadsworth Publishing.

WHITE, B.Y., & HOROWITZ, P. (1987, March). *Thinker-Tools: Enabling Children to Understand Physical Laws.* (Report No. 6470). Cambridge, MA: BBN Laboratories Incorporated.

WILDMAN, T.M., & BURTON, J.K. (1981). Integrating learning theory with instructional design. *Journal of Instructional Development, 4*(3), 5–14.

WILKINSON, A.C. (Ed.). (1983). *Classroom Computers and Cognitive Science.* New York: Academic Press.

WITTROCK, M.C. (1974). Learning as a generative process. *Educational Psychologist, 11*(2), 87–95.

WYDRA, F.T. (1980). *Learner Controlled Instruction.* Englewood Cliffs, NJ: Educational Technology Publications.

YUEH, J-S., & ALESSI, S.M. (1988). The effect of reward structure and group ability composition on cooperative computer assisted learning. *Journal of Computer-Based Instruction, 15*(1), 18–22.

2

TUTORIALS

In the previous chapter we maintained that successful instruction should include the following four activities.

1. Information is presented or skills are modeled
2. The student is guided through initial use of the information or skills.
3. The student practices for retention and fluency.
4. Student learning is assessed.

Tutorial lessons aim to satisfy the first two components of instruction, and usually do not engage in extended practice or assessment of learning. Some tutorials do not even guide the student through the information, but only present it. However, we contend that a good tutorial should include both presentation and guidance, while extended practice and assessment are the domain of other methodologies.

Tutorials are used in almost every subject area from the humanities to the social and physical sciences. They are appropriate for presenting factual information, for learning rules and principles, or for learning problem-solving strategies (Gagne, Wager, & Rojas, 1981).

Figure 2–1 shows the structure and sequence of a typical tutorial. It begins with an introductory section which informs the student of the purpose and nature of the lesson. After that a cycle begins. Information is presented and elaborated. A question is asked which the student must answer. The program judges the response to assess student comprehension, and the student is given feedback to improve comprehension and future performance. At the end of each iteration, the program makes a sequencing decision to determine what information should be treated during the next iteration.

The cycle continues until the lesson is terminated by either the student or the program. At that point, which we call the closing, there may be a summary and closing remarks. Although not every tutorial need engage in all these activities, most *effective* ones include these or similar components.

Our treatment of tutorials and the other methodologies will focus on a

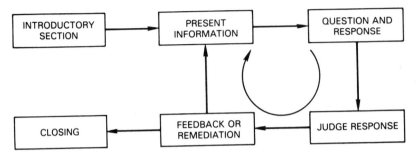

Figure 2-1 The general structure and flow of a tutorial.

number of *factors*. By factors we mean those characteristics under the designer's control which affect appearance and effectiveness.

There are many instructional factors relevant to tutorial instruction, and we organize our discussion by grouping them according to the following aspects of a tutorial:

> *Introduction* of the tutorial
> *Student control* of the lesson
> *Motivation*
> *Presentation* of information
> *Questions* and *responses*
> *Judgment* of responses
> *Feedback* about responses
> *Remediation*
> *Sequencing* lesson segments
> *Closing* of the tutorial

Computer-based instruction methodologies other than the tutorial have many of the above components as well. Many of the factors discussed in this chapter are therefore relevant to the methodologies discussed in the following chapters. Although we will not repeat all the relevant factors in the other chapters, the reader should remember that they are applicable.

INTRODUCTION OF THE TUTORIAL

The factors relevant to the introduction of a tutorial are:

> The title page
> Presentation of objectives
> Directions
> Stimulating prior knowledge
> Pretesting

The Title Page

All tutorials begin with a title page (Figure 2–2) or similar device to attract the student's attention, to create a receptive attitude, and to indicate in a general way what the lesson is about. Title pages vary from a simple title and author's name, to elaborate pages with multi-colored animated graphics. A title is essential to inform the student that a new lesson is about to begin, and what its contents are. How much more should be on a title page is controversial. Gagne & Briggs (1979) indicate that doing something more to motivate the student is important. However, long, complicated, or humorous text and graphics are frequently annoying to students. Flashy title pages are greeted with smiles and amusement the first time, but with impatience on subsequent uses of the lesson.

Figure 2-2   A title page in *General Chemistry* (Smith & Chabay, 1983). *(Courtesy of COMPress)*

Presentation of Objectives

After the title page, there is frequently a statement of the objectives for the lesson (see Figure 2–3). The behavioral school of psychology, which spawned the instructional systems design model of instructional development, encourages the use of behavioral objectives (Mager, 1962). While many lessons do inform the student of objectives in purely behavioral form, many do not strictly adhere to this practice. The following are examples of behavioral objectives.

> After this lesson you will be able to multiply two-digit numbers.
> At the end of this lesson you will be able to state the causes of the Civil War.
> This lesson will teach you to determine whether a painting is of the Classic, Impressionist, or Modern period.

Such objectives are characterized by indicating what the student will be able to do, say, or write at the completion of the lesson. The actions words *multiply, state,* and *determine* label these statements as behavioral. A more complete behavioral objective will include

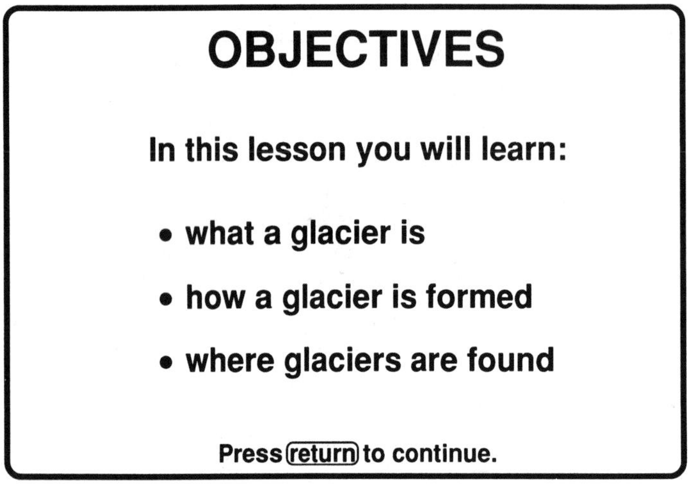

Figure 2-3 Objectives for a tutorial.

OBJECTIVES

In this lesson you will learn:

- **what a glacier is**
- **how a glacier is formed**
- **where glaciers are found**

Press return to continue.

A statement of conditions under which the behavior should occur
A description of the behavior
A criterion for acceptable performance

For example, the first example above would be restated as follows.

When presented with twenty 2-digit multiplication problems, you will be able to solve at least eighteen correctly in twenty minutes.

Some educators discourage the use of behavioral objectives (Atkin, 1968), or believe they should be used in conjunction with other forms of objectives. The following are non-behavioral objectives.

After this lesson you will understand the events that led up to the Civil War.
You will learn to distinguish and appreciate paintings of different periods.

A major objection to behavioral objectives is that they focus student attention on only those things stated in the objectives. The use of non-behavioral objectives, it is argued, will enhance both specific and non-specific learning from a lesson. Other objections are that behavioral objectives are hard for students to read, especially at the beginning of a lesson; and that they are difficult to write for some subjects.

Although there is evidence that presenting objectives, whether behavioral or not, enhances learning and satisfaction, not all tutorials do so. There are sometimes good reasons for omitting them, such as when the students are very young and cannot comprehend them. However, in most cases, objectives are omitted because of oversight. When objectives are not given to the student, it is useful to have them in a printed document for instructors.

Objectives can serve another important function, that of motivating students. Keller & Suzuki (1988) maintain that four functions enhance motivation: attention, relevance, confidence, and satisfaction. Well-written objectives can demonstrate the relevance of material to the student.

Our recommendation is that a tutorial should have a concise and accurate statement of objectives, not necessarily in behavioral form. It should be stated in terms the students can understand and be able to motivate the students by demonstrating relevance to their needs. The major exception to this recommendation is for young students, especially non-readers using lessons that are primarily pictorial.

Directions

Directions are essential to the effectiveness of any computer-based lesson. A lesson without directions is likely to fail while one with some directions at least has a chance to succeed. Figure 2–4 shows short but sufficient directions from a tutorial that is controlled completely by the keyboard. Figure 2–5 shows directions for a tutorial controlled primarily by mouse-sensitive buttons on the screen.

DIRECTIONS

Press (return) after answering a question, or for the next page.

Press (esc) to return to the menu and to exit.

Press (ctrl-h) for help.

Press (ctrl-b) to to back to a previous page.

Press (return) to continue.

Figure 2-4 Directions for a keyboard-controlled lesson.

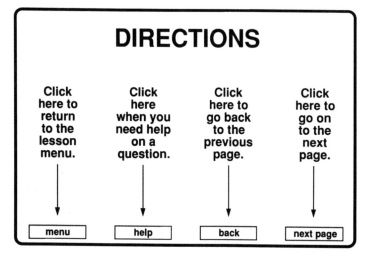

DIRECTIONS

| **Click here to return to the lesson menu.** | **Click here when you need help on a question.** | **Click here to go back to the previous page.** | **Click here to go on to the next page.** |

| menu | help | back | next page |

Figure 2-5 Directions for a mouse-controlled lesson.

At the start of a lesson, directions are frequently made optional for the student. However, for students in a lesson for the first time this is not advisable. Many will not notice the option to read directions, or will try to save time by skipping them. The speed at which information can be displayed on most microcomputers is so great that it is just as fast to show a page of directions as it is to ask the student if directions are desired. When directions pertain to keypresses or other information that is difficult to remember, a method should be provided to return to the directions from any point in the lesson.

Directions must be more carefully constructed when student control uses the keyboard rather than the mouse. Mouse control is more natural and places little demand on memory, thus having less need for directions.

Stimulating Prior Knowledge

Research on human learning indicates that students will learn more if they can relate new information to what they already know (Anderson, 1977; Adams & Bruce, 1980; Rumelhart & Ortony, 1977). A tutorial should not review prior knowledge in detail, but may provide a brief synopsis of related information studied previously (Gagne, Wager, & Rojas, 1981). A student about to study glacial formation, for instance, may be prompted to think about snow on sidewalks turning into ice. Often the use of prior knowledge is extended throughout a tutorial, as when an extended analogy is used. For instance, in introducing the parts and functions of a computer, a tutorial might relate each component in turn to a part of the human body and its corresponding functions, such as the central processing unit to the brain, the input to the eyes, and the output to the mouth. Long sections relating prior knowledge to the lesson content should not be in the introduction, but in the primary presentations of the lesson.

Pretesting

Some tutorials give a pretest in the introductory section. This is a short diagnostic test designed to ascertain if the lesson is appropriate for the student. There are three possible outcomes of such a test:

> The student is not ready for this lesson.
> The student is ready for and should study this lesson.
> The student already knows the information and should skip the lesson.

On one hand, we believe pretests that determine student readiness and need for a lesson are worthwhile. It makes sense for students to skip a lesson on known material, and it does not make sense for them to study things they are not prepared for. On the other hand, it is not good for a pretest to be built *into* a tutorial. It is better for a pretest to be in a separate program to be used *before* the tutorial program. It is also possible to put the pretest in a program with an option for the instructor to turn it on or off, although this is more complicated to implement. For simplicity as well as flexibility, putting pretests in separate lessons is generally advised.

There are several advantages to doing this. First, you may already know that the lesson is appropriate for a particular student or group of students. For example, your students have just completed addition and subtraction, and all per-formed well on a test over that material. You are sure they can begin learning about multiplication. In this situation, it is not necessary to have students do a pretest.

In the case where you know that your students need to study the lesson, it may be detrimental to give them a pretest. The pretest will have many questions about material they have not studied, and they will probably do poorly. This may damage their attitude, make them apprehensive about the difficulty of the new subject, or make them feel like failures. If the pretest is a separate program, you have more flexibility to use it for some students (those you are uncertain about) and not for others.

Another reason for having the pretest in a separate program is to make the tutorial more generally useful to a larger number of teachers. Some teachers may like having a pretest, some may not. If the pretest is separate, you satisfy both. If integral to the tutorial, teachers not wanting or needing the pretest are likely to avoid using the lesson altogether.

In summary, pretests should be used only when necessary, generally with adult learners or when you do not know if a student is ready for or needs a lesson. Pretests should be separate from tutorials, should be short, and include only items that test the necessary prerequisites or major goals of a lesson.

STUDENT CONTROL OF THE LESSON

One of the most complex aspects of designing lessons is student control. There are two considerations in this regard, *what* control to give to the student and the *method* of control.

What Control to Provide

Considerable research has been done on student control in computer-based instruction. It has been suggested (even before the existence of microcom-puters) that students can make better sequencing decisions than teachers (Bruner, 1966a,b).

Based on a belief in student control, a major CBI system, the TICCIT sys-tem (Merrill, Schneider, & Fletcher, 1980), provides almost complete student con-trol of lesson sequence and other lesson parameters. The student using TICCIT (which is designed primarily for adult education and stands for *Time-*shared, *In-*teractive, *Computer-*Controlled, *Information Television*) decides what part of a curriculum to study, and whether to see rules, to practice with problems, the diffi-culty of practice problems, and when to take a test. All of these decisions are easily made with a special keyset having keys labeled *rule, example, practice, easy, hard,* and *help.*

However, studies investigating student control have shown that students do not make good decisions and that the more control is given to the student the more learning suffers (DiVesta, 1975; Steinberg, 1977, 1989; Tennyson & Rothen, 1979). Student control is more beneficial when students receive specific feedback regarding their progress and the success of their decisions (Tennyson, 1981) or when they receive explicit instruction on proper control of lessons.

Hannafin & Phillips (1987) have suggested that there are at least four types of *locus of control:* student control, program control, adaptive control, and adaptive advisement. Student control allows the student most control without instruction or feedback. Program control allows the student some simple controls (such as forward progression or asking for help) but determines sequence, completion, and other important factors by rules the lesson author has programmed. Adaptive control is a combination of lesson and student control attuned to each student's needs, with the amount and type of student control determined by performance in the lesson. Learner control with advisement gives students the most control but also provides instruction and ongoing advice about what to do, which students may follow or ignore.

Generally, studies have found simple student control to result in the poorest performance. Lesson control and adaptive control tend to be the best, dependent on variables such as student maturity, subject matter, and lesson methodology. The procedures for adaptive control and learner control with advisement, however, are complicated to program and time consuming for the student, who generally begins the lesson with a lengthy pretest.

Although further research will provide more effective types of student and lesson control, the best current approach is to intelligently provide *some* student control for appropriate aspects of a lesson depending on the educational level of the student and lesson complexity. Following are some general rules for student control in tutorials, based upon research evidence.

> Give adults more control than children.
> Always allow control of forward progression.
> Allow review, especially backward paging, whenever possible.
> For general capabilities like directions, help, comments, glossaries, and temporary termination; provide *global* control—available everywhere and in the same manner.
> Always allow temporary termination.

When a tutorial has more than one part, menus are often used to control sequence. For example, a lesson on glaciers might include instruction explaining what a glacier is, how glaciers form, where glaciers are found, and the role of glaciers in the ice ages. Figure 2–6 shows menu control of such a lesson. Clicking with a mouse on a section title takes the student to that section. Several general rules for menus can also be made:

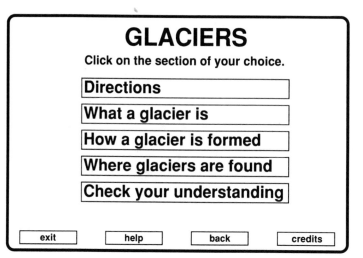

Figure 2-6   Menu control of a
lesson.

Provide menus if section sequence is not critical.

Provide menus more for adults than for children.

Use a "progressive menu" (Figure 2–7) for *review* without *skipping*.

If menus are used, they should always be accessible.

Give menus a good header name, not *menu* (Figure 2–7).

Give advice and progress information on the menu (Figure 2–7).

Keep menu choices simple and few in number (Shneiderman, 1987).

Keep menu levels few in number (Shneiderman, 1987).

For simple content, allow advanced students menu control.

For complex content, either do not provide initial choice or provide a few simple choices. Complex lesson structures may be more readily explained with a picture, such as a flowchart, a block diagram, or a map.

Menus should include options to return to directions and to exit.

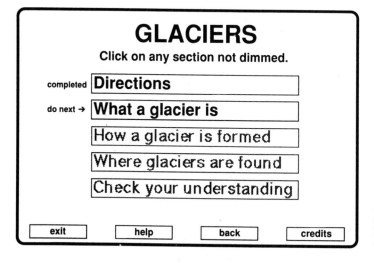

Figure 2-7   Progressive menu.
Review is allowed, but not skipping.
Progress information and advice is
also provided.

Some other valuable recommendations for design of control procedures, based on Hannafin (1984) are:

Use learner control with advisement for older or more able students.
Use lesson control with younger or less able students.
Use lesson control for procedural learning and low-order skills, like memorizing.
Use learner control for high-order skills, such as problem solving.
Use lesson control for mastery learning and unfamiliar content.
With learner control, include advice and procedures to catch students who are doing poorly.
If learner control is ineffective, switch to lesson control, or vice versa.

Method of Control

For those things the student does control, the methods used will determine the ease of use and consequently the extent to which students use them. Method of control may be subdivided into techniques and modes. Techniques are more under the author's control. For example, providing sequence control via menus versus commands, either of which are always possible. Mode, the physical manner in which the student makes choices, is constrained by computer hardware. Whereas all computer systems have keyboards, not all have special function keys, mice, touch panels, or other input devices.

Let us consider modes of control first. Traditionally, CBI has utilized the keyboard for student control. This has always been problematic, for the keyboard is also used for interactions such as answering questions. Thus answers must be distinguished from requests by the student, such as for help or to exit. For this reason compound keys such as ⟨control-x⟩ have been used. These tend to be hard to remember, necessitating screen prompts that clutter the display, directions which the student can retrieve, or off-line quick-reference cards.

Some CBI systems, such as PLATO and IBM InfoWindow, use touch panels as a means of control (as well as for other interactions). Unfortunately, touch panels have been notoriously inaccurate and unreliable.

The introduction of the computer mouse has greatly improved the quality of human interaction with computers. Mice are accurate, reliable, reasonably easy to learn and use, and quickly becoming available on most microcomputers. We strongly encourage the inclusion of a mouse on any computer system intended for CBI and recommend its use for many kinds of user actions previously done by keyboard.

Other modes are available or will become increasingly available. Joysticks, graphics tablets, and light pens are useful for some special purposes, but, all being pointing and drawing devices, have largely been replaced by the mouse. Speech input is new, expensive, and inaccurate, but may become much more common in the future as an alternative mode for verbal commands.

Techniques.   The primary two techniques of student control are menus and commands. Menus are typically used for initial control, sequence selection, and review. Commands are typically used for control of forward progression, local review (paging backwards), and special requests such as to go to menus, help, glossaries, and to exit. Either menus or commands may be keyboard or mouse-oriented.

Figures 2–8 through 2–10 show three keyboard oriented menus. Figure 2–8 uses letters, Figure 2–9 uses numbers, and Figure 2–10 uses cursor control keys. Each has advantages. The first two require fewer keypresses and are faster. Cursor control is less prone to error, providing better visual feedback of the option being chosen. Figure 2–11 shows a mouse-oriented menu. We prefer this menu if a mouse is available. It is the easiest and least error prone. Preferably, the option clicked will be highlighted but the actual branch will not occur until the mouse button is released.

Figure 2–12 illustrates *command* controls, in this case key presses for student control. If a lot of difficult controls are necessary, the technique shown in Figures 2–13 and 2–14 is preferred. In Figure 2–13 there is just one command,

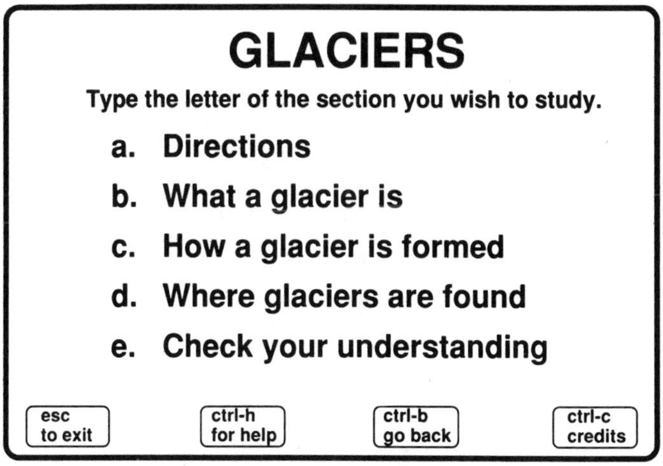

GLACIERS
Type the letter of the section you wish to study.

- a. **Directions**
- b. **What a glacier is**
- c. **How a glacier is formed**
- d. **Where glaciers are found**
- e. **Check your understanding**

`esc to exit` `ctrl-h for help` `ctrl-b go back` `ctrl-c credits`

Figure 2-8 Letter menu

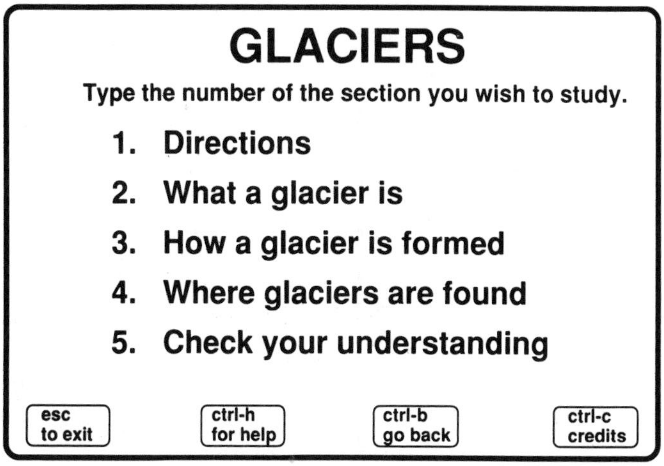

GLACIERS
Type the number of the section you wish to study.

- 1. **Directions**
- 2. **What a glacier is**
- 3. **How a glacier is formed**
- 4. **Where glaciers are found**
- 5. **Check your understanding**

`esc to exit` `ctrl-h for help` `ctrl-b go back` `ctrl-c credits`

Figure 2-9 Number menu.

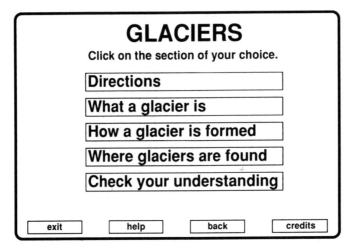

GLACIERS

Use the arrow keys to indicate the section
you wish to study. Then press (return).

Directions

→ **What a glacier is**

How a glacier is formed

Where glaciers are found

Check your understanding

| esc
to exit | ctrl-h
for help | ctrl-b
go back | ctrl-c
credits |

Figure 2-10 Cursor menu.

GLACIERS

Click on the section of your choice.

| Directions |
| What a glacier is |
| How a glacier is formed |
| Where glaciers are found |
| Check your understanding |

| exit | help | back | credits |

Figure 2-11 Mouse-oriented menu.

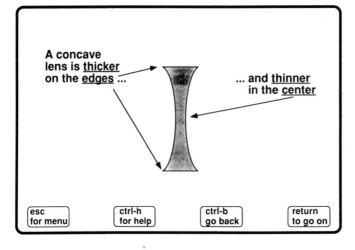

A concave
lens is <u>thicker</u>
on the <u>edges</u> ...

... and <u>thinner</u>
in the <u>center</u>

| esc
for menu | ctrl-h
for help | ctrl-b
go back | return
to go on |

Figure 2-12 Key commands on
presentation display.

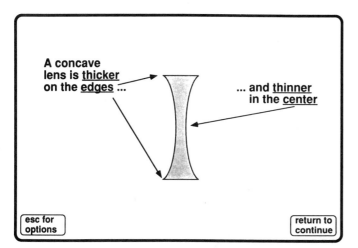

Figure 2-13 ⟨Esc⟩ for a list of control options.

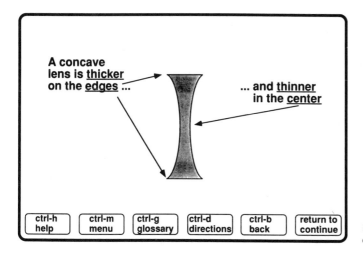

Figure 2-14 The menu of control options reached.

press ⟨esc⟩ for a list of options. This combines the command and menu methods. It is advantageous because with a lot of options, commands will either be hard to remember or will clutter the screen.

A similar feature on mouse-oriented computers, such as the Macintosh, is the pull-down menu (Figure 2–15). Pull-down menus allow many student control options to be available at all times without cluttering the screen. Although they are a little harder to use initially, students quickly learn and become accustomed to their use. Pull-down menus are particularly good for global controls, those that should always be available.

Figure 2–16 shows command controls using mouse-sensitive buttons. These do not require student memory or a secondary menu. Although the buttons consume some screen space, they require less text and space than describing the functions of various keypresses, and are easier to use and less prone to error.

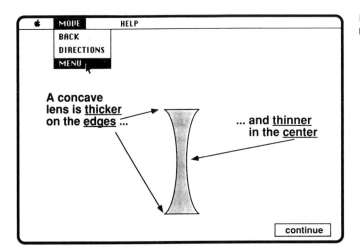

Figure 2-15 Mouse-controlled pull-down menu.

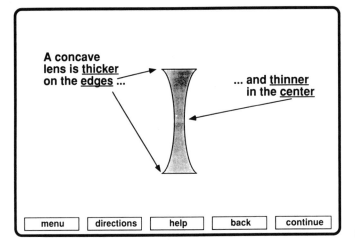

Figure 2-16 Mouse controls on presentation display.

A last consideration for user control functions, and in general for directions to the student, is that they should *be visible only when available.* In many lessons one sees user control buttons on the display even when they are not functional. In questions it is common to see directions such as "Type your answer and press ⟨return⟩" visible even after the student has given a response and received feedback. Directions and control options should be erased when no longer valid.

Functional Areas. Heines (1984) recommends that designers pay careful attention to the definition of functional areas. This means allocating sections of the screen to specific purposes, such as directions or orienting information. It is common, for example, to put page numbers and section titles at the top of the display, main lesson content in the middle, and directions or control options at the bottom, as in Figure 2–16. On the Macintosh, pull-down menus are usually placed along the top line of the display. Although software such as *Hypercard* has recently encouraged mouse buttons and pull-down (or pop-up) menus everywhere on the display, we recommend buttons consistently placed on the bottom and pull-down menus at the top.

MOTIVATION

In the previous section we discussed issues relating to student control of a lesson. Student control, although not often improving learning, is generally found to improve student attitude and motivation. For that reason alone it is often recommended. However, there are other ways to increase motivation which may be implemented independently of student control.

Intrinsic versus Extrinsic Motivation

Lepper (Lepper, 1985; Lepper & Chabay, 1985; Lepper & Malone, 1987) has argued that motivators may be either intrinsic or extrinsic. Extrinsic motivators are those which are independent of the instruction, such as paying or otherwise rewarding the student with things they consider desirable. Lepper's research has provided evidence that when extrinsic motivators are used, student interest in learning is diminished because the student's goal becomes the reward rather than learning.

Intrinsic motivators, in contrast, are things inherent in the instruction that motivate the student. Put in common terms, instruction is intrinsically motivating if students consider it to be "fun." Lepper and his associates make several suggestions which they claim will generally enhance intrinsic motivation:

Use game techniques.

Embellishments (such as visual techniques) should increase student intensity of work and attention and should encourage deeper cognitive processing.

Use exploratory environments.

Give the student personal control.

Challenge the student.

Arouse the student's curiosity.

Give encouragement, even when errors are made.

Additionally, they point out that techniques for maintaining motivation should be considered at both the macro and micro level. The macro level refers to the instructional strategy level, such as their suggestion to use gaming techniques. The micro level refers to specific elements of a lesson, such as the use of graphics and animation. Lastly, they emphasize that motivation techniques must be individualized, because different students find different things interesting.

Malone's Motivation Theory

In his early research on motivation Malone (1981) suggested three relevant factors: challenge, curiosity, and fantasy. In his more recent work (Malone &

Lepper, 1987) he has added student control. We summarize these four factors below.

Challenge. The most important principle is that the challenge should be adjusted for the student. A lesson should not be too easy, but also not too difficult. Setting challenging goals at the start of the lesson is beneficial. Having uncertain outcomes, wherein the student is not sure if they are attainable or not, increases challenge. Varying the difficulty of material as student performance improves will maintain challenge throughout the lesson.

Curiosity. Malone distinguishes sensory curiosity and cognitive curiosity. Sensory curiosity is aroused by visual or auditory effects which are surprising or which attract attention. Cognitive curiosity is aroused by information which is surprising in that the information conflicts with the student's existing knowledge or expectation, is contradictory, or is in some way incomplete. These situations encourage the student to seek new information that remedies the conflict.

Control. Three rules are relevant to student control: contingency, choice, and power. According to the contingency rule, what the lesson does should be clearly a result of the student's actions and responses. Lessons which give feedback as a function of specific responses, or which follow different paths through the content based on student performance, follow the contingency rule. The choice rule encourages procedures, such as menus and global branching options, that permit the student to determine sequence or lesson parameters such as difficulty. The notion of power is that lessons in which students' actions have "powerful effects" will be very motivating. Such lessons include environments in which the student creates computer programs or uses computer tools such as graphics programs.

Fantasy. Fantasy situations are those which encourage the students to imagine themselves in a situation or which include vivid realistic images of an imaginary context or event. Although fantasy is usually just associated with games, there are many ways it may be incorporated in tutorials and other instructional methodologies. Suggesting to the students in a typing lesson that they are taking a test for a high paying executive secretary position may increase involvement and effort. In an astronomy lesson about the constellations, the fantasy that the students are lost at sea and will use knowledge of the stars to return home may be similarly effective. In any lesson, it may be valuable to encourage the students to envision themselves in a situation where they can really use the information they are learning.

Keller's ARCS Motivation Theory

Another set of suggestions for increasing student motivation comes from the work of Keller (Keller & Suzuki, 1988). Keller's general point of view is that the instructional designer must be proficient at motivation design as well as instructional strategy and content design. Keller indicates four design considerations relevant to creating motivating instruction: Attention, relevance, confidence, and satisfaction, hence the ARCS model.

Attention must not only be gained early in the lesson, but maintained throughout it. Curiosity, as in the Malone theory, is one way to do so. Perceptual and content variety also maintain attention.

Relevance means showing the students that what they are learning will be useful to them. The examples just given for encouraging fantasy, or similar ones, are also examples of showing relevance. A more direct way is for content and examples to be those of interest or importance to the student. In a math lesson, engineering students are more likely to find math problems relevant if they are about engineering problems, while education students are more likely to find the problems relevant if they are classroom grading problems.

Confidence is increased by making expectations for learning clear to the student, by providing reasonable opportunity to be successful in the lesson, and by giving the student personal control. These are similar to Malone's notions of providing challenge and student control.

Satisfaction is increased through activities which enable students to use what they have learned in ways which are real and useful, by providing positive consequences following progress, encouragement during times of difficulty, and by being fair. Fairness is accomplished through lesson consistency, through activities in keeping with stated objectives, and through intelligent and consistent evaluation of student actions.

Motivation in Moderation

We are in agreement with these authors on the importance of designing with student motivation in mind. Motivation is an essential aspect of instruction. A lesson may be perfectly sequenced and worded, yet still fail to teach if students become bored. Although the recommendations made in the above theories are supported by research, they must still be applied intelligently and in moderation. The designer must keep in mind, for example, that although student control is motivating, too much control has been demonstrated to impede learning because students make poor decisions. Similarly, the designer must not go overboard in encouraging fantasy or providing positive consequences. Instructional design is always a series of compromises, balancing competing factors (such as motivation versus program control) to create lessons which are effective. We will return to the importance of motivation when we discuss Drills and Games.

PRESENTATION OF INFORMATION

Mode of Presentations

Mode of presentation means whether information is presented to the student as text, graphics, sound, or a combination of these. Text is the most common way to present information in computer-based instruction. Graphics are the next most common method, and include any visual information which is not text: such as pictures, line drawings, cartoons, bar graphs, line graphs, photographs, and animated images. Graphic presentations greatly enhance instruction about spatial relationships, about objects or procedures that can be visually depicted, or for modeling (showing a student how to do something). Animations allow the computer to demonstrate changes, processes, and procedures in a way few other media can.

Sound is a presentation mode quite different from either text or graphics, both of which are visual. The use of sound in computer-based instruction is not as advanced as the visual modes. Its most common use is for primitive sound effects such as beeps or explosions. The use of sound for music or speech, though useful, is more difficult and less frequent.

Recent advances in computer technology permit easier recording of voice and other sounds for use in lessons. This recording is called *digitization,* because the actual sounds are converted to the digital signals (ones and zeros) of the computer. *Digitized* sound is easier to produce and more realistic than *synthetic* sound, in which program code creates sounds. However, digitized sound consumes more storage space and is less flexible. Some of the newer microcomputers have digital sound capabilities built into them as a standard feature.

Sound is necessary when the information itself is of an aural nature, such as learning music or bird calls, or where the student must be spoken to, as in early reading instruction. Sound is also useful for conveying temporal information such as poetic meter, while visual information is better for spatial information such as maps. Sound is also good for attracting attention even if the student is not looking at the screen. Sound has the *disadvantage* of being ephemeral. When sound is used for important information it should be repeatable.

Research on human learning (Fleming & Levie, 1978) indicates that dual modalities tend to enhance learning. Fleming and Levie were referring primarily to dual sensory modalities (visual, auditory, and tactile), but some other research (Rigney & Lutz, 1976) indicates that correctly combined visual modalities also enhance learning. This is illustrated by the typical method of video instruction, wherein a narrator explains how to do something while the procedure is demonstrated.

Length of Text Presentations

A critical factor affecting the quality of a tutorial is the length of information presentations. The length of a presentation is whatever occurs between two successive student responses. This may mean the length of a passage between questions or the number of successive pictures between problem-solving exercises.

Presentations should be short to increase the frequency of student interaction. The more complex information is, the more important it is to break it into steps with student activity for each step. A science lesson teaching six ways of identifying rocks (such as color, hardness, fracture, and so on) should present one method at a time with questions after each method, rather than presenting all six methods followed by a series of questions.

Appropriate length depends on the subject matter and the age and level of the student. More mature students can generally deal with longer presentations without losing interest or becoming confused. Extended texts of more than a page or two should alert you to potential problems. They may overload memory, cause confusion, or decrease interest.

Most computer displays hold less information than a piece of paper. The display limitations are not much of a disadvantage with text, which is easily split up into pieces. But they frequently present problems for graphics, which may lose their effectiveness when fragmented. Although authors must be aware of them, these limitations probably serve to increase the quality of lessons by preventing authors from displaying too much information at one time.

Layout of Text

Scrolling should always be avoided. Scrolling means adding new text lines to the bottom of the display, and having everything else "jump" up a line to make room for it, with the top line eventually disappearing off the top of the display. Paging, the display of new information from top to bottom, should be used instead. Scrolling is discouraged for many reasons. Most people find it hard to read text when it is scrolling. Scrolling is disconcerting because when text is moving it is hard to distinguish the boundary between new information and old. Lastly, with scrolling, information at the top of the display disappears automatically with the result that important information is sometimes erased unintentionally.

Sentences and paragraphs should be well formatted. This means that lines should not end in the middle of words, and that paragraphs should not begin on the last line of the display, or end on the first line of the next display. Consistent use of indentation or blank lines to indicate new paragraphs should be used. Text should not be squeezed into half of the display leaving the rest almost empty. In general, all of these considerations are the same as for text on paper, but authors of computer-based lessons often do not show the same concern for well-formatted text. Figures 2–17 and 2–18 illustrate a poorly formatted and a well-formatted display, respectively.

Spacing between lines has an effect on the readability of text. Some computer displays have very little blank space between lines. When this is the case double spacing improves the readability of text. Some programming languages provide control over "leading," the space between successive lines. When available it should be adjusted to make text readable and attractive. Newer microcomputers are better in this regard.

Figures 2–17 and 2–18 illustrate a number of the format considerations we have been discussing. Figure 2–17 contains text which is all in upper case, single spaced, crowded to the left side of the display, splits words across lines, uses inconsistent paragraphing conventions, and ends the page in the middle of a sentence. Figure 2–18 corrects all of these errors leaving a display that is much easier to read.

When a combination of text and graphics appear on a display, it is useful

WHERE GLACIERS ARE FOUND

MANY PEOPLE THINK
GLACIERS ARE ONLY FOUND
NEAR THE NORTH AND SOUTH
POLES. IN FACT, GLACIERS
ARE FOUND AT ALMOST EVERY
LATITUDE, FROM THE POLES
TO NEAR THE EQUATOR.

NEAR THE EQUATOR GLACIERS
FORM IN TALL MOUNTAINS. IF
A MOUNTAIN IS VERY TALL, TH
E TOP OF THE MOUNTAIN IS VE
RY COLD AND IT MAY BE
COVERED WITH SNOW ALL

Figure 2-17   A poorly formatted display.

**WHERE GLACIERS
ARE FOUND**

Many people think glaciers are only found
near the north and south poles. In fact,
glaciers are found at almost every latitude,
from the poles to near the equator.

Near the equator glaciers form in tall
mountains. If a mountain is very tall, the top
of the mountain is very cold and it may be
covered with snow all year long.

Figure 2-18   A well-formatted display.

to enclose the primary text in a box, as in Figure 2–19. Many other ways of emphasizing particular segments of text are available, as illustrated in Figure 2–20. Underlining and alternate typefaces are common methods, but not particularly
effective. Blinking text (not illustrated) should never be used. It is annoying and
makes text very difficult to read (Smith & Goodwin, 1972). All capital letters or
inverse writing also make text difficult to read. Boxes and arrows are more effective methods. An excellent technique is the use of large letters. Isolation (Figure
2–21) is also very effective. Remember that any emphasis technique should be
used in moderation or it will cease to be effective.

There is some difference of opinion among computer-based education
developers as to whether text layouts should remain consistent or vary throughout
a lesson. Proponents of varying layouts (Minnesota Educational Computing Con-

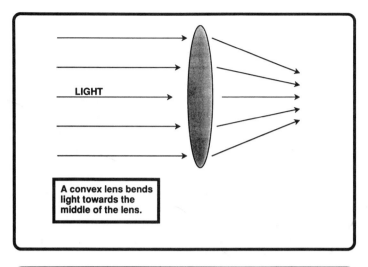

LIGHT

A convex lens bends light towards the middle of the lens.

Figure 2-19 Block of text outlined by a box.

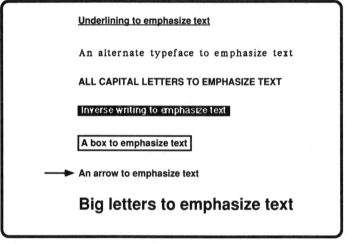

Underlining to emphasize text

An alternate typeface to emphasize text

ALL CAPITAL LETTERS TO EMPHASIZE TEXT

Inverse writing to emphasize text

A box to emphasize text

An arrow to emphasize text

Big letters to emphasize text

Figure 2-20 Methods of emphasizing text.

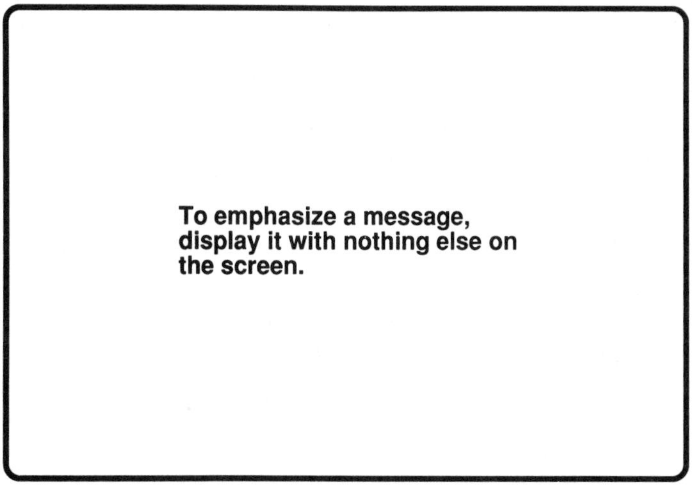

To emphasize a message, display it with nothing else on the screen.

Figure 2-21 Emphasizing text by isolation.

sortium, 1981a) claim that it makes a lesson more interesting and increases the student's attention. We maintain that consistency is more important. Motivation and attention can and should be maintained, but through vehicles other than variable text layout. Readers become comfortable with the conventions of a book or a program, and changes cause them to slow down or become confused. Considerable advantage can be gained with conventions that clearly indicate when new topics are being introduced, where to look for directions, or how to answer questions. A few such conventions are:

Put control options or mouse buttons on the bottom of the display.

Use a consistent prompt for student responses, such as, "Type your answer here."

Start a new display for a change in topic and label it accordingly.

Make it clear when a student key press will add to a display, in contrast to erasing a display and beginning a new one.

Use consistent key presses for frequent actions, such as ⟨return⟩ to move forward. Some programs cause confusion by switching between ⟨return⟩ and ⟨spacebar⟩ for moving forward.

Use consistent margin and paragraph conventions.

Graphics and Animation

New software for microcomputers makes it increasingly easy to produce graphs, pictures, and animations. As a result more and more tutorials use them. The result has been both positive and negative. Dwyer (1978) presents substantial research evidence that, when properly used, pictorial information enhances learning. However, this is not always true, and if used improperly is detrimental.

A major consideration regarding the effectiveness of graphic information is the importance of the information presented. The student is generally attending to *something*. Attention should be focused on the important information in a lesson rather than the unimportant information (Fleming & Levie, 1978). Pictures, especially animated ones, capture attention more than text. Thus, graphic presentations should be chosen based on what is important in the text. Unfortunately, authors frequently produce graphics that are artistically excellent, but are not instructionally useful.

There are many ways graphics should be used in lessons. Three primary uses of graphics during the presentation part of a tutorial are:

As the primary information

As an analogy or mnemonic

As a cue

Figure 2–22 shows a presentation in which a picture is the source of primary information. To explain what a triangle and its parts are without pictures would require textual explanations beyond the reading ability of most children.

Graphic analogy is illustrated in Figure 2–23. The picture of the mountain is is a way of making the main concept, concavity, clearer and more memorable.

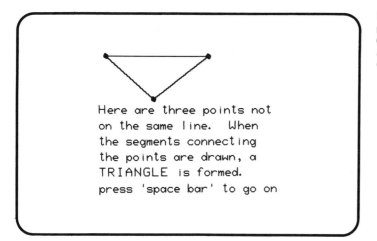

Figure 2-22 Graphics as the primary information in *Triangles* (MECC, 1981b). *(Courtesy of Minnesota Educational Computing Consortium)*

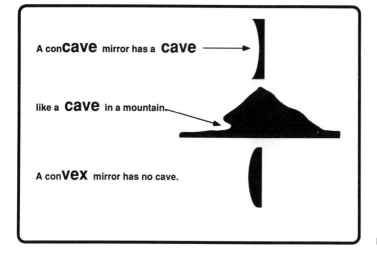

Figure 2-23 Graphic analogy.

Figure 2–24 shows graphics used as a cue, focusing attention on important information, which in this case is text. Similarly, Wilcox, Merrill, & Black (1981) demonstrate the power of graphics to make the content organization clear to students. We will illustrate other uses of graphics when we discuss questions and feedback, and in the chapters about other instructional methodologies.

Let us now consider some general recommendations about the proper use of graphics in lessons. Graphic information should be consistent with and integrated into the rest of the instructional message. For instance, a lesson teaching about the water cycle in nature is enhanced by a diagram oriented around a circle to emphasize the nature of the water cycle. Figure 2–25 is an example.

Excessive detail or realism should be avoided in graphics. Details can overload memory and confuse the student, who will not know what to focus on. Realistic pictures generally contain more details than simplified ones. Simple line

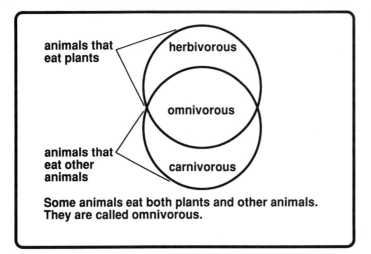

Figure 2-24 Graphics as a cue for important text information.

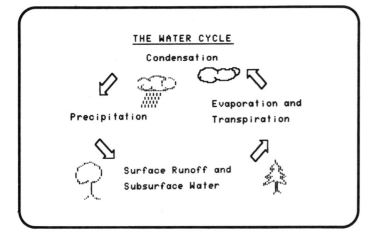

Figure 2-25 Graphics depicting circular nature of a process. *(Courtesy of Minnesota Educational Computing Consortium)*

drawings may demonstrate a point more clearly than realistic pictures (Dwyer, 1978).

Graphics containing a lot of information should be broken down, if possible, into simpler parts. It is not as easy to break up graphics as it is text. A useful technique is to produce *part* of a graphic, allowing the student to inspect or read about that first, and then to *overlay* the next part or add details, gradually building up a large or complex presentation. Figures 2–26 through 2–28 show a series of pictures in which the parts of a laboratory apparatus are overlaid until the complete device is assembled.

Students should control the length of time they look at graphic presentations. Pictures should not disappear after a specific number of seconds, but when the student presses a key indicating readiness to go on. This is more difficult to accomplish for animations, which by their nature change. These should end with an option to repeat the sequence.

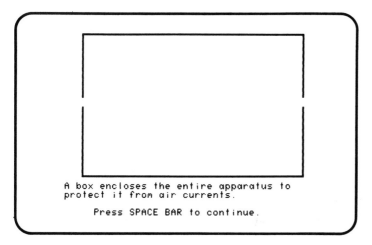

A box encloses the entire apparatus to protect it from air currents.

Press SPACE BAR to continue.

Figure 2-26 First part of a graphic overlay in *Electron Charge* (MECC, 1982). *(Courtesy of Minnesota Educational Computing Consortium)*

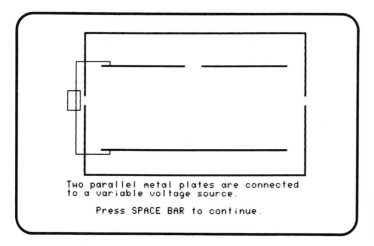

Two parallel metal plates are connected to a variable voltage source.

Press SPACE BAR to continue.

Figure 2-27 New graphic information added to the display. *(Courtesy of Minnesota Educational Computing Consortium)*

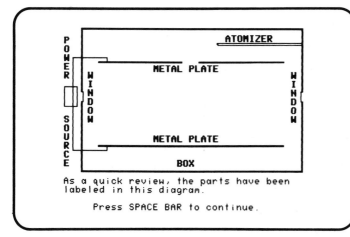

As a quick review, the parts have been labeled in this diagram.

Press SPACE BAR to continue.

Figure 2-28 The final form, after a number of graphic overlays. *(Courtesy of Minnesota Educational Computing Consortium)*

Pictures should be presented simultaneously with related text, so the student can inspect the illustration and the explanation together, as in Figure 2–22. Changing pages between an illustration and its textual description makes comprehension more difficult. See Merrill & Bunderson (1981) for further suggestions on the proper use of graphics.

Color and Its Use

The use of color is closely akin to that of graphics. As with graphics, new hardware and software make the use of color increasingly easy. While there is some evidence that color can enhance learning (Dwyer, 1978), it does not appear to be as powerful as some other techniques, such as animation (Baek & Layne, 1988). Also like graphics, color is easily misused so as to be ineffective or even detrimental.

Color is effective for attracting attention. However, the more color is used the less it will do so, because attention is always drawn to what is novel.

Color may increase the information capacity of a display. Imagine a graph with lines showing the effect of the economy on the earnings of several businesses. With more than about five lines, it is difficult to distinguish one line from another. Using dotted, dashed, crossed, and other types of lines just increases confusion. Colors make the lines clearly distinguishable.

The attention-getting effect of color can and should be used, like that of graphics, to attract attention to important information. For example, a lesson may present corrective feedback in bright yellow. This technique can be easily overdone. Imagine a lesson in which primary information is displayed in green, corrective feedback in yellow, directions in red, hints in blue, and section titles in orange. The student will forget what each color is for and will ignore them.

There is always a danger when using color graphics that the information may be lost on students who are color blind, about one person in fifteen. When possible, use color as a redundant cue. This means when using color to convey information, try to convey the information in another way as well. If different lines on a graph are drawn with different colors, label them with text as well. An exception is when the objective of the lesson deals with color, as in an art lesson. In such a case it is difficult to convey the essential information in any way other than with color.

Some colors, especially those near the center of the visible spectrum such as yellow and green, are easier to perceive than others (Durrett & Trezona, 1982; Silverstein, 1987). Colors at the extremes of the visible spectrum, the reds and blues, are the most difficult colors perceptually and should be avoided for text or detailed pictures. Furthermore, some color combinations are better than others. One should avoid red with green, blue with yellow, green with blue, and red with blue. More than four to seven simultaneous colors should be avoided (Smith, 1987), especially for beginning students.

The use of color in a tutorial should be consistent with common usages in society. Using green to mean "stop" and red for "go" will result in errors. Do not show businessmen graphs in which red indicates profits and black indicates losses.

For more discussion of color in computer software, consult Durrett (1987) and Shneiderman (1987).

Text quality

Leanness.   Burke (1982) uses the word *leanness* to describe an important quality of a tutorial. The program should say just enough to teach what is desired, and no more. This applies not only to text descriptions, but to examples of concepts, sample applications of rules, pictures for demonstration purposes, and so on. In support of lean presentations, Reder & Anderson (1980) demonstrated that students learn the main points of a textbook better from summaries of the main points than from the text itself. This was even true when the main points in the textbook were underlined.

In addition to this evidence, it should be obvious that students will require less time to study such a lesson. Furthermore, validation and revision of a lean program is easier. If you evaluate a long program and find that it teaches well, you will not know what parts of the program were most responsible for learning. It will be difficult to shorten the lesson and increase its efficiency. If a lean program works well, however, you have no need to shorten it. If it does not teach well enough, you will have less concern about adding material to improve it.

Transitions.   Maintaining a clear flow of ideas in a computer tutorial is more difficult than in textbooks. Limited display capacity requires changing pages more frequently. It is difficult for a student to distinguish a change in display that represents a continuation, from one that represents changing to an entirely different topic, the equivalent of changing chapters in a book. A good tutorial uses clear transition statements such as, "Now that you know what glaciers are, we discuss the way in which they are formed." Similarly, a lesson should inform the student whether a key press or mouse click will cause a continuation or a change in topic. Contrast these two directions.

> Press ⟨return⟩ to continue.
> Press ⟨return⟩ for the next section: HOW GLACIERS ARE FORMED.

Clarity.   A lesson should avoid ambiguous language and should use consistent terminology. Ambiguity occurs frequently in technical areas, in which specific technical terms have come into everyday usage with less specific meanings. When using such terms in their technical sense, it may be necessary to point that out so students do not assume the common usage. Ambiguity is also caused by using pronouns with unclear referents. Consider the following directions from a chemistry laboratory. "The liquid is then poured into a beaker. It must be heated." It is not clear whether the liquid is heated before being poured into the beaker, if the beaker is supposed to be heated before the liquid is poured into it, or if heating takes place after pouring.

Use of consistent terminology means two things. First, more than one word should not refer to the same thing. The reader may think there is some subtle difference between the two. Secondly, the same word should not be used at different times to mean different things, which produces ambiguity.

Reading Level. The reading level of a tutorial must be suited to the students who will use it. It is common to find beginning arithmetic lessons, to be used by first grade students, with directions and questions at the third grade level. Readability formulas are useful to determine the approximate reading level of a lesson or segments of it.

Mechanics. Mechanics is a characteristic of text quality which should not be a factor at all. It refers to the use of correct grammar, spelling, and punctuation. Unlike clarity, there are established standards for mechanics, and it remains only for authors to follow them. When a lesson has poor mechanics, students view the author of the lesson as less of an authority, and do not take the instruction as seriously. They may also learn poor mechanics themselves.

Type of Information and Text Organization

Organization should be a function of the nature of what is being taught. Four common types of information are:

Verbal information
Concepts
Rules and principles
Skills

Verbal Information. Verbal information may present many kinds of relationships: temporal (do A after you do B), causative (A causes B), categorical (A is a member of B), exemplary (A is an example of B), characteristic (A is a characteristic or property of B), or comparative (A and B are compared for their similarity and differences). To teach verbal information, the individual elements must be presented in a logical order and the relationships between them stressed. Organizational summaries listing the elements and their relationships are important. Such summaries may be textual, in the form of lists of points or outlines (Figure 2–29), or pictorial, with textual information arranged spatially, and connected with arrows or other symbols to show the relationships (Figure 2–30).

Concepts. Conceptual information includes concrete concepts such as "cat" or "circle," and defined concepts such as the chemical concept "oxidation" or the social concept "city." Some concepts are very difficult to define (for students and teachers alike) such as the concepts "love," "sentence," or "theme of a short story."

A concept is a class of things with common characteristics that are distinguished from other things not sharing those characteristics. Much of what we learn is concepts. Tutorials teaching concepts typically use the following organization.

Figure 2-29 A text summary.

Summary of lesson COMMAS

Commas are used:

- to separate items in a series,

- following introductory phrases,

- preceding coordinating conjunctions which link main clauses, and

- to separate parenthetical elements in a sentence.

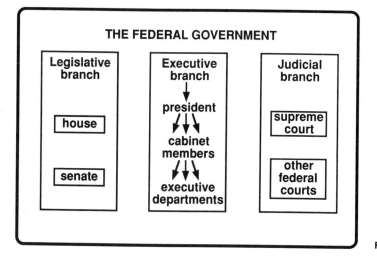

Figure 2-30 A graphic summary.

First the characteristics which define the concept are taught. These are called the *relevant features*. Teaching the characteristics of a concept is frequently done by stating a definition in terms of the relevant features.

Next, simple instances of the concept are given, such as a dog being an instance of the concept "animal." Simple instances are those which contain all or many of the relevant features, and few or no irrelevant features or incidental features. Irrelevant features are neither necessary nor commonly possessed by instances of a concept. Incidental features are those commonly possessed but not necessary to a concept.

Simple non-instances of the concept are given for contrast. Non-instances are those things not of the class. Simple non-instances contain few or no relevant or incidental features, and many irrelevant features.

After the student has learned the concept at the level of simple instances and non-instances, difficult instances and non-instances are introduced. Difficult instances are those with few relevant features and many irrelevant and incidental features. Difficult non-instances have many relevant and incidental features and few irrelevant features.

To teach the concept "animal" a lesson would begin with cats and dogs (simple instances) and contrast them to pencils and books (simple non-instances). After the child masters the classification of simple cases, the lesson might introduce insects (difficult instances for a child) and stuffed teddy bears (difficult non-instances because they share many of the features of real animals).

This technique for teaching concepts has proven very effective. For more information see Engelmann (1969, 1980), Fleming & Levie (1978), Klausmeier & Feldmann (1975), Tennyson & Park (1980), Merrill and Tennyson (1977), and Ali (1981). Concepts will be discussed further in Chapter 8.

Rules and Principles. Rules and principles, which play an important role in the mathematical, physical, and social sciences, are taught in one of two ways. The more common method is the *Rule-Example* or expository method. Using the Rule-Example method, the rules or principles and their foundations are directly stated and then demonstrated, after which the student is guided in their application. The *Example-Rule* approach, on the other hand, demonstrates applications, and leads the student to infer or discover the rule or principle. Advocates of the Rule-Example approach claim that it works better for most students. Advocates of the Example-Rule approach claim it leads to better understanding. Research evidence appears to support the Rule-Example approach (Klausmeier, Ghatala, & Frayer, 1974; Klausmeier & Feldman, 1975; Koran, 1971; Merrill, 1974), although there is some contrary evidence (Lahey, 1981).

Skills. Skills are generally taught using step-by-step descriptions, demonstrations, and modeling of the activity the student is to learn. Most skills can be broken down into component subskills. When that is the case, presentations and modeling of the component subskills are usually done first. As the student learns the subskills, the more complex skills are described, demonstrated, and practiced.

J.R. Anderson (1976, 1982) contends that the acquisition of *procedural knowledge* depends on the student first learning *propositional knowledge* (verbal information, concepts, rules, and principles), and then converting that into procedural knowledge, primarily through practice. Wilson (1985) recommends the following steps in designing procedural learning:

Perform a path analysis to determine steps, sequence, and decisions.
Begin with a simple example of the procedure.
Provide help on the difficult steps.
Give an overview or summary of the steps.
Teach the principles that underlie the procedure.

Content Structures.   Hannum (1988) discusses how different subject matters have different inherent organizations. Three common structures are hierarchical (Figure 2–31), web (Figure 2–32), and the classification matrix (Figure
2–33). Not only does determining the structure help suggest a good teaching sequence, but demonstrating the structure to students (as with Figures 2–31 through
2–33) will help them understand the organization and increase their learning.

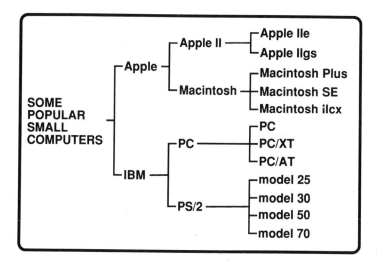

Figure 2-31   Hierarchical structure.

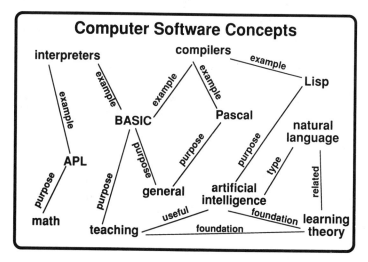

Figure 2-32   Web structure.

Instructional Prompts

Prompts are used to guide the student and provide hints. Examples of
prompts are emphasis of important words, suggestions to the student to carefully
inspect a picture, or telling the student that "the next point is very important."

Programming Language Characteristics

	Pascal	C	BASIC	Lisp
Method	compiled	compiled	interpreted and compiled	compiled
Purpose	general	general	general and teaching	artificial intelligence
Structured	yes	yes	no	yes
Difficulty	hard	hard	easy	very hard
Power	good	very good	poor	good

Figure 2-33 Classification matrix structure.

Analogy is an effective type of prompt. Analogy uses previous knowledge to make new information more comprehensible, such as explaining the parts and functions of a computer system by comparing them to the parts of the human body and their functions. Other prompting techniques are the use of mnemonics for remembering lists (such as the mnemonic HOMES, which cues the first letters of the names of the five Great Lakes), and aphorisms for remembering rules (such as the old weather predictor, "red sky at morning, sailor take warning, red sky at night, sailor's delight").

Prompts are classified as either *formal* or *thematic* (Markle, 1969). Formal prompts aid the student by pointing out the form of the answer to a question or of an action the student should make. Underlining important words is a common formal prompt. In contrast, a thematic prompt is one that tells the student about the theme, or topic, of the answer. Following an incorrect answer, the hint, "Try again, the answer has to do with entropy" is a thematic prompt, while the hint, "Try again, the answer has five letters" deals with the form of the answer and is a formal prompt. Analogies are thematic prompts, while mnemonics are usually formal prompts. Thematic prompts generally enhance comprehension while formal prompts aid recall.

Instructional prompts in a tutorial are usually "faded" as the lesson progresses. That is, fewer and fewer prompts are given until eventually the student must respond without them. Some tutorials are based on the strategy of frequent prompting at the beginning, and fading all prompts toward the end. This method is very effective for teaching information that must be memorized, such as foreign language vocabulary.

For prompts to be effective they must be salient. Salience is increased through attention-getting devices such as color, animation, large letters in text, and pointing with arrows. Salience is also affected by physical placement. Information is more salient toward the center of the computer display than at the corners. Information is also more salient when surrounded by empty space, rather than by other information. Excessive detail in graphics will decrease the effectiveness of prompts, because they will not be as salient.

Providing Help

Students should be able to get help when using a lesson. They frequently need help of two types, procedural and informational. Procedural help is essential, and refers to help operating the lesson, such as changing pages. This information is usually provided in the directions, so procedural help may send the student back to the directions.

Informational help means help with the content. This includes accessing more detailed descriptions, more examples or sample problems, or explanations worded more simply. Other informational helps include glossaries, references, and diagrams. While a lesson should always provide procedural help, provision for informational help depends on the nature and difficulty of the lesson.

When help of either sort is provided, it must be easy for students to access. If a student does not remember how to get help, its usefulness is completely lost. The best way to access help is with a mouse sensitive button (Figure 2–34). Although keys are often used for help (such as the *?*, *esc,* or *control-h* keys, or a key labeled *help*) students forget or do not use them. Mouse buttons are easily used and appear on the screen as constant reminders when help is available.

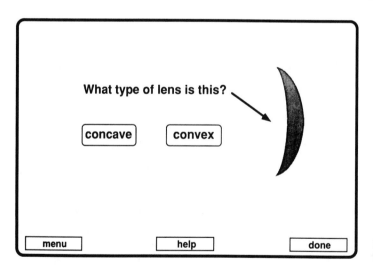

Figure 2-34 A mouse sensitive button for requesting help.

QUESTIONS AND RESPONSES

The Function of Questions

A lesson which presents information without demanding interaction with the student will not be successful. In tutorials, the most common method of interaction is to pose questions that the student must answer. Although some educators maintain that tutorial instruction relies too much on asking questions (Jonassen, 1988) or that the effects of questions on learning are still unproven (Andre, Mueller, Womack, Smid, & Tuttle, 1980), a sizable amount of research supports the facilitative effect of questions in instruction (Anderson & Biddle, 1975; Hall, 1983). Questions serve several important purposes (Wager & Wager, 1985). They keep the student attentive to the lesson, provide practice, encourage deeper processing, and assess how well the student remembers and understands information. Lastly, by virtue of assessing recall and comprehension, questions provide a basis for lesson sequencing. That is, a program determines what information to present next based on a student's responses.

Frequency of Questions

Questions (or similar interactions) should occur frequently. As discussed previously, long information presentations are best divided with interspersed questions. The student reads or inspects small amounts of information and then answers a question, thus enhancing comprehension and recall. The more the student interacts with the program in this way, the more attention will be maintained, the more the student will enjoy the lesson, and the more learning will be facilitated.

Types of Questions

Questions can be categorized into two basic types. Alternate-response questions are those in which the student chooses the correct response or responses from a list. These include true/false, matching, multiple-choice, and marking questions. Constructed-response questions require the student to produce rather than select a response, and in computer-based instruction are most frequently completion or short-answer questions.

Alternate-Response Questions. Although all four types of alternate-response questions are used in computer-based instruction, we recommend the use of multiple-choice and marking questions. True/false questions are less reliable because the student has a good chance of answering correctly by guessing and a correct response is not a strong indication that the student has learned the material. Matching questions tends to be complicated in format even if the information tested is simple. The directions needed for a student to enter responses to matching questions may be long and difficult to comprehend, although matching questions using the mouse are better than those using the keyboard (Figure 2–35). A matching question can always be divided up into a number of multiple-choice questions. Figure 2–36 shows a multiple-choice question constructed from the matching question in Figure 2–35.

Multiple-Choice Questions. Multiple-choice questions are the most common type of alternate-response question. Several considerations ensure their quality.

Figure 2-35 A matching question using the mouse.

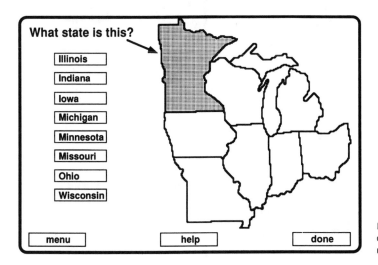

Figure 2-36 A multiple-choice question made from the previous matching question.

Multiple-choice questions may use letter keys (Figure 2–37), number keys (Figure 2–38), a moving cursor (Figure 2–39), or a mouse to select options (Figure 2–40). The best method is the mouse, assuming one is available. It is easiest to learn and least error prone. Number choices are often confused with numeric answers. Letter choices tend to be error prone. And the moving cursor requires a lot of key pressing.

The incorrect alternatives (called foils) of a multiple-choice question must be plausible. The student should not be able to determine the correct answer simply by eliminating obviously wrong ones. A good way to develop a multiple-choice question is to first construct a short-answer question, try it out on students, and then use the most common wrong responses as the foils in the multiple-choice form of the question.

What is the largest organ in the human body?

a. the brain

b. the liver

c. the lungs

Type a letter and press (return).

Figure 2-37 Multiple-choice question with letter choices.

What is the largest organ in the human body?

1. the brain

2. the liver

3. the lungs

Type a number and press (return).

Figure 2-38 Multiple-choice question with numeric choices.

What is the largest organ in the human body?

the brain

● the liver

the lungs

Use the arrow keys to raise (↑) or lower (↓) the marker (●) to your choice. Then press (return).

Figure 2-39 Multiple-choice question with moving cursor choices.

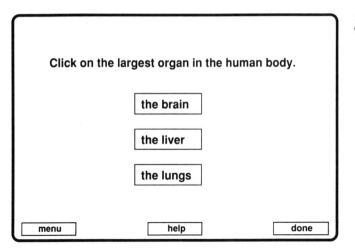

Figure 2-40 Multiple-choice question with mouse selection.

About four alternatives should be given. Although a greater number of alternatives decreases the likelihood of guessing, it also makes a question more difficult to construct and more confusing.

The correct answer should not be given away by irrelevant features of the alternatives. Common errors are for the correct answer to be the longest one, or for incorrect alternatives to contain grammatical or spelling errors.

The stem of the question (that part above the alternatives) should be a complete sentence. A question should not begin "The law of conservation of matter and energy means:". Rather, it should begin "What does the law of conservation of matter and energy mean?"

There should only be one correct answer among the alternatives. Related to this, questions should avoid alternatives such as "none of the above" and "all of the above."

Marking Questions.   Marking questions (Figures 2-41 and 2-42) require the student to respond by marking parts of the display. The question in Figure 2-41 is like a multiple-choice question with more than one correct answer. Figure 2-42 shows a question testing similar content, but in the more natural context of a regular sentence. As in these examples, marking questions are easiest to answer with a mouse, rather than the keyboard.

Constructed-Response Questions.   There are three major types of constructed-response questions: completion, short-answer, and essay questions. Only the first two are common in computer-based instruction. Even with today's sophisticated microcomputers, it is impossible for a program to analyze an essay response and determine if the student understands the material.

Completion Questions.   Completion questions (Figures 2-43, 2-44, and 2-45) have one or more missing words that the student must fill in. The primary

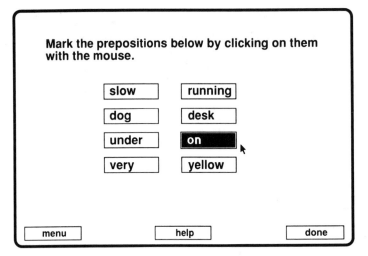

Mark the prepositions below by clicking on them with the mouse.

slow	running
dog	desk
under	**on**
very	yellow

| menu | help | done |

Figure 2-41 A marking question, much like multiple-choice. The student selects with the mouse.

Mark the prepositions in the sentence below by clicking on them with the mouse.

The boy ran **over** the hill and under the bridge **on** his way home.

| menu | help | done |

Figure 2-42 A marking question in the context of a sentence. The student selects with the mouse.

Complete this statement.

The three [_____] of rocks are sedimentary, [_____], and metamorphic.

Click on a box to type a word into it.

| menu | help | done |

Figure 2-43 A completion question.

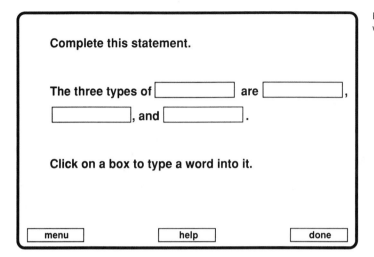

Figure 2-44 A completion question with too much missing information.

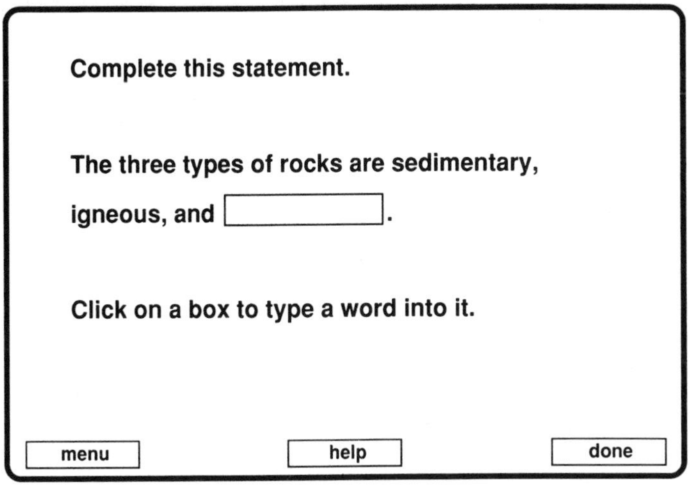

Figure 2-45 A good completion question, having one missing word at the end.

considerations for completion questions are the importance of the missing words, the number of missing words, and their location.

Only words of significance should be blanked out, such as key concept names. Questions will be artificially difficult if details or unimportant words are missing. Furthermore, students assume that the missing words are important, and begin to focus on that information.

There should not be too many blanks in a question. With many blanks, the entire meaning of a statement is lost. Figure 2–45 illustrates a better question than Figure 2–44 because there are fewer blanks. The blanks should be near or at the end of the question. Blanks near the beginning of a statement force the student to hold the location of the missing information in mind until the end of the sentence, thus making it less comprehensible. Figure 2–45 is the best of the three examples because it has only one blank at the end of the statement.

Short-Answer Questions.   Short-answer questions require the student to type words or numbers (Figures 2–46, 2–47, and 2–48). Figure 2–46 shows a short-answer question that requires the student to enter a single word. A single-word response is much easier for a computer program to judge than the multiple-word response required in Figure 2–47. Figure 2–48 shows a problem-solving question which requires a numeric response. Such questions are common in computer-based math and science lessons. The length of expected responses in short-answer questions should be reasonably short, both to prevent typographical errors and to facilitate judging.

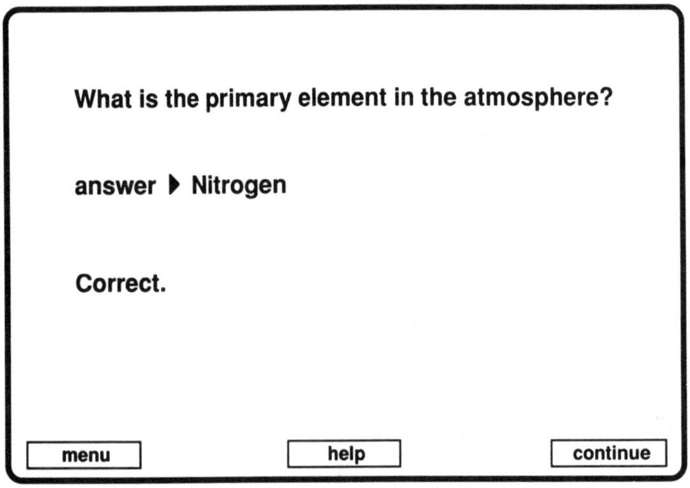

What is the primary element in the atmosphere?

answer ▶ Nitrogen

Correct.

menu		help		continue

Figure 2-46   A single-word short-answer question.

What principle allows the branches of the Federal Government to prevent any one branch from exerting too much control?

answer ▶ checks and balances

Correct.

menu		help		continue

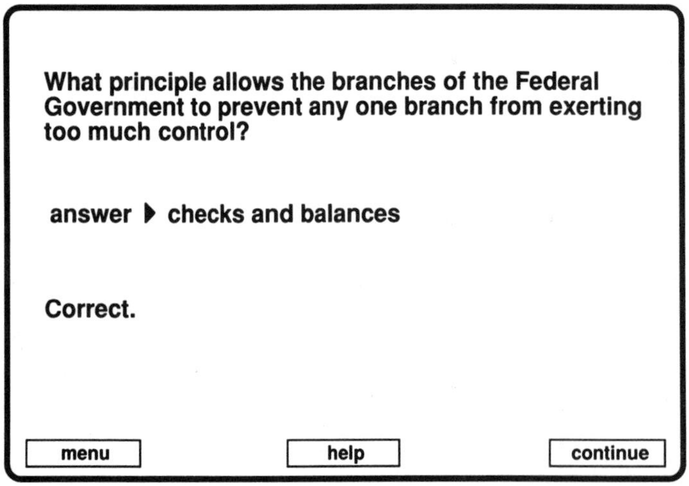

Figure 2-47   A multiple-word short-answer question.

A 5 kilogram weight is at rest. Then a force is applied which accelerates it at a rate of 20 meters per second squared.

What will the weight's displacement be after 10 seconds?

Give your answer in meters.

answer ▶

Type a number and press (return).

Figure 2-48 A numeric short-answer question.

Advantages of the Different Types of Questions.   Alternate-response questions are generally easier to program and require little typing to respond. Students are less likely to make errors unrelated to the instructional content, such as spelling errors. In contrast, constructed-response questions are easier to write, and reduce student guessing. Many educators maintain that alternate-response questions primarily test recognition of the correct answer, while constructed-response questions test recall, which is more important in most real-life situations. Although this is generally true, the most important issue is whether questions test comprehension, in contrast to either recognition or recall. This issue is addressed in the next section.

Other Factors Affecting Quality

Assessing Comprehension.   According to R.C. Anderson (1972), questions frequently test recall or recognition, although they are intended to test comprehension. This happens because many questions are merely statements from the text rephrased into question form, called *verbatim questions,* having the same key words as the original text. The student can answer such questions by remembering key words, rather than by understanding the meaning. To test comprehension, three types of questions are recommended: *paraphrase, new-application,* and *categorical* questions.

Paraphrase questions rephrase statements in the presentations using synonyms. This makes it impossible for the student to answer based on recall of key words. New-application questions require the student to apply a rule or principle to a new situation. If the student has just learned about the effects of supply and demand in the United States economy, a new-application question might deal with the effects of supply and demand in the British economy. Categorical questions require the student to apply rules or principles to subordinate or superordinate classes. If a lesson has presented information about respiration in mammals, a superordinate question would ask about respiration in animals, and a subordinate question would ask about respiration in primates.

Reading Level.   The difficulty of answering a question is not just a function of the difficulty of the lesson's information. Many of the factors we have discussed determine how difficult the question itself is to read and comprehend. The reading level of the text in a question is another such factor. Readability formulas provide an estimate of question adequacy in this regard.

Abbreviations.   Abbreviations generally increase the difficulty of a question. Abbreviations should be defined the first time used in presentations, and should be avoided in questions.

Negative Words.   Negative words should be avoided in questions. The question in Figure 2–50 is preferable to that in Figure 2–49.

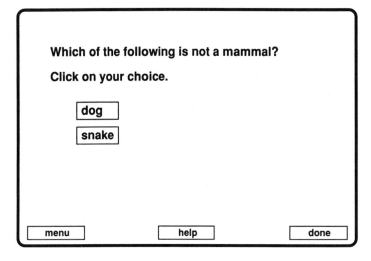

Figure 2-49   A poor question, having negative words.

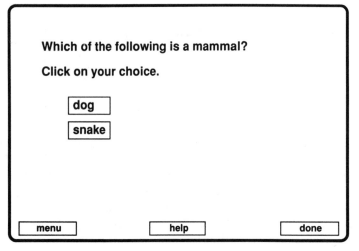

Figure 2-50   A good question, having no negative words.

Scrolling. Scrolling should never occur in questions. In some lessons, when a student gives multiple incorrect responses to a question and receives feedback a number of times, the various responses and feedback messages fill the display and cause scrolling. When this occurs, the question typically disappears from the screen. Erasing old responses and feedback and displaying new ones in the same place permits any number of attempts without scrolling.

Use of Graphics in Questions

Few authors capitalize upon the potential for graphics in questions. There are two main ways graphics may be used in this regard: as the context of the question, and as a hint or prompt.

Graphics as the Context. Figure 2–51, from a lesson entitled *Interpreting Graphs* (Dugdale & Kibbey, 1983), shows a question in which a picture of a graph is the context of the question. That is, the answer lies in the student's comprehension of the picture. Figure 2–52, from a lesson entitled *Decimal Darts* (Control Data Corporation, 1981), which deals with identifying decimal numbers on the number line, also uses graphics as the context of questions. Not only must the student understand the picture, but the student response consists of manipulating the picture by specifying numbers, and thus shooting darts at the balloons. A third example is shown in Figure 2–53, a lesson about reading the micrometer. Again, the essence of the question is to understand the picture, which in this case is a simplified picture of a tool the student must learn to operate.

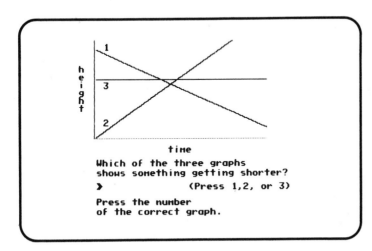

Figure 2-51 Graphics as the main context of a question in *Interpreting Graphs*. (Courtesy of Sharon Dugdale, Dave Kibbey, and the publisher, *CONDUIT, The University of Iowa*)

Graphics as a Prompt. Figure 2–54, from a lesson about the symbolic names of chemical elements, shows the use of graphics as a prompt. The goal is to teach the shorthand symbols for the elements (H for Hydrogen, He for Helium, Li for Lithium, and so on). This could be accomplished without a picture of the periodic table. However, by asking questions with the periodic table in view, the stu-

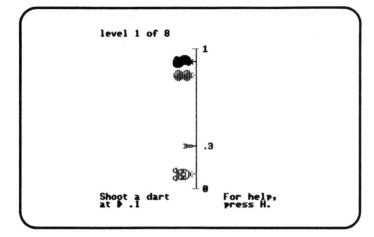

Figure 2-52 Graphics as the main context of a question in *Decimal Darts. (Courtesy of Control Data Corporation)*

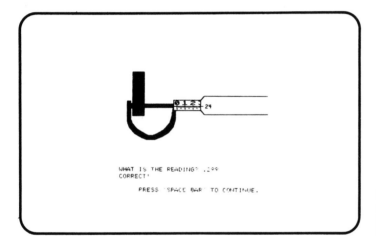

Figure 2-53 Graphics as the main context of a question in *Micrometer* (MECC, 1980). *(Courtesy of Minnesota Educational Computing Consortium)*

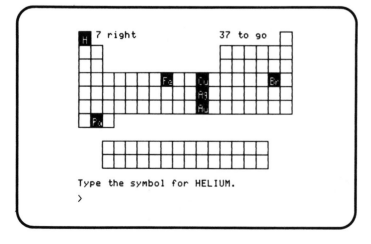

Figure 2-54 Graphics as a hint in *General Chemistry* (Smith & Chabay, 1983). *(Courtesy of COMPress)*

dent who understands the structure of that diagram receives an additional hint for answering the questions. For instance, at the 19th element the student might not recognize the abbreviation K. But seeing that its position is below that of Sodium, the student may remember that it is Potassium, an element with similar properties.

Question Relevance

Questions should require the student to deal with important information. Questions about details, used merely to keep the student active, will focus attention on unimportant information. If the student is to learn general concepts, questions about general concepts must be asked. Although most authors realize this, they frequently ask questions about unimportant information because they are easier to write.

Placement of Questions

Questions may appear before or after the information assessed. Questions prior to presentations are rhetorical questions which motivate the student to search for the answer. Research indicates that questions asked before presentations will facilitate learning the information they cover, while questions asked after presentations facilitate the learning of all the material presented (Anderson & Biddle, 1975). It may be beneficial to use questions in both ways; prior to presentations to focus attention on important information, and afterwards to enhance general attention and provide practice.

When a question appears that must be answered (in contrast to a rhetorical question), students will typically apply themselves to responding, and other information on the display tends to be ignored. For this reason, if information must be read prior to answering a question, it should be displayed prior to the appearance of the question.

Mode of Response

The mode of response defines the way in which the response is entered into the computer. Our illustrations have assumed that responses are entered by typing on a keyset or clicking with a mouse. The advantage of the keyset is its flexibility. It can be used for both short alternate-response questions and long constructed-response questions. The problem with the keyset is that it requires typing skill; most students make many typing errors. Typing also forces most students to look away from the computer display to see the keyboard. Important changes on the display may occur during this time and not be noticed as the student types.

The mouse is superior for pointing and drawing. It does not require typing skill and keeps attention focused on the screen. Less common devices for pointing and drawing responses are touch panels and light pens. Both are similar to the mouse and easier to learn to operate, but not as accurate or reliable. Any of these pointing devices is superior for questions that require multiple selection.

Contrast the question in Figure 2–55, with complicated directions for the keyboard, with the same mouse-oriented question in Figure 2–56.

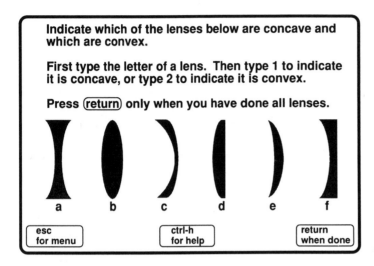

Figure 2-55 Keyboard question with complicated directions.

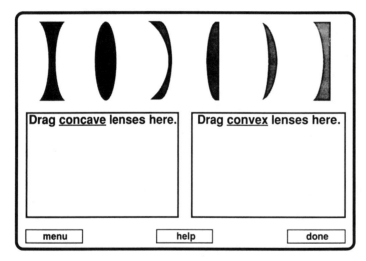

Figure 2-56 Mouse question with simple directions.

Since the mouse has become very popular on microcomputers, some other pointing devices, notably the touch panel, light pen, and graphics tablet, have become less common. Pointing devices have been classified into two types, direct and indirect (Whitefield, 1986). Direct devices such as the touch panel and light pen are those in which the student's physical act of pointing is toward the display itself and the actual display object. Indirect devices (mice and graphics tablets) are those in which the student's physical action is to move a device which is not oriented toward the display but rather is beside the computer on the desk. An icon on the computer screen, usually a small arrow, moves as the pointing device is moved and shows the part of the display being pointed at. Direct devices tend to be easier to learn. But indirect devices are more accurate, reliable, and do not obscure the user's view of the display while pointing.

Another response mode is speech. At this time, speech input is very primitive. Most devices allow only limited vocabularies for one or a few individuals. Inexpensive and effective speech input devices are under development, and this promises to be an important response mode in the future. It will be especially useful for people not yet proficient with writing or typing. Programs utilizing speech presentations should also benefit from speech input. Instruction in elementary reading requires speech input of a quality computers do not yet possess. Speech may also pose problems, for speech is imprecise and tends to be more wordy than necessary (Dear, 1987).

Response Economy

The amount of typing or other physical activity required to produce a response should be as little as necessary. Multiple-choice questions have high response economy. Pointing devices like the mouse tend to facilitate response economy. When it is necessary for a question to be answered with words or phrases, the amount of typing can still be kept to a minimum. Short responses prevent input errors and are easier to judge.

Longer responses may be improved by splitting them into parts. Rather than asking "What are Newton's three laws of motion?" a program may ask three questions: "What is Newton's first law of motion?" "What is Newton's second law of motion?" and "What is Newton's third law of motion?"

The Response Prompt

A response prompt is a symbol which indicates that the computer is waiting for a response. When a response prompt is displayed, anything the student types will appear immediately to the right of the prompt. The most common are a flashing box, a flashing underline character, or a question mark. Usually a response prompt immediately follows a phrase describing what the student is to type, such as "Type your answer" or "Press the letter of your choice."

The response prompt signals the exact place on the screen that the student response will appear. It is important that students see their responses as they are typed to be sure they are not making spelling or format errors. The placement of the prompt is therefore important, because the student must clearly see it. Some authors feel that the prompt should appear immediately to the right of a question (Minnesota Educational Computing Consortium, 1981a), as shown in Figure 2–57. In this example, the student's response would appear next to the triangle, which is the response prompt for this question.

Our preference is to put the response prompt, which should not flash, a line or two below the question and near the left margin. A word or short phrase may precede the prompt for clarification, as shown in Figure 2–58. This method

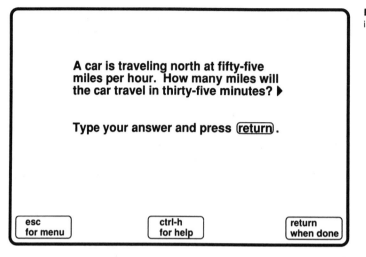

Figure 2-57 The response prompt is difficult to notice in this display.

A car is traveling north at fifty-five miles per hour. How many miles will the car travel in thirty-five minutes? ▶

Type your answer and press (return).

| esc for menu | ctrl-h for help | return when done |

A car is traveling north at fifty-five miles per hour. How many miles will the car travel in thirty-five minutes?

answer ▶

Type your answer and press (return).

| esc for menu | ctrl-h for help | return when done |

Figure 2-58 The response prompt properly placed, below the question and near the left side.

makes the response prompt more noticeable. It also leaves more room for typing longer answers.

For pointing at responses with a mouse, it is important to make the selection areas obvious. A message indicating a mouse response is awaited (Figure 2-59) is also beneficial, otherwise students are likely to wait for something to happen.

Other Types of Student Interaction

We have placed the emphasis here on questions and student responding. Historically this has been the primary kind of interaction in CBI tutorials. It is also the easiest for the novice developer to produce. However, CBI professionals agree that questions answered by students alone do not fully utilize the computer's

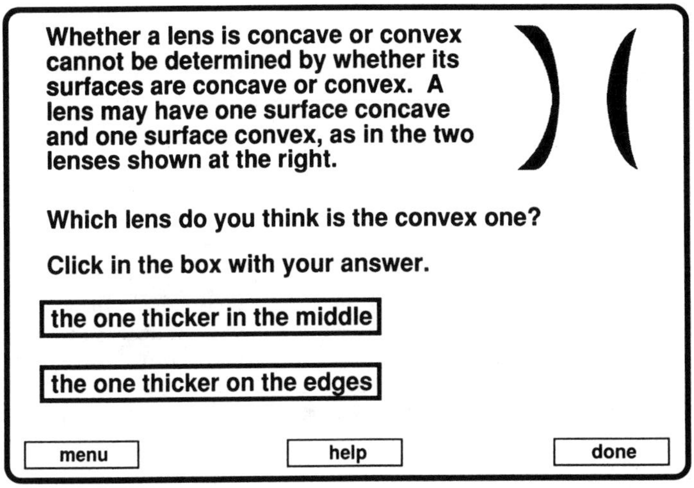

Whether a lens is concave or convex
cannot be determined by whether its
surfaces are concave or convex. A
lens may have one surface concave
and one surface convex, as in the two
lenses shown at the right.

Which lens do you think is the convex one?

Click in the box with your answer.

the one thicker in the middle

the one thicker on the edges

menu   help   done

Figure 2-59 Highlighting mouse responses and indicating that a mouse response is required.

power and probably do not facilitate student thinking as much as some other types of interaction. While we disagree with Jonassen's (1988) contention that questions have not been proven to facilitate learning (c.f. Anderson & Biddle, 1975), we agree that other methods are important as well. Allowing students to ask questions, to take notes, to construct diagrams, and to generate analogies are some of Jonassen's recommendations. To this we add interactions between students. Tutorial programs need not be constructed for use by just one student at a time. Lessons may assume two students working together and promote interactions between the students, asking each other questions and discussing answers. Another technique is for the computer to ask an open-ended question, have one student answer it, and have the other student judge if it is correct and enter that into the computer. The second student acts as the eyes and ears for the computer—allowing complex-response types and storing or branching on the results. Designers should strive for more creative interactions.

JUDGMENT OF RESPONSES

Judging is the process of evaluating a response in order to give feedback, to make lesson sequence decisions, and to store performance data. The goal is to judge the response as well as a teacher would. A teacher is capable of hearing or seeing a response and picking out the important information, ignoring extra words, recognizing synonyms, noting spelling errors, and finally making a rational decision that the response is correct or incorrect. It is much more difficult for a computer to engage in this kind of "intelligent judging," but it is the goal you should strive for.

Types of Judgments

There are a number of possible judgments for a response. They are as follows:

The response is correct.

The response contains an expected error. It is frequently the case that certain errors can be predicted. If a child has just begun learning multiplication and the program asks for the product of 3 times 6, some students are likely to add and respond 9. Such errors should receive special feedback, which requires recognizing them when they occur.

The response contains an unexpected error.

The response is partially correct. This means it contains some but not all the correct information, or it contains expected or unexpected errors in addition to correct information.

The response is neither right nor wrong. An example is when the program asks for the student's name. The response is not right or wrong; it is just accepted as the student's name. Similarly, if the program requires the student to draw a picture and the student responds by asking for the directions for drawing, the response is neither right nor wrong. The program should give the directions and continue to await a response.

Answer Types

A judgment is produced by searching the student's response for correct answers and optionally for incorrect answers. The difficulty of this searching depends primarily on the type of answers. Seven major answer types, in order of increasing judgment difficulty, are:

A single selection, such as a multiple-choice question

Multiple selections, such as a marking question

A numeric answer, such as for an arithmetic problem

A single-string answer, such as a word

A multiple-string answer, such as a phrase or sentence

A numeric-plus-string answer, such as a physics problem requiring the response "35 meters"

Dragging and drawing (mouse-oriented responses)

We now consider what is involved in judging each of these answer types.

Single-Selection Answer. This is the easiest type of judgment. The response mode may be clicking with the mouse, pressing a key, touching the screen, or moving a cursor to select a line or other section of the display. A letter or number is stored as a result of the student response and is compared to the answer, which is also a single letter or number. The response will be either correct, incorrect, or improper. An example of an improper response is choosing the letter *e* on a four-option multiple-choice question. Such a response should be considered a format error and the student prompted to note the directions and try again.

Multiple-Selection Answers. This type of judgment is only slightly more difficult. The response modes and the response-answer comparison are basically the same as for the single-selection case, but the mouse is preferred for ease of use and simplicity of directions. Now, however, the response may be correct, incorrect, improper, or partially correct. A partially correct response means that although some correct selections were made, either some incorrect selections were included, or not all correct selections were made. For example, a question requires the student to underline the nouns in a sentence containing two nouns. Underlining both nouns would be correct. Underlining anything but the nouns, such as two verbs, would be incorrect. Underlining one noun, a noun and a verb, or two nouns and a verb, would all be partially correct responses.

Numeric Answers. Math and science problems frequently require numeric responses. They typically involve a single number and are easy to judge. The mode of such responses is almost always via the keyboard. The response is judged by comparing it to the correct number and optionally to one or more anticipated incorrect numbers. Responses may be correct, expected incorrect, unexpected incorrect, partially correct, or improper. Improper responses are usually the result of using letters instead of digits, or using punctuation (such as commas or dollar signs). An example of an expected incorrect response was already discussed; the case when the student was to multiply two numbers but added instead. Other examples would be when the student forgets to carry during addition or borrow during subtraction.

Numeric questions sometimes allow a tolerance. This is most common in science problems. Suppose a problem requires the student to calculate how long it will take a falling object to reach the ground and the correct answer is 14 seconds. You may want to accept as correct a response in the range 13.5 to 14.5 seconds. A response outside of that range would be considered incorrect.

Single-String Answer. This judgment is required in sentence-completion and short-answer questions. Many more judging considerations are important for this and the following response types. The considerations are:

Does the correct string appear in the response?
Does a synonym for the correct string appear in the response?
Is the correct string spelled correctly?
Is the case (upper or lower) of the string correct?
Do any expected incorrect strings appear in the response?
Are there any unnecessary words?
Is there any punctuation in the response, and if so, does it affect the answer?

How these questions are treated determines how strictly the response is judged. A response is judged most strictly when only a single word is considered correct, it must be spelled perfectly, and no extra words or punctuation are allowed. A response is judged very leniently when any one of a number of synonyms is considered correct, and when small spelling errors, punctuation, and extra words (other than explicitly wrong ones) are ignored. Based on these considerations the response may be judged correct, partially correct, expected incorrect, unexpected incorrect, or improper. Examples of improper responses in this situation are a single letter when at least a word is expected, or a response which is over some permissible length.

Judging is done in this case by searching the student's typed response for one or more correct strings, for one or more expected incorrect strings, and applying various rules that recognize errors in spelling, punctuation, extra words, and capitalization.

Multiple-String Answer.   A sentence-completion or short-answer question may require the student to produce a response with more than one word. In the case of the single-string answer, only one word was required, although the student might have typed more. In this case, the student's response will probably consist of more than one word. Once again, the student response is searched for the correct and incorrect answer strings, and a number of rules are applied to consider or ignore spelling errors, punctuation, extra words, and capitalization. Synonyms may or may not be considered for either correct or expected-incorrect strings.

A last consideration, which was not relevant for previous response types, is word order. The required correct strings (or their synonyms) might be required in a specific order, allowed in any order, or allowed in several specific orders. All of these considerations combine to make multiple-string answer judging very difficult. That is why it is preferable to construct questions that do not require many words in the response.

Numeric-Plus-String Answer.   Science problems typically require responses like "25 meters," which combine the numeric answer with the single-string answer. The simple numeric judging considerations (the most complicated of which is allowing a tolerance) must be combined with the many difficult string judging considerations. In addition to these, the response-judging machinery must distinguish the numeric and the string parts of the response, and must allow for both parts to be correct, both parts to be incorrect, or one part correct and one part incorrect. Because units in science problems are frequently abbreviated, correct treatment of synonyms is essential. If combined units are necessary, such as in "25 feet/second," a numeric answer is now combined with a multiple-string answer, and considerations of word order and punctuation become relevant.

Dragging Screen Objects.   The mouse can be used to position screen objects by *dragging*. This means clicking on an object, holding the mouse button, moving the mouse with the object following, and releasing the button to "drop" the object. Dragging is a useful type of interaction. Words can be dragged to label a picture, construct a sentence, answer a matching exercise, or alphabetize a list. Pictures may be dragged to construct an apparatus, create a map or diagram, or match pictures to words. Although the question which permits dragging may be complex to program, judging is usually easy, requiring only that you note the beginning and ending screen coordinates of the mouse.

Drawing. Drawing with a mouse opens up a range of very powerful and beneficial interactions. Currently, however, computer judging of drawings ranges from difficult to impossible. Judging a simple drawing like a line or circle is difficult while judging complex pictures is nearly impossible. Drawing may allow students to create diagrams ("Draw and label the parts of a drill press"), demonstrate visual knowledge ("What is the shape of the stomach?"), or modify other pictures ("Where would you put the first surgical incision for open heart surgery?").

Although judging drawings is difficult for computers, it is easier for people. A student may be instructed to draw, then be shown a correct drawing overlaid for comparison, then asked to indicate if his or her response was close to the overlay. With two students working together, one may draw and the other may evaluate the drawing.

General Judging Considerations

The following judging considerations are relevant for several or all of the response types discussed above.

Length. In all text judging situations a limit should be set on the permissible length of a student response. For a multiple-choice question this is a single character. For a sentence-completion question expecting a single word, the length limit might be ten or fifteen letters. A short-answer question might allow thirty or more letters. In all cases, if the student exceeds the permissible length, the program should not judge the response incorrect, but should inform the student of a format problem and await a response of correct length.

Time Limits. We discourage a time limit on answering questions in tutorials. If a long response latency indicates a problem, such as the student not knowing what to do, we recommend the program ask if help is needed, rather than considering the lack of response to be incorrect.

Help and Escape Options. Whenever the student is at a question, global options such as asking for help or to leave the program should be provided. Consequently, the judging machinery must recognize certain mouse positions, key presses, or words, as special requests rather than as responses. It is common for lessons which otherwise have good global controls to omit them in questions, simply because they are harder to program within question sequences.

Conclusion

Given the many considerations involved in judging, it should not be surprising that most computer-based lessons do it poorly. Our two main recommendations regarding judging are as follows. First, strive for a program which judges responses the same way a teacher would. Second, design questions which foster response economy, thus making judgment easier.

FEEDBACK ABOUT RESPONSES

Feedback is the reaction of a program to the student's response and may take many forms, including text messages and graphic illustrations. Its most common function is to inform the student about the appropriateness of a response. Following correct responses, it may also provide reinforcement for the student. Following incorrect responses, it should provide correction, with the purpose of improving future performance. In tutorial programs especially, feedback should encourage the student to think and comprehend the information better (Schimmel, 1988).

As discussed in the previous section, there are several judgments possible for a response. Let us consider the feedback appropriate for each.

Feedback Following Format Errors. A format error is an error of form rather than content, such as using letters instead of numbers. Feedback should prompt the student to correct the format and to try again. For example, feedback should say, "Please use numerals only. Press ⟨return⟩ to try again," rather than saying, "Your answer is wrong, try again." Figure 2–60 shows feedback for a format error.

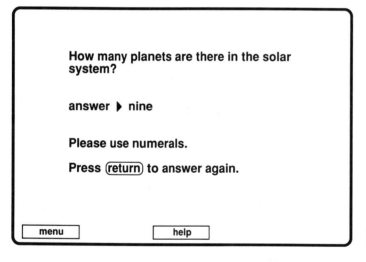

How many planets are there in the solar system?

answer ▶ nine

Please use numerals.

Press (return) to answer again.

menu   help

Figure 2-60 Feedback for a format error.

Feedback Following Correct Responses. When a response is correct a short affirmation is made, usually with a single word such as "good" or "correct." Many programs randomly select different "correct" words for the sake of variety. Figure 2–61 demonstrates feedback after a correct response. Lessons for children frequently engage in procedures to reinforce correct responses as well. This may be done with encouraging words such as "You're doing a great job!" or with an interesting picture or animation. However, such reinforcers should have variety and should not be too time consuming, especially if they occur frequently.

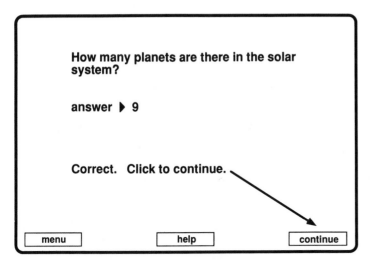

Figure 2-61   Feedback for a correct response.

How many planets are there in the solar system?

answer ▶ 9

Correct. Click to continue.

| menu | help | continue |

Feedback Following Neutral Responses.   A response may be neither right nor wrong, as when you are asked for your name. Feedback such as "Thank you. Press ⟨return⟩ to continue" is appropriate in this case.

Feedback Following Content Errors.   A response may be incorrect or only partially correct. Feedback following errors has a great effect on the success of instruction, and the remainder of this section deals with the nature of feedback in this situation.

Positive and Corrective Feedback

Feedback should be positive. It should avoid negative statements, sarcasm, and should never demean the student. Jokes should not be made at the student's expense. While some students may find such jokes humorous, not all students will. The slowest students, whose confidence and attitudes are already low, will suffer the greatest discouragement. Research on the effectiveness of humor in instruction is inconclusive (Vance, 1987).

Feedback should be corrective. It should provide the student with information to improve future performance. Simply saying "incorrect" after a response is not corrective.

A potential danger of corrective feedback is that it may increase student errors. Simple corrective feedback, such as "No, the correct answer is Abraham Lincoln," does not generally act as a reinforcer. However, when feedback following errors is much more interesting than that following correct responses, the student may be stimulated to make errors intentionally, in order to see the interesting effects. Although it is important to correct errors, it is also necessary that the corrections not be so entertaining that they encourage more errors.

Timing of Feedback

Timing of feedback refers to whether feedback occurs immediately after an error, or is delayed. In research studies, immediate feedback is not always more beneficial than delayed feedback, but is almost always better than no feedback (Gaynor, 1981; Surber & Anderson, 1975; Kulhavy & Anderson, 1972). The proper timing of feedback depends on the nature of what is being learned and how it is being learned. In a review of the literature on timing of feedback, Kulik & Kulik (1988) maintain that in studies where the nature of learning was similar to that of taking a multiple-choice test with feedback, delayed feedback showed an advantage. But studies where the nature of learning was more like a typical CBI lesson showed an advantage for immediate feedback. They recommend that immediate feedback always be used in CBI lessons.

Additionally, research showing an advantage for delayed feedback, has generally demonstrated it for propositional knowledge (verbal information, knowledge, principles). It is likely that learning procedural knowledge (J.R. Anderson, 1982) will be enhanced more by immediate feedback. Irrespective of its effects on learning, immediate feedback is easier to administer in tutorials than is delayed feedback. It may also be the case, as Gaynor (1981) found, that students believe the computer is not working properly when feedback is delayed. In general, we recommend immediate feedback in tutorials.

Types of Feedback

Text Feedback. The most common type of feedback is to give the correct answer in text form, below the student's incorrect response. For completion questions this is usually the word or phrase most preferred in the blank. For alternate-response questions, it is some indication of the correct alternative, such as the correct letter for a multiple-choice question. For completion questions, feedback in the form of the correct answer may be inserted directly into the blank (or blanks) in the original question. Although aesthetically pleasing, feedback of this type might go unnoticed by the student.

Text feedback need not supply the correct answer. It may supply a hint so the student can try again. Common ways of providing a hint are:

Rewording the question or problem, highlighting key words or parts
Showing the solution for a similar problem
Giving the student *part* of the answer

Graphic Feedback. Very effective feedback can be given graphically. Extended verbal explanations may sometimes be eliminated in favor of a well-placed arrow or picture. Figure 2–62 shows a display from *Decimal Darts* (Control Data Corporation, 1981), in which the student must identify points on a number line by indicating the numbers where balloons are located. When the student gives a correct number a dart flies across the screen and pops a balloon. If the student gives an incorrect number, a dart flies across the screen and sticks in a part of the num-

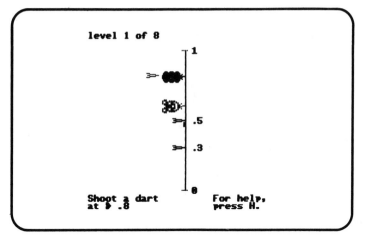

Figure 2-62 Graphic feedback. Answering correctly pops a balloon. *(Courtesy of Control Data Corporation)*

ber line where there is no balloon. It is immediately obvious to most students when their response is correct, too large, or too small. The simple location of the dart with respect to the balloons conveys all of this information.

Markup. Another form of graphic feedback is answer markup, which is used when a response is partially correct. Special symbols indicate errors and missing information. Consider Figure 2–63, which demonstrates the automatic markup facility of *EnBASIC* (Tenczar, Smith, & Avner, 1982). In the first response the symbols indicate that a word (Thomas) is missing. In the student's second attempt, the symbols indicate that the last name is spelled incorrectly. On the third try the response is correct. Markup of this sort with several symbols of different meanings is difficult for students to interpret and we do not generally recommend it.

Figure 2–64 demonstrates a different kind of markup facility called

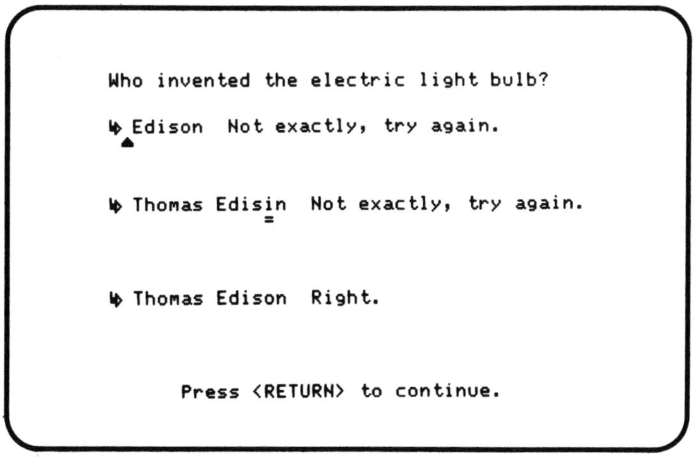

```
Who invented the electric light bulb?

↳ Edison  Not exactly, try again.
  ▲

↳ Thomas Edisin  Not exactly, try again.
                =

↳ Thomas Edison  Right.


        Press <RETURN> to continue.
```

Figure 2-63 Response markup in *EnBASIC. (Courtesy of COMPress)*

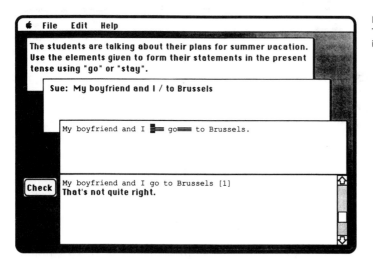

Dasher (Pusack, 1990). Correct letters in the response remain on the display and incorrect or missing letters are replaced with dashes. The response prompt is positioned at the first dash. The student corrects the response by typing in the missing or incorrect letters, rather than retyping the entire word. Because it only uses one markup symbol, this method is simple to understand and use. It also fosters response economy. We recommend it especially for multiple-string response judging.

Error-Contingent Feedback

Feedback tailored to the nature of the student's error is called *error-contingent feedback*. Answer markup is an example, because different symbols indicate specific errors in the response. Answer markup is usually employed when the response is partially correct. However, even when a response is totally wrong, feedback specific to the error is useful. Consider the examples in Figures 2–65 and 2–66. In the second example the student is probably adding instead of multiplying, which was not the case in the first example. The feedback given recognizes the special nature of the error. The responses and feedback in Figures 2–67 through 2–70 also illustrate error-contingent feedback.

Subsequent Attempts

After a response error and feedback, the student may be given another chance to answer the question. Tutorials vary widely in this regard, from allowing just one try to requiring the student to try until correct. The purpose of a tutorial is not to test achievement but to guide the student in its acquisition. Tutorials should therefore give the student more than one attempt. The other extreme, requiring the student to try until correct, is not beneficial either. Being unable to produce a correct response will be very discouraging, and may require the student

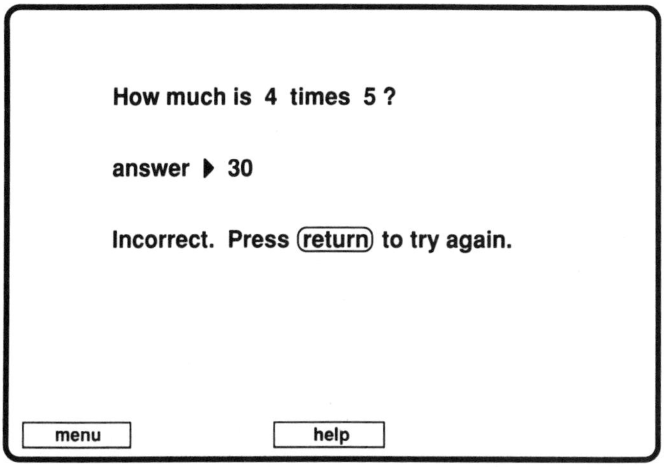

How much is 4 times 5 ?

answer ▶ 30

Incorrect. Press (return) to try again.

menu   help

Figure 2-65 Feedback *not* contingent on the answer.

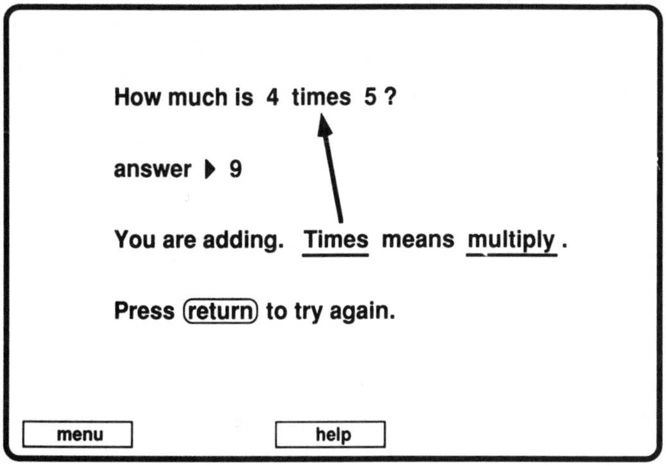

How much is 4 times 5 ?

answer ▶ 9

You are adding. <u>Times</u> means <u>multiply</u> .

Press (return) to try again.

menu   help

Figure 2-66 Error-contingent feedback.

Who invented the electric light bulb?

answer ▶ Alexander Graham Bell

No, he invented the telephone.

Press (return) to try again.

menu   help

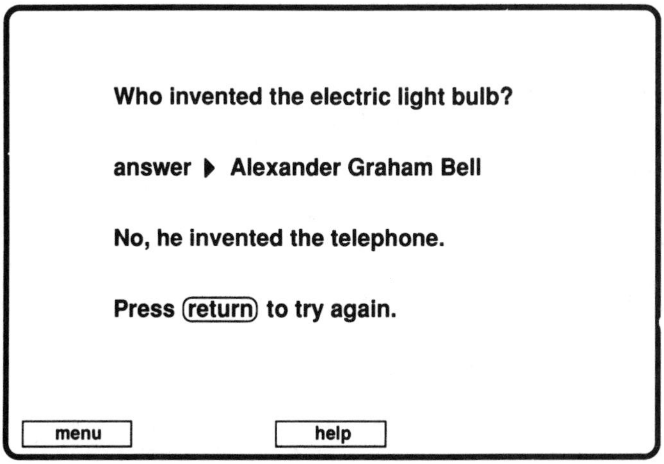

Figure 2-67 Error-contingent feedback for the first error.

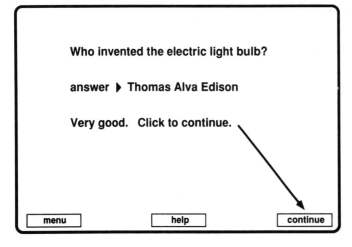

Who invented the electric light bulb?

answer ▶ Samuel Morse

No, he invented the telegraph.

Press (return) to try again.

| menu | help |

Figure 2-68 Error-contingent feedback for the second error.

Who invented the electric light bulb?

answer ▶ Thomas Edison

Almost perfect. Try again, using his middle name as well.

Press (return).

| menu | help |

Figure 2-69 Error-contingent feedback for a partially correct answer.

Who invented the electric light bulb?

answer ▶ Thomas Alva Edison

Very good. Click to continue.

| menu | help | continue |

Figure 2-70 Feedback when the answer is finally correct.

to leave the program. A tutorial should give the correct answer after a reasonable number of attempts (about three), or should permit requesting the answer.

REMEDIATION

While feedback is generally concise information about a response, *remediation* refers to the more extensive presentation of information for the student who is not learning the material. Tutorials vary from giving no remediation to giving remediation following each student response error. The types of remediation used in lessons are those used by most teachers in classroom instruction.

The most common remediation procedure is to repeat information already seen. Although this is not elegant, it is effective, for example, for students who were not reading carefully. A similar technique is to provide restatements of information with new and simpler wording.

Providing new information or repeating old information with more detail also aids the student who was paying attention, but who did not understand the initial presentation. This may take the form of more examples, pictures, sample problems, or practice with simpler parts of the material.

A computer lesson will not always be effective for all students. A remediation technique that should not be overlooked is having the student use other media (textbooks, workbooks, films) or work with a teacher.

SEQUENCING LESSON SEGMENTS

Linear Lessons

The simplest type of lesson sequence in tutorials is linear. The lesson progresses from one topic or concept to the next, presenting information and asking questions. Figure 2–71 depicts a linear lesson. First a description of glaciers is presented. Then the student answers a few questions about the characteristics of glaciers. Next are some presentations about how glaciers are formed, followed by a question about that information. All students go through the presentations and questions in this order, and the order does not change regardless of whether students answer questions correctly or incorrectly. Although common, this structure does not take advantage of the computer, does not adapt to individual students, and is not very creative or interesting.

Hierarchical Sequence. The sequence in a linear lesson is determined by the author. One way the author may do this is according to a hierarchy of information. For example, in math, being able to do addition is necessary before you can do multiplication. Addition, subtraction, and multiplication are all needed to learn long division. Thus, most arithmetic curricula begin with addition, followed by subtraction, multiplication, and division.

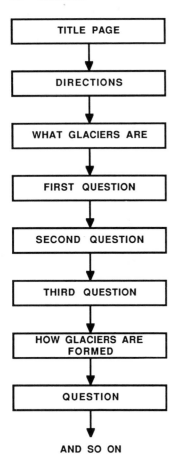

Figure 2-71 Sequence in a linear tutorial.

Familiarity and Difficulty. Sequence may also be determined based on the familiarity or the difficulty of the information. Vocabulary instruction usually begins on words with a higher frequency of usage, and follows with words which are progressively less common. Reading instruction begins with easier reading skills, such as picking out facts from a story, and follows with determining the theme of a story or making inferences from it. Instruction on punctuation puts the rules for the use of periods before the rules for commas, and both of those before colons and semicolons.

Branching Lessons

In branching tutorials, sequence is affected by student performance and choice. Such lessons are much more likely to be effective than simple linear lessons. The flowchart in Figure 2-72 is a variation of that in Figure 2-71. It has been supplemented with three decision points, labeled *Branch 1, Branch 2,* and *Branch 3,* which may cause sequence to be altered.

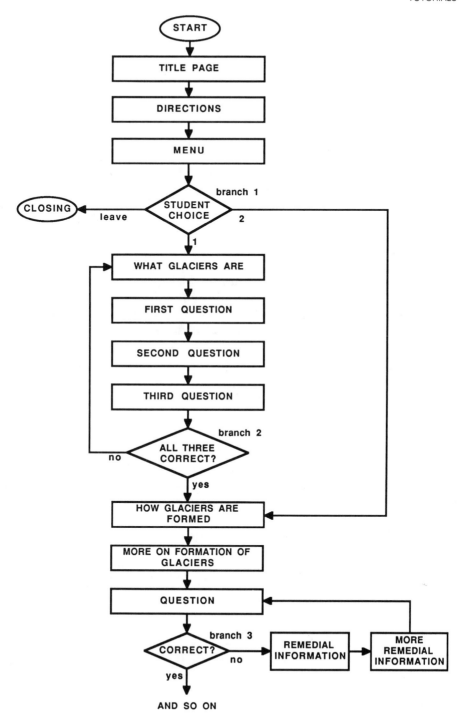

Figure 2-72 Sequence in a branching tutorial.

Amount of Branching. The amount of branching in a tutorial may vary considerably, from occasional branch points to branching after every student response. In Figure 2–72, branching does not occur after every question, but does occur frequently.

Criteria for Branching. Branching may occur based on individual performances, cumulative performance, or student choice. In Figure 2–72, Branch 3 is based on the result of a single question, Branch 2 is based on cumulative performance over three questions, and Branch 1 is based on the choice made by the student on the initial menu. Branching may be based on performance on a pretest, either at the beginning of a lesson or prior to it.

Direction of Branching. Branching may be forward, meaning the student skips information that most students see; backward, meaning the student is returned to repeat instruction; or sideways, meaning the student is exposed to information that most students skip. In our illustration, Branch 1 is a forward branch. If the student chooses to go directly to the second topic, the information and questions in the first topic are skipped. Branch 2 is a backwards branch. If performance on the three questions was not adequate, the student is returned to repeat the information and answer the questions again. Branch 3 is a sideways branch. If the student answers the question incorrectly, new information is presented before the question is repeated.

Assessing Student Level and Adjusting Difficulty Level

Many tutorials teach a single concept or skill and hence do not have branching from one topic to another. Instead, they teach information in depth, and sequencing progresses from easier to more difficult problems. An example would be a spelling lesson about a particular rule, which begins with words obeying the rule and later teaches exceptions to the rule. If a student using the lesson spells all the regular words correctly, the lesson will move on to the exceptions. Another example is an arithmetic lesson which begins with single-digit addition and progresses to two- and three-digit addition. When a student is successful with all single-digit addition problems, the program begins two-digit addition. The flowchart in Figure 2–73 demonstrates how program difficulty level may be based on student level of performance.

Restarting

To *restart* means to return to an unfinished lesson at the approximate point you last reached, like using a bookmark to return to the section of a book where you left off. Never assume students will finish a lesson in one session. Restarting students at the beginning of a lesson when they return can be very frustrating, and frequently diminishes both student and instructor satisfaction with a lesson.

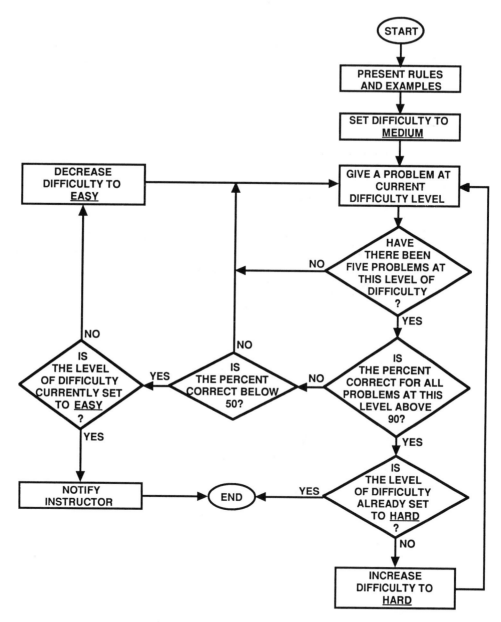

Figure 2-73 Sequence in a tutorial that adjusts difficulty based on student performance.

It is not necessary to return students to the exact point they left off. It is preferable for students to return to the beginning of the subsection they were studying. Restarting at the exact point is like picking up a textbook in the middle of a chapter. Most people prefer to return to the start of the interrupted chapter when they begin reading again.

To illustrate, imagine a tutorial on chemistry's three laws of thermodynamics. Let us say a student has studied the first two laws and must leave the lesson while studying the third. When the student returns the next day, a lesson with restarting will send the student to the beginning of the section about the third law, rather than the beginning of the entire lesson. Additionally, the lesson might give the student the *option* of starting at the very beginning, at the second law, or at the third law. This could be accomplished with a menu, as in Figure 2–74.

THERMODYNAMICS

Yesterday you stopped at the third law.

Click the section you would like now.

> First law of thermodynamics
> Second law of thermodynamics
> Third law of thermodynamics

| quit | help | credits |

Figure 2-74 A menu for restarting.

Restarting automatically requires storing data on disk or some other permanent device. If that is undesirable, restarting by using a menu should be used. When the student chooses to leave during the section on the third law of thermodynamics, a display as in Figure 2–75 could inform the student what menu option to choose when returning.

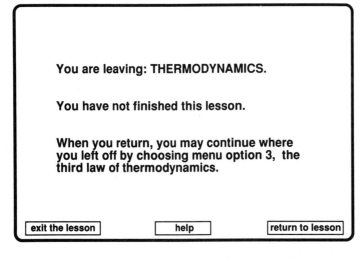

You are leaving: THERMODYNAMICS.

You have not finished this lesson.

When you return, you may continue where you left off by choosing menu option 3, the third law of thermodynamics.

| exit the lesson | help | return to lesson |

Figure 2-75 Giving the student information for restarting at a later time.

Automatic restarting (based on stored data) may present a problem for new students. A lesson must be able to distinguish returning students from new ones so that returning students may restart where they left off, and new students may start at the beginning. This may be accomplished by asking the student, when they begin, if they are returning; or by asking for the student's name and checking for stored restart data for that student. We recommend that any lesson lasting more than ten minutes have some restarting facility.

CLOSING OF THE TUTORIAL

When to End a Lesson

A tutorial may be ended either temporarily, such as when the student must leave but intends to return later, or permanently, when all required parts have been completed. The option to leave temporarily should *always* be available, while the end of the lesson should be based on successful completion.

Ending a lesson does not mean that the student *must* leave the lesson. Rather, it means that the student has completed the program requirements and probably should go on to something new. The option for the student to review the lesson can still be provided.

Temporary Ending

If there is to be restarting where the student left off, data must be stored on disk about what the student has completed. Alternatively, the student might receive a message indicating how to return to the point left off.

Permanent Ending

For a permanent ending, data may be required for two purposes: to provide information for the instructor, and to guide sequencing in future lessons. Both of these require permanent storage.

A permanent ending may provide some statement of transition into the lesson or lessons that will follow. Most commercial programs, however, attempt to be independent of other lessons and provide no such transition statements. Programs that are part of larger curricula are more likely to have them.

More commonly, when a tutorial is about to end permanently, it provides summary statements about the information in the lesson. A summary might be a list of major points or a paragraph summing up the purpose of the lesson. If the program has been collecting data about student performance, the student may be given a summary of performance and recommendations for further study.

According to some educators, after presenting all its information, a tutorial should provide activities to enhance retention and transfer of learning (Gagne & Briggs, 1979; Gagne, Wager, & Rojas, 1981). We believe that retention and transfer are best promoted by instructional methodologies other than tutorials—namely drills, simulations, games, and tests. All of these methodologies enhance retention. Simulations and games are especially effective for promoting transfer of learning. Multiple instructional methodologies need not be in separate lessons. A single lesson may contain a tutorial, followed by a drill or simulation, and end with a practice test. However, it is beneficial to keep sessions relatively short (twenty or thirty minutes). Within that time frame it is difficult to introduce new material and to enhance retention and transfer.

The Final Message

When ending temporarily or permanently, a lesson should always have a message making it clear that the student is leaving the program. Figure 2–76 illustrates such a message. Many programs do not do this. Often, the last piece of information presented in the lesson is left displayed on the computer screen, giving the impression that the tutorial is not really over. It is important to clean up the display at the end. Any text and pictures should be erased, and the final message displayed.

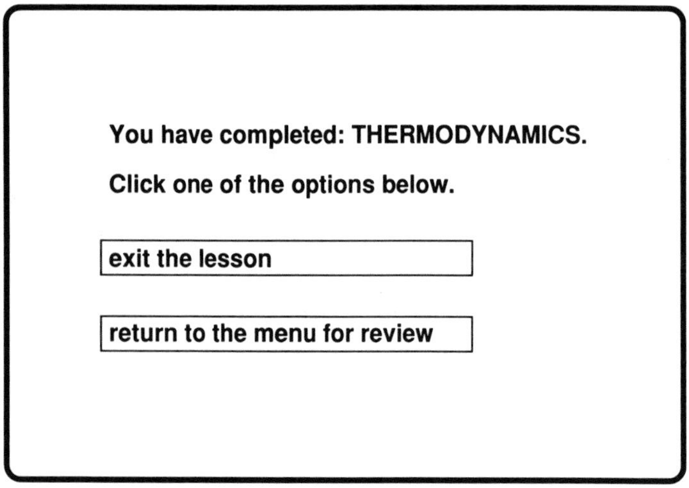

```
You have completed: THERMODYNAMICS.

Click one of the options below.


 exit the lesson

 return to the menu for review
```

Figure 2-76 The final message in a tutorial.

Exiting the Program

Clicking the *exit* option at this point should take the student to an appropriate place. If students enter the tutorial from a system or curriculum menu page, that is where they should return. If they enter the tutorial by typing the program name at an operating system prompt, they should return to the operating system prompt. If the lesson is one in a predetermined sequence of lessons, students should proceed to the next lesson in the sequence. In all cases, the student should be allowed to choose whether to go on immediately or to return later.

CONCLUSION

The factors we have discussed affect the outward appearance of a lesson and its quality. Familiarity with these factors has two purposes. It provides a basis for reviewing and evaluating instructional programs you may buy, and it provides a basis for designing your own lessons. The lesson designer should be aware of these factors and their influence, and make *deliberate* decisions about them when planning lessons.

We have devoted many pages to the analysis of the instructional factors relevant to tutorials. Many of the factors we have discussed in detail in this chapter are important to other methodologies as well, but will not be repeated when those are discussed. In the chapters to come, we will discuss new factors specific to those methodologies. Occasionally we will refer back to factors already discussed, but only when a factor takes on a new meaning or importance.

In the next chapter we discuss computerized drills. This ordering, tutorials followed by drills, is intentional. The first three instructional activities, *present, guide,* and *practice,* are well provided by having students use tutorials followed by drills on the same material.

REFERENCES AND BIBLIOGRAPHY

ADAMS, M., & BRUCE, B. (1980). *Background Knowledge and Reading Comprehension.* (Reading education report number 13). Urbana, IL: Center for the Study of Reading, University of Illinois at Urbana-Champaign.

ALI, A.M. (1981). The use of positive and negative examples during instruction. *Journal of Instructional Development, 5*(1), 2–7.

ANDERSON, J.R. (1976). *Language, Memory, and Thought.* Hillsdale, NJ: Lawrence Erlbaum.

ANDERSON, J.R. (1982). Acquisition of cognitive skill. *Psychological Review, 89,* 369–406.

ANDERSON, J.R., & KOSSLYN, S. (1984). *Tutorials in Learning and Memory.* San Francisco: W.H. Freeman.

ANDERSON, R.C. (1972). How to construct achievement tests to assess comprehension. *Review of Educational Research, 42,* 145–170.

ANDERSON, R.C. (1977). The notion of schemata and the educational enterprise. In R.C. Anderson, R.J. Spiro, & W.E. Montague (Eds.), *Schooling and the Acquisition of Knowledge.* Hillsdale, NJ: Lawrence Erlbaum.

ANDERSON, R.C., & BIDDLE, W.B. (1975). On asking people questions about what they are reading. In G. Bower (Ed.), *Psychology of Learning and Motivation* (Vol. 9). New York: Academic Press.

ANDRE, T., MUELLER, C., WOMACK, S., SMID, K., & TUTTLE, M. (1980). Adjunct application questions facilitate later application, or do they? *Journal of Educational Psychology, 72*(4), 533–543.

ATKIN, J.M. (1968, May). Behavioral objectives is curriculum design: A cautionary note. *The Science Teacher,* pp. 27–30.

BAEK, Y.K., & LAYNE, B.H. (1988). Color, graphics, and animation in a computer-assisted learning tutorial lesson. *Journal of Computer-Based Instruction, 15*(4), 131–135.

BLACK, J.B., SWAN, K., & SCHWARTZ, D.L. (1988). Developing thinking skills with computers. *Teachers College Record, 89*(3), 384–407.

BORG, W.R., & SCHULLER, C.F. (1979). Detail and background in audiovisual lessons and their effect on learners. *Educational Communication and Technology Journal, 27,* 31–38.

BRUNER, J.S. (1966a). *Towards a Theory of Instruction.* Cambridge: Harvard University Press.

BRUNER, J.S. (1966b). Some elements of discovery. In L.S. Shulman & E.R. Keislar (Eds.), *Learning by Discovery: A Critical Appraisal.* Chicago: Rand McNally.

BURKE, R.L. (1982). *CAI Sourcebook.* Englewood Cliffs, NJ: Prentice-Hall.

CONTROL DATA CORPORATION. (1981). *Decimal Darts.* (In *Decimal Practice.*) [Computer Program]. Minneapolis, MN: Control Data Corporation. (Adapted from Dugdale, S., Kibbey, D., & Leung, H. [1974]. *Decimal Darts.* Urbana, IL: University of Illinois Computer-based Education Research Laboratory.)

DEAR, B.L. (1987). AI and the authoring process. *IEEE Expert, 2*(2), 17–24.

DiVESTA, F.J. (1975). Trait-treatment interaction, cognitive processes, and research on communication media. *AV Communication Review, 23,* 185–196.

DUGDALE, S., & KIBBEY, D. (1983). *Interpreting Graphs.* [Computer Program]. Iowa City, IA: CONDUIT.

DURRETT, H.J. (Ed.). (1987). *Color and the Computer.* Orlando, FL: Academic Press.

DURRETT, H.J., & TREZONA, J. (1982). How to use color displays effectively: The elements of color vision and their implications for programmers. *Pipeline, 7*(2), 13–16.

DWYER, F.M. (1978). *Strategies for Improving Visual Learning.* State College, PA: Learning Services.

ENGELMANN, S. (1969). *Conceptual Learning.* Sioux Falls, SD: Adapt Press.

ENGELMANN, S. (1980). *Direct Instruction.* Englewood Cliffs, NJ: Educational Technology Publications.

FLEMING, M., & LEVIE, W.H. (1978). *Instructional Message Design: Principles from the Behavioral Sciences.* Englewood Cliffs, NJ: Educational Technology Publications.

GAGNE, R.M., & BRIGGS, L.J. (1979). *Principles of Instructional Design.* New York: Holt, Rinehart, and Winston.

GAGNE, R.M., WAGER, W., & ROJAS, A. (1981, September). Planning and authoring computer-assisted instruction lessons. *Educational Technology,* pp. 17–21.

GAYNOR, P. (1981). The effect of feedback delay on retention of computer-based mathematical material. *Journal of Computer-Based Instruction, 8,* 28–34.

HALL, K.A. (1983). Content structuring and question asking for computer-based instruction. *Journal of Computer-Based Instruction, 10*(1), 1–7.

HANNAFIN, M.J. (1984). Guidelines for using locus of instructional control in the design of computer-assisted instruction. *Journal of Instructional Development, 7*(3), 6–10.

HANNAFIN, M.J. (1987). The effects of orienting activities, cueing, and practice on learning of computer-based instruction. *Journal of Educational Research, 81*(1), 48–53.

HANNAFIN, M.J., & PHILLIPS, T.L. (1987). Perspectives in the design of interactive video: Beyond tape versus disc. *Journal of Research and Development in Education, 21*(1), 44–60.

HANNUM, W. (1988). Designing courseware to fit subject matter structure. In D.H. Jonassen (Ed.), *Instructional Designs for Microcomputer Courseware.* Hillsdale, NJ: Lawrence Erlbaum.

HEINES, J.M. (1984). *Screen Design Strategies for Computer-Assisted Instruction.* Bedford, MA: Digital Press.

JONASSEN, D.H. (Ed.). (1982). *The Technology of Text (Volume 1): Principles for Structuring, Designing, and Displaying Text.* Englewood Cliffs, NJ: Educational Technology Publications.

JONASSEN, D.H. (Ed.). (1985). *The Technology of Text (Volume 2): Principles for Structuring, Designing, and Displaying Text.* Englewood Cliffs, NJ: Educational Technology Publications.

JONASSEN, D.H. (1985). Generative learning vs. mathemagenic control of text processing. In D.H. Jonassen, (Ed.), *The Technology of Text, (Volume 2): Principles for Structuring, Designing, and Displaying Text* (pp. 9–45). Englewood Cliffs, NJ: Educational Technology Publications.

JONASSEN, D.H. (1988). Integrating learning strategies into courseware to facilitate deeper processing. In D.H. Jonassen (Ed.), *Instructional Designs for Microcomputer Courseware.* Hillsdale, NJ: Lawrence Erlbaum.

KELLER, J.M., & SUZUKI, K. (1988). Use of the ARCS motivation model in courseware design. In D.H. Jonassen (Ed.), *Instructional Designs for Microcomputer Courseware.* Hillsdale, NJ: Lawrence Erlbaum.

KLAUSMEIER, H.J., & FELDMAN, K.V. (1975). Effects of a definition and a varying number of examples and nonexamples on concept attainment. *Journal of Educational Psychology, 67,* 174–178.

KLAUSMEIER, H.J., GHATALA, E.S., & FRAYER, D.A. (1974). *Conceptual Learning and Development: A Cognitive View.* New York: Academic Press.

KORAN, M.L. (1971). Differential response to inductive and deductive instructional procedures. *Journal of Educational Design, 62,* 300–307.

KULHAVY, R.W., & ANDERSON, R.C. (1972). The delay-retention effect with multiple-choice tests. *Journal of Educational Psychology, 63,* 505–512.

KULIK, J.A., & KULIK, C-L.C. (1988). Timing of feedback and verbal learning. *Review of Educational Research, 58*(1), 79–97.

LAHEY, G.F. (1981). The effect of instructional sequence on performance in computer-based instruction. *Journal of Computer-Based Instruction, 7*(4), 111-116.

LEPPER, M.R. (1985). Microcomputers in education: Motivational and social issues. *American Psychologist, 40,* 1–18.

LEPPER, M.R., & CHABAY, R.W. (1985). Intrinsic motivation and instruction: Conflicting views on the role of motivational processes in computer-based education. *Educational Psychologist, 20*(4), 217–230.

LEPPER, M.R., & MALONE, T.W. (1987). Intrinsic motivation and instructional effectiveness in computer-based education. In R.E. Snow & M.J. Farr (Eds.), *Aptitude, Learning, and Instruction, III. Conative and Affective Process Analysis.* Hillsdale, NJ: Lawrence Erlbaum.

MAGER, R.F. (1962). *Preparing Instructional Objectives.* Belmont, CA: Fearon Publishers.

MALONE, T.W. (1981). Towards a theory of intrinsically motivating instruction. *Cognitive Science, 5,* 333–369.

MALONE, T.W., & LEPPER, M.R. (1987). Making learning fun: A taxonomy of intrinsic motivations for learning. In R.E. Snow & M.J. Farr (Eds.), *Aptitude, Learning, and Instruction: III. Conative and Affective Process Analysis.* Hillsdale, NJ: Lawrence Erlbaum.

MARKLE, S.M. (1969). *Good Frames and Bad: A Grammar of Frame Writing.* New York: John Wiley and Sons.

MERRILL, J. (1987). Levels of questioning and forms of feedback: Instructional factors in courseware design. *Journal of Computer-Based Instruction, 14*(1), 18–22.

MERRILL, M.D., SCHNEIDER, E.W., & FLETCHER, K.A. (1980). *TICCIT.* Englewood Cliffs, NJ: Educational Technology Publications.

MERRILL, M.D., & TENNYSON, R.D. (1977). *Teaching Concepts: An Instructional Design Guide.* Englewood Cliffs, NJ: Educational Technology Publications.

MERRILL, P.F. (1974). Effects of the availability of objectives and/or rules on the learning process. *Journal of Educational Psychology, 66,* 534–539.

MERRILL, P.F., & BUNDERSON, C.V. (1981). Preliminary guidelines for employing graphics in instruction. *Journal of Instructional Development, 4*(4), 2–9.

MINNESOTA EDUCATIONAL COMPUTING CONSORTIUM. (1980). *Micrometer.* [Computer Program]. St. Paul, MN: Minnesota Educational Computing Consortium.

MINNESOTA EDUCATIONAL COMPUTING CONSORTIUM. (1981a). *Designing Instructional Computing Materials.* St. Paul, MN: Minnesota Educational Computing Consortium.

MINNESOTA EDUCATIONAL COMPUTING CONSORTIUM. (1981B). *Triangles.* [Computer Program]. St. Paul, MN: Minnesota Educational Computing Consortium.

MINNESOTA EDUCATIONAL COMPUTING CONSORTIUM. (1982). *Electron Charge.* [Computer Program]. St. Paul, MN: Minnesota Educational Computing Consortium.

PAAP, K.R., & ROSKE-HOFSTRAND, R.J. (1986). The optimal number of menu options per panel. *Human Factors, 28,* 377–385.

PUSACK, J.P. (1990). *Dasher.* [Computer Program]. Iowa City, IA: CONDUIT.

REDER, L.M., & ANDERSON, J.R. (1980). A comparison of texts and their summaries: Memorial consequences. *Journal of Verbal Learning and Verbal Behavior, 19,* 121–134.

RIGNEY, J.W., & LUTZ, K.A. (1976). Effects of graphic analogies of concepts in chemistry on learning and attitude. *Journal of Educational Psychology, 68,* 305–311.

RUMELHART, D.E., & ORTONY, A. (1977). The representation of knowledge in memory. In R.C. Anderson, R.J. Spiro, & W.E. Montague (Eds.), *Schooling and the Acquisition of Knowledge.* Hillsdale, NJ: Lawrence Erlbaum.

SCHIMMEL, B.J. (1988). Providing meaningful feedback in courseware. In D.H. Jonassen (Ed.), *Instructional Designs for Microcomputer Courseware.* Hillsdale, NJ: Lawrence Erlbaum.

SHNEIDERMAN, B. (1987). *Designing the User Interface: Strategies for Effective Human-Computer Interaction.* Reading, MA: Addison-Wesley.

SILVERSTEIN, L.D. (1987). Human factors for color display systems: Concepts, methods, and research. In H.J. Durrett (Ed.), *Color and the Computer.* Orlando, FL: Academic Press.

SMITH, S., & CHABAY, R. (1983). *General Chemistry.* [Computer Program]. Wentworth, NH: COMPress.

SMITH, S.L., & GOODWIN, N.C. (1972). Another look at blinking displays. *Human Factors, 14,* 345–347.

SMITH, W. (1987). Ergonomic vision. In H.J. Durrett (Ed.), *Color and the Computer.* Orlando, FL: Academic Press.

STEINBERG, E.R. (1977). Review of student control in computer-assisted instruction. *Journal of Computer-Based Instruction, 3,* 84–90.

STEINBERG, E.R. (1989). Cognition and learner control: A literature review, 1977-1988. *Journal of Computer-Based Instruction, 16*(4), 117-121.

SURBER, J.R., & ANDERSON, R.C. (1975). Delay-retention effect in natural classroom settings. *Journal of Educational Psychology, 67,* 170–173.

TENCZAR, P., SMITH, S., & AVNER, A. (1982). *EnBASIC.* [Computer Program]. Wentworth, NH: COMPress.

TENNYSON, R.D. (1981). Use of adaptive information for advisement in learning concepts and rules using computer-assisted instruction. *American Educational Research Journal, 18,* 425–438.

TENNYSON, R.D., & PARK, O.-C. (1980). The teaching of concepts: A review of instructional design research literature. *Review of Educational Research, 50,* 55–70.

TENNYSON, R.D., & ROTHEN, W. (1979). Management of computer-based instruction: Design of an adaptive control strategy. *Journal of Computer-Based Instruction, 5,* 63–71.

TUFTE, E.R. (1983). *The Visual Display of Quantitative Information.* Cheshire, CT: Graphics Press.

VANCE, C.M. (1987). A comparative study on the use of humor in the design of instruction. *Instructional Science, 16.* 79–100.

WAGER, W., & WAGER, S. (1985). Presenting questions, processing responses, and providing feedback in CAI. *Journal of Instructional Development, 8*(4), 2–8.

WALKER, D.F., & HESS, R.D. (Eds.). (1984). *Instructional Software: Principles and Perspectives for Design and Use.* Belmont, CA: Wadsworth.

WHITEFIELD, A. (1986). Human factors aspects of pointing as an input technique in interactive computer systems. *Applied Ergonomics, 17*(2), 97–104.

WILCOX, W.C., MERRILL, M.D., & BLACK, H.B. (1981). Effect of teaching a conceptual hierarchy on concept classification performance. *Journal of Instructional Development, 5*(1), 8–13.

WILSON, B.G. (1985). Techniques for teaching procedures. *Journal of Instructional Development, 8*(2), 2–5.

SUMMARY OF TUTORIALS

INTRODUCTION

Use a short title page.

State the lesson goals or objectives briefly, except with children.

Give accurate directions and make them available to the student at all times.

Relate what the student will study to previous knowledge.

Do not put pretests in a tutorial. Use pretests only when you know they are needed, and use them in separate computer programs.

STUDENT CONTROL

Give adults more control than children.

Always allow control of forward progression and backward review.

Allow global controls, rather than occasional control, as much as possible.

Always allow temporary termination.

When menus are used, they should always be available.

Use the mouse for student control if one is available.

MOTIVATION

Use intrinsic motivation whenever possible.

Consider motivation at the macro level (strategies) and micro level (lesson characteristics).

Use an appropriate level of challenge.

Arouse curiosity.

Enhance imagery and involvement through fantasy.

Use an appropriate level of student control.

Arouse and maintain attention throughout the lesson.

Content should be relevant to the student and the relevance should be clear.

Lessons should provide opportunity for success and satisfaction through appropriate goals, reinforcement, and fairness.

Motivational techniques should be applied in moderation, intelligently, and in harmony with other instructional factors.

PRESENTATION OF INFORMATION

Presentations should be short.

Layouts should be attractive and consistent.

Avoid scrolling.

Use conventions in paragraphing, key presses, directions, and response prompts.

Use graphics for important information, analogy, and cues.

Keep graphics simple.

Use color sparingly and for important information.

Avoid color in text.

Text should be lean, clear, and have good mechanics.

Stress clear transitions between presentations on different topics.

Use appropriate organizational methods for verbal information, concepts, rules and principles, and skills.

Don't over prompt, and use thematic prompts when possible.

Provide procedural help and make it easy to request.

QUESTIONS AND RESPONSES

Ask frequent questions, especially comprehension questions.

Consider inputs other than the keyboard, if available.

The response prompt should be below the question, near the left margin.

Questions should promote response economy.

Ask questions about important information.

Allow the student more than one try to answer a question.

Do not require the student to get a correct answer (without help) to proceed.

Give help on response format whenever necessary.

Alternate-response questions are harder to write, easier to judge, and allow guessing.

Constructed-response questions are easier to write, harder to judge, and prevent guessing.

Foils on multiple-choice questions should be plausible.

Fill-in questions should have the blanks near the end.

Be aware of whether you should be testing recall or comprehension, and use appropriate question types.

Reading difficulty should be appropriate to the student's level.

Avoid abbreviations and negatives in questions.

Questions should never scroll out of view.

Questions should appear after information in a lesson and below information on a particular display.

JUDGING RESPONSES

Judge intelligently, as a teacher would. Allow for word order, synonyms, spelling, and extra words.

Look for both correct responses and expected incorrect responses.

Allow as much time as the student desires for a response.

Allow the student to ask for help, and to escape.

PROVIDING FEEDBACK ABOUT RESPONSES

If response content is correct, give a short affirmation.

If response format is incorrect, say so and allow another response.

If response content is incorrect, give corrective feedback.

REMEDIATION

Provide remediation for repeated poor performance. This might be a recommendation to restudy or see the instructor.

SEQUENCING LESSON SEGMENTS

Overall sequence should be hierarchical or based on difficulty.
Avoid simple linear tutorials. Provide branching based on performance.
The student should control progression. Never use timed pauses.
Provide restarting capability.
Give sequence control to mature students.
Always permit temporary ending based on student choice.
Permanent ending should be based on student performance.

CLOSING

Store data for restarting.
Clear the screen.
Make the end obvious with a short final message.
Return the student to wherever he or she started from before the tutorial.

3

DRILLS

INTRODUCTION

In Chapter 2 we discussed tutorial instruction, an instructional methodology that is frequently used to accomplish the first two activities of instruction, presenting information and guiding the student. Now we turn to computerized drills, a methodology used primarily for the third aspect of the instructional process, providing practice.

Computer-based drills receive a lot of criticism. Some of this is deserved and some is not. Many educators claim drills do not capitalize upon the power of the computer (for example, Gravander, 1985; Jonassen, 1988; Slesnick, 1983; Streibel, 1986) and that drills can as easily be accomplished through workbooks or flashcards. We maintain that this is an unjust criticism. While it is true that most *existing* drills do not capitalize on the computer's power, it is also the case that the computer can be used to produce drills of much greater effectiveness than workbooks, flashcards, or teacher-administered drills. The characteristics of such drills will be discussed in this chapter.

Another unjust criticism is that there are too many drills. The fact is there are not enough good drills. (There are also not enough good tutorials, simulations, games, or tests!) The *practice* phase of instruction is very important. Drills, in combination with tutorials and other methodologies, provide practice and are necessary for learning information in which fluency is required, such as basic math skills, foreign languages, spelling and English usage, and vocabulary. Authors should not avoid developing drills in order to develop lessons of other types. We need more of all types, all of which should be of better quality.

Another criticism is that drills do not teach but merely provide practice with the assumption the student is already familiar to some degree with the subject matter. This is true. Drills are not *intended* to teach. The problem arises when teachers assume a drill is capable of teaching new information and use it thus. Drills should always be preceded by instructional methodologies that present the information and guide the student through initial learning. In computer-based instruction this might mean preceding the drill with an appropriate tutorial or simulation. It might also mean preceding the computer-based drill with readings in a textbook, a classroom lesson, or a group discussion.

A valid criticism is that most computerized drills are of low quality. Most do not incorporate good instructional principles, and most do not collect useful information to show the instructor how well the student is progressing. In addition, the response-judging procedures are frequently poorly programmed so that correct responses are sometimes judged to be incorrect.

APPLICATIONS OF DRILLS

Many people believe drills are useful only in limited areas such as arithmetic and spelling. However, the function of drills is to provide practice, and they are applicable to all types of learning, assuming that initial presentation and guidance has already occurred.

Drills may be applied to simple paired-associate learning, such as spelling or foreign language word translation; to verbal information, such as definitions, historical facts, or scientific concepts and principles; to simple problem solving, such as arithmetic facts; and to complex problem solving, such as problems in the physical and social sciences.

BASIC DRILL PROCEDURE

Figure 3–1 illustrates the general procedures of a drill. Like a tutorial, there is an introductory section, followed by a *cycle* which is repeated many times. Each time the cycle is repeated the following actions generally take place.

An item is selected.
The item is displayed.
The student responds.

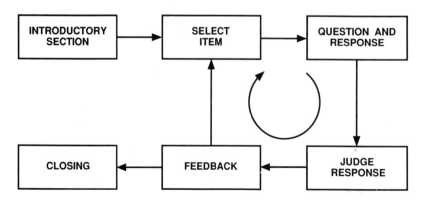

Figure 3-1   The general structure and flow of a drill.

The program judges the response.

The student receives feedback about the response.

After a number of items the program terminates. This procedure differs from that for tutorials (see Figure 2–1) in one major way. There is usually no presentation of information in a drill. In drills that step is replaced with the *item selection* step.

Although most drills follow this basic procedure, there are many variations. Some select items randomly while others select them in a specific order. Some terminate the drill after a hundred items, some after thirty minutes, and some after student performance reaches an acceptable level of quality.

As with tutorials, we classify these differences in terms of the instructional factors relevant to drills. Many factors relevant to tutorials are important in drills as well. In this chapter we discuss those *new* factors relevant to drills, which we categorize into the following topics:

The introduction of a drill

Item characteristics

Item selection procedures

Feedback

Item grouping procedures

Motivating the student

Data storage

THE INTRODUCTION OF A DRILL

Initial Student Control

Many drills incorporate methods of initial student control which probably *decrease* their quality. Some, for instance, allow the student to decide how many items will be presented. This particular decision is one that students are not capable of making in a fashion that truly enhances learning. It is better made by the author and should be based on the student's performance in the drill. Similarly, we do not recommend allowing the student to choose the difficulty level of items. This too should be based on student performance. Many authors give too much choice to the student because they themselves do not know how many items the student should receive, nor at what difficulty level to begin.

A more appropriate type of student control in a drill is the ability to select the type of information practiced. For instance, a drill might have two sections, one on using formulas to calculate the area of common geometric figures such as triangles and squares, and another for using the formulas for determining perimeters of the same figures. The student would be allowed to determine which to do first, but once that choice was made, the program should determine which items to administer.

ITEM CHARACTERISTICS

Item Types

The reader has probably noticed that in discussing drills we have used the word *item* where we previously used the word *question.* This is in keeping with standard practice when discussing this subject. One reason people refer to drill *items* instead of drill *questions* is because in many cases drills do not administer questions of the usual sort, but present a display demanding a response in a way unlike most tutorial questions.

An example of this is the *paired associate.* A paired associate is any pair of related words or events. The English word *dog* and the Spanish word *perro* are paired associates. In a translation drill, the response to *dog* would be *perro* and the response to *perro* would be *dog.* Other paired associates are a musical tone and its name (c-sharp, for instance), or a musical tone and its pictorial representation on a musical scale. Pictures of objects and the English words identifying them, the names of chemical elements and their abbreviations, a spoken word and its spelling, countries and their capitals, and numbers and their square roots are all examples of paired associates. Many of these represent simple translation of modality, such as sound-to-text (hearing a word and spelling it) or picture-to-name (seeing a picture of an object and typing the noun that represents it).

Other kinds of items are used in drills in addition to paired associates. Many of these are standard questions, such as multiple-choice, sentence-completion, and short-answer questions. For simplicity's sake we will use the word item to refer to all questions in drills.

Graphics in Drill Items

Graphics may enhance drills considerably when used as described in Chapter 2. Graphics may be used as the context for an item, such as the balloons on the number line in *Decimal Darts;* as a prompt for an item, such as the periodic table for a drill on the symbols of the elements; and as feedback, such as the popping balloons in *Decimal Darts.*

Graphics may also be used as a motivator to make a drill more enjoyable. Drills are less interesting than other instructional methodologies and can quickly become boring. Furthermore, if a student is not performing well in a drill, it can become frustrating. Graphics provide one way to increase motivation. The graphic feedback in *Decimal Darts,* for example, serves to motivate students. It also has the advantage of reinforcing correct responses with interesting feedback and following incorrect responses with uninteresting feedback.

Item Difficulty

In a given drill, the items will not all be of the same difficulty. Thus, from one item to the next, difficulty of responding can vary. The way it varies can be an important factor in the effectiveness of a drill. The most common treatment of this factor is to ignore it. That is, the author does not consider the possibility of different item difficulties, and thus its variation in the drill is random. This can cause problems, such as student frustration due do difficult items appearing at the start of the drill. We encourage authors to treat the difficulty factor in one of the following ways.

Keep difficulty constant. That is, select items which are all of equal or approximately equal difficulty.

Increase difficulty based on student performance. That is, start out with easy items and, as the student masters them, present more-difficult items.

Group items by difficulty. In this method, items of similar difficulty are put in groups. The student must master the items in an easy group before moving on to a new group of more difficult items. The student may also be sent back to an easier group if performance on a difficult group is poor.

Pacing

Drills often emphasize fluency, a part of which is speed of responding. Speed is usually facilitated by using items that do not take long to read and answer (if you know the information). Thus, leanness and clarity are more essential in drill items than in tutorial questions.

Pacing means giving the student a limited amount of time to respond. We have frequently said that timed displays are to be avoided and in general that the student should have as much time as desired to read and look at information. We amend our position somewhat for drills, because the major goal of some drills is speed and accuracy. It is of no benefit to translate an English word into French if it takes thirty seconds. The student will never be able to read or converse in French if word recognition takes so long. Similarly, most math teachers would not consider a student to know the arithmetic facts if more than a few seconds are required to respond. Thus, it is frequently appropriate in drills to require a quick response for it to be correct. The author should be careful, however, in choosing the time limit. Too short a time limit will frustrate many students. A drill may dynamically alter the time limit, requiring faster responses as the student becomes more proficient.

Pacing is not the only way to increase fluency. Salisbury (1988) suggests both speeded responding and the use of a secondary task. A secondary task means requiring the student to pay attention to some other task which may be unrelated to the items (pressing a key whenever the computer beeps) or related to them (responding to items in the context of a complex game).

Item Lists and Item Generation Algorithms

Drills use two major methods to present items. The most common method is to *select* items from a list. The method used primarily for math drills and science problem solving is *generation* of items using an algorithm.

List Selection. Most drills, such as vocabulary, translation, spelling, multiple-choice questions, single-word response questions, and some science problem solving, select items from a list. By that we mean that all the items which may be presented to the student are constructed ahead of time by the author and put into a list or library in the computer's permanent storage. The drill program then selects items from the list and presents them to the student. Answer keys are usually stored in the same list. For long drills, the storage of such lists of items may require considerable space. Language vocabulary drills, for instance, are likely to fill many diskettes.

Generation by an Algorithm.　Drills involving mathematics frequently use an algorithm to generate items. An algorithm is a procedure (a set of rules) to produce an item. A simple algorithm for an addition facts drill is illustrated in Figure 3–2.

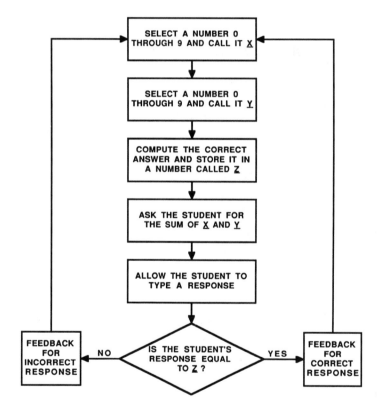

Figure 3-2　A simple item generation algorithm.

　　The program first selects two numbers and calculates their sum. Then it presents the numbers to the student and asks the student to type the sum. The student responds, and the program compares the number typed to the number calculated internally and indicates if the student was correct or incorrect. The procedure is then repeated and another addition problem with different numbers is presented. This type of algorithm together with a rule for when to stop provides a way for a computer to produce many items from a simple set of rules.

Some programs combine list procedures with generation by an algorithm. Instead of a list of questions, the program contains a list of algorithms. Each algorithm produces a particular type of item. For instance, an arithmetic drill could contain algorithms for four types of items, addition, subtraction, multiplication, and division. During each iteration of the drill cycle, an item *type* is selected, and the corresponding algorithm produces a specific question.

ITEM SELECTION PROCEDURES

In a drill that uses selection from a list, the selection procedure is a crucial factor. The selection procedure refers to the rules the program follows to select an item (or algorithm) for each iteration of the drill cycle. This is the most neglected factor in drill development. Most commercially produced drills utilize random item selection which, unfortunately, is the least efficient and least effective item selection method. Selecting specific items based on student performance, on the other hand, will improve any drill and is to be encouraged in all drill development.

Drills generally rely on the principle of repetition to enhance recall. Considerable research has supported the theory that we have two forms of memory, short-term and long-term memory. Information just encountered is easily stored in short-term memory, but also easily lost (Miller, 1956). Recall is enhanced by moving information from short-term memory into long-term memory. Item selection procedures should be designed in recognition of this process and of the limited nature of short-term memory.

Random Selection

In this procedure, each item is randomly selected from a list or randomly generated. The result is an inefficient drill. The student may answer a question incorrectly, be told the correct answer, but forget it before it is selected and presented again. Thus the student does not practice giving the correct response. Furthermore, the student may be given correctly answered questions more frequently than incorrectly answered ones, when in fact the student should get more practice on items causing difficulty than on those whose answers are known. A better item selection procedure is one which selects items frequently (while still in short-term memory) when they are answered incorrectly and infrequently when they are answered correctly.

Organized Queuing

Organized *queuing* techniques attempt to solve this deficiency. A queue is an ordered list. In a drill, that means an ordered list of items. Queuing therefore means determining ahead of time the order in which items will be presented. Two organized techniques are *flashcard queuing* and *variable interval performance queuing.* Both are methods in which the selection of items is determined by past performance. Other techniques of organized queuing are described by Salisbury (1988), including what he calls two- and three-pool drills, increasing ratio review drills, and progressive state drills. These are variations on the types of queuing we now discuss.

Flashcard Queuing. Flashcard queuing, which is similar to Salisbury's two- and three-pool drills, is so named because it is similar to the way people use flashcards. If you had a deck of flashcards with Spanish words on one side and English translations on the other, you would probably use a procedure like that illustrated in Figure 3–3.

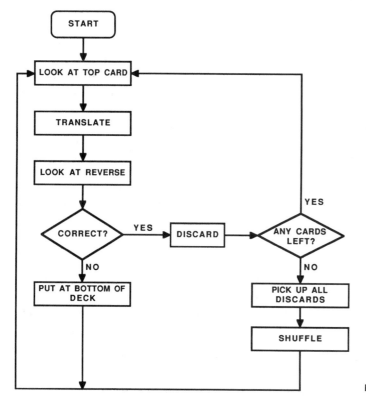

Figure 3-3 Flashcard queuing.

You would look at the top card and translate it. You would then look at the other side and, if correct, would discard it from the deck. If you were wrong you would put it at the bottom of the deck. When all cards are discarded, you would shuffle them and begin again.

You would continue doing this until you felt comfortable with all the words. Perhaps you would do it until you could go through the entire deck of cards without error. However, at the start of the drill, before any items are discarded, it may be a long time between missing an item and seeing it again. Thus, the student is likely to forget the response before it is presented again. Elimination of errors is still slow and difficult. Nevertheless, computer programs that use this procedure increase the frequency of items missed by the student, thus providing more practice with them than random selection.

Variable Interval Performance Queuing. The basic principle of variable interval performance (VIP) queuing, similar to Salisbury's three-pool drill with increasing ratio review, is that when an item is answered incorrectly it is positioned, or *queued*, at a number of new positions in the "future order of presentations," or *future queue.* By future queue we mean the organized list of all remaining items in the drill. This queue changes continuously as each item is administered. The first new position will generally be soon enough that the item will be readministered while still in the student's short-term memory, thus facilitating transfer of the information into long-term memory.

Notice we said that when an item is answered incorrectly it is queued at a *number* of *new* positions. For example, if an item is answered incorrectly, it is first deleted from its remaining *old* positions in the future queue and might then be placed in positions 3, 8, and 17. In other words, two different items will be administered, after which the missed item would reappear. Then four items will be administered, after which it would again reappear. Then eight other items will be administered followed by the question missed. Notice in our example that the number of intervening items grows. First there are 2, then 4, and then 8 intervening items. The item is queued in *variable* intervals, specifically in *increasing* intervals. Thus, after an item is missed, it is presented again fairly soon, but then gets presented increasingly *less* frequently, assuming it is answered correctly on successive presentations. The item is first *deleted* from its old positions so that if it is missed a number of times, the drill does not become excessively repetitive. Indeed, if the item were not first deleted, it would soon appear in adjacent positions in the future queue.

Consider a concrete example. Suppose we are administering a Spanish translation drill on ten words and are using the VIP queuing technique with positions of 2, 6, and 14. These numbers mean that after an error there will be 1, 3, and 7 intervening items. Suppose also our intention is to go through the initial list twice. At the start of the drill a random initial order is created for the ten words and then is repeated once. Assume the list is as follows:

       word 7
       word 3
       word 9
       word 1
       word 4
       word 10
       word 5
       word 8
       word 2
       word 6

word 7
word 3
word 9
word 1
word 4
word 10
word 5
word 8
word 2
word 6

Now the first item, *word 7*, is presented and the student responds with the correct translation. The new future queue is shown below.

word 3
word 9
word 1
word 4
word 10
word 5
word 8
word 2
word 6
word 7
word 3
word 9
word 1
word 4
word 10
word 5
word 8
word 2
word 6

The first item was deleted, and the future queue comprises the remaining nineteen items.

The next item presented is *word 3*. Suppose the student responds *incorrectly* to this item. The new future queue is created by deleting all instances of *word 3*, and then inserting it at positions 2, 6, and 14. When an item is inserted at a position, the item previously at that position and all other items below it are forced down one position. The future queue is now as follows.

word 9
word 3
word 1

word 4
word 10
word 3
word 5
word 8
word 2
word 6
word 7
word 9
word 1
word 3
word 4
word 10
word 5
word 8
word 2
word 6

The inserted item *word 3* is boldface to make its new positions more prominent. Count the lines and you will see that *word 3* now occupies the second, sixth, and fourteenth positions in the list.

This procedure would be repeated for each item. Whenever an item is correctly answered, the new future queue is produced by removing the top question. Whenever an item is missed, the future queue is produced by first removing the item missed from all positions it occupies and then inserting it in positions 2, 6, and 14, pushing down the items already in those positions. The reader should practice how this works by continuing this procedure and rewriting the future queue when the student makes the following responses for the next five items.

The next item is answered correctly.
The next item is answered correctly.
The next item is answered incorrectly.
The next item is answered incorrectly.
The next item is answered correctly.

The resulting five future queues appear below from left to right.

word 3	word 1	word 4	word 1	word 4
word 1	word 4	word 1	word 4	word 10
word 4	word 10	word 10	word 10	word 3
word 10	word 3	word 3	word 3	word 5
word 3	word 5	word 5	word 5	word 4
word 5	word 8	word 1	word 4	word 1
word 8	word 2	word 8	word 1	word 8
word 2	word 6	word 2	word 8	word 2

word 6	word 7	word 6	word 2	word 6
word 7	word 9	word 7	word 6	word 7
word 9	word 1	word 9	word 7	word 9
word 1	word 3	word 3	word 9	word 3
word 3	word 4	word 4	word 3	word 4
word 4	word 10	word 1	word 4	word 1
word 10	word 5	word 10	word 1	word 10
word 5	word 8	word 5	word 10	word 5
word 8	word 2	word 8	word 5	word 8
word 2	word 6	word 2	word 8	word 2
word 6		word 6	word 2	word 6
			word 6	

This procedure results in items the student finds difficult being repeated more frequently. Conversely, as the student's performance on an item improves, it is selected less frequently. There are many variations that can be made on the procedure. The particular positions (2, 6, and 14) might be different, although they are reasonable numbers for a list of ten words. The *number* of new positions (in this case three) might also be different; the greater the level of mastery required, the larger the number of new positions needed. The VIP queuing technique is summarized in the flowchart in Figure 3–4.

Retirement Criteria

When a student responds correctly to an item a number of times, we can assume that he or she knows the correct response. An efficient drill will stop presenting such an item and give greater emphasis to those items with a poor performance history. The criterion for taking an item out of the list is what we call the retirement criterion. Consider the previous example. The queue was originally created with the list of ten words presented once, then repeated once for a total of twenty items. If an item was correctly answered the first two times, it would have been retired from the queue. The retirement criteria began as *two* correct responses in a row. Whenever a word was missed, it was placed at three new positions in the queue. Thus, once an item was missed, its retirement criterion changed to *three* correct responses in a row. In the final future queue shown above, *word 1* will need to be answered correctly twice in a row to be retired (it appears twice in the future queue), while *word 4* still needs to be answered correctly three times before it will be retired.

Different retirement criteria are possible. We might have begun with the original list repeated three times (thirty items in the queue), in which case the retirement criterion would have started out at three correct. Similarly, we might have begun with the list just once, in which case a single correct response would retire an item.

Retirement can also be based on something other than number of successive times an item is answered correctly, for example, the speed of responding.

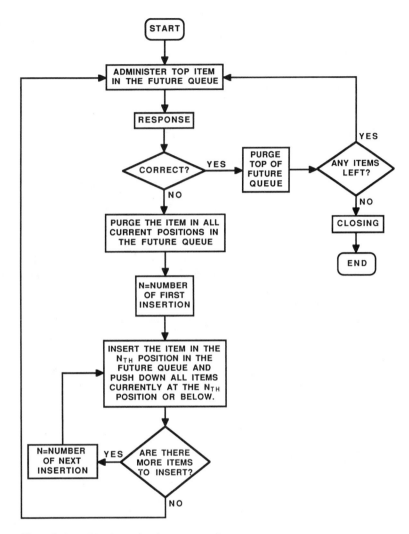

Figure 3-4   Variable interval performance queuing.

The criterion should, however, always be based on student performance. An item should not be retired because it has been administered three times, ignoring how the student responds. An item should not be retired because the student has indicated he or she does not like the item. We recommend retirement based on number of correct responses, with a slightly more difficult retirement criterion once errors are made.

Choice of Queuing Parameters

Insufficient research has been done on queuing techniques to advise designers on the correct number of insertions, their positions, retirement, and other parameters. They are likely to vary based on item difficulty, item type, number of items, and mastery required. The drill designer must determine reasonable numbers for particular content and students through pilot testing.

Termination

Termination means the decision to end the drill. As with tutorials, we distinguish *temporary termination,* in which the student must stop but intends to return and study more later, from *permanent termination,* where the student has completed the drill and will proceed to another lesson.

Temporary Termination. The student should be able to terminate the drill session temporarily at any time. A simple procedure should always be available for the student to do this, such as clicking on a mouse-sensitive *exit* button. The method must be well advertised, so when needed the student will know exactly what to do. Directions for termination should be given at the beginning of the drill. If keypresses are used and if there is room on the display, repeating those directions on each item display is a good idea. A mouse-sensitive *exit* button is the easiest and clearest method. If students do not remember how to terminate a drill correctly, they will probably turn off the computer, remove the diskette, or just walk away, in which case performance and restart data will be lost.

In addition to allowing the student to terminate temporarily at any time (which we consider essential), the *program* might also decide to terminate temporarily or suggest to the student to terminate temporarily, based on other considerations. For instance if the student has worked for an abnormally long time on a drill and is making many errors, it might be better to continue on the following day, rather than persisting and becoming frustrated. Drills of more than fifteen to thirty minutes can be very tiring, and performance will decrease as the student becomes fatigued.

Permanent Termination. Permanent termination of a drill should be based on student performance. This might be indicated by a message to the student that he or she has mastered all the items and now has the option of terminating the drill permanently. Or, when the student has mastered all items, the program may terminate permanently with a message, with no choice for the student to continue. Either method may be appropriate. More important is the criterion that defines permanent termination.

A criterion we discourage is student choice. Some drills allow the student to define how many items will be presented or to say at any time that he or she has had enough. Although this is appropriate for temporary termination, it is not good for permanent termination. The purpose of a drill is to enhance fluency and retention, and many students will end a drill because it is too hard, which is exactly the opposite of what they should do. When the student finds the drill too hard, it is obviously the case that the student *needs* the drill. It might be fine to stop for today, but fluency has not yet been achieved for the drill items. They have not been mastered.

Other criteria we discourage are absolute time in the drill and absolute number of items presented. Some authors use these criteria because they do not want students to become discouraged and to stop using the drills altogether. Again, we feel these criteria are good for temporary termination, which can prevent student discouragement. But if students are to learn the information, permanent termination should be based on performance only.

If a drill retires items as the student responds correctly to them, it may terminate when all items have been retired. This appears a natural and logical termination criterion. If implemented as such, however, it has one difficulty. After all but a few items have been retired, the drill will become very repetitious with the same two or three items being repeated over and over. Without many intervening items, the student may be responding to them based on short-term memory and not really be mastering them at all. There are two ways to correct this problem, *resurrection* and *premature termination.*

Altering the Queuing Parameters.   As the number of remaining items becomes less, two things may be done. The number of times an item is reinserted following an error may be decreased or the number of intervening items between insertions may be decreased. Assume we began a drill with three reinsertions following errors, with insertions as positions 2, 7, and 15. Eventually the length of the future queue will drop below 15. Using the first method, we would subsequently do only two reinsertions after errors, still at positions 2 and 7. Using the second method we would still do three insertions, but with fewer intervening items, say at positions 2, 5, and 10. The two methods may be combined so that as the future queue becomes very short, both the number of reinsertions and the number of intervening items decrease to a minimum of one reinsertion after one intervening item.

Resurrection.   Resurrection means taking items that have been previously retired and using them again in the future queue. In our previous example we began with ten items. At some point we would retire all but three items, let us say *word 3, word 1,* and *word 7.* We would resurrect a few retired items to use as spacers between these items. Presumably the student will respond correctly to resurrected items. But if not, the items would be treated like any others and be queued accordingly. Using the resurrection technique, the drill would never have fewer than about five items and so would not be too repetitious at the end.

Premature Termination.   Premature termination means that when all but a small number of items are retired, the drill is terminated despite there still being some un-retired items. For example, we might terminate the drill when there are five items left un-retired. This is simpler than the resurrection technique but it appears to create another problem, namely that some items are unmastered and the student will not receive further practice with them. This need not be the case, however. Most subject areas are such that there is enough material to construct many drills. Spanish vocabulary contains many thousands of words. You would not want to construct a 100,000-word Spanish vocabulary drill. Rather, you would probably construct many small drills of about twenty Spanish words each. Since this is usually the case, the un-retired items at the end of a drill may be carried over and added to the items of later drills. We will elaborate on this in a later section of the chapter. Premature termination may also be used in conjunction with the previous two techniques.

There are other ways in which student performance may define drill termination. For example, the author may define termination as occurring when the student answers ten items correct in a row, regardless of what the items are. The termination criterion might also be defined as "when overall performance is 80 percent correct." If particular items are in themselves unimportant, these criteria may be appropriate. But when the student should master all items, termination based on item retirement is more appropriate.

FEEDBACK

Most of the factors concerning feedback in tutorials apply to drills as well. An additional factor which is more important in drills than in tutorials is feedback following discrimination errors. A discrimination error is an error caused by confusion between similar things. Mistaking a cat for a dog, as children often do, is a discrimination error. Mistaking a rectangle for a square may also be a discrimination error. Although such errors occur in tutorials, they are not a primary concern because in tutorials, which are meant for initial exposure to information, we are not as concerned with mastery of all questions. It is usually not important if at the end of the tutorial a student cannot answer every question correctly. In drills, we are usually interested in the student being able to answer all items correctly, and sometimes rapidly as well.

When beginning a drill, let us say on twenty Spanish words, the student will make many random errors. The student will respond to English words with letter combinations that are not Spanish words at all. As the drill progresses, the student's errors will be different. Becoming more familiar with the words, the student will begin to confuse some of the possible Spanish words. Suppose a drill consists of the following English to Spanish translations.

dog	perro
much	mucho
beach	playa
hit	pegar
until	hasta
wood	madera
happy	faliz
chair	silla
every	cada
noise	ruido
thin	delgado

warm	caliente
servant	sirviente
north	norte
owl	luchuza
foot	pie
bad	malo
but	pero
nose	nariz
tired	cansado

It is likely that the student will confuse *pero* (meaning *but*) with *perro* (meaning *dog*). However, it is also the case that the student will make many other errors, responding to *foot* with *nariz* even though the correct response, *pie,* does not look or sound anything like *nariz.* This occurs because the student is learning to respond to some questions with *nariz,* but has not fully learned *when* that response is appropriate. Although *pie* and *nariz* are not similar in spelling or sound, they are confusable in this drill because they are both possible correct responses to particular stimuli (parts of the body) in the drill.

Researchers investigating paired-associate drills have theorized that such learning occurs in two stages (Underwood, Runquist, & Schultz, 1959). First is the response learning stage in which the student learns the responses themselves. During this stage the more random errors tend to occur. Second is the associative stage in which students link the responses to the correct stimuli. During this stage discrimination errors become common.

To summarize, when beginning a drill a student will make errors that are simply wrong. Words that are not Spanish words at all will be given as responses. But gradually, as the student learns the set of appropriate Spanish words, this type of erroneous non-word response will disappear and the errors that predominate will be Spanish words from the list given in response to the wrong English words. These errors are much more difficult to eliminate because they receive positive feedback in *some* situations. As the student attains near-mastery of the material, these confusions will be the last ones to be eliminated.

For drills on a small number of paired associates (one of the most common types of drills), it is convenient to define a discrimination error as a response which is a correct response to some *other* item in the list. The response, although wrong, is in the list of correct responses, so we call it a *within-list error.* In other words, if a response is a correct response for some other item in the drill, it is a discrimination error. In contrast, an *out-of-list* error, namely a response that is not a correct response for any item in the list, is not a discrimination error. Any Spanish word not being practiced in this particular drill is not considered a discrimination error, even if its spelling or sound is confused with the correct response. For example, in the above drill *faliz* would be a discrimination error in response to any English word in the list except *happy,* to which it is the correct response. Similarly *cada* is a discrimination error for every English word in the list except *every,* to which it is the correct response. On the other hand, *zoro* (the Spanish word for *fox*) is not in this drill list at all, so it would be an ordinary (out-of-list) error in response to any item in the list.

This operational definition of discrimination error is useful because it is easy to program the computer to recognize whether a word is in a particular list. It is harder to program a computer to recognize "how similar" two words are in spelling. It is *very* difficult to program a computer to recognize that two words *sound* similar.

Following a regular error, a drill will indicate the response was incorrect and give the correct response. For example, if the student is presented with *nose* and responds *oreja* (which means *ear*) the feedback would be

No, the Spanish word for *nose* is *nariz*.

Following a discrimination error, we should not only indicate that the response is incorrect and give the correct response, but should also point out that the response is the correct one to another stimulus in the drill. It is best to present all of this information at the same time so that the student may inspect the two stimulus-response pairs and observe similarities and differences. For instance, if the student responds to *nose* with *pie,* feedback emphasizing the discrimination error would be

No. *Pie* means *foot.*
The Spanish word for *nose* is *nariz.*

This procedure will make the student more aware of the type of errors made and will reinforce the associations between the correct words.

ITEM GROUPING PROCEDURES

Subdrill Grouping

Any single drill session should be about fifteen minutes to avoid boredom or fatigue. However, few subject areas will be even partially covered in this time. In a single drill, for instance, we might master ten or twenty Spanish words, but there are many thousands more.

The usual way of dealing with drills for a large amount of subject matter is to divide the material into many subdrills. The list of twenty English/Spanish words listed previously was one possible subdrill for English to Spanish word translation. Many more subdrill lists would be necessary. In grouping items into subdrills there are four relevant factors: group size, the method of assigning items to groups, selecting groups within a drill session, and review of items from old groups.

Group Size. Group size should be selected to produce a subdrill that can be mastered in a drill session of about fifteen minutes. This usually allows about ten to twenty items, depending on the difficulty of items, the length of time needed to respond to items, and the likelihood of discrimination errors. For language drills on word meaning or translation, in which discrimination errors are likely and responses are based primarily on memory, about twenty items is a good rule of thumb. Language drills on grammar or punctuation, in which responses are based on rules or a combination of rules and memory, may require a smaller number of items. Simple arithmetic drills may allow for more items. Problem-solving drills in the sciences or mathematics, which require more reading and thinking, call for a smaller number of items. In general, aim for a drill that takes about fifteen minutes to complete.

Assigning Items to Groups. Two criteria are relevant to grouping items in the same subdrill. The first criterion is grouping by difficulty. A math drill, for example, should consist of questions of approximately equal difficulty. If items of very different difficulty are necessary in the same drill session, the drill should introduce the difficult items after the student masters the easier ones.

The second criterion is to select items based on the likelihood of discrimination errors. We have indicated that a major impediment to mastering a drill list is discrimination errors. However, research evidence currently gives a mixed picture for the advantage of grouping versus separating confusable items. Alessi & Shih (1989) found that grouping items with confusable *responses* (the answer portion of the items) resulted in more errors during initial learning. But the results suggested that later recall might be better. Similarly, Nesbit & Yamamoto (1990) found that grouping items with confusable *stimuli* (the question part of the items) resulted in better performance on a recall test given soon after the drill session. Further research must assess the long-term effects.

While it appears that grouping confusable items makes it harder to learn them, the discriminations must eventually be learned, so such a grouping might be better in the long run. It remains to be determined if such grouping should occur earlier or later. Our current thinking is that for very new material, confusable items should be separated into different drill sessions. Later, such as during review, confusable items should be grouped. For example, with beginning students studying foreign-language translation drills, we would put phonetically dissimilar words together. In our previous Spanish drill, the choice of *perro* and *pero* in the same drill might have been a poor one (although we did it to illustrate a point). All other words in that list would be reasonable in the same group, because they are not inherently confusable.

In contrast to phonetic or orthographic similarity, some research has indicated that grouping by semantic similarity improves learning (Underwood Runquist, & Schultz, 1959). This is demonstrated in the classroom, for example, when a language instructor introduces words which all relate to foods and eating.

Group Selection. Having grouped items into subdrills we would usually use just one subdrill in a drill session. In some cases, however, a drill might select items from different groups in a single session. This may be done continuously, meaning that each time an item is to be selected the selection procedure also makes a decision about what *group* to select an item from. It might, however, be done only occasionally, for example, when we want a drill session to increase in difficulty. In that case the drill begins with a group of easy items and, as performance improves, switches to a group of more difficult items. Although these techniques may be useful in certain circumstances (especially mathematics and science), they are more difficult to develop. In most cases we recommend the use of drill sessions with a single subdrill of equal difficulty items.

Review of Items.   If we group items into subdrills, we face another instructional problem. Because the student masters a particular subdrill, such as our list of twenty English/Spanish words, we should not assume that the student will remember them forever. Indeed, without practice we can be assured that the student will forget them. Periodic review is necessary for retention. Review is needed especially for the items which the student finds the most difficult or uses the least often in situations outside of instruction. One way to accomplish this is to collect permanent data on all items indicating how difficult they were for the student to master.

When discussing item retirement and drill termination, we pointed out a problem that item retirement creates. Near the end of a drill session there are few items and the drill becomes very repetitious. One suggested solution was premature termination, such as terminating the drill when all but five items are retired. Those un-retired items are prime candidates for inclusion in later drill sessions along with new items. Item review by this or any method incorporates the important instructional principle of spaced practice, namely, that information will be better retained if practiced a little bit at a time over many occasions, instead of a lot on a few occasions. (For example, see Greeno, 1964.)

The Endless-Continuum Technique

This method is in direct contrast to grouping items into subdrills. It is related to the progressive state drill described by Salisbury (1988), but is different in operation. The procedure treats the subject matter (Spanish words, for instance) as one long, ordered list. In the first drill session, the program begins administering the first ten or twenty items according to a VIP or similar queuing technique. However, whenever an item is retired it is immediately replaced with a new item—the next one on the continuous list. The student gradually masters and retires items from the beginning of the list and moves on to items further down on the list.

Using this technique the number of "active" items is always the same. The drill is never terminated permanently. Each session is terminated either when a certain number of old items have been retired or when a specified amount of time (about fifteen minutes) had been spent on that day's session. We recommend the latter termination criterion.

The drill list is not really endless, but for a subject like Spanish vocabulary or calculus problem solving, it is for all practical purposes. It will certainly take a long time before a student completes the entire list. The ordering of the items in this long list is important. The list should be of increasing difficulty. Depending on level of the students, potentially confusable items might be kept separated in the list (to minimize discrimination errors for beginners). According to these considerations, a poor way to order Spanish words would be to list them alphabetically. This would randomize difficulty, because alphabetically adjacent words may have vastly different frequencies of usage. It would also maximize discrimination errors, because all items would be similarly spelled. A better way would probably be to first order all Spanish words by frequency of usage and then to make minor changes in the order by separating similarly spelled words.

An advantage of the endless-continuum technique is that it prevents the previously mentioned problem of repetitious drill endings due to item retirement. The number of items is always the same because whenever an item is retired a new one is added. This also simplifies use of the VIP queuing technique, for there are always sufficient items in the future queue to be placed between items that have been queued due to errors. Another advantage is that items which a student finds difficult to master may stay in the drill for a long time, until eventually mastered, without causing any particular drill sessions to be abnormally long. Review of retired items can be as easily incorporated into the endless-continuum technique as into the subdrill-grouping technique.

A last advantage of the endless-continuum technique is that it eliminates the problem of deciding how many items to include in a subdrill list to produce a drill session of reasonable length. There are no subdrills, and all drill sessions may be of a predetermined reasonable length because the drill always terminates temporarily, and termination may be based on time in the session or on student choice.

There are a few disadvantages to the endless-continuum technique. Storage of long lists on diskette-based microcomputers is difficult, and the algorithms needed to process long lists are more difficult to program. These are not insurmountable problems but a matter of increased program development time. With modern microcomputers using hard disk drives or networks, long item lists present little difficulty.

The endless-continuum technique may also have an adverse effect on motivation. Students may suffer a loss of motivation because the drill never seems to end, but goes on and on. Using the subdrill-grouping technique, the student is periodically told that the current group has been mastered and it is time to go on to a new group. Such milestones are encouraging to students. Slower students especially need the reinforcement of being told they have completed something successfully, even if there are more difficult things still to be done. Although this reinforcement may be lacking in the endless-continuum technique, the program may give the student information about progress in some other way, such as keeping track of the number of retired items, or the improvement in percent correct from one session to the next. Other ways of motivating the student in drills will be discussed in the next section.

To summarize this section, there are two techniques for drill item grouping, subdrill-grouping and the endless-continuum technique. In subdrill-grouping, groups should be constructed to require about fifteen minutes for mastery, to keep difficulty constant, and possibly to minimize discrimination errors. A single session should consist of a single subdrill containing items of equal difficulty. Spaced practice should be incorporated through review of items from past sub-drills.

In the endless-continuum technique, the list should be ordered to increase gradually in difficulty and possibly to minimize discrimination errors in any particular session. A session should have a constant number of active items and terminate based on time in the session or on student choice. Extra attention may need to be paid to student motivation when using the endless-continuum technique.

MOTIVATING THE STUDENT

As we have noted several times, the motivational quality of drills is inherently low. This is because drills are repetitious in nature: asking the same or similar questions over and over, requiring the same response format most of the time, and giving the same type of feedback after all responses. It is not surprising that teachers reviewing commercially available, computer-based instructional materials criticize the preponderance of drills. The majority of the drills are very poor. The reason most teachers do not like them, whether they are aware of it or not, is because they find them boring. There is good reason to expect that students will also find them boring. In the previous chapter we discussed several methods for increasing student motivation. We now consider some additional motivation techniques which have particular relevance in drills.

Competition

Four main types of competition that can be used to increase the student's motivation in a drill are:

Competition against other students
Competition against the computer
Competition against oneself
Competition against the clock

These are arranged in order of decreasing motivational quality for the average student. That is, most people compete the hardest against other people, a little less hard against a computer, and least hard against one's own previous performance or against the clock.

Competition between students can be accomplished in two ways. Two students may use a drill simultaneously, or the computer may store data on a number of students so that each can see how their performance compares to the others. This is sometimes done by showing a rank ordered list of student performance. The problem with competition among students is that while it serves as a powerful motivator for students who do well, it may be a punishment and embarrassment for those who do poorly. Many teachers avoid the use of competition among individual students for this reason. The use of handicaps, or competition between teams that are generally more evenly matched than individuals, can make competition between students less punishing for poor students.

Competition against the computer has the advantage of allowing all students to succeed and receive reinforcement. It is possible to adjust the difficulty of the computer's competitiveness so that against the best students the computer is very competitive and against the poorest students it is least competitive. In this way, the drill program can motivate each student to work at his or her best. When the student does so, success is beating the computer. The problem with computer competition is that it is not meaningful in some situations, such as a spelling drill.

Competition against oneself means trying to improve your previous performance on each use of a drill. This may mean answering more items correctly or responding more quickly. This type of competition is applicable to any kind of drill (unlike competition against the computer), and allows all students the chance of success (unlike competition between students). However, it is somewhat less motivating for students than the previous methods.

Competition against the clock is usually a variation of competition against oneself, for the clock time to beat is usually based on the student's own previous performance (although the student may not know it). The clock time may also be set as a function of other students' performance or the average performance of other students, in which case it is a variation of competition among students that may be more motivating.

Multiple Modes and Display Variety

Display and response variety may also increase student motivation. That is, presentations may utilize text, graphics, color, or sound; and responses may be made with a mouse, game paddles, joysticks, touch panels, light pens, and graphics tablets.

Goal Setting and Scoring

This method is somewhat akin to competition against oneself, although it may be used even for the student's first time in a drill. Simply indicating how many "points" the student needs to master the drill and periodically indicating the number of points earned so far can be motivating for most students. For younger students who would not be able to interpret the meaning of their score, simplified messages like "You're halfway there!" are an effective motivator as well.

Adjunct Reinforcement

This method of enhancing motivation applies to any instructional program as much as it applies to drills. The idea is to follow successful completion of the drill with some other activity the student finds enjoyable. In a computer-based education setting, this can be done by allowing the student to play a computerized game after successful completion. The computerized game may be instructional in nature or may be pure entertainment. This method is only effective if you pick activities that the student finds enjoyable. Do not assume that all students like computerized games.

When using this technique, the student must know the criterion for obtaining the adjunct reinforcement. It may be earning a specified number of points, retiring a specified number of items, or completing an entire subdrill. Data must be stored so that an instructor may ascertain that the student did indeed reach the required goal. While computerized games may be the most easily implemented reinforcer in the computer-based instruction environment, many other reinforcers are possible, such as playing basketball, reading a leisure book, leaving class early, or listening to records in the library.

Drill Session Length

We end this section by reminding the reader that the longer students work on a drill, regardless of what the material is, the more bored they will get. The length of drill sessions should be chosen in accordance with how repetitious the items are, how inherently interesting they are, and what other motivators are present. With other motivators present, drill lengths of thirty minutes to a maximum of about forty-five minutes are possible. Without such motivators, drill sessions should be about fifteen minutes to avoid the boredom which prevents students voluntarily coming back for more.

DATA STORAGE

Data storage in computer programs is an advanced topic. Our intention here is to indicate the purposes for storing data during drills and to describe the different kinds of data that must be stored for each purpose.

Data may be stored on a temporary basis, meaning in memory; or on a permanent basis, on computer disks or other magnetic media. When we say "permanent" we do not really mean forever. We mean that the data will not disappear when the student leaves or when the computer is turned off. The instructor may delete permanent data when desired, as long as the author has provided a way for the instructor to do so. For each type of data to be described, we will indicate whether, in general, the data should be stored permanently or temporarily.

The most important purpose for data in a drill is for item selection. If a randomized item-selection procedure is used, no data may be necessary, but we recommend more efficient procedures such as the VIP queuing technique. For this kind of item selection, the author must store data defining the future queue at any point in time. This may simply be a list of item identification numbers in the order indicated by the future queue. These data need only be temporarily stored. They must be in memory (rather than on disk), because they are constantly changing and must be accessed quickly every time an item is completed and a new one is to be selected.

If the type of procedure we have advocated is used, data for item retirement will be inherent in the data stored for the future queue, because an item is retired when it no longer appears in the future queue. If one uses other criteria, such as retiring an item after a certain number of presentations, additional data will be needed. If a resurrection procedure is used, or retired items are to be periodically reviewed, data must be stored about performance on such items.

If you define termination as exhausting the future queue, only data pertaining to the queue are necessary for determining termination. If you use another item selection procedure or a different termination criterion, other data may need to be stored. Total number of items presented, number of minutes in the drill, total correct or percent correct, number of items retired, and number of items left to be retired are all types of data that may be stored and used for the decision to terminate. These data are stored temporarily, as were the previous two classes of data.

Some data must be stored permanently. These include data for instructors indicating student performance on the drill, and data for restarting if the drill is being terminated temporarily. Restarting means to leave the drill and to come back at a later time. During the intervening time, other students may use the computer or the computer may be turned off, so data stored in memory will be lost. The easiest data to store for restarting is the future queue at the time of temporary termination. When the student restarts, the future queue is retrieved from disk and placed back in memory as temporary data for the purpose of item selection, retirement, and termination decisions.

To inform students of their progress in a drill, the program must store data temporarily and perhaps permanently. Temporary storage is needed if students receive progress reports during the drill, such as percentage of drill items completed. For that purpose the same data used for item retirement and termination may be sufficient. The future queue itself may be sufficient if all you want to do at any time is tell the student how many items remain in the list. A permanent record of performance requires storing some of the same data permanently.

Instructors sometimes need data for grading and other purposes. Similarly, authors need data to evaluate the effectiveness of their drills and to make improvements. Both require the collection of permanent data. For the instructor, summary data are usually required, such as the final score for each student or the time each required to complete a drill. Authors need more detailed data, such as item analysis information, in order to determine which items to keep or eliminate when revising a drill. The most common item data to collect are the errors on an item. One may also collect the average number of presentations required to retire an item.

Other kinds of data may be useful, but it is easy to get carried away and collect a lot of data that nobody will ever look at. Collect only data you need.

ADVANTAGES OF COMPUTER-BASED DRILLS

We began this chapter by pointing out that computerized drills are frequently criticized. We also took the point of view that much of the criticism is unjustified. We now summarize the advantages of computerized drills.

Drills of any sort, with workbooks, flashcards, or a teacher, are not very interesting. Computer-based drills can be made more interesting through competition, the use of graphics, informing the student of progress, and introducing variety. Some of these may admittedly be used for drills in other media as well.

The use of interactive graphics can be used to increase the effectiveness of drills in ways not possible with workbooks or flashcards. The use of graphics as a prompt, as a context, as a motivator, and as feedback can all serve to make computerized drills more effective than other types.

The sophisticated queuing methods possible on a computer, which emphasize practice on difficult items, have great potential for increasing drill efficiency and effectiveness. These methods are practically impossible to implement using flashcards or workbooks. The computer's computational power makes them possible and its unfailing memory makes possible the periodic review of retired items. This too is difficult or impossible with noncomputerized drills.

Some software packages are available that allow developers to produce drills incorporating these principles without programming the details of queuing and data storage, such as *DrillShell* (Alessi & Schwaegler, 1984), *DrillMaker* (Schwaegler, 1986), and *IMPART* (CMC Limited, 1989).

Immediate corrective feedback is possible with flashcards but not with most workbooks. Some workbooks give the answers on the next page or at the end of a chapter. However, flashcards and books with answers permit the lazy student to peek at the answers. If you peek at the answers in a computerized drill, meaning that you ask to see the answer, the program considers your answer wrong and you will be forced to practice that item more. Thus, it is not possible to get through computerized drills the lazy way, assuming a good queuing technique is used. Computerized drills can also provide special feedback for discrimination errors, which requires sophisticated response judging and list searching, which is difficult or impossible for other media.

Lastly, the computer is very good at storing different types of data automatically and effortlessly. This permits better methods of item queuing, retirement, and drill termination. It also permits permanent records for the student, the teacher, and the author about student performance and item quality.

REFERENCES AND BIBLIOGRAPHY

ALESSI, S.M., & SCHWAEGLER, D.G. (1984). *DrillShell.* [Computer Program]. Iowa City, IA: CONDUIT.

ALESSI, S.M., & SHIH, Y-F. (1989). Discrimination Errors and Learning Time in Computer Drills. In the *31st ADCIS Conference Proceedings.* Bellingham, WA: Association for the Development of Computer-Based Instructional Systems.

ATKINSON, R.C., & CROTHERS, E.J. (1964). A comparison of paired-associate learning models having different acquisition and retention axioms. *Journal of Mathematical Psychology, 1,* 285–315.

CALFEE, R.C., & ATKINSON, R.C. (1965). Paired-associate models and the effects of list length. *Journal of Mathematical Psychology, 2,* 254–265.

CMC LIMITED. (1989). *IMPART.* [Computer Program]. Secunderabad, India: CMC Limited.

FUSON, K.C., & BRINKO, K.T. (1985). The comparative effectiveness of microcomputers and flash cards in the drill and practice of basic mathematics facts. *Journal of Research in Mathematics Education, 16*(3), 225–232.

GRAVANDER, J.W. (1985). Beyond "drill and practice" programs. *Collegiate Microcomputer, 3*(4), 317–332.

GREENO, J.G. (1964). Paired-associate learning with massed and distributed repetitions of items. *Journal of Experimental Psychology, 67,* 286–295.

JONASSEN, D.H. (1988). Integrating learning strategies into courseware to facilitate deeper processing. In D.H. Jonassen (Ed.), *Instructional Designs for Microcomputer Courseware.* Hillsdale, NJ: Lawrence Erlbaum.

KEPPEL, G. (1964). Facilitation in short- and long-term retention of paired associates following distributed practice in learning. *Journal of Verbal Learning and Verbal Behavior, 3,* 91–111.

LEPPER, M.R. (1985). Microcomputers in education: Motivational and social issues. *American Psychologist, 40,* 1–18.

MERRILL, P.F., & SALISBURY, D. (1984). Research on drill and practice strategies. *Journal of Computer-Based Instruction, 11*(1), 19-21.

MILLER, G.A. (1956). The magical number seven, plus or minus two: Some limits on our capacity for processing information. *Psychological Review, 63,* 81–97.

NESBIT, J.C., & YAMAMOTO, N. (1990). *Sequencing Confusable Items in Paired-Associate Drill.* Unpublished manuscript. Tsukuba, Japan: University of Tsukuba.

PETERSON, L.R., WAMPLER, R., KIRKPATRICK, M., & SALTZMAN, D. (1963). Effect of spacing presentations on retention of a paired associate over short intervals. *Journal of Experimental Psychology, 66,* 206–209.

SALISBURY, D.F. (1988). Effective drill and practice strategies. In D.H. Jonassen (Ed.), *Instructional Designs for Microcomputer Courseware.* Hillsdale, NJ: Lawrence Erlbaum.

SALISBURY, D.F. (1990). Cognitive psychology and its implications for designing drill and practice programs for computers. *Journal of Computer-Based Instruction, 17*(1), 23–30.

SALISBURY, D.F., & KLEIN, J.D. (1988). A comparison of a microcomputer progressive state drill and flashcards for learning paired associates. *Journal of Computer-Based Instruction, 15*(4), 136–143.

SALISBURY, D.F., RICHARDS, B.F., & KLEIN, J.D. (1985). Designing practice: A review of prescriptions and recommendations from instructional design theories. *Journal of Instructional Development, 8*(4), 9–19.

SCHWAEGLER, D.G. (1986). *DrillMaker.* [Computer Program]. Iowa City, IA: CONDUIT.

SIEGEL, M.A., & MISSELT, A.L. (1984). An adaptive feedback and review paradigm for computer-based drills. *Journal of Educational Psychology, 76,* 310–317.

SLESNICK, T. (1983). Hold it: You're using computers the wrong way. *Executive Educator, 5*(4), 29–30.

STREIBEL, M.J. (1986). A critical analysis of the use of computers in education. *Educational Communication and Technology Journal, 34*(3), 137–161.

UNDERWOOD, B.J., RUNQUIST, W.N., & SCHULZ, R.W. (1959). Response learning in paired-associate lists as a function of intralist similarity. *Journal of Experimental Psychology, 58*(1), 70–78.

UNDERWOOD, B.J., & SCHULZ, R.W. (1959). Studies of distributed practice: XIX. The influence of intralist similarity with lists of low meaningfulness. *Journal of Experimental Psychology, 58,* 106–110.

SUMMARY OF DRILLS

Use a short title page.

Provide complete directions and allow the student to return to them at any time.

Use item types which both enhance response economy and accomplish your aims. Single-word or numeric answers are usually good.

Consider mixed mode presentations and responses.

Item presentations should be lean, have good layout, and use proper spelling, grammar, and punctuation.

Use graphics as context, prompts, feedback, and a motivator.

Keep item difficulty fairly constant in a drill session.

Use variable interval performance (VIP) queuing for item or algorithm selection.

Retire items based on mastery, such as elimination from the future queue in VIP queuing.

Terminate drills permanently based on performance, such as complete exhaustion of the future queue.

Allow temporary termination at any time based on student request, and allow restarting.

Allow help requests and requests to see the answer.

Judge intelligently.

Give format feedback when format is wrong. Don't consider the response incorrect; rather, give another try.

Use answer markup for constructed responses which are partially correct.

Give a short confirmation when the response is correct.

Give immediate corrective feedback when the response content is incorrect.

Keep feedback short and positive.

Provide special feedback for discrimination errors.

If subdrill-grouping is being used, keep drill sessions to about fifteen minutes. Select items for the subdrill based on equal difficulty and to minimize discrimination errors. In a drill session, select items from a single subdrill group except for some review items from completed subdrills.

The endless-continuum technique may be used as an alternative to subdrill-grouping. It avoids the problems of repetitious drill endings and adjusting session length. Drill sessions should be terminated at about fifteen minutes and students should be kept informed of progress.

Increase motivation with competition, setting reasonable and relevant goals, and progress reporting. Limit drill sessions to about fifteen minutes. Be careful that competition does not discourage poorer students.

In this summary, we include several recommendations from our discussion of tutorials that are also important in drills, although they were not repeated in this chapter.

4

SIMULATIONS

INTRODUCTION

In an educational context, a simulation is a powerful technique that teaches about some aspect of the world by imitating or replicating it. Students are not only motivated by simulations, but learn by interacting with them in a manner similar to the way they would react in real situations. In almost every instance, a simulation also simplifies reality by omitting or changing details. In this simplified world, the student solves problems, learns procedures, comes to understand the characteristics of phenomena and how to control them, or learns what actions to take in different situations. In each case, the purpose is to help the student build a useful mental model of part of the world and to provide an opportunity to test it safely and efficiently.

Simulations differ from interactive tutorials, which help the student learn by providing information and using appropriate question-answer techniques. In a simulation the student learns by actually performing the activities to be learned in a context that is similar to the real world.

The model of teaching discussed earlier had four phases: presenting the student with information; guiding the student in acquiring the information or skills; providing practice to enhance retention and fluency; and assessing learning. Tutorials generally engage in the first two of these instructional phases, and drills almost always deal with the third. Simulations, in contrast, may be used for any of the four phases; that is, they may serve for initial presentation, for guiding the learner, for practice, for assessing learning, or for any combination of these. Simulations that assess learning usually do not incorporate any of the other phases, while when the other phases are present it is usually in combination.

For the purpose of this discussion, it is convenient to divide simulations into two main groups, those that teach *about* something and those that teach *how to* do something. The *about* group has two subcategories, namely *Physical* and *Process*. The *how to* group also has two subcategories, namely *Procedural* and *Situational*. This can be summarized as follows:

> *About* simulations
>> Physical
>> Process
> *How to* simulations
>> Procedural
>> Situational

This classification is useful because there is widespread confusion as to what is meant by simulation. The word *simulation* has very different connotations to people of different disciplines. When civil engineers or economists refer to a simulation, it is very likely they mean what we call a process simulation. Educators, on the other hand, normally deal with situational simulations, and training professionals with physical or procedural simulations.

Although a framework for understanding the differences between these categories is beneficial, there is also the potential drawback of creating the impression that the categories are clearly distinct. In fact, most simulations do not fall neatly into just one of these categories, but rather are a combination or synthesis of more than one type. Nevertheless, a classification system does help clarify some of the existing confusion.

PHYSICAL SIMULATIONS

In a computer-based *physical* simulation, a physical object or phenomenon is represented on the screen, giving the student an opportunity to learn about it. Typical examples are simulations of the movement of glaciers, of light through lenses and prisms, or of the transmission of electricity through power lines.

A typical physical simulation, for example, is one of a mechanics experiment in which the student propels an object out of a cannon with varying velocity, angle, and other parameters. The program shows the path of the object and graphs other information. The student can investigate, for example, what cannon angle results in the object going farthest. Figure 4-1 illustrates such a program, called *Mechanics—Physics Simulations I* (Cabrera, 1986). The benefit of doing this experiment through a simulation is that the student can complete many more trials with less effort than could be done in a laboratory with real objects. The student can easily compare the relative paths under different conditions. In a real laboratory, the student can only deal with a limited range of velocities, cannot manipulate friction or other parameters, and cannot easily observe the resulting path of a projectile.

Another typical physical simulation is that of the movement of molecules under constraints of temperature, pressure, and volume. A simulation is an ideal way for a student to explore the relationships among these as expressed in the Gas Laws. In the simulation the student can change the volume of a container in which a fixed amount of gas is trapped and see the effect this has on the temperature and pressure. Figure 4-2 shows a screen from *Chem Lab Simulation #2—Ideal Gas Law* (High Technology Software, 1979). The benefit in this case is that the student can

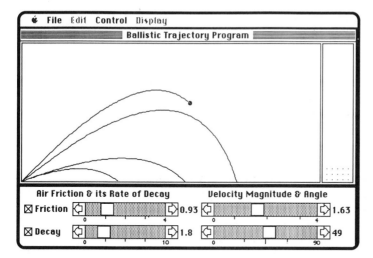

see the movement of the molecules and the rate at which they collide with the sides of the container—things normally invisible to the naked eye. This visualization of what is happening facilitates learning.

A third physical simulation is *Standing Waves* (Lane, 1984). This is a completely user-controller simulation of wave motion in physics. The user can choose the wave shape, amplitude, frequency, and a variety of other parameters. Then, as the wave progresses, the user can slow it down, freeze it, decompose it into component parts, integrate relativistic effects, and so on. *Standing Waves* can be used by an instructor as an electronic blackboard demonstration or by students as a labo-

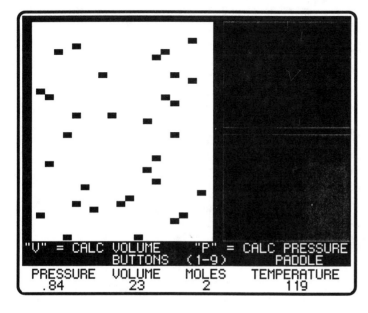

ratory to investigate wave motion on their own. Figures 4–3a and 4–3b show some of the controls for *Standing Waves,* and a complex wave with its component parts superimposed.

There are also physical simulations of more common phenomena, such as the movement of stars and planets or of the development of weather systems (look at the weather segment on the television news for examples of this). Other simulations show how an internal combustion engine works or how an earthquake affects the earth's surface.

Physical simulations, then, are generally used to inform students about some phenomenon. Students learn from the simulation by manipulating some aspect of the world they are working with (such as in the Gas Law program) or

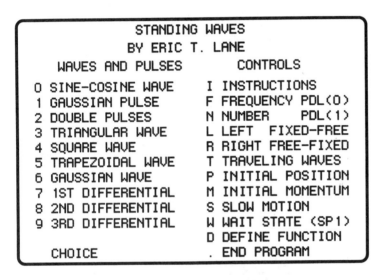

Figure 4–3a A physical simulation of wave motion. *(Courtesy of CONDUIT)*

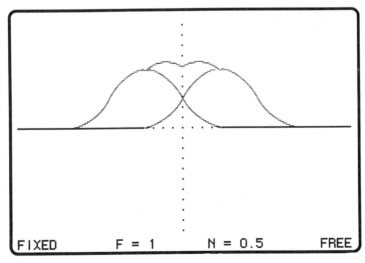

Figure 4–3b

merely by observing how change occurs over time (as in an engine simulation or a program showing the course of glaciers).

PROCESS SIMULATIONS

Process simulations are quite similar to *physical* simulations in that they attempt to teach *about* something. Process simulations are generally used to inform students about a process or concept that does not manifest itself visibly, such as how the economy works, or how the laws of supply and demand affect pricing, or how populations grow and decline. Physical and process simulations differ from other simulations in that they are not as interactive. Instead of participating as in situational simulations, or constantly manipulating as in procedural simulations, the student selects values of various parameters at the beginning of the simulation, and then watches the process occur without intervention. The student then resets some of the initial values and repeats the process. Learning comes from observing the effect of changing values on the outcome.

Economists, for example, use process simulations for forecasting. At the beginning of a simulation to determine how much revenue will be available for appropriation, the economist would select values for such parameters as unemployment rate, gross national product, labor productivity, income tax rates, and so on. The simulation would then be run. The result is an estimate of how much revenue would be available given the circumstances defined at the beginning. Learning occurs by repeating the process a number of times with different beginning values for the parameters, and comparing the results.

Another distinguishing feature of process simulations is that they are an accelerated or slowed-down version of the real process. That is, they change the rate at which the process occurs in reality to one that enhances the learning process. Some actions happen too fast to see, such as the movement of electrons or the passage of light. Others take so long that it is difficult to gain a perspective of the process, such as the dynamics of a country's economy over a year or the growth of populations. It is much easier for a student to conceptualize what is occuring when it is presented in a time frame that highlights the changes. Once the student understands the process, the true rate of occurrence can be introduced, together with its ramifications.

Catlab (Kinnear, 1982), is an example of a process simulation. The student chooses initial physical characteristics of a female and a male cat, such as fur color and pattern. The cats mate and have kittens, a process which is speeded up so that the kittens arrive a few seconds after mating, rather than after the normal nine weeks. The student then has a litter of kittens with characteristics derived from their parents, according to the laws of genetics. That is, the kittens are not identical to the parents, but share some of their characteristics.

The process is then repeated, with the student choosing to mate two new cats from any available. These include the original parents and all generations of their offspring, which are assumed to mature immediately. The purpose of the simulation is for the student to become familiar with genetic research and the laws of genetics. This is accomplished by generating hypotheses about how physical characteristics of cats are inherited, and by testing each hypothesis through observation of the results of each mating. Many generations of kittens have to be produced before the student has enough information to understand how the genetic laws of inheritance operate. In the simulated world, this can be accomplished in a matter of minutes.

There are a number of biological simulations similar to *Catlab*. Other simulations mate fruit flies or raise strains of bacteria in jars. Some simulations deal with the migration of animals due to changes in their environment and the effect of such changes on population. In a program called *Balance: A Simulation of Predator/Prey Relationship* (Luncsford, Rivers, & Vockell, 1981), the student makes choices about the initial number of wolves and deer in a forest, the number of wolves shot annually by hunters, and similar factors. The simulation begins and the student can observe how the numbers of wolves and deer increase or decrease each year. The student can then choose different initial populations to see how the annual figures change as a result. Figures 4–4a, 4–4b, and 4–4c illustrate part of this program.

```
SIZE OF DEER POPULATION AT TIME ZERO
?750
SIZE OF THE WOLF POPULATION AT TIME ZERO
?15█
```

Figure 4-4a A process simulation in ecology. *(Courtesy of Diversified Educational Enterprises, Inc.)*

```
            TYPE OF ENVIRONMENT
            1.  FOREST
            2.  BRUSH
            3.  MEADOW
        SELECT 1, 2, OR 3 ?2█
```

Figure 4-4b

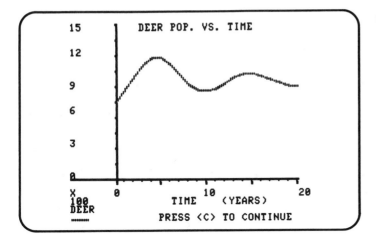

Figure 4-4c

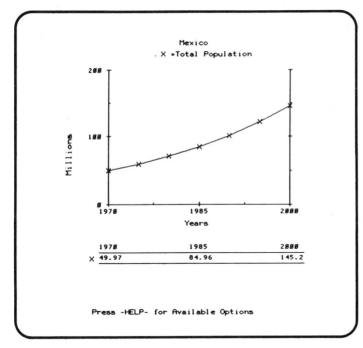

Figure 4-5 A process simulation about human population showing a graph of the population of Mexico from 1970 to the year 2000. *(Courtesy of the Board of Trustees, University of Illinois)*

Similar simulations of human populations help students study the effects of various factors on population growth. In such simulations, the student may select initial fertility rates, average age of marriage, average age of death, infant mortality rates, and so on. On running the simulation, it is possible to observe how the population changes over a number of years based on those factors. Figure 4–5 shows a graph produced by such a simulation, *Population Projections* (Population Dynamics Group, 1976), showing the predicted population of Mexico from 1970 to the year 2000, given that the underlying factors present in 1970 do not change unexpectedly.

PROCEDURAL SIMULATIONS

The purpose of most procedural simulations is to teach a sequence of actions that constitute a procedure. Common examples are operating a hand-held calculator or telephone, performing a titration, diagnosing an equipment malfunction, or landing the space shuttle. Procedural simulations frequently contain simulated physical objects because the student's performance must imitate the actual procedures of operating or manipulating some physical entity. However, it is important to distinguish between the role that the physical objects play in this type of simulation in contrast to that in physical simulations. Here the simulation of the various physical objects is necessary to meet the procedural requirements, whereas in physical simulations the objects themselves are the focus of the instruction. The purpose of a distillation simulation, for example, is to teach science students how to obtain measurements for calculating the required results, not to show what the apparatus looks like, although it may serve this function too. In other words, the primary objective of a procedural simulation is to teach the student how to do something, while a physical simulation is designed to teach how something works.

An important type of procedural simulation is the "diagnosis" simulation. The student is presented with a problem to solve and must follow a set of procedures to determine the solution. Typical of these simulations are medical situations in which the student must diagnose a patient's problems and prescribe appropriate treatments. Other simulations involve diagnosing electronic or automotive faults, or identifying unknown substances or minerals. In the latter case, the student applies the correct sequence of tests to determine the nature or composition of the object or substance, just as a chemist or geologist would do. Figure 4–6 shows a display from a program, *Trouble Shooting Fuel Systems* (Dare, 1973), that teaches automotive fault finding. Each test that you make and each action taken has a "flat time charge." That is, you are charged this amount no matter what the outcome. Part of the incentive is to repair the fuel system as inexpensively as possible.

In all of these procedural simulations, whenever the student acts, the computer program reacts, providing information or feedback about the effects the action would have in the real world. Based on this new information, the student takes successive actions and each time obtains more information. For example, consider a medical diagnosis simulation. The student is told that a patient has been admitted to the hospital with certain symptoms such as a high temperature, skin coloration, and a feeling of general weakness. The student must take some action, such as choosing from available medical tests: blood test, tissue samples, throat cultures. The simulation provides the test results: for example, the blood and tissue are normal, but the throat culture is not. Based on these results, the student selects further tests and obtains more results. This procedure continues until the student feels confident enough to enter a diagnosis into the computer. The program then provides feedback about the accuracy of that diagnosis.

A primary characteristic of procedural simulations is that there is one or more correct or preferred sequences of steps which the student should learn to perform. However, there may be many different ways of reaching the same con-

```
The engine cranks but will not start.

What do you want to do?

Select a letter, then press NEXT.

POSSIBLE CHECK                          FLAT TIME CHARGE
a.  Check the fuel tank.                   2 minutes
b.  Check the fuel gauge.                  1 minute
c.  Check the in-tank fuel filter.        10 minutes
d.  Check the tank-to-pump fuel line.      8 minutes
e.  Check the fuel pump output.            5 minutes
f.  Check the pump-to-carb fuel line.      1 minute
g.  Check the in-line fuel filter.         2 minutes
h.  Check the in-carburetor fuel filter.   5 minutes
i.  Check the carburetor output.           2 minutes
POSSIBLE CORRECTIVE ACTION
j.  Fill the tank.                         5 minutes
k.  Replace the in-tank filter.            5 minutes
l.  Replace the tank-to-pump fuel line.    5 minutes
m.  Replace the fuel pump.                10 minutes
n.  Replace the pump-to carb fuel line.    5 minutes
o.  Replace the in-line fuel filter.       2 minutes
p.  Replace the in-carburetor fuel filter. 4 minutes
q.  Replace the carburetor.               15 minutes
r.  CRANK THE ENGINE.                      no charge

If you want to see the drawing again, press the HELP key.
                   >

   So far, you would have taken   9 minutes.
```

Figure 4-6 All the choices available in *Trouble Shooting Fuel Systems*, together with their associated costs. *(Courtesy of Board of Trustees, University of Illinois, and Frank Dare)*

clusions, not all of which are equally efficient. A procedural simulation provides the opportunity to explore these different paths and their associated effects.

SITUATIONAL SIMULATIONS

Situational simulations deal with the attitudes and behaviors of people in different situations, rather than with skilled performance. Unlike procedural simulations, which teach sets of rules, situational simulations usually allow the student to explore the effects of different approaches to a situation, or to play different roles in it. In virtually all situational simulations, the student is an integral part of the simulation, taking one of the major roles. The other roles may be taken by students who interact with the same program, or by the computer playing the role of a person.

An example of a situational simulation is *School Transactions* (Lunetta, 1984), a program for prospective teachers that simulates difficult situations in classroom management. In this simulation, you are confronted with a variety of classroom management problems, such as a note being passed during class or equipment disappearing from your chemistry laboratory. For each situation you must make a decision about what to do. In the example of the note being passed, you could ignore it, confiscate it and put it away, read it aloud, and so on. As a consequence of your action, the situation may be resolved, may worsen, or may be unaffected. Resolution of the situation requires a number of actions. In each case, feedback is based on your decisions and the resulting outcomes. The instructional benefit is that the situation may be used many times to experiment with different approaches to the same problematic situation with no penalty of failure. Figures 4–7a, 4–7b, and 4–7c show three displays from the *School Transactions* program.

```
You are a science teacher in a school
of moderate size.

This class has had no serious behavior
problems, but after the students left
the room yesterday you noticed that a
small amount of lab material was
missing.  You had no opportunity to
resolve the problem during the rest of
the day.

Some time ago, you ordered an important
film to show to the class today.  Class
is about to begin.

What do you do?



          Press RETURN to continue.
```

Figure 4–7a A situational simulation, *School Transactions*, showing choices and outcomes. *(Courtesy of CONDUIT)*

```
1.   Confront the issue immediately.
'There will be NO further labs until
the materials are returned.'  Then
proceed with the work of the day.
2.   To deal with the minor problem will
cause too much disruption. 'Those kids
are already too anxious to waste
valuable time.'  Ignore the incident.
3.   Inform students that materials
cannot continue to disappear. They must
be CHECKED IN at the end of each lab.
4.   Discard your plans and confront the
issue. 'We cannot have labs if
materials disappear.' Ask the class to
suggest ways to resolve the problem.
5.   Confront the issue by telling the
class to return after school. Then
proceed with the work of the day.

Enter the NUMBER of your response. 1
```

Figure 4–7b

```
The missing materials are not
returned,

and you have told the class there will
be no further labs until the materials
are returned.

What do you do now?


          Press RETURN to continue.
```

Other role-playing simulations deal with such diverse topics as choosing careers, international affairs, or operating a business. In a simulation entitled *Biznes* (Schenk, 1983), for example, the student plays the role of a company executive making annual decisions about the number of employees, capital outlays, production, and sales. The simulation determines revenue and profit for the year.

```
                     Year 0
Labor hired             5.
  Cost/unit          8000.
Capital used            5.
  Cost/unit         12000.
Amount produced        99.
  Price/unit         1000.
Amount sold            86.

Total revenue       86000.
  Revenue/unit        868.69
Total cost         100000.
  Cost/unit           1010.1
Profit             -14000.
  Profit/unit         -141.41
Marginal product
  of labor             12.88
  of capital            7.13
Demand elasticity       8.66

Here is the report that last year's
management received.

     Press RETURN to continue.
```

Figure 4–8a A situational simulation, *Biznes*, showing choices the student can make. *(Courtesy of CONDUIT)*

Figure 4-7c

```
                    Year 0        Year 1       Figure 4-8b
Labor hired           5.            7.
  Cost/unit         8000.
Capital used          5.           10.
  Cost/unit        12000.
Amount produced      99.          158.
  Price/unit       1000.
Amount sold          86.

Total revenue     86000.
  Revenue/unit       868.69
Total cost       100000.
  Cost/unit         1010.1
Profit            -14000.
  Profit/unit       -141.41
Marginal product
  of labor            12.88
  of capital           7.13
Demand elasticity      8.66

What price would you like to
charge? 1100
```

You can modify your choices for each year and compare profits to determine effective combinations to make your company grow and profit. The simulation teaches the complex interactions of running a business and the problem-solving inherent in running a business successfully. There is no single way to make a profit. Rather there are a number of strategies that may be successful. The simulation allows you to explore different strategies without having to lose real money. Figures 4–8a and 4–8b show two displays from *Biznes*.

Some types of games may also be classified as situational simulations, particularly adventure and gambling games. These will be discussed along with other types of games in the next chapter.

ADVANTAGES OF SIMULATIONS

We divide our discussion on the advantages of simulations into two parts—why using a simulation is frequently a better instructional vehicle than the real world, and why simulation offers more instructionally than other methodologies.

Simulation versus Reality

There are a number of advantages that simulation has as an instructional tool as compared to using the real world as the classroom. These range from being able to enhance safety, to provide experiences not readily available in reality, to modify the time frame, to control the complexity of the learning situation for instructional benefit, and to save money.

Consider the case of teaching someone how to operate a nuclear power plant. For safety reasons it is not appropriate to use a real plant for teaching novices about the complexities of operation. If the student were to make a mistake, the results could be catastrophic. Similarly, nobody would consider teaching a future Boeing 747 pilot how to deal with the failure of a couple of engines on takeoff by actually cutting the power at lift-off in a real airplane.

Sometimes simulation provides the only way of providing certain types of instruction. In a history course, for example, it is impossible for students to actually witness events in the past. However, through simulation they can gain a good impression of what happened and often can play the role of one of the participants. Similarly, in an economics course, simulation would be the only way for students to relive the events of the Great Depression.

Another attribute of simulations is that one can control aspects of reality that would ordinarily make learning difficult. A good example is the control of time for instructional benefit. In some circumstances it is helpful to accelerate the passing of time. For example, in the simulations mentioned above in which cats or fruit flies are bred, it is very useful having successive generations arrive in seconds rather than hours or months. Similarly, in the study of the movement of glaciers, simulations can compress years or even centuries into minutes. Sometimes it is very useful to slow down time. In studying the movement of molecules, for example, it is helpful to manipulate time so that the student can see the movement.

Consider the videodisc program *Assessment of Neuromotor Dysfunction in Infants* (Blackman, Lough, & Huntley, 1984). It provides access to several pediatric disorders that occur so seldom that most medical students (and even qualified physicians) would never encounter them. Filmed over an extended period, it provides visual documentation of these disorders together with simulated diagnosis.

There are other ways in which simulations can enhance learning. The most common of these is by providing the learner with an environment that is more conducive to learning than the real one. This is very often the case, because real-world situations are inevitably filled with distractions. Consider again the task of learning how to fly an airplane. The cockpit of a modern airplane is one of the worst learning environments possible. Not only are there many instruments facing the novice pilot, but there are messages being relayed to and from the traffic controllers from all planes in the vicinity, requiring careful attention to what is being said. The novice pilot is usually very apprehensive about being up in the air and is also concerned about other aircraft nearby. All this creates a situation in which most attention is being concentrated on aspects actually irrelevant to the immediate task at hand, which is learning to control the plane. With attention thus divided, it is not surprising that it takes a long time to learn how to fly when the actual plane is used as the vehicle for learning.

On the other hand, the initial learning could take place in an appropriate simulator, which is usually a computer-controlled, mechanical device that looks like an airplane cockpit that gives the student the impression of flying a real airplane. In reality, of course, it never really leaves the ground. Most of the extraneous intrusive factors, such as air-traffic conversation, noise, and fear, do not exist in the simulation, or at least can be controlled by the instructor. Thus, the student pilot is able to pay greater attention to the objectives of a particular lesson, making the hours of simulator time at the beginning of a person's training considerably more productive than the same time spent in a real airplane.

In some ways *computer-based* simulators can offer benefits not found in ordinary mechanical ones. Conventional simulators are most effective when used with an instructor, who can manipulate the environment, such as wind and turbulence, and provide feedback on performance. A computer-based simulator can do more than simulate the physical world. It can also simulate the instructor. That is, it can monitor performance just as an instructor does, then identify errors, and attempt to diagnose why they occurred. Prescriptive feedback can then be given to the student. The advantage of this is that a simulated instructor is always vigilant and is infinitely patient. A simulated instructor is also always available.

Trollip (1979) used a computer-based simulation to teach pilots how to fly holding patterns. Since this task is primarily a cognitive one rather than one of controlling the airplane, using a simulation results in numerous benefits. For example, the instruction is highly efficient because the simulated airplane can be repositioned for each sequence of instruction, whereas, of course, a real airplane would have to fly to the appropriate starting position each time. In this simulation, students flew holding patterns using simulated instruments in a variety of conditions. At the end of each pattern a simulated instructor analyzed the pattern flown, compared it to the ideal pattern for the given set of conditions, and provided both informational feedback ("Your inbound leg was more than ten degrees to the left of where it should be.") and prescriptive feedback ("You must adjust the outbound heading more for the crosswind.").

A different type of complexity is the number of variables in a phenomenon. For example, *Catlab* (Kinnear, 1982) deals with only seven characteristics of cats and *Biznes* (Schenk, 1983) with only three major decisions in running a business. Real cats and real businesses have many more variables than have been simulated in these programs. This simplification of reality is often beneficial pedagogically, because students would be confused if they had an array of variables to control.

Simulations are also more convenient than their real counterparts, in such ways as costing less, being available at any time, or being repeatable. For instance, a simulation of flying an airplane is certainly less expensive than actually flying an airplane and can be used anytime, day or night, irrespective of weather conditions. Furthermore, if the instructor is also simulated, a student does not have to coordinate with a real instructor and can even learn at home. A simulation of diagnosing a particular disease in a patient can be done at any convenient time, whereas in reality the student may have to wait for a patient with the required disease to enter the hospital. The first year of teaching happens only once in real life, but in a simulation can be repeated, hopefully improving the real experience when it occurs. Similarly one can repeat the treatment of a sick patient until the appropriate tests and treatments are learned. In reality finding patients with identical symptoms is rare.

Simulations are also generally more controllable than reality. As mentioned before, simulations are not only imitations of reality, but are also simplifications of it. This is necessary because reality is impossible to imitate in all its detail. Simplification, moreover, is instructionally advantageous. A person will generally learn faster if details are eliminated at the beginning of instruction. For instance, in an automotive diagnosis simulation, differences between engines, such as age, quality of spark plugs, and months since the last tune-up, can be ignored or eliminated, and the instruction focused on the particular problems to be diagnosed. If real engines were to be used for training, the student may be distracted or misled by the minor, but irrelevant, problems all engines have.

In general, simulations such as this facilitate initial learning by simplifying the phenomenon. As the student becomes increasingly competent in dealing with the simple case, the simulation may then add detail to bring the student closer to reality.

Simulation versus Other Methodologies

Simulations typically have three major advantages over conventional tutorials, drills, and tests. The first is that they enhance motivation; the second is that they have better transfer of learning; and the third is that they are more efficient.

Motivation. That simulations enhance motivation is well known and not surprising. One would expect a student to be more motivated by being an active participant in a learning situation than by being relatively passive. It is more interesting to fly a simulated airplane, for example, than it is to read about flying it. It is more exciting to try to save a simulated patient than it is to read a medical textbook. Although the "learning by doing" philosophy has been advocated for a long time (Anzai & Simon, 1979; Bruner, 1973; Papert, 1972, 1980, for example), the introduction of computers into the educational field is beginning to make its implementation more widespread.

Transfer of Learning. Transfer of learning refers to whether skills or knowledge learned in one situation apply in other situations (Clark & Voogel, 1985). We say that simulations have good transfer of learning, because what was learned in the simulation results in improved performance in the real situation. It is easy to understand why a simulation of growing a rose garden, for example, in which one manipulates soil acidity, the exposure to sunlight, and the amount of watering, would result in better transfer than would reading a gardening book. The simulation gives the student practice in growing roses, and the opportunity to try out different combinations of conditions. The book, however, only provides information and hints on how to do it. We would expect the student who had used the simulation to be better prepared.

Efficiency.   The idea of transfer of learning can be taken a step further. Not only can one measure how effectively knowledge, skills, or information transfers from one situation to another, but one can also measure how efficient the initial learning experience is with respect to the transfer. This is best illustrated with a hypothetical example.

Assume that you have two different sections in a chemistry course. To one class you give a series of interesting and informative lectures dealing with a specific laboratory procedure. To the other you give a computer program that not only provides the same information but also has a simulation of the laboratory. On completing its respective form of instruction, each section performs the procedure in a real laboratory. Your observation of the two groups convinces you that there is no difference in performance, and that both perform well. On the basis of this information you would be forced to say that both instructional methods have the same transfer of learning. However, if the lecture series took ten hours, and the average time to completion of the simulation were only five hours, you would also have to say that the simulation was more efficient. That is, more transfer occurred per unit of learning time with the simulation than with the lectures. (See Roscoe, 1971, 1972; Povenmire & Roscoe, 1973; and Carter & Trollip, 1980, for more information on transfer of training.)

Phases of Instruction

As can be seen from the discussion above, simulations are very powerful learning tools. They encourage active learning by demanding student participation and are efficient both logistically and instructionally.

It was mentioned earlier in the chapter that simulations usually satisfy more than one of the four major phases of instruction. In fact, they usually satisfy two: either initially presenting the material and guiding the student through it; or guiding the student through previously learned material and providing practice in it. Assessing learning is usually not combined with other phases. It is rare to find simulations that provide three or all four phases in the same lesson.

Laboratory simulations, such as *Chem Lab Simulation #2—Ideal Gas Law* (High Technology Software, 1979), assume the student has had an introduction to the laboratory, and are primarily a vehicle for the guidance and practice phases. Other simulations, such as *School Transactions* (Lunetta, 1984), introduce the student to new situations and are intended as initial instruction and guidance.

When simulations do provide initial instruction, they frequently do so by a "discovery" or "experimentation" approach. That is, by interaction with the system or situation, the student learns about it. In using the *School Transactions* simulation, for example, the student teacher "experiences" interactions with students, and by virtue of those experiences develops skills about working in the social system of the classroom. In a similar fashion, by repeatedly breeding cats in *Catlab* (Kinnear, 1982), the student learns about the genetic laws as they apply to particular observable features of cats.

Not all simulations teach in this way, however. Many combine instructional strategies in an attempt to optimize learning. They may begin much like a tutorial, showing the student a drawing of a telephone, for example, and providing information on how to operate it. Then the program may have the student make calls on a simulated telephone, providing guidance at first by correcting errors or by reminding the student to pick up the receiver before dialing. Later, the program may allow the student to practice dialing using the simulated telephone, giving little or no guidance or feedback. The simulated telephone, at this point, would operate just like a regular one, providing busy signals and recorded messages for incorrect dialing.

A simulation about road signs and driving laws may introduce the signs and rules, guide the student in their use, and provide practice by letting the student use the simulation over and over until very familiar with the laws. Many simulations have this characteristic. If used once, the simulation presents information and guides the student in its acquisition. If used repeatedly, it takes on the characteristics of a drill. Of course, some simulations are in fact drills, requiring the student to continue until proficiency is demonstrated.

Finally, simulations may be used as tests. Flying a simulated airplane may be the test that determines if the student is ready to fly real planes. If the student "crashes" in a flight simulation, more practice is probably needed in the simulated environment. If the simulated flight is successful, the student is perhaps ready to fly in a real airplane—with an instructor of course. Another benefit of using simulations as tests is that they are often more valid than other alternatives. For example, a paper-and-pencil test with multiple-choice items is unlikely to provide the same information about a student's ability to perform a chemistry experiment as would requiring the student to perform the experiment via a simulation.

In summary, simulations may be used for any of the first three phases of instruction. Most frequently they include initial presentation of information and guidance, or guidance and practice, rather than all three. If the first type of simulation is used repeatedly, it may also serve as practice, whether or not that was intended. Additionally, simulations may be used as tests and often have considerable advantages when used in this way. We continue the discussion on this topic in Chapter 6 on Tests.

FIDELITY IN SIMULATIONS

Fidelity refers to how closely a simulation imitates reality. An airplane simulator with a sophisticated visual and motion system provides a high-fidelity simulation of flying. A computer-based simulation, such as *Flight Simulator* (Artwick, 1983) has much lower fidelity. *Transfer of learning* refers to the extent a student can apply what is learned in instruction to a new situation, usually intended real performance. In this section we discuss an extremely important design consideration, namely the relationship between fidelity and transfer of learning.

Historically people believed that increasing fidelity in an instructional setting led to better transfer. However, research has demonstrated that the relationship between the two is more complex than this and depends on the instructional level of the student (Ruben & Lederman, 1982; Wolfe, 1985; Schneider, 1985). Alessi (1988) proposes that the fidelity/learning function may be represented by Figure 4–9.

For a novice student, while low-fidelity instruction produces learning, some increase in fidelity might yield better learning. For example, a student pilot would learn from reading a text about flying an airplane but might learn more from watching a film with narration. The same student might learn less, however, from a very high-fidelity experience such as a mechanical simulator. And putting the novice student in a real airplane, the highest possible level of fidelity, may be so confusing and stressful as to result in no learning at all.

The experienced student learns more for even higher levels of fidelity, such as in a mechanical simulator. In a real airplane, that student may learn less than in a simulator, but more than the novice student.

For the expert, such as an experienced pilot learning to fly a new airplane, a high-fidelity simulator might be very effective and the actual airplane could be even more effective.

The line labeled *best learning* is plotted through (or near) the maximum point of each curve, the point of best learning for that level student. For increasingly sophisticated students it reflects increasingly high-fidelity instruction. However, that line does not represent the best level of fidelity in terms of other training factors. The line labeled *most cost-effective* intersects the curves where they begin to exhibit diminishing returns. Beyond that point great increases in fidelity and expense are required for small increases in learning. An efficient curriculum would train at levels of fidelity along the *most cost-effective* line, increasing along it

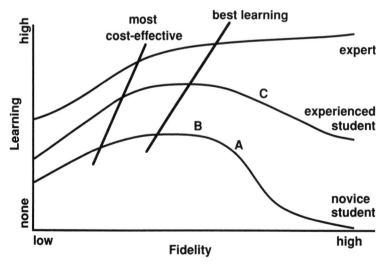

Figure 4-9 Hypothesized relationship of fidelity and learning. *(By permission of the Journal of Computer-Based Instruction and The Association for the Development of Computer-Based Instructional Systems)*

as students increase in experience. Methods of measuring and deciding upon the most cost-effective combinations of media and instructional fidelity are discussed in Roscoe (1971, 1972), Povenmire and Roscoe (1973), and Carter and Trollip (1980).

Figure 4-9 describes the effect of fidelity on learning *at the time of instruction.* How does that relate to *transfer?* Transfer is a complicated function which includes not only initial learning at the time of instruction, but also the *similarity* of the instructional situation to the performance environment, the *perceived* similarity of the instructional situation to the performance environment, and the student's level of *motivation.* These factors are not independent. Actual similarity affects perceived similarity, which affects motivation. Neither are they identical. It is possible that while point *A* on Figure 4-9 yields less initial learning for that student than *B,* it may still yield higher transfer. However, point *C* for a more advanced student, which represents higher fidelity and higher initial learning, should yield better transfer than either *A* or *B.*

In summary, it appears we are faced with a dilemma in simulation design. Increasing fidelity, which theoretically should increase transfer, may inhibit initial learning which in turn would inhibit transfer. On the other hand, decreasing fidelity may increase initial learning, but what is learned may not transfer to the application situation if too dissimilar.

The solution to this dilemma lies in ascertaining the correct level of fidelity based on the student's *current* instructional level. As a student progresses, the appropriate level of fidelity should *increase.* So, for a novice student initial learning is emphasized and for an advanced student transfer is emphasized. This is what we do by choosing points along the *best learning* line in Figure 4-9, or in recognition of economic and time limitations, along the *most cost-effective* line. This solution has been suggested for instruction generally in Bruner's spiral curriculum (Bruner, 1966) and Reigeluth's elaboration model of instruction (Reigeluth, 1979).

FACTORS IN SIMULATIONS

The underlying flow of a simulation is shown in Figure 4-10. As with both previous methodologies, there is an introduction, followed by a cycle which is repeated. For each cycle the following occurs.

> A scene is presented.
> The student is required to react.
> The student reacts.
> The system changes in response to this action.

Depending on the nature of the simulation, the cycle may repeat very frequently, as in a flight simulation, or infrequently, as in a process simulation where the cycle may occur only once after the student chooses the initial parameters.

As with tutorials and drills, we discuss the factors that affect the nature of simulations and influence their effectiveness. However, we will not deal again

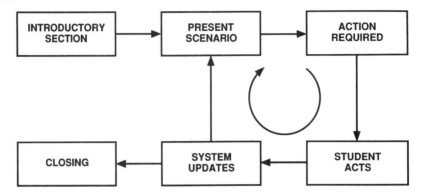

Figure 4-10 The general structure and flow of simulations.

with factors that were discussed in previous chapters. We break our discussion into three broad areas, namely

the introduction
the presentations and interactions
the completion of the simulation

INTRODUCTION TO THE SIMULATION

Objectives

Because students are generally less familiar with simulation methodology than they are with tutorials, drills, and tests, greater emphasis should be placed on introducing the student to the objectives of the simulation and to the instructional goals. For example, to inform students that a lesson is about "the Civil War" is not likely to excite them. For many students it would conjure up memories of history books filled with dry facts about the Civil War and dates to be remembered. If the lesson states, however, that "You will play the role of advisor either to General Grant or General Lee. You will help make decisions about purchasing weapons, food, medical supplies, and about strategy, which will effect the outcome of the war," the student is likely to be more interested in the lesson.

One needs to exercise some caution, however, because a statement like the one above is so different from students' usual educational experiences that they might still wonder about the purpose of such a lesson. Consequently, a lesson should not only state what will happen in the simulation, but should also make clear what is the purpose of the activity. The above example might continue by explaining that "This simulation will acquaint you with the social, political, and economic situations in the middle nineteenth century, and how they influenced the outcome of the Civil War." Keller and Suzuki (1988) include as a part of their theory for maintaining motivation in CBI that relevance of the lesson to the student's needs should be clear. More than in other methodologies, objectives in simulation can make relevance clear.

Directions

Clear and complete directions are more important in simulations than in most methodologies, because students engage in activities that are more complicated and varied. For example, there is greater use of devices other than the keyset for inputting information. The most common of these are mice and joysticks. If the lesson uses such devices, their operation should be carefully explained in the directions, and perhaps practice provided to master their use. If the use of the device is crucial to the successful operation of the simulation, you may even want to ensure the skill level by requiring proficiency before the student is allowed to start the simulation.

The Opening

After the title page, objectives, and directions, a simulation needs to establish the scenario for the lesson. This is usually accomplished with what has been called an "opening scene" (Dennis, 1979). This generally describes the context of the simulation, paying particular attention to the physical entities the student will manipulate, the procedures the student will engage in, the situations which the student will encounter, or the processes to be studied. In *Fractional Distillation Experiment* (Smith, 1975), the opening is very verbal (Figure 4–11). However, the succeeding display is almost entirely made up of graphics (Figure 4–12).

The opening of a simulation merely sets the stage. It by no means determines all that the simulation will do. In the distillation simulation, for example,

```
            Fractional Distillation


This program provides a simulation of a fractional
distillation.  First you will be asked to assemble
the apparatus by touching the parts illustrated and
then putting them on the distillation column by
touching the correct location on the apparatus.


After the equipment has been assembled, you will
be asked to separate a 50:50 mixture of pentane,
bp 36°C, and hexane, bp 69 °C.  To do this you
will have to control the temperature of the heating
bath so the liquid in the distillation pot continues
to boil.  Note that as the pentane is removed the
boiling point of the residue keeps going up so you
will have to slowly increase the bath temperature.
```

Figure 4-11 The verbal opening of *Fractional Distillation Experiment. (Courtesy of Board of Trustees, University of Illinois, and Stanley Smith)*

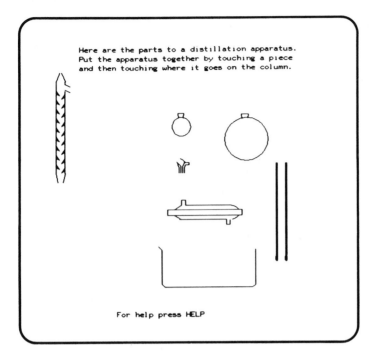

Here are the parts to a distillation apparatus. Put the apparatus together by touching a piece and then touching where it goes on the column.

For help press HELP

Figure 4-12 The graphic page following the opening page in *Fractional Distillation Experiment.* *(Courtesy of Board of Trustees, University of Illinois, and Stanley Smith)*

the assembly of the apparatus is just the beginning. After the assembly is completed, the student must heat parts of the apparatus, cool other parts, take temperature readings, and empty containers as they fill up. After collecting sufficient samples, the student must perform some mathematical calculations to determine the outcome of the experiment.

THE BODY OF THE SIMULATION

Simulations are not as easily divided into parts like tutorials and drills, because they are usually a more integrated whole. However, for the sake of descriptive convenience, it is useful to describe the main body of the simulation in terms of four components:

> the underlying model
> the presentations
> the student actions
> the system reactions or feedback

The Underlying Model

The underlying model of the simulation is the representation of the system or phenomenon being simulated. It is the way of depicting the physical entity, the procedure, the situation of which the student is a part, or the process which the program mimics.

Computer models underlying simulations are primarily of three types: continuous, discrete, and logical. Continuous simulation models are those that represent phenomenon that change continuously over time. Most phenomenon in the physical and many in the social sciences are of this sort. The model under-lying motion of a falling object, growth of animal populations, and cycles of an economy all are based on continuous simulation methods.

The mathematics used to represent such systems is differential equations, and the solutions that enable one to program the model are based on numerical integration. The program for a continuous simulation will include the initial con-ditions for relevant variables, their rates of change, and the time period and incre-ments over which they are examined.

If you are building a program to simulate plant growth, for example, vari-ables might include sunlight intensity, air temperature, water and mineral avail-ability, chlorophyll content of the plant, and plant tissue mass. The initial values of each of these would be necessary along with formulae indicating how each changes over time and the values of other variables and constants. Given this in-formation, a continuous simulation calculates the change in these variables for each time increment (for example, every hour).

The mathematics underlying this type of simulation is complicated, but software exists to aid the designer in development. For Apple II and IBM comput-ers *MicroDynamo* (Pugh-Roberts Associates, 1982), and for Macintosh computers *Stella* (High Performance Systems, 1987) and *Extend* (Diamond, 1988), allow the developer to enter initial conditions, rates of change, and time parameters, and the software solves the equations.

Discrete simulations are less common in education. They represent phe-nomenon in which quantities vary by discrete amounts over time. Common exam-ples of discrete simulations are queuing simulations which represent things waiting in line. Systems such as automobile and air traffic, check out lines in a grocery store, and production on an assembly line are examples amenable to dis-crete simulation.

The mathematics of discrete simulations is probability and statistics. Such phenomenon are characterized by objects arriving for some kind of ser-vice (cars, airplanes, or people), waiting in line for service, being served, and finally leaving the system. The solution and program depends on knowing the distribution representing arrival of objects, and the patterns and time required to serve them.

Although considerably easier to solve and program than continuous sim-ulations, discrete simulation development is also facilitated by simulation systems and languages. Both *Stella* and *Extend* include commands for discrete simulation models.

Logical simulations are very common in computer-based instruction, though uncommon in other uses of simulation, such as for research and develop-ment. Logical models are those represented by sets of *if-then* rules in a computer program. Systems represented by logical models include the operation of machines, decisions in running a business, and many social interactions. For example, a machine starts to operate *if* the power switch is depressed. A camera takes a picture *if* there is film and it is properly advanced and you press a button. Sales take place *if* it is a work day and there is inventory to sell.

Continuous and discrete simulation methods have long been used by scientists and engineers for research and development. They often used these simulations to understand how various physical phenomenon work and to design systems based upon them. Logical simulation methods are of greater interest to educators. However, many simulations, especially educational ones, are a combination of these methods. Most simulations in science education, for example, include a combination of continuous and logical simulation methods.

The underlying model includes a number of factors which determine both the nature of the simulation and the nature of the student's interactions with it. These factors are:

the objects
the precision
the type of reality
the sequence
the number of solutions
the time frame
the role of the student
the involvement of the student

Objects. The objects of the simulation are any physical entities, pictured or described. Examples are an airplane, chemical apparatus, a telephone, spaceships, hospital patients, automobile engines, unknown substances, a job application, road signs, school principals, animals, corporations, and countries. Some simulations may deal with a single object, such as a piano, while others may deal with many, such as the teachers and students in an elementary school.

Having a larger number of objects does not necessarily make the simulation more complicated, either to program or to use. Rather, it is usually the presence or absence of *people* as objects that increases complexity. The rules governing the behavior of people are far less understood than those governing the behavior of airplanes, pianos, and animals.

Precision. Precision refers to how well what is being simulated is understood. The precision of the real phenomenon is closely related to the presence or absence of people as objects. The most precise subjects are those involving strict mathematical, physical, or chemical laws. It is well known what happens when a distillation apparatus is heated or when a 5-kilogram weight is dropped from 3 meters. However, even things that follow physical or chemical laws may have elements of probability or chance. That is, some of the factors that influence reality are either unknown or impossible to determine.

An automobile engine, for example, probably follows physical and chemical laws completely, but deciding why an engine runs poorly is still a difficult matter because there are so many physical and chemical influences on the many parts of the engine. There are also many unknown influences as well, such as the care the engine has received in the past, or how fast the owner normally drives the car. Thus, the operation of an engine is based on chance or probabilistic considerations, as well as scientific or mechanical ones. The more chance is involved, the less precise the model is and the harder it will be to program the simulation.

The extreme case occurs when people are involved. Very little is really understood about individual human behavior, which makes predicting it almost impossible. Simulations that include humans as objects, therefore, usually incorporate a great deal of chance, and consequently are the least precise and most difficult to program.

It is useful to keep in mind that simulations require a description or prediction of the behavior of the various objects in them. So, when trying to determine how difficult a simulation will be to program, think about how predictable the various objects are. Pianos, for example, are very predictable, because pressing a particular key will always result in the same sound. Automobile engines are less predictable. When you turn the ignition key on a cold morning, they do not always start. People are very unpredictable, although the degree of predictability varies from one individual to another. Thus, simulating a piano is easier than simulating an automobile engine, which in turn is easier than simulating a person.

Type of Reality.   The type of reality of a simulation refers to whether what is depicted is one that occurs in the real world. There are three levels of reality: subjects that do occur as simulated, which include most simulations described so far; subjects that do occur but not exactly as simulated, such as when a student pretends to be a fish in a lake or doubles the birth rate of a country at will; and imaginary subjects, which do not occur at all, such as castles with dragons, or battles between spaceships. Realistic subjects are neither better nor worse than imaginary ones. They simply have different purposes and advantages.

Sequence.   Sequence refers to whether the events which occur do so in a linear, cyclic, or more complex fashion. The events of a titration, for instance, are essentially linear. There is basically one way in which a titration should be performed. The events of driving and obeying road signs are cyclic. We periodically approach a road sign and engage in appropriate behavior, such as slowing, stopping, and looking. The same scenario occurs repetitively as we drive.

Many phenomena are complex, by which we mean that the order of events is not strictly definable or that there are many different possible orders, some perhaps preferable to others. For example, there are many ways to fill out a job application, land an airplane, diagnose problems in an automobile engine, or run a business. There are many unpredictable events that occur in one's first year of teaching, or in treating a hospital patient. In general, including unpredictable events makes the sequence of a simulation more complex. Although complexity is a function of reality, the underlying model of the simulation is usually simplified in order to make it easier to design and program, and to make learning easier for the student.

Number of Solutions.   Reality varies a great deal with respect to the number of solutions available. Sometimes there is no solution because there is no right or wrong. An example of this is the effect of mating different cats on the characteristics of the offspring. Another is measuring the time it takes for objects to reach the ground when dropped from different heights.

Other subjects, particularly procedural ones, have one preferred sequence of events. Examples of these are performing a titration, playing a particular song on a piano, or properly obeying a series of road signs encountered on a road. Finally some subjects have many correct or incorrect paths, especially situations such as diagnosing a patient's disease, the first year of teaching, or running a business.

When designing a simulation, the number of solutions possible in the real subject is usually reduced in the model for convenience or efficiency.

Time Frame.   The time frame of a subject is the period of time over which it normally takes place. An event in optical physics, such as light moving through a lens, occurs in a billionth of a second. A titration may take from ten minutes to an hour. Diagnosing a rare disease takes days or weeks. Breeding and raising cats takes many months. Doubling the population of a country takes decades. The formation of mountains and rivers takes a million years. Models can be built to simulate all of these things, but the more extreme the time frame of the real phenomenon, the less realistic the model will be on this dimension. Nevertheless, it is precisely those events that occur extremely fast or very slowly that simulations excel at teaching. Students cannot in reality observe the motion of light through a lens, or the growth of a mountain, but they can do so through simulation.

Role of the Student.   The role of the student refers to whether the student using the simulation is considered to be one of the objects in the model or is external to it. Being a part of the model, however, does not necessarily mean the student is a person in it; the part may be an animal or physical object. Usually, however, people are people. In a situational simulation, the student is usually a part of the simulation. For physical, procedural, or process simulations, the student generally manipulates and observes them from outside.

The Involvement of the Student.   In the real world, sometimes a person is the primary actor to which objects react. In contrast, objects may be the primarily actors to which people react. Sometimes neither take the primary role, but act and react in equal ways. In a titration simulation, the student is the primary actor and controls the apparatus and the experiment. This is also the case for the piano simulation and for most process simulations. In a road signs simulation, however, the student must react correctly when a particular road sign comes into view. The student has no control over the signs, and thus is the reactor. The student is also the reactor when filling out a job application.

The most challenging simulations to design are those in which both the student and the model act and react because this makes the underlying model more complex. In a medical simulation, the patient shows symptoms, the physician performs tests, the test results come back. The physician prescribes a treatment, new symptoms begin to develop in the patient, and so on. Each change in symptoms causes a reaction in the physician (the user of the simulation), and each choice or decision by the physician, such as giving medication, causes reactions in the patient and other aspects of the simulation. Situational simulations usually include equal action and reaction by both the model and the user of the simulation. This is seen in *School Transactions* (Lunetta, 1984), in which decisions made by the teacher cause reactions by the students. Their reactions in turn shape subsequent actions of the teacher.

Summary.   In this section we have looked at some of the factors that affect the nature and complexity of the model underlying a simulation. We use the term *completeness* to refer to the extent to which the important components of reality exist in the simulation. All simulations simplify reality by eliminating objects or other components which are not essential to the instructional goals. A flying simulation for a beginner will not present all the instruments nor will require interaction with air traffic controllers or other airplanes. Only those objects contributing to the task at hand would appear in the display. As proficiency increases and the simulation becomes more complex, other instruments may be added.

When designing a simulation, the completeness of the underlying model should be assessed against the instructional needs of the learner rather than merely against reality.

We turn now to a discussion of how the simulation appears to the student.

Presentations

This section deals with how the simulation is presented to the student and discusses what the student sees and hears as well as how faithfully objects of the simulation are represented.

Whether the Subject Is Visual or Conceptual.   Physical subjects are usually visual in nature, situational subjects are usually conceptual in nature, and procedural or process subjects are commonly either or both. The nature of reality influences the manner in which it is depicted. It is easier to depict road signs by showing pictures of them than it is by describing them in words. Conversely, it is easier to depict the first year of teaching by describing it as in a story rather than by trying to draw it. Depicting a visual subject pictorially is usually more realistic, but not necessarily better from a pedagogical point of view. Sometimes it is just not possible to use anything other than text.

Types. There are four major types of presentations, and are usually all present to varying degrees in every simulation. They are:

choices to be made
objects to be manipulated
events to react to
systems to investigate

Choices to be made are often textual, because they involve the selection of one option from among many (Figure 4–13). However, as authoring systems make greater use of icons, choices are more frequently being accomplished by selecting an appropriate icon. Objects to be manipulated, such as the controls of an airplane or pieces of chemical apparatus, are frequently pictorial, as in Figure 4–14. Events to which the student must react can be of any mode. Thus, the student may be told that a patient's vital signs have deteriorated; a student pilot may see a

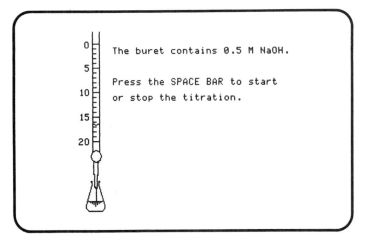

```
INFORMATION CHOICES:

 1  Opinion leadership (7 days)
 2  Newspaper exposure (7)
 3  Radio exposure (7)
 4  Meeting attendance (7)
 5  Demonstration attendance (7)
 6  Literacy (3)
 7  Feedback (2)
 8  Longer descriptions of choices
Enter the number of your request: _
```

Figure 4-13 Choices are usually made on textual displays. *(Courtesy of Christopher H. Lovelock, Charles B. Weinberg, and the publisher, CONDUIT)*

```
The buret contains 0.5 M NaOH.

Press the SPACE BAR to start
or stop the titration.
```

Figure 4-14 When objects are to be manipulated, the displays are normally graphic. *(Courtesy of COMPress)*

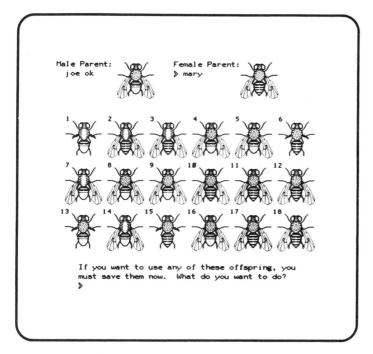

Male Parent:
joe ok

Female Parent:
》 mary

1 2 3 4 5 6

7 8 9 10 11 12

13 14 15 16 17 18

If you want to use any of these offspring, you
must save them now. What do you want to do?
》

Figure 4-15 Textual or graphic displays are common when the student must react. This display is from *Drosophila Genetics* and mixes text and graphics. *(Courtesy of Board of Trustees, University of Illinois, and Gary Hyatt, David Eades, Paul Tenczar, and J. Denault)*

change in the instruments; or a young musician may hear a note played by the computer. Systems to be investigated also typically use mixed modes. *Balance: A Simulation of Predator/Prey Relationship* (Luncsford, Rivers, & Vockell, 1981) describes the numbers of animals numerically and graphically, while *Drosophila Genetics* (Hyatt, Eades, Tenczar, & Denault, 1968), a simulation of fruit fly genetics, draws pictures of each new generation of fruit flies on the screen (Figure 4–15).

Realism.   In the previous section we indicated that most simulations make compromises with respect to reality, usually through the process of simplification. The result of such changes is a decrease in the fidelity of the simulation. It is important to remember that such a decrease in fidelity does not necessarily mean that the effectiveness of the simulation has also decreased. To the contrary, it is usually beneficial to simplify the context.

The realism of the simulation refers to the degree to which a particular component appears like its real counterpart. Once again increased realism is not necessarily tied to increased effectiveness. In a program about weather, it may be important to draw a cumulo-nimbus cloud quite accurately, showing its anvil shape, and giving details about growth rate, height, and intensity. However, in a program about cross-country flying it may only be necessary to show that there are clouds in the vicinity of the airplane. In a chemistry lab simulation, if the purpose of a simulation were to introduce chemical apparatus, it could be important to include details such as volume markings, stoppers, and correct size. If the simulation merely uses the apparatus as part of some experiment, simple silhouettes would suffice.

The most common error made in the design of simulation is believing that increased realism leads to improved learning. Particularly among novice designers, there is almost a compulsion for high fidelity. The level of realism must be determined by instructional effectiveness.

Summary. It is important to analyze the instructional requirements of the visual presentations carefully because bad decisions will have a big impact on effectiveness and cost. Objects that appear with inappropriate fidelity can often affect learning adversely. It is important to remember, too, that increasing fidelity always costs more, but does not always improve learning. We will discuss this topic later in the chapter.

Student Actions

Simulations are very interactive in nature. That is what makes them both appealing and effective. Because they require a great deal of input from the student, it is necessary to look at these student actions from a design perspective.

Mode. Simulations incorporate more varieties of input modes than other instructional methodologies. In addition to the keyset, the mouse is frequently used. Devices such as touch panels, light pens, and speech input and output are also used, and may be seen or used in increasing numbers of simulations. The use of mice, trackballs, and touch panels is particularly useful in simulations that require the student to manipulate objects on the screen. Designing input for handicapped students requires careful thought. You certainly do not want to provide more obstacles for them. We recommend you consult with experienced people before finalizing your decisions.

The keyset is easier for inputting information, but as always, the age and typing ability of the student is a major design consideration. Mice are very good for selecting, drawing, and moving objects. However, if they are to be used, you should ensure that they are available on the computers where the simulation is to be used and that there is enough space on the desk to use them. If you are using a touch panel, having keystroke equivalents is recommended because panels are not very reliable. Furthermore, if the monitor is placed high relative to the user, too much touching will cause fatigue. Finally, the use of several modes within a lesson probably enhances interest and stimulates more learning than would the use of a single mode (Rigney & Lutz, 1976).

Types. Earlier, four types of presentations were introduced and discussed: choices to make, events to react to, objects to manipulate, and systems to investigate. Each has its own student action associated with it. They are, respectively, making a choice, manipulating objects, reacting to an event, and asking for or collecting information.

Making choices is usually accomplished by typing the number or letter of a choice, by selecting or manipulating an appropriate icon, or by typing out a request in a subset of English. Thus, "increase the temperature" is an example of a choice made by the student. The same choice could be made in a different way, as illustrated in Figure 4–16.

Manipulations are usually made by pressing keys or using one of the external devices, usually a mouse or touch screen. In the distillation simulation, the student touches a picture of a thermometer and then touches the place on the screen to which it should be moved. The same is true for all other parts of the apparatus. Contrast this manner of assembling the apparatus with having to type "put the thermometer inside the beaker."

Typical examples of simulations that require the student to react are stopping at a stop sign, keeping an airplane flying at constant altitude, or taking disciplinary action when students pass notes around the classroom. Such reactions may be indicated in a wide variety of ways. The student may react by pressing an appropriate key to make an immediate choice or may use the mouse to move an object on the screen. In some cases the reaction will not be overt, but will influence future decisions. For example, in a chemistry simulation the student may notice the temperature of a flask to be rising too quickly. If the temperature had not yet reached a dangerous level, the student may take no immediate action, but would rather monitor the status more carefully, and eventually reduce the heat.

Finally, when a simulation allows a student to investigate a system, rele-

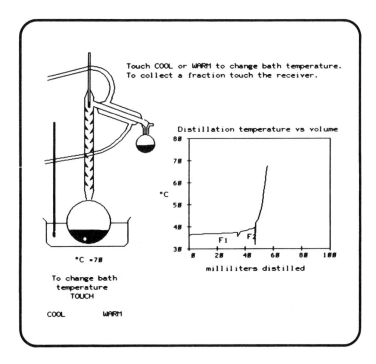

Figure 4-16 In this simulated experiment from *Fractional Distillation Experiment,* heat is controlled by touching the appropriate words on the screen. *(Courtesy of Board of Trustees, University of Illinois, and Stanley Smith)*

vant information is usually entered via the keyboard on older simulations and via the mouse on newer ones. This is most common in process simulations, in which the student learns by selecting parameters for the process and observing the results. The student may ask to see the graph of the population of Mexico for the following ten years based on a change in the average age of marriage, or can ask to see the sex of each cat in a new litter.

Realism. Student actions, like presentations, have varying degrees of realism. This means that the similarity between the student's action and the action of a person in the real situation varies. In this context, fidelity may refer either to the mode of action or the type of action. Typing in the desired rotation speed of a motor is of lower fidelity than dialing a simulated knob to achieve the same end. Multiple-choice questions are not common in the real world as a means for diagnosing why an automobile will not start in the morning, whereas touching the buttons of a simulated telephone is similar to the actual activity.

Student Control of the Simulation

The amount of control a student has in a simulation depends largely on its type. Most control exists in process simulations, somewhat less in physical simulations, still less in procedural simulations, and the least in situational simulations. Examples of the kinds of control the student may have are:

> initial choices
> obtaining directions
> restarting within the simulation
> terminating
> restarting after termination

Initial choices and returning to remake initial choices are essential in process simulations. They are the vehicle for determining process parameters and for rerunning the process with different parameters each time. Restarting within the simulation means to begin a procedural, situational, or physical simulation over again. It is frequently useful to allow such an option when the student takes an action which causes a failure, such as crashing the airplane into a mountain. Restarting after termination, in contrast, means choosing to use the simulation again having terminated the program on a previous occasion. Restarting simulations cannot always be done in the same way as for tutorials and drills, however, where a marker may be left where the student will continue working. Because of the holistic nature of simulations, the student must sometimes start again from the beginning. Procedural or situational simulations that are very long are more likely to incorporate markers for restarting than are physical or process simulations. In the latter types, the student usually has more control over the simulation anyway, so restarting capabilities are not as necessary.

It is important to analyze the different types of actions students will have to take in the simulation. Sometimes it is important to create an environment that allows the student action to approximate reality. Other times it has no adverse instructional impact if you design the action for convenience only. More will be said of this later in the chapter.

System Reaction or Feedback

We have just discussed the actions of the student. Now we look at the actions of the simulation. This usually takes two forms: reaction to student actions and feedback on student performance.

Natural and Artificial.   After taking an action, something usually happens as a reaction. This is a form of feedback, although often quite different to that found in tutorials and drills where feedback is usually immediate, corrective, and positive. In simulations, this is frequently not the case, because of the presence of a new factor, which is whether the feedback given is similar to the real world, or similar to what we previously described for tutorials and drills. The former we call *natural* feedback, and the latter *artificial.* Which one is used determines the fidelity of the feedback.

In the real world, if you fly an airplane into the clouds and become lost, you are given no message to that effect or about the fact that there are mountains in the vicinity. Natural feedback may come in the form of never reaching your destination or of crashing into the mountain. In a simulation of such a flight, the same type of natural feedback could be provided with the simulated airplane crashing. However, in such a simulation artificial feedback could also be given, which would be a written or spoken message, such as "You have just crashed."

Consider a simulation in which a mechanic is working on an engine that will not start. If the mechanic diagnoses the problem incorrectly, and decides to replace the spark plugs instead of cleaning a blocked fuel line, which is the real cause of failure, natural feedback would be an engine that still does not start. Artificial feedback would be a message, such as "The old spark plugs were fine. Try something else."

Natural feedback in a simulation, therefore, is very similar to what would occur in reality. On the other hand, artificial feedback may provide the same information, but does so in a way that does not occur naturally.

Immediate and Delayed.   Feedback about any action may be given immediately or at some later stage. In the examples above, for instance, the feedback was delayed. In the case of the airplane that flew into the clouds, no feedback was provided when it first penetrated. Rather, the feedback was delayed until the inevitable happened. An alternative would have been to inform the student the moment visibility was lost, thus preventing the crash. In the case of the mechanic fixing the engine, it would have been possible to give a message as soon as the decision was made to change the spark plugs, rather than waiting for them to be replaced and the attempt made to start the engine.

Natural feedback, as in these two examples, was delayed. This is true even though it occurred at exactly the time as it would have in reality. It is described as delayed because it occurred some time after the initial action which led to it, which is the way real-world feedback often is. Thus, the student may not discover the consequences of an action until a considerable time after the action. It is not true, however, that natural feedback is always delayed. In the same flight in which the feedback is delayed about the decision to fly into the clouds, each movement of the joystick results in immediate changes in the flight instruments. In a simulation of playing the piano, playing an incorrect chord is immediately displeasing to the ear.

Sometimes no feedback is given at all, which is often the case with reality. For example, if you do not notice a stop sign while driving along a road and drive through it, you may never know that you had done so. The only possible natural feedback would be a terrified shout from a passenger, an obscene gesture from a passing motorist, or a ticket from a lurking patrol car.

Regardless of the situation in the real world, simulations provide the option of giving natural, artificial, or no feedback. The main reason for artificial feedback is to give immediate, more understandable feedback. The advantages, on the other hand, of using natural feedback, are that it has greater face validity, is usually more interesting, and often results in better transfer of learning. Immediate verbal feedback about actions helps correct them before the student becomes hopelessly lost and confused. Natural feedback is more like the real world, and sometimes better prepares the student for performing in it.

In light of these considerations, our recommendation is to use immediate corrective feedback, even it if is unnatural, when a student first begins using a simulation or when the simulation's purpose is initial presentation and guidance. In contrast, when a more advanced student uses the simulation, especially when it is used for practice or as a test, it should give natural feedback as much as possible, whether delayed or immediate. A good simulation might start the student out with very helpful, immediate, and corrective feedback. As the student progresses and improves performance, it could reduce the amount of artificial feedback, replacing it with more natural feedback.

In general, student actions fall into four major categories: good or desirable, unnecessary or neutral, bad, and critical. The feedback that is provided should be appropriate to the nature of the student action and to the intention of the instruction. When a student action is necessary or good, which helps progress toward a goal, immediate feedback is least necessary, and natural feedback is suitable in most cases.

In any situation, it is possible to take actions that have no effect on the attainment of the goal. For instance, looking at your watch will not make your flight to New York arrive any earlier. When such an action is taken in a simulation, immediate feedback is probably unnecessary.

An action may be negative, causing the student to move further from the goal or possibly preventing its attainment unless corrective action is taken. An example of this would be deciding to fly an extra hundred miles when low on fuel.

For beginning students, future performance in a situation like this may be enhanced by using immediate feedback, even if it is artificial.

Finally, an action may be critical, causing the goal to be permanently unreachable. That is, overall performance would be regarded as a failure. Continuing to fly with the fuel gauge on empty would be an example. In such circumstance, future performance is enhanced when the student receives immediate artificial feedback, and is shown how to avoid the destructive consequences.

The examples above are meant only to illustrate the kinds of considerations involved in choosing feedback. They are not rules to be followed blindly. Artificial, natural, delayed, and immediate feedback can always be used, and may be used in various combinations. Each situation must be analyzed to determine which type of feedback will best help students attain the objectives of the simulation.

Sequence of the Simulation

The sequence of events in a simulation is a function of the sequence in the real context, although usually a simplification of it. A context with a linear sequence is the easiest to develop. It generally has a single path with a fixed number of steps. The titration experiment is an example of a reasonably linear simulation. Cyclic contexts, in which events are repeated (perhaps slightly differently each time), are fairly easy to simulate in the same way. Flying a plane in a holding pattern, and breeding cats in *Catlab* (Kinnear, 1982) are examples of cyclic simulations.

Contexts with complex sequences are the most difficult to simulate. They must usually be simplified a great deal before programming. Complex sequences usually have multiple paths with variable number of steps. The paths and number of steps depend on the actions of the user, and so may change at any time. Procedural simulations like the diagnosis simulations, situational simulations like *School Transactions* (Lunetta, 1984), and process simulations like a game-migration simulation, are examples of complex sequences.

Just as the simulation of student actions affects learning, so does how you handle the way in which the system reacts and provides feedback. As a designer you can control these variables to the benefit of the student.

COMPLETION OF THE SIMULATION

Completion means the student has succeeded or failed in a particular run through the simulation. In process simulations, for example, this simply means the process has run to completion. Process simulations are typically short and the student repeats them many times. The student may choose to begin it again or not. In physical, procedural, and situational simulations, completion usually means the student has followed either a successful path, or one that has led to failure. In either case, it does not necessarily mean the student terminates the simulation. The student may choose (if the option is available) to do the simulation again immediately. If the student does not choose to do so, the simulation is either temporarily or permanently terminated.

A TAXONOMY FOR FIDELITY ANALYSIS

In the prior sections we have raised many issues to consider when designing simulations. If you look back you will see that the discussion on the body of the simulation had four parts: the underlying model, the presentations, user actions, and system reaction and feedback. In this section we take the discussion a step further and create a taxonomy of these issues across the four types of simulation. What this implies is that each of the four types of simulation has a different set of criteria for determining fidelity. The factors in a physical simulation for which the level of fidelity is most important are different from those in process simulations.

Figure 4–17 (from Alessi, 1988) contains an initial taxonomy of what factors are most critical to the fidelity of each simulation type.

The columns represent four aspects of simulations to which fidelity is relevant. In the first column, the underlying model, fidelity considerations emphasize the *objects* inherent in the phenomenon and the *rules* underlying their behavior. In the second column, presentations, primary considerations are the visual and audible *stimuli* and the *time frame* in which events occur—most simulations slow down or speed up events. In the third column, user actions, fidelity concerns the *number* and *type* of actions, the student may engage in. In the fourth column, system feedback, considerations include whether there is any *feedback,*

	UNDERLYING MODEL	PRESENTATIONS	USER ACTIONS	SYSTEM FEEDBACK
PHYSICAL	number of objects cause-effect relationships time frame	detail/realism of presentations visual versus textual presentations illusion of motion	user control versus natural progression of the phenomenon	mode of feedback immediacy of feedback whether there is any feedback at all exaggeration of feedback magnitude

PROCESS	number of variables in the math model
	
	accuracy of variables in the math model
	
	time increment for recalculation
		what variables are:
		  unknown
		  known but not manipulated
		  known and manipulated
		
		speeding or slowing the time frame
			setting initial variables
			
			high level of user control between runs of the simulation
				mode of feedback (text or pictorial)
				
				whether there is any feedback at all

PROCEDURAL	number of possible solution paths nature/complexity of solutions number of objects cause-effect relationships	mode of display (text, graphic, real) realism & completeness of images or descriptions	number of possible actions mode of actions (e. g. typing a word versus moving a joystick)	mode of feedback (text, pictorial, real) immediacy of feedback whether there is any feedback at all
SITUATIONAL	number of persons in the simulation probabilistic nature of human behavior behavior a function of multiple events level of precision of theory accuracy of theory chance events	mode of display (text, graphic, real) completeness of a scenario	number of possible actions flexibility of actions (e. g. multiple choice versus constructed response)	immediacy of feedback probabilistic feedback

Figure 4–17   Taxonomy of simulation fidelity considerations. *(By permission of the Journal of Computer-Based Instruction and The Association for the Development of Computer-Based Instructional Systems)*

whether it is *immediate* or *delayed,* and whether it is *natural* or *artificial.*

Let us look at examples of fidelity analysis for each type of simulation, based on the theory and taxonomy above.

Physical Simulations

In a physical simulation, for example, of teaching about gravitation and the orbits of satellites around the earth, a primary decision is what objects to include in the domain. For all students the satellite and the earth would be necessary. At an advanced level of instruction and fidelity it would include the sun and the moon. Similarly, the mathematical equations governing the satellite and other bodies can be programmed with varying degrees of accuracy. Given few objects for beginning learners, simplified equations would be used.

For the presentations in the same simulation, the scale of the pictures, the realism of the earth and the satellite, the speed with which the satellite moves, and the extent that the images are labeled and explained all have potential for variation. Beginning students would learn faster given greater labeling and distortion of scale. In contrast, high-fidelity of the speed at which the satellite moves would not benefit anyone—it would be much too slow.

Fidelity of user actions in this example and many physical simulations should not vary much even for different phases of instruction. Physical simulations usually give considerable user control such as to start, stop, and slow down, but do not allow changing the physical laws which are the object of the lesson.

Feedback correcting input errors would be an instructional technique decreasing fidelity but appropriate for any level student. Feedback for actions that lead to catastrophic results (the satellite crashing to earth) might help prevent them for beginning students while being more realistic and allowing them for advanced students. However, preventing such events is not as important in physical simulations as in procedural simulations, where the instructional objective is the correct procedure. It is typical for the fidelity of models to be more critical for physical and process simulations, while fidelity of presentations, actions, and feedback to be more critical in procedural and situational simulations.

Process Simulations

An example of a process simulation is *Catlab* (Kinnear, 1982), which we mentioned before. It is a genetics simulation in which the student mates cats and investigates the laws of genetics by observing the characteristics of the parents passed on to the offspring. Considerable variation in the underlying model is possible, from dealing with just one or two genetic traits through a large number. In simulations in which rates of change are of major importance, such as economics or population growth, the size of the time increment for recalculating equations affects the accuracy of the simulation with regard to reality.

Process simulations usually deal with multiple variables and which of those variables can be observed and changed is important to student learning. Students using *Catlab* are often observed to become confused and frustrated because too many variables may be considered and they try to manipulate too many at the same time. Additionally, students never see the cats' genotypes—the underlying genetic codes. They see only the phenotypes—the visible characteristics of the cats—and can only manipulate those for the original parent cats. A newer simulation called *Catgen* (Kinnear, 1986) also permits modification of genotypes, but with a corresponding increase in simulation complexity.

Procedural Simulations

Flight Simulator (Artwick, 1983) is a well-known procedural simulation. It is a particularly instructive example for discussing fidelity. Variation of the underlying model is not as important as the previous types of simulations. The model should be faithful to reality and will not affect student learning much if the other aspects of fidelity are properly chosen.

The fidelity of the presentations and actions are more important. The program confronts the student with a bewildering array of instruments, views out different windows, and controls to manipulate. The beginning student has considerable difficulty attending and reacting to the relevant visual information. The task of operating the simulated airplane is much easier if a subset of the instruments and controls are present and the wide variety of visual stimuli from outside the airplane is reduced to just a few. But advantageous as this is for the beginner, the advanced student must be facile with all the instruments, controls, and outside stimuli such as other airplanes, thunderstorms, and tall buildings. Indeed, it is essential that a student pilot be able to do so when flying a real airplane.

Fidelity of feedback has even greater importance in procedural simulations for it affects whether incorrect actions are corrected in the future. In a flight simulation, low-fidelity feedback warning of dangerous actions may be very beneficial during initial instruction, but should be faded during practice and assessment.

Situational Simulations

School Transactions (Lunetta, 1984), as mentioned previously, is a situational simulation for student teachers dealing with classroom management and behavior problems. Individual human behavior is very complex and difficult to predict. That complexity and lack of predictability makes it difficult to model in a computer program, but is can be done to varying degrees. Different numbers of individuals may be included in such a simulation as may be different degrees of variation in their behavior. The behavior of real people is not a function of immediately preceding events but of all their experience. A simulation's fidelity may be varied in terms of the degree to which individual behavior is based upon multiple past events rather than just the preceding event.

As with procedural simulations, a critical issue is the number of actions the student can make. A real teacher faced with misbehaving students can take a wide variety of actions. In *School Transactions* a limited number of actions are provided in multiple-choice format. Users of the simulation often think of actions not included among the programmed alternatives.

Because the emphasis is on the student learning what to do, feedback fidelity is again very important. Beginning students should profit from artificial feedback which corrects inappropriate actions or prevents unfortunate outcomes. Transfer to the real world requires that more advanced students learn the consequences of their behavior within social systems (see also Reigeluth & Schwartz, 1989).

SIMULATION SYSTEMS AND LANGUAGES

There are a variety of simulation languages and systems to aid in simulation development. Examples are *MicroDynamo* (Pugh-Roberts Associates, 1982) for IBM and Apple II microcomputers; and *Stella* (High Performance Systems, 1987), and *Extend* (Diamond, 1988) for the Macintosh. *MicroDynamo* allows the developer to enter simple equations for the initial values of variables and how they change over time based on each other. The Macintosh examples allow the developer to create a diagram in which variables are represented by display icons, and lines connecting them are equations representing how they affect each other over time. All of them generate either tables of numbers or graphs that describe system behavior over time and under various circumstances.

Figures 4–18 through 4–21 show examples from *Stella*. The rectangles in Figure 4–18 represent the primary variables in the system, in this case the amount of snow and ice in a glacier. The circles with hollow arrows on top of them represent the rates at which these variables increase or decrease. The plain circles represent other variables or constants which affect the system, such as the amount of precipitation and air temperature. The plain arrows indicate which variables or constants affect which other ones.

The relationships, as the diagram shows, can be many. The software automatically figures out the necessary equations and their solutions, shown in the "equations" window of Figure 4–19. When the simulation is run, the software pro-

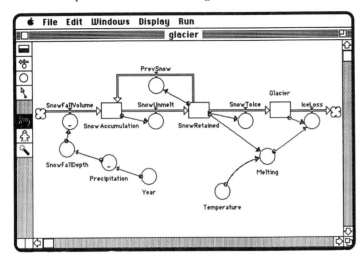

Figure 4-18 The flow diagram describing a simulation in *Stella*. *(Courtesy of High Performance Systems, glacier model by James Quinn and Jay Cook)*

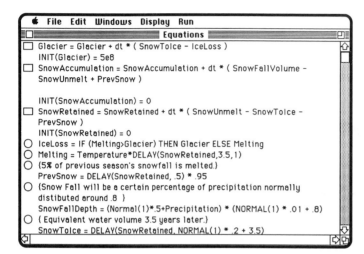

Figure 4-19 The equations generated by the flow diagram in *Stella. (Courtesy of High Performance Systems)*

gressively increments time and calculates changes in all variables for each time increment. The results are shown as a graph in Figure 4–20 and as a table of numbers in Figure 4–21. The developer can easily change the relationships of variables and initial values and see the changes in equations and system behavior.

Software like this has obvious utility for the CBI developer. The equations, graphs, or tables may be generated and then used in other development software to deliver a student-controlled simulation which includes animation, text, your own pictures, and so on. *Stella* even has a companion product, *Stella Stack* (High Performance Systems, 1989), which allows one to incorporate the complete model directly into a Macintosh Hypercard stack.

In addition to incorporating it into your own lessons, such software has another instructional value. As described in the *Stella* manual (Richmond, Peterson, & Vescuso, 1987) and in the textbook written for the *MicroDynamo* programs (Roberts, Andersen, Deal, Garet, & Shaffer, 1983), a valuable instructional meth-

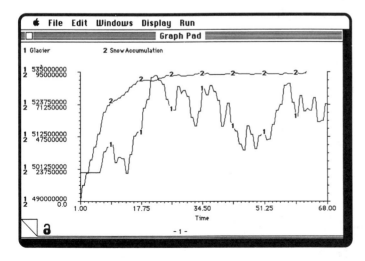

Figure 4-20 A graph generated by running a *Stella* simulation. *(Courtesy of High Performance Systems)*

```
 File  Edit  Windows  Display  Run
╔══════════════════════════ Table ══════════════════════════╗
║   Time  │  SnowAccumulation │  SnowRetained │   Glacier     ║ ⬆
║   1.00  │             0.0   │         0.0   │  500000000    ║
║   2.00  │      12000000     │         0.0   │  500000000    ║
║   3.00  │      21000000     │   3000000.0   │  500000000    ║
║   4.00  │      30600000     │   5400000.0   │  500000000    ║
║   5.00  │      40080000     │   7920000.0   │  500000000    ║
║   6.00  │      49584000     │   10416000    │  500000000    ║
║   7.00  │      59083200     │   9916800.0   │  503000000    ║
║   8.00  │      65733360     │   9866640.0   │  507452416    ║
║   9.00  │      70673328     │   9006672.0   │  508890208    ║
║  10.00  │      73561336     │   7702665.5   │  509794144    ║
║  11.00  │      74488536     │   8858667.0   │  503476896    ║
║  12.00  │      76282136     │   9198427.0   │  505539968    ║
║  13.00  │      77950104     │   10523783    │  504905120    ║
║  14.00  │      80460176     │   12311050    │  499878208    ║
║  15.00  │      84040624     │   11871929    │  506438400    ║
║  16.00  │      86308800     │   12405327    │  512759104    ║
║  17.00  │      88516664     │   11673684    │  514161920    ║ ⬇
╚════════════════════════════════════════════════════════════╝
```

Figure 4-21 A table of numbers generated by running a *Stella* simulation. *(Courtesy of High Performance Systems)*

odology is to have students investigate systems by creating their own simulations. The process of determining what variables are relevant, which ones affect each other, and how they vary with time is a valuable problem-solving and learning experience. Learning about a system by creating simulations is akin to the notion of practicing problem solving through Logo programming or, as will be described in Chapter 15, learning by creating expert systems. The current generation of simulation software is so easy to use that this idea is practical for classroom use.

CONCLUSION

Simulation is an instructional methodology that uses the full power of the computer for instruction. Simulations improve on tutorials and drills through enhanced motivation, transfer of learning, and efficiency. They have the advantages of convenience, safety, and controllability over real experiences, are a good precursor to real experiences, and are useful for giving students experiences that would not otherwise be possible. One further advantage is that they can be used for any of the four phases of instruction.

REFERENCES AND BIBLIOGRAPHY

ALESSI, S.M. (1988). Fidelity in the design of instructional simulations. *Journal of Computer-Based Instruction, 15*(2), 40–47.

ANZAI, Y., & SIMON, H.A. (1979). The theory of learning by doing. *Psychological Review, 86,* 124–140.

ARTWICK, B.A. (1983). *Flight Simulator II.* [Computer Program]. Champaign, IL: subLOGIC Corporation.

BLACKMAN, J.A., LOUGH, L.K., & HUNTLEY, J.S. (1984). *Assessment of Neuromotor Dysfunction in Infants.* [Videodisc and Computer Program]. Coralville, IA: Cognitive Design Technologies, Limited.

BORG, W.R., & SCHULLER, C.F. (1979). Detail and background in audiovisual lessons and their effect on learners. *Educational Communication and Technology Journal, 27,* 31–38.

BRUNER, J.S. (1966). *Toward a Theory of Instruction.* Cambridge, MA: Harvard University Press.

BRUNER, J.S. (1973). *Beyond the Information Given.* New York: Norton.

CABRERA, B. (1986). *Mechanics—Physics Simulations I.* [Computer Program]. Palo Alto, CA: Stanford University.

CARTER, G., & TROLLIP, S.R. (1980). A constrained maximization extension to incremental transfer effectiveness, or, How to mix your training technologies. *Human Factors, 22,* 141–152.

CLARK, R.E., & VOOGEL, A. (1985). Transfer of training principles for instructional design. *Educational Communication and Technology Journal, 33*(2), 113–123.

CORMIER, S.M., & HAGMAN, J.D. (Eds.). (1987). *Transfer of Learning: Contemporary Research and Applications.* San Diego: Academic Press.

DARE, F.C. (1973). *Trouble Shooting Fuel Systems.* [Computer Program]. Urbana, IL: University of Illinois Computer-based Education Research Laboratory.

DENNIS, J.R. (1979). *Computer Simulation and Its Instructional Uses.* Report #8e, The Illinois Series on Educational Applications of Computers. Urbana, IL: Department of Secondary Education, University of Illinois at Urbana-Champaign.

DIAMOND, B. (1988). *Extend.* [Computer Program]. San Jose, CA: Imagine That, Inc.

DOERNER, D. (1980). On the difficulties people have in dealing with complexity. *Simulation & Games, 11*(1), 87–106.

DUKE, R. (1980). A paradigm for game design. *Simulation & Games, 11,* 364–377.

GAGNE, R.M. (1954). Training devices and simulators: Some research issues. *The American Psychologist, 9,* 95–107.

GAGNE, R.M., FOSTER, H., & CROWLEY, M.E. (1948). The measurement of transfer of training. *Psychological Bulletin, 45,* 97–130.

HIGH PERFORMANCE SYSTEMS. (1987). *Stella.* [Computer Program]. Lyme, NH: High Performance Systems.

HIGH PERFORMANCE SYSTEMS. (1989). *Stella Stack.* [Computer Program]. Lyme, NH: High Performance Systems.

HIGH TECHNOLOGY SOFTWARE. (1979). *Chem Lab Simulation #2—Ideal Gas Law.* [Computer Program]. Oklahoma City, OK: High Technology Software.

HYATT, G., EADES, D., TENCZAR, P.J., & DENAULT, J. M. (1968). *Drosophila Genetics* [Computer Program]. Urbana, IL: University of Illinois Computer-based Education Research Laboratory.

KELLER, J.M., & SUZUKI, K. (1988). Use of the ARCS motivation model in courseware design. In D.H. Jonassen (Ed.), *Instructional Designs for Microcomputer Courseware.* Hillsdale, NJ: Lawrence Erlbaum.

KINNEAR, J.F. (1982). *Catlab.* [Computer Program]. Iowa City, IA: CONDUIT.

KINNEAR, J.F. (1986). *Catgen.* [Computer Program]. Iowa City, IA: CONDUIT.

LANE, E.T. (1984). *Standing Waves.* [Computer Program]. Iowa City, IA: CONDUIT.

LUNGSFORD, D.M., RIVERS, R.H., & VOCKELL, E.L. (1981). *Balance: A Simulation of Predator/Prey Relationship.* [Computer Program]. West Lafayette, IN: Diversified Educational Enterprises.

LUNETTA, V.N. (1984). *School Transactions.* [Computer Program]. Iowa City, IA: CONDUIT.

MERRILL, M.D. (1980). Learner control in computer-based instruction. *Computers in Education, 4,* 77–95.

PAPERT, S. (1972). Teaching children to be mathematicians versus teaching about mathematics. *International Journal of Mathematics Education and Science Technology, 3,* 249–262.

PAPERT, S. (1980). *Mindstorms.* New York: Basic Books.

POPULATION DYNAMICS GROUP. (1976). *Population Projections.* [Computer Program]. Urbana, IL: University of Illinois Computer-based Education Research Laboratory.

POVENMIRE, H. K., & ROSCOE, S.N. (1973). The incremental transfer effectiveness of a ground-based general-aviation trainer. *Human Factors, 15,* 534–542.

PUGH-ROBERTS ASSOCIATES. (1982). *Micro-DYNAMO.* [Computer Program]. Reading, MA: Addison-Wesley.

REIGELUTH, C.M. (1979). In search of a better way to organize instruction: The elaboration theory. *Journal of Instructional Development, 2*(3), 8–15.

REIGELUTH, C.M., & SCHWARTZ, E. (1989). An instructional theory for the design of computer-based simulations. *Journal of Computer-Based Instruction, 16,* 1–10.

RICHMOND, B., PETERSON, S., & VESCUSO, P. (1987). *An Academic User's Guide to Stella.* Lyme, NH: High Performance Systems.

RIGNEY, J.W., & LUTZ, K.A. (1976). Effect of graphic analogies of concepts in chemistry on learning and attitude. *Journal of Educational Psychology, 68,* 305–311.

ROBERTS, N., ANDERSON, D., DEAL, R., GARET, M., & SHAFFER, W. (1983). *Computer Simulation: A System Dynamics Modeling Approach.* Reading, MA: Addison-Wesley.

ROBERTS, N., FRIEL, S., & LADENBURG, T. (1988). *Computers and the Social Studies: Educating for the Future.* Menlo Park, CA: Addison-Wesley.

ROSCOE, S.N. (1971). Incremental transfer effectiveness. *Human Factors, 13,* 561–567.

ROSCOE, S.N. (1972). A little more on incremental transfer effectiveness. *Human Factors, 14,* 363–364.

RUBEN, B.D., & LEDERMAN, L.C. (1982). Instructional simulation gaming: Validity, reliability, and utility. *Simulation & Games, 13*(2), 233–244.

SCHENK, R.E. (1983). *Biznes: A Simulation of a Firm.* [Computer Program]. Iowa City, IA: CONDUIT.

SCHNEIDER, W. (1985). Training high-performance skills: Fallacies and guidelines. *Human Factors, 27,* 285–300.

Simulation & Games: An International Journal of Theory, Design, and Research. Beverly Hills, CA: Sage Publications.

SMITH, S. (1975). *Fractional Distillation Experiment.* [Computer Program]. Urbana, IL: University of Illinois Computer-based Education Research Laboratory.

TROLLIP, S.R. (1979). The evaluation of a complex, computer-based flight procedures trainer. *Human Factors, 22*(1), 47–54.

WOLFE, J. (1985). The teaching effectiveness of games in collegiate business courses: A 1973–1983 update. *Simulation & Games, 16*(3), 251–288.

SUMMARY OF SIMULATIONS

Use simulations instead of actual experience when the latter is unsafe, costly, very complex, or logistically difficult.

Use simulations instead of other CBI methodologies when there is need to increase motivation, transfer of learning, or efficiency.

Use a short title page.

Give objectives, including the instructional purpose of the simulation.

Give complete and clear directions, and allow the student to return to the directions at any time.

Use graphics, color, and sound for important information.

Do not use overly detailed graphics. Provide just as much detail as is necessary to convey the necessary information.

Be clear about the simulation's purpose—to teach *about* something or to teach *how to do* something.

Thoroughly understand the phenomenon before you try to develop an instructional simulation.

Use simulation languages to refine the underlying simulation model.

Use modes of presentation and student action that enhance fidelity.

Use lower fidelity for beginning students.

Use higher fidelity for advanced students.

Use immediate feedback (regardless of fidelity) for beginning students.

Use natural feedback (regardless of immediacy) for more advanced students.

In physical and process simulations, analysis of the fidelity of the underlying model and presentations is usually more critical.

In procedural and situational simulations, analysis of the fidelity of the student actions and system reactions is usually more critical.

Allow the student to return to initial choices.

Allow internal restarting.

Allow temporary termination at any time.

Provide restarting after temporary termination.

Clear any displays and give a final message at the end.

Ensure the student knows what to do next.

5

INSTRUCTIONAL GAMES

Games are a powerful instructional tool that are becoming more prevalent with the proliferation of computers in schools. They are very much like simulations, and are often discussed together because of their similarities. The purpose of both simulations and games is to provide an environment that facilitates learning or the acquisition of skills. Simulations attempt to do so by mimicking reality; many simulations are also quite entertaining, but entertainment is not one of their distinguishing features. Conversely, games may or may not simulate reality, but they are nearly always characterized by providing the student with entertaining challenges. Our discussion focuses primarily on those games that have an instructional component, in contrast to those whose sole purpose is to entertain.

DEFINITION

It is difficult to define games precisely. Consequently, it may be helpful to have games define themselves by example. The instructional games described below vary considerably in purpose, content, and target population. Reading their descriptions, however, should allow a rough definition to emerge.

Decimal Darts

Decimal Darts (Control Data Corporation, 1981) is an elementary school arithmetic game designed to teach about points on the number line. At each level, a wall is displayed representing a number line. On the wall are several balloons. The objective of the game is to estimate where on the number line each balloon is located. The estimate is entered, and a dart flies across the screen. If the estimate is accurate, the dart pops the balloon; if inaccurate, the dart sticks into the wall. Figure 5–1 illustrates this. As can be seen, the limits of the number line are shown, as are several unpopped balloons. The dart on the left is about to pop the balloon at location 0.4. The difficulty of the game can be varied by requiring greater precision. Figure 5–2 shows a more difficult set of problems, with greater precision being required of each estimate. For the player, the motivation is to keep popping the balloons.

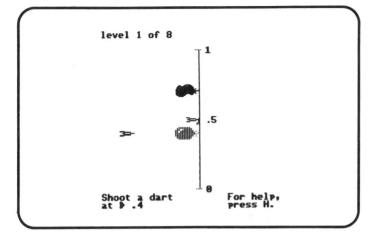

Figure 5-1 A dart flies toward the balloon at the specified location. Some tolerance is allowed. *(Courtesy of Control Data Corporation)*

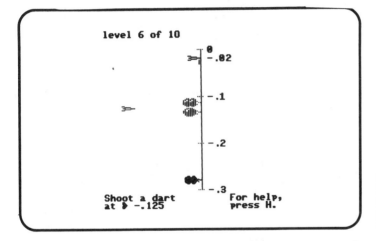

Figure 5-2 A dart aimed at popping two balloons simultaneously. No tolerance is allowed in this case, and greater accuracy is required. *(Courtesy of Control Data Corporation)*

How the West Was Won

How the West Was One + Three × Four[1] (Seiler & Weaver, 1976) is a board game depicting a race between a stagecoach and a railroad engine. The race starts in Tombstone and ends in Red Gulch, passing through six towns on the way. Progress is initiated each turn by combining three numbers that have been randomly generated and displayed on spinners (see Figure 5-3). On each turn, the player may use each of the four basic arithmetic operations ($+$, $-$, $\times$, and $/$) only once, and parentheses. Thus, the numbers on the spinners in Figure 5-3 could be combined in many different ways, such as $(2 \times 2) - 1$, $(2 + 1) \times 2$, or $2 + 2 - 1$. After entering the combination, the player must evaluate the expression and input the answer. If correct, the player's piece advances the appropriate number of units; if incorrect, the player loses the turn.

---

[1] For convenience, we shall refer to this game as *How the West Was Won.*

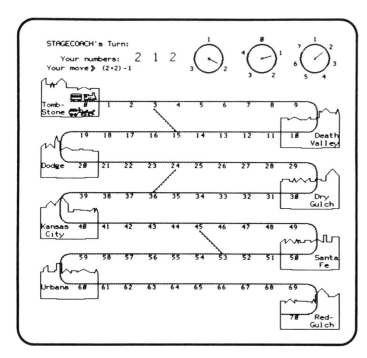

Figure 5-3 The playing board of *How the West Was Won,* showing the players' pieces, the route to be traversed, and the spinners. *(Courtesy of the Board of Trustees, University of Illinois, and B. Seiler and C. Weaver)*

There are some other important rules. If a piece lands in a city, it automatically proceeds to the next city—a bonus. If it lands at the top of a shortcut, such as the one from position 3 to 15, it takes the shortcut—another bonus. The weapon of each player is landing exactly where the opponent is. If this happens, the opponent is sent back two towns (see Figure 5-4). Each player's goal is to reach Red Gulch first by creating combinations of numbers that both maximize forward progress and retard the opponent's progress. Play alternates between the two players.

Ordeal of the Hangman

Ordeal of the Hangman (Michael, Berger, Dennis, & Jones, 1976) is a guessing game with a difference. The computer selects a word from its vocabulary and informs the student how many letters it has. The student has to guess what the word is by selecting one letter at a time. If the letter is in the word, it is shown in its correct position or positions. If it is not part of the word, a human body begins to take shape (Figure 5-5). Once the body is completed, the next incorrect guess causes the person to be hanged (Figure 5-6). Of course, the victim is you! The purpose of the game is to teach the student to infer from the available letters what the word is. One way of increasing difficulty is by lengthening the hidden word

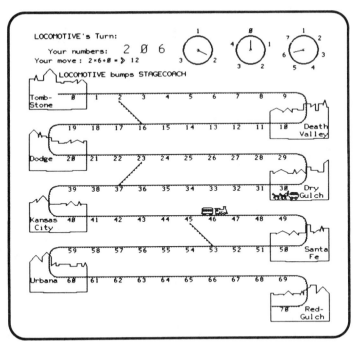

Figure 5-4 The stagecoach has sent the locomotive back two towns by landing at the same place. *(Courtesy of the Board of Trustees, University of Illinois, and B. Seiler and C. Weaver)*

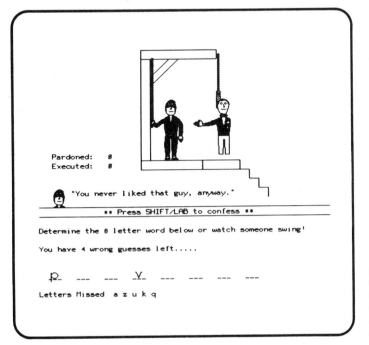

Figure 5-5 As letters are guessed that are not in the hidden word, the victim's body is built up. *(Courtesy of the Board of Trustees, University of Illinois, and G. Michael, M. Berger, D. Dennis, and D. Jones)*

without giving the victim more parts; that is, the number of guesses remains constant. Another way is by reducing the number of guesses allowed.

Rocky's Boots

Rocky's Boots (Robinett, 1982) is one of a series of programs designed to teach logical reasoning to young children. Throughout the lesson, the student builds logic machines, using animated AND, OR, and NOT gates (the basic logic circuits of computers), together with other devices that recognize colors or shapes. For example, the student may be asked to design a machine that recognizes green crosses, or one that recognizes purple or green diamonds. After the machine is designed, a series of different symbols of different colors is passed through the machine. For each symbol recognized correctly, which is illustrated by having Rocky's boot kick it out of the machine (Figure 5–7), points are scored. The higher the score, the better the machine works. Machines can be designed that are logically correct, but that have intermittent malfunctions (glitches) due to the use of too many gates or too lengthy wiring.

Archaeology Search

Archaeology Search (Snyder, 1982a) is a game whose purpose is to teach elements of the scientific method of inquiry. It does so by having student teams work

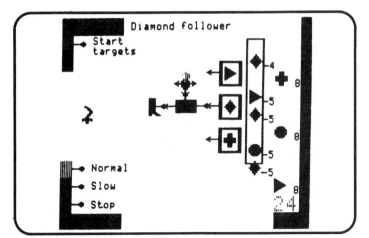

Figure 5-7 When the machine correctly identifies a symbol as it passes through, Rocky's boot kicks it out. *(Courtesy of The Learning Company)*

together on an excavation at a simulated archaeological site. Each team can move about the site, can make decisions about whether to do a shallow or deep dig, or can ask questions of the computer about the site and its contents. Shallow digs inevitably yield artifacts (usually uninteresting ones), while deep digs have a lower probability of finding something. Of course, when something is found on a deep dig, it is usually a valuable find. Different decisions take different amounts of time to implement, and the goal for each team is to spend the time in the most productive way. As each team gains more information about the site, it has to piece together these clues to make the subsequent decision.

Phizquiz

Phizquiz: A Problem-Solving Test in Elementary Mechanics (Peterson, Smith, & Kane, 1973) is a program that poses common problems in mechanics without providing all the information necessary to answer them. The student can purchase information at $2.00 a piece, obtain a list of all relevant equations for $5.00, or obtain help for $5.00. The purpose is to solve the problem using as little money as possible. Figure 5–8 shows an initial problem presentation. A cannon in a field fires a shell. The problem is to calculate the horizontal distance traveled. The student decides to buy information (Figure 5–9) for $2.00, asking what the muzzle velocity of the shell was, and is told that it was 200 meters per second. The student also asks the initial trajectory of the shell and is told that it was 20 degrees. Figure 5–10 shows the display when the student spends $5.00 for help. Figure 5–11 shows the initial display augmented by the information bought. The student continues in this fashion until enough information has been accumulated to answer the questions, or until funds run out.

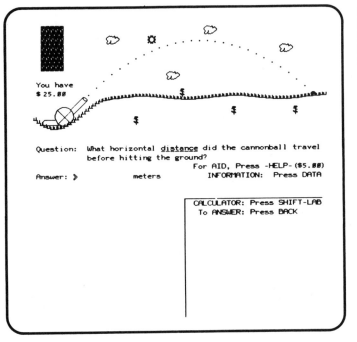

Figure 5-8 The initial problem page in *Phizquiz*, presenting the problem in both words and pictures. *(Courtesy of the Board of Trustees, University of Illinois, and J. Smith and D. Kane)*

Figure 5-9 Information is bought—in this case the muzzle velocity of the shell. *(Courtesy of the Board of Trustees, University of Illinois, and J. Smith and D. Kane)*

You have
$ 18.00

First we must find the time the cannonball is in
the air. We find this from our knowledge that the
vertical component of velocity equals 0 at the
top of the path. Remember that this is only half
of the total time of flight.

Since the horizontal component of the velocity is
constant (why?), we can use it and the time to
find the distance.

Press -BACK- to return from here.

Figure 5-10 Additional help is bought for $5.00. *(Courtesy of the Board of Trustees, University of Illinois, and J. Smith and D. Kane)*

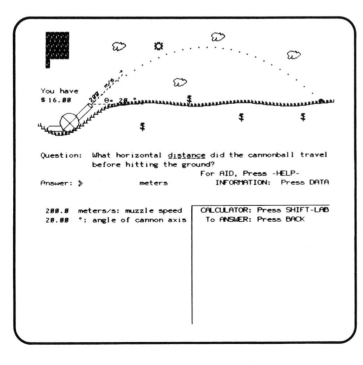

Figure 5-11 The initial problem is redisplayed with all the information that has been bought. *(Courtesy of the Board of Trustees, University of Illinois, and J. Smith and D. Kane)*

Four-Letter Words

Four-Letter Words (Luster, 1983) is a vocabulary game that asks the player to create as many four-letter words as possible from four given letters. These letters may either be specified by the player, may be constrained by having a specific letter in a specified position in the word, or may be given by the computer. Each letter may be used as many times as required. In Figure 5–12, the player chose the four letters *o, k, l,* and *m,* and was able to produce only four acceptable words (*loom, look, kook,* and *loll*). The computer then filled in the remaining words from its dictionary and assigned a score (57%). In a sense this is an automated *Scrabble* (Selchow and Righter) game without the interaction of an opponent.

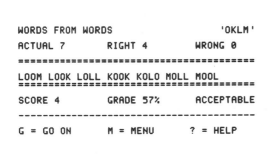

```
WORDS FROM WORDS              'OKLM'
ACTUAL 7        RIGHT 4       WRONG 0
=====================================
LOOM LOOK LOLL KOOK KOLO MOLL MOOL
=====================================
SCORE 4         GRADE 57%     ACCEPTABLE
-------------------------------------
G = GO ON       M = MENU      ? = HELP
```

Figure 5-12 A display from *Four-Letter Words,* showing the words that can be made from the letters at the top right. *(Courtesy of Robert G. Luster and the publisher, CONDUIT)*

MAJOR CHARACTERISTICS OF GAMES

All the games described above are intended to be instructional. It is also possible for a game that was initially intended for entertainment to be used instructionally, such as *Monopoly* (Parker Brothers) as an introduction to the real estate and financial markets. Although we occasionally make reference to such games to illustrate a point, we generally discuss only games whose purpose is intentionally instructional.

Although no definition of games is completely satisfactory, an examination of the examples above indicates that common features are present to varying degrees. The degree to which these are present in an instructional setting gives a good indication of how gamelike the instruction will be.

Goals

Every game, for instance, has a *goal* that is either stated or inferred. This is the end to which each player strives. In some games it is scoring points, in others it is popping balloons, solving mysteries, discovering unknown lands, guessing words, or solving problems.

Rules

These define what actions are allowed within a game and what constraints are imposed. Their distinguishing feature is that they are artificial. That is, rules are artifacts of our imagination even though they may sometimes attempt to simulate reality. Rules can be changed, and frequently are, to meet changing needs. Each year, for example, some rule of basketball or football is changed in an attempt to eliminate a perceived weakness in the nature of the game, or to make the game more interesting.

Competition

Games usually involve some form of competition, either against an opponent, against oneself, against chance, or against time. Many games combine these elements. Football involves competition against both an opponent and time; *Space Invaders* (Taito America) against opponents, in the form of invaders, and oneself, in attempting to better the previous highest score; and *Monopoly* or bridge against opponents and chance. Games may combine these features in different ways.

Challenge

One of the most appealing aspects of games is that they provide some sort of challenge. This differs from the goal in that the challenge is what one has to accomplish to reach the goal. For example, in *Decimal Darts* the goal is to pop the balloons. This remains constant. The challenge, however, can be increased by demanding that the student specify with greater and greater precision the location of the balloons. For instance, once a student has mastered the game using numbers with one decimal place, the challenge can be increased by demanding two decimal places. In *Ordeal of the Hangman*, the goal is to guess a word before being hanged; varying the length or difficulty of the hidden words, or changing the number of guesses allowed, will alter the degree of challenge of the game.

Fantasy

Games often rely on fantasy for motivation. The degree of fantasy can range anywhere from a close representation of reality (a computer-based basketball game representing a real game, for instance), to a more distant representation (*Decimal Darts* depicting a real darts game), to a totally imaginary one (princes slaying magic dragons).

Safety

Games can provide a safe way of acting out a more dangerous reality, such as in war games, computerized contact sports, or investment games. This in turn encourages the players to explore alternative approaches in the game with the knowledge that failure at worst means losing the game. There are no real consequences.

Entertainment

Almost all games are entertaining, although not necessarily as their primary purpose. Instructional games, while primarily intended to teach, use their entertainment appeal to enhance motivation and learning.

Although a complete and precise definition remains elusive, the essence of games becomes clearer in light of each of the features described above. The presence of these features, either singly or in combination, is not sufficient to define a game. Nevertheless, the greater their presence, the more likely instruction will be regarded as a game.

TYPES OF GAMES

There have been many attempts to classify games (Abt, 1968; Ellington, Adinall, & Percival, 1982). For our purposes we classify them by an overall generic description such as combat games; adventure games; card, board, or logic games; role-playing games; and psychomotor games. This is the easiest way to discuss games, because the categories are widely understood. In many cases a game will play several of these roles simultaneously. The following is a list of games classified by type. Where a game has multiple roles, it is classified in several categories.

Adventure Games

An adventure game is one in which the player assumes the role of a character in a situation about which little is known. The player must use existing information and resources to solve the problems posed for the character by these situations. The purpose of an instructional adventure game is usually to teach problem-solving skills, deductive reasoning, or hypothesis testing.

Oregon (Minnesota Educational Computing Consortium, 1983) is typical of such games. In it the student plays the role of a settler in the Wild West, traveling across America to the frontier lands. The settler and family have limited resources and are confronted by a variety of difficult situations, such as hostile raiders, mountain passes, lack of food, and frigid winters. The settler has to make decisions continuously about the available resources. These decisions are always of the nature of a trade-off. Should food be bought instead of ammunition? Should one buy medical supplies or conserve money for warm clothing? When riders approach should an attempt be made to flee? Figure 5–13 shows two displays from the game. The resources that remain are given at the top.

Another typical instructional adventure game is *Snooper Troops* (Snyder, 1982b), which is classified as an adventure game because the player takes the role of a detective who has to determine whom to accuse of the crime. The detective can interrogate people and inspect clues to obtain information from which the identity of the criminal must be deduced. Often the information given to the detective is false. In Figure 5–14, you are driving in your Snoopmobile to a suspect's house, and in Figure 5–15, you are asking questions.

```
MONDAY- APRIL 26,1847            MILES= 441
-------------------------------------------------
 FOOD  BULLETS  CLOTHING    MISC.    CASH
 128    2484      100        25       75
-------------------------------------------------


RUGGED MOUNTAINS
THE GOING IS SLOW

BLIZZARD IN MOUNTAIN PASS--TIME AND
SUPPLIES LOST
```

Figure 5-13a Two displays from *Oregon.* (Courtesy of Minnesota Educational Computing Consortium)

```
MONDAY- APRIL 26,1847            MILES= 441
-------------------------------------------------
 FOOD  BULLETS  CLOTHING    MISC.    CASH
 128    2484      100        25       75
-------------------------------------------------


RIDERS AHEAD...THEY
LOOK HOSTILE.

TACTICS -

1. RUN
2. ATTACK
3. CONTINUE
4. CIRCLE YOUR WAGONS

WHICH NUMBER?
```

Figure 5-13b

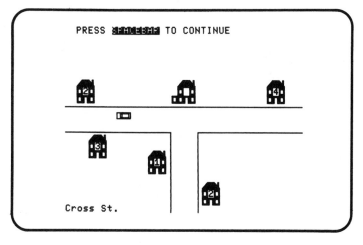

Figure 5-14 The detective drives to a suspect's house in the Snoopmobile. *(Courtesy of Spinnaker Software)*

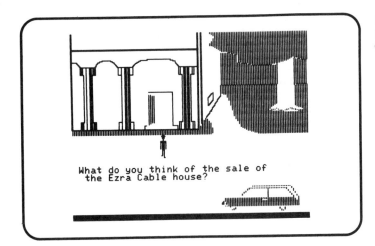

Arcade-type Games

As a vehicle for instruction, arcade-type games are similar to those found in an amusement arcade. Examples of these are *Decimal Darts*, described above, and *Pinball* (Dugdale, Kibbey, & Leung, 1975), which uses a simulation of a pinball machine to teach arithmetic facts. Four bumpers are put on the screen, each with a problem in it. The ball bounces from one bumper to another, stopping only a short time at each. During this time the answer to the problem must be entered to score the points associated with the bumper. If the student fails to answer in time, no points are scored and the bumper is no longer active. Furthermore, as each problem is correctly answered, the time to answer becomes shorter. Figure 5–16 shows a display from the game. One bumper is inactive.

Board Games

Board games are often computerized versions of existing games. Chess, checkers, *How the West Was Won*, and *Hurkle* (Minnesota Educational Computing Consortium, 1980) are examples of computerized board games. In a sense, most adventure games are similar to board games. *Hurkle* is a game designed to teach young children the elements of two-dimensional space. To start the game, a Hurkle (a small, friendly creature) hides itself in a field that is marked as a grid. The player types in the two numbers designating where he or she thinks the Hurkle is hiding. If the chosen position is incorrect, the Hurkle provides feedback like "Go North-east" or "Go South." Using this feedback, the player chooses another position on the field and enters its coordinates. Play continues until the Hurkle is located in as few guesses as possible.

Card or Gambling Games

These are generally characterized either by the existence of a large element of chance or by the use of money as a motivator. Any game that has random

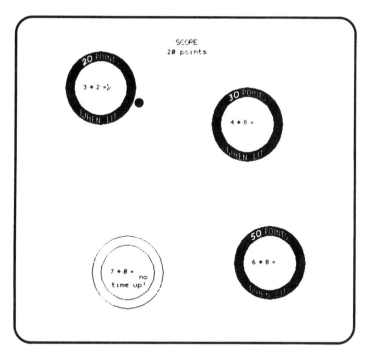

Figure 5-16 The ball indicates which problem must be answered in *Pinball.* An incorrect answer or an answer entered too slowly has already turned one bumper off. *(Courtesy of the Board of Trustees, University of Illinois, and S. Dugdale, D. Kibbey, and H. Leung)*

fluctuations falls into this category, as do games such as *Phizquiz,* in which the student has to use money for information. Typical of such games is *Casino Reading* (Stevens, Reichmann, & Liu, 1982), a game designed to help children develop their comprehension of stories. At the beginning a short extract of a simple story is put on the screen (Figure 5–17a). This is usually a single sentence. The student then has the option of either buying a new sentence for $3.00, or betting on which of a set of alternatives comes closest to telling what the story is about. In Figure 5–17b, the student has already spent $6.00 on two purchases of new sentences, and has decided to bet $15.00 on which of the sentences at the bottom best summarizes the story. At each stage, the player has to decide whether to spend more money to obtain further information, which depletes the amount of money available for betting. There is obviously an incentive to decide what the story is about as quickly as possible.

Combat Games

Many games use combat or violent competition as their primary motivator. In these, players are pitted against each other, often one on one, and compete until there is a clear winner and loser. We advise that you exercise caution when considering these games. Although they help to motivate, we believe that the type of motivation may be detrimental in that winning becomes the primary goal rather than what is to be learned. In addition, there is growing concern that violence in games, instructional or recreational, may contribute to violence outside

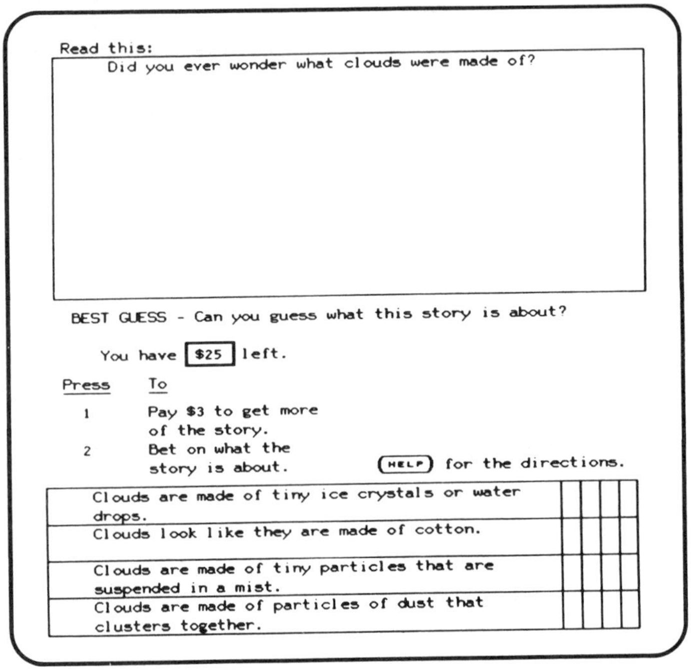

Read this:

Did you ever wonder what clouds were made of?

BEST GUESS - Can you guess what this story is about?

You have $25 left.

Press   To

1   Pay $3 to get more
         of the story.
2   Bet on what the
         story is about.   (HELP) for the directions.

Clouds are made of tiny ice crystals or water drops.			
Clouds look like they are made of cotton.			
Clouds are made of tiny particles that are suspended in a mist.			
Clouds are made of particles of dust that clusters together.			

Figure 5-17a *Casino Reading. (Courtesy of the Board of Trustees, University of Illinois, and R. Stevens, L. Reichmann, and A. Liu)*

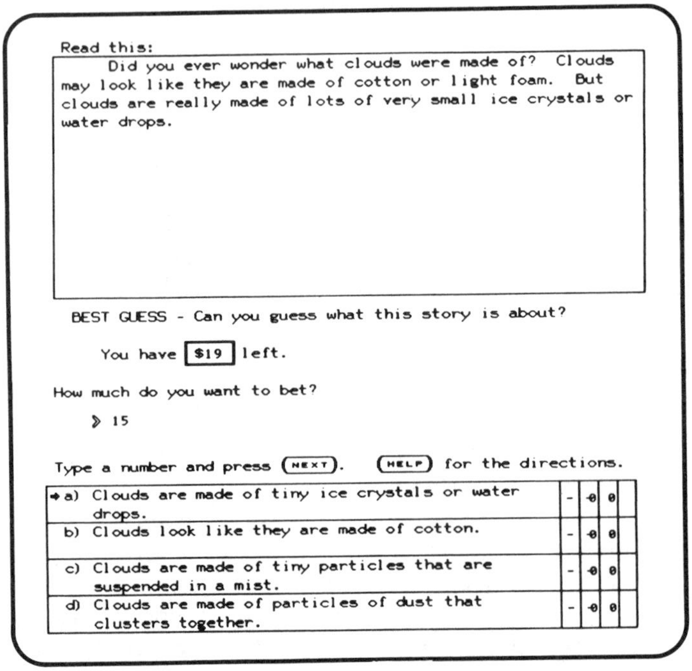

Read this:

Did you ever wonder what clouds were made of? Clouds may look like they are made of cotton or light foam. But clouds are really made of lots of very small ice crystals or water drops.

BEST GUESS - Can you guess what this story is about?

You have $19 left.

How much do you want to bet?

⟩ 15

Type a number and press (NEXT).   (HELP) for the directions.

→ a) Clouds are made of tiny ice crystals or water drops.	-	0	0
b) Clouds look like they are made of cotton.	-	0	0
c) Clouds are made of tiny particles that are suspended in a mist.	-	0	0
d) Clouds are made of particles of dust that clusters together.	-	0	0

Figure 5-17b

of the gaming situation. Some combat games, such as *Moonwar* (Bloomfield, 1973), which teaches the laws of reflection, are good instructional games. This game was designed to be played by two players at different terminals. Each player sees on the screen the world in which they are playing—the edges of the screen and several mountains. Hidden on the screen is the enemy. Each player attempts to shoot the other with a laser, which can bounce off the edge of the screen but which is absorbed by mountains. The purpose is to maneuver your own ship into a position from which you can shoot your opponent, either directly or indirectly, off the edges (Figure 5–18). The idea is to use the laws of reflection to maximize your chances. In a sense, games such as *Oregon* and *How the West Was Won* are also combat games.

Logic Games

Logic games are those that require the player to use logical problem solving to succeed. *Rocky's Boots,* discussed earlier, is a good example. Others are *Baffles* (Spain, 1983), chess, and most mathematical strategy grid games, such as the *Battleships* game, played originally with pencil and paper the world over. *Baffles* is very much like *Battleships* and *Hurkle* in that the goal is to locate hidden objects. Players are given a closed box that contains a number of baffles set at 45 degrees to the edges of the box. One can shoot a laser beam through the box from any one of the forty marked locations (Figure 5–19). If the beam hits a baffle it is reflected and can continue to be reflected until it reaches the edge of the box, at which point it

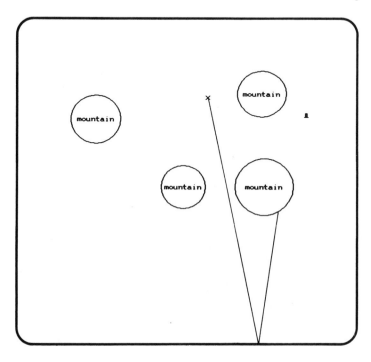

Figure 5-18   A player uses the edge of the screen to bounce a laser shot toward the opponent. *(Courtesy of the Board of Trustees, University of Illinois, and D. Bloomfield)*

reappears. If it misses all baffles, the beam reappears immediately opposite the point it went in. In Figure 5–19 a beam entered the box at position 15 and emerged at position 27. Hypothesizing that there was a baffle at this position (15,27), the player used the laser at position 7, only to find it emerging at position 38, which did not positively confirm the hypothesis. Play would continue in this fashion until certain of the location of a baffle. Then the player could tell the program to draw it where it should be. Figure 5–20 is an X-ray (which the student cannot normally see) of the box in Figure 5–19, showing the location of the baffles. As can be seen, the laser entering at position 7 actually reflected off three baffles before emerging at location 38.

Psychomotor Games

Psychomotor games are those that combine intellectual and motor skills. Most of these are noninstructional, for example, virtually all space games and the

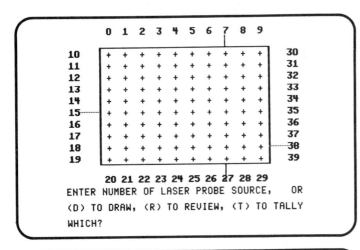

Figure 5-19 The closed box in *Baffles*, showing where two laser beams entered and left. *(Courtesy of James D. Spain and the publisher, CONDUIT)*

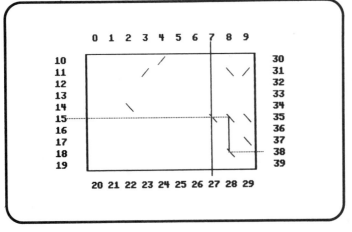

Figure 5-20 An X-ray of the box showing the location of the hidden baffles. *(Courtesy of James D. Spain and the publisher, CONDUIT)*

computerized versions of popular sports like tennis, baseball, or basketball. Some instructional games have psychomotor components, such as *Rocky's Boots,* which calls for manipulating objects on the screen, and *Moonwar,* which requires moving one's own spaceship while entering angles at which to fire one's lasers. Very often these games make use of the joystick or game paddles for input.

Role-Playing Games

Role-playing games are those in which the student assumes the guise of a character and acts out that role. By doing so, the student learns about the character's environment and problems, and how to solve these problems. We have already described *Archaeology Search, Oregon,* and *Snooper Troops,* all of which can be classified as role-playing games. Another is *Diffusion Game* (Lovelock & Weinberg, 1981), in which you visit an unknown village (Figure 5–21) to sell a new product. Before the game starts, you decide how long to stay and set a goal for the percentage of the village that will buy the product before you leave. At any stage in the game you can obtain factual information about the various avenues of communication available, such as newspapers, radio, or public meetings (Figure 5–22); about who the influential leaders are in the village; and about the way the village is divided into cliques (shown by numbers on the map). Based on this information, you can choose different diffusion methods to inform the public of the product. Some choices are to influence a powerful leader, to buy radio or newspaper advertising, to talk to residents at random, or to hold public meetings.

Each piece of information you request takes time to obtain, as does the effect of any diffusion method. The purpose of the game is to accomplish your stated goals successfully within the length of your visit. Naturally there are always trade-offs. More successful advertising media, such as radio, take longer to prepare and to have an effect. Setting up meetings with powerful leaders takes more time than with those who have less influence. In addition, all decisions and actions are subject to chance occurrences. Your Jeep may run over a powerful leader's

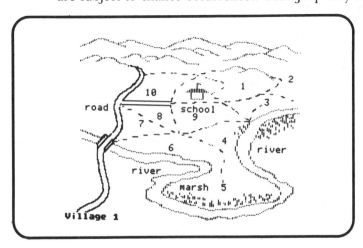

Figure 5-21 The map of the village in *Diffusion Game,* showing the locations of cliques (shown by the numbers). *(Courtesy of Christopher H. Lovelock, Charles B. Weinberg, and the publisher, CONDUIT)*

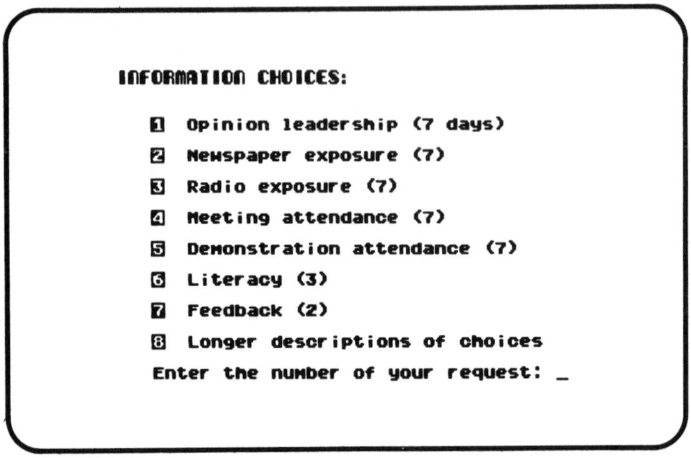

```
INFORMATION CHOICES:

  1  Opinion leadership (7 days)
  2  Newspaper exposure (7)
  3  Radio exposure (7)
  4  Meeting attendance (7)
  5  Demonstration attendance (7)
  6  Literacy (3)
  7  Feedback (2)
  8  Longer descriptions of choices
Enter the number of your request: _
```

Figure 5-22 Sources of information in *Diffusion Game. (Courtesy of Christopher H. Lovelock, Charles B. Weinberg, and the publisher, CONDUIT)*

dog, partially nullifying the effect of your sales presentation, or an unexpected turn of events may give you better results than anticipated when using a low density medium, such as a public meeting.

A series of programs of this nature has been built around a mythical character *Carmen Diego,* for example, *Where in the World Is Carmen Diego?* (Bigham, Portwood, & Elliott, 1985). In each of these, Carmen or one of her associates commits a crime. It is the student's goal to locate and arrest the guilty person. The student is given clues about the location, intentions, or appearance of the suspect and from these must make decisions about where to look for further clues or for whom to obtain an arrest warrant. The series is good in that it forces the player to use external resources, such as a world almanac, to make sense of some of the clues. For example, a clue may be "The plane he left on had a flag with a golden lion." To decide where the suspect was headed for, the student must locate which country's flag has such an emblem. Making wrong decisions causes you to lose time or go off on a wrong track.

TV Quiz Games

These instructional games take the form of an ordinary television quiz game. Typical of these is *Meet the Presidents* (Versa Computing, 1982). Here, the student is given clues about the identity of a president of the United States, and must guess who it is. The clues come in two forms. First, a detailed computer picture of the president in question slowly appears on the screen. Second, as this happens, clues as to his identity are flashed at the bottom of the screen. At any time the player may type in a guess. The sooner the correct name is entered, the higher the number of points awarded. Figures 5–23a, 5–23b, and 5–23c show how the picture of the particular president becomes more and more discernible, until the answer is given at the bottom. Two of the verbal clues are also shown.

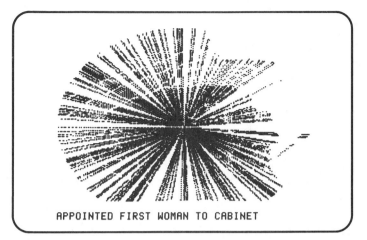

APPOINTED FIRST WOMAN TO CABINET

Figure 5-23a Three displays from *Meet the Presidents,* showing how verbal clues are given, while a graphic clue becomes more recognizable. *(Courtesy of Versa Computing, Inc.)*

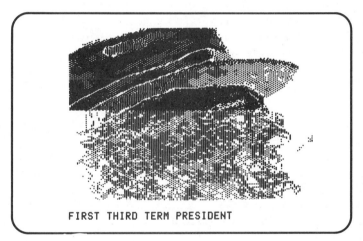

FIRST THIRD TERM PRESIDENT

Figure 5-23b

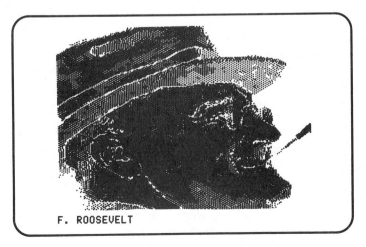

F. ROOSEVELT

Figure 5-23c

Word Games

Word games either teach about words or use words as the basis of the game. Many games that teach foreign vocabulary fall into this category, as do *Four-Letter Words* and *Ordeal of the Hangman*, which we described earlier. *Ordeal of the Hangman* is often used, in fact, in foreign language instruction as a vocabulary exercise.

Templates

Before concluding this section on the types of games, we want to mention the idea of templates, or template games. These are games whose form lends itself to being used in a variety of areas. Many adventure games, board games, combat games, and word games can be easily adapted to teach almost any subject matter.

Ordeal of the Hangman, for example, is usually associated with spelling. The same game, however, can be employed in any number of contexts: foreign language drill, arithmetic examples, shape or musical note recognition. In fact, whenever a question or problem is answered incorrectly, the potential victim's body could be augmented. In this way, by using the *Ordeal of the Hangman* template, it becomes relatively easy to create a game for any circumstance. Thus, the long and difficult process of designing, redesigning, and testing a new game can be avoided.

THE PURPOSE OF USING GAMES IN INSTRUCTION

Games are becoming more popular in the instructional setting because teachers are beginning to appreciate their potential for motivating students to learn. Obviously, the overriding purpose of instructional games is to teach, and they can be successfully used to convey a variety of information, such as (from Maidment & Bronstein, 1973; Nesbitt, 1971):

> Facts and principles
> Processes, such as titration or real estate acquisition
> The structure and dynamics of systems
> Skills, such as problem solving, decision making, or the formulation of strategies
> Social skills, such as communication
> Attitudes

A variety of incidental learning may also occur such as the nature of competition, how people cooperate, the dynamics of social systems, the role of chance, and the fact that penalties often have to be paid for just or unjust reasons.

Teachers find that games have advantages over most traditional instruction because games tend to motivate students and focus their attention on the goal of the game (Schild, 1968). This often leads to more efficient learning, for the student is less easily distracted by classmates, daydreams, or external events. Maidment and Bronstein (1973) also postulate that games enhance the learning environment because the teacher plays a less dominant role and is not the only judge of performance. In fact, by constructively discussing with the student how to perform better, the teacher may well be perceived as an ally. This encourages many students to interact more freely with the teacher.

When used properly, instructional games are very powerful learning tools and should be given consideration as an alternative to more conventional options. Of course, games should not be used just because they are games, but because they will achieve some positive outcome. An effective instructional game maintains the student's interest and encourages the acquisition and development of the desired knowledge or skills.

THE STRUCTURE OF GAMES

Games are much like simulations in their basic structure, as can be seen by comparing the flow of a game (Figure 5-24) with that of a simulation (Figure 4-10 in Chapter 4). The only difference is the addition of an optional input by an opponent. Otherwise it has the same cyclic nature. Games can be divided into three main parts: the introduction, the body of the game, and the conclusion. In the following sections we discuss the instructional factors relevant to each part, once again omitting those we have discussed under other methodologies.

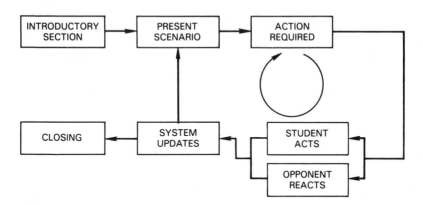

Figure 5-24 The general structure and flow of games.

FACTORS IN THE INTRODUCTION OF A GAME

The purpose of the introduction is to set the stage for the game, and to ensure that the student understands what to do, and how to do it. If the game is poorly introduced it may lose much of its instructional benefit, because the student may have to concentrate on solving unimportant problems rather than on playing the game.

Goal

The goal of a game is the target towards which each player aims. In most cases this goal is clearly stated. In some cases it is the same for all players; in other instances it may vary from one player to another. Sometimes the goals of the person playing the game will differ from the stated goals of the game itself. For example, in *How the West Was Won* the stated goal is to reach the final destination before your opponent. For most people this is the only goal. Some players, however, may have the private goal of winning by an ever increasing margin. In a game of poker, the goal is to leave the table with more money than when you arrived. A private goal may be to bankrupt all the other players.

In an instructional game, the goals need to reinforce the intended objectives. To teach well, an instructional game should ensure that success comes about by the application of the skills or knowledge to be learned, rather than by luck, tricks, or unintended skills. Progress towards the game's goals should always follow progress towards instructional objectives. Learning is enhanced most if progress is an immediate reward for learning and is perceived as such by the student.

Rules

The rules of a game define its nature and the role each player will take. As mentioned earlier, these rules are essentially artificial and can be changed whenever necessary. In traditional games, such as *Monopoly* or *Scrabble,* this is done quite often to suit local circumstances. In computer-based games, however, it is usually impossible to alter the rules other than by rewriting the program. Because of this, it is rare for such games to be played differently from the way they were intended.

The rules usually define the players, the equipment used, the permissible procedures, the constraints imposed, and the possible penalties.

Players

The rules govern what role each of the players will assume (bankers, clients, generals, star fleet commanders). Rules also designate, in terms of both minimum and maximum numbers, how many players of each type can participate. Also stated is whether the computer will or can play the role of one of the participants, particularly in those games that normally have two opponents, such as *How the West Was Won* or chess. One of the advantages of many computer-based multiplayer games is that an individual can still play even if alone.

Equipment

Rules always include a statement about the equipment required to play the game. For computer-based games, this is usually restricted to joysticks, game paddles, or particular hardware requirements, such as size of memory or number of disk drives. In noncomputerized games it includes such items as boards, dice, and cards.

Procedures

The procedures of a game detail how to set it up, how it proceeds, how it ends, and what happens when a winner emerges. Also included are procedures for handling disagreements between players, such as instances of two players claiming that each was the first to do something or to be somewhere, or of more than one player claiming the same property or money.

Constraints

In addition to the procedures that tell what actions are allowed, there are also constraints that stipulate the boundaries and limitations of those actions, such as the number of houses one may have on a property, the number of cards one may exchange, the number of consecutive turns allowed, or the quantity of resources that one can accumulate or use. In *Ordeal of the Hangman*, for example, the number of attempts allowed at guessing letters in the hidden word is a constraint. In *Four-Letter Words* the length of word is a constraint. Constraints may further specify particular actions that are disallowed entirely. In *How the West Was Won*, the student is not allowed to use powers or roots when combining numbers for the next move, nor can the student use the same arithmetic operator more than once.

Penalties

The penalties of a game are the actions taken if a player violates the rules or procedures. Sometimes the penalties are stated explicitly, for example, that a turn is forfeited if a player plays out of turn or fails to respond within a given time limit. In other cases, the penalties are implicit; occasionally the players themselves make them up. Traditional games, like *Monopoly* and *Scrabble*, frequently have local rules specifying the penalties for cheating or improper behavior. Computer-based games are generally not amenable to such informal penalties.

Directions for Use

Rules, procedures, and penalties tell the player what actions to take to play the game; directions inform the player about the logistics of performing these particular actions. In *How the West Was Won*, the rule is that spinners provide three random numbers, each of which has to be used in an expression in which each arithmetic operator can appear no more than once. The directions tell you how to activate the spinners. In a word game, like *Four-Letter Words*, the rules dictate that as many words as possible have to be made from a given pool of letters. The directions tell you how to obtain the pool and what to do with the words made up. Other examples include instructions on how to test game paddles if required, how to enter each person's name or identifier, how to set the level of difficulty of a game, how to specify the number of players, or how to request information. Frequently, directions appear in an accompanying booklet rather than in the game program itself. Since nearly all software is accompanied by written directions on how to load the program into the computer and make it operational, including the directions in a booklet makes sense logistically.

Choices

A player often makes many of the important choices prior to the start of the game. These choices may include whether the computer will be one of the players and, if so, at what level of proficiency it should play. In *Decimal Darts*, for example, the difficulty can be specified by changing the precision required in the answer, or whether both positive and negative numbers are to be included. In some games you are given the choice of changing the length of words to be selected, as in *Ordeal of the Hangman*. Other games also allow you to select an option in which the computer can play against itself, with you acting as a spectator.

Another common choice involves time, in one of two ways. Either you can select how long the game is to continue (that is, when it is to terminate), or how fast it is to take place. Speed of action is closely related to the level of difficulty, with increased rate of movement or reaction usually being associated with greater difficulty.

Other common choices include the name by which you want to be known within the game, such as Lord Avatar, Babe Ruth, or Jackie Stewart, depending on the game. One can frequently select the piece that represents you, such as a car, locomotive, or stagecoach, or the shape and color of your spaceship. Such choices are important, particularly in multi-player games, to discriminate between players.

FACTORS IN THE BODY OF THE GAME

Games have a structure very much like simulations, and they are just as difficult to divide into distinct parts. For purposes of discussion, however, it is convenient to deal with the following categories.

The scenario
The level of reality
The cast
The role of the players
The presence of uncertainty
The presence of curiosity
The nature of the competition
The relationship of learning to instructional objectives
Skill versus chance
Wins and losses
Choices
The information flow
Turns
Types of action
Modes of interaction

Scenario

The scenario of a game is the "world" in which the action takes place. Scenarios include interstellar space populated by friendly and hostile spaceships, a casino, a country with particular economic and political conditions, a map of an archaeological dig, a maze, a wall covered with balloons, and so on. The scenario determines the type of game in which the instruction is embedded: an adventure, space, card, or board game, to name but a few. For example, if the object of instruction is simple arithmetic operations, such as addition and subtraction, a variety of scenarios may be employed to teach this. *How the West Was Won* uses a race between a stagecoach and railroad engine as the scenario. *Beehive* (Dugdale, Kibbey, & Leung, 1978) allows the player to let bees in and out of a hive, each time asking how many remain in it (Figure 5–25). Other games have the player buying and selling things, each time calculating the remaining funds. In each of these, addition and subtraction are being used, but the scenario is different.

There are 8 bees in all.

How many bees are in the hive? ⊳ 5   Good!
Press NEXT.

Figure 5-25 The game *Beehive* uses a natural scenario for simple arithmetic drills. *(Courtesy of the Board of Trustees, University of Illinois, and S. Dugdale, D. Kibbey, and H. Leung)*

Scenarios comprise three dimensions: realism versus simplification; concentration versus comprehensiveness; and emotion versus intellect (adapted from Abt, 1968). Each of these involves trade-offs. The more realistic the scenario, the harder it usually is to play the game, because of detail and complexity. On the other hand, the greater the simplification the further it is from reality, which can lower the transfer of knowledge to real life. Likewise, the more the game focuses on a topic, the less perspective the player will get of that topic in the broader context. Increasing the comprehensiveness of the scenario can lead to loss of important realism and detail. Finally, the greater the presence of emotional involvement or reward, such as in space battles where the enemy always threatens, the less likely the player is to analyze the situation from a detached perspective. Likewise, games that have only intellectual appeal frequently are low in motivation.

Scenarios can be further classified by where they fall on the relationship triangle. This triangle has three vertices representing intrinsic, related, and arbitrary relationships between the context or scenario and the instructional goals.

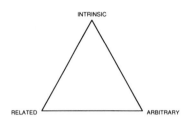

An example of an *intrinsic* scenario is *Archaeology Search*. In this game, the team of students explores an archaeological site in search of ancient relics. They do so by asking the computer questions. They then use the answers either to formulate new questions or to begin excavating. As they move through the ruins, the students see different features, and would find different artifacts if they started digging. Because the purpose of the game is to teach the scientific method of archaeology, and the scenario of the game is an archaeological site that the student can explore, the scenario is called intrinsic. Each student action is dependent on a reaction from the scenario. Likewise, the response from the scenario depends on where the student is within it, and what questions are asked. Many role-playing games are highly intrinsic.

Decimal Darts falls closer to the *related* vertex of the relationship triangle. It does so because, although throwing darts at balloons has nothing to do with number lines, the position of the balloon directly influences the response of the student. Likewise, the student action affects the scenario. If the estimate of the balloon's position is accurate, the balloon pops.

An *arbitrary* scenario is one in which there is no relationship or interaction between the scenario and what is being learned. In *Ordeal of the Hangman*, for instance, the creation and the hanging of the victim have no relationship to guessing the hidden words other than to act as a motivator. Certainly, student actions affect the scenario, but the scenario (how close the victim is to death) has no influence at all on future guesses. Many games that accumulate points or money as a reward for good performance have a high arbitrary value.

Another measure of the arbitrariness of a game is the lack of a cause-and-effect relationship between the student actions and the real scenario depicted in the game. Thus, in reality, when a student performs badly at guessing hidden words, no one actually is hanged. This also makes the *Ordeal of the Hangman* scenario arbitrary.

Malone (1980) claims that games with high intrinsic qualities are generally the most interesting and instructional. This implies that clothing instruction in a game format is unlikely to improve the instruction a great deal, unless the scenario of the game is directly involved with what is being learned. So, when the scenario is used merely to provide a gaming environment, it is less likely to enhance learning.

Level of Reality

Three basic types of scenarios—real, unreal, and fantasy—can be incorporated into a game. A *real* scenario is one that exists in real life. An example is the game *Pinball,* in which a child plays a simulated pinball machine in order to learn various math facts. A pinball machine, which is the context of the game, actually exists in the real world.

An *unreal* scenario represents something that exists in real life but in a different form. Many examples of these abound; chess has a board representing a battlefield and pieces representing different ranks of soldiers and nobles; *Monopoly* has a board representing the real estate of a city, paper money representing real money, and a shuffled deck of cards representing the vagaries of everyday luck or misfortune; *Snooper Troops* allows the student to play the role of a detective, searching houses, questioning suspects, and making accusations. Each of these represents a real situation, but in a detached or abstract way.

A *fantasy* game is one in which the scenario is purely a figment of the imagination. A game like *Dungeons and Dragons* (TSR Hobbies) is a good example. Here the player has to negotiate a passage through a complicated assortment of rambling hallways, imaginary animals, unworldly people, and impossible situations to reach an elusive goal. Another type of fantasy game is one in which a part of the scenario is imaginary. An example of this is *Oregon.* Certainly the Wild West existed and the problems encountered by the player are realistic. However, to a twentieth-century person, it is only fantasy to be transported back in time.

Cast

Every game has a cast of players. In some games the cast may be one person, in others, many. In some games, all the players may be people, in others the computer may also become a player. Sometimes a player or the computer or both can play several roles simultaneously. In *How the West Was Won,* for example, the student may play either against another person or against the computer. In addition, the student can choose to watch the computer play against itself.

Role of the Players

A computer-based game can often define or constrain the roles of the participants more than a traditional game. For example, in a normal board game it is possible for a player to cheat by rolling the dice, picking them up very quickly before the other players can see them, announcing a preferred sum, and moving accordingly. A player could accidently move a piece an incorrect number of spaces merely by miscounting. In a noncomputer game, one of the other players would have to be alert to notice either action.

With computer-based games, it is possible to police such situations automatically. Because the computer rolls the dice, for instance, it can also total their points, and move the player's token automatically, precluding illegal moves. However, programming a game on a computer can lead to an inflexibility of rules that could change the nature of the game. For example, in a game like *Monopoly*, part of the entertainment is the formation of alliances between players in an attempt to corner the market. This usually involves loans of money from one to another to optimize resources. If a computerized version were only to allow the purchase of new property when the player landing on it had enough money, this practice of alliance would be curtailed. This could well reduce the overall appeal of the game.

Finally, each player's role and that of the computer must be made clear. All players can have identical roles, different roles, or additional duties, as the banker does in *Monopoly*. Whatever the case, all players must know their own roles, and, if appropriate, the roles of the other players as well.

Presence of Uncertainty

Malone (1980) and others (Kagan, 1978; Eifferman, 1974) believe that for a game to be challenging, the attainment of its goal must be uncertain. Malone (1980, p. 50) says this can be accomplished in a number of different ways:

Variable difficulty level
Multiple level goal
Hidden information
Randomness

Variable Difficulty Level.   Within each game there should be situations that require varying levels of effort by the player. Some situations should be easily mastered; others should be difficult. In this way the player is provided both with reward and with continuing challenge. A simple example of this is incorporated into *Decimal Darts*. Normally a small tolerance is allowed when hitting a single balloon. Sometimes, however, when two balloons are adjacent, it is possible to pop both simultaneously—but only if the dart is perfectly positioned. No tolerance is allowed in this case.

Multiple Level Goal.   This means that the game has adjustable levels of difficulty, which are set either by the player or by the game itself. A game may, for example, adapt its level of difficulty to the performance of the player, thus making it constantly a challenge. As a player improves, the harder the game gets; if a player is not performing well, the game becomes a little easier. This is the case in *Decimal Darts.* In contrast, it is the player in *Rocky's Boots* who chooses the level of difficulty, by selecting the complexity of the machine to build.

Hidden Information.   A game is more challenging if each player operates with incomplete or hidden information. The attraction of a game is increased if each player is uncertain about some facts needed to attain the goal. Thus, the game of *Battleships* has always fascinated children. Each player hides a fleet of ships in the ocean. The ships are of different sizes, and their location has to meet several constraints. Each player in turn "shoots" at a particular coordinate on the ocean, and is told whether the shot was a hit. From the pattern of hits and misses, the player must infer where ships are and try to sink them.

In this game, it is seldom certain where the ships are. Furthermore, because ships are of different sizes and are aligned differently, it is impossible to predict from a single hit where the rest of a ship is, or what type of ship it is. Success results from being able to develop good problem-solving strategies. A hypothesis about the location of enemy ships must be developed given the available information and a strategy developed for testing it. The attraction of the game resides in the fact that a player often has to wait some time before knowing whether the hypothesis was correct. *Baffles,* a game we described above, is designed on the same principle as *Battleships,* but is much more difficult and intriguing.

Randomness.   This involves the extent to which random fluctuations or chance play a role in the game. Games that depend on the roll of dice or the dealing of cards have a high element of randomness. So do games like *Snooper Troops* and *Diffusion Game,* in which random events affect the outcome, such as the owner of a house returning while you are snooping in the basement, or your Jeep breaking down on the way to address a meeting. Some arcade video games have hostile spacecraft flying with a degree of randomness to their motion. This unpredictable behavior makes it more difficult to create and master optimal strategies for winning. However, if luck is the only factor that is important in winning, a game is likely to be less appealing than one in which the player perceives, rightly or wrongly, that strategy influences the outcome.

Presence of Curiosity

Curiosity motivates us to learn more than we currently know, or to explore further than we have come. It compels us to seek new knowledge. Games depend on the curiosity of the player as part of the motivation for playing. Of course, curiosity and challenge are closely related, the challenge of a game frequently being how to satisfy curiosity. Malone (1980, p. 60) has proposed:

> . . . environments (*scenarios*) can evoke a learner's curiosity by providing an optimal level of informational complexity (Berlyne, 1965; Piaget, 1952). In other words, the environments should be neither too complicated nor too simple with respect to the learner's existing knowledge. They should be novel and surprising,

but not completely incomprehensible. In general, an optimally complex environment will be one where the learner knows enough to have expectations about what will happen, but where these expectations are sometimes unmet.

Curiosity generally comes in two forms, *sensory* and *cognitive*. Sensory curiosity involves ways in which the senses are aroused: sight and hearing being the most prominent in computer games. Frequent alterations in what is seen on the screen helps maintain our attention, either through use of different colors or by means of changing the scene. This is the reason that television commercials are always active and rapidly changing. Similarly, it is the reason why many computer or arcade games make extensive use of sounds of different pitches and durations.

Cognitive curiosity is the desire to know, and it is aroused by different means. One common method is to prevent or prolong the natural ending or closure of whatever is happening. When closure is not reached, we become highly motivated to do whatever is necessary to obtain it. For example, if there is a television transmission problem during the last two minutes of an exciting football game, people become highly motivated to find out the result. They turn on the radio or call the newsroom at the television station or local newspaper. Similarly, if the last few pages of a thrilling detective story are missing from the book, many readers will go to great lengths to learn the ending.

Curiosity is also frequently aroused by inconsistency in a person's view of the world. Malone uses the example that students may be told that plants require sunlight to activate necessary processes for survival. On the other hand, other plants, such as mushrooms, can live in the dark. This apparent contradiction motivates a person to explore the reasons for the phenomenon more fully. The appeal of *Snooper Troops* is based on the arousal of curiosity. As more clues are found, some of which are inconsistent, the more eager the player becomes to piece them together into a meaningful pattern.

How curiosity motivates people has ramifications for the design of games. An enjoyable game will arouse a person's curiosity and provide a means for satisfying it if performance is adequate or sufficient.

Nature of Competition

The nature of competition in a game is defined by three major components: the number of participants, whether play is individual or in teams, and against whom or what the players compete.

The number of players in a game can vary from one to many, and often includes the computer. Usually each participant acts individually, but there are some games, such as *Archaeology Search,* in which players are encouraged to form teams. Games like *Decimal Darts, Rocky's Boots, Ordeal of the Hangman*, and *Phizquiz* have only one player. *How the West Was Won* and most combat games require more than one player. Sometimes the role of the other player or players can be taken by the computer. In *Oregon* the computer always plays, while a player can choose to play against the computer in chess or *How the West Was Won*. In some games, such as *Snooper Troops*, the computer plays many roles.

Often players compete against themselves. This is particularly true of games in which some numerical measure of performance is kept. Good examples of this in traditional games are golf or bowling. Examples of instructional games of this type are *Decimal Darts*, *Rocky's Boots*, and *Phizquiz*. In each of these, the player strives to improve performance against some absolute standard. In other games the competition is directly with the computer, as in *Oregon* and other games in which the computer can be chosen as the opponent. In games such as *Pinball* or *Type Attack* (Sirius Software), which is a typing skill game, the players compete against time. Of course, in most games the nature of the competition is determined by combinations of these various factors.

Relationship of Learning to Instructional Objectives

The learning that takes place in an instructional game can either be *intended* or *unintended*. If what is learned is intended, there is a very strong relationship between it and the instructional objectives. Conversely, if learning is unintended, there is no relationship, and we call it *incidental.*

In almost every educational setting it is impossible, and undesirable, in our opinion, to have the students learn only what was specified in the objectives. Students learn all sorts of unspecified skills and knowledge as a by-product of their formal learning; examples include social interactions, the fact that beakers heated over Bunsen burners can cause severe burns on fingers, that careless use of electricity can cause painful shocks, or that reference to particular situations or people can cause anxiety or excitement in teachers or classmates. All of these are examples of incidental learning.

Sometimes it is possible for learning to be intended by the teacher, but from the student's perspective to be incidental. That is, the student is unaware of all the goals of the instruction. For example, most sports are very good at teaching how to exercise self-control when both winning and losing—a skill that is valuable outside the sporting arena. It is clear, however, that in terms of the game itself such a benefit is incidental. A good game can foster such things as cooperation between team members or ethical behavior without obviously doing so.

Skill versus Chance

A game is more likely to be entertaining and to continue to be entertaining if there is a balance of skill and chance. Chance increases the unexpected, which can increase the challenge. However, if chance is overdone, the student may not be sufficiently skilled to overcome its effects. Similarly, if only skill is required to master the game, the uncertainty is eliminated, and the game may lose its appeal.

Wins and Losses

There are two major ways to determine whether a player wins in a game. One is when a specific goal has been attained, either reaching an explicit target or defeating an opponent.

Other games have a less explicit way of determining whether there is a winner. Some people, for example, regard themselves as winners if they perform better than they ever have before. One bowler may be disappointed with scoring 190, while another may be ecstatic. Golf, in particular, evokes this type of reaction, as do various arcade games. Similarly, improving performance in an instructional game can also be regarded as winning. In *Oregon,* for instance, a player traveling farther along the trail than ever before may be a winner. Guessing the hidden word in *Ordeal of the Hangman* in fewer attempts than before can be regarded as winning, as can calculating the answer to a problem in *Phizquiz* using less money. In all of these, the player does not attain a perfect score and so cannot be judged a winner in any absolute sense. However, relative to previous scores or performance, the player is a winner. Computer games make it particularly easy to keep track of each person's prior performance, and to make one a winner if he or she exceeded it.

It is also important to consider what constitutes losing, because its effects are more critical than those of winning. Harm seldom comes from winning, but a single devastating loss or a series of persistent losses can demoralize a student.

There are different ways of losing. You can fail to reach a clearly stated objective, or can be defeated in head-to-head combat, as in chess, *Moonwar,* or *How the West Was Won.* You can be one of several losers, as in team games like *Archaeology Search,* or can fail to reach a self-imposed level of performance, as in *Pinball* or *Decimal Darts.* It is important for the future motivation of players to ensure that losing does not create ill will or feelings of anger or inferiority. In such cases, it may be very difficult to recapture the interest and attention of the student.

The final aspect of winning and losing is the nature of what is won or lost. This can sometimes be crucial to the success of the game. Poker, for example, which is America's most popular game, has very little appeal to most people if played for tokens rather than money. The level of stake is very important. If too low, there is little incentive to be cautious when betting or bluffing. If too high, anxiety can detract from the pleasure of playing. Computer games are generally different in this respect. Because there are generally no material rewards or losses, winners usually take with them only the pleasure of success, while losers lose only the game, and not money or possessions.

Choices

There are typically four types of choices that occur in the body of a game:

Informational
Strategic
Assistance
Leaving

Informational. Many games require access to information on which strategic decisions are based. Consequently, it must be clear to the player how to access such information. Typical of such information is the necessary data and the relevant equations for solving problems in *Phizquiz*, as illustrated in Figure 5–26. In *Snooper Troops* the player constantly needs information from witnesses and suspects, and access to evidence and clues collected previously. In an air combat game, the screen may be filled for most of the game with simulated flight instruments. However, at any time the pilot (the player) must be able to access information detailing the amount of fuel remaining, or the number of missiles left. The ability to access this information should be well documented and easy to accomplish.

Strategic.   Strategic choices are usually the central part of a game. These are the choices that a player makes to manipulate the context or to participate in the action of the game. How the various choices are to be accomplished must be easy to learn and readily accessible. Sometimes these are discrete events, such as the entry of a number, answer, or course of action. Sometimes the choices are apparently continuous, such as when using a game paddle or joystick to direct some moving object on the screen. Whatever the type, it must be clearly stated how to make the choice.

Assistance.   It is difficult for a new player and often for seasoned players to remember how to do everything in a game, particularly when there are many variables to alter, or when players take different roles. As the number of options

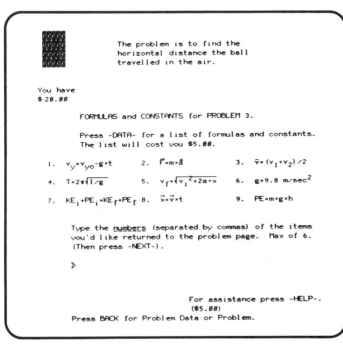

Figure 5-26 The necessary equations for solving *Phizquiz* problems. *(Courtesy of the Board of Trustees, University of Illinois, and J. Smith and D. Kane)*

increases, it becomes more important to provide easy access to the directions of the game, or to help on both content and strategy. Games can be programmed to provide strategic assistance to beginners, for instance, as an instructional device. Such assistance must be easy to obtain, preferably through a minimal number of keystrokes if on-line, or in an easily read manual if not. *Rocky's Boots* uses an interesting technique. Whenever players need information, they must go to a "directions room" where assistance is available (Figure 5–27). Most instructional games are very weak in providing ongoing access to directions, and they often require players to remember large amounts of information.

Leaving. There are two instances when a player may want to leave a game, and two possible future actions. A player may want to leave once the game has been completed, in which case the usual choice is whether to play again or to leave. A player also may want to leave the game before it is finished. This can be because the game has lost its appeal, the player does not want to lose, or time has run out.

In the case when the player leaves while playing, two other possibilities arise. Either the player wants to end involvement in the current game, or wishes to be able to return to the same point and continue. When the player wants to return later, the nature of the game will dictate whether this is possible. Games in which there is only one player usually pose no problem. The game may be frozen and restarted later. In such a case all the relevant information must be stored from one session to another to allow this to happen. Both *President Elect* (Hernandez, 1981), a game that teaches about election strategies, and *Snooper Troops* allow the current state of the game to be stored on disk. This is useful because both games can take a long time to complete.

Games in which more than one player participates are more difficult to arrange. Certainly games like chess or checkers can be frozen as long as the participants agree to return. However, the greater the number of opponents the less likely it will be to make such an arrangement.

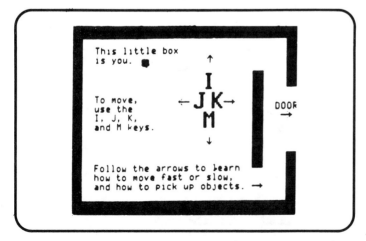

Figure 5-27 The directions room in *Rocky's Boots. (Courtesy of The Learning Company)*

Whatever options a game offers, it must be clear to all players how to invoke them. Furthermore, the ramifications of choosing each option should be known. If the player can return to continue playing, explicit instructions must be provided as to the procedure to follow. Most of these directions need not appear during the game but can be specified at the beginning. The only ongoing piece of information the player needs to know is the procedure to initiate departure—usually a special key press, such as ⟨ESC⟩⟨q⟩.

The interaction of a player with a game is the most important component once the game has started. Thus, it is essential that the choices available be known and easily implemented.

Information Flow

In all games the player needs information on which to make choices. In this section we discuss information, what it is, when it must be provided, and how it can be given.

Types of Information Given.   Throughout a game, each player obtains information either automatically or on request. What type of information it is can directly influence the progress of the game and the chances of the player's success. There are several types: accurate, misleading, partial, and false. Each can be embodied into the pictorial, textual, or audible modes.

If continuation of a game is dependent on information being accurate, then that is what should be provided. Examples of this are whether a student's answer to a question is correct or incorrect, that the value for the acceleration due to gravity is approximately 9.8 meters/second/second, or that a particular equation is the correct one to use in a given problem. There would be little benefit to the student if such information were incorrectly supplied.

There are cases, however, when the use of misleading information heightens the challenge by increasing the uncertainty of the player. This can have positive motivational effects. For example, in *Snooper Troops*, a player can never be certain how correct the information is when interviewing witnesses or suspects. Every piece of information has to be verified from other sources. This type of game requires the student to have a type of meta-view of the game. Knowing that information is not always true can influence a player's strategies throughout a game, even though false data may only appear occasionally.

Partial information can have a similar motivating effect. In *Phizquiz*, for instance, the student has to solve problems on mechanics. In each only partial information is given. The rest has to be calculated from available information, inferred, or bought with play money. Because one of the goals is to solve the problems spending as little money as possible, there is considerable motivation to obtain the information without buying it.

Giving false information should be avoided, unless the student knows that this is a possibility, in which case it is usually being used as a motivator, as in *Snooper Troops*. One other occasion involving false information occurs when the computer cheats when playing one of the roles in a game. This raises some ethical issues. For instance, in a board game, it is possible for the computer to purposely adjust the seemingly random generation of numbers on its turn so as to give the computer an added advantage. One purpose of such a subterfuge would be to make the game as challenging as possible for the student by having the computer be continually competitive. If the student moves rapidly, the computer generates higher numbers for itself; if the student does not progress quickly, the computer appropriately slows down. From a motivational perspective, this practice may be successful. Nevertheless, it can also engender an attitude in students, particularly if young, that computers either always cheat, which is not true, or should never be trusted, which may be true.

Our stance is that if the computer is going to cheat, in the sense described above, the student should be made aware of that fact. We believe it is better to potentially damage some of the motivational attributes of a game than it is to lead a student to believe that the computer's performance is honest when it is not.

Source of Information.   Most information during a game comes from the computer, and includes directions on how to play, the results of each player's actions, questions or problems to be answered, and feedback on performance. Most computer games supply all the necessary information to play. There are some, however, that also provide information in a manual or booklet supplied with the game. Sometimes this information is a duplicate of that contained in the game itself; sometimes it is new information that cannot be obtained from anywhere else, such as maps or charts. Most frequently it is initial information on how to load the program into the computer.

Information can also come incidentally from other players. Although not an instructional game, *Monopoly* serves to illustrate the point. Not only does the game provide information, such as how many houses are on a property or what the penalties are for landing on it, but the other players do also. It is useful to remember who owns what properties or to know how much money each player has. This type of information can lead to different strategic decisions about the acquisition of new property or the negotiation of property exchanges. Most computer games do not have the same capacity for providing information of this sort, because they tend to deal with players in a way that prevents the information from being accessed by others.

Computer games can themselves inadvertently provide useful information to the player that knows where to look. For example, experienced players use information not immediately apparent to the novice, such as slight variations in sound signaling the approach of a particular type of hostile craft, or of an imminent change of circumstances. Similarly, by doing an analysis of the random generator used by a computer, it may be possible to alter one's perception of the odds. So, for instance, if an analysis of many throws of dice indicated that instead of each of the six numbers appearing with approximately equal frequency, 6 appeared twice as frequently as 1, this would allow a player to increase the perceived probability of 6 appearing and would almost certainly affect the strategies in playing or betting.

When Information Is Provided.   Some information is always supplied at the beginning of a game. This includes the rules, directions, and any other information necessary to start the game. As the game progresses there is a constant flow of information. Sometimes it is provided immediately in response to a player's action, the passage of time, or as a result of a player failing to act. At other times, information about an action is delayed in the same way as feedback can be delayed in simulations. In *Rocky's Boots*, for example, the student can assemble many components in an attempt to construct a machine that meets the required specifications. After each component is added, the student has immediate visual confirmation that it is attached properly. However, it is only after all the components have been assembled and the machine tested that the student obtains the necessary information to decide whether the machine's design meets the specifications.

At the end of a game, the student may know how well he or she performed, but may have to wait to obtain information about performance relative to other players. For example, at the end of each problem in *Phizquiz*, the student knows how much money was spent solving the problem, but it may be several days before the same student found out how that matched the performance of classmates.

How Information Is Provided.   Information can be provided either explicitly, such as in a message to the player, or implicitly, as in the relative movement of various pieces or tokens. Furthermore, information can be transmitted by means of words, sounds, movements, pictures, colors, or the actions of opponents. It can also be provided from both off-line or on-line sources.

Turns

Players can interact in different ways in games. They can take turns in a specified sequence, as in *Archaeology Search* or *How the West Was Won*; they can react at will to another player's actions as in *Moonwar;* they may react simultaneously, as in many conflict games; or they may do nothing at all.

In many games each player completes an entire game at a time, awaiting completion by other players for information on relative standing. In other games, players can act independently of each other, with each action potentially influencing future actions of other players.

As with all possible player involvement, it must be made clear what the various options are so that the player is not penalized by the difficulty of manipulating the system.

Types of Action

Playing a game involves a variety of different actions on the part of a player. In instructional games, the most common are moving things on the screen, answering questions, choosing from options, attacking or defending, turning machines or switches on or off, and seeking information. Most games use combinations of these, employing different types at different points in the game, and for different reasons.

Modes of Interaction

Given the types of actions that will occur in a game, a number of possible modes can be used to implement each action. The usual modes available are through the keyboard, by touching the screen, by means of a joystick or game paddle, or with increasing frequency through speech recognition. Each has advantages and disadvantages with respect to each action.

If the game requires the student to answer questions about a topic, the student can recall the answer and type it in using the keyboard, or can choose, using either keyboard, mouse, or joystick, one of several multiple-choice alternatives. The advantage of the former is that the student has nothing on the screen that acts as a prompt or hint. The drawback, however, is that it assumes the student can type with some proficiency. Selecting among alternatives is easier for a student to do, but this may not elicit the same information. Touch panels have the advantage over keyboards in that people of all typing skills can use them, and that one does not have to look away from the screen in order to respond or act. Disadvantages include the fact that not all computers have touch panels and that they are less reliable than keyboards. Mice provide the best option, being easy to use and reliable.

Summary

This section has been devoted to the various factors that make a game what it is, and how each factor influences the nature of the game. We have discussed the various forms each factor can take and the effects each has on a game. Often there are no clear distinctions between these factors, and many interact strongly, which means that altering one may have extensive ramifications. In all instructional games, the primary goal should always be to meet the instructional objectives rather than merely to produce an enjoyable game.

FACTORS IN THE CONCLUSION OF THE GAME

The four factors associated with the conclusion of a game are:

> Recognizing the winner
> The reward
> Providing information
> The final message

Recognizing the Winner

At the end of a game it is important to recognize the winner, if there is one. In most games this is accomplished by a verbal message or an appropriate graphic display seen only by the current players. In some games, however, this is taken further. If a person's score or performance ranks in the top 10 or 20 of all previous games, this is recognized by being placed on a scoreboard containing the best scores. If this is automatic, rather than at the winner's choice, mention should be made of it before the game starts, particularly if the player's real name is being used. This can prevent embarrassment for someone who does not want to appear on such a list.

It is motivating for all players if the computer not only recognizes the winner but also congratulates all players whose scores exceeded their previous best. Of course, this requires storing data on performance from one session to another.

The Reward

The reward for winning a game varies greatly. It can be specific, such as money, goods, or free additional games; or more subtle, such as when a player merely knows that performance was improved. Whenever possible the reward should not become the end in itself; rather it should be another factor that can be manipulated to create a good instructional environment. The promise of a large reward certainly does not ensure motivation and rarely will negate the detrimental effects of an uninteresting game. If the game piques curiosity, external rewards are often totally unnecessary.

Providing Information

It is appropriate once the game has ended to provide feedback to each player on the progress of the game and on individual performance. It is also a good time to supply information about better ways to play the game or to solve the problems embedded in it. Some games, such as *Green Globs* (Dugdale & Kibbey, 1983), which is a two-dimensional version of *Decimal Darts*, save the entire game when the score is high so others can review the strategies of better players. There are also times when the strategic solution or the answer to the puzzle can be given, although this is usually done only if the player will not return to the game.

Final Message

The student may choose (if the option is available) to play the game again immediately. If the student does not choose to do so, it is appropriate to display a message stating that the program is ending. Do not end abruptly without such a message because the student may wonder if the program has malfunctioned.

ART OF GAME DESIGN

In the sections above we have detailed the various attributes present in games and how their presence or absence can affect instructional effectiveness. We are compelled to point out, however, that designing and implementing successful instructional games is difficult—far more so than any other methodology. There is definitely an art to game design, and even if a game is technically well designed, it may not work. We have seen many attempts by our students and professional designers, adhering to accepted design guidelines, to create instructional games. We have seen few that are interesting or motivating.

One implication of this is that you should be cautious when deciding that games are a methodology that you want to embrace. It is easy to spend hundreds of hours preparing a game, only to find that it has no appeal. We recommend testing your game on paper before implementing it on the computer, if at all possible. From this you should be able to sense whether it has a chance of success.

CONCLUSION

Games are a powerful instructional tool if used appropriately. It is clear that they have a strong motivating influence on children and adults alike. However, it is important to remember that instruction clothed in game format does not necessarily make the instruction effective. It is not the game format itself that appeals to people, it is the challenge or enjoyment of a particular game. For a game to be successful, it must be enjoyable *and* satisfy your instructional requirements.

REFERENCES AND BIBLIOGRAPHY

ABT, C.C. (1968). Games for learning. In S.S. Boocock & E.O. Schild (Eds.), *Simulation Games in Learning*. Beverly Hills, CA: Sage Publications.

ABT, C.C. (1970). *Serious Games*. New York: Viking Press.

BERLYNE, D.E. (1965). *Structure and Direction in Thinking*. New York: John Wiley and Sons.

BIGHAM, D., PORTWOOD, G., & ELLIOTT, L. (1985). *Where in the World Is Carmen Sandiego?* [Computer Program]. San Rafael, CA: Broderbund Software.

BLOOMFIELD, D. (1973). *Moonwar*. [Computer Program]. Urbana, IL: University of Illinois Computer-based Education Research Laboratory.

BOOCOCK, S.S., & SCHILD, E.O. (Eds.). (1968). *Simulation Games in Learning*. Beverly Hills, CA: Sage Publications.

CARROLL, J.M. (1982). The Adventure of Getting to Know a Computer. *Computer, 15* (11), 49–58.

CONTROL DATA CORPORATION. (1981). *Decimal Darts*. (In *Decimal Practice*.) [Computer Program]. Minneapolis, MN: Control Data Corporation. (Adapted from Dugdale, S., Kibbey, D., & Leung, H. (1974). *Decimal Darts*. Urbana, IL: University of Illinois Computer-based Education Research Laboratory.)

CRAWFORD, C. (1984). *The Art of Computer Game Design*. Berkeley, CA: Osborne/McGraw-Hill.

DUGDALE, S., & KIBBEY, D. (1983). *Green Globs*. In *Graphing Equations*. [Computer Program]. Iowa City, IA: CONDUIT.

DUGDALE, S., KIBBEY, D., & LEUNG, H. (1975). *Pinball*. [Computer Program]. Urbana, IL: University of Illinois Computer-based Education Research Laboratory.

DUGDALE, S., KIBBEY, D., & LEUNG, H. (1978). *Beehive.*

[Computer Program]. Urbana, IL: University of Illinois Computer-based Education Research Laboratory.

EIFFERMAN, R.R. (1974). It's child's play. In L.M. Shears & E.M. Bower (Eds.), *Games in Education and Development*. Springfield, IL: Charles C. Thomas.

ELLINGTON, H., ADINALL, E., & PERCIVAL F. (1982). *A Handbook of Game Design*. London, UK: Kogan Page.

GIBBS, G.I. (1974). *Handbook of Games and Simulation Exercises*. Beverly Hills, CA: Sage Publications.

GREENBLAT, C.S., & DUKE, R.D. (1975). *Gaming-Simulation: Rationale, Design, and Applications*. New York: Halstead Press.

HERNANDEZ, N. (1981). *President Elect*. [Computer Program]. Palo Alto, CA: Strategic Simulations, Inc.

KAGAN, J. (1978). *The Growth of the Child*. New York: Norton.

LEPPER, M.R. (1985). Microcomputers in education: Motivational and social issues. *American Psychologist, 40,* 1–18.

LOVELOCK, C.H., & WEINBERG, C.B. (1981). *Diffusion Game*. [Computer Program]. Iowa City, IA: CONDUIT.

LUSTER, R.G. (1983). *Four-Letter Words*. [Computer Program]. Iowa City, IA: CONDUIT.

MCVAY, P.O. (1980). *Tapping the Appeal of Games in Instruction*. Technical Report Number 6. Bedford, MA: Digital Equipment Corporation Educational Services.

MAIDMENT, R., & BRONSTEIN, R.H. (1973). *Simulation Games: Design and Implementation*. Columbus, OH: Charles E. Merrill.

MALONE, T.W. (1980). *What Makes Things Fun to Learn?*

Study of Intrinsically Motivating Computer Games. *Cognitive and Instructional Sciences Series CIS-7* (SSL-80-11). Palo Alto, CA: XEROX Palo Alto Research Center.

MALONE, T.W. (1981). Towards a theory of intrinsically motivating instruction. *Cognitive Science, 5,* 333–369.

MICHAEL, G., BERGER, M., DENNIS, D., & JONES, D. (1976). *Ordeal of the Hangman.* [Computer Program]. Urbana, IL: University of Illinois Computer-based Education Research Laboratory.

MINNESOTA EDUCATIONAL COMPUTING CONSORTIUM. (1980). *Hurkle.* [Computer Program]. Minneapolis, MN: Minnesota Educational Computing Consortium.

MINNESOTA EDUCATIONAL COMPUTING CONSORTIUM. (1983). *Oregon.* [Computer Program]. Minneapolis, MN: Minnesota Educational Computing Consortium.

NESBITT, W.A. (1971). *Simulation Games for the Social Studies Classroom.* New York: Foreign Policy Association.

PARKER BROTHERS. *Monopoly.* Beverly, MA: Parker Brothers.

PETERSON, S.B., SMITH, J.H., & KANE, D. (1973). *Phizquiz: A Problem-solving Test in Elementary Mechanics.* [Computer Program]. Urbana, IL: University of Illinois Computer-based Education Research Laboratory.

PIAGET, J. (1952). *The Origins of Intelligence in Children.* New York: International University Press.

RACE, P., & BROOK, D. (1980). *Perspectives on Academic Gaming and Simulation 5.* London, UK: Kogan Page.

ROBINETT, W. (1982). *Rocky's Boots.* [Computer Program]. Portola Valley, CA: The Learning Company.

SCHILD, E.O. (1968). The shaping of strategies. In S.S. Boocock & E.O. Schild (Eds.), *Simulation Games in Learning.* Beverly Hills, CA: Sage Publications.

SEILER, B.A., & WEAVER, C.S. (1976). *How the West Was One + Three × Four.* [Computer Program]. Urbana, IL: University of Illinois Computer-based Education Research Laboratory.

SELCHOW and RIGHTER. *Scrabble.* Bay Shore, NY: Selchow and Righter.

Simulation & Games: An International Journal of Theory, Design, and Research. Beverly Hills, CA: Sage Publications.

SIRIUS SOFTWARE. *Type Attack.* [Computer Program]. Sacramento, CA: Sirius Software.

SNYDER, T. (1982a). *Archaeology Search.* [Computer Program]. New York: McGraw-Hill.

SNYDER, T. (1982b). *Snooper Troops.* [Computer Program]. Cambridge, MA: Spinnaker Software.

SPAIN, J. (1983). *Baffles.* [Computer Program]. Iowa City, IA: CONDUIT.

STEVENS, R., REICHMANN, L., & LIU, A. (1982). *Casino Reading.* [Computer Program]. Urbana, IL: University of Illinois Computer-based Education Research Laboratory.

TAITO AMERICA. *Space Invaders.* [Computer Program]. Elk Grove, IL: Taito America Corporation.

THIAGARAJAN, S., & STOLOVITCH, H.D. (1978). *Instructional Simulation Games.* Englewood Cliffs, NJ: Educational Technology Publications.

TSR HOBBIES. *Dungeons and Dragons.* Cambridge, UK: TSR Hobbies.

VERSA COMPUTER. (1982). *Meet the Presidents.* [Computer Program]. Newbury Park, CA: Scholastic Inc.

SUMMARY OF GAMES

Use a short title page.

Give objectives, including the instructional purpose of the game.

State the rules clearly and allow the student to return to them any time.

Give complete directions and allow the student to return to them any time.

Choose a scenario that will capture the student's attention.

Pilot the game in a noncomputerized way first, to make sure it is interesting.

Relate the scenario to what is being learned.

At every level of difficulty allow the student some success.

Make the game challenging.

Use sensory and cognitive curiosity to maintain motivation.

Incorporate worthwhile instructional interactions.

Reward learning rather than luck.

Make sure that interesting feedback follows correct rather than incorrect performance.

Seek to design intrinsic rather than extrinsic motivators.

Make the game the motivator, not the reward.

Minimize the use of violence.

Provide all necessary information.

Employ multiple input and output modes.

Recognize the winner.

Clear any display and give a final message at the end.

Ensure the student knows what to do next.

6

TESTS

Assessment, the fourth phase of our instructional model, is an essential aspect of all instruction. It is used for a variety of purposes: determining what a student knows and does not know; rank ordering students in terms of performance; deciding who should be employed; assigning grades; admitting to college; diagnosing mental problems. It can take the form of an informal quiz or a strictly monitored examination where admission is by reservation only. Test results can range from being of little consequence to changing the course of a person's career. This chapter first analyzes the factors of computer-based tests and then presents an extended example of one. The chapter ends with a discussion of several testing techniques that can *only* be implemented in a computer environment.

There are two major ways to incorporate computers in the testing process: using the computer as an aid to construct the test, and using the computer to administer the test. Computerized test construction utilizes the computer to generate, print, and score tests that students write on paper. Additionally, with the proliferation of microcomputers and mainframe computers with networks of terminals, it is now feasible to administer tests directly to students right at the computer or terminal. Both techniques offer advantages and both have limitations. Wisely used, however, both can save a substantial amount of time without sacrificing quality, and can frequently improve the quality of testing.

COMPUTERIZED TEST CONSTRUCTION

For many years, computers have been used to help construct and score tests. Such help takes a variety of forms. For example, once you have written test questions, the computer can store them in pools (called item banks) that can be accessed whenever tests are needed. Typically, once the instructor has decided which questions to use, they are printed, duplicated, and distributed to students. Frequently, the students record their answers on machine-readable forms for computerized scoring.

There are many alternative ways to assemble questions into test form. For example, on one test the questions could appear in the same order as stored in the computer. In a later test, they could be chosen at random before printing and duplicating. Another alternative is to order the questions randomly for each student so that each answers the same questions but printed in different orders. Another method is to construct the test by selecting questions from a larger pool, so that each student receives a different set of questions on the test. With a computer it is relatively easy to change the method by which questions are selected. We recommend trying out these alternatives to determine which is the most appropriate for your environment.

A second way a computer can assist in test construction is by *generating* items. Rather than storing every question exactly as it would appear on a test, the computer stores a general format or template of the question, together with a procedure for providing the details. Thus, to generate ten questions, each asking the student to calculate the area of a triangle, it is more efficient to store the general form of the question (Figure 6-1) and have the computer substitute different numbers for each new question than it is to store all ten questions separately. Figure 6-2 shows how the question looks to the student as printed on the test form.

```
You are given a right triangle ABC
with angle A being the right angle.

   If side AB =     inches, and
      side AC =     inches,

then calculate the length of side AC
and the area of the triangle.
                    (6 points)
```

Figure 6-1 The template for questions on triangles.

```
You are given a right triangle ABC
with angle A being the right angle.

   If side AB =   6 inches, and
      side AC =   9 inches,

then calculate the length of side AC
and the area of the triangle.
                    (6 points)
```

Figure 6-2 A particular question generated from the template.

Another way to use computers to construct tests is to extend the idea of large pools of questions, as discussed above, into a larger context. Rather than having instructors or schools creating their own pools of questions, there are advantages in them sharing a pool. All the schools in a district, for example, could share a large pool of questions covering topics from American history. Whenever teachers in the district wanted to give a history test, they could access the pool and select the questions they wanted. Such access is accomplished through a terminal or microcomputer located at the school and connected to the central computer facility by telephone line. Once the questions had been selected, they could be printed out at the individual school for duplication. For example, a teacher could ask for twenty questions on Brown's *American History Alive* Chapter 12, or could specify "Items 12-5-1, 12-5-6, 12-5-8, 12-5-9, and 12-5-13 through 12-5-28."

This system has several advantages. By having many teachers provide questions to the pool, individual teachers could have instant access to a larger number of questions than they ordinarily would have. This would allow them to construct different tests each time, thus minimizing the risk of questions becoming public knowledge. Furthermore, because so many people would be preparing questions, the burden on any one teacher would be reduced. There would be less duplication of effort, and possibly greater collaboration between teachers in different schools. Finally, if such large pools were administered properly, appropriate data could be gathered to evaluate each question. Bad questions could be eliminated from the pool and good ones retained, thus improving the overall quality of each teacher's tests.

Two pieces of equipment have made this form of computerized testing very appealing. The laser printer allows the integration of complex graphics into the printed test and the production of the machine readable forms themselves. Optical scanners can read these forms after the students have recorded their answers and can record not only the answers but also comments. When scoring is done like this, the central system can automatically update item and test statistics.

The system also has some disadvantages that arise not from the system itself but from its potential for misuse and abuse. A teacher, for instance, because of the convenience of the system, could construct a test without paying proper attention to whether the questions selected actually tested the objectives taught. It would be easy to assume that any question in the pool is appropriate. This is an example of misuse. Similarly, it would be easy to assume all questions were of high quality, whereas some may have only been recently added to the pool, and were untested. Finally, any system that allows access from remote sites is prone to having security problems. To date, no simple system has been devised that cannot be abused.

We believe that the advantages of shared pools of questions outweigh the disadvantages and that such resources have been under-utilized. Great care must be taken in their implementation, however, and caution exercised in their use. Lippey (1974) and his contributors provide a thorough discussion of the benefits and problems of using computers in this way. Note, however, the book is dated and refers mainly to mainframe-based systems.

COMPUTERIZED TEST ADMINISTRATION

Increasingly, computers are being used not only to construct tests, but also to administer them; the student sits in front of a computer terminal, and enters directly into the computer answers to questions that appear on the screen. In this way, the entire test becomes automated, with the computer assuming much of the conventional instructor's role. Of course, the human factor is still essential in determining the content and conduct of the test.

The advantages of administering tests via computer are similar to those of providing computerized instruction. Testing can often be individualized, allowing students to take a test when ready rather than at a fixed time. The content of the test can also be tailored to suit each individual, or the same test can be constructed differently for each student.

Computerized tests also offer advantages to the instructor. Whether correct or incorrect, each student's answers can be stored for use in improving the questions in a pool. For the same purpose, it is easy to accumulate individual and group data about questions, time to completion, response patterns, or frequency of seeking help. All these data provide useful information to the instructor who is committed to improving the testing process.

There are, of course, also disadvantages to computerized testing. If scoring is to be automated, then the types of questions that can be asked successfully are currently restricted to multiple-choice, matching, or short-answer format. Computers have difficulty in judging extended or open-ended responses well.

The administration of tests to large numbers of students can also raise severe logistical problems, such as having sufficient terminals or microcomputers, or providing back-up procedures in case of computer or power failure. Allowing students to take tests at their convenience may create the necessity for providing proctored facilities at all times of the day, or for writing questions whose answers are difficult to obtain by cheating. Administering tests at geographically separate locations raises the same issues.

Finally, most tests cause anxiety in students. If the software administering the test is difficult to use, this may result in increased anxiety and hence scores that do not accurately reflect the students' knowledge.

Student reaction to computer-administered tests is generally very positive if the testing program is well designed. In particular, students like to be given immediate feedback on how they performed. When asked, most students indicate they would take and recommend to others to take exams via computer rather than by conventional paper-and-pencil (Trollip & Anderson, 1982).

FACTORS IN TESTS

The discussion of the factors in tests is a little different from the other instructional methodologies, because two separate issues have to be considered: the nature and content of the test, and the manner in which it is presented. The latter is an issue because tests play such an important role in a student's education that how they are administered is a major factor in their success or failure. Additionally, of all the instructional methodologies, testing most lends itself to the construction or use of a software package that can handle many different tests—an approach we recommend. It is far easier to use a testing system each time you want to build a test, than it is to write a new program. Consequently, a testing system should cater to different needs at different times. Currently there are a number of both mainframe and microcomputer-based test packages available on the market.

Characteristics of the Test

The process of testing has two major phases: determining the characteristics of the test, and administering the test. In this section we discuss the factors that relate to the first phase.

Purpose.   The first step in the creation of any test is to determine exactly what its purpose is and what content it will cover. A test can be interpreted correctly only if these are known. One common use of tests is called *criterion-referenced* testing, which acts as a learning aid both for the instructor and the student. Here the instructor uses the results either to find out what the student does not know, so that appropriate information can be provided, or as an indication of how good the instruction is. For the student, such tests are an opportunity to discover misunderstandings of the subject matter and to be given instructive feedback to clarify these.

Another common form of testing is called *norm-referenced* testing, because its purpose is to rank order people with respect to whatever the test measures. Most standardized tests belong to this group, because they attempt to indicate the relative standing of the student with respect to all others who have taken the test. Common examples of these are the Graduate Record Examination (GRE) and the Scholastic Achievement Test (SAT). Both rank the student's predicted success at college relative to all other examinees.

It is important to point out that the same test may be used for different purposes and, consequently, should be interpreted according to its purpose. A real estate license examination, for example, is generally used by licensing authorities as a criterion-referenced examination. If a student demonstrates that a given proportion of the information is known, the license is issued. The same test could be used, however, by someone teaching a real estate course as a tool to decide which areas of knowledge need more coverage. In this case, it is not so much the score that counts, but rather which questions were answered incorrectly. Finally, the local association of realtors could use the results of the test to give an award to the best student, based on the examination score. In this case, the score would be used normatively to determine relative abilities. In the foregoing example, three different groups used the same test for different purposes. There are hazards to this, and you should always try to determine what the original purpose of a test was. If a test is originally designed for criterion-referenced testing, it may not be good for assessing normative ranking, and vice versa.

One final determination needs to be made, namely the perceived importance of the test to both instructor and student. It is generally the case that the greater the perceived importance to the student, the greater the test anxiety. Consequently, closer attention should be paid to those aspects of the test that affect anxiety (for excellent coverage of this issue, see Sarason, 1980). For example, it is taken for granted in a paper-and-pencil test that the student can erase an answer and change it. Many computerized tests we have seen, however, do not give the student this capability, although newer testing systems usually offer this as an option. Thus, if the test has important ramifications, such as obtaining a license or gaining entrance to college, students will be very anxious if this capability is not available. On the other hand, they will be less concerned about this in a short, classroom test.

The implication of this is that the program that administers a test must meet the requirements and expectations of the students. If all your tests are going to be short and informal, there will be less need for a sophisticated testing system. If the outcomes are important, the system must provide the flexibility students are accustomed to. Because a flexible system can be used in all circumstances and a constrained one cannot, our discussion assumes that flexibility may be required.

Objectives.   The single most important feature of any test is the specification of its objectives. You must be clear as to what you want the test to cover. The objectives of a test are usually closely related to the objectives of current instruction, or to the objectives of a syllabus or curriculum. Some tests cover only a few objectives; others, such as final tests or certification examinations, deal with the objectives of whole or major portions of curricula.

It is useful to list the instructional objectives in order of importance. Doing this accomplishes two things. First, they are an invaluable reference from which to work, eliminating any doubt or uncertainty as to the goals of the test. Second, having them in order of importance will help decide how many questions to allocate to each objective. Because all tests have some time limit, you will have to make compromises as to how well each objective is tested. Knowing the relative importance of the objectives makes this easier. When compromising, however, you should never sacrifice test quality for the sake of time. If the test you want to give will take more time than is available in class, break it into two shorter tests to be administered in consecutive classes, rather than eliminating questions on important objectives.

Length.   The length of a test is determined by how many questions are needed to satisfy its purpose and whether these questions can be given in one session. Generally, classroom tests have severe time constraints, which means that a long test may have to be split into more than one part. However, if the test is to be used for a final in class, for example, then it may be important to cover all related content in one session, allocating whatever time is needed for students to complete it.

Another factor that influences test length is the nature of those taking the test. As with the amount of information that can be presented at a time, it is usually the case that the younger the student the shorter the test must be. Motivation, reading level, and even physical environment can also influence the length. The decision as to how many questions will be administered in each session must be made early in the process, because many features of the testing program will depend on it.

Item Banking or Item Generation. As we have mentioned, there are two ways of producing questions. The first is to draw from a pool of questions previously stored in the computer. The second is to generate items, a method that is usually associated with numeric examples. For instance, if you wanted to give your students ten questions covering simple multiplication, you could generate these questions by using a generalized algorithm or procedure that substituted particular values for each question presented. These values could be previously stored or could be generated randomly as each question appeared.

Size of Item Pool. If the testing situation requires a pool of items from which the test is to be constructed, the test can either present all the questions in the pool or can sample from it. This issue does not really affect the student at all, because the number of questions on the test remains the same. It does affect the instructor, because the sampling method will require creating more questions.

Usually there is no need in informal testing to have large pools. However, if the test is to be used for grading or certification purposes, then there is always an incentive for students to pass questions on to others who will take the test in the future. If the test is drawn from a large pool, the likelihood is diminished that two students would be given the same items. Having a larger pool also means that you can create different tests each semester or year, thus discouraging the dissemination of questions. Naturally, the disadvantages of item banking are that it is more difficult to ensure the statistical reliability of tests and to keep test difficulty the same.

The Questions. For any test to measure what it is supposed to measure, the questions must provide the correct stimulus to elicit the desired response. To do this each question must satisfy at least two criteria. First, the question must test the stated objectives and not unrelated information or skills. In the present context, facility or familiarity with a computer may be critical. There are many people whose intimidation by computers would decidedly affect their performance—test anxiety compounded by computer anxiety.

Second, the question must be written in such a way that the student only has to answer the question, rather than also having to decide *how* to answer it. Too often students who know the answer to a question are judged to be incorrect because they failed to input the answer in exactly the way the test program required. For example, if an item asked for the name of the first president of the United States, and a student answered "George Washington" instead of "Washington," or "washington" (with no capital) instead of "Washington," it would be grossly unfair to score these answers as incorrect. A test should measure knowledge of subject matter and not the student's ability to decipher the instructor's programming quirks. Finally, as with all tests, questions must be clearly written and unambiguous.

Writing good questions is a very difficult task, taking far longer than most people are willing to allot. It is wise to set aside approximately one hour to produce a single multiple-choice question, including writing, testing, and revising. We discussed in detail many aspects of questions in Chapter 2.

Feedback. Feedback can be provided or omitted depending on the type of test. While most tests, formal or informal, provide some feedback, some, such as the Graduate Record Examination, provide no information at all about the answers to questions. Other tests do not provide *immediate* feedback as to whether the student passed or failed. Rather, they delay such feedback until the test has been officially reviewed.

If the computer can score items automatically, then it is possible to provide feedback. If this is the case, its timing is important. Each question can either be scored as it is answered, and feedback provided immediately, or scoring and feedback can be delayed until the student has completed the entire test. The timing depends largely on the purpose of the test. The general practice is to delay feedback on more important tests until the entire test has been completed. On the other hand, less formal classroom tests often provide feedback immediately. If security is an issue, feedback is also usually delayed.

The third feature relating to feedback concerns its content. It can merely indicate correctness (that is, "correct" or "incorrect"), or it can provide an explanation as well. Computerization provides an increased opportunity to make the most formal tests educationally more beneficial. If a student must sit for three hours, sweating over an important test, why not provide useful information about specific matters of content? Because of the capability of the computer to grade tests immediately, it is possible to provide explanations to the student while the content is still fresh in mind.

Passing Score. If it is appropriate for the purpose of the test, there will be a passing score. There are no convincing arguments for any one cutoff score; rather, the content, purpose, and type of student will determine the passing level. It will also depend on your intentions for the test. A mastery test will have a very high pass mark as will a certification test enabling a person to operate in a dangerous environment, such as a nuclear power station. An ordinary quiz or classroom test is likely to be less stringent. Sometimes a test may have no passing grade at all, as when its intention is to locate areas of weakness and direct subsequent instruction rather than to categorize or grade students.

Timing. In general we are opposed to imposing on a test a time limit that may adversely affect student performance. This usually refers to criterion-referenced tests. Certainly there are always logical reasons for restricting the time spent, but if such a restriction is imposed the content of the test should be adjusted so that time is not an important factor. Many people do not perform well under the pressures of time, so unless the presence of this pressure is part of the test's objective, it should be avoided. One example where time may be part of the test's objective is in a foreign language class, where the speed at which a person translates is a good indication of fluency.

The Federal Aviation Administration, for example, has taken a very sensible approach to the time limit imposed on applicants to its written examinations. It allows students four hours to complete the sixty multiple-choice questions on the Private Pilot Written Exam. Of a sample of 120 applicants, the mean time to completion was 2.1 hours, with the shortest time being 1.0 hours and the longest 3.7 (Anderson & Trollip, 1982). Virtually everyone has enough time to complete the test, but in the case of an exceptionally slow student, the instructor must terminate the test after four hours. It appears, in this case, that the limit is for the protection of the instructor rather than a real limitation on the student.

Most of the standardized tests used for college admission, on the other hand, are power tests; that is, they require you to answer as many questions as possible in a rigid time limit. This is typical of most norm-referenced tests.

Data to Be Collected.   The features discussed above relate to nature of the test, its content, length, time and passing score. Another important feature is the type of data to collect for instructors. Some possibilities are the final score, individual answers to each question, time taken, changes to answers, and requests for on-line assistance. However, we caution you against collecting data just because it is easy to do so with a computer. Instead, analyze what data are necessary for improving the test or related instruction, or what data you need to determine performance, and collect only those.

Presentation of Results.   Two different types of results can be presented. First, there is the information given to the student at the end of the test. Traditionally this would include the score obtained, whether it was a passing score, and feedback, as discussed above. Second is the information for instructor use. This typically includes the results of all students and the summary statistics for the test.

Implementation of the Test

All the features already discussed are related to the *characteristics* of the test. Once you have established these, you will know exactly what the test is to do, what questions will be presented and in what order, what feedback and results will be made available to the student, and what information will be stored and made available to the instructor. At this point you have conceived the test. The next step is to *implement* it, deciding how it will look on the screen, how it operates, the options available to both instructor and student, and the safeguards against unexpected occurrences.

We have based our discussion on three important principles around which we believe all tests should be designed (Anderson & Trollip, 1981, 1982). They are stated as follows:

1. Ensure easy access to needed information.
2. Maximize user control.
3. Install safety barriers and nets.

Easy Access to Needed Information. The first principle states that the user should have easy access to needed information. There are two parts to this: It is first necessary to decide what information is needed; then one must make that information easily accessible. Generally, the more important the information, or the more frequently it is used, the easier it should be to access. An instructor, for example, typically needs easy access to the test results. A student usually needs directions on how to use the testing system, or which questions still need to be answered.

Maximize User Control. The second principle seeks to maximize user control. By this we mean that the user (either instructor or student) should decide what to do next and when to do it rather than having the testing system make that decision. From the student's perspective, the compelling reason for including this principle is that many testing situations generate a great deal of anxiety. Giving the student control over the testing situation frequently helps minimize anxiety. An example of this would be allowing the student to answer questions in any order, or to change answers to questions. A testing system with poor user control would force the examinee to answer questions in a specific order without the possibility of changing answers. Another example of poor control would be not allowing the student to review the test directions at any time. In both of these last two examples, the testing system constrains what the student would like to do.

Safety Barriers and Safety Nets. The third principle involves the inclusion of both safety barriers and safety nets into the testing system. A safety *barrier* is a mechanism that makes it difficult to do something accidently. An example is requiring the instructor to press an unusual combination of two or three keys to delete some records (Figure 6-3). It can cause grave problems if records are destroyed accidently. Requiring an unusual action usually prevents it from happening.

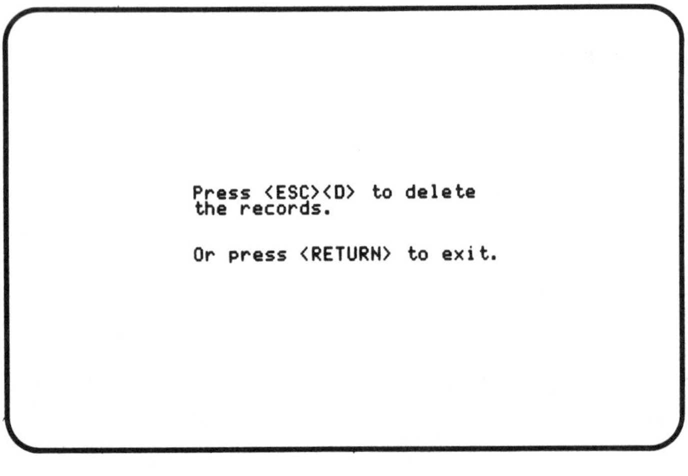

```
Press <ESC><D> to delete
the records.

Or press <RETURN> to exit.
```

Figure 6-3 An example of a safety barrier—in this case an unusual combination of keys to be pressed simultaneously.

Because the consequences of unwanted scoring of the exam or deletion of records can be so disruptive, we also advocate the installation of safety *nets*. These are procedures that operate even if the safety barrier has been surmounted. Thus, if an instructor does press the keys to delete records, an appropriate safety net would be a question asking whether, in fact, this action was desired. Only on affirmation would the records actually be deleted. Figure 6-4 illustrates a safety net.

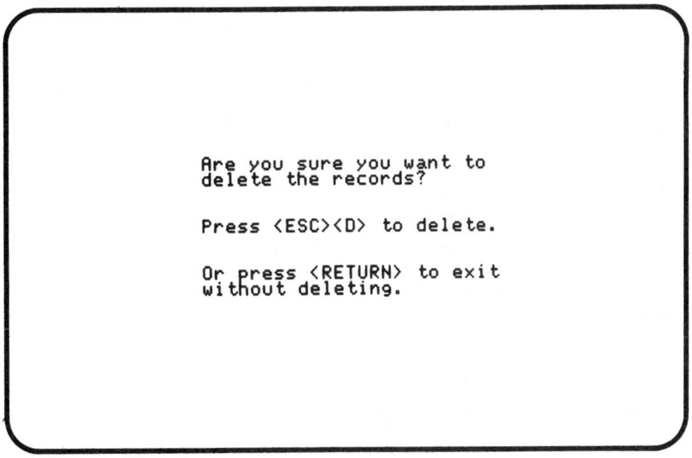

```
Are you sure you want to
delete the records?

Press <ESC><D> to delete.

Or press <RETURN> to exit
without deleting.
```

Figure 6-4 An example of a safety net—the user must press an unusual combination of keys again.

These three principles provide a framework for designing a testing system. Adherence to them will ensure flexibility and ease of use, while at the same time preventing accidental occurrences.

Based on these three principles, we now discuss factors relevant to test implementation. We have divided our discussion into the three natural phases: before, during, and after the test. Within each phase we examine both the student's and instructor's role in the process.

Before the Test—The Instructor's Role

The time before the test is the most crucial from the instructor's standpoint, because this is when the parameters for the test are established. Typically, the instructor must make decisions about who has access to the test, the number of questions, the passing score, the time limit, and the order of presentation of the questions or items. Most of these features have already been discussed. However, we did not discuss the features of a testing program that would allow the instructor to change any of these parameters. We also introduce several new factors.

Access. In most testing situations, it is important to ensure that the correct people take the test. In one sense you do not want Sue Smith taking a math test when she should be taking a physics test. In another sense, you want to be certain that Sue Smith is actually the person who takes the test, and not Pepe Garcia. The first situation can be handled in several ways. The program can be designed to check that the correct test is given to the person whose name is typed into the system. Thus, to enter the testing program, a student types in his or her name or identification number. The program then checks this against a list previously entered, and administers the correct test.

Another common practice is to handle access manually rather than automatically. One way of doing this is to have the instructor hand the student a floppy disk containing the correct questions. Although this generally requires more work by the instructor, it also is a method that is less prone to error. Of course, if everyone is to take the same test, and only one version of it exists, then there is no problem of a student taking the incorrect one.

Controlling cheating is much more difficult. If all students are at one site, the problem is no different from traditionally administered tests. However, if one has a network system that permits access at scattered locations, it is essential that the testing program precludes unauthorized use. Validating the identity of people at remote sites may be impossible, unless there are proctors available to check identification, or unless there is some type of sophisticated optical scanning system in operation. Fortunately, most testing applications do not require such stringent measures, either locally or at a distance, so the security issue may not be a big issue.

Changing Test Parameters.   Some testing systems provide the instructor with the option of changing the parameters of the test, such as the length of the test and the order of presentation of the questions. For example, the instructor can decide whether the questions should be presented at random, at the student's choice, or in a predetermined sequence. A decision also has to be made for timed tests. If your microcomputers do not have clocks, the question is moot, and the proctor does the timing. For systems with clocks, you may want to automate timing and termination.

If the instructor can change test parameters, it must be made clear what options are available. The options should be readily accessible with the most important or most frequently used ones being the easiest to access. The directions for making changes must be unambiguous. The program should also either check for unreasonable entries or require confirmation of all changes. For instance, if an instructor wants to change the number of questions on a test from 40 to 50 and incorrectly enters the number 5 (instead of 50), the program should query the small number of questions or have the instructor answer a confirming question in the affirmative. Figure 6–5 illustrates this.

Testing the Test.   A desirable procedure is for the instructor to try out the test in its entirety before students use it. If allowed, any data collected must either be deleted or properly interpreted. It would not be proper to include the answers to questions or the final score, for instance, in any summary statistics. Another alternative is not to collect data at all when the test is taken by an instructor. Testing the test ensures that all aspects of the test are working properly. We strongly recommend this procedure for all tests.

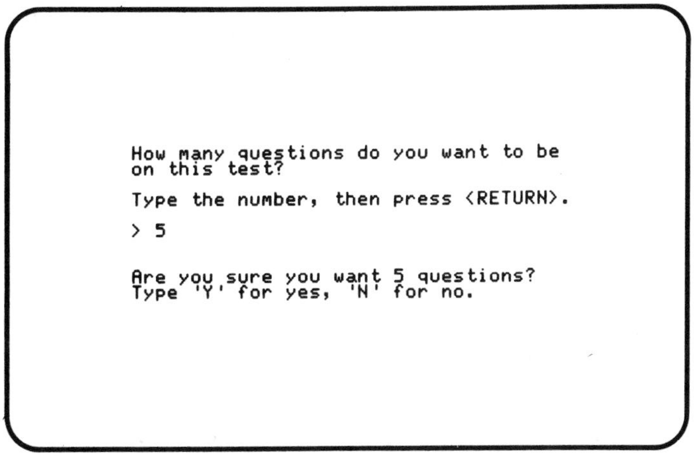

```
How many questions do you want to be
on this test?
Type the number, then press <RETURN>.
> 5

Are you sure you want 5 questions?
Type 'Y' for yes, 'N' for no.
```

Figure 6-5 Another type of safety net. The user must answer a confirming question affirmatively.

Before the Test—The Student's Role

The time just prior to the start of the test is very important, because it is then that the student has first contact with the testing system. This is when anxiety is heightened or reduced. If the system appears to be easy to use, and if there is ample opportunity to practice using the computer and the testing system, experience indicates that students will respond positively to the exam.

Test Directions.   At the beginning of an exam, a student needs three types of information. First, there should be clear directions on how to use the computer and the testing system. Second, any restrictions affecting the administration of the test should be clearly stated, such as how much time is allowed, when timing starts, and what resources, if any, are permitted. Third, if the situation demands it, the student should be given all the details concerning the exam, including the content to be covered, how many questions are on the exam, and the passing score, if applicable.

This information should be clear, concise, and organized for easy reference. The directions should be presented step by step, in order of occurrence, with the most important information highlighted. In addition, if the test is not already on the screen when the student arrives, it should be made obvious how to accomplish this. The student should not have to find an instructor for directions on how to start.

Practice.   When reading the instructions, the student should have ample opportunity to practice using the computer, particularly the keyboard. Practice questions should be available to answer, so that the procedures for taking the test are also well known. This practice should be self-paced, and the student should decide when to start the test. If the test is to be timed, this should not start until the first question appears. During the test, the student should be able to review any of the instructions as many times as required.

Appropriate safety barriers and nets should be in place to prevent the student from accidently starting the test before being ready, or leaving the testing system prematurely. Figure 6–6 illustrates a safety barrier (SHIFT-F10) in place to prevent accidental starting.

```
┌══ EXAMINATION OPTIONS ═══════════════════════════════════┐
│                                                           │
│  Before you begin your examination you can learn how to use the │
│  system.  When you are ready to begin the examination, press    │
│  SHIFT-F10.  Press a key to indicate your choice:               │
│                                                           │
│  1 - General Instructions                                 │
│                                                           │
│  2 - Try out a sample examination                         │
│                                                           │
│  ESC - Return to the previous display                     │
│                                                           │
│  SHIFT-F10 - Begin the examination                        │
│                                                           │
└───────────────────────────────────────────────────────────┘
┌───────────────────────────────────────────────────────────┐
│  Total time allowed in minutes:            20             │
└───────────────────────────────────────────────────────────┘
```

Figure 6-6 A safety barrier (SHIFT-F10) to prevent accidental starting of a test. *(Courtesy of Stanley R. Trollip and Gary C. Brown)*

During the Test—The Instructor's Role

There is very little the instructor has to do during the test especially if the computers are not networked. Consequently, this phase really only requires consideration of what happens if there is a problem during the administration of the test.

Cheating.   There are two situations that may require instructor intervention. The first is the case when the student is caught cheating and the instructor wants to terminate the test. Some mechanism should be incorporated whereby this can be accomplished without loss of information. That is, the answers to questions already answered should be stored permanently. The details of the incident would most probably be recorded on paper rather than on the computer.

Accidental Termination.   The second situation that may happen is the accidental termination of the test, usually due to a power interruption or a computer malfunction. In this situation, the instructor needs to reestablish access for the person taking the test. It is important to realize that the unexpected interruption of a test can cause great anxiety and generate very negative feelings if not handled properly. It is aggravating to a student, for instance, to be nearly finished with an exam only to have the computer fail. It is almost intolerable, however, if all those questions previously answered have to be re-answered because the responses were not stored.

The mechanism for terminating or restarting an exam should be readily accessible to the instructor, and it should be protected with safety barriers and nets to prevent accidental action.

Other Issues. If the computers are networked, the instructor can have some other options. It is possible to list the students by name on the screen with some indication of their status, such as which test they are taking, the number of items answered, time remaining, and so on. If the instructor wants to communicate with some or all of the students, this can be done quietly via electronic mail. For example, if the instructor notices a typographical error in an item, the students can be alerted automatically.

During the Test—The Student's Role

For the person taking the test or exam, answering the questions is the most crucial phase. Needed information includes continued access to the directions; the text of each question, all of which should be displayed at once; the identity of all unanswered questions, as well as those marked for review; and the time remaining, if a time limit is imposed. This information should be readily available and easily accessible. Movement between the various components of the system should be completely at the discretion of the student and not constrained by the system.

Flexibility of Responding. In some applications, it is appropriate to require the student to answer each question as it is presented, while in others it is better to give the option to respond or not to respond. Giving the option not to respond is essentially the same as permitting the student to browse through all the questions before answering them. In adaptive tests (see the discussion later in the chapter) students are usually required to answer an item as it appears. In most conventional tests, browsing is desirable. If unsure about what to do, provide as much flexibility as possible.

There are two stages at which a student might want to change the answer to a question: while the question is still on the screen, or later, after other questions have been answered. If a student incorrectly enters an answer, it should always be possible to erase it immediately and to change it. An added option is to allow the student to return to a question and change the answer. Allowing this has important implications. It means that no question is graded until all questions have been answered or until the student indicates that he or she does not want to continue. It also implies that the student may browse among the questions, moving through them as desired. That is, it would be possible to read a question without answering it.

A related option is to provide the facility for the student to tag any question for later review. If the facility is available, the student should be able to access these marked questions very easily, rather than having to cycle through the whole test item by item searching for them.

Appropriate Feedback.   It is important to provide the student with appropriate feedback if the response entered contains a format error rather than being wrong. For example, if the alternatives of a multiple-choice question are labeled with numbers and the student enters a letter, feedback should be provided immediately that a format error has been made. It is not the case that the response is wrong; it is just given in the wrong fashion. This is illustrated in Figure 6–7.

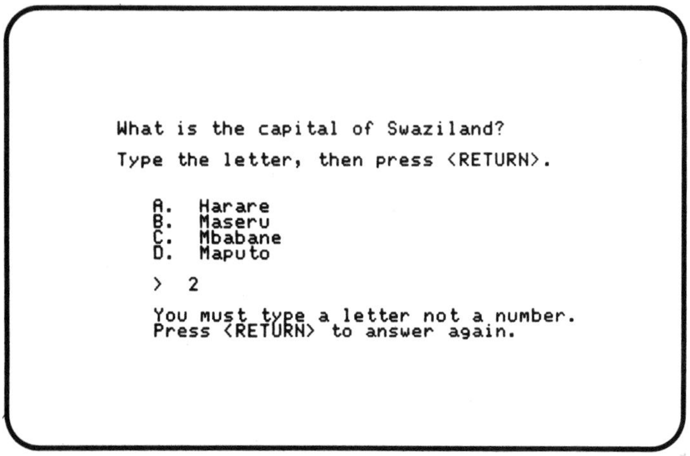

```
What is the capital of Swaziland?
Type the letter, then press <RETURN>.

   A.   Harare
   B.   Maseru
   C.   Mbabane
   D.   Maputo

   >  2

   You must type a letter not a number.
   Press <RETURN> to answer again.
```

Figure 6-7   Appropriate feedback after a format error.

Student Comments.   A useful feature during this stage of the test is the provision for the student to make comments. Although for children or nontypists it may not be possible, we prefer this to be on-line. However, having paper available next to the terminal will suffice. The purpose of this is twofold. First, it enables information to be gathered about the content of the exam or the functioning of the testing software. Such information is invaluable for the continued improvement of the test. Second, it provides a way that the student can express irritation or frustration about the test. The more important the ramifications of the test, the more important it is to provide a vehicle by which the student can raise objections or complaints. These comments are then sent to the instructor or person responsible for the examination to be taken into consideration as the exam is graded. Thus, if a student felt that a question could be interpreted in more than one way, explaining the interpretation taken in answering the question could change the way in which the answer was scored (assuming that the interpretation were valid, of course).

Termination of the Test.   If each question is to be graded as soon as it is answered, the test terminates automatically after the last question. However, when the student can move between questions at will, or can choose not to answer questions when first presented, the student must decide when to terminate. If the test has a time limit, it must obviously be terminated when this limit is reached if the student is still working. The program may give periodic warnings as the limit approaches.

Precautions against Accidents.   The most elaborate precautions in terms of accidents are needed while the student is taking the test. The presence of safety nets and barriers is crucial, particularly if the test is important. Obviously, it must be difficult either to leave the testing system or to terminate the test accidently. If the barriers in the system are circumvented, such actions need to be confirmed by a positive answer to a question. In addition, before a test is scored, the student should be provided with a list of questions that have not yet been answered, or which remain marked for review. The student can then decide to return to the questions or to continue.

Finally, should the student succeed in leaving the test accidently (in contrast to requesting it to be scored), or should the computer system fail in the middle of the exam, procedures should be available to restart the test without loss of information. That is, answers to questions already answered should have been stored and should still be available for scoring. Furthermore, if the time is being kept by the computer, the time remaining should also be stored so that if the test is restarted the student is not penalized.

After the Test—The Instructor's Role

Although preparing the test is the most crucial for the instructor, in some ways the most important phase of the testing cycle for the instructor occurs after the student has finished the test. Typically the information required at this point includes student results, data on the test, and access to any comments made by the student about the test. A convenient way of accessing this information is by means of a menu or list of options.

Display and Storage of Results.   You should be cautious about the storage and display of results. Access to these data may be governed by law (for example, The Privacy Act). Consequently, you should understand your legal position in this issue.

In general, you should not provide access to personal records to anyone who is not authorized. It is not always easy to prevent such access, especially when you use microcomputers and have the records stored on floppy disks. Because it is so easy to read what is on a disk, the disks should be protected by passwords, securely locked away, or there should be some foolproof method of preventing the data being read from disk, such as having the data encrypted.

Results can be displayed in different formats. Typically, students are allowed only to see their own data, while instructors can access data on each individual, such as final scores or detailed information on each question. It is also usual to provide summary information on group performance. In addition, most instructors want access to data gathered about the items, such as classical item analysis data. What data are available should be clearly displayed so an appropriate choice can be made.

Deleting or Manipulating Data.　An instructor may also want the capability for deleting or manipulating the data. Generally data are not kept forever, so being able to destroy them is essential. Of course, providing the power to destroy data immediately implies that one should have appropriate safety barriers and nets in place to prevent the accidental deletion of needed information. Similarly, when data can be manipulated, perhaps for statistical purposes, it is good practice to keep the original data intact, and to manipulate a copy. Access to such data should be appropriately protected. If such manipulation will change the nature or format of the data, you should warn the user before it happens, not afterwards.

Printout of Results.　A common option in testing software is to print out the results on paper. Most people are satisfied with having the results on the screen for informal tests, but need a printout when the test is important. Often the school system or testing authority requires a permanent printed record of all tests. It is also convenient for the instructor to have the summary statistics on paper.

After the Test—The Student's Role

Results.　The most important information the student needs after completing the test is the results of the test along with appropriate feedback. In general, these should be readily available. However, if there is a compelling reason not to provide results, ensure that the student cannot get access to them.

Printout of Results and Leaving.　Most test-takers like to have a record of their performance on an exam. Thus, providing printed results is usually desirable. Once the results have been displayed and printed, there should be clear directions for leaving the testing system and computer. It should also be clear how to return to the computer and view the results again, if such a facility is offered. As we have mentioned before, a student should be permitted to view only his or her own results, and should not be able to access anyone else's. However, you may provide information about the relative standing.

Helpful Resources.　A useful feature is to provide the student with a list of appropriate resources available both on-line and off-line that relate to the subject matter. If any of these resources are on-line, such as instruction programs or drills, it is convenient if the student can access them without having to go through some complicated rigmarole. If such programs are accessible through a simple menu, for example, their use will increase. This topic is also discussed in Chapter 13 on Computer-Managed Instruction.

Conclusions

It is always important to analyze the requirements of the student and the instructor when designing a testing system. Regard testing as a three-phase process: the phase before the student takes the test, the phase during testing, and the phase after the test. Both instructor and student play different roles in each of these phases and require different information from each. The program must not only meet these needs but also prevent accidents disruptive to both.

From the student's perspective the most important times are before the test and during the test. Before the test, the student needs to become comfortable with all aspects of the testing system in a way that does not heighten test anxiety. During the test, the student should be able to concentrate on answering questions and not on the procedures of the testing software.

The discussion above has raised a number of issues that apply to tests in general. We now present a specific application to illustrate the principles we have suggested.

AN EXAMPLE OF A TESTING PROGRAM

Computer-based test construction and administration began on mainframe computers and is still widely used in this form today, such as *Exambase* (Trollip, Entwistle, & Anderson, 1983). Due to the explosion in numbers of personal computers in recent years, microcomputer-based systems are becoming more common. As an example of these, we will design and implement a test on a system called *The Examiner* (Trollip & Brown, 1989).

The Examiner is designed for use both in formal, certification environments and in informal, classroom situations. It is also designed to be used by instructors and students who have little or no computer background. For our example, we will create a short geography test and will discuss the software from both the instructor's and the student's perspective in each of the three phases of testing.

Before the Test—The Instructor's Role

The most important time from the instructor's point of view is before the test because this is when the details of the test are established. Once access to the system has been accomplished, which is done by supplying the correct passwords (Figure 6–8), the instructor must supply the necessary information. This is stored in a *profile* and comprises two distinct sets of information: the *parameters* of the test and a description of *which items* are to be administered (Figure 6–9).

The parameters include the number of items, the passing score, the time, and the difficulty of the exam (Figure 6–10). Another parameter is the order of presentation of the alternatives within an item. Here the instructor can specify whether the alternatives in a multiple-choice item appear in the same order as initially entered into the system, or whether they are randomized for each student. Similarly the instructor must specify the order of presentation of items. Normally, easy items are presented at the beginning of a test, but if good reason exists to

```
┌═ DATABASE PASSWORD ACCESS ═══════════════════════════════════┐
║                                                               ║
║ C:\EXAMINER\CLASS                                             ║
║                                                               ║
║ Press a number to enter the database at the described level.  ║
║                                                               ║
║                                                               ║
║ 1. Director Access:   Access not allowed - needs password.    ║
║                                                               ║
║ 2. Edit Access:       Allowed.                                ║
║                                                               ║
║ 3. View Access:       Allowed.                                ║
║                                                               ║
║ ═════════════════════════════════════════════════════════════║
║                                                               ║
║ F2  -    to enter a password, or change the current password. ║
║                                                               ║
║ ═════════════════════════════════════════════════════════════║
║                                                               ║
║ F1  -    Help.                                                ║
║                                                               ║
║ ESC -    Previous display.                                    ║
║                                                               ║
└───────────────────────────────────────────────────────────────┘
```

Figure 6-8 Passwords protect the testing software from unauthorized access. *(Courtesy of Stanley R. Trollip and Gary C. Brown)*

```
┌───────────────────────────────────────────────────────────────┐
│ Profile:   geography Last edited on:   8:47:59 Thr 28 Dec 1989 │
│ Avg. Examination Difficulty:     ---     Avg. Examination Score:   --- │
│ ═════════════════════════════════════════════════════════════ │
│ Press a key to select an option:                               │
│                                                                │
│ 1   -   Set examination parameters.                            │
│                                                                │
│ 2   -   Set item selection options.                            │
│                                                                │
│ 3   -   Select text frames for use in an examination.          │
│                                                                │
│ 4   -   Review this profile.                                   │
│                                                                │
│ 5   -   Copy an existing profile.                              │
│                                                                │
│ ═════════════════════════════════════════════════════════════ │
│                                                                │
│ SHIFT-F7 -  Delete this profile.                               │
│                                                                │
│ F1  -       Help.                                              │
│                                                                │
│ F5  -       Store this profile.                                │
│                                                                │
│ ESC -       Return to the main menu without storing any changes.│
└────────────────────────────────────────────────────────────────┘
```

Figure 6-9 The main menu page for creating a profile of an exam. *(Courtesy of Stanley R. Trollip and Gary C. Brown)*

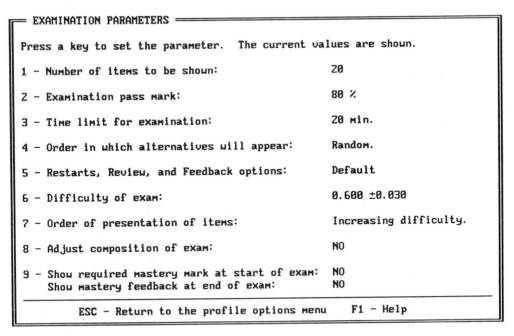

```
┌─ EXAMINATION PARAMETERS ════════════════════════════════════┐
│                                                              │
│  Press a key to set the parameter.  The current values are shown.  │
│                                                              │
│  1 - Number of items to be shown:          20               │
│                                                              │
│  2 - Examination pass mark:                80 %             │
│                                                              │
│  3 - Time limit for examination:           20 min.         │
│                                                              │
│  4 - Order in which alternatives will appear:   Random.    │
│                                                              │
│  5 - Restarts, Review, and Feedback options:   Default     │
│                                                              │
│  6 - Difficulty of exam:                   0.600 ±0.030     │
│                                                              │
│  7 - Order of presentation of items:       Increasing difficulty. │
│                                                              │
│  8 - Adjust composition of exam:           NO               │
│                                                              │
│  9 - Show required mastery mark at start of exam:  NO       │
│      Show mastery feedback at end of exam:         NO       │
│  ──────────────────────────────────────────────────────    │
│      ESC - Return to the profile options menu    F1 - Help  │
└──────────────────────────────────────────────────────────┘
```

Figure 6-10   The instructor can set a variety of parameters governing the administration of the exam. *(Courtesy of Stanley R. Trollip and Gary C. Brown)*

alter this, such as presentation by subject matter area or by random selection, this can be easily changed. The instructor must also decide whether students should be told what the pass mark is before the test starts and whether they passed once the test is scored. If the instructor is in any doubt about what an option means, context-specific help is available on-line at all times (Figure 6–11).

Figure 6–10 illustrates that our test will have twenty items with a pass mark of 80%. The test will have a difficulty within the range 0.57 to 0.63. (The difficulty of an item is the number of times students have answered it correctly divided by the number of times they have attempted to answer it. Hence the smaller the number the more difficult the item. The difficulty of a test is the mean of item difficulties.) There is a time limit of twenty minutes for the test and items will be presented in order of increasing difficulty. Furthermore, for multiple-choice items, the alternatives will be randomized before presentation.

The second set of information that the instructor must specify before the exam is which items will be given to each student. The instructor is given great flexibility to do this, being able to specify that some items will appear on all students' exams while others will be drawn at random from one or more specified pools of items. This means that different students can be given exams of equivalent difficulty containing some identical items and some different items. To accomplish this, the instructor is given a logical outline of the database containing all the items. At each point in the outline, the instructor indicates what is to be done with items below that point. So it is possible to create a pool from which

```
╔════ EXAMINATION PARAMETER HELP - PAGE 1 OF 2 ════════════════════╗
║                                                                   ║
║  The previous display allows entry of the parameters that control the║
║  generation of the exam.  Here is what each entry means:          ║
║                                                                   ║
║  1 - Number of items.  This is how long the examination will be.  ║
║      Examinations can be from 1 to 500 items long.                ║
║                                                                   ║
║  2 - Pass mark.  This is the mark required for examination mastery.  It║
║      can be in the form of an absolute number of points or as a per-║
║      centage of total examination points.                         ║
║                                                                   ║
║  3 - Time limit.  Examinations can have no time limit or one from 0 to║
║      600 minutes.                                                 ║
║                                                                   ║
║  4 - Order of alternatives.  This allows the selection of the order of║
║      presentation of the alternatives in a multiple choice item.  ║
║      Alternatives can be presented as they were entered, in a random║
║      order, or in the alternative order specified within the item.║
║                                                                   ║
║  5 - Set the availability of item feedbacks, user-controlled exiting of║
║      examinations, and the ability of users to change answers.    ║
║  ───────────────────────────────────────────────────────────────║
║          F1 - more help            ESC - previous display         ║
╚═══════════════════════════════════════════════════════════════════╝
```

Figure 6-11   The instructor can access help directly on the computer screen. (*Courtesy of Stanley R. Trollip and Gary C. Brown*)

items are to be drawn that contains all items in the database, or one that just contains items related to a small subset of the database. Different subsets can also be combined into larger pools.

Figure 6–12 illustrates the item selection process. The tree structure represents the structure of the content in the database whose name is CLASS. At the top level there are three entries *Geography, Physics,* and *Aviation.* Geography is broken down into two areas, namely *Land* and *Oceans and Seas.* Land is further subdivided into *Islands* and *Countries,* while Oceans and Seas has subdivisions *Northern Hemisphere* and *Southern Hemisphere.* The test we want to give has twenty items which are selected as follows: All items below *Islands* form a pool from which six are drawn at random. Four specific items will be included from *Countries.* The remaining items will be drawn from a pool containing all items from *Southern* and *Northern Hemisphere.*

As mentioned above, the description of a test is stored in a *profile,* which resides in the system until deleted. Only descriptions of exams are stored, not the exams themselves. This enhances the security of the exam. Figure 6–13 shows the summary of a profile and Figure 6–14 the summary of the item selection procedures. The notation ↓↓↓**1.0.0.0** indicates that the section of the database in Figure 6–13 below node 1.0.0.0 (Geography) has been further defined for item selection. ↓↓↓**1.1.0.0** indicates that the section of the database labeled *Land* has been further defined. **(6) 1.1.1.0** means that six items will be selected randomly from all items below *Islands.* ↓↓↓**1.1.2.0** shows that *Countries* has been defined further and ▶ ▶ ▶ **1.1.2.1** through ▶ ▶ ▶ **1.1.2.7** illustrate that these specific items will be included on all tests. ↓↓↓**1.2.0.0** indicates that *Oceans and Seas* has been defined further for

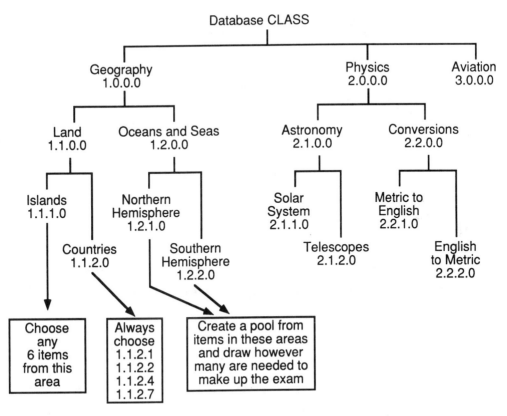

Figure 6-12   Selecting the items to be included in the geography test. The database of items deals with other subjects as well (for example, physics and aviation).

item selection. *** **1.2.1.0** and *** **1.2.2.0** are the symbols indicating that all items below the nodes *Northern Hemisphere* and *Southern Hemisphere* are to be pooled. The system will draw as many items as needed to make up the balance of the test from this pool. All other parts of the database are ignored.

When the instructor is ready to administer the test, the profile is recalled and activated, and a choice made between a paper-and-pencil test or one for computer-administration. The latter is usually put onto a floppy disk that can be shipped to remote locations. One of the options available to the instructor during the exam creation process is to restrict access to the exam to specified dates and times or only to people with a specified password. This provides the instructor with control over the administration of the exam. Items for the exam that are stored on the floppy disk are encrypted, so that if a disk is stolen there is little risk that the items can be deciphered and publicized.

Before the Test—The Student's Role

Once the instructor has produced the floppy disk, the student can take the exam at the times specified by the instructor. It is essential that the student has

```
┌─────────────────────────────────────────────────────────────────────────┐
│  Profile Summary for: geography        Database: class                    │
│  ═══════════════════════════════════════════════════════════════════     │
│                                                                           │
│  Number of items to be shown:         20                                  │
│  Examination pass mark:               80 %                                │
│  Time limit:                          20 min.                             │
│  Alternative presentation order:      Random.                             │
│  Examination difficulty:              0.600 ±0.030                        │
│  Item presentation order:             Increasing difficulty.              │
│  Item selection method:               As selected.  (ENTER for details.)  │
│  Show mastery at examination Start: NO          End: NO                   │
│                                                                           │
│  EXCLUDE:                                                                 │
│                                                                           │
│  Introductory frames:  ----                                               │
│  Instruction frames:   ----                                               │
│  Exam start frames:    ----                                               │
│  Scoring frame:        ----          Scoring key:                         │
│                                                                           │
│  ═══════════════════════════════════════════════════════════════════     │
│      ESC - leave      F3 - print      ENTER - Item selection lists.       │
└─────────────────────────────────────────────────────────────────────────┘
```

Figure 6-13   The system provides a summary of the parameters. Notation at the bottom of the display deals with aspects of the system not discussed here. *(Courtesy of Stanley R. Trollip and Gary C. Brown)*

```
┌─────────────────────────────────────────────────────────────────────────┐
│   Profile:    book                           ↓↓↓   1.0.0.0                │
│   Database:   class                          ↓↓↓   1.1.0.0                │
│   ─────────────────────────────────────      (6)   1.1.1.0                │
│   The list on the right specifies the items  ↓↓↓   1.1.2.0                │
│   from which the examination will be drawn.   ►►►   1.1.2.1                │
│                                               ►►►   1.1.2.2                │
│   ***  All items below added to pool.         ►►►   1.1.2.4                │
│                                               ►►►   1.1.2.7                │
│   ↓↓↓  Refined further - exclude others.      ↓↓↓   1.2.0.0                │
│                                               ***   1.2.1.0                │
│   **↓  Refined further - include others.      ***   1.2.2.0               │
│                                                                           │
│   (22) Include this number in pool.                                       │
│                                                                           │
│   ↓↓9  Include this number, then refine.                                  │
│                                                                           │
│   ►►►  This item will appear in the exam.                                 │
│   ─────────────────────────────────────                                   │
│   Press F3 to print this and the previous list.                          │
│   ─────────────────────────────────────                                   │
│   Arrow keys scroll the list.                                             │
│   ESC - previous display.                                                 │
└─────────────────────────────────────────────────────────────────────────┘
```

Figure 6-14   A summary of how items are selected. The various symbols indicate different item selection methods. *(Courtesy of Stanley R. Trollip and Gary C. Brown)*

ample opportunity to become familiar with the system, especially when the exam is an important one, because unnecessary anxiety can impair performance. *The Examiner* (Trollip & Brown, 1989) provides both written directions on how to use the system and a practice test that the student can take to get used to how the system works. The student may practice for as long as needed without penalty.

When ready to take the test, the student is given one last chance to return to the practice before starting (see Figure 6–6).

During the Test—The Instructor's Role

As mentioned before, the instructor has very little to do while the test is in progress. Depending on how the examination was specified, it is possible that the instructor may be called upon to restart a student's exam should they decide to leave in the middle. Similarly, if a student is cheating, the instructor will have to terminate the test. In the microcomputer environment, it is more difficult to monitor student progress unobtrusively than it is on a mainframe.

During the Test—The Student's Role

As soon as the first question appears on the screen, timing of the exam begins in this example. On each item display, the main options available to the student are visible. As can be seen from the bottom of the screen in Figure 6–15, the student may advance or go back an item with a single key press. Furthermore,

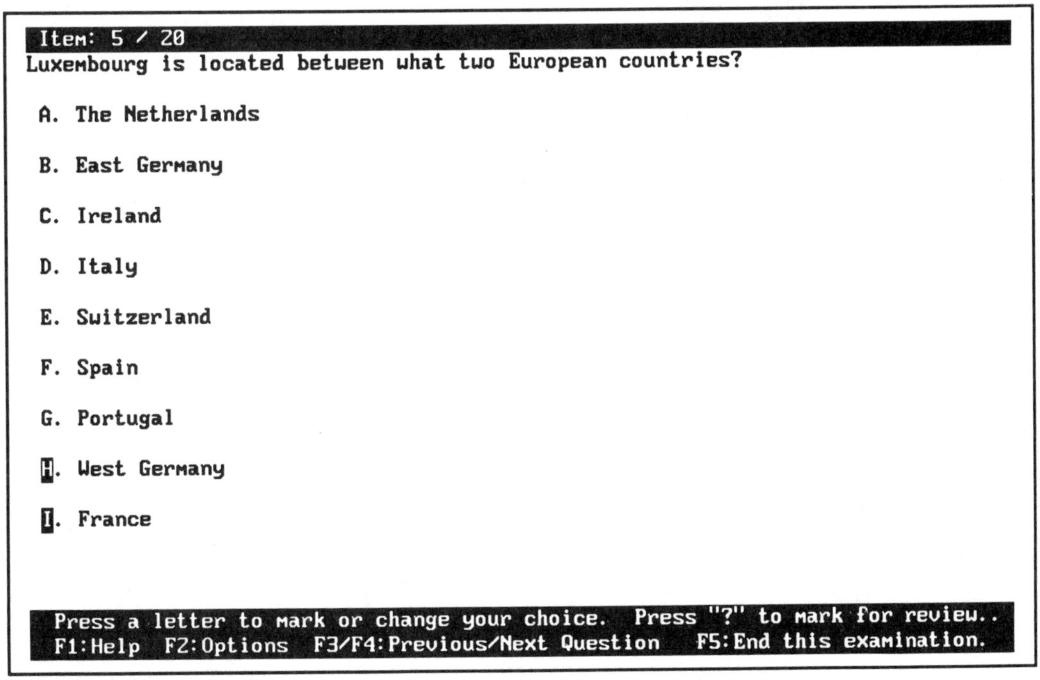

```
 Item: 5 / 20
Luxembourg is located between what two European countries?

 A. The Netherlands

 B. East Germany

 C. Ireland

 D. Italy

 E. Switzerland

 F. Spain

 G. Portugal

 H. West Germany

 I. France




   Press a letter to mark or change your choice.  Press "?" to mark for review..
   F1:Help  F2:Options  F3/F4:Previous/Next Question   F5:End this examination.
```

Figure 6-15 A question as it appears to the student. The options available are listed at the bottom.
(Courtesy of Stanley R. Trollip and Gary C. Brown)

items can be answered or not answered, and answers may be changed at any time. These features allow the student as much flexibility as a paper-and-pencil test, providing the browsing capability so frequently demanded by students. In addition, directions for using the system are readily available by pressing a single key, as is an overview of progress in the exam. If the student elects to see how the exam is progressing, Figure 6–16 appears.

```
═ EXAMINATION INFORMATION ═══════════════════════════════════

  Total items in exam:           20              1
  Minutes left in examination:   18.7            2
  You have answered:             6               3
  Marked for review:             2           ???  4
  You have NOT answered:         14          ???  5
                                                  6
                                                  7
                                                  8
                                                  9
  ────────────────────────────────────────        10
  The list at the right shows ALL the items in     11
  the examination.  Use the arrow keys (↑↓) to     12
  move the list up and down.  To go DIRECTLY       13
  to an item enter the number at the prompt        14
  and press the ENTER key.                         15
                                                   16
  >                                                17
                                                   18
  ???    Means marked for review.                  19
  [2]    Answered question is highlighted.         20

  ────────────────────────────────────────
  Press:  F5 to end the examination.
          ESC for the item you just left.
```

Figure 6-16 An overview of a long test is very helpful. This display gives the student a complete status report. *(Courtesy of Stanley R. Trollip and Gary C. Brown)*

In this overview display, the time remaining is shown near the top of the left column, while on the right is a display showing the status of every item. Shaded numbers indicate that the item has been answered. Question marks indicate that the item has been marked for review, and unshaded numbers indicate unanswered items. During an exam, a student marks an item for review by typing a question mark with or without a response to the item. If time is short, the student may quickly access items marked for review or unanswered items by pressing appropriate keys that bypass other items.

At any stage the student may request that the exam be scored. Before the system scores the exam, however, the student is told if there are any items unanswered or marked for review, as well as how much time remains. Scoring only takes place when an unusual combination of keys is pressed (⟨SHIFT-F10⟩) (Figure 6–17). This safety barrier is designed to prevent an exam being scored before the student is ready.

```
┌─ SCORING WARNING ══════════════════════════════════════════════════════════╗
║                                                                              ║
║ Number of items:          20                                                 ║
║                                                                              ║
║ Items answered:           6                                                  ║
║                                                                              ║
║ Items marked for review:  2                                                  ║
║                                                                              ║
║ Minutes left to complete all items: 18.5                                     ║
║                                                                              ║
║ You have requested scoring.  Once scoring has been completed, you cannot     ║
║ change any of your answers.                                                  ║
║                                                                              ║
║ ─────────────────────────────────────────────────────────────────────────  ║
║                                                                              ║
║ Press:            SHIFT-F10 to score.                                        ║
║                                                                              ║
║                   Press ESC for the previous display.                        ║
║                                                                              ║
╚══════════════════════════════════════════════════════════════════════════════╝
```

Figure 6-17 A safety net appears before the test is scored. The student may re-enter the test at this point or have the test scored. *(Courtesy of Stanley R. Trollip and Gary C. Brown)*

After the Test—The Instructor's Role

Once the test has been completed, all the examination data are read into the database. This process updates all item statistics and stores a complete description of the student's performance. This description includes the specific answers to items, as well as the amount of time spent on each item and on the test. These data can be accessed whenever needed (by someone with the appropriate passwords) in either summary (Figure 6–18) or complete form (Figure 6–19). In addition, they can be printed or transferred electronically to another program, such as a student records program.

After the Test—The Student's Role

In our example, once the exam is scored, the results are given to the student (Figure 6–20). This option can be turned off if necessary. In many situations, the student is then automatically taken by a routing program to another computer-based program, such as for remediation when test results are unsatisfactory. This capability is possible because *The Examiner* (Trollip & Brown, 1989) can be accessed and run from within external programs. A student management system can use the system as its assessment vehicle, using the results to route students to appropriate resources.

This short example illustrates the versatility that is typical of good off-the-shelf testing systems. If you are going to administer tests frequently, doing so via computer can bring some appealing benefits. We recommend that you explore various packages to see which suits your needs the best.

```
┌── EXAMINATION RECORDS ═══════════════════════════════════════════════════════┐
║                                                                              ║
║  Use the cursor keys to scroll through the examination records.  All the     ║
║  data that was gathered for this examination is shown.  If the examination   ║
║  history you are looking at is in the current database you can view the      ║
║  item by entering the record number and pressing ENTER.                      ║
║                                                                              ║
║  View record:        >           F1 - Help   F3 - Print   ESC - previous display ║
║  ─────────────────────────────────────────────────────────────────────────── ║
║  Detailed History File                                                     ↑ ║
║                                                                            ▓ ║
║  Candidate: patrick a. brown                                               ▓ ║
║  ID: 123 45 6789                                                           ▓ ║
║  Examination time and date: 8:54:15 Thr 28 Dec 1989                        ▓ ║
║  Database: class Profile: geography                                        ▓ ║
║  Examination Number: 39                                                    ▓ ║
║                                                                            ▓ ║
║                                                                            ▓ ║
║  Pass grade = 80 percent which is 16 point(s) out of 20 total.             ▓ ║
║  With 16 point(s), the candidate passed.                                   ▓ ║
║                                                                            ▓ ║
║  For the complete examination, the candidate passed.                       ▓ ║
║                                                                            ▓ ║
║  The user took 2.4 minutes on the examination.                             ↓ ║
└──────────────────────────────────────────────────────────────────────────────┘
```

Figure 6-18   A summary of results is available to the instructor. This figure illustrates a short summary given on the computer. *(Courtesy of Stanley R. Trollip and Gary C. Brown)*

OTHER TESTING APPROACHES IN THE COMPUTER ENVIRONMENT

The example above revolved around the administration of traditional tests by computer. This section discusses other testing approaches that cannot be accomplished without the computer. That is, if you are going to use the computer for testing, not only can you automate existing tests, but you can explore and use tests that cannot readily be implemented outside the computer environment.

Simulations

The first area in which computerization can benefit the testing process is in simulations. In Chapter 4, we alluded to the fact that simulations can be used for testing. One example we gave was that of a student pilot who could be tested in a simulation of the cockpit before actually flying a real airplane. Similarly, students can be tested on laboratory procedures, salesmanship, or many other areas by means of appropriate simulations.

Testing via simulations makes a great deal of sense. We would feel more confident that nuclear power plant operators could perform safely, for example, if they were certified after successfully operating a simulation of the relevant equipment than if they passed a multiple-choice test on the topic.

The difficulty in using simulations for testing generally lies in the automation of the evaluation process. It is relatively easy, for example, to write a simula-

Detailed History File

Candidate: stan trollip
ID: 123 44 1234
Examination time and date: 11:02:59 Mon 26 Feb 1990
Database: class Profile: book
Examination Number: 40

Pass grade = 80 percent which is 16 point(s) out of 20 total.
With 14 point(s), the candidate failed.

For the complete examination, the candidate failed.

The user took 1.7 minutes on the examination.

==
What follows is a detailed listing of the candidate's responses
on the examination. Shown is the item number, followed by database
item identifier. Next is an identifier of question type, and then
the candidate's response.

==
 1 (13): 01.01.01.01 Passed MULTIPLE A
 2 (14): 01.01.01.02 Passed MULTIPLE A
 3 (15): 01.01.01.03 Passed MULTIPLE B
 4 (17): 01.01.01.04 Passed MULTIPLE B
 5 (16): 01.01.01.05 Passed MULTIPLE B
 6 (18): 01.01.01.06 Passed MULTIPLE B
 7 (1): 01.01.02.01 Passed ALPHA mexico
 8 (2): 01.01.02.02 Failed MULTIPLE EI
 9 (4): 01.01.02.04 Passed NUMERIC 48
10 (3): 01.01.02.07 Passed ALPHA wellington
11 (7): 01.02.01.01 Passed MULTIPLE A
12 (10): 01.02.01.02 Failed MULTIPLE C
13 (11): 01.02.01.03 Failed MULTIPLE A
14 (12): 01.02.01.04 Passed MULTIPLE D
15 (6): 01.02.01.05 Failed MULTIPLE C
16 (5): 01.02.02.01 Failed MULTIPLE B
17 (8): 01.02.02.02 Passed MULTIPLE DF
18 (9): 01.02.02.03 Passed ALPHA indian
19 (19): 02.01.01.03 Passed MULTIPLE E
20 (20): 02.02.01.01 Failed NUMERIC 2.2

Figure 6-19   A complete summary of results is also available. This is an example of one provided
on paper. *(Courtesy of Stanley R. Trollip and Gary C. Brown)*

tion that allows a student to fly an airplane under instrument conditions. However, it is far more difficult to make it assess the student's performance automatically (see Trollip, 1979).

    The automated assessment of performance in simulations requires two
distinct and difficult steps. First, you must establish what constitutes acceptable
performance. As you go through this process, it is likely that your own views of

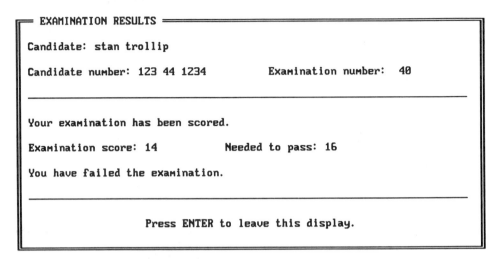

Figure 6-20 A summary of results can be shown to the student if desired. *(Courtesy of Stanley R. Trollip and Gary C. Brown)*

acceptable performance will change. As a flight instructor you may initially say that if the student can perform all the maneuvers necessary for the test keeping within 50 feet of a specified altitude, within 5 degrees of a given heading, and within 5 knots of a given airspeed, then the student has performed satisfactorily. On the surface this seems reasonable. However, if a student in a real airplane met all these requirements but manipulated the controls in a very abrupt manner, a flight instructor would normally fail the student. So the original set of standards would have to be modified to include control smoothness—which is much more difficult to quantify.

   Once a set of standards has been established, the evaluation routines must be implemented on the computer. This too can be difficult, particularly if the simulation is to provide feedback as to why something was wrong. Multiple-choice tests are easy to evaluate because the range of expected answers is small and discrete. In most simulations, the range of possibilities is very large and often continuous. That is, flying an airplane around a holding pattern must be monitored continuously for four or five minutes; evaluating how a doctor treats an emergency room patient may take even longer and involve a number of different but acceptable solutions. For example, it may be acceptable to take the pulse before the blood pressure or vice versa.

   Another difficulty of using simulations as tests is deciding the degree of fidelity required for valid testing. In Chapter 4 (Simulations) we discussed the issues of fidelity in *instructional* simulations. Gagne (1954) points out that while fidelity should often be low for *instructional* purposes, it should be higher for *assessment*, where validity is important. Remember that the validity of a simulation test is its ability to predict performance in the real situation.

   Despite these difficulties, we are confident as computers become increasingly used for traditional testing that their potential for non-traditional testing will be realized and exploited. We encourage the use of simulations and even games in the testing process, and advocate research to establish their reliability and validity in comparison to traditional tests.

Adaptive Testing

The second testing methodology that can be administered only via computer is adaptive testing. Strictly speaking, any test that selects items based on the student's previous responses is an adaptive test.

Many computer-based instruction programs have incorporated informal forms of adaptive testing. At the end of a module of instruction, the computer switches to testing mode. A question is presented to the student. If answered correctly a second question is administered. If answered wrongly, however, the computer selects a second question related to the first that is designed to probe more deeply into the student's understanding of the topic. This is a type of adaptive test because the sequence of items is based on prior responses.

In contrast to the "informal" adaptive testing mentioned above are various more formal or rigorous ones. Most literature on adaptive testing is based on what is called latent trait theory, item characteristic theory, or item response theory. Some of the benefits of these arise from the fact that traditional testing methods have some inherent problems. For example, normal item analysis data are dependent on the population from which they were gathered. So if a test on basic algebra were given to a group of 14 year olds, the item analysis data would be very different from those gathered from university freshman. That is, for traditional item analysis data to be useful, one has to know precisely the nature of the original population.

Latent trait or item characteristic theories are not population dependent. That is, the data associated with any item apply to all populations. These data can be depicted graphically as in Figure 6–21. The horizontal axis represents the ability or knowledge in a particular area, such as algebra. The vertical axis represents the probability of answering this item correctly. The curve, therefore, shows the probability of answering the item correctly for all levels of ability. As would be expected, the lower the level of ability (for example, at position A) the lower the probability of answering the item correctly, and vice versa.

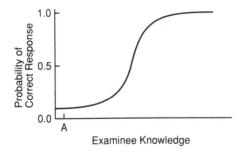

Figure 6-21 An item characteristic curve showing the relationship between a student's knowledge or ability level and the probability of answering the item correctly.

The curves can be of different shapes as seen in Figure 6–22, but all retain the same basic shape. Two characteristics of the curve are of greatest interest. The first is the point of inflection, which indicates how difficult the item is. The further to the right the point of inflection is, the harder the item. So Figure 6–22a represents two items with different difficulties (Item 1 is more difficult than Item 2).

The second is the steepness of the curve at the point of inflection, which indicates how well the item discriminates between people with abilities slightly above and below the point of inflection. The items represented by the curves in Figure 6–22b discriminate differently (Item 3 discriminates more than Item 4). Consider students with knowledge levels C and D. When given Item 3, for example, students at C will almost certainly answer it correctly (the probability is very close to 1.0), while students at D will have a probability of about 0.1 of answering correctly. The difference in these probabilities for Item 3 is approximately 0.9. That is, the item discriminates well between students of the two levels. On the other hand for Item 4, students at C have a probability of answering correctly of about 0.75, and students at D about 0.25, giving a difference of 0.5. That is, Item 4 does not differentiate as well. It is useful to note that both items shown in Figure 6–22a have the same discrimination, while both items in Figure 6–22b have the same difficulty.

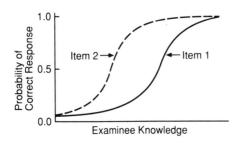

Figure 6-22a Two item characteristic curves with different difficulties.

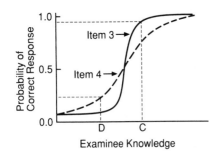

Figure 6-22b Two item characteristic curves with different abilities to discriminate.

The difficulty and discrimination of an item can be combined mathematically to determine the amount of information an item provides at each point along the knowledge axis. Figure 6–23 shows the information functions of the two

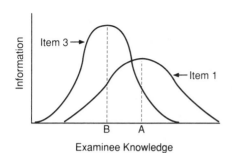

Figure 6-23 Two information curves showing how different items provide different amounts of information about students.

solid-line items in Figures 6-22a (Item 1) and 6-22b (Item 3). As can be seen, Item 1 provides more information for higher knowledge levels than Item 3. So if a student is of knowledge level *A*, Item 1 would provide more information than Item 3. However, the reverse is true for students of knowledge level *B*.

When implemented on a computer, an adaptive test works as follows. Remember, the purpose of the test is to find out what the student knows of a subject—in other words, we want to estimate the student's knowledge level as accurately as possible. First, the computer estimates the student's knowledge. This is usually done on the basis of past experience by assuming the average for previous students or from specific information from the particular student, but can be done purely at random. The computer then searches through all the items in its database, looking for the one that provides the greatest amount of information at the estimated knowledge level. This item is administered. If the student responds correctly, the system adjusts its estimate upwards; if the response is incorrect the estimate is adjusted downward. The computer then searches its database for the item that provides the greatest information at the new estimated level and administers it. On the basis of the response, a new estimate is made and the process repeated. This is depicted in Figure 6-24.

Figure 6-24 An illustration of how an adaptive test constantly changes its estimate of the student's knowledge level. The process is generally convergent.

Associated with each estimate is an *error of estimate*. That is, whenever the system makes an estimate, it is unlikely to be exactly correct. However, it is possible to give a range in which the estimate is likely to fall for a specified degree of confidence. This range decreases as more items are administered, which makes sense, since one's confidence in an estimate is likely to increase as one gathers more information. The system will eventually stop administering items when the error estimate is acceptably small. That is, the system stops presenting questions when it is confident that the estimate given is close enough to the student's real knowledge level.

Adaptive testing of this type has been shown to have two major benefits.

First, the estimate of ability is usually more accurate than traditional testing procedures; and second, the number of items you must administer to reach the estimate is substantially fewer on the average.

It makes intuitive sense for an adaptive test to require fewer items than a traditional one. If students are very good, you know before the test begins that they will answer all easy items correctly. Similarly, weak students will get all difficult items wrong. If this is true, why administer those items? An adaptive test administers only those items necessary to form its estimate. In an adaptive test, a good student would be given few, if any, easy items, and a poor student would never see the difficult ones. Thus, adaptive testing is intrinsically efficient.

In a study at the University of Illinois Aviation Research Laboratory (Trollip, Anderson, & Strandmark, 1983), the standard sixty-item Private Pilot examination was administered via computer to 125 applicants. Their responses were recorded for use in a simulation of an adaptive test. In the simulation, when the adaptive test administered an item, we answered it with the same answer as the real applicant. On average, the adaptive algorithm was able to predict accurately whether an applicant would pass or fail the examination in approximately sixteen items instead of sixty—a dramatic savings in time.

Adaptive testing has, of course, some constraints. The most notable of these are that an adaptive test, by assumption, can measure only one type of knowledge. That is, it is not appropriate to use a single adaptive test to measure algebra and geometry together, or history and geography. If you need to test more than a single knowledge domain, two or more adaptive tests can be merged into a single administration. However, the testing system then has to keep track of all the data for each separately. Second, in order to obtain an item characteristic curve (as shown in Figure 6–21, for example) that is stable and accurate, each item needs to be administered several hundred times to students with a broad range of knowledge levels before it can be used reliably in an adaptive test.

If these constraints can be met, adaptive testing may have a lot to offer and should be considered. More detailed information can be obtained by reading Weiss 1982; Trollip & Anderson, 1982; Warm, 1978; and Lord, 1980.

Admissible Probability Measures Testing

One of the criticisms leveled at multiple-choice tests has been that they do not provide useful information to either student or instructor as to what precise problems a student is experiencing. Certainly, they give a summary of what the student knows within the area tested, but little more. A student can answer an item correctly or incorrectly—there is no capability for partially correct answers. Yet students rarely know all or nothing about the subject of the item. Typically they have some knowledge, part of which may be accurate, part faulty. Traditional multiple-choice tests cannot tease out this partial information because they do not cater to partial answers.

Using computers, it is possible to implement a technique known either as Admissible Probability Measures testing (APM) (Bruno, 1987) or Information Referenced Testing (IRT) (Bruno, Holland, & Ward, 1988) that does in fact allow partial answers, or at least allows the determination of whether the student knows part of the answer. The method can be administered via paper-and-pencil and scored on a computer, or administered and scored directly on a computer.

Unlike traditional tests, APM (IRT) tests are built on the assumption that there is a continuum of how well people know the answer to an item, such as being well informed, misinformed, or uninformed, rather than merely knowing or not knowing. Historically, testing specialists have attempted to capture the notion of this continuum by having students select an answer to a question and then indicate the level of confidence they have in their answer. So a student selecting the correct answer with a confidence level of 60 out of 100 is likely to know less overall than a student selecting the same answer with a confidence of 90 out of 100. This type of testing has never really become popular and is not often encountered.

The APM method uses a different method for capturing the information it needs for providing its feedback. First all questions have three possible answers rather than the more traditional four. These three answers can be represented as the vertices of a triangle (see Figure 6–25). If students think answer *A* completely answers the question, they would mark *A* on the triangle on the answer sheet. Similarly with answers *B* and *C*. This is the same as traditional testing. However, if students think that answers *A* and *B* are equally likely to be answers to the question, they would mark *H*. If, for example, they think that *B* and *C* are answers to the question and that they have more confidence in *B* than in *C*, they would mark *J* as their answer. If students are unable to choose between any of the three choices or if they think each alternative is equally correct, they mark *M* (in the middle of the triangle, equidistant from each option).

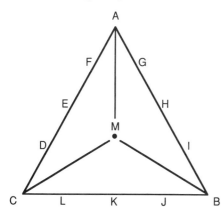

Figure 6-25 An Admissible Probability Measures answer sheet has a triangle with multiple points for the student to represent the answer. *(By permission of the Journal of Computer-Based Instruction and the Association for the Development of Computer-Based Instructional Systems)*

Once the student has answered the question, points are allocated as follows: points are *deducted* in varying amounts for differing degrees of confidence in a wrong answer; points are *awarded* in varying amounts for differing degrees of confidence in a correct answer. Confidence is determined by the distance of the student's mark from each of the vertices. The closer the mark is to a vertex, the greater the confidence that the vertex represents the correct answer.

In Figure 6–25, assuming that *A* is the correct answer, a student who marks the triangle at position *A* has great confidence that *A* is the correct answer (which it is) and is awarded a large number of points. If the student chooses position *E*, the confidence is lower that *A* is correct and so the student is awarded fewer points. If position *D* is chosen, this represents reasonably high confidence that *C* is correct (which it is not), and hence the student is quite heavily penalized. Similarly choosing positions *B* or *C* represents the fact that the student is very confident of selecting the correct answer (but has actually selected an incorrect one), and is thus penalized substantially. Figure 6–26 shows how points are awarded when the student chooses the different points on the triangle assuming *A* is the correct answer (Bruno, 1987).

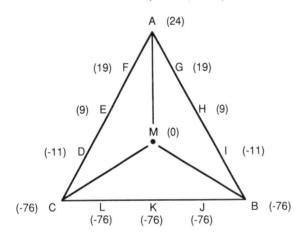

Figure 6-26 Point allocation on an Admissible Probability Measures answer sheet when *A* is the correct answer. (*By permission of the Journal of Computer-Based Instruction and The Association for the Development of Computer-Based Instructional Systems*)

Figure 6–27 illustrates how students may be classified on this basis. A student who has low confidence in the correct answer *A* (or conversely, high confi-

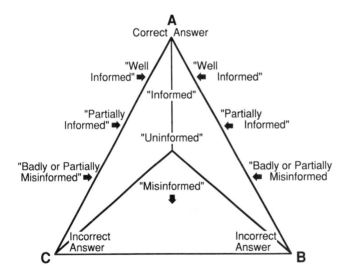

Figure 6-27 Verbal description of choosing various points on the Admissible Probability Measures answer sheet. (*By permission of the Journal of Computer-Based Instruction and The Association for the Development of Computer-Based Instructional Systems*)

dence in the incorrect answer *B* or *C*) is labeled as Misinformed; a student who has relatively high confidence in the correct answer is Well Informed; and a student who has complete confidence in the correct answer is regarded as being Informed. Other categories are Partially Informed, Partially Misinformed, and Uninformed. It is possible to equate these APM categories with traditional grades.

The benefits of APM testing are that it provides more sensitive information about what to do with students. For example, Informed students can be advanced to the next grade or topic; Partially Informed students can be given a review of the information; and Uninformed students would most probably require instruction. Misinformed students (in contrast to uninformed students) require *re-education* rather than being re-instructed. That is, the Misinformed student has the wrong concept of the subject matter, while the Uninformed student has no concept at all.

In his studies on APM testing, Bruno has found a far greater acceptance of the method among students than traditional Right-Wrong testing. Teachers, too, like the method because it provides more useful information about what to do with students than traditional testing.

For a more detailed explanation of this technique, read Bruno (1986).

CONCLUSION

Assessment of learning is a crucial part of the instructional process. Tests are the primary means we have for assessment. Because they can have such a strong influence on a student's future, tests need to be constructed with great care. The content has to be relevant to the instruction it follows, or must meet the goals of the test. The questions must cover all objectives thoroughly, and the integrity of the test should not be compromised because of perceived time constraints. The administration of the test also has to be faultless, minimizing student anxiety and ensuring that logistical considerations do not interfere with content knowledge. Finally, using computers to administer tests not only can provide relief to instructors but also can improve the overall quality of traditional tests. Furthermore, computers provide the opportunity to administer new types of tests that may be more valid, reliable, or efficient than the multiple-choice ones we rely on so much. Computer-based testing is still in its infancy but has exciting possibilities that are worth exploring.

REFERENCES AND BIBLIOGRAPHY

ANDERSON, R.I., & TROLLIP, S.R. (1981). *Humanizing Computer-Administered Tests: Satisfying the Needs of Both Teachers and Learners.* Annual Conference of the Illinois Association of Educational Data Systems, Champaign.

ANDERSON, R.I., & TROLLIP, S.R. (1982). A computer-based private pilot (airplane) certification examination: A first step towards nation-wide computer-administration of FAA certification exams. *Journal of Computer-Based Instruction, 8*(3), 65–70.

ASSESSMENT SYSTEMS CORPORATION (1989). *Microcat.* [Computer Program]. St. Paul, MN: Assessment Systems Corporation.

BROWN, D., & SILVEIRA, M. (1989). *Microtest II.* [Computer Program]. San Diego: Chariot Software Group.

BRUNO, J. (1986). Assessing the knowledge base of students: An information theoretic approach to testing. *Journal of Measurement and Evaluation in Counseling and Development, 19*(3), 116–130.

BRUNO, J. (1987). Admissible probability measures in instructional management. *Journal of Computer-Based Instruction, 14*(1), 23–30.

BRUNO, J., HOLLAND, J., & WARD, J. (1988). Use of information referenced testing for enhancing effectiveness of academic support programs. *Journal of Measurement and Evaluation in Counseling and Development, 21*(1), 5–15.

GAGNE, R.M. (1954). Training devices and simulators: Some research issues. *The American Psychologist, 9,* 95–107.

GRONLUND, N.E. (1977). *Constructing Achievement Tests.* Englewood Cliffs, NJ: Prentice-Hall.

GRONLUND, N.E. (1981). *Measurement and Evaluation in Teaching.* New York: Macmillan.

LIPPEY, G. (Ed.). (1974). *Computer-based Test Construction.* Englewood Cliffs, NJ: Educational Technology Publications.

LORD, F. (1980). *Applications of Item Response Theory to Practical Testing Problems.* Hillsdale, NJ: Lawrence Erlbaum.

RECKASE, M.D. (1989). Adaptive testing: The evolution of a good idea. *Educational Measurement: Issues and Practice, 8*(3), 11–15.

ROID, G.H., & HALADYNA, T.M. (1982). *A Technology for Test-Item Writing.* New York: Academic Press.

SARASON, I.G. (1980). *Test Anxiety: Theory, Research, and Applications.* Hillsdale, NJ: Lawrence Erlbaum.

SARASON, I.G. (1987). Test anxiety, cognitive interference, and performance. In R.E. Snow & M.J. Farr (Eds.), *Aptitude, Learning, and Instruction: III. Conative and Affective Process Analysis.* Hillsdale, NJ: Lawrence Erlbaum.

TROLLIP, S.R. (1979). The evaluation of a complex, computer-based flight procedures trainer. *Human Factors, 22*(1), 47–54.

TROLLIP, S.R., & ANDERSON, R.I. (1982). An adaptive private pilot certification examination. *Aviation, Space, and Environmental Medicine, 53*(10), 992–995.

TROLLIP, S.R., ANDERSON, R.I., & STRANDMARK, N. (1983). *Computerized Adaptive Testing—Final Report.* Report prepared for the Office of Personnel Management under contract number OPM-29-80.

TROLLIP, S.R., & BROWN, G.C. (1989). *Examiner, V 2.1.* [Computer Program]. Mendota Heights, MN: Media Computer Enterprises.

TROLLIP, S.R., ENTWISTLE, W., & ANDERSON, R.I. (1983). *Exambase.* [Computer Program]. Savoy, IL: University of Illinois Aviation Research Laboratory.

WARM, T.A. (1978). *A Primer of Item Response Theory.* Technical Report CG-941278, U.S. Coast Guard Institute.

WEISS, D. (Ed.). (1982). *Proceedings of the 1982 Item Response Theory and Computerized Adaptive Testing Conference.* University of Minnesota Computer Adaptive Testing Laboratory.

WEISS, D.J. (Ed.). (1983). *New Horizons in Testing: Latent Trait Test Theory and Computerized Adaptive Testing.* New York: Academic Press.

WISE, S.L., & PLAKE, B.S. (1989). Research on the effects of administering tests via computers. *Educational Measurement: Issues and Practice, 8*(3), 5–10.

WISE, S.L., PLAKE, B.S., EASTMAN, L.A., BOETTCHER, L.L., & LUKIN, M.E. (1986). The effects of item feedback and examinee control on test performance and anxiety in a computer-administered test. *Computers in Human Behavior, 2,* 21–29.

SUMMARY OF TESTS

BEFORE THE TEST:

Give clear directions.
Give the purpose of the test.
Give the constraints.
Give an opportunity to practice.
Let the student decide when to start the test.
Inform the student of time constraints.

DURING THE TEST:

Keep each question on one display.
Keep question format consistent.
Provide easy access to the questions.

Provide capability to change responses.
Provide capability to mark questions for review.
Provide capability to browse through the questions.
Do not penalize format errors.
Provide restart capability.
Provide a way for the student to make comments.
Ensure feedback is consistent with the purpose of the test.
Let the student know how much time remains.
Provide safety barriers and nets.

AFTER THE TEST:

Give the results immediately.
Give detailed feedback.
Provide the option for printed results.
State how to leave testing system.
Provide a way for the student to make comments.
Store all necessary data.
Prevent unauthorized access to results and data.
Provide safety barriers and nets.

7

PREPARATION

INTRODUCTION TO DEVELOPMENT OF CBI

Part 1 of this book discussed the major instructional methodologies used to deliver instruction on computers. The discussion was organized around the relevant characteristics of each methodology and the instructional factors that determine their effectiveness in a lesson. Being familiar with these methodologies is also a necessary part of developing computer-based lessons, because you must be able to make decisions about which methodologies to use and how to implement them.

While an understanding of the instructional methodologies and their various factors is important for developing high-quality lessons, it is not sufficient by itself. Part 2 of our book discusses and demonstrates the other activities that constitute the development of instruction. The model we describe applies only to the methodologies discussed in Part 1. Other educational applications of computers, such as the advanced topics of Part 3, are not treated in this development model.

We begin with a brief overview of our development model. This model is oriented directly towards computer delivery of instruction, so it includes not only designing a lesson on paper, but implementing it on a computer and finally evaluating it. Because the model is oriented towards the novice instructional developer, we simplify some of the activities involved. We have also tried whenever possible to present the model in a general way so it applies to most subject areas.

Many of the procedures in this model are similar to components of the Instructional Systems Design (ISD) approach. Our intention is to take those parts of the ISD approach that are specifically related to individual lesson design, simplify them for the beginning instructional developer, add to them those procedures necessary for delivery by computer, and incorporate into them procedures that will enhance the creative use of the computer.

For the student interested in reading more about Instructional Systems Design, several references are listed. O'Neil's works (1979a, b) are good introductions to the topic. Other general references on instructional design and design for computer-based instruction are included in the references and bibliography.

Our model is flexible and we expect that as you gain experience you will mold it to your own individual needs and style of work by reordering, adding, or deleting steps. If you aspire to become a professional developer of computer-based instruction, you must go beyond this introduction.

There are several important features this model embodies. First is that it is empirically based. By that we mean development is based on a cycle of draft, evaluate, and revise until the product works. While there is much research in learning and instruction to guide us in developing instruction, the best guarantee that a lesson will teach well is to try it out on students, revise it, try it out again, and so on until you get it right. Our model incorporates evaluation at several intermediate steps as well as having a thorough evaluation as the last step.

A second important feature of the model is that it is driven by principles of cognitive psychology. These are the same principles discussed in Chapter 1: perception and attention, memory, comprehension, active learning, motivation, locus of control, transfer of learning, and individual differences. The summaries supplied with each instructional methodology chapter contain reminders of learning principles that affect student outcomes.

A third important feature is an emphasis, included early in the development process, on creativity. We believe that poor CBI is often developed as a result of cookbook-style instructional design wherein the developer never engages in activities resulting in creative ideas. Creativity is necessary in this new field, and without it, it is unlikely that the computer's capabilities will be fully exploited.

A fourth important feature is the progression from discussion to paper ideas to implementation on a computer. With the increasing availability of microcomputers and the profusion of "integrated" tools, it is tempting to start working on the computer too soon. We encourage the designer, especially the novice, to spend considerable time first discussing and planning with other people, then drafting ideas on paper, before implementing the plans on a computer. Our experience with many students has convinced us some initial design on paper is still essential.

The fifth and last feature is that we encourage a team-oriented approach. In our experience, and that of other designers (Roblyer, 1988), courseware is always better when several people collaborate. This is true for two reasons. First, more skills and knowledge are involved in a development effort than one person typically has. A project team should include people with expertise in instructional design, programming, graphics arts, and the subject matter. Second, several people working together raise the expected standard of acceptable quality. An individual is not good at criticizing his or her own ideas or work. A team generally has more creative ideas than an individual and is collectively more critical.

Our model for developing computer-based instructional materials comprises the following ten steps:

1. *Determine **needs** and **goals***
   In this step you determine the goal of a single lesson. The goal of a lesson includes what the student should know or be able to do after completing the lesson. The primary consideration affecting definition of goals is the entry knowledge of the student. Determining goals therefore includes assessing the characteristics and instructional needs of your intended students.

2. *Collect* **resources**

Resource materials are relevant to the subject matter, instructional development, and the instructional delivery system, in this case computers. Useful subject-matter resources include textbooks, reference books, original source materials, films, and most importantly, other people knowledgeable in the area. Resource materials for instructional design include texts on instructional design (such as this book), storyboarding sheets, graphics arts materials, a word processor, and if at all possible, persons who have experience in instructional design. Resource materials for the delivery system include the computer itself, its operating manuals, software reference guides, and people experienced with the computer and software you intend to use during development.

3. **Learn** *the content*

The person developing a CBI lesson will either be a subject-matter expert who must learn about CBI design or a designer who must learn the content. Even when working in conjunction with a content expert, the designer must learn the content. To a lesser extent, the content expert will also learn about instruction. For the designer, learning the content includes interviewing the expert, reading texts and other instructional materials, and generally becoming a student again. You cannot develop effective instruction which challenges the student in creative ways unless you become thoroughly familiar with the content. Shallow understanding can only produce a shallow lesson.

4. **Generate** *ideas*

This step consists of brainstorming to generate creative ideas. Generating ideas via brainstorming is very important, and we suggest procedures for encouraging creative ideas in the development process. Many designers get stuck at this early point, either spending too much time trying to come up with the perfect idea or, more frequently, giving up and proceeding with a mediocre idea. With brainstorming, the designer, with assistance from others, pursues the goal of generating as many ideas as possible, suspending any judgment of their quality or feasibility until a later time. We are strong advocates of brainstorming because it has proved to be a method that facilitates creativity and quickly produces a list that will include some interesting and good ideas.

5. **Design** *instruction*

The outcome of brainstorming is a long list of ideas that range in quality from very bad to very good. You must eliminate the worst ideas and then begin ordering, detailing, and refining the ideas that are good. This is done by performing concept and task analyses on the content. Regardless of the nature of the content, such analyses bring to bear principles of learning to assemble a plan for an effective lesson. This includes preliminary choices about instructional methodologies and factors.

It cannot be emphasized enough that good instructional development incorporates evaluation throughout the process, not just at the end. This is reflected in the model by incorporating explicit evaluation and revision activities as part of several steps. After the design step, evaluation includes review and discussion by the content experts, instructional designers, and clients. Revision may require reassessment of goals, collecting more resources, learning more about the content, generating more ideas, correcting task analyses, changing the methodology, and so on. After revision the evaluation should be repeated. Evaluation and revision form a cycle which progresses until all concerned parties are agreed that the quality is sufficient to progress to the next step.

6. **Flowchart** *the lesson*

A flowchart is a series of diagrams describing the operations a computer performs. Flowcharting is important because computer-based instruction should be interactive, and interactions are best depicted as a visual representation of decisions and events. While the flowchart does not include the actual text and pictures for your lesson, it should include their sequence. The flowchart includes information about when the computer will draw or animate pictures, what happens when the student makes mistakes, and when the lesson should end.

Flowcharting can be done in varying amounts of detail. We recommend different amounts of detail for different instructional methodologies. For simpler methodologies (tutorial, drill, and tests) we recommend simple flowcharts giving an overview of the lesson's scope and sequence. For complex methodologies, such as simulations and instructional games we recommend more detailed flowcharts that include the algorithms underlying the simulation models, game rules, and so on. Regardless of the amount of detail, we suggest producing flowcharts in a series of drafts.

7. *Storyboard* *displays on paper*

Storyboarding is the process of preparing textual and pictorial displays so they will fit within the display limitations of your computer. While the flowcharts depict the sequence and decisions of a lesson, the storyboards depict its content and presentations. This step includes drafting the actual instructional messages students will see, such as information presentations, questions, feedback, directions, prompts, pictures, and animations.

At this point the draft lesson on paper should be carefully evaluated and revised until members of the project team agree on its quality. It is important to use more than content experts and instructional designers for this review. The materials should also be looked at by potential students and persons not already knowledgeable about the content. This uncovers ambiguities, confusing or missing content, and material that is too easy or too hard.

8. *Program* *the lesson*

This is the process of translating what you have on paper into a series of instructions understandable to the computer. We use the word "programming" in a more general sense than has been used in the past. Historically, programming has referred to writing code in a standard language such as BASIC or Pascal. We use it to mean *any* way of producing a lesson on the computer. As the state of the art of computer-based instruction advances, an increasing variety of methods for producing programs are becoming available. We discuss the relative advantage of different kinds of programming languages, authoring languages, authoring systems, and tools. We make a number of suggestions on how to go about programming, how to avoid errors, checking your program for errors, and making changes until it does exactly what you want.

9. *Produce* *supporting materials*

Computer-based instruction is rarely sufficient without some supporting materials. We discuss four kinds: student manuals, instructor manuals, technical manuals, and adjunct instruction. Teachers and students have different needs, and materials for them should be quite different. Teachers need information about setting up programs, accessing student data, and integrating the materials into their curriculum. They also need summary information, both for determining whether to use a particular program and also to aid students going through programs. Students primarily need help running a program and moving around in it. Technical manuals are necessary when setting up a lesson is complicated or requires sophisticated devices such as local area networks. Adjunct instruction includes worksheets, diagrams, exams, photographs, and assignment sheets.

10. *Evaluate* *and revise*

Finally, the lesson and support materials should be evaluated with emphasis on how the lesson looks and works. You will determine how well the lesson looks by using it yourself and having other people with design experience go through it. We call this procedure lesson review. You will assess how well the lesson works by observing the results of real students studying the lesson and assessing how much they learn. These students should be representative of those for whom the lesson is intended. This step includes both pilot testing and validation.

Although we recommend that you do the design and development process in this order, we recognize that deviations will sometimes be necessary and helpful. First, there will be many cases where you need to switch the order of the steps. For example, it is sometimes useful to collect resource materials before you can define your goals. Second, progression through the sequence of steps is not linear. After each of the evaluation steps a developer must typically go back and redo part or all of a previous step. The development of high quality lessons can occur only if the developer takes the view that lesson production is not linear, but cyclic and empirical.

As you read this and following chapters, keep in mind that our goal is to teach a model of *lesson* development. When we talk about a lesson, we mean a segment of instruction that deals with one or at most a few concepts and that requires fifteen to sixty minutes for a student to complete. This definition is not all encompassing but should suffice to give you the general idea of our use of the term.

THE TELEPHONE EXAMPLE

This and the next five chapters describe these ten steps in detail. To illustrate the model, we use a hypothetical lesson about the telephone, imagining that we have the goal of teaching people how to use it properly. In the first seven steps we use this example to illustrate the procedures necessary to develop such a lesson.

You may wonder why we choose as our illustration something that everyone knows and which certainly does not require a computerized lesson. There are three reasons. First, because every reader of this book is familiar with the operation of the telephone, all of our instructional design examples will be clear to everyone. If we were to give examples from mathematics, some readers would undoubtedly be confused by the content. If we were to use examples from language arts or American history, there would be others, unfamiliar with those subjects, who would be confused. Since the object of this book is not math, language arts, or American history, but instructional design, our example needs to be a commonplace one with which all readers are familiar. In that way, you should be able to focus on the real content—instructional design for the computer—and not be distracted by the subject matter. Second, as will become clear as the examples progress, a lesson on telephone operation can utilize any one or a combination of instructional methodologies such as tutorial, drill, or simulation. Finally, a lesson on telephone operation illustrates both textual and pictorial information displays.

COMPUTER TOOLS

In the past few years many computer software products have become commercially available to aid in the development of instructional software. Software is available that can support any of the ten steps just summarized or combinations of steps. Much useful software comes from the standard collection used in business. Word processing can aid in many of the early phases (planning and learning content) and later in developing manuals and supplementary materials. Spreadsheets can aid in budgeting, in evaluation analyses, and in designing mathematical models for simulations. Databases can be used for cataloging resources. Graphics programs are useful for storyboarding, program development, and manual production. Project management software helps schedule the members of a development team and assures meeting important deadlines. Desktop publishing programs can decrease the time and cost of manual production, while greatly increasing quality.

In addition to these standard business tools, there is a growing list of other software that can be very useful. Flowcharting programs reduce the difficulty and tedium of producing flowcharts. Statistical software is useful in all the evaluation steps. Mapping software and outlining programs aid in organizing the content. One expert system we know of, *Problem Analysis* (Wells & Ebersberger, 1987), facilitates the analysis phase, suggesting to the developer what kind of task or instructional analysis is most appropriate.

Central to CBI development are design and programming tools. Design tools include software for program scripting and storyboarding. Programming tools include programming languages, authoring languages, and authoring systems, all of which support the difficult process of transforming ideas on paper into a functioning computer program. We will discuss many of these tools in this and the chapters that follow.

Two important issues must be considered at the start. The first is the issue of whether to use several independent tools for different steps, or to use a set of integrated tools that facilitate development across steps.

The issue of individual versus integrated tools exists outside the field of instructional design and is of wide concern. For example, one can purchase individual business tools such as word processors, spreadsheets, graphics packages, and databases; or one can purchase an integrated package that does all four. The advantage of the integrated package is that it is easy to move information between the functions. You can incorporate a picture into your letter and send the letter to all the addresses listed in a database. The disadvantages of the integrated approach is that each of the separate functions may not be accomplished as well as by independent programs. In contrast, independent programs do not make the exchange of information between functions as easy. However, you can choose the best word processor, the best spreadsheet, and so on, and any time a new and better product comes on the market you can switch to it. Thus, in large part, the issue is whether to maximize the power of individual functions or to maximize exchange of information between functions.

When looked at in this fashion, it becomes apparent that a related issue is the type of computer and operating system you use. Older microcomputers, such as the Apple II series, do not provide the power or operating-system capabilities to move information between different programs. Although information can be transferred, it requires a level of computer programming expertise few instructional developers have.

The earlier IBM microcomputers provide a more powerful operating system, especially in terms of speed and memory, but still do not provide for ease of information sharing. Both the early Apple II and IBM-compatible microcomputers have the same major flaw that most hampers their ease of data sharing—the provision of different display modes. The IBM-compatible computers not only have different display modes, text versus graphics, and different levels of graphics resolution, but also different monitors for each. This hardware difference frequently makes information sharing between programs even harder than on the older Apple II.

The introduction of the Macintosh computer provided the first widespread example of a computer and operating system that *foster* data sharing to a high degree. The Macintosh integrates text and graphics in all programs. Graphics resolution is always the same, and the system provides specific tools, the "clipboard" and the "scrapbook," which facilitate transfer between programs. On a Macintosh, almost any picture can be clipped out of a graphics program and inserted into a letter in a word processor. Text in any word processor can be incorporated into the display of a CBI lesson developed with an authoring system. Data collected about student performance in a lesson can be copied into a spreadsheet for evaluation analysis.

More recently, operating system software has been developed for Apple II and IBM-compatible computers that emulates the integrated text and graphics environment of the Macintosh. However, such software only works on machines with considerable mass storage and memory. More importantly, thousands of old software packages for those computers will not work in the new operating systems. In contrast, most software ever written for a Macintosh can exchange text, graphic, and numeric information with relative ease. As a result, integrated packages have some advantage on Apple II and IBM-compatible computers. But on Macintosh computers (and some very new systems such as the NeXT computer), independent tools generally work together very well and provide the greatest power for individual steps.

Although the preponderance of CBI developed to date has been for Apple II microcomputers, and although the most common microcomputers in business and industry are IBM-compatible, the integrated environment and development tools available for the Macintosh computers make it, in our estimation, the most powerful microcomputer for most CBI development. In particular, the newer model Macintosh II computers with color capability both facilitate development and provide for high quality delivery of instruction. Unfortunately, their cost is still considered prohibitive by many schools.

The issue of integrated tools versus independent tools with exchangeable information may well change in the future. The goal of some instructional technologists is a complete authoring system that facilitates every step of the analysis, design, and production process. Such a system will clearly have advantages for all developers, especially novices, as long as the power for any particular step is not sacrificed.

The second important issue is to decide when you *should* do design activities on a computer, given that they *can* be done that way.

Two good examples are flowcharting and storyboarding. Several programs exist explicitly for flowcharting. Because of the difficulty of drawing and revising flowcharts by hand, we have found computer flowcharting programs to be fruitful right from the first draft of a flowchart.

Storyboarding stands in contrast to this. Many computer graphics programs exist that can be used for storyboarding. Those computer graphics can, especially in integrated environments, be incorporated into computer programs during a later stage of development. Additionally, the newest generation of authoring systems allows for on-line storyboarding and refinement such that storyboards are gradually transformed into the actual lesson.

On-line storyboarding has the advantage that is allows one to directly incorporate color, text fonts and sizes, screen dimensions, perhaps even animation and sound capabilities into the storyboards. But we have found that going on-line with storyboards too early is detrimental. The developer begins to think of the storyboards, which should just be a part of program design, as the actual program and consequently resists major design changes. Furthermore, a designer's inexperience with a computer program may force constraints on design that would not occur when using paper and pencil.

Lastly, although there may be long-term efficiency, on-line storyboarding can be slow compared to doing a paper-and-pencil sketch. On paper a person can sketch and write as he or she thinks, which enhances creativity. The computer novice may be slowed down using a computer drawing program, thus interrupting thought processes and creativity. For storyboarding, we suggest that the initial draft be done on paper. Later drafts or parts of a design that require color, special fonts, animation, or sound, may be prototyped with on-line storyboarding tools. Some day we may have tools available that are so fast and easy that they facilitate creativity at an early stage, but we do not believe current software tools are at that level.

Computer tools can and should be used during all steps of the design process. However, discussion, paper, and chalkboards should also be used. As we discuss each step in the chapters that follow, we will point out useful software, showing when we believe it should be used.

In the remainder of this chapter we discuss the first four steps of the model which are in preparation for design and development. For these and the following three steps (through storyboarding) we will discuss the issues involved; suggest specific procedures; describe useful computer software; and demonstrate the procedures with an example of a lesson about telephone operation.

STEP 1—DETERMINE NEEDS AND GOALS

Definitions and Issues

By defining goals we mean determining what you want your students to know or be able to do at the end of your lesson. Some instructional designers (Mager, 1962) recommend a complete specification of specific learning objectives for both the end of a lesson (terminal objectives) and intermediate points during the lesson (intermediate or enabling objectives). In keeping with our belief that computer-based instruction demands the infusion of creativity early in the design process, we suggest that the designer produce only general objectives or goals at this point. Plotting out specific intermediate or enabling objectives occurs in the fifth step, *design*. The instructional designer must engage in considerable planning and learning before beginning to design. Furthermore, it is important that the infusion of creativity occurs early in the development process, before the lesson's structure is decided.

Another part of this step is needs assessment. This means charting out the characteristics, current competencies, and needs of your expected students. This will be useful for a number of purposes. It will clarify the appropriate content and methodology of your lesson and will give you a sense of the range of abilities in the student population.

Procedures

State Your Goal.   The first activity is to state a general goal, the subject area you want your students to learn. This is easy and usually presents no problem. The next statement is a little more difficult. Recognizing that you are developing a single lesson, and that it should teach just a few concepts in about fifteen to sixty minutes, state the particular aspect of the subject you intend to teach. This more refined goal may arise out of a particular interest you have always had, an area your students always have trouble learning, a need specified by a curriculum committee, or material your employer has instructed you to teach. If you have difficulty defining your purpose in this way, we recommend you go immediately to Step 2, *collecting resource materials,* and assemble information that can help you decide on a reasonably sized goal for a lesson.

Produce a Chart of Student Characteristics.   Next you should collect and chart out information about your intended students. Instructional designers usually base learning and teaching goals on what they know about their students' learning needs. It is useful, however, to get a more complete picture of the students' characteristics, competencies, limitations, and familiarity with the subject area.

Students are not all identical. Some will have more familiarity with the subject material than others. Some are older than others. It is impossible, and probably not even useful, to delineate the unique characteristics of each student. Recognizing that your lesson should be appropriate for a certain range of students, describe the range by writing down the characteristics of students at the *low* end of the range, in the *middle* of the range, and at the *high* end of the range.

The information in the chart should include general student characteristics such as age, educational level, reading proficiency, and motivation. It also should include information relevant to the subject material, such as proficiency in the prerequisite skills for the current lesson and interest in the lesson content. Furthermore, because you are interested in teaching with a computer, it is useful to ask some questions about the students' facility with a computer; indeed, about whether they have ever used one. Because student-computer interactions involve some typing, an important question is how well the students type.

It is useful to produce a chart with the student characteristics listed in rows down the left-hand side of the page and with columns representing the low-ability, average, and high-ability students. The characteristics selected will depend on the subject area and instructional methodology. Figure 7–1 illustrates such a chart. The bottom row and the two partial columns on the right-hand side will be discussed later.

Some cells in this chart will require very little written in them. For typing ability, you can probably say "none," or "some," or "touch typists." For experience in the subject, you should provide a more complete description. If your current lesson deals with the multiplication of fractions, experience in the subject should indicate whether the student has mastered the more fundamental aspects of fractions, such as addition and subtraction of integers.

State Your Terminal Goal and Add It to the Chart of Student Characteristics. So far you have stated your general goal (for example, multiplication of fractions), you have stated what part of that you intend to teach (multiplication of proper fractions in numeric form, for example), and you have begun charting out information about your students' characteristics. Now you should add your terminal goal (what you want your students to know or be able to do at the end of the lesson) to the bottom of the chart and fill in all the columns for that goal. For each of the columns representing the range of students, indicate whether they can attain the goal without further instruction. Then estimate the time it will take to teach the students you have defined and estimate how difficult the students will find the topic. The two columns on the right only apply to the rows added at the bottom for your instructional goals.

Keeping in mind that a lesson should not be longer than an hour, when you fill in the time and difficulty columns you may find the goal is too ambitious. Possibly, if you changed your goal to something smaller, such as "multiplying fractions with single-digit numerators and denominators" and filled in the chart for that goal, you might decide that this is more reasonable given the characteristics of your students and the breadth and difficulty of the topic.

A lesson may have more than one goal. If so, it is even more important to put all the goals on the chart, together with their respective teaching times and difficulty levels. The sum of the teaching times must be reasonable for a single lesson. This procedure will aid you in avoiding a common problem, trying to teach too much in a single lesson. You should not be dismayed that it may take a long time to attain even single goals. Remember that goals, if complex, can always be split into smaller subgoals that are reasonably sized.

Computer Tools

One of the earliest development activities during the first step of setting goals is planning the schedule for a project and what each team member should do. Teamwork requires good coordination and adherence to schedule. Time-line

	LOWEST LEVEL STUDENTS	AVERAGE LEVEL STUDENTS	HIGHEST LEVEL STUDENTS	TIME REQUIRED TO TEACH	DIFFICULTY TO LEARN
AGE					
EDUCATIONAL LEVEL					
READING PROFICIENCY					
GENERAL MOTIVATION					
EXPERIENCE IN SUBJECT					
INTEREST IN THE SUBJECT					
COMPUTER FAMILIARITY					
TYPING ABILITY					

Figure 7-1   Chart of student characteristics.

programs such as *Harvard Project Manager* (Software Publishing, 1988) on the IBM and *MacProject* (Claris, 1989) on the Macintosh allow a team to plot out individual responsibilities, critical dates, and interdependencies such as whose product must be completed before another person's can begin. Scheduling programs make such information available to all members and in some cases allow tracking of projects and recording what has and has not been completed. A related planning activity is drafting and refining a budget, a process facilitated by computer spreadsheet programs such as *1-2-3* (Lotus Development, 1985) for the IBM, possibly the best selling of all microcomputer software, or *Excel* (Microsoft, 1988) for Macintosh computers.

Developing a chart of student characteristics and goals with associated information about difficulty and time can be a tedious process with pencil-and-paper. Adding cells of new information can necessitate rewriting a whole page, and often information does not fit in the space available on a piece of paper. Some word processors and most spreadsheet programs provide good facilities for producing charts. For example, *Microsoft Word Version 4* (Microsoft, 1989) on the Macintosh permits easy addition of rows and columns and editing information within any cell, adjusting the entire chart as the information in any cell changes.

Telephone Example

The following represents Step 1 of our development model for the lesson about telephone operation.

State the General Goal.   This is quite easy. Our goal is to teach people how to operate telephones.

State What You Intend to Teach in a Single Lesson.   In our lesson we will teach the student how to make telephone calls. Note that there are many activities concerning telephone operation that this goal does not include, such as answering telephone calls. More importantly, there are many aspects of telephones that might be subsumed under this goal or be prerequisite to attaining it, although we are not yet sure. Will we include making calls from pay phones, for example? However, any further definition should wait until later.

Produce a Chart of the Characteristics of Intended Students.   This chart is shown in Figure 7–2 and is based on the premise that our students will be foreign students who have just arrived in the United States. Although their education is quite high, very few people in their native country have telephones. English is a second language to them, so their reading level in English is below their general educational level. They know telephones are very useful devices so they have high interest in learning how to operate them. Lastly, they have no experience with computers or typewriters.

State a Terminal Goal for the Lesson.   Our goal is that given a telephone number, the student will be able to use the telephone to call it. We have stated our

	LOWEST LEVEL STUDENTS	AVERAGE LEVEL STUDENTS	HIGHEST LEVEL STUDENTS	TIME REQUIRED TO TEACH	DIFFICULTY TO LEARN
AGE	20	25	35		
EDUCATIONAL LEVEL	GRADE 9	GRADE 12	COLLEGE		
READING PROFICIENCY	GRADE 5	GRADE 8	GRADE 12		
GENERAL MOTIVATION	HIGH	HIGH	HIGH		
EXPERIENCE IN SUBJECT	NONE	NONE	NONE		
INTEREST IN THE SUBJECT	HIGH	HIGH	HIGH		
COMPUTER FAMILIARITY	NONE	NONE	NONE		
TYPING ABILITY	NONE	NONE	SOME		

Figure 7–2 Chart of student characteristics. Information about the students has been entered.

	LOWEST LEVEL STUDENTS	AVERAGE LEVEL STUDENTS	HIGHEST LEVEL STUDENTS	TIME REQUIRED TO TEACH	DIFFICULTY TO LEARN
AGE	20	25	35		
EDUCATIONAL LEVEL	GRADE 9	GRADE 12	COLLEGE		
READING PROFICIENCY	GRADE 5	GRADE 8	GRADE 12		
GENERAL MOTIVATION	HIGH	HIGH	HIGH		
EXPERIENCE IN SUBJECT	NONE	NONE	NONE		
INTEREST IN THE SUBJECT	HIGH	HIGH	HIGH		
COMPUTER FAMILIARITY	NONE	NONE	NONE		
TYPING ABILITY	NONE	NONE	SOME		
GIVEN PHONE NUMBER THE STUDENT WILL CALL IT CORRECTLY	CANNOT DO	CANNOT DO	CANNOT DO	1 HOUR	MEDIUM

Figure 7-3 Information about the goal of the lesson is now included in the chart.

goal in this way because we are not including instruction about telephone books, nor do we presume our students can use telephone books.

Add the Terminal Goal to the Chart. Figure 7–3 shows the chart reproduced with an added line, the terminal goal. Our educated guess is that the terminal objective will require about thirty minutes to one hour to learn, and that the task is of medium difficulty.

STEP 2—COLLECT RESOURCE MATERIALS

Definitions and Issues

Resource materials include every item or source of information that is essential to or can aid the instructional development effort. There are three kinds of resource materials: those relevant to the subject matter; those relevant to the instructional development and teaching processes; and those relevant to the delivery system for your lesson, in this case, the computer and lesson development software you intend to use.

Most instructional developers collect some resource materials. When developing instruction on a computer almost everyone has the necessary equipment and manuals on hand. A smaller number of developers collect subject-matter materials such as textbooks. Some people believe it is important to "do it their own way" and do not wish to have their ideas influenced by the instructional methods others have used. However, only a few developers systematically collect resource materials regarding the instructional development process itself.

The risks in not collecting materials are many. These include the comparatively minor problem of lacking organization and, consequently, taking longer than necessary to complete the lesson design; the problem of reinventing the wheel because you did not know someone else had already produced the same lesson; and the major problem of producing a poor program because you did not have sufficient information about the subject area or about good instructional methods.

The primary reason for collecting resource materials is organizational. Upon completing this step you will have all the necessary information on hand to use in later steps of the development process. These materials are particularly necessary for the next three steps, learning the content, generating ideas, and designing instruction. Also, as already mentioned, if you have difficulty trying to define your purpose, it is useful to go ahead and collect resource materials as an aid before doing Step 1.

Subject Resources. Resource materials relevant to the subject matter include any item that contains information about the subject or that demonstrates ways in which it may be taught. These items include textbooks, other computer-based instruction programs, original sources, reference materials, technical manuals, films and television programs, tapes and slides, actual equipment such as a typewriter if you intend to teach typing, equipment operation manuals, and, most importantly, the names and locations of accessible people knowledgeable about the subject. People who have taught the subject themselves or have developed instructional materials about it are particularly useful.

Instructional Design Resources. Resource materials relevant to the instructional development process include texts and manuals about instructional design, plenty of scratch paper and graphic arts materials, and the materials in the Appendix of this book, such as the lists of relevant instructional factors for each of the major methodologies discussed previously. These lists figure prominently in the generation of ideas, the organization of ideas, and the production of lesson displays. The listing of instructional design textbooks in the bibliography at the end of the chapter is an adequate selection for most people's needs.

Computer software to aid in the design and development process should also be located at this time. Useful software tools are discussed for each step of our development model. For example, in the previous step we briefly discussed timeline programs, spreadsheets, and word processors. Although a few specific products are named, many more are available. At this time the designer should do research to locate the tools most suitable for the project and available computer hardware.

The final instructional development resource is again the most important, namely a list of accessible people familiar with the design and development of instructional materials. It is best if they also have experience in the development of computer-based instruction.

Media Resources. Resource materials relevant to your delivery system include the computer itself, its operation manuals and references, the development software you intend to use, manuals and textbooks for the development software, and a list of accessible people experienced with the same computer and software.

Procedures

We have said that many developers do not systematically engage in the collection of resource materials. This is surprising in light of the fact that it is the easiest step in the development process. There is always the temptation to save time by omitting this step until the need for particular materials arises. Unfortunately, if you do not know what resources exist, you will probably never recognize the need for them, even when you run into difficulty. In the long run, your time will be well spent if you systematically seek out all available materials early in the process. Begin by generating a list of subject matter, instructional development, and instructional media resources. The most important ones were described in the previous section. While collecting these you will usually be led to others. For example, as you collect instructional design or programming language reference books, their bibliographies will contain other resources that may be useful.

If you do not know where to begin this step or have no idea what resources exist, go to the resource people on your list and ask them for a list of resources. This holds true regardless of the step you are performing, whether it be defining goals, collecting resources, generating ideas, organizing ideas, producing lesson displays, flowcharting, programming, or evaluating a lesson. If you are not sure what to do, where to begin, or what resources to consult, go to a knowledgeable person for assistance.

The two primary uses of subject-relevant materials are as a source of the actual content and as a source of experts' overall organization of the content. Unless you are an expert in the subject area yourself, you should become familiar with the tables of contents of textbooks and references to ensure that you have neither omitted essential information nor included incorrect or nonessential information. Further, organizing the information into the best possible presentation for the student is often a difficult task, even for an expert. You will, of course, organize the content of your lesson to meet your own particular needs, but the organization used by others in the subject area is always a reasonable place to begin.

We indicated previously that if you encountered difficulty trying to define your purpose, you should skip ahead to the collection of resource materials. The table of contents of a good textbook will give you a picture not only of the breadth of topics in the subject area, but also of the way in which subject matter experts break the subject into topics, and of how they order them. Keeping in mind the characteristics and needs of your student population, examine the table of contents in a number of representative textbooks to determine what topics are appropriate for your intended students. By these we mean topics that they need to learn and have the necessary background to study. You can estimate whether your students have the necessary background information by examining earlier topics in the table of contents. To the extent that your students are familiar with earlier topics, they will have the necessary background. Having located one or more topics in this way, return and continue the definition of purpose as before.

Computer Tools

Collecting resources for later use is only beneficial if the resources are well organized and cataloged. The use of computer databases is beneficial in this regard. Textbooks and articles relevant to the content, instructional design, and the delivery medium may not only be cataloged on a database, but their contents cataloged and described so that the information can be quickly located when needed. Although this procedure may sound unnecessary, as the number and variety of resources grows, the harder it is to remember and find them when needed.

Even more important to catalog are resources that are known but not at hand, such as knowledgeable people, books in the library, or equipment that might be purchased or rented at a future time. These "out-of-sight–out-of-mind" resources are unlikely to be used when needed if team members are not reminded of their existence. A good computer database, if asked, for example, "What resources do we know of for connecting an IBM microcomputer to an oscilloscope?" can quickly provide appropriate library call numbers and names and addresses of people with expertise or companies that have interface products.

Telephone Example

To demonstrate the process of collecting resources for our lesson on telephone operation, we include three lists. The first shows resources regarding the telephone itself. The second shows resources regarding the instructional development process, and the third shows resources assuming our lesson will be on an Apple Macintosh computer using an authoring system.

These represent a fairly complete listing of resources for our lesson on the telephone, although no doubt you can think of others we did not include.

Subject Matter Resources for a Lesson on Telephone Operation

a telephone and pictures of telephones

a telephone book (especially the first twenty or so pages)

a telephone bill

pamphlets available from the telephone company

a person who uses telephones frequently

a telephone operator

a telephone company service representative

Federal Communications Commission documents about phone service

a store where a variety of telephones are sold

the directions listed at the top of a pay phone

Instructional Design Resources for a Lesson on Telephone Operation

the appendix of this book

instructional design books in the bibliography of Chapter 7

lots of paper, both lined and unlined

pencils, colored pencils, rulers, and other art materials

transparent plastic for tracing and reproducing pictures

index cards and bulletin board for storyboarding and flowcharting

computer graphics software for storyboarding

a flowcharting template or flowcharting software

a person who has designed instruction for computer presentation

Delivery System Resources for a Lesson on Telephone Operation

Macintosh SE computer

book on programming with an authoring system

book on operation of the Apple Macintosh SE computer

a friend who has used the Macintosh with this authoring system

STEP 3—LEARN THE CONTENT

Definitions and Issues

One of the common and grave errors we see novices commit is to develop a lesson with only a surface level understanding of the content. A good lesson should facilitate thorough comprehension by the student. This simply cannot be done if the developer does not also have thorough knowledge of the content. Surface familiarity with the content can only result in a shallow lesson. Students will undoubtedly get more out of a good book on the subject.

It is rare for the designer of a lesson to be completely familiar with the content to be taught. On a development team, the designer must usually learn the content before much design can be done. Learning the content is usually accomplished by a combination of interviewing and working with subject matter experts, reading textbooks on the subject, consulting reference works and original sources, and so on. In essence the designer must become a student again. The difference between studying the content for design, however, and studying in the usual sense, is that the designer must always have the design of a lesson in mind. That means, for example, that if the designer finds a particular element of the content difficult and confusing, it is likely that students will have the same trouble. The designer should not only try to learn that difficult content any way possible, but should note the fact that it caused a problem and that it is a likely area of difficulty for students. In other words, the designer should not only take notes on the content being learned, but on the process of learning it. What is easy and what is difficult? How long does it take to learn particular segments? What are the better information sources? Which instructional techniques in textbooks are good and which are not?

It is also important to emphasize learning the structure of content rather than the details. Hannum (1988) points out that different subject areas have different kinds of structure, and that instruction should be designed in keeping with the structure. This requires that the designer learn the structure explicitly and well.

Hannum divides types of learning into five domains (similar to Gagne, 1985): information, intellectual skills, motor skills, attitudes, and cognitive strategies, and gives examples for the first three, which are usually the ones dealt with by the instructional designer. According to Hannum, the structure of knowledge in the information domain is generally the semantic network, in which *nodes* represent pieces of information and *lines* between nodes represent the relationships between information. Some semantic networks may be shown as a *web* where any piece of information may be related to any other through a variety of relationships, or as a *hierarchy* where any node tends to be related to one superordinate node and one or more subordinate nodes.

A hierarchy is really a specific type of web, in which the types of relationships and connections between nodes are few and very specific. Another type of web structure discussed by Hannum is the *classification matrix*. This is appropriate where nodes represent different dimensions, and every node in one dimension has a relationship with every node on the other dimension or dimensions. For example, if you were to teach about the chemical elements, one dimension (side) of the matrix would be the elements and the other would be characteristics such as atomic number, atomic weight, type of element, natural state (gas, liquid, or solid), and so on.

Motor skills are generally characterized by a procedural structure. Visually this often is shown as a flowchart depicting sequence and decision points that affect sequence.

The domain of intellectual skills, according to Hannum, is represented by a prerequisite structure. A typical diagram depicts what knowledge or skill is necessary before more advanced knowledge or skills can be acquired. We maintain that in many cases both prerequisite and procedural structures will be relevant.

Procedures and Computer Tools

The obvious procedures in this step are to read textbooks and other materials, to interview and talk with content experts, and, if the object is to learn how to use equipment or follow some procedure, to practice that activity yourself. The less obvious activity is to submit to some kind of test, preferably by the content expert who will evaluate your performance, to determine when you know the content sufficiently well to design instruction about it.

As we have said, this step of instruction essentially requires the designer to become a student to learn the new material. In this step there are many computer tools of which the designer can and should take advantage. *Thinktank* (Winer & Bierman, 1987), *More* (Winer, Baron, Winer, & Bierman, 1987), and many word processing programs such as *Microsoft Word* provide computerized outlining capabilities to take notes on subject matter content. *Design* (Albright & Snow, 1987) and *Learning Tool* (Kozma & Roekel, 1986) (Figure 7–4) are examples of programs that let you draw a free-form web diagram showing arbitrary relationships between nodes. Flowcharting tools such as *MacFlow* (Bertrand & Terpstra, 1988) (Figure 7–5) and *Easyflow* (Farnell & McDowell, 1987) are useful for learning and describ-

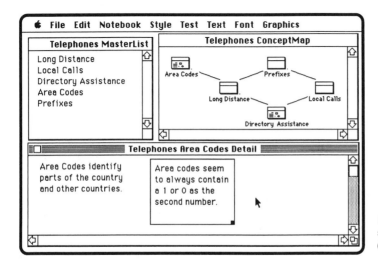

Figure 7-4 A conceptual map of some content using *Learning Tool*. *(Courtesy of Arborworks, Inc.)*

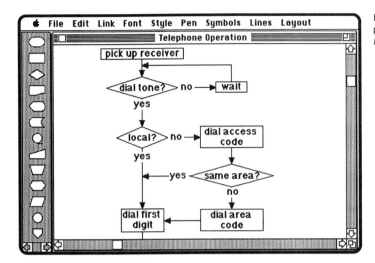

Figure 7-5   A flowchart showing procedural information using *MacFlow. (Courtesy of Mainstay)*

ing procedural knowledge and intellectual skills. More general programs such as *Hypercard* (Apple Computer, 1988) (Figure 7–6), and standard applications such as databases, spreadsheets, and word processors are useful for learning and describing content organization. Gayeski (1989) describes a computer program to guide the instructional designer when interviewing subject matter experts.

Telephone Example

It might appear at first glance that there is little the instructional designer needs to learn about telephones. In this regard, our telephone is a good example because even a simple topic like telephones contains many details unknown to most people. Do you know how to initiate international telephone calls? How are telephone numbers structured? What should you do if a telephone fails to work?

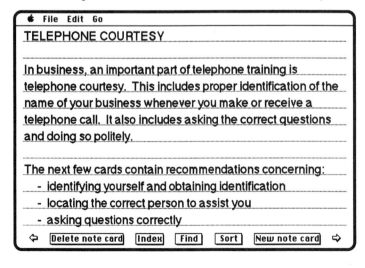

Figure 7-6   Note cards with subject matter content in *Hypercard. (Courtesy of Apple Computer, Inc.)*

What are the regulations concerning purchasing your own phone and connecting it to the telephone system? What specialized equipment can be connected to home phones? How do you buy and use one of the new cellular telephones for a car?

Although many of these topics may not be necessary or appropriate for our telephone lesson, we can only make good decisions of what to include or not include if we are thoroughly familiar with the content. Thus, at this point, we would read literature from the telephone company, from companies making telephone-related equipment, and talk to customer service agents at the phone company, all the while taking notes and organizing what we learn. Figures 7–4 through 7–6 show examples produced by some computer tools of maps, diagrams, and note cards we made to assist us in learning the topic.

STEP 4—GENERATE IDEAS

Definitions and Issues

At this point in the design process many instructional developers have difficulties. This is true even of experienced designers. It is far easier to decide what to teach, that is, to define the purpose of instruction, than it is to decide how to teach it well. Many existing models of instructional design do not foster much creativity. The activity in this step is therefore designed to help the developer generate good, creative ideas, and to do so quickly.

The procedure we recommend is known as brainstorming. This is not an idea that originated in the field of instructional development, but one that has been used for many years in other fields such as business for solving problems and producing creative ideas. Brainstorming is a process in which a number of people work as a group to rapidly produce as many ideas as possible in a non-evaluative way. Typically, someone voices an idea, then other group members immediately say what comes to their minds. Ideas might include problems, potential solutions, additions to other group members' solutions, and so on. The group continues to produce as many ideas as possible until the frequency of new ideas decreases and people are only repeating old ones.

In the context of instructional design, the intent is for a small group of people to generate as many ideas as possible about instructional content and methodology, without regard for quality, feasibility, difficulty, relevance, uniqueness, or any other criteria. The emphasis at this stage is on *quantity* rather than quality. This does not imply that we are unconcerned with quality or the relevance of ideas for the lesson. We simply want to postpone decisions concerning quality and relevance until later. This simple process of producing ideas prevents the developer from having no ideas, or only poor ones, with which to work. It also increases to a surprising degree the probability of generating very good and creative ones. Another benefit of this non-evaluative approach is that anyone can participate in the process and make valuable contributions without being threatened by others' judgmental comments. The process of selecting and refining the best ideas is done later.

After defining their goals, most instructional developers produce just a few ideas for a lesson, sometimes only one. They then develop that idea as the basis for a whole lesson. For experienced instructional developers, this idea is often good. For inexperienced instructional developers, however, it is frequently not. The prevailing practice of using the first idea that comes to mind does not produce consistently high quality results. Our purpose is to enable even the inexperienced developer to consistently produce enough ideas for a good lesson design. We believe that *the more ideas you generate early in the design process, the more likely it is that at least one of them will be an exceptionally good one.* This is the underlying principle of brainstorming.

Procedures

There should be two brainstorming sessions: one to generate ideas about what information to teach, using the previously defined goals and subject matter resource materials from Steps 1 and 2; the second to generate ideas about how to teach the information, using the lists of instructional methodologies and their respective instructional factors as discussed in Part 1 and summarized in Appendix A. In addition to the resource materials, you will need plenty of blank paper, pens or pencils without erasers, and two to four other people. You should use pens or pencils without erasers, because erasing implies correction or evaluation, whereas the emphasis should be only on producing ideas.

Brainstorming is done in small groups, because people almost always get ideas by listening to those of others. Three to five people is a good number for brainstorming. Try to include at least one highly creative person, such as an artist or actor.

The first brainstorming session proceeds as follows. Gather the group of people around a single small table. Give each person pencil and paper, a written copy of the previously defined lesson goals, and copies of the subject-matter resource materials. Select one person to be responsible for deciding when to stop brainstorming. Begin by generating ideas about *what* information you will teach. Any individual can start off by suggesting an idea. The idea can be a specific fact, concept, principle, or rule to be taught. Everyone then *writes it down immediately*. Do *not* be judgmental. Do *not* discuss whether it is a good idea or not. Do *not* question its relevance or its similarity to a previous idea. Just write it down. Now the goal of each person in the group is to scan the available resources and the ideas just written down and *be the first one to voice the next idea.* The next idea may be very similar, on a totally different track, the complete opposite of the first idea, or a slight variation of the first idea. It does not matter. Once voiced, each group member writes it down, then immediately tries again to be the first to produce the next idea.

This procedure is repeated over and over, with group members continually scanning the assembled resource materials, defined goals, and ideas generated so far to produce more ideas. One person, appointed at the start, is responsible for stopping this process. In general, the generation of ideas will start out slowly. Then production will accelerate and reach a peak. Finally, the rate will taper off and the ideas will become repetitious. The selected person monitors the ideas when writing them down and stops the process when the rate drops considerably or when there is excessive repetition. It is important not to terminate the session too soon; usually the group hits a low point with few ideas, but then perks up again and enjoys a renewed period of activity. When the rate slows and the group produces few or no new ideas for a minute or more, it is time to stop.

The most important caution, which cannot be overemphasized, is to avoid the temptation to criticize ideas. Any form of judgment or analysis of ideas slows the creative process.

When you have completed brainstorming about content, repeat the process for *instructional methods.* If the first session was long and tiring, you may want to have the second on the following day. Give each person a copy of the list of instructional factors corresponding to each of the instructional methodologies (Appendix A) and other instructional design resource materials collected in Step 2. Start writing ideas on a different sheet of paper to keep the *subject-matter* ideas and *instructional method* ideas separate. Again, any person may begin by suggesting a method to teach any of the ideas on the first list, and everyone then writes down the idea. Immediately scan the resource materials, the list from the previous brainstorming session, the list of methodologies and factors, and the previous idea just generated in this session, and try to produce the next idea. Continue as in the first brainstorming session.

Try to experiment this time, combining each of the instructional methodologies with each of the ideas about what information to teach. Keep scanning the lists of instructional factors to generate specific details about the teaching process, such as types of questions to ask, pictures to show the student, or remedial sequences after the student makes errors. As before, one person is designated to decide when to stop. In the second brainstorming session, you should not stop until you have produced at least a few ideas corresponding to *each* of the ideas on the first brainstorming list.

When the brainstorming sessions are over, you will have two complete lists, identical to each other person's lists, of all ideas about potential subject matter and teaching methods. It is sometimes productive to spend some time alone, reflecting on the final lists, to see if you can come up with any more ideas.

Computer Tools

During brainstorming a word processor with a large screen projector may facilitate the process. Instead of each person writing down everything, one person may serve as secretary. Everyone can see the projected image, can put effort into generating ideas rather than writing, and the list may be printed out when copies are needed. Tape-recording the session is also a good way to prevent ideas from being lost.

Telephone Example

Below are lists of the ideas generated by a brainstorming session on our lesson on telephone operation. The first list contains ideas about information that we might teach. The second list contains ideas concerning how we might teach the topics on the first list.

Both of these lists are examples of the output of brainstorming sessions. They are likely to be quite different from the list other people would generate, although the contents would be similar. Typically, the second list is much longer, because there are many factors about which we might generate ideas. You should by now have a good picture of the amount and variety of ideas that are possible and that you should strive for. In closing, note that *many of the ideas are irrelevant to our previously stated goals,* or, for one reason or another, will not be used. In the next step, *design,* we will begin by paring down these lists to a few of the best and most relevant ideas.

List 1: Ideas about Information That Should Be Taught

dialing a telephone
recognizing a telephone
answering a telephone
recognizing the dial tone
knowing that the telephone is working
using a touch-tone phone
knowing what a telephone is used for
using a telephone book
getting a telephone book
getting a telephone
telephone bills
paying telephone bills
dialing long distance calls
dialing local calls
dialing collect calls
answering collect calls
dialing for information
asking for information
dialing for long-distance information
dialing the operator
dialing person-to-person
dialing overseas
credit card calls
using pay telephones
using pay telephones with credit cards
understanding area codes

---

how the zero works differently if you pause or keep dialing

what to say when someone answers your call

distinguishing ringing and busy signals

different types of busy signals

what to do if nobody answers your call

what to do if you get a wrong number

what to do if you get a busy signal

how to use extension telephones

how to use party lines

party lines and emergencies

telephone courtesy

what to do if you get annoying or obscene phone calls

toll-free telephone numberspolice and other emergency numbers

hanging up

hanging up before you finish dialing

what to do if you don't get a dial tone

looking up a person's telephone number

using the yellow pages

how telephone bills are calculated

what to do if your telephone bill is incorrect

what to do when the phone is not working

unlisted telephone numbers

history of the telephone

List 2: Ideas about How to Teach the Topics in List 1

give a tutorial about the purpose of the telephone

tutorial on dialing local calls

simulation of dialing local calls

simulate dialing a touch-tone phone with a touch-sensitive screen

simulate dialing a touch-tone phone with a mouse

drill, given numbers, on dialing the numbers

draw a picture of a telephone on the display

draw a picture of a dial telephone

draw a picture of a touch-tone telephone

draw a picture of a coin-operated telephone

drill on dialing a simulated touch-tone telephone

questions and answers about using the telephone

tutorial on long-distance dialing

have the student use a real telephone

tutorial on the telephone book

test using the real telephone book

simulate a telephone book and have the student look up numbers

simulate ringing, dial tone, and busy signal and test the student on each

tutorial and demonstration of collect calls and person-to-person calls

connect a real telephone to the computer and have student use the computer controlled phone

have the student answer the telephone and carry on a conversation

have the student answer the telephone when it is a wrong number

tutorial on area codes and the structure of phone numbers

tutorial on phone bills and charges

drill on phone bills and charges

tutorial and test on paying phone bills

tutorial on ordering a phone

use simulation to make overseas calls

use simulation to make toll-free calls

drill on distinguishing local, long distance, and overseas numbers

tutorial on what to do when you dial incorrectly

tutorial on party lines and extension phones

tutorial on what to do when the phone does not work properly

tutorial and test on telephone courtesy

videotape of someone using telephones

require the student to both look up and dial numbers

student uses the phone simulation to discover what happens when you dial different numbers

have the student dial touch-tone by touching the computer screen

give the student immediate feedback whenever dialing errors are made

don't give student feedback, just let the phone simulation do whatever a real phone would do

carry on a simulated conversation with text on the display

use a synthetic voice device to carry out a simulated vocal conversation

tell the student what the objectives of the lesson are at the start

have the student read in a tutorial first and use a simulation later to practice dialing

use a color coded picture of the phone to teach the names of the parts of the phone

have the simulated phone ring by the computer actually ringing

have the simulated phone ring by displaying "ring-ring" on the display

ask student lots of multiple-choice questions of the variety "what will happen if I dial this?"

as the student masters each goal, move on to harder goals

begin with dialing locally, then long distance, then operator assisted

have drills with all text questions

have drills using the simulated phone

drill the student until he/she can dial correctly nine times out of ten

do discrimination training of dial tones, busy signals, and ringing

have a game in which the student must make phone calls to gather clues in a mystery

have a game in which the student must look up and dial numbers as rapidly as possible

have a game in which two students race each other to make phone calls

CONCLUSION

In this chapter we have outlined the first four steps in our instructional design model. When you have completed them, you will have gathered all the resources necessary for the project, established the goals for the lesson, determined the nature of your student population, obtained a good grasp of the content, and generated lists of ideas about content and ways of teaching it. The steps to this point have provided you with the information, resources, and perspective to create an interesting and effective lesson. In the next chapter we describe the process of moving from this point to having a detailed lesson plan.

REFERENCES AND BIBLIOGRAPHY

ALBRIGHT, R., & SNOW, J. (1987). *Design.* [Computer Program]. Cambridge, MA: Meta Software.

APPLE COMPUTER. (1988). *Hypercard.* [Computer Program]. Cupertino, CA: Apple Computer, Inc.

BERTRAND, P.A., & TERPSTRA, D. (1988). *MacFlow.* [Computer Program]. Los Angeles: Mainstay.

BRIGGS, L.J. (Ed.). (1977). *Instructional Design: Principles and Applications.* Englewood Cliffs, NJ: Educational Technology Publications.

CLARIS. (1989). *MacProject.* [Computer Program]. Santa Clara, CA: Claris Corp.

CRISWELL, E.L. (1989). *The Design of Computer-Based Instruction.* New York: Macmillan.

FARNELL, C., & MCDOWELL, R. (1987). *Easyflow.* [Computer Program]. Kingston, Ontario, Canada: Haventree Software.

GAGNE, R.M. (1985). *The Conditions of Learning and Theory of Instruction. 4th ed.* New York: Holt, Rinehart and Winston

GAGNE, R.M., & BRIGGS, L.J. (1979). *Principles of Instructional Design.* New York: Holt, Rinehart, and Winston.

GAGNE, R.M., WAGER, W., & ROJAS, A. (1984). Planning and authoring computer-assisted instruction lessons. In D.F. Walker & R.D. Hess (Eds.), *Instructional Software: Principles and Perspectives for Design and Use.* Belmont, CA: Wadsworth Publishing.

GAYESKI, D. M. (1989). Interviewing content experts—a new software tool. *Instructional Delivery Systems, 3*(2), 25–27.

HANNAFIN, M.J., & PECK, K.L. (1988). *The Design, Development, and Evaluation of Instructional Software.* New York: Macmillan.

HANNUM, W. (1988). Designing courseware to fit subject matter structure. In D.H. Jonassen (Ed.), *Instructional Designs for Microcomputer Courseware.* Hillsdale, NJ: Lawrence Erlbaum.

KEARSLEY, G. (1988). Beyond authoring: Software tools can help manage program development. *Instructional Delivery Systems, 2*(3), 15, 18–20.

KEMP, J.E. (1985). *The Instructional Design Process.* New York: Harper & Row.

KOZMA, R.B., & ROEKEL, J.V. (1986). *Learning Tool.* [Computer Program]. Ann Arbor, MI: Arborworks, Inc.

LOTUS DEVELOPMENT. (1985). *1-2-3.* [Computer Program]. Cambridge, MA: Lotus Development Corp.

MAGER, R.F. (1962). *Preparing Instructional Objectives.* Belmont, CA: Fearon Publishers.

MICROSOFT. (1988). *Excel.* [Computer Program]. Redmond, WA: Microsoft Corp.

MICROSOFT. (1989). *Microsoft Word.* [Computer Program]. Redmond, WA: Microsoft Corp.

MORRISON, G.R., & ROSS, S.M. (1988). A four-stage model for planning computer-based instruction. *Journal of Instructional Development, 11*(1), 6–14.

O'NEIL, H.F. (Ed.). (1979a). *Issues in Instructional Systems Development.* New York: Academic Press.

O'NEIL, H.F. (Ed.). (1979b). *Procedures for Instructional Systems Development.* New York: Academic Press.

O'NEIL, H.F. (Ed.). (1981). *Computer-Based Instruction: A State of the Art Assessment.* New York: Academic Press.

REIGELUTH, C.M. (Ed.). (1983). *Instructional-Design Theories and Models: An Overview of Their Current Status.* Hillsdale, NJ: Lawrence Erlbaum.

REIGELUTH, C.M. (1987). *Instructional Theories in Action: Lessons Illustrating Selected Theories and Models.* Hillsdale, NJ: Lawrence Erlbaum.

REIGELUTH, C.M., & STEIN, F.S. (1983). The elaboration theory of instruction. In C.M. Reigeluth (Ed.), *Instructional-Design Theories and Models: An Overview of Their Current Status.* Hillsdale, NJ: Lawrence Erlbaum.

ROBLYER, M.D. (1988). Fundamental problems and principles of designing effective courseware. In D.H. Jonassen (Ed.), *Instructional Designs for Microcomputer Courseware.* Hillsdale, NJ: Lawrence Erlbaum.

SOFTWARE PUBLISHING. (1988). *Harvard Project Man-*

ager. [Computer Program]. Mountain View, CA: Software Publishing.

TRAINING AND DOCTRINE COMMAND. (1975, August). *Interservice Procedures for Instructional Systems Development.* TRADOC Pamphlet 350–30. Fort Benning, GA: Combat Aims Training Board.

WELLS, J., & EBERSBERGER, W.S. (1987). *Problem Analysis.* [Computer Program]. La Jolla, CA: Park Row Software.

WINER, D., & BIERMAN, R. (1987). *Thinktank.* [Computer Program]. Mountain View, CA: Living Videotext.

WINER, P., BARON, D., WINER, D., & BIERMAN, R. (1987). *More.* [Computer Program]. Mountain View, CA: Living Videotext.

ZEMKE, R., & KRAMLINGER, T. (1987). *Figuring Things Out: A Trainer's Guide to Needs and Task Analysis.* Reading, MA: Addison-Wesley.

SUMMARY OF THE FIRST FOUR STEPS

STEP 1: DETERMINE NEEDS AND GOALS

State the general goal, the subject area.

State what part of the subject area you intend to teach in a single lesson.

Produce a chart of the characteristics of intended students.

State a terminal goal for the lesson.

Add the terminal goal or goals to the chart and estimate how much time it will take to teach and how difficult it will be to learn.

STEP 2: COLLECT RESOURCES

Produce a list of resource materials you intend to collect for the subject matter, for instructional development, and for the operation and programming of your computer. Be sure to include knowledgeable people in each category. If you do not know of many resources, go to the resource people for help in generating a list.

Collect textbooks, reference books, manuals, films, videotapes, and other materials reflecting the content of the subject and its organization. Be especially watchful for organizational summaries, indices, tables of contents, charts, and graphs.

Prepare copies of Appendix A of this book and collect other instructional design textbooks. Use their bibliographies to locate other useful resources.

Collect paper and various graphic arts materials such as graph paper, clear plastic, and a ruler.

Research and obtain suitable computer tools to aid in all design and development steps.

Have your intended computer available and collect manuals for it and the programming language or authoring tools you intend to use.

STEP 3: LEARN THE CONTENT

Read texts, references, and original source material.

Talk to and interview content experts.

Use actual equipment and practice the procedures students must learn.

Take tests, evaluated by content experts, to assess your learning.

STEP 4: GENERATE IDEAS

Gather three to five people around a small table.

Provide each person with the instructional goals, resource materials, paper and pens.

Produce as many content ideas as possible without being judgmental.

Stop when few new ideas are being generated.

Give each person a list of instructional methodologies and factors.

Repeat the process to generate ideas about how to teach the things listed in the first brainstorming session.

Stop when few new ideas are being generated. Try to have several ideas for each idea on the first list.

Save the two lists of ideas for the next step, organizing ideas.

8

DESIGN

The first four steps in the instructional process are designed to prepare you for the design step. At this point you should have all the resources necessary for the project and have a good idea both of who your students are and what you will be teaching them. You will also have lists of content and instructional ideas. Step 5 of our model synthesizes what you have and produces the specifications for the lesson. This step has the following four sub-steps:

> Elimination of ideas
> Task and concept analysis
> Preliminary lesson description
> Evaluation and revision of the design

ELIMINATION OF IDEAS

Procedures

The first activity in this step is to eliminate ideas from both lists produced when brainstorming. There are four bases for doing this:

> characteristics of the student population
> the relationship of ideas to the subject matter and goals
> the amount of time needed to teach the content
> the restrictions of your instructional delivery system

The chart of student characteristics produced earlier in Step 1 should now be retrieved and used to consider the suitability of ideas. The primary considerations are the students' age, prerequisite skills, reading ability, typing ability, and probable interest in the ideas. For example, if your students are very young or have no typing ability, you will definitely eliminate ideas whose presentation depend on a lot of reading or typing. A more complicated consideration is whether your students have the prerequisites to learn the content. We might not retain ideas concerning telephone bills if our students have not yet learned about writing checks. Very few people have party lines, so we can assume our student would have little interest to learn about that idea, therefore it can be eliminated.

Next, consider how each idea in the first brainstorming list relates to the subject matter and your goals. Remember that in the previous step we were trying to be non-judgmental. As a result, many ideas were generated that were only remotely related to the subject area or to the original instructional goals. Now is the time to eliminate those ideas. You will recall that we did *not* discard those ideas earlier, even if they were obviously of little relevance or importance, because their presence on the list during brainstorming could have sparked some other very *relevant* and *good* ideas.

Individual ideas relate to the subject matter in terms of their relevance, their importance, and their difficulty level. The last consideration primarily refers to the number of other ideas that must be understood first. On our list, answering a telephone is not advanced because it only requires recognizing a telephone, discriminating a telephone ring from other sounds, and knowing the meaning of a ringing telephone. In contrast, dialing long-distance information is much more advanced. It requires recognizing a telephone, knowing its purpose, understanding the concept of long distance, understanding area codes, knowing how to dial, understanding access codes, looking up area codes in the telephone book, and so on. You should now eliminate ideas that are likely to be too advanced for your students or are already known by them. For example, recognizing a telephone may be a skill all your students have. You should eliminate those ideas that are not relevant to the subject or your goals, such as laws regarding annoying phone calls, and those that are simply not important, such as how to use party lines.

With respect to how much time an idea will require in a lesson, there are two main considerations. First, the total allotted lesson time is a variable that will constrain how many of your instructional ideas can be included in the lesson. Second, the time required for any particular idea must be weighed against the importance of that idea. The most important and relevant idea deserves a large proportion of the total available time. Tangential ideas, even if interesting, should be eliminated if they require a lot of the student's time; however, if time is available you may decide to include them. Of course, if only a few ideas have to be covered, each can be allotted more time. If you generated many ideas that you feel are very good and important, you should consider producing two or more lessons with a few ideas in each.

To aid in the time-allotment process, you should now list all ideas on the chart of learner characteristics that have not been eliminated. In the columns for low, medium, and high level students, indicate whether each group already knows the idea; then put estimates in the columns for time and difficulty. Note also the relative importance of each idea. Once again, you may eliminate ideas that you believe most of your students know. As the list lengthens, the comparative time required and the importance of each idea will indicate which ideas should remain and which should be eliminated or saved for another lesson.

As items are removed from the first list, which contains ideas about *what* to teach, the associated ideas can be automatically eliminated from the second list, which contains ideas about *how* to teach them. If, for example, we eliminate the idea of teaching about long distance information, we can eliminate ideas in the second list that suggest using a tutorial for that purpose.

Lastly, we must eliminate some ideas because of the restrictions and limitations of our instructional delivery system, a computer. These restrictions and limitations include the computer's input capabilities, software capabilities, and the complexity of implementing an idea. In this regard we are concerned with the list of *how* to teach, since it is the teaching methodology that is affected most directly by the delivery system.

Considerations of student input to the computer are straightforward. Most computers currently rely on the keyset and mouse for input, although touch-sensitive screens, graphics tablets, game paddles, and voice-recognition devices are available as well. If you have generated ideas that depend on such devices and your computer does not have them, those ideas must be eliminated. One of our ideas for the telephone was to use a touch-sensitive computer screen to simulate operating a touch-tone phone. Since we plan to use a Macintosh computer, such a device is not likely to be available. That particular idea must be eliminated. But a similar idea, to operate a touch-tone telephone simulation using the mouse, may be retained.

In some subject areas such as beginning reading, it is very likely that certain ideas will require voice input. Very few computers are capable of high-quality voice input at this time, so ideas requiring this input mode must be eliminated unless a viable alternative can be found.

Restrictions due to the output capabilities of the computer are also straightforward. You should become familiar with the display capabilities of your computer. How many lines and columns can it display? Can it produce circles and lines? What colors can it produce? How fast can it draw a full-screen picture? Ideas requiring screen output that exceeds the amount of text display possible, that exceeds the color or picture drawing capabilities, or that demands animations exceeding the speed at which you can move pictures around may all need to be eliminated. Ideas requiring output of speech or music may need to be eliminated if your computer does not have these capabilities.

Even though you might have special input or output devices for your computer, they may be worthless if your programming language does not have commands to utilize them. Experiment with your programming language or authoring system to determine whether it can control printers, speech synthesizers, light pens, color, or animation. If the software cannot do what you want, you must either acquire new software or eliminate ideas that are software dependent.

There is one other important consideration about input, output, and computer software. You must be concerned not only with the capabilities available on *your* computer, but also with what facilities your potential *users* will have available. If you develop a program that requires a voice-input device, *you* may be able to use it, but very few other people will. If you hope to sell your lesson, this should be a serious concern. Using non-standard hardware or software will severely limit your market.

The skills of the person doing the programming is also an important consideration. Simulations and games are usually much more difficult to program than tutorials and tests. Drills fall somewhere in between. A telephone simulation that allows long distance calls will be more difficult to program than one that can accept only local calls. A simulation that includes operator-assisted calls will be harder still. Most people tend to underestimate the difficulty and time involved in programming an idea.

Keep in mind that if good ideas must be eliminated because they are not possible on your computer, those ideas may still be worthy of implementation using other delivery systems.

Having eliminated many of the ideas generated during brainstorming, a short list of the best and most important ideas remains. This includes *content* ideas and *teaching method* ideas. These remaining ideas should be listed on your chart of student characteristics with estimates of students' familiarity with the topic, the time required to teach the topic, and the difficulty of the topic.

Telephone Example

For most of the remaining activities we will not include a *complete* script of the process for our example, as it would be very long. A sample will suffice to illustrate our points.

The first activity of this step is the elimination of ideas. You may wish at this point to refer back to Lists 1 and 2 of ideas generated about telephone operation and how to teach this information. The following are *some* of the ideas eliminated from those lists and the reasons for eliminating them.

Idea Eliminated	Reason for Elimination
recognizing a telephone	too easy, probably known
answering a telephone	too easy
how to use party lines	rarely needed
what to do when the phone is not working	rare
using pay telephones	not needed yet, advanced
credit card calls	not needed
telephone bills	would take too long, will be taught in another lesson
history of the telephone	not of interest to students and not useful for phone operation
simulate dialing a touch-tone phone with a touch-sensitive screen	not possible on delivery system
use a synthetic voice device to carry out a simulated vocal conversation	not possible on delivery system

TASK AND CONCEPT ANALYSIS

Definitions and Issues

The remaining ideas must now be analyzed to determine a suitable teaching sequence and to produce the necessary details of the lesson. There are many ways to determine sequence and detail, and we will not attempt to cover all of them. For more details on analysis in instructional design we recommend Briggs (1977), Fleming & Levie (1978), Anderson & Faust (1973), and Merrill & Tennyson (1977). We will describe two methods of analysis that are frequently useful, namely task analysis and concept analysis. Task analysis is a procedure for analyzing the things a student must learn to *do,* such as behaviors and skills. Concept analysis is a procedure for analyzing the content itself, the information the student must *understand.*

Most subject matter benefits from task analysis or concept analysis or both. We are usually interested in students understanding particular content, for which concept analysis is useful. We are also interested in most cases with students developing specific skills related to the information, for which task analysis is useful. However, these methods are not applicable in all situations. Furthermore, the task and concept analysis procedures vary from one application to another and differ according to the person doing the analysis. The following two sections should be considered a general introduction to these procedures. We encourage you to become familiar with the details and variations of these analytic methods by reading the works of other educators.

Procedures

Task Analysis.   Task analysis is an integral part of the ISD and similar instructional design models (Gagne & Briggs, 1979; Briggs, 1977; and Anderson & Faust, 1973). Its purpose is to break complex skills down into component skills, so as to determine an effective teaching sequence. A good teaching sequence should first teach skills that only require the student to use and combine skills they already have. The teaching sequence should proceed to combine these new skills to teach more complex ones, continuing in this fashion until the student finally learns the skills which comprise the terminal objective of the lesson. To teach a student to operate a new type of camera, for instance, you might begin by teaching how to load the film, how to adjust the f-stop, how to focus, and how to snap the shutter. Later in the teaching sequence these skills would be combined, and eventually the student would learn to "use the camera to take pictures."

Although the goal of a task analysis is to determine an efficient sequence for teaching the content, we actually begin at the end with the terminal skills and break them down into component skills. We then break those skills down further, and so on, until we reach a collection of skills that the student has already acquired or that the student can perform simply by being asked. These are often called the entering skills or behaviors for the lesson.

Let us illustrate the process with an example. Suppose you are preparing a lesson for a cooking class. The goal of the lesson is to teach how to make a loaf of bread. First, state the terminal objective, *make a loaf of bread.* Then ask whether that is a skill the students already possess. If the answer is no, break it down into its component or enabling skills. We do not mean the lowest level skills or the smallest steps possible, but the largest sub-steps that are still smaller than the objective of making a loaf of bread. A reasonable division might be *prepare the dough* and *cook the dough.* Now ask whether each subskill is one that the student already possesses, and if not, repeat the process.

At the next level, for example, you could break down *prepare the dough* into *assemble ingredients, mix ingredients, knead dough,* and *let the dough rise.* Similarly, you could break down *cook dough* into *prepare the oven, prepare the pan,* and *bake the dough.* Written on paper, your analysis resembles a tree. Actually it is an upside-down tree, with the single trunk—the terminal objective—at the top, the main branches—the first subdivisions— extending from the trunk, and with successively more and smaller branches developing farther down. Figure 8–1 shows the tree so far.

For each branch, repeat the process of asking whether these are skills the student already possesses or can do without instruction. Circle skills that can be done to signify that they need not be analyzed further into component skills. All circled skills, then, indicate students' previously acquired *entry-level skills.* Skills that students cannot currently perform should be broken down further. *Assemble ingredients* can be subdivided into *purchase ingredients* and *measure ingredients. Mix ingredients* can be broken down into a number of other steps such as *checking the quality of the yeast,* and *sifting together dry ingredients. Let the dough rise* can be subdivided into *where to raise dough,* and *testing to see if dough is completely risen. Prepare the oven* can be broken into *preheating* and *steaming the oven. Preparing the pan* is subdivided into *selecting a pan, greasing the pan,* and *placing dough in the pan. Baking dough* is subdivided into *placing properly in the oven, timing, testing whether cooked,* and *removal from the oven.* Figure 8–2 shows the task analysis tree after another subdivision of skills.

Continue this process until *all* branches end with circled entry-level skills for your expected students. For the example of baking bread, these might be skills like *buying flour, measuring dry ingredients, measuring liquid ingredients, mixing water and yeast, kneading, greasing a bowl,* and *reading the thermometer.*

Another task analysis method is to produce a flowchart that illustrates what someone must do to perform an activity. This analysis method is very useful

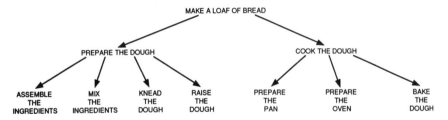

Figure 8-1 The beginning of a task analysis for making bread.

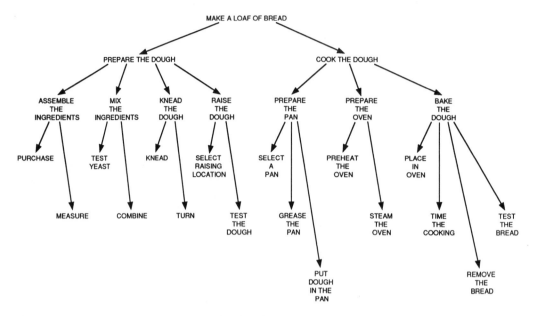

Figure 8-2 The task analysis of baking bread continued another step.

following the one just described. Figures 8–3 and 8–4 show flowcharts which describe parts of the process of making bread. While Figures 8–1 and 8–2 show the analysis into components of the skill, Figures 8–3 and 8–4 show the integration of the components into the complete skill as the student must learn to perform it.

In summary, a task analysis begins with the most superordinate skill, your terminal objective. You break this down into successively subordinate skills, continuing to do so until you reach the entry-level skills you expect that your students already possess. The lesson itself will proceed in the opposite direction, teaching the student to combine entry-level skills into successively more complex skills, and eventually the terminal objective. Producing a flowchart of how the skills will be acquired helps determine the sequence of instruction.

Concept Analysis. Concept analysis may be used like task analysis to analyze the skills we wish to teach. However, it is primarily used to analyze the content. Proponents of concept analysis for instructional design argue that while there are many ways for information to be organized, the best way is to view content as concepts and their interrelationships. Instructional sequences, then, are centered around the teaching of important concepts.

For instance, there are many ways to subdivide the subject of world history. It can be subdivided into time periods, such as years or centuries; geographical areas, such as countries or continents; or famous people, such as Alexander the Great, Napoleon, or George Washington. Looking at world history from a conceptual point of view, you might subdivide history into concepts such as *govern-*

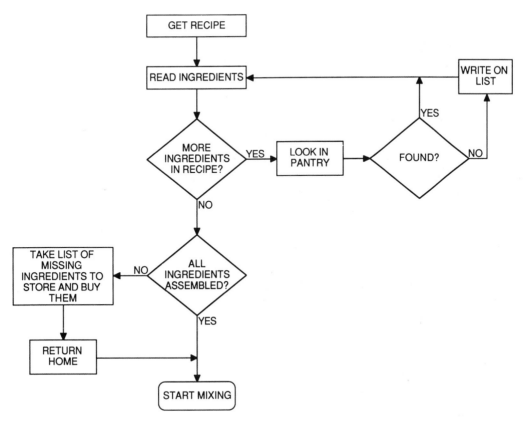

Figure 8-3 Task analysis flowchart for one aspect of making bread—assembling ingredients.

ment, colonization, war, and *trade.* Although a concept analysis of world history would certainly include the history of particular countries and the chronological structure of history in the final instruction, it might emphasize the ways in which concepts like governmental form and colonization have shaped history. Teaching students the major concepts of a field of study is assumed to be essential to their understanding of that field.

The value of concept analysis is easy to see. Regardless of how you subdivide and teach a subject, you will invariably encounter concepts the student must learn. Some of the ideas listed during a brainstorming session will usually be concepts or contain concepts, and concept analysis is a way to produce effective teaching sequences for those ideas. Concepts from the telephone example brainstorming session include *telephone, busy signal, dial tone, ring, touch-tone phone, coin-operated phone, phone number, area code, local,* and *long distance.* Some of these may already be familiar to the student and need not be taught. Some, such as *dial tone,* may not be familiar, but are easy to teach and do not require a lengthy analysis. Others, such as *local number* versus *long-distance number,* may be more complex or more easily confused with other concepts, and therefore require analysis. The process of concept analysis will often help to produce teaching sequences for such ideas.

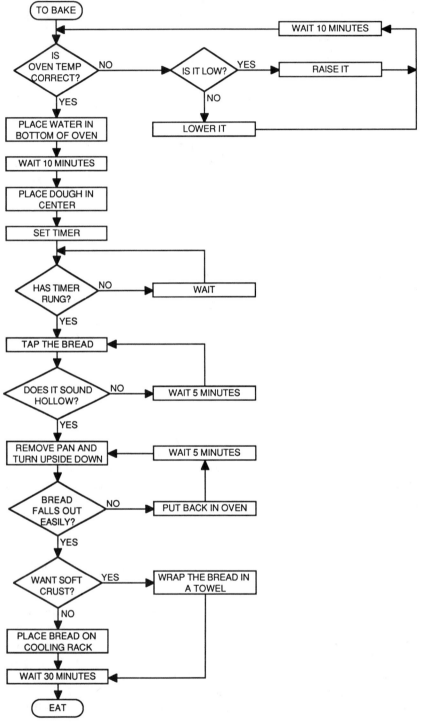

Figure 8-4 Task analysis flowchart for another aspect of making bread—baking.

The following description conveys the general procedure of concept analysis. Again, the reader should realize that different instructional developers do concept analysis in different ways, and that a concept analysis will vary from one situation to another.

In order to identify concepts in your subject matter it is important to know what a concept is. A concept is defined as a group of objects, events, or relationships that all share a set of common features. Examples of concepts are *telephone, man, woman, adjective, running, circle, above, war, sad, love, away, work,* and *cold.*

Each individual member of a class, or concept, has a number of characteristics. Those characteristics that are common to all instances of a concept and are essential to being an instance of the concept are called the *relevant features.* The entire set of relevant features is what distinguishes the particular instances of a concept (those things belonging to the class) from the non-instances of a concept (those things not belonging to the class). For example, all telephones share a set of essential features that includes a mouthpiece that receives your voice, a speaker through which you hear the other person's voice, a dialing mechanism for choosing a number to call, a bell or similar signaling device, and are used for communication with other people who have telephones.

It is important to realize that many instances of a concept may have other shared characteristics that, although they may be important, are not the features that define the concept. Most telephones are plastic, but that is not what makes them telephones. Similarly, they usually have a common shape. These features may be classified as incidental or irrelevant. Incidental features are those that many and perhaps all instances of a concept possess, but which are not necessary. Irrelevant features may be possessed by instances of a concept, but are neither necessary nor common. The relevant, irrelevant, and incidental features of a concept are not always obvious and not always constant. At one time a rotary dial might have been considered an essential feature of a telephone, but with the introduction of touch-tone telephones this has become an irrelevant feature. Similarly, being connected with wires could have been regarded as an essential feature, but this too is no longer true.

The purpose of identifying relevant, irrelevant, and incidental features is to help students discriminate instances and non-instances of a concept. We would not want students mistaking radios for telephones, which is possible if our concept definition were faulty. Like telephones, radios are used for two-way audio communication over a distance. However, telephones have an additional feature—the communication can be targeted. That is, a radio transmission is accessible to anyone on the same frequency, but each telephone has a uniquely identifying number.

As you can see, different concepts may be confused because they possess shared features. Defining concepts so they are unambiguous to students is not easy. It is not just a matter of stating what the relevant and irrelevant features are. You must teach the range and limits of these features as well. Telephones may vary in color, price, shape, construction materials, the sound of their ring, and the dialing mechanism. You want your students to recognize all of these as being telephones despite these differences. Conversely, you do not want students identifying radios and doorbells as telephones. Although they are similar in some ways, they do not share all the essential features of telephones.

Knowing the concept *telephone* requires both recognizing a wide variety of very different looking objects as being telephones, and recognizing some things that are very similar to telephones as *not* being telephones. As discussed in Chapter 2, the presence of many relevant features makes instances of a concept more clear and non-instances less clear, while the presence of many irrelevant features makes instances less clear and non-instances clearer. The presence of many incidental features tends to make both instances and non-instances less easy to classify. It is a useful exercise to try to define a telephone so that all telephones would be included and all other devices excluded as examples of the concept.

Before doing concept analysis you must identify concepts that require teaching. Words or ideas that are likely to be confused or seen as similar by students are the best candidates. Examples in telephone dialing would be area code and access code.

The first activity in a concept analysis is to identify the relevant and irrelevant features. All other features may be considered incidental features. Next you should identify a number of instances and non-instances of the concept. Some of these should be clear, while others should be less clear. A clear instance of a telephone is a typical plastic desk telephone. An unclear instance might be a telephone that looks like Mickey Mouse. Although these are telephones, novices might not recognize them as such, hence their classification as being unclear instances.

A clear non-instance of a telephone is a book. There is little about a book that would cause a novice to confuse it with a telephone. Needless to say there are plenty of clear non-instances of telephones. An unclear non-instance of a telephone is a radio, an intercom, or a doorbell. These are not telephones, but because they have similar characteristics novices may confuse them with telephones. To teach most concepts, it is useful to have all four of these: clear instances, clear non-instances, unclear instances, and unclear non-instances.

After doing the concept analysis you must produce a teaching sequence. In general this is done by sequencing examples and non-examples while identifying them as such. In some cases it is useful to tell the student at the start what the relevant features are. First show a number of clear instances, identifying them as examples of the concept, and a number of clear non-instances, in order to focus attention on the presence or absence of relevant features. After the student can demonstrably discriminate between clear instances and non-instances, such as telephones from books, present unclear instances and then unclear non-instances, identifying them as such. For instance, we would show things like Mickey Mouse telephones and radios until the students could correctly classify them.

For more information about concept analysis and its place in the instructional design process, see Engelmann (1969, 1980) and Merrill and Tennyson (1977).

Computer Tools

Several computer tools can facilitate task and concept analysis. *Problem Analysis* (Wells & Ebersberger, 1987) is a small expert system for IBM microcomputers based upon Zemke & Kramlinger's (1987) *Figuring Things Out: A Trainer's Guide to Needs and Task Analysis,* which helps the developer choose among analysis techniques. The *Spectrum Job Task Analysis Database* (Dufault & Trollip, 1989) was designed for doing task analysis on a large number of hierarchically related tasks. Figures 8–5 and 8–6 show examples from *Problem Analysis,* and the *Spectrum Job Task Analysis Database.*

Telephone Example

Some of these ideas may be subjected to a task analysis. As an example, consider an analysis of *dialing a local number.* This skill can be split into *preparing to*

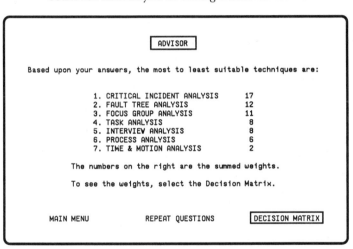

Figure 8-5 *Problem Analysis.*
(Courtesy of Park Row Software)

```
                          ┌─────────┐
                          │ ADVISOR │
                          └─────────┘

Based upon your answers, the most to least suitable techniques are:


            1. CRITICAL INCIDENT ANALYSIS      17
            2. FAULT TREE ANALYSIS             12
            3. FOCUS GROUP ANALYSIS            11
            4. TASK ANALYSIS                    8
            5. INTERVIEW ANALYSIS               8
            6. PROCESS ANALYSIS                 6
            7. TIME & MOTION ANALYSIS           2

        The numbers on the right are the summed weights.

        To see the weights, select the Decision Matrix.



    MAIN MENU          REPEAT QUESTIONS      ┌─────────────────┐
                                             │ DECISION MATRIX │
                                             └─────────────────┘
```

```
                    ┌────────────────────────┐
                    │ ADVISOR Decision Matrix │
                    └────────────────────────┘
                                Ans  TA  T&M  PA  CI  FTA  FG   In
Job/Task/Product well-defined    Y    5   5    5  -5   3   -5   -1
Large amount of diversity        Y   -3  -3   -3   5   1    3    5
Lots of decision-making          N   -1  -1    5   3   3    1    1
Speed an important part          N    0   5    1   0   0    0    0
Intuition an important part      N    0  -3   -3   3   1    1    1
Task is repetitious              Y    0   3    1   0   0    0    0
Study focus: problems, errors    Y    1   1    3   3   5    3    1
Focus: performance differences   Y    1   0    0   5   0    3    1
Focus on quantitative data       N   -1   5   -1  -1   5   -1    1
Information providers scarce     N    0  -1   -1   1   0    5    1
Info. providers distributed      N    0  -1   -1   3   0   -1    5
Skilled analysts conduct study   Y    5   1    5   5   5    5    1
Involvement is important         N    0   0    0   0   0    0    3
Time available is limited        N   -1  -1   -1   1  -1    2    2
Budget is limited                N   -1  -1   -1   1  -1   -1    1


    If you want to change answers or weights, select the change option.
    If you want the new values to be permanent, select the save option.

┌──────────┐
│ RANKINGS │    QUESTIONS    CHANGE VALUES    SAVE VALUES    MAIN MENU
└──────────┘
```

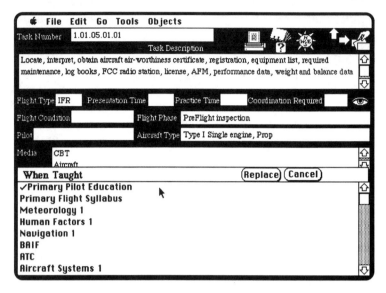

Figure 8-6 *Spectrum Job Task Analysis Database. (Courtesy of the University of North Dakota Center for Aerospace Sciences)*

dial and *dialing. Preparing to dial* can be split into *lifting the receiver, listening for the dial tone,* and *knowing the number to dial. Dialing* can be split into *placing the finger, turning the dial,* and *releasing the dial.* Some of these subskills can be further split up but we will continue with only one. *Listening for dial tone* could be divided into *holding the correct part of the receiver to the ear* and *discriminating the dial tone from other tones.* At some point, we will have subskills which are already known to the student, such as reading the number to dial or subskills which the student can easily do on direct command, such as putting the finger in the hole or touching the button with the correct number. The task analysis is then complete.

Some ideas may benefit from a concept analysis. A simple example is the concept *operator.* The essential features are that the operator is a person who is reached by dialing *0.* Irrelevant features are the sex of the operator, that you hear a voice, or that operators are helpful. A clear instance is a woman you talk to when you dial *0.* A clear non-instance is your brother. An unclear instance is an operator who is a man (although this is becoming less of an unclear example). And finally an unclear non-instance is the person you get when you dial directory assistance (411 in the United States).

PRELIMINARY LESSON DESCRIPTION

Definitions and Issues

The previous activities have served to analyze content and instructional ideas into small pieces. For a lesson to come together and work as a whole, these ideas must still be integrated. Furthermore, they must be integrated in light of what we know about how people learn. Hoffman & Medsker (1983) suggest an activity they call *instructional analysis* that promotes such integration. Instructional analysis includes identification of types of learning, of procedures students must learn, of subordinate and supportive skills, and integration of all of these in a learning map. The learning map shows the rough structure and sequence of a lesson with types of learning, procedures, and skills identified. To this idea of instructional analysis and building a learning map we add a few components, namely choosing a lesson methodology and making decisions about instructional factors as identified in the methodology chapters of Part 1. The learning map thus becomes a *preliminary lesson description* of the content, sequence, and characteristics of a lesson in pictorial form.

Procedures

Identifying Types of Learning. Gagne (1985) has identified several types of learning (verbal learning, motor skills, problem solving, rule learning, concept learning, attitudes, and cognitive strategies) and maintained that they require different instructional techniques. Thus, identifying types of learning within the content will help determine the methodologies and other instructional factors. A good way to identify the types of learning is to ask what it is the students are learning to do (Hoffman & Medsker, 1983). Verbal learning is demonstrated by students being able to *state* information. Attitudes are demonstrated by students *choosing* to do something. Problem solving is represented by students *generating* solutions or procedures to find solutions. Rule learning is demonstrated by students *applying* rules and *demonstrating* principles. Concept learning is demonstrated by students being able to *label* or *classify* things as members or non-members of a class.

Choosing a Methodology. The next activity is to make some final decisions about instructional methodology. You may already have made this choice in the process of eliminating ideas in the previous step. If you eliminated enough ideas, the decision about methodology may be complete.

If a decision about a methodology has not yet occurred, it should be finalized now. At this point the decision will be a function of 1) the ideas previously generated, 2) your observations about the limitations of your delivery system, 3) considerations about student level and motivation, and 4) the types of learning involved. We do not wish to give strict rules for deciding on a methodology. As we have said before, we consider it important to be creative concerning the design of computer-based instruction. However, any decision should be based in part on how the various methodologies serve the four phases of instruction.

Recall from Part 1 that tutorials generally provide for the first two phases of instruction (presentation and guidance); drills for the third phase (practice); tests for the fourth phase (assessment of learning); simulations for any combination of the four phases, usually either presentation and guidance, practice, or testing; and games for the third phase (practice). The type or types of learning expected is also critical. Tutorials are most used for concept and rule learning, drills and games for verbal learning, and simulations for skills and attitudes. Simulations also appear to be most effective for enhancing transfer of learning while games for enhancing student motivation. Lastly, lessons that *combine* methodologies will have a greater likelihood of being effective.

Identifying Procedures and Required Skills.

Even when learning consists primarily of concepts, rules, or verbal information, there are likely to be procedures and associated skills necessary for success in a lesson. In the sciences, problem solving is usually accompanied by mathematical procedures. In the arts and humanities, creative design or writing is often necessary. Hoffman & Medsker suggest that the designer should distinguish simple procedures from complex ones (which combine different kinds of learning) and determine prerequisites (usually motor skills or intellectual skills). Using a method similar to what we suggested under task analysis, the designer should identify the subordinate or superordinate relationships between procedures and other information.

Factor Decisions.

The next activity should be very rigorous. Having decided on a methodology or combination of methodologies for different parts of your lesson, you should now systematically make decisions about your treatment of all of the factors relevant to the chosen methodologies. At this point in the design process you would consult Appendix A to review those factors and perhaps reread sections of Part 1 to review our recommendations regarding them. Pay particular attention to those factors that are important in all methodologies and to those which we have indicated have received the most research attention. Some of the most important factors are feedback, question types, directions, student control, motivation, judging, simulation fidelity, and the use of graphics.

Sequence Description.

The last activity in organizing ideas is to produce a preliminary description of the sequence of the lesson. Hoffman & Medsker's *learning map* (Figure 8–7) is one kind of preliminary description. The nature of this depends on the methodology. For a tutorial it should include the general order in which students will encounter directions, presentations, interactions, remediation, and the closing. It need not contain the details such as branching based on student performance, which will be elaborated in detail in a later step. The preliminary sequence for a drill should indicate most of the same information as for tutorials, with additional information about the order of events for each item and a simple description of how items will be selected. The preliminary sequence for simulations and games will be more complicated. For simulations it should include the directions, opening scene, presentations, student interactions, and the closing. For games it should also include the presentation of rules, events which enhance competition or the entertaining aspects of the game, and what happens when someone wins or loses the game. The preliminary sequence for tests should include the order in which students encounter the directions

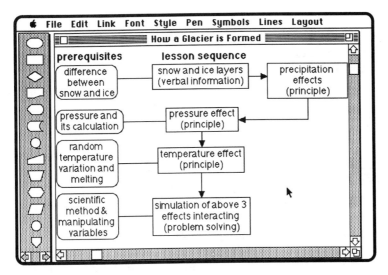

Figure 8-7 A preliminary sequence description using *Mac-Flow,* similar to Hoffman & Medsker's learning map. *(Courtesy of Mainstay)*

and practice items, enter the test, receive real items, leave the test, and receive the results of the test.

Rather than writing the preliminary sequence description, we recommend drawing a diagram, such as a simple flowchart, to describe the preliminary sequence. The major events of the lesson may be briefly depicted as boxes in a flowchart with arrows indicating the order in which the student will encounter them. The preliminary sequence description is a greatly simplified draft version of the final lesson sequence. Its purpose is to integrate the analysis which has occurred so far, and to serve as a transition into producing a flowchart.

Computer Tools

Computer tools that can facilitate the preliminary lesson description are the flowcharting and diagramming tools such as *Design* (Albright & Snow, 1987), *Learning Tool* (Kozma & Roekel, 1986), *MacFlow* (Bertrand & Terpstra, 1988), and *EasyFlow* (Farnell & McDowell, 1987). All are useful for generating a preliminary lesson sequence diagram or learning map. Figure 8–7 shows a preliminary sequence description using *MacFlow.*

Telephone Example

The next activity in our example is identifying the types of learning relevant to the ideas that remain. The following table shows *some* of the remaining ideas and the types of learning they represent.

Remaining Ideas	Types of Learning
dialing local calls	simple skill
dialing long-distance calls	complex skill
dialing for information	concept and procedure learning
understanding area codes	concept learning
distinguish ringing and busy signals	concept learning
telephone courtesy	attitude learning
using the yellow pages	intellectual skill
looking up a telephone number	intellectual skill

We next choose a methodology for our intended lesson. Because we want to introduce students to telephones and to provide practice using them, we have decided to use a combination of methodologies, a tutorial followed by a drill-simulation. By drill-simulation we mean that we will have the computer simulate a telephone for the purpose of drilling the student on various aspects of its operation. We will alternate between short tutorials and drill-simulations, starting with simple tasks such as dialing the operator, progressing to harder ones such as dialing a local number, and ending with the most difficult such as dialing a long distance number.

Next we exhaustively consider the instructional factors relevant to our chosen methodologies and make decisions about them. We demonstrate this with a few of the factors relevant to *drills* for those parts of the lesson where the student practices dialing the simulated telephone.

Factor	Decision
getting initial attention	draw a phone on the screen and have it ring
directions	text directions at the bottom of the screen directing the student to use the mouse to dial
mode of presentation	pictorial and sound, number appears textually as it is dialed
color	black and white for standard Macintosh
timing of feedback	not immediate; natural feedback such as wrong number or no connection
response type	pointing at numbers to dial
response mode	pointing with a mouse
provision for help	yes, by pointing at a HELP button

. . . and so on for all factors.

Making decisions about all factors is time consuming, but is very important. By doing it you will find out many of the details of the lesson's operation and content that you have overlooked until this time, and that many designers overlook completely.

Lastly we produce a preliminary sequence that will aid in the later steps of flowcharting and storyboarding. Figure 8–8 shows a preliminary sequence which includes some of the elements recommended by Hoffman & Medsker (1983).

In Figure 8–8 we see the preliminary sequence: begin with a tutorial, assess learning in the first section, demonstrate dialing, allow dialing practice with a simulation, give a tutorial about long-distance dialing and seeking help from an operator, assess what the student has learned about long-distance dialing, and end with a segment on telephone courtesy. We also see that certain parts of the lesson are identified as verbal learning, concept learning, attitude learning, and procedures. Prerequisite skilis are identified and noted where they are relevant.

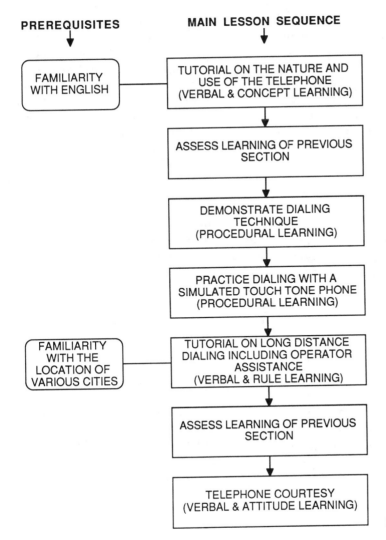

PREREQUISITES

MAIN LESSON SEQUENCE

FAMILIARITY WITH ENGLISH

TUTORIAL ON THE NATURE AND USE OF THE TELEPHONE (VERBAL & CONCEPT LEARNING)

ASSESS LEARNING OF PREVIOUS SECTION

DEMONSTRATE DIALING TECHNIQUE (PROCEDURAL LEARNING)

PRACTICE DIALING WITH A SIMULATED TOUCH TONE PHONE (PROCEDURAL LEARNING)

FAMILIARITY WITH THE LOCATION OF VARIOUS CITIES

TUTORIAL ON LONG DISTANCE DIALING INCLUDING OPERATOR ASSISTANCE (VERBAL & RULE LEARNING)

ASSESS LEARNING OF PREVIOUS SECTION

TELEPHONE COURTESY (VERBAL & ATTITUDE LEARNING)

Figure 8-8 A learning map.

EVALUATION AND REVISION OF THE DESIGN

Definitions and Issues

The activities of task or concept analysis, identifying learning, and describing preliminary sequence are usually done in some form by most instructional developers. The activity of making decisions about instructional factors is one of our methods of quality control. In Part 1 we discussed these instructional factors in detail and showed how, in large part, they determine the instructional effectiveness of any particular lesson. Again, we stress that it is important to make deliberate decisions about these factors in light of the information presented in Part 1. If you fail to make deliberate decisions, you are nevertheless making decisions. Frequently, such a non-decision results in the same poor methodology that many other computer-based instruction developers have used with lessons in the past.

Making deliberate decisions about instructional factors only increases the probability of producing a good first draft. It does not guarantee it, and certainly does not guarantee that the lesson will successfully teach. That guarantee comes through evaluation and revision—the empirical approach to instructional development.

At the start of the development process, the products available for review are few and rather vague. Thus, the evaluation procedures are general in nature. It is nevertheless essential that evaluation takes place. A poor learning sequence is easy to discard if discovered early. If discovered later after a lot of development has taken place on the computer, revision will be time-consuming and difficult.

Procedures

The primary method of evaluation at this point is peer review. The content should be reviewed by subject-matter experts who assess if the goals chosen are appropriate and if the content in the learning map is accurate and likely to accomplish those goals. Other instructional designers should assess if the sequence depicted in the learning map will facilitate learning, if the methodology and media chosen are appropriate, if the ideas remaining after brainstorming and idea elimination are good ideas, if all prerequisite skills and knowledge have been identified, and if good decisions were made about instructional factors.

Computer Tools

The computer tools useful during revision of the design are the same ones used in the previous steps. More importantly, it should be emphasized that the extent to which computer tools are used in earlier steps will determine the ease with which revision can take place. If documents have been drafted with a word processor and learning maps with a graphics program, the process of revising and improving them will be easier and faster. If additional brainstorming, task analysis, or learning about the subject matter are required, the same tools for writing, learning, and organizing that were used previously are used again.

Telephone Example

For design evaluation and revision, we give our preliminary lesson sequence (learning map) and intermediate documents such as the brainstorming lists and description of goals, to several people. These include a content expert (for example, a secretary-receptionist who is very familiar with telephone operation and use), an instructional designer, and our client, the person who is paying us to develop the lesson or who is typical of people we believe will want to purchase and use the lesson.

We go over these documents together, encouraging criticism and new ideas. From the content expert we seek evidence of any content errors. We are informed that there have been many changes in area codes necessitated by the growing number of telephones. There are also changes in dialing information and the use of access codes for long-distance calling. We are also told that some operators today are not people, but a computer with a synthesized voice. Because of this we might need to make modifications since our students cannot get the same kind of help from a computer that they can get from a human.

Going over our plans with another instructional designer we are told that our introductory section should include a description of different types of phones and our simulation section should emphasize access codes. The instructional designer also suggests using digital sound and that the final assessment should be done as a simulation rather than as a set of questions.

Our clients inform us that their major concern is that their employees are able to use telephones for long distance, and they do not see this sufficiently addressed in the instruction. This is a problem with our definition of goals and requires that we revise Step 1.

Subsequently, we add goals, which requires more brainstorming, we collect more and newer resources, we learn more about the content, and we redo our analyses, including a new preliminary lesson plan. Having made more than just minor changes, we return to our peer evaluators for another review. The cycle of steps 1 through 5 *must* continue until all our evaluators, especially our clients, indicate that the plan looks good. Only then can we proceed with confidence.

CONCLUSION

The design step is critical to the effectiveness of the lesson. During this step we eliminate ideas on content and methodology from our brainstorming lists. We analyze the content and skills we want to teach and establish and map the relationships between the various parts of the content. We outline the content and sequencing of the lesson, and we have our plan reviewed by colleagues and clients.

This step is not complete until all reviewers are satisfied with the lesson plan and content. It is always worth the effort to complete this step properly. Too much haste will inevitably result in a less effective product or in unnecessary time being wasted later. It is much easier to revise things on paper than to revise a computer program.

REFERENCES AND BIBLIOGRAPHY

ALBRIGHT, R., & SNOW, J. (1987). *Design*. [Computer Program]. Cambridge, MA: Meta Software.

ANDERSON, R.C., & FAUST, G.W. (1973). *Educational Psychology: The Science of Instruction and Learning.* New York: Dodd, Mead and Company.

BERTRAND, P.A., & TERPSTRA, D. (1988). *MacFlow.* [Computer Program]. Los Angeles: Mainstay.

BRIGGS, L.J. (Ed.). (1977). *Instructional Design: Principles and Applications.* Englewood Cliffs, NJ: Educational Technology Publications.

CARLISLE, K.E. (1983). The process of task analysis: Integrating training's multiple methods. *Journal of Instructional Development, 6*(4), 31–35.

DUFAULT, G., & TROLLIP, S.R. (1989). *Spectrum Job Task Analysis Database.* [Computer Program]. Grand Forks, ND: University of North Dakota Center for Aerospace Sciences.

ENGELMANN, S. (1969). *Conceptual Learning.* Sioux Falls, SD: Adapt Press, Inc.

ENGELMANN, S. (1980). *Direct Instruction.* Englewood Cliffs, NJ: Educational Technology Publications.

ENGELMANN, S., & CARNINE, D. (1982.). *Theory of Instruction: Principles and Applications.* New York: Irvington Publishers.

FARNELL, C., & McDOWELL, R. (1987). *Easyflow.* [Computer Program]. Kingston, Ontario, Canada: Haventree Software.

FLEMING, M., & LEVIE, W.H. (1978). *Instructional Message Design: Principles from the Behavioral Sciences.* Englewood Cliffs, NJ: Educational Technology Publications.

FOSHAY, W.R. (1983). Alternative methods of task analysis: A comparison of three techniques. *Journal of Instructional Development, 6*(4), 2–9.

GAGNÉ, R.M. (1985). *The Conditions of Learning and Theory of Instruction. 4th ed.* New York: Holt, Rinehart and Winston.

GAGNÉ, R.M., & BRIGGS, L.J. (1979). *Principles of Instructional Design.* New York: Holt, Rinehart and Winston.

HOFFMAN, C.K., & MEDSKER, K.L. (1983). Instructional analysis: The missing link between task analysis and objectives. *Journal of Instructional Development, 6*(4), 17–23.

JONASSEN, D.H., & HANNUM, W.H. (1986). Analysis of task analysis procedures. *Journal of Instructional Development, 9*(2), 2–12.

KEARSLEY, G. (1988). Beyond authoring: Software tools can help manage program development. *Instructional Delivery Systems, 2*(3), 15, 18–20.

KOZMA, R.B., & ROEKEL, J.V. (1986). *Learning Tool.* [Computer Program]. Ann Arbor, MI: Arborworks, Inc.

MERRILL, M.D., & TENNYSON, R.D. (1977). *Teaching Concepts: An Instructional Design Guide.* Englewood Cliffs, NJ: Educational Technology Publications.

MERRILL, P.F. (1978). Hierarchical & information processing task analysis: A comparison. *Journal of Instructional Development, 1*(2), 35–40.

RODRIGUEZ, S. R. (1988). Needs assessment and analysis: Tools for change. *Journal of Instructional Development, 11*(1), 23–28.

WELLS, J., & EBERSBERGER, W.S. (1987). *Problem Analysis.* [Computer Program]. La Jolla, CA: Park Row Software.

ZEMKE, R., & KRAMLINGER, T. (1987). *Figuring Things Out: A Trainer's Guide to Needs and Task Analysis.* Reading, MA: Addison-Wesley.

SUMMARY OF DESIGN

Eliminate ideas based on student characteristics, subject matter, time, and delivery system limitations.

Analyze the ideas that remain to fill out the details of the lesson.

Identify types of learning that will be required in the lesson.

Choose a methodology or combination of methodologies based on the types of learning involved and the motivation of the student.

Identify procedures and skills that will be required of or learned by the students.

Make decisions about treatment of all the instructional factors for the methodologies employed and the ideas they will be applied to in the lesson.

Integrate the results of the above four activities in a preliminary lesson description and sequence diagram.

Have content experts and clients evaluate the content.

Have instructional designers evaluate the brainstorming lists, factor decisions, and preliminary lesson description.

Revise the results of previous steps until content experts and instructional designers are satisfied with the quality of the design.

9

FLOWCHARTING

DEFINITIONS AND ISSUES

The previous step ended with the evaluation of a draft plan for a lesson and a graphic or textual description of the content, methodology, and sequence. This chapter describes Step 6, flowcharting, while the next one describes Step 7, storyboarding. Flowcharts are a bird's-eye view showing the structure and sequence of the lesson, while storyboards show the details, what students see. We therefore recommend flowcharting first to lay out the complete plan and follow with storyboarding to fill in the details. In practice, the order of events is more fluid. Flowcharting and storyboarding may occur simultaneously because changes in one require modifications to the other.

A flowchart, as its name implies, is a chart or diagram of how the lesson progresses or flows. It should depict not merely the lesson sequence from beginning to end, but all possible decisions throughout. Flowcharts are not the only way of diagramming a computer program (see Pace & Pace [1987] for several others), and there is disagreement as to the degree to which flowcharting improves program development (Shneiderman, Mayer, McKay, & Heller, 1977). However, we have found flowcharting to be especially useful for CBI programs, which are in many ways different than other computer applications such as business or scientific tools. We find them especially useful for novice or occasional programmers, which instructional designers typically are. We therefore encourage flowcharting as an integral part of CBI development.

Detailed flowcharting can be very difficult. For this reason we suggest a procedure of creating flowcharts in a series of increasingly elaborated forms. A Level-1 flowchart is a one-page overview of lesson sequence and method. A Level-2 flowchart adds essential decisions and branching. A Level-3 flowchart adds all storyboard references, calculations, branching, information management, and user control.

Not all CBI programs require the detail of a Level-3 flowchart. The level of detail required depends on the complexity of the lesson being developed, on whether you are using computerized flowcharting software, and on the tools you will be using to implement the lesson on the computer.

Simple lessons, such as a tutorials, generally require only Level-1 and Level-2 flowcharts, because many of the sequences and procedures are repetitious. In such cases it is sufficient to show the overall sequence and primary decisions such as menu choices or requests for help.

Drills and tests are slightly more complex. In addition to basic procedures common to all lessons, such as the opening, directions, and data management, they follow a single algorithm over and over. Such an algorithm uses a set of rules to choose the next item, administer it, judge the student response, administer feedback, and store data. The algorithm repeats itself until no items remain and lesson closing procedures are called. For such a program, the flowchart must describe not only the basic procedures but the primary algorithm as well. Drills and tests require a Level-2 flowchart with extra detail for the primary algorithm.

Simulations and games are more complicated. As we have seen, simulations must contain a model of some phenomenon such as a physical process or social interaction. This is typically a complex set of mathematical or logical rules describing phenomenon behavior under various circumstances. In addition, the usual aspects of lesson sequence, user control, data management, and so on are present. Simulations require a Level-3 flowchart, describing in much greater detail the internal model and all computerized decisions, calculations, displays and interactions.

Games can vary from being moderately to very complex. As we have seen, some are simply drills with an entertaining context. These, like drills, require only a Level-2 flowchart. The flowchart must include elements such as the rules, scorekeeping, and turn-taking. Others are *simulations* with an entertaining context. These have all the complexity of a simulation plus rules, directions, scorekeeping, determining turns, and deciding the winner. These require a detailed, Level-3 flowchart.

Also relevant to the level of flowcharting is whether you will be using computerized flowcharting tools. *Easyflow* (Farnell & McDowell, 1987) on the IBM and *MacFlow* (Bertrand & Terpstra, 1988) on the Macintosh are two such programs. They facilitate creating and revising flowcharts in the same way a word processing program facilitates writing and revising text. Flowcharting by hand is *very* tedious. Any small change in a flowchart requires a lot of erasing and rewriting. Flowcharting software makes the process less tedious, so it is more reasonable to use such a tool if you have to go to a greater level of detail.

The type of computer tools you will use in the next step, storyboarding, also affects the level of flowchart detail necessary. Some storyboarding software, such as *Scripter* (Huntley & Low, 1986) or *IVD Toolkit* (Electronic Vision, 1987), incorporate detailed branching information. If they are to be used, less detail is necessary in the flowcharting step. If storyboards are to be produced on paper or with a standard computer graphics program, more flowchart detail is useful.

The method by which you implement the lesson on a computer will also determine the amount of flowcharting necessary. Programming with a standard language such as BASIC or Pascal requires great detail because such languages do not have built-in procedures for the type of activities typical in computer-based instruction. Authoring systems include typical instructional procedures such as answer judging and feedback, user control, answer storage, and animation. Less flowchart detail is therefore necessary if you will implement your lesson using an authoring system. Some of the new *icon-oriented* authoring systems provide built-in flowcharting as the means for defining lesson sequence, so even less flowchart detail may be necessary in such cases. Examples are *Authorware Professional* (Authorware, 1989), *Course Builder* (Appleton, 1987), and *IconAuthor* (AIMTech, 1988).

We will first describe the process of flowcharting as if it were being done on paper. We then describe the characteristics and advantages of computer tools for flowcharting and of flowcharting within authoring systems. The flowcharting procedures will be illustrated with the telephone example.

PROCEDURES

As stated, we recommend an iterative flowcharting process with up to three stages, starting with a simple linear sequence, progressing through a more complex flowchart giving an overview of the entire lesson structure. In some cases these should be followed by a highly detailed flowchart that specifies every aspect of the lesson.

The Level-1 flowchart is a simple diagram of how the lesson will proceed. It contains no branches and no explicitly stated decisions. You may think of it as an executive summary, in schematic form, of your instructional plans. The Level-2 flowchart is more elaborate, showing the major decision points and what happens at each of them. The minute details do not appear in it, but the major strategies do. The Level-3 flowchart is a very detailed blueprint of the lesson including all the details another person would need to implement the lesson on a computer.

The basic symbols used in flowcharting are shown in Figure 9–1. The first four symbols show basic lesson components and flow, the start and end of the lesson (circles), each lesson segment (rectangles), and the sequence from one thing to the next (arrows). The fifth symbol, the diamond, represents decisions. These are generally internal decisions the computer program makes, but in some cases they represent decisions by the student. The sixth symbol, several examples of which are shown in Figure 9–2, represents reference to what is called a subroutine. In a lesson or other computer program, a subroutine is a group of commands that stands by itself and is accessed from different parts of the program.

Level-1 Flowchart

To illustrate the process of flowcharting, we use a very simple guessing game that is played all over the world in some form or another. In it, one player chooses a number in a specified range, say 1–100 inclusive, and the other player has to guess it. After each guess, the original player has to say whether it is too high, too low, or correct. The player using the fewest attempts to guess the other's number is the winner. Assume that we want to program this little game onto the computer, with the computer choosing the number and providing the feedback. Our flowchart shows how the guessing game would be implemented.

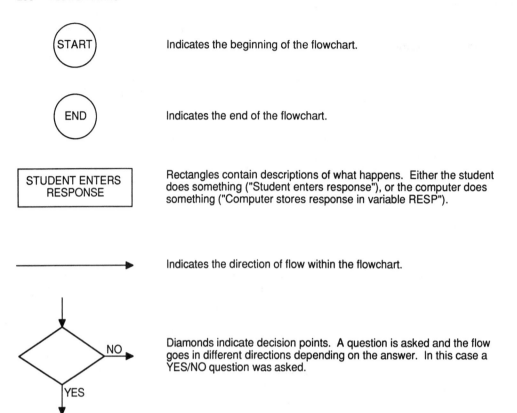

START — Indicates the beginning of the flowchart.

END — Indicates the end of the flowchart.

STUDENT ENTERS RESPONSE — Rectangles contain descriptions of what happens. Either the student does something ("Student enters response"), or the computer does something ("Computer stores response in variable RESP").

Indicates the direction of flow within the flowchart.

Diamonds indicate decision points. A question is asked and the flow goes in different directions depending on the answer. In this case a YES/NO question was asked.

Figure 9-1 Basic flowchart symbols.

Figure 9–3 is our Level-1 flowchart of the game. It is a very simple depiction of what the game is about. There are no branches or decision points and it is simple enough for someone to understand the nature of the game just by looking at the flowchart. It is unnecessary at this stage to incorporate any detail. Note that the flowchart starts and ends with the appropriate circular symbols, and that actions are described in the rectangles. The flow from one part of the flowchart to another is shown by arrows.

Level-2 Flowchart

After completing the Level-1 flowchart, the next step is to elaborate it to the level of being able to grasp what the lesson will look like when used by a student. This second-level flowchart should give a comprehensive overview of the structure of the lesson and include most of the pedagogical attributes. It should contain major branches, such as what happens if a student passes or fails a test, and where major reviews occur. It should not contain detailed programming decisions, such as internal branches for data storage or retrieval.

Figure 9–4 is the Level-2 flowchart of the guessing game. Compare it to the first-level flowchart (Figure 9–3). Several decision points have been incorpo-

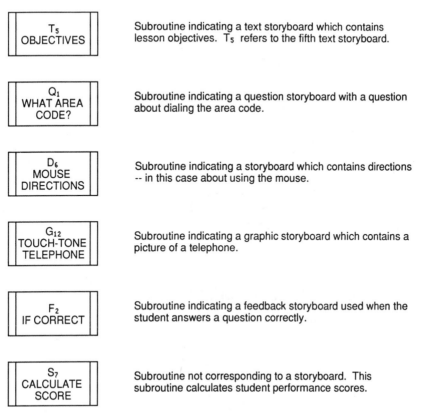

Subroutine indicating a text storyboard which contains lesson objectives. T_5 refers to the fifth text storyboard.

Subroutine indicating a question storyboard with a question about dialing the area code.

Subroutine indicating a storyboard which contains directions -- in this case about using the mouse.

Subroutine indicating a graphic storyboard which contains a picture of a telephone.

Subroutine indicating a feedback storyboard used when the student answers a question correctly.

Subroutine not corresponding to a storyboard. This subroutine calculates student performance scores.

Figure 9-2 Flowchart subroutine symbol.

rated. The first of these ("See Rules?") asks whether the user would like to read the rules of the game. On the flowchart, each of the possible user responses is listed next to the arrow related to that choice. In this case, the only possible replies are "Yes" or "No." Based on the user response, the computer program will branch accordingly.

In the second decision, after the player has entered a guess, the computer compares it with the number the computer chose at the beginning of the game. There are three possible outcomes to this comparison: the guess is too high, too low, or correct. Depending on which of these is the case, the flow through the lesson changes. In the game, it is the feedback provided to the player that changes depending on the magnitude of the guess. Thus, the decision diamond has three paths leaving it, appropriately tagged "high," "low," and "correct." As before, flow is indicated by the arrows.

Level-3 Flowchart

For so simple a game a Level-3 flowchart might not be necessary. However, if a standard programming language is being used, and someone other than

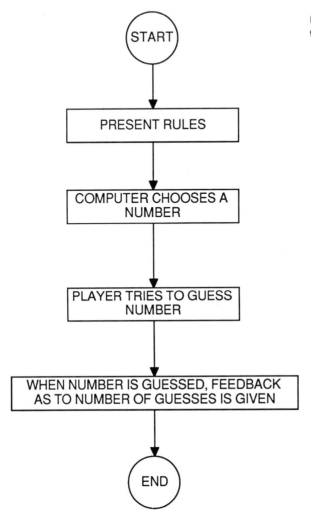

Figure 9-3   Level-1 flowchart of the guessing game.

the designer is doing the programming, it is a good way to convey all the necessary details to the programmer. We show a Level-3 flowchart for completeness.

Depending on the complexity of the lesson, there may be two stages to producing the third-level flowchart. The first is augmenting the second-level flow-chart with details such as what information needs storing and where to store it. The second stage involves the creation of new subsidiary flowcharts that map out the flow of subroutines used by the main flowchart. These are typically computational procedures that are necessary for the operation of the lesson but which do not appear visibly on any storyboard. Most standard programming languages and authoring languages have subroutine capabilities. Not all authoring systems do, so the use of subroutines and subroutine symbols may be dictated by the capabilities of the development software you use.

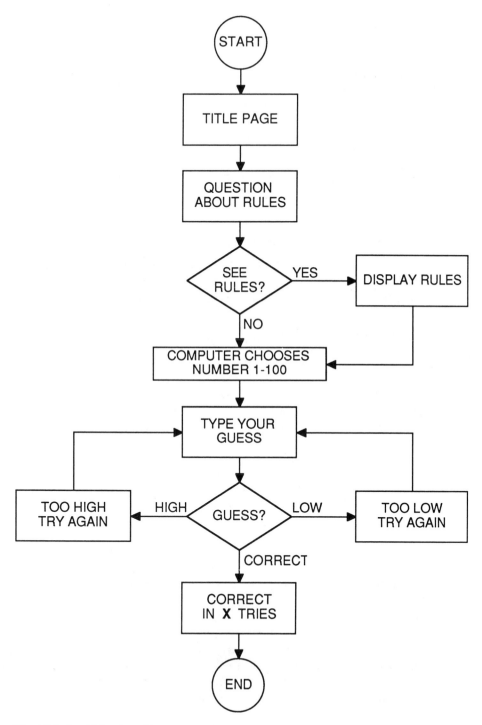

Figure 9-4 Level-2 flowchart of the guessing game.

For example, Figure 9-5 shows the Level-3 flowchart for the guessing game. As you can see, it differs only in the level of detail from the Level-2 flowchart (Figure 9-4). Figure 9-6 illustrates the addition of a useful subroutine. In this and most programs, whenever the student is reading a display and may press a key to continue, a single subroutine may take care of pausing while the student reads, determining what key is pressed (which may include other user control keys such as to quit the program), and erasing part of the current display as the program goes on to the next display. All of these actions, repeated several times throughout the program, are accomplished by the *pause and erase* subroutine of Figure 9-6.

Level-3 flowcharts may be much more complex than this one, as will be seen in the third-level flowcharts for the telephone lesson, shown later.

Dry-Running the Flowchart

The common problem with detailed (Level-3) flowcharts is correctly specifying what the lesson should do. If you give the programmer a faulty flowchart, a faulty lesson will almost certainly result. The process of checking a flowchart is called *dry-running,* and is essential to the efficient production of good programs when using programming or authoring languages.

Dry-running is the process whereby you pretend that you are the computer and follow all the instructions given in the flowchart. Thus, you would start at the beginning and follow the flow of the flowchart for a variety of different situations. For each situation or for each decision that is made, the flow should take you to the correct place.

In complicated flowcharts, you should keep track of the changing values of variables by writing them down on paper. In a typical instructional lesson, you will have to keep updating such variables as "the number of questions answered correctly" or "the number of questions answered incorrectly" or "the number of attempts at this question" or "the number of attempts at question number 4." You should keep track of these because they form the basis for branching decisions. For example: "If student has fewer than six questions correct out of ten, go to a review section; otherwise continue to the next tutorial segment." To know which branch to follow, you must keep track of the contents of relevant variables.

There are two broad categories of errors in flowcharts: typographical and logical. Typographical errors usually occur when connectors are misnumbered. Thus, you may want flow to progress from some point to connector number 8 for example, but inadvertently direct flow to connector 6. The only way to find such a mistake before programming starts is to dry run the flowchart several times, each time taking different paths. An easy way to keep track of which parts of the flowchart you have tested is to mark the flow through the flowchart in red ink as you go through it. If you do this each time, it becomes very easy to see which parts have not yet been tested. When dry-running instructional lessons, it is important to test each question and its feedback by answering it correctly, incorrectly, not at all, and with nonsense in different runs through the flowchart. In each case, the flow-

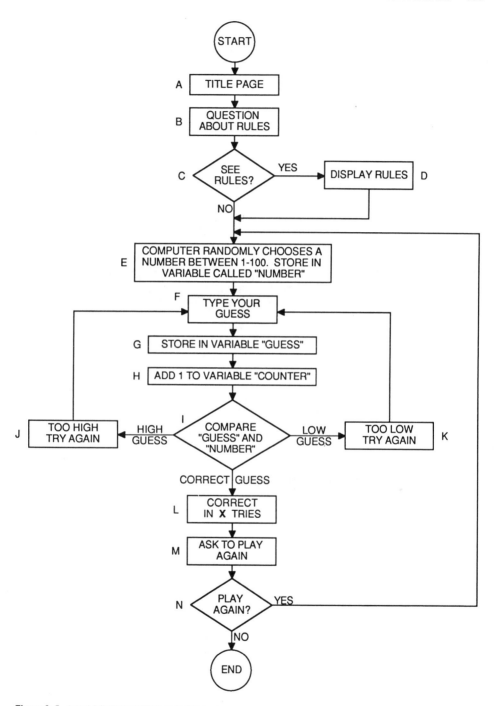

Figure 9-5 Level-3 flowchart of the guessing game.

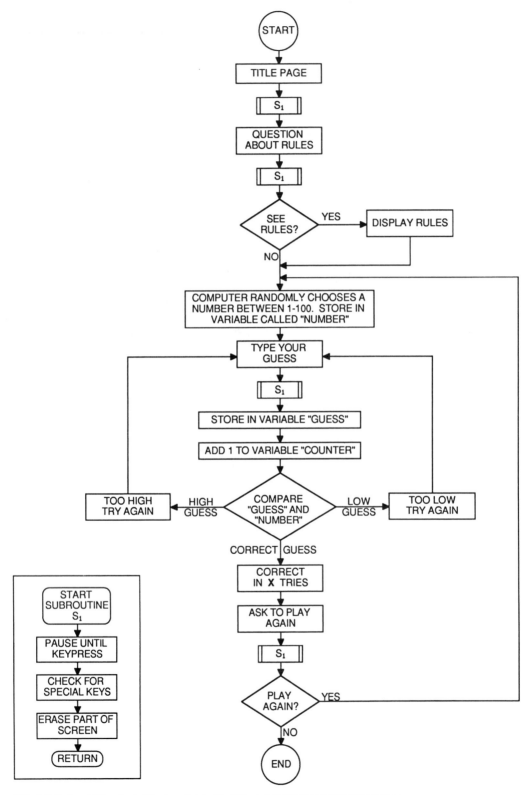

Figure 9-6 Level-3 flowchart of the guessing game using a subroutine for pausing and erasing.

chart should give the correct feedback and take you to the appropriate next action.

The second type of error is a logical one. This is where you have incorrectly conceived the flowchart. Once again, dry-running the flowchart will bring such errors to light. The dry-running process should be thorough, exploring the unusual occurrences as well as anticipated ones. Flowcharts are usually correct for the likely flow of a student through a lesson, but frequently fail for those situations where the student performs unexpectedly or where your instructions to the student are ambiguous, unclear, or nonexistent.

To illustrate the process of dry-running a flowchart, we return to the Level-3 flowchart of the guessing game (Figure 9–5). Before continuing, dry run this flowchart to ensure that it works properly. Do it now.

If you were thorough with your dry-running, you will have found that the flowchart has a logical error in it. Although it performs as desired for the first game, it does not do so for subsequent ones. Let us see why. On the left side of the text below is the letter labeling the relevant part of Figure 9–5. In the middle column is a commentary of what we would do or look for. In the right column, we keep track of the contents of three variables: NUMBER, GUESS, and COUNTER.

A	Title page appears on screen.	NUMBER	=	0
		GUESS	=	0
		COUNTER	=	0
B	Player asked to see rules: types <n>.	no change		
C	Flow goes to E.	no change		
E	Computer chooses random number, say 34.	NUMBER	=	34
	Stores it in variable NUMBER.	GUESS	=	0
		COUNTER	=	0
F	Player inputs guess, say 50.	no change		
G	Store guess in variable GUESS.	NUMBER	=	34
		GUESS	=	50
		COUNTER	=	0
H	Add 1 to counter. This keeps track of number of guesses.	NUMBER	=	34
		GUESS	=	50
		COUNTER	=	1
I	Compare GUESS and NUMBER. Guess is high. Flow goes to J.	no change		
J	Computer tells player guess is too high.	no change		
F	Player inputs guess, say 30.	no change		
G	Store guess in variable GUESS.	NUMBER	=	34
		GUESS	=	30
		COUNTER	=	1
H	Add 1 to counter. This keeps track of number of guesses.	NUMBER	=	34

		GUESS	=	30
		COUNTER	=	2
I	Compare GUESS and NUMBER. Guess is low. Flow goes to K.	no change		
K	Computer tells player guess is too low.	no change		
F	Player inputs guess say 34.	no change		
G	Store guess in variable GUESS.	NUMBER	=	34
		GUESS	=	34
		COUNTER	=	2
H	Add 1 to counter. This keeps track of number of guesses.	NUMBER	=	34
		GUESS	=	34
		COUNTER	=	3
I	Compare GUESS and NUMBER. Guess is correct. Flow goes to L.	no change		
L	Computer congratulates player, and informs number of guesses is 3.	no change		
M	Computer asks whether another game is to be played. Player answers "no."	no change		
N	Flow goes to end.	no change		

You may wonder at this stage why we said there was a logical error in the flowchart. It is apparent from the dry-running above that everything works as planned. But that is true only for the first game. Because we provide the opportunity to play more than one game, we should test that option too. We continue the process by changing the last answer from a "no" (no more games) to a "yes." Thus the last action becomes:

M	Computer asks whether another game is to be played. Player answers "yes."	no change		
N	Flow goes to E.	no change		

And continuing:

E	Computer chooses random number, say 69. Stores it in variable NUMBER.	NUMBER	=	69
		GUESS	=	34
		COUNTER	=	3
F	Player inputs guess, say 50.	no change		
G	Store guess in variable GUESS.	NUMBER	=	69
		GUESS	=	50
		COUNTER	=	3
H	Add 1 to counter. This keeps track of number of guesses.	NUMBER	=	69

		GUESS	=	50
		COUNTER	=	4

Now it is obvious where the problem lies. After the first guess of the second game, the counter has 4 in it instead of 1. We forgot to reset the counter to zero after the game. Notice, however, that it was not necessary to reset the variable containing the computer's number or the player's guess. This is because the contents of those two variables were *replaced* by new numbers, whereas the contents of variable COUNTER were *augmented.* This is a typical logical error, and errors of this kind occur frequently. For your information we have included a corrected flowchart (Figure 9–7), adding program steps to correct the problem found above.

As you can see from the very simple example above, dry-running a flowchart may not be an easy task. To expedite it and to ensure that you test it adequately, it is usually best to prepare a plan before starting. Decide what paths you want to check and create scenarios that will accomplish that. For instance, on one pass through the flowchart assume the student taking the lesson performs well. On further passes, assume students of different abilities. Planning carefully helps eliminate oversights and usually reduces the amount of time you have to spend as well. If you do make revisions to the flowchart on the basis of the dry-running, you should repeat the process with the new version to ensure both that the problems were eliminated and that no new errors were inadvertently introduced.

The more complex and detailed your flowcharts are, the more important it is to dry run. If you give a programmer a flowchart containing errors, the program that is written will contain the same errors.

COMPUTER TOOLS

Even though many software designers recognize that a well-constructed and dry-run flowchart usually increases the quality of the subsequent program, most consider flowcharting laborious and tedious. However, availability of flowcharting software makes the process much easier. Just as a word processor eases the revision of textual material, flowcharting software allows revision and expansion of a flowchart without a lot of redrawing and rewriting by hand.

MacFlow (Bertrand & Terpstra, 1988) on the Macintosh is typical of flowcharting programs. Flowchart symbols are easily moved around (by dragging them with the mouse), inserted, and deleted. Arrows are quickly rerouted to change program sequence. And of course, at any time a printout may be made of the current state of the flowchart. Portions of a flowchart may be nested within individual flowchart symbols to facilitate hierarchical program organization. Figure 9–8 shows a display in which a flowchart is being edited using *MacFlow.*

EasyFlow (Farnell & McDowell, 1987) for IBM microcomputers has the same basic capabilities as *MacFlow.* The flowcharts in *EasyFlow* are more structured, but tend to look more professional and are easier to modify when very

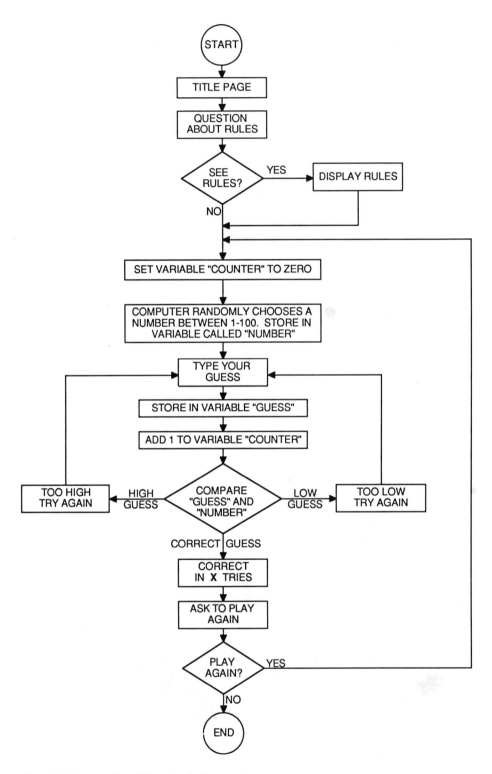

Figure 9-7 Corrected Level-3 flowchart for the guessing game.

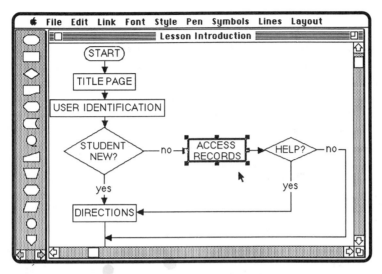

Figure 9-8 Flowcharting with *MacFlow. (Courtesy of Mainstay)*

large. Although it uses a mouse, moving symbols is not as easy as dragging on the Macintosh. Figure 9–9 shows a flowchart being created using *EasyFlow*.

MacFlow and *EasyFlow* are "stand-alone" flowcharting programs. That is, their purpose is creating, editing, and printing flowcharts. There is an increasing number of software products whose purpose is development of computer software which include flowcharting capabilities as a part of the design process. These include authoring systems such as *Authorware Professional* (Authorware, 1989), illus-

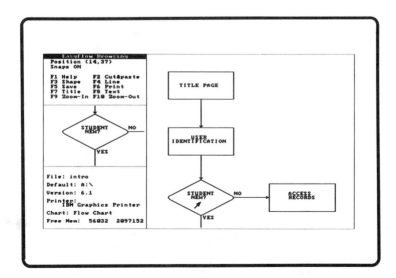

Figure 9-9 Flowcharting with *EasyFlow. (Courtesy of Haventree Software)*

trated in Figure 9–10; *Course Builder* (Appleton, 1987); and *IconAuthor* (AIMTech, 1988). They also include more generic development systems such as *Visual Interactive Programming* (Lienart, 1987), illustrated in Figure 9–11, which are becoming known as CASE tools, for Computer-Assisted Software Engineering. We have found, however, that these products do not allow flowcharting in as free-form a fashion as is desirable at this stage. Even if you will use such software for development in the programming step, we recommend flowcharting at this point with stand-alone flowcharting software or by hand.

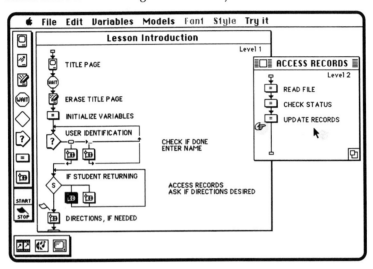

Figure 9-10   A flowchart in *Authorware Professional. (Courtesy of Authorware)*

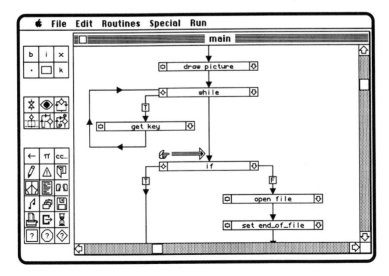

Figure 9-11   A flowchart in *Visual Interactive Programming. (Courtesy of Mainstay)*

TELEPHONE EXAMPLE

Let us now consider the flowcharting step for our lesson on the telephone. Because of the length of the lesson, we do not show a complete set of flowcharts but rather choose pertinent excerpts.

Figure 9–12 is the Level-1 flowchart for the computer lesson on telephone operation. By looking at this flowchart, it is possible to obtain a good idea of what the lesson would be like in final form. For most people, it is unnecessary and wasteful to have too detailed information about the branching strategies and similar instructional aspects of the lesson. All the relevant information is contained in the flowchart, including brief details of the various components of the lesson. Although there are no decision points, the flow through the lesson is clearly depicted.

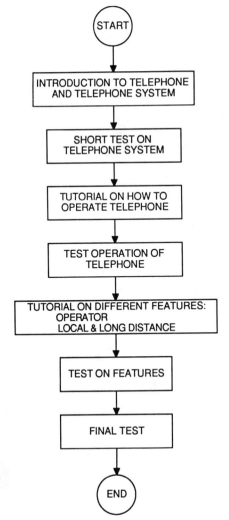

Figure 9-12 Level-1 flowchart for the telephone example.

The Level-2 flowchart for the telephone example is shown in Figures 9–13a, b, and c. This flowchart has grown considerably. It also contains two unfamiliar features: the use of an interrupt and the use of connectors.

In two places, the flowchart indicates that a subroutine is available *on interrupt.* An interrupt is anything that interrupts the current processing of the les-

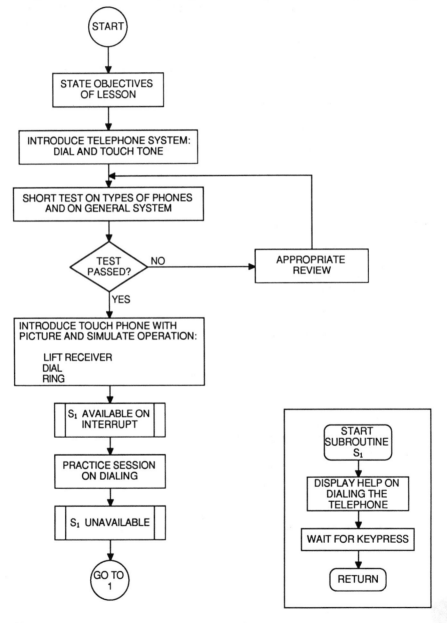

Figure 9-13a   Level-2 flowchart for the telephone example.

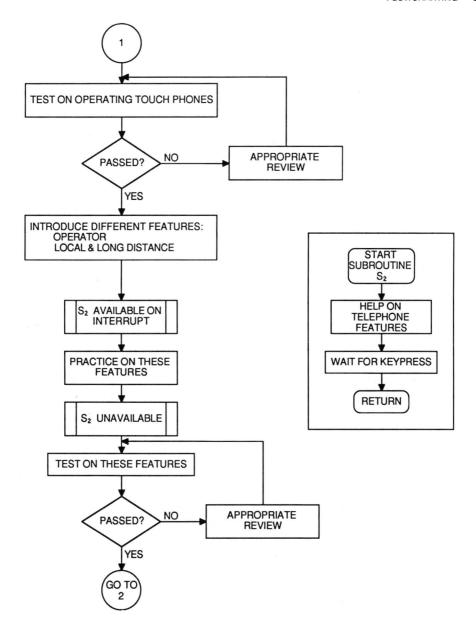

Figure 9-13b

son. Pressing the ⟨esc⟩ key or clicking a mouse button may cause this to happen. In the telephone example, for instance, after the introduction to the simulated telephone, there is opportunity to practice using it. If the student interrupts this practice by clicking on the **help** button on the screen, the information contained in subroutine HELP is put onto the screen. When the subroutine ends, the pro-

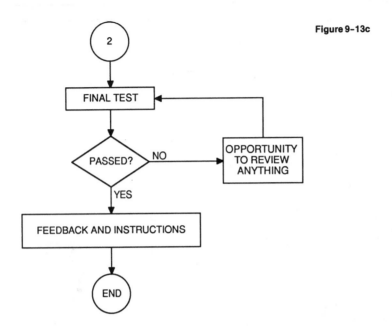

Figure 9–13c

gram continues at the point in the practice session at which **help** was clicked. Notice the different way in which the review routines are handled. They are built into the structure of the lesson, leaving the student little or no choice about going through them. Poor performance on a test automatically branches the student through the review sequence.

The second new feature on this flowchart is the use of the connecting symbol. As you can see, the flowchart is too large to fit on a single page. Consequently, it is necessary to overflow onto continuation pages. To ensure that it is easy to follow the flow, numbered connectors are used. The same number should not be used more than once within a flowchart as a destination. By this we mean that it is acceptable, and usually necessary, to go to a single destination within a flowchart from multiple points. In Figures 9–14a, b, c, d, for example, there are several places which go to connector number 6. However, there is only one connector number 6 from which flow emanates. Having more than one would cause confusion.

The Level-3 flowchart shown in Figure 9–14 depicts only the small part of the total flowchart which deals with the simulated phone. It shows the subroutine that charts the flow of how the simulated phone works. It has been designed to work the same way as a real telephone. For convenience, we have not shown all parts of this subroutine and have omitted several important subsections, such as what happens when *0* is dialed. Nevertheless, the level of detail is very great.

CONCLUSION

A flowchart is a graphic depiction of the lesson, which shows what happens in the lesson under all possible circumstances. Together with the storyboards, which are

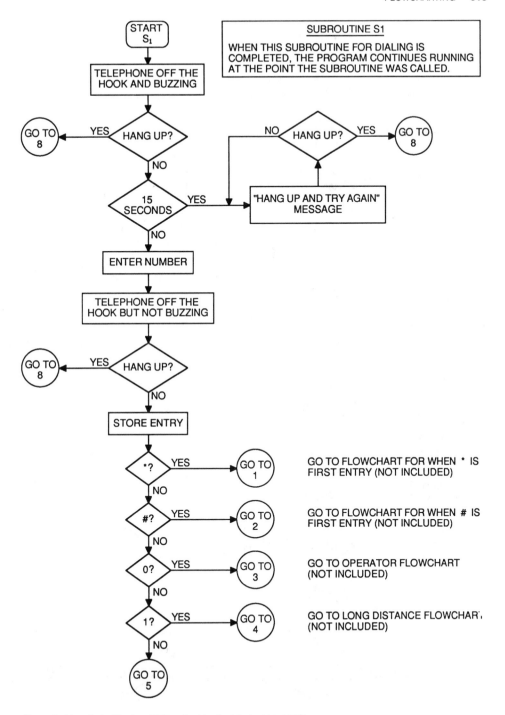

Figure 9-14a Part of the Level-3 flowchart for the telephone example.

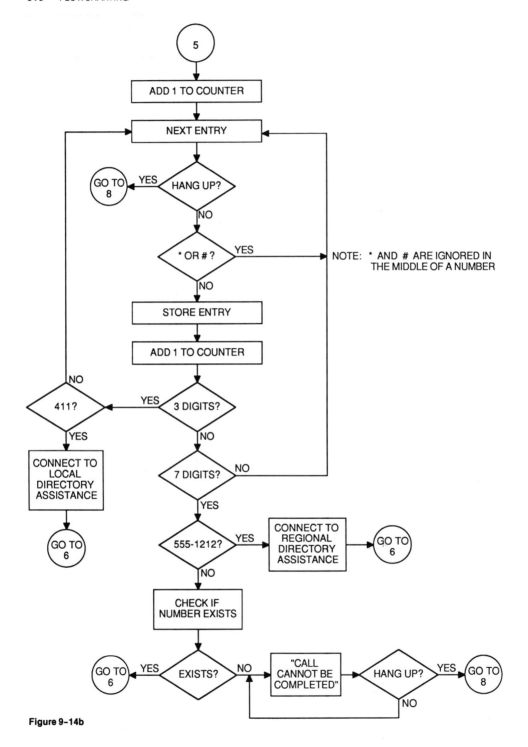

NOTE: * AND # ARE IGNORED IN THE MIDDLE OF A NUMBER

Figure 9-14b

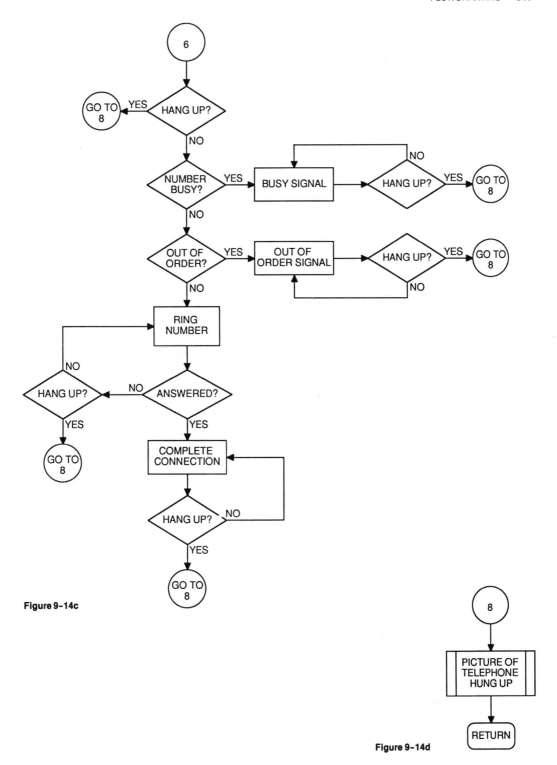

Figure 9-14c

Figure 9-14d

produced next, they provide a complete description of the lesson content and sequence. The production of a clear and detailed flowchart is facilitated by adopting an iterative approach, beginning with a very brief overview and progressing to the level of detail necessary for your lesson. Simple lessons like tutorials require little detail while complex lessons like simulations require considerably more. We end this chapter by emphasizing our belief that the more time spent on flowcharting, the less time you will spend later correcting program errors.

REFERENCES AND BIBLIOGRAPHY

AIMTech. (1988). *IconAuthor.* [Computer Program]. Nashua, NH: AIMTech Corp.

Appleton, W.C. (1987). *Course Builder.* [Computer Program]. Knoxville, TN: TeleRobotics International.

Authorware. (1989). *Authorware Professional.* [Computer Program]. Minneapolis, MN: Authorware, Inc.

Bertrand, P.A., & Terpstra, D. (1988). *MacFlow.* [Computer Program]. Los Angeles: Mainstay.

Electronic Vision. (1987). *IVD Toolkit.* [Computer Program]. Athens, OH: Electronic Vision.

Farnell, C., & McDowell, R. (1987). *Easyflow.* [Computer Program]. Kingston, Ontario, Canada: Haventree Software.

Huntley, J.S., & Low, N. (1986). *Scripter.* [Computer Program]. Coralville, IA: Cognitive Design Technologies, Limited.

Lienart, D. (1987). *Visual Interactive Programming.* [Computer Program]. Agoura Hills, CA: Mainstay.

Pace, P., & Pace, L. (1987). *Logic Tools for Programming.* Albany, NY: Delmar.

Shneiderman, B., Mayer, R.E., McKay, D., & Heller, P. (1977). Experimental investigations of the utility of detailed flowcharts in programming. *Communications of the ACM, 20*(6), 373–381.

Stern, N.B. (1975). *Flowcharting: A Tool for Understanding Computer Logic.* New York: John Wiley and Sons.

SUMMARY OF FLOWCHARTING

PREPARE THE FLOWCHART

Draw a simple flowchart without decision points.
Add important decisions to create a Level-2 flowchart.
Create Level-3 flowcharts for simulations or complex lessons.
Whenever possible put repeated routines in subroutines.
Ensure that connector numbers are not ambiguous.
Ensure that decision outcomes and direction of flow is clear.

DRY RUN THE FLOWCHART

Plan several paths through the flowchart.
Note which paths were taken at each decision point.
As you dry run the chart, keep track of the values of variables.
Check that the flowchart takes you where you expect to go.
Check that all variables have the values you expect.
If there are errors, revise the flowchart.
If you revise the flowchart, dry run the new version.

10

STORYBOARDING

In Chapter 9 we discussed Step 6 of our model, Flowcharting. In it we outlined the various levels of complexity that can be required of flowcharting. The flowcharts that come out of Step 6 do not contain details of the actual screen displays that the student will ultimately see. In this chapter we discuss Step 7 of the model, called Storyboarding, which is where you produce these displays.

The products of this step are lengthier and more specific than previous ones, and thus will take more time to complete. Also, you will become much more concerned with the medium of delivery, the computer and its capabilities and constraints, although you may not actually use the computer for storyboarding.

As with some previous steps, we break storyboarding into a number of component sub-steps. We do this to bring order to what might look like a very disorderly array of events and to prevent the novice from omitting essential activities. The seven sub-steps of storyboarding are:

> Write and revise primary text.
> Write and revise secondary text.
> Produce storyboards.
> Check the fit of overlaying displays.
> Draw and revise graphic displays and plan other output.
> Check graphics and simultaneous text for fit.
> Review the flowcharts and storyboards.

We now describe these sub-steps. Following that we briefly illustrate the process with examples from our hypothetical lesson about the telephone.

WRITE AND REVISE PRIMARY TEXT

In this sub-step you write the actual instructional messages that students will see in the lesson. We use the phrase *text displays* to distinguish them from *graphic displays* or other outputs such as computer-generated sound, even though graphics displays usually contain some text. *Primary* text displays refer to the text displays that contain the essential instructional content. In tutorials primary text usually comprises new information, such as definitions, descriptions, and principles, the questions asked, and the feedback given after responses. In drills the primary text displays are the stimuli to which students respond and the feedback they receive. In simulations and games, the primary text includes any description of the phenomenon and the ongoing information about changes in it. In tests the primary text displays are the test questions themselves.

Primary text displays do *not* include directions, help messages, hints, or cues. These are contained in *secondary* text displays which are written after the primary text displays, upon whose content they are usually dependent.

At this stage primary text displays may be written as continuous text rather than as individual screen displays. Writing the first draft as screen displays can waste time because the ongoing editing process requires reorganizing the text into new screen boundaries with each revision. For efficiency, therefore, ignore the fact that you will later split the text into segments to fit on the computer screen and write primary information, questions, and feedback as continuous text.

While writing the primary text information, keep in mind the following instructional factors as discussed in Part 1. Presentations should be concise and to the point rather than wordy and repetitive. Emphasize what is important; do not spend pages describing the trivial and only a sentence or two on difficult or hard-to-explain concepts. Use special text features such as large letters, underlining, or color to draw attention to the important information, but do not overuse such techniques or they will lose their attention-getting ability. Make use of sound teaching principles: arrange information in lists when appropriate, state rules, use analogy and metaphor, and incorporate frequent and active student participation. Organize the content so it is clear. Writing a hierarchical outline first encourages a well-organized sequence of text. State information clearly and include brief but obvious statements of transition when changing the topic or moving from one logical point to another. Consider incorporating the *occasional* use of humor or colorful language, but at the same time be wary of overuse, of being sarcastic or insulting, or of being so subtle that students miss the point. Be attentive to grammar, spelling, and sentence construction. Use vocabulary familiar to your intended students and maintain a general writing style appropriate to their reading level. In simulations and games keep in mind the phenomenon or context and its desired level of fidelity.

When writing questions and feedback, consider the appropriateness of different question types such as completion, multiple-choice, or matching, and consider introducing some variety. Ask clear, concise questions about important information only. Also make sure the method of responding will be clear to the student. Seek response economy.

At this stage it is useful to decide on the criteria for judging student responses. Make parenthetical or marginal notations about these criteria. When writing feedback, consider giving feedback about both the *form* and the *content* of the response. Feedback should be clear, concise, and positive for both correct and incorrect responses. Feedback for incorrect responses, although it may be more informative, should not be more entertaining than feedback for correct responses. When appropriate, use error-contingent feedback.

Once you have produced drafts of the primary text information, reread them paying attention to *all* the instructional factors relevant to the chosen methodology. Have others review the text also and make revisions as needed.

WRITE AND REVISE SECONDARY TEXT

Having completed the primary text, write the secondary text messages, which are supportive of the primary text. Writing secondary text is much easier when you have completed the primary information, and includes directions, menus, transitions, prompts, hints, review material, help, score and progress information, entertainment messages (most frequently found in instructional games), and lesson exit messages.

As with primary text, remember that you are now writing information that students will eventually see, so be complete, clear, accurate, and concise; in short be attuned to the principles of good writing. All of the considerations we suggested for primary text writing apply to secondary text as well. In addition, pay attention to the salience of instructional cues or prompts (that is, the degree to which they are brought to the student's attention), to the clarity and accessibility of help messages, to the types of remediation used, and to the use of color and other attention devices. As before, the text is written in whole paragraphs, without regard to the fact that it will be split up later to fit on a computer screen.

When finished writing the secondary text, review it with regard to relevant instructional factors and have colleagues review it as well. Make revisions where necessary.

PRODUCE STORYBOARDS

Upon completion of sub-steps 1 and 2, both primary and secondary texts will be written in draft form. However, computer display characteristics are quite unlike those of paper. The most notable difference that concerns us at this stage is capacity. A long paragraph, which fits easily on paper, frequently will not fit on a computer display. While the display capacity of microcomputers is constantly being expanded, for most current microcomputers it is less than paper with respect both to line and page length. While ordinary 8-1/2″ by 11″ paper can accommodate about eighty characters per line and sixty-six lines, older microcomputers still in common use permit only forty characters to a line and only twenty to twenty-five lines. Newer microcomputers typically allow eighty-character lines, but still only about twenty-five lines. Most computer screens have between one-half to one-sixth the display capacity of a piece of paper. Primary and secondary text displays must therefore be divided to accommodate your computer display capacity.

There are also educational reasons for reorganizing text into smaller segments. As discussed in the chapter on tutorials, long segments of text may lose some students' attention while providing little or no student involvement or interaction with the instructional topic. Frequent breaks in text are useful for asking questions, displaying pictures, and giving the student the choice of progressing to new material or of returning to review previous material. In most cases, you would not even want to utilize the entire capacity of the computer screen. It is instructionally more beneficial to fill just half the screen and then engage in some student activity, than it is to fill the screen with text with no student interaction.

Storyboarding is the process of rewriting the information onto pieces of paper, with each piece corresponding to a separate computer screen display or part of one. The first aspect of storyboarding is the purely practical consideration of choosing the appropriate medium for the work. There are several approaches to consider. Many developers use paper with the same dimensions as the computer screen and print on it with letters the same size as the computer produces. Others use paper scaled down to a more manageable size, such as 4″ by 5″ index cards with appropriately reduced print. A third option is to use computer graphics software and do storyboarding on the computer.

Storyboarding Grids

Storyboarding grids are pieces of paper approximately the size of the computer display, with horizontal and vertical lines showing the actual character dimensions across and down the page. Appendix C contains storyboard grids for several popular computers' formats.

There are two main advantages to using storyboard grids over blank index cards. First, the grid provides greater ease in centering and spacing text and precludes writing too much text on a line, which often leads to making unnecessary adjustments later. The second advantage pertains to graphics production. Graphic displays *can* be drawn on scaled-down paper, but it may be better to put them on paper of exactly the same dimensions as your computer screen. This allows later "tracing" directly onto the computer, a procedure which is difficult with anything but 1-to-1 scale drawings. If a graphics scanner is used, shrinking a large paper image results in a better computer display than expanding a small image. The disadvantage of using full-size storyboards, in contrast to index cards, is size. It is difficult to assemble all of your storyboards to get the big picture. In contrast, with index cards, an entire lesson may be assembled on a bulletin board for evaluation. Lastly, storyboarding grids are less useful on computers which use proportional fonts, such as the Macintosh.

Storyboarding Software

An increasingly viable storyboarding option is to use computer graphics software on the same computer for which your lesson is intended. Graphics art programs such as *Canvas* (Deneba Software, 1988) on the Macintosh, and *PC Paintbrush* (ZSoft, 1987) on IBM-compatible computers are examples. Both allow the developer to draw pictures with the mouse, type text with the keyset, and easily arrange parts of the display, align the parts, change colors and sizes, and produce paper copy of the displays. Two programs designed specifically for storyboarding interactive video programs are *Scripter* (Huntley & Low, 1986) and *IVD Toolkit* (Electronic Vision, 1987). Figure 10–1 shows storyboards being produced with *Canvas*.

   File   Edit   Text   Object   Layout   Effects   Macro   Windows

Canvas:Telephone Picture

Lift the
receiver
before
you
start
dialing.

(217) 555-2331

COPY

1:1   Layer #1   X 1'-1"   Y 2'-5"

Figure 10-1   Storyboarding with *Canvas* (*Courtesy of Deneba
Software*)

There are several advantages to storyboarding on the computer (Sampath
& Quaine, 1990). It is easy to create displays with just the right amount of text or
other information that will fit within the screen dimensions. It is easy to incorporate and show the styles of text, the colors, and character and line spacings, and all
other display variables of the computer you are using. As with any computerized
tool, you may make changes and effortlessly obtain new printouts whenever
changes are made. In some cases, the computerized storyboards may be "im-
ported" to your final lesson and altered there, reducing effort later in the programming step. With some software, it is even possible to prototype animation,
sound, and control of peripherals as a part of your storyboards.

There are also some disadvantages to using storyboarding software. At an
early stage, it can cause the designer to begin thinking about details when the big
picture is not yet complete. This can be a waste of time, because as whole sections are
added and deleted, many details may be eliminated or changed. If storyboarding software is available and considered desirable, our recommendation is to do very sketchy
storyboarding on paper first, followed by a second draft on the computer.

Whatever storyboarding method is used, some paper copy will be produced at various stages. The paper storyboards should have a margin for notations
that will not actually appear on the display for the student, but that will be useful
for reference. The most important of these notations is an identifying number for
each display so that you can refer to each without a long description of its contents. A coding scheme is useful, with T1, T2, T3, and so on for text storyboards,
Q1, Q2, Q3 for questions, D1, D2, D3 for directions, G1, G2, G3 for graphics, and
F1, F2, F3 for feedback. As you create storyboards, add these identifying numbers
to your flowcharts, which should already contain short descriptions in each symbol. Such labels should *not* be the *only* identifiers on a flowchart; that makes the

flowchart very difficult to understand and evaluate. Other marginal notations include the identification numbers of overlaying displays, answers to questions, criteria for judging students' responses, storage of the students' performance data, keys that are active and what happens when the student presses them, and identifying numbers of destination storyboards when branching.

Having chosen a storyboard medium, you next rewrite the primary and secondary text to fit on them. This task requires patience and ingenuity, because you will find that computer displays are smaller than you would like them to be. Your main objective is to determine suitable points at which to break the text. Decisions should be based not on the size of the storyboards, but on the ideas in the text. There are several guidelines to facilitate this process. First, always err in the direction of putting too little information on a display rather than too much. Second, avoid shortening or otherwise changing the text to make it fit; it is usually preferable to try to split it into pieces. Third, leave room for the addition of text that might be necessary at a later time. Keeping these guidelines in mind, continue until all primary and secondary text displays are suitably divided and rewritten onto storyboards.

CHECK THE FIT OF OVERLAYING DISPLAYS

Many of the separate storyboards will be "overlaid" on single computer displays. A common example occurs when asking the student a question. One storyboard contains the questions as well as the space in which the student will type a response. Another storyboard contains a feedback message presented when the student gives an incorrect response. During the actual lesson presentation these two displays may appear on the screen at the same time. Why then are they not written on the same storyboard? There are a number of reasons. First, different messages appear on the screen depending on whether the student answers the questions correctly or incorrectly. Since each of these messages appear on the screen, we obviously cannot put them on the same storyboard in the same place. Instead they are placed in identical locations on separate storyboards, thus ensuring that each message will fit simultaneously with the original question.

A second reason for using separate storyboards is that the same message may be used as feedback for *different* questions. To write it on each question would be very inefficient. Just as you probably would not write separate program code for each presentation of the feedback, so it should be for storyboard displays. Finally, it is generally a good idea to establish a one-to-one correspondence between storyboards and segments of a lesson, such as subroutines, as we will discuss later. Because computer displays in a lesson are frequently programmed by putting together "pieces," it is best to storyboard the pieces on different cards.

At this point, you should check that pieces appearing together in a single display, such as a question and its feedback, will indeed fit in the space provided on the computer screen. Be sure to avoid not only overlapping, but also overcrowded screen displays. Crowding is not just a function of how much information is presented in a display, but of how the information is arranged and of how much space is left between different pieces of information. This process is facilitated if your storyboarding medium is the computer itself, using a graphics program.

Storyboard overlays occur primarily in question-answer-feedback displays; in user control messages; in directions or help message displays that may supplement text or questions; in incremental text—text that is not presented on the screen all at once, but rather is added a little at a time; and in replaced text—a portion of text that is erased from a larger display and replaced with a different one. Consequently, these are the main places you should look for potential problems. Checking for overcrowded or overlapped text is simple if you use storyboards which have grids and are all the same size, or if you storyboard on the computer. When using paper grids, an easy method is to hold displays that will occur together up to the light so their images actually overlay just as they would on the screen. Look for any overlapping or overcrowded information. Be certain to test all possible combinations that may be overlaid in the actual lesson. It is easy to forget, for example, that a particular set of directions may appear at the same time as a particular question.

DRAW AND REVISE GRAPHIC DISPLAYS AND PLAN OTHER OUTPUT

Graphic displays refer to a variety of non-text presentations. Simple line drawings, more complicated pictures, cartoons, animations, geometric figures, and bar and line graphs are all graphic displays. Sometimes it is necessary or useful to consider special cases of text as graphics, especially when such text is very large, is enclosed in boxes, or is otherwise highlighted.

Other output comprises any presentation that does *not* appear on the computer screen. The most frequent and important of these is sound.

Graphic displays are treated quite differently from text displays. In particular, they are not produced and then later split up into storyboards. Graphics are more unified entities than text and, once drawn, cannot always be broken up into pieces as can text. The value of most pictures lies in seeing the whole and the relationship of the parts to one another. Therefore, when developing graphic displays, do so directly on storyboards the size of your computer screen, or directly on the computer.

Animations require special consideration because it is difficult to capture the nature of movement on paper. In addition to producing the essential elements in still form, make marginal notations that include a description of *what parts* change and the *nature* of the change, such as direction, size, how far, and how fast. Sometimes it is necessary to draw a few different still pictures to show the change at different stages. For instance, a science lesson containing an animation of a frog hopping might show the frog with legs bent, the frog with legs half extended, the frog with legs fully extended, and the frog landing with legs again bent. A description such as "The frog's legs will straighten and then bend again, while the frog moves across the screen" might be insufficient to describe the animation for programming.

Sound also requires special consideration because it is difficult to describe on paper. A storyboard for sound would consist entirely of marginal information describing the sound in terms of its nature such as music or speech, its content such as what is played or said, and its duration. A marginal notation identifying a tape recording containing the precise sounds is the best information to include, such as "the sounds on tape number 25 are heard during this display." However, because some people will not have access to the tape recording, a written description is also recommended.

All graphic portions of your lesson should be storyboarded with the following considerations. First, graphics should be used to present or elaborate important information. Second, they should be clear and contain no unnecessary detail or ambiguous parts. Color can be very effective for distinguishing different parts of pictures or graphs or for emphasizing important features, but avoid using too many colors simultaneously. Always allot space for simultaneous text. In simulations and games, produce each graphic component with regard to the phenomenon or context and the level of fidelity desired.

When all of the graphic displays have been storyboarded, they should be reviewed with regard to the relevant instructional factors and revised as necessary. When dealing with pictures, it is frequently the case that you will reduce or enlarge them based on display constraints. This can be done with a photocopying machine that can change the size of the original, or with a graphics scanner and computer graphics software which will expand or shrink images. Remember that shrinking a large image generally looks better than expanding a small image. Do not put any text on your original graphic storyboards, because you may want to reuse them at different times in the lesson. Producing graphics with a computer program is useful because they may be easily modified, magnified, or reduced.

CHECK GRAPHICS AND SIMULTANEOUS TEXT FOR FIT

Graphic displays, like text displays, are sometimes overlaid either with each other or with other text. As with text, you should check that there is no overlapping or overcrowding in the composite displays. Text that usually appears with graphics includes explanations or labels for the graphics and directions for student control. Although occasionally necessary, it is usually bad practice to make the student switch back and forth between different displays, one containing graphics, for example, and the other containing its description or directions for student control. Graphics and corresponding text should be displayed simultaneously, and it is important that they do so correctly.

Checking for overlap or crowding can be done in the same way as before, holding simultaneous storyboards up to the light. Once again, this is very easy if a single-size storyboard grid is used. With good computer graphics software, it is usually easy to superimpose two storyboards on one another to check for fit.

If there is a problem with overlap or crowding, revisions can be made in a variety of ways. Graphics can be changed in size, an advantage not always possible with text. Alternatively, the graphics and text displays can be moved further apart or closer together as needed. If necessary, the amount of detail in a graphic may be decreased. Text may be paginated by breaking it into smaller pieces appearing one at a time on different pages, while the graphic part remains unchanged. On newer computers having a variety of high quality text sizes and styles, text may be sized to accommodate display constraints.

REVIEW THE FLOWCHARTS AND STORYBOARDS

Until now, we have not paid much attention to sequencing the storyboards, nor to looking at the lesson as a whole, but rather to many individual segments. For reviewing you must assemble all the pieces into a reasonable order.

Assemble the Flowcharts and Storyboards and Review Them Yourself

This procedure involves assembling all of the completed storyboards in the *approximate* order they will occur in the lesson, as indicated by the flowcharts. They should be laid out side by side, rather than in a stack, so that you can see them all at once. The best way to assemble them is to tack them up on a large bulletin board. An average length lesson is likely to have so many individual storyboards that you can easily fill a bulletin board. This method is useful because it is easy to change the order. If possible, leave some space between storyboards when initially tacking them up in order to facilitate moving them around into different positions later. Alternatively, storyboards may be taped to a chalkboard or a wall, or laid out on a large table. If storyboarding has been done on a computer, printouts should be made for this step. Flowcharts should also be printed and available for inspection along with the assembled storyboards.

Place all of the storyboards in view in the order that the typical student will probably encounter them in a lesson. Naturally no student will see all of the displays. However, imagine that your average student answers each question both correctly and incorrectly and encounters all of the appropriate presentations, choices, questions, hints, feedback messages, and remediation. Do not be concerned that most students will go through your lesson in an order different from the one you now produce.

Now review the flowcharts and complete storyboard layout with regard to overall sequence, style, completeness, student control, and length. Imagine that the lesson is in operation on a computer in front of you, and assume the role of a student. Proceed from card to card, interacting with the lesson, making choices, sometimes giving incorrect answers and receiving corrective feedback, other times answering correctly and receiving positive feedback. You should do this a number of times, so as to ensure that you make all choices and answer all questions both correctly and incorrectly.

As you do this, locate and take notes on problems, the most frequent of which include:

Missing or incomplete directions
Directions that are unavailable when needed
Lack of student interaction
Topics inadequately discussed
Overlapping, overcrowded, or poorly spaced displays
Seldom or never-used displays
Redundant or irrelevant displays
Displays that emphasize minor points
Question loops in which students may get stuck
Poor transitions
Poor student control, such as displays that cannot be reviewed
Text passages that could be enhanced with graphics

The purpose of this sub-step is to find and take notes on these problems, not to fix them. Do not attempt to correct problems at this point, since you will have the opportunity to do so later.

Have Experts Review the Flowcharts

The flowcharts should be reviewed by other instructional designers, content experts, your client, and programming professionals to assess pedagogical quality, correctness of content and sequence, attainment of objectives, and suitability for the computer hardware and software to be used. The storyboards may be referred to for clarification of flowchart symbols or descriptions.

Have Experts and Students Review the Storyboards

Both experts and students should review the storyboards. The experts are the same people who reviewed the flowcharts. They are now concerned with the details, pedagogy, content accuracy and completeness, sequence, display aesthetics and clarity, and hardware and software suitability.

Students should help you assess wording (too hard or too easy), clarity of text and pictures, and whether the lesson is interesting.

When someone else reviews the storyboard assembly, do not provide too much advance information about the lesson and how it *should* work. Doing so often inhibits the person from asking questions and noting problems. See if your reviewer can understand the information from what is presented in the storyboards. You should instruct reviewers to imagine they are seeing these displays on a computer, and ask them to think out loud, noting information that is missing, confusing, or unnecessary. They should feel free to ask questions, and you will certainly have to help them and explain things, such as when a segment of text refers to a figure that is on another storyboard. Take complete notes about their questions and comments, but avoid becoming defensive if they are critical. This inhibits further comments. The more you have to answer questions or give assistance, the more improvement your plan requires.

Make Revisions

Based on your own and your reviewers' comments, you should make revisions. Do not be concerned with minor improvements such as spelling. These are better done at a later time. Be more concerned with major changes such as removing or replacing whole storyboards, adding more questions, or changing lesson sequence as indicated on the flowcharts.

TELEPHONE EXAMPLE

Since a complete set of telephone lesson storyboards would number well over a hundred, only representative examples are presented for each of the seven substeps.

Write and Revise Primary Text

Below are examples of the primary text written in its original continuous form. Notice that there was no attempt to organize the text into screen-size segments; rather, the emphasis is on content. The first example is for the introductory part of the lesson.

> This lesson will teach you about the use of telephones. The telephone system in the United States is a very complicated electronic system that allows people to call from one side of the country to the other in seconds. This is made possible by having computers in control of the system, which means that everything can be handled automatically.
>
> The basis of the system is telephone numbers that uniquely identify each telephone line. Therefore, every phone line has its own number. In the first section of this lesson we will discuss these numbers. In the second section of this lesson we will discuss the two main types of dialing: rotary-dial and touch-tone.

The next example is for the part of the lesson dealing with the structure of telephone numbers.

> Every telephone in the United States is uniquely identified by a ten-digit number. However, it is not always necessary to dial all ten digits to call another telephone. The country is split up into over one hundred "areas." Within each area all telephones have the same first three numbers. The first

three numbers of every telephone are called its "area code." In Chicago *all* telephone numbers begin with the digits 312. In Miami, Florida, they all begin with the digits 305. In Los Angeles all phone numbers begin with the digits 213.

When you call a telephone in your own area you *do not* use the area code. You dial only the *last seven* numbers. When you dial a telephone that is *not* in your area, it will not have the same area code as your own and you must dial the entire ten-digit number: the three-digit area code and the seven-digit *local* number.

The last example is a question that tests the student's understanding of telephone numbers.

If you live in Chicago and wish to call a friend who lives in Los Angeles, California, do you need to use the area code?
(answer: yes)

In reviewing the above question, we decided the answer was too obvious. Furthermore, the method of answering the question was dissimilar to the activity being taught, namely dialing. Consequently, we developed a slightly different question whose answer reflected the skill needed in making a telephone call. The following is the revised question and answer.

Imagine that you live in Miami and your telephone number is 555-3396. You have a friend who lives in Los Angeles, California, and her telephone number there is 555-3955. What number must you dial to call your friend? Type the number without dashes and press⟨return⟩.
(answer: 2135553955)

Write and Revise Secondary Text

During one lesson segment, a picture of a touch-tone telephone appears on the screen, and the student practices making simulated calls by clicking with the mouse on the receiver to lift it and hang it up and on the simulated telephone buttons to dial. The corresponding text segment is a short list of directions to tell students how to do this. HELP and EXIT are mouse-sensitive buttons for requesting help and leaving the lesson.

Using the mouse:
Click on   the hung receiver to lift it UP
                 the lifted receiver to put it DOWN

1 to dial 1
2 to dial 2
3 to dial 3
4 to dial 4
5 to dial 5
6 to dial 6
7 to dial 7
8 to dial 8
9 to dial 9
0 to dial 0
HELP for HELP
EXIT to leave the lesson

Although these directions appear at the bottom of the screen, invariably some students will begin to dial a number without first lifting the receiver. When nothing happens, some will remember the necessary sequence and lift the receiver, but others will have to click on HELP. The next example illustrates the text of the help message.

Before you can click the buttons to dial the telephone you must pick up the receiver and wait until you get a dial tone. To pick up the receiver, click anywhere on it with the mouse. To hang up the receiver, click anywhere on it again.

TRY AGAIN   EXIT

Eventually, the student will click the EXIT button to leave the simulation. Because this is easily done by accident, the following secondary text is included as a safety net.

You clicked EXIT to leave the simulation. Are you sure?

RETURN TO THE LESSON   EXIT

After reviewing the secondary text displays, a few changes seem appropriate. First of all, the directions for using the keyset are longer than necessary because of the repetitive directions for all ten digits. Also, directions for the help and exit buttons are probably unnecessary. We modified the directions as follows.

Click the receiver to lift it up or put it down, or 0-9 to dial.

HELP   EXIT

There are probably many other ways you can think of to improve the directions even more.

Produce Storyboards

After writing the primary and secondary text displays, they are rewritten onto storyboards. Figures 10–2 and 10–3 illustrate some of the primary text rewritten and divided into smaller segments. The identifying labels on the storyboards are also added to our previously written flowcharts. This clarifies the relationship between the flowchart symbols and particular storyboards. It also helps to prevent you from deviating radically from your original plan, or from forgetting important storyboards.

Note the changes from the original text to Figure 10–2. The lines are shortened to accommodate the computer. Note also the marginal notations for overlays such as for a directions storyboard saying "Click here to continue."

Figures 10–4, 10–5, and 10–6 show how a question about dialing the telephone and the separate feedback messages for correct and incorrect answers appear on the storyboards. If we were really preparing this lesson, we would also have first prepared the feedback messages in "long" form when writing primary text (sub-step 1).

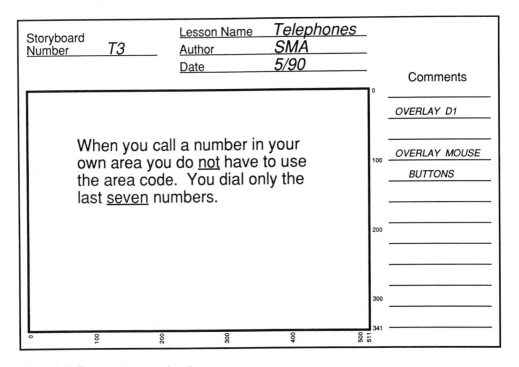

Figure 10-2 Text entered on a storyboard.

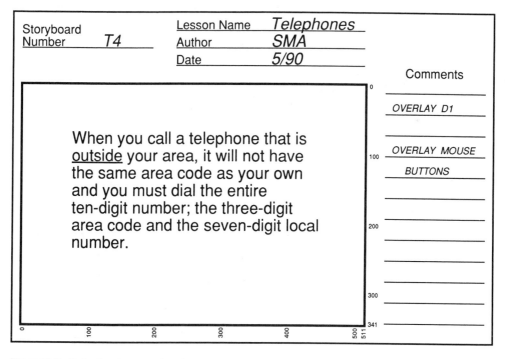

Figure 10-3 Text entered on a storyboard.

Check the Fit of Overlaying Displays

In looking through the storyboards for those combinations of displays that will appear simultaneously, it is obvious that the questions and related displays must be checked. Thus, the storyboards in Figures 10–4, 10–5, and 10–6 are examined for overlap and overcrowding. As currently designed, the question, correct feedback, and mouse buttons at the bottom will not all fit. Either the question or the feedback displays must be changed. One way to correct the problem is to reformat the feedback. Figure 10–7 shows the revised storyboard.

Draw and Revise Graphic Displays and Plan Other Output

In one section of the lesson students practice dialing on a simulated telephone. This requires some pictures of a telephone. On a Macintosh computer it is also possible to reproduce the sounds of a telephone (ringing, dial and busy tones) fairly easily. Figures 10–8, 10–9, and 10–10 show a touch-tone telephone with the receiver down, with the receiver lifted and a marginal notation for a dial tone, and with the receiver up and a marginal notation to stop the tone (dial tones stop when you begin dialing). The number being dialed appears at the right.

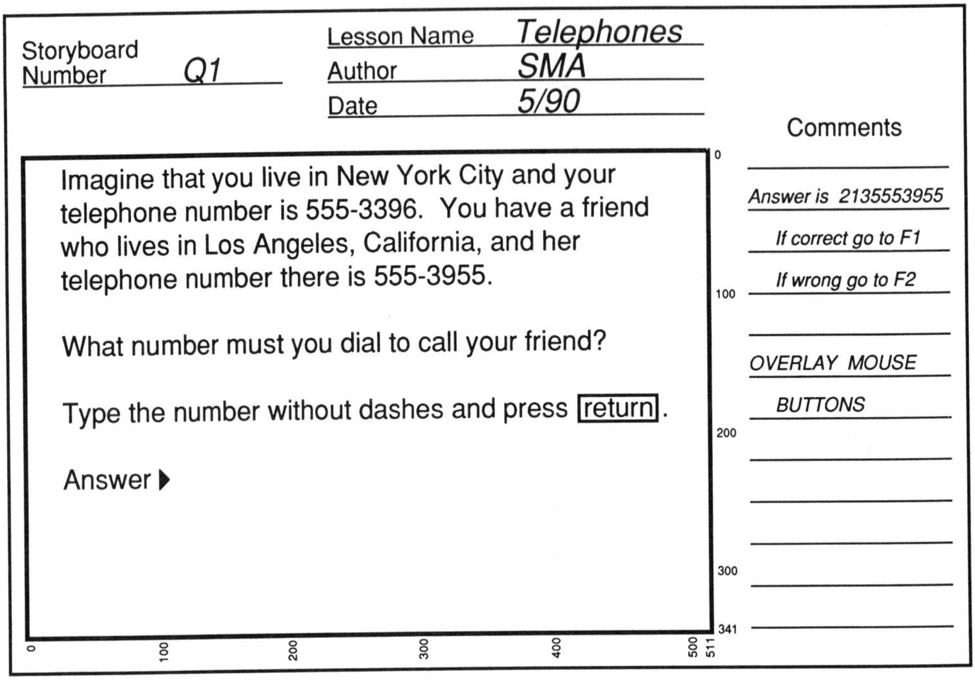

Storyboard Number ___Q1___	Lesson Name ___*Telephones*___
	Author ___*SMA*___
	Date ___*5/90*___

Comments

0

Imagine that you live in New York City and your telephone number is 555-3396. You have a friend who lives in Los Angeles, California, and her telephone number there is 555-3955.

What number must you dial to call your friend?

Type the number without dashes and press return .

Answer ▶

Answer is 2135553955

If correct go to F1

If wrong go to F2

100

OVERLAY MOUSE

BUTTONS

200

300

341

0   100   200   300   400   500   511

Figure 10-4 Question entered on a storyboard.

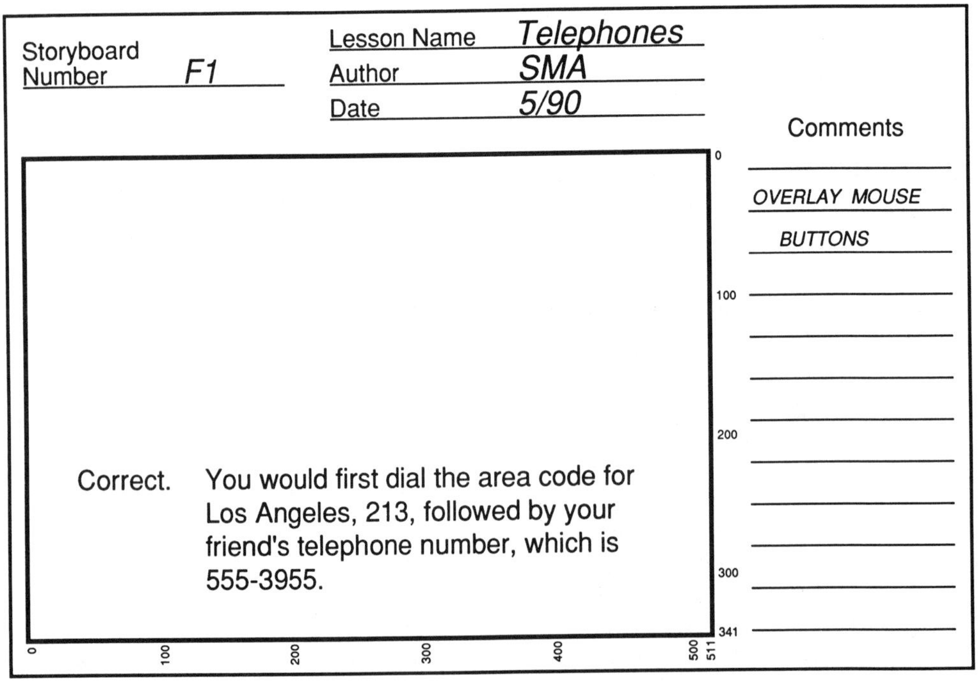

Storyboard Number ___F1___	Lesson Name ___*Telephones*___
	Author ___*SMA*___
	Date ___*5/90*___

Comments

0

OVERLAY MOUSE

BUTTONS

100

200

Correct.   You would first dial the area code for Los Angeles, 213, followed by your friend's telephone number, which is 555-3955.

300

341

0   100   200   300   400   500   511

Figure 10-5 Feedback for correct response on a storybord.

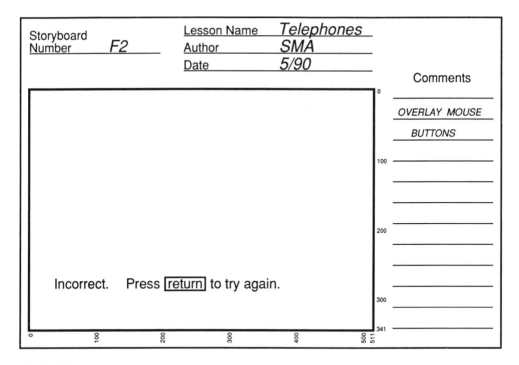

Storyboard
Number   *F2*   Lesson Name   *Telephones*
                            Author   *SMA*
                            Date   *5/90*

                                                            Comments

                                                            OVERLAY MOUSE

                                                            BUTTONS

Incorrect.   Press return to try again.

Figure 10-6   Feedback for incorrect response on a storyboard.

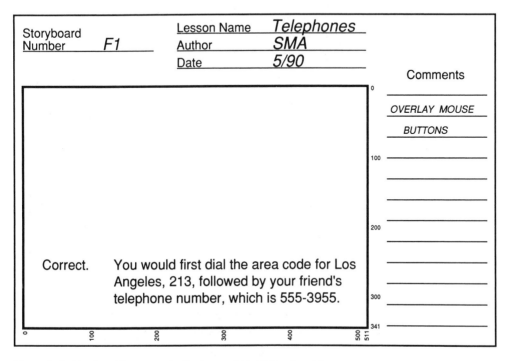

Storyboard
Number   *F1*   Lesson Name   *Telephones*
                            Author   *SMA*
                            Date   *5/90*

                                                            Comments

                                                            OVERLAY MOUSE

                                                            BUTTONS

Correct.   You would first dial the area code for Los
             Angeles, 213, followed by your friend's
             telephone number, which is 555-3955.

Figure 10-7   Storyboard F1 corrected to fit when overlaid with Storyboard Q1.

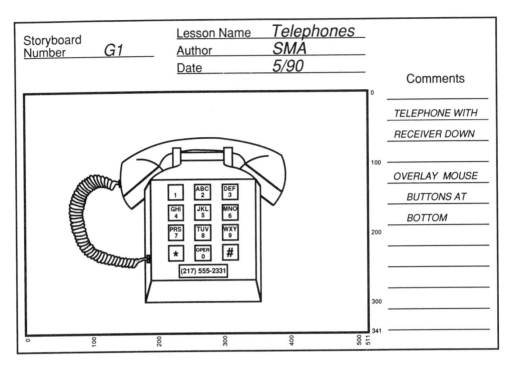

Figure 10-8   The telephone with the receiver down.

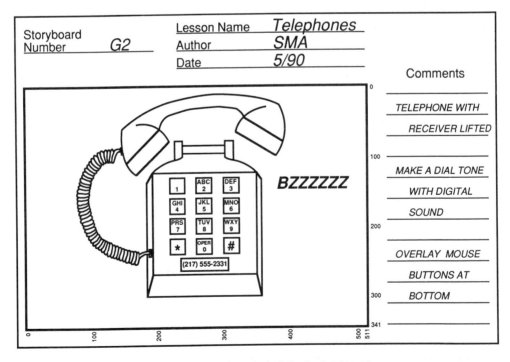

Figure 10-9   The telephone with the receiver up and marginal notation for digital sound.

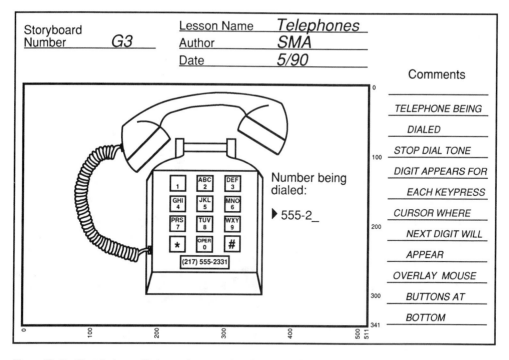

Storyboard Number *G3*	Lesson Name *Telephones* Author *SMA* Date *5/90*	

Comments

TELEPHONE BEING

DIALED

STOP DIAL TONE

DIGIT APPEARS FOR

EACH KEYPRESS

CURSOR WHERE

NEXT DIGIT WILL

APPEAR

OVERLAY MOUSE

BUTTONS AT

BOTTOM

Number being dialed:

▶ 555-2_

(217) 555-2331

Figure 10-10   The telephone with the receiver up and numbers appearing at the right as the student dials.

Check Graphics and Simultaneous Text for Fit

In checking each telephone picture and its respective text it appears that some will not fit due to the vertical size of the display. For example, Figure 10–10 allows too little room for the accompanying directions and the number that the student will dial. This problem can be corrected in a variety of ways, such as moving the picture to a different location on the display, eliminating or changing some of the text, or reducing the size of the picture. In this case, it seems preferable to reduce the size of the picture so that all textual material fits as it is, provided, of course, that the smaller picture is still clear and legible. All of the pictures will need to be reduced, because we would not want lifting the receiver to cause a change in the size of the telephone.

Review the Flowcharts and Storyboards

The flowcharts are now spread out on a table and all completed text and graphic storyboards are tacked to a bulletin board in an order approximating that which will appear to students. Figure 10–11, which simply labels the contents of each storyboard, gives an idea of the storyboard layout for the telephone lesson.

The title page is followed by two pages of introduction, stating the objec-

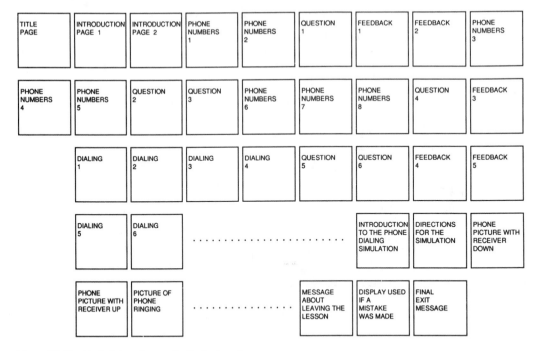

Figure 10-11 A bulletin board covered with storyboards.

tives and giving instructions about how to proceed through the lesson. Next are two pages about the structure of telephone numbers (storyboards T1 and T2), a question (storyboard Q1), and possible feedback messages (storyboards F1 and F2).

The layout continues with information, questions, and feedback about telephone numbers; then information, questions, and feedback about dialing. Later in the lesson the student reads the introduction and directions for the dialing simulation and can then practice dialing. The layout finally ends with the closing messages of the lesson. The box labeled "message about leaving the lesson" asks if the student really wishes to leave. If not, the next storyboard appears and then the lesson returns to the practice simulation. If the student indeed wishes to leave, the display labeled "final exit message" signals the end of the lesson.

In this example, many storyboards are omitted for the sake of brevity. In a real design effort, all presentations, questions, feedback, help messages, directions, and so on would need to be included.

Now we review the storyboards, pretending to be a student seeing these displays on a computer screen and reacting accordingly. While doing this, take notes on any problems, such as poorly worded presentations, missing directions, unclear questions, demeaning feedback, spelling errors, or crowded displays.

Other instructional designers now review our flowcharts. Overall sequence, pedagogy, and motivation are discussed. A content expert should pay particular attention to the simulation of dialing to determine if it will perform correctly under all reasonable circumstances. It is best for the flowchart symbols to contain both coded reference to storyboards and short text descriptions. This allows quick reference to a storyboard if the reviewer wants to see details, but does not require reference to every storyboard to understand the flowchart.

It is important to have other people review your flowcharts. Review of one's own storyboards seldom produces a very complete list of errors. Problems are more likely to be noticed by people who were not involved in their production.

When two or three people review the storyboards, many additional problems will come to light. One person may ask about hanging up in the middle of dialing a number, and although this should work, you may not have planned for it. Another person may want to review the directions at the beginning of the lesson, but there is no way to do this. A third person wishes to leave halfway through the lesson, and wants to be able to come back later and start again exactly where leaving off; there is currently no way to do that either.

Collect as many opinions as is reasonably possible. A good rule of thumb is to stop the process when a reviewer does not point out any new problems. Remember to write down everything that reviewers say, even if you disagree or their comments seem trivial. If several reviewers dislike something, *you* are probably wrong.

In checking all of the reviews, if it is determined that there are some major problems, such as missing directions or no means of "hanging up" during the simulation, you should fix the major problems before proceeding to the next step. On the other hand, revision of minor problems, such as a crowded display or poor wording, can be postponed until the next step (programming) when other minor problems will undoubtedly surface.

CONCLUSION

Having completed flowcharts and storyboards, you are ready to begin implementation of your lesson on a computer. Care in generating and evaluating these preliminary design materials ensures an easier time in the final production and evaluation steps. We reiterate the warning to avoid skipping these steps. Many people, with only an instructional idea in their head, attempt to sit at a computer and create a lesson. This usually results in an inferior lesson. While the detail of flowcharts and the artistic quality of storyboards need not be great, it is important to generate a concrete plan for everyone involved to view and discuss. You should not go on to the final steps until you and others are satisfied with the plan.

REFERENCES AND BIBLIOGRAPHY

DENEBA SOFTWARE. (1988). *Canvas*. [Computer Program]. Miami, FL: Deneba Software.

DWYER, F.M. (1978). *Strategies for Improving Visual Learning*. State College, PA: Learning Services.

ELECTRONIC VISION. (1987). *IVD Toolkit*. [Computer Program]. Athens, OH: Electronic Vision.

FLEMING, M., & LEVIE, W.H. (1978). *Instructional Message Design: Principles from the Behavioral Sciences*. Englewood Cliffs, NJ: Educational Technology Publications

HEINES, J.M. (1984). *Screen Design Strategies for Computer-Assisted Instruction*. Bedford, MA: Digital Press.

HUNTLEY, J.S., & LOW, N. (1986). *Scripter*. [Computer Program]. Coralville, IA: Cognitive Design Technologies, Limited.

MARKLE, S.M. (1969). *Good Frames and Bad: A Grammar of Frame Writing*. New York: John Wiley and Sons, Inc.

SAMPATH, S., & QUAINE, A. (1990). Effective interface tools for CAI authors. *Journal of Computer-Based Instruction, 17*(1), 31–34.

WALKER, D.F., & HESS, R.D. (Eds.) (1984). *Instructional Software: Principles and Perspectives for Design and Use.* Belmont, CA: Wadsworth Publishing Company.

WILEMAN, R.E. (1980). *Exercises in Visual Thinking.* New York: Hastings House, Publishers.

ZSOFT CORP. (1987). *PC Paintbrush.* [Computer Program]. Marietta, GA: ZSoft Corporation.

SUMMARY OF STORYBOARDING

Write and revise primary text, which includes information, questions, and feedback.

Write and revise secondary text, such as directions, hints, and end-of-lesson messages.

Produce storyboards, in which you rewrite all of the materials from the previous two sub-steps to fit on your computer display.

Check the fit of overlaying displays, such as questions and feedback, or information and directions, to make sure that nothing overlaps and that displays are not too crowded.

Draw and revise graphic displays and plan other output, which includes pictures, graphs, cartoons, sounds, music, and voice. Graphics should be done, if possible, in the actual size they will appear on the computer display.

Check graphics and simultaneous text for fit. Pictures and their descriptions or directions, for instance, should be coordinated to eliminate overlap or crowdedness, as in sub-step 4 above.

Assemble the flowcharts and storyboards on a bulletin board, blackboard, or large table so they can all be seen at one time.

Review the flowcharts and storyboard assembly yourself, looking for errors, checking for completeness, and getting, for the first time, the whole picture of the lesson.

Have experts review the flowcharts. Write down *all* comments.

Have experts and students review the storyboard assembly. Write down *all* comments.

Make revisions. Fix real problems, but not little details. There will be more changes to come in the next two steps.

11

PROGRAMMING AND SUPPORT MATERIALS

STEP 8—PROGRAMMING

The next step is the implementation of your plan on the computer. This has become known as programming because in the past one generally used a programming language such as BASIC or PASCAL to generate the lesson. Today there are more options available, but we retain the term *programming* for lack of a better one.

Because implementation is very different depending on the type of software used, we cannot give a step-by-step list of procedures and examples as for previous phases. Rather, we will discuss the alternatives, their advantages, and the activities common to all of them.

Authoring Alternatives

Several years ago it was common to describe the software options for developing lessons according to the continuum shown in Figure 11-1.

Programming *languages*, such as BASIC, were the most common alternative. Standard programming languages usually provided the greatest control of the computer, and thus maximum power and flexibility in lesson development. It was also the least costly alternative, since some programming language would generally come as standard with a computer. However, learning a programming language is hard and time consuming.

Authoring languages, such as TUTOR (Schaefges, Eisenberg, & Stock, 1982) or PILOT (Apple Computer, 1980), were easier to learn. They provided routines necessary for computer-based instruction, such as combining text and graphics, answer judging, and student control functions, that were typically missing or difficult to use in standard programming languages. But authoring languages still required typical programming activities, writing lines of computer commands. They were also uncommon and more expensive, and it was often difficult to find support because there were fewer expert users than for standard languages.

Authoring *systems* were first introduced in the late 1970's and were software packages claiming to permit CBI development without programming. They

The Authoring Tools Continuum

Programming Languages	Authoring Languages	Authoring Systems
greater power and flexibility lower cost expertise more widely available faster execution of lessons more transportable among platforms		easier to learn easier to use faster development facilitate more phases of development

Figure 11-1 General authoring tools continuum with relative advantages.

typically consisted of a *prompting editor* which asked the developer questions about presentations, questions, and branching, and then generated a lesson. Some used editors for creating graphics or text displays. Early authoring systems were very primitive and limited the developer to simple tutorial and drill programs. They were more expensive than authoring languages and even less common. As a result not many developers used them.

In the second half of the 1980's considerable improvement was made in authoring languages and systems. Most authoring languages added features previously found in systems, such as graphics editors. Authoring systems in turn became much more powerful. Some added the ability to write code as well as to use editors and prompters, thus providing more flexibility and power. Some added animation editors and other features for simulations and games. Some of the most recent systems have added a flowchart component to describe sequence and decision points.

Thus, it is now useful to look at the original continuum in a new way, combining authoring languages and systems (the right two thirds of Figure 11–2) into a single continuum (Figure 11–2) with three general types of systems: code-oriented, frame-oriented, and icon-oriented.

Code-oriented systems are those in which a substantial part of the development is programming of the classic type, writing lines of computer commands that depict input, output, branching, and data manipulation. They typically have editors to easily generate and edit text and graphic displays, animations, and sounds. Examples of code-oriented systems for IBM microcomputers include *IMSATT-2000* (IMSATT, 1988), *PC/PILOT* (Kheriaty, 1984), *TenCORE* (Computer

The Authoring Systems Continuum

Code-oriented Systems	Frame-oriented Systems	Icon-oriented Systems
greater power and flexibility faster execution of lessons		easier to learn easier to use faster development

Figure 11-2 Authoring system continuum with relative advantages.

Teaching Corporation, 1985), and *Unison* (Courseware Applications, 1988). These systems retain most of the advantages of standard programming languages and authoring languages as described before. They are powerful, allowing the developer to access all the capabilities of the computer. They are good for all kinds of CBI lessons, from simple drills to sophisticated simulations. However, they are more difficult and time consuming to learn than the other types of systems. Figure 11–3 shows an example of writing code in *Unison.*

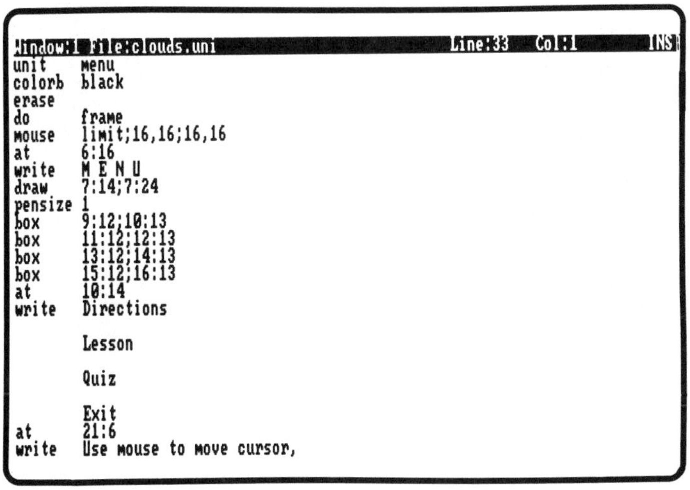

```
Window:1 File:clouds.uni                          Line:33   Col:1        INS
unit    menu
colorb  black
erase
do      frame
mouse   limit;16,16;16,16
at      6:16
write   M E N U
draw    7:14;7:24
pensize 1
box     9:12;10:13
box     11:12;12:13
box     13:12;14:13
box     15:12;16:13
at      10:14
write   Directions

        Lesson

        Quiz

        Exit
at      21:6
write   Use mouse to move cursor,
```

Figure 11-3 A segment of code in the *Unison* system. *(Courtesy of Courseware Applications)*

Frame-oriented systems are those which are centered around a powerful display editor that includes capabilities for combining text, graphics, sound, and animation. They are typically "what-you-see-is-what-you-get" or WYSIWYG (pronounced wizz-e-wig) editors. The way you arrange things on the display is how they will look to the student. Usually, the display is easily arranged with a mouse or other pointing device. Frame-oriented systems generally require an editor for branching and data manipulation that is more like programming, requiring the use of special commands, logic symbols, and data variables. These systems are generally easier to learn and use than code-oriented systems but less powerful for the creation of complex lessons. Examples of frame-oriented systems for IBM microcomputers are *SAM* (Learncom, 1986) and *Quest* (Allen Communication, 1985). Figure 11–4 shows the display and branching editors in *SAM,* which stands for System for Authoring Microtraining.

Code-oriented and frame-oriented systems are to some extent growing together. As the manufacturers of code-oriented systems try to increase their ease of use, they add more and better display editors. As the manufacturers of frame-oriented systems try to increase the power of their systems, they add the ability to "drop down" to the code level and write code for simulations and other methodologies. Such combinations are called *hybrid* systems (Fairweather & O'Neal, 1984). Several of the systems referenced above are becoming hybrid.

Icon-oriented systems are the newest breed of authoring systems. These

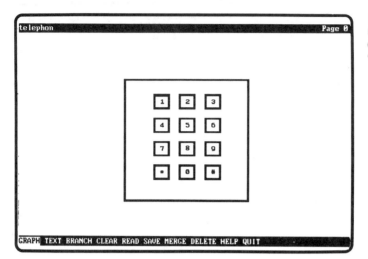

Figure 11-4 The display and branching editors in the *SAM* system. *(Courtesy of Technology Applications Group, Inc. and Sandy Corporation)*

allow the developer to describe the entire lesson plan—its parts, sequence, and branching decisions—by creating a flowchart. Then the developer specifies the details of each flowchart element, which may be text and graphics displays, calculations, animations, control of other devices connected to the computer, student control of the lesson, input and output. Such systems typically work only with computer operating systems that provide integrated text and graphics and a "windowed" environment, such as the Macintosh, Apple IIgs, IBM microcomputers using *Microsoft Windows* (Microsoft, 1985), or the new *OS/2* operating system (International Business Machines, 1988). Icon-oriented systems generally are the easiest type of system to use, yet come close to code-oriented systems in power. Although they need more improvement for the development of commercial courseware, we believe that they are the best kind of authoring tool for the novice

CBI developer. Icon-oriented systems for IBM and compatible computers are *Icon-Author* (AIMTech, 1988), *ProPi* (ASYS Computer Systems, 1989), and *PCD-3* (Control Data Corporation, 1988). Examples for the Macintosh are *Authorware Professional* (Authorware, 1989) and *Course Builder* (Appleton, 1987). Figure 11–5 shows the flowchart for a short lesson being created in *Authorware Professional*. Each small icon represents a display, a question, some feedback, a calculation, or other lesson component.

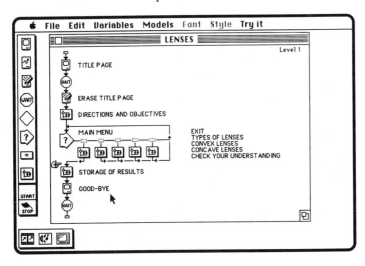

Figure 11-5 A short lesson flowchart in *Authorware Professional*. *(Courtesy of Authorware)*

By clicking on an icon the developer "opens it" to put in the details. In Figure 11–6 a display icon has been opened and a display is being created. In Figure 11–7 a decision icon has been opened and a looping structure is being created. There are also icons for animation, erasing, pausing, questions, calculations, video, sound, and for "grouping" lesson segments.

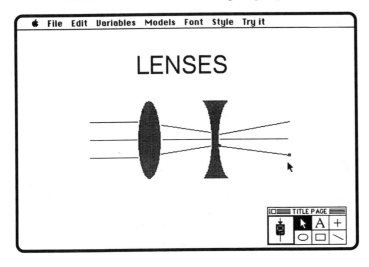

Figure 11-6 Creating a display in *Authorware Professional. (Courtesy of Authorware)*

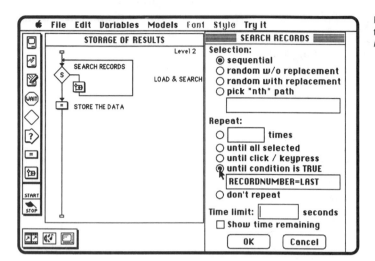

Figure 11-7 Creating a loop using the decision icon in *Authorware Professional. (Courtesy of Authorware)*

Choosing Appropriate Authoring Software

Given the many alternatives available for authoring, it is obvious that an important decision before you begin programming is to select the best tools for the job. That decision must be a function of hardware and cost constraints, instructional strategies desired, and experience of the developers. Familiarity with a variety of software tools is advisable for it enables you to make better choices with less research for each new job. Although there is no single comprehensive source evaluating authoring software, there are several articles and books with summary information, in-depth treatments of particular authoring software, and guidelines to aid in selection (Barker, 1987; Burger, 1986; Crowell, 1988, 1989; Hannum, 1986; Huntley & Alessi, 1987; Kearsley, 1984a, 1984b, 1988; Locatis & Carr, 1985; Lommel, 1986; T.H.E. Journal, 1988).

If you intend to distribute software you develop, an overriding factor may be license fees. Most authoring systems and languages charge fees for distributing lessons developed with their systems. In contrast, most standard programming languages do not charge such fees. Along with your budget and computer hardware, such logistical constraints often take precedence over other considerations. After those constraints, the instructional strategies and methodologies you desire should be the primary considerations. Simulations and games typically require the greater power and flexibility of standard languages. Tutorials and drills are more easily constructed with authoring languages or systems. Computer-based tests are best implemented with the testing systems described in Chapter 6.

While ease-of-use is the primary reason for choosing authoring systems, we place it lower in importance than those considerations already discussed. It is of no benefit that a tool is easy to use if it does not do what you want. All other things being equal (cost and hardware constraints, power required) ease-of-use may be considered. The two situations where ease-of-use should take precedence *over* power and cost are for prototyping lessons and for students learning CBI development. In the latter case, the ease-of-use of icon-oriented authoring systems allow the novice developer to pay more attention to instructional design considerations and less to the details of programming.

Rules for Good Programming

Regardless of the authoring alternative to be used—whether it is a standard programming language or an icon-oriented authoring system—there are several practices that the developer is encouraged to follow to ensure that a lesson works properly and to increase the efficiency of development.

Refer to a Flowchart. A flowchart is not only useful for conceptualizing and designing a lesson, but for guiding programming. This is especially true when using a standard programming language or code-oriented system. With these tools it is very easy to get lost in a long program and to write an erroneous program that does not do what you intended. When using a language, a detailed Level-3 flowchart is advisable. For frame-oriented and icon-oriented authoring systems a briefer Level-2 flowchart is sufficient. However, even with these newer development tools, producing and carefully following at least a Level-2 flowchart is very beneficial. Not doing so will usually lead to omissions and errors in your work.

Off-line Organization. Not many years ago, when computers were much more expensive and fewer in number, it was necessary to plan one's computer program in detail on paper, then enter it into the computer. Today, computers are no longer a scarce resource and most developers are likely to have one on their own desk. Thus there is the temptation to begin implementation on the computer sooner than one should. If one is writing standard program code, such as BASIC, there is the temptation to create the first draft right on the computer. Regardless of the type of development software you use, we strongly encourage careful off-line planning. If you use a programming language, this means writing code or pseudo-code on paper. If you use a frame-oriented or icon-oriented authoring system, this means planning the structure of the lesson, its parts, decisions, branching, user control, and so on. Although an experienced developer may create a first draft interactively on a computer, knowing from experience how to structure the lesson, novices attempting to do so invariably create a first draft that is so disorganized and erroneous that it must often be thrown out and completely redone. We strongly encourage careful planning on paper.

In the off-line plan, we do not advocate that you write out all the text and questions you will use; you can make reference to the appropriate storyboards for this. The off-line details should emphasize those things not in the storyboards such as sequence, calculations, file manipulations, and student control.

The benefits of off-line coding diminish the more you use programming tools, such as graphics packages and automated answer judging routines. These often require interactive procedures to implement or test, which can only be done on-line. As more of these tools become commonplace, there will be less to gain from off-line preparation.

Using Existing Materials.   Many parts of a lesson are similar and much of what you create can be copied to speed up the production process. Thus, if you have already entered one question and have established how the lesson will handle the data collection, answer judging, and branching, it is advantageous to copy the question segment as many times as needed. On each copy, all you have to do is change the wording, judging details, and branching destinations.

This reproduction technique is even more useful when using a programming language that requires that you write all the code for everything you want the program to do. This onerous task of writing instructions in the minutest detail may be eased if you can use segments of code you have written before, either from within the same lesson or from previous ones.

Copying and modifying existing materials can save a great deal of time. In fact, we recommend you establish libraries of often-used routines for yourself and anyone else to access and copy. You should encourage colleagues to contribute to the library. To make the library more useful, maintain a comprehensive, up-to-date listing of what is available and ensure the entries are easily accessible, both off-line and on-line.

For the more popular programming languages, a good source of code is libraries, either traditional ones that have computer software, or specialized computer libraries that allow subscribers to use or copy any of the materials. Other sources are colleagues, local computing clubs, and published computer science books with examples of common routines. Of course you should pay attention to copyright law and courtesy in this regard. Copyrighted code should not be used without permission and anything copied, even public-domain material, should give credit to the creator of the material.

Modularization.   A programming technique that can lead to major savings in time and effort is modularization. This is concerned with the overall structural design of the lesson. In general, this means adopting a *top-down* approach. The lesson should have a central section, such as a student-choice menu, which calls the various parts of the program. These parts in turn share common procedures, such as question and feedback, help, or data storage procedures.

Shared procedures of this sort are called subroutines in most programming and authoring languages. In some newer languages, which are known as object-oriented languages, they are called objects. A major problem with many frame-oriented and icon-oriented authoring systems is that they do not provide for creating subroutines and thus hinder modular design.

Many of the storyboards produced earlier can be regarded as subroutines. We suggested that repetitive presentations, such as feedback or directions, be put on one storyboard card and overlaid when needed. This facilitates organization of the lesson into subroutines and consequently a modular form.

Judging. Judging a student response is one of the most difficult parts of a lesson to implement. It takes care and experience to create good judging routines that are flexible and that provide the necessary information about the student response for making decisions about feedback and sequencing. The process is eased by using an authoring system that provides good judging routines. These are routines that analyze the response according to given rules and criteria, and that automatically provide information about the response. *Authorware Professional,* for example, provides a question icon which allows processing student responses made by typing single letters, typing words and phrases, clicking parts of the screen with the mouse, and dragging objects on the screen with the mouse. Text responses can deal fairly flexibly with capitalization, punctuation, word order, and spelling variation.

If you are using a programming language and must write judging routines yourself, it is worth the effort to plan them in advance to be as context-free as possible. That is, if you can generalize these routines in any way, then you can use them repeatedly in the form of a subroutine. For example, if you write a judging routine that provides information about the student's response to the question "Who was the first president of the United States?" it would be better in the long run to develop it to compare *any* response with *any* answer rather than only with "Washington." This routine could then be used for many other situations requiring comparison of two words.

Producing Graphics. Graphics production used to be one of the most difficult aspects of implementation but has become one of the easiest. Regardless of what computer and implementation software you are using, there will be a variety of compatible graphics programs from which you can choose. The better programs are referred to as "object oriented" (not to be confused with object-oriented programming languages) or as "draw" programs. These programs, of which *MacDraw* (Claris, 1988) is very typical, allow you to create pictures by drawing or tracing with the mouse and typing with the keyset. A display is composed of many individual objects, such as sentences, boxes, circles, and arrows. Individual objects are easily moved, changed in size or color, duplicated, or deleted. The way the display appears in the graphics program is very much what it will look like to the student. Programming languages and authoring systems alike are increasingly providing the ability to import and use displays created in this way. The Macintosh computer's operating system is very good in its ability to move text and graphic information between different software packages.

Other tools to facilitate graphic production are the graphics scanner and video digitizer. A graphics scanner is a device that can take a graphic image from a piece of paper and convert it into computer graphics inside a graphics creation program. You may then modify it for use in your lesson. Video digitizers allow you to connect a television camera to a computer so that any image the camera can see can be converted to a computer graphic image. Graphics scanners can be purchased for as little as $200. Video digitizers cost more but generally have the capability to produce color images and images of greater realism.

As with copying and modifying existing code, the increasing ease of taking an existing image and incorporating it into your own program still requires the developer to pay attention to the laws of copyright and courtesy.

Internal Documentation. The purpose of putting documentation inside a lesson is to make it easier to understand how it functions. The nature of documentation varies depending on the type of development software used. In a programming language or code-oriented system, it consists of comments that relate to lines or sections of code, notes on how the program is structured or where related sections of code are to be found, and other devices that organize or describe the program or make it easier to read. In an icon-oriented system the icons themselves, labels on icons, and comments inside them are the primary means of documentation.

Documentation is helpful both during the initial implementation of a lesson and when it has to be revised. It is particularly useful when someone other than the original person has to make revisions, or when revisions must be made a long time after the original programming. It can be an impossible task to change or maintain a complex lesson that has no helpful comments describing what different parts of the program do and how they function. Documentation can also be useful to you even during initial implementation. You would be surprised how difficult it is to understand a section of a large program you have not worked on in the past week.

Good documentation takes up a considerable amount of disk space and memory. This may cause problems. For example, if the lesson has to be written onto several disks because internal comments lengthen the program, you may want to have two versions—a multiple-disk version with all the comments for developers, and a single-disk version without comments for student use. A problem with that, however, is that you must remember to update both versions every time you make a program change. Some software, such as standard language compilers and some authoring systems, automatically strip out comments when a student version of a lesson is produced.

When using a language, indentation is a form of documentation. It is a simple process for making code more readable. If you have hundreds or thousands of lines in a program, it is frequently very difficult to find your way about it or to distinguish one section from another. If the programming language allows it, an easy way is to use indenting to differentiate sections. This allows you to see which commands are associated with each section. This technique is particularly useful if you have nested IF. . . THEN or ON. . . NEXT command structures. A related technique is to place blank lines throughout the program, marking off related sections of code, which helps to visually illustrate the program's structure.

Unfortunately, it is common to leave documentation to the end of the implementation cycle. This is a mistake, because when the program is functioning correctly there is little incentive to devote the time necessary for adequate documentation. Other tasks suddenly assume higher priorities and documenting is seldom completed. Write comments as you implement your lesson. They will be clearer if done at this time and will also be more helpful to you and those that follow.

Error Detection and Correction

Once the lesson has been written it must be checked for errors. This testing is often called *debugging*—a most descriptive example of computer jargon. Errors are called "bugs" because they are usually small, annoying, and elusive. Our recommended method of debugging is to test independent segments of a lesson as they are developed. Obviously, this is facilitated by adhering to the principle of modular design. So, for example, as soon as a subroutine to judge student responses has been drafted, you should test it to check that it functions as desired. By checking parts individually as they are produced, you will know when an error appears that it is probably in the *newest* section of your program.

There are two major types of bugs: those that you are given information about and those you have to discover yourself. The former are much easier to find and fix than the latter.

This first type of bug, more common with programming languages and code-oriented systems, usually appears in one of two forms: the syntax error and the execution error. Typical examples are misspelled commands (such as PRNIT, instead of PRINT), references to nonexistent lines or routines, and inappropriate use of command syntax, such as leaving out periods or commas. The computer itself locates these errors before the lesson is even run and points their location out to you. Sometimes a suggestion is made for how to eliminate the error.

The second type of known bug is called an execution error because it causes a malfunction during execution of the lesson. These errors satisfy the basic syntax rules but fail to operate properly because they attempt to do something impossible or which the computer cannot do because of missing information. The most common examples are in expressions such as X/Y, when $Y = 0$, or the square root of Z, when Z is negative. The expressions themselves, X/Y and square root of Z, are both valid. However, under certain conditions they cannot be evaluated, in this case when Y is zero and Z is negative. Most programming languages suffer an execution error when this type of situation occurs.

Execution errors usually manifest themselves quite obviously, because the program ceases to function. Fortunately, most programs will give some indication of the reason for the failure, although the error message may not be very clear or directly helpful. This type of bug is more difficult to locate than a syntax error because it may only occur in an unusual set of circumstances. That is, the program may function correctly for a long time until this set of circumstances arises. Only then will the program fail.

A more difficult type of bug to correct is that which you are given no information about, unknown errors. These are usually logical and occur when the program executes properly but does not do what *you had intended* it to do. An example of this would be a calculation to determine test scores using an incorrect formula. Such a lesson might be acceptable to the computer, but on running would produce incorrect results. So, if you had written a program to calculate a class's average test score and you multiplied rather than divided the summed scores by the number of students, your program would generate the wrong result. Other examples include constructing an algorithm that produces erroneous output; branching on the basis of the wrong variable; mistyping the correct answer in an answer-judging sequence; or recording incorrect data. These errors appear only when the program is running. Some are easy to find because their results are immediately apparent. Others occur so rarely and in such unlikely combinations of circumstances that they are very difficult to locate and correct.

An unknown bug may be a carryover from errors in your flowchart. If your flowchart branches to incorrect parts of the lesson, so will the program if you followed your flowchart carefully. If the flowchart has a faulty algorithm for generating questions, so will the program. These errors will be less frequent if you dry run your flowcharts well.

Debugging Techniques.   The best way to minimize the existence of errors is by prevention. Debugging is trivial if there are few or no errors. As we have mentioned before, the best preventive measure is a good flowchart that has been thoroughly tested. Still, bugs do creep in and need to be found and fixed.

There are several stages in debugging a lesson. First, run it with carefully selected information, such as a predetermined selection of correct and incorrect answers. On the basis of these responses, you should be able to determine what the lesson should do next, such as what feedback it will provide. If there is any discrepancy between the actual and expected output, you have uncovered a bug.

A second stage is going through the lesson entering unusual answers. These may be negative numbers or zeroes when the program expects a positive number, numerals when it expects letters, or pressing ⟨return⟩ without typing anything. Once again, the lesson should function predictably and sensibly. The third stage is to press different keys at points in the lesson when there is no need to press them. Only keys that are advertised to have some function should have an effect.

Unfortunately, noting that a bug exists does not necessarily mean that you know what it is or where it occurs. The more complicated the lesson, the less likely it is that the cause of the error is where you first notice it. So, for example, in a lesson that is used by many students, which summarizes all the data collected for the instructor, an error that appears in the summary may reflect a problem with the routines that do the summarizing or may be caused by poor data-collection routines during instruction. There are several techniques, however, that can help in locating these bugs.

Step-by-Step Execution.   Most languages and some systems have the facility of running a program one line or segment at a time, allowing you to monitor execution. The best way to use such a facility is to enter carefully constructed responses so it is easy to know the value of relevant variables at any stage in the lesson. The contents of these variables should either be temporarily displayed on the screen or be easily accessible. By comparing the contents of these variables with predicted values, you can usually determine at what point a problem occurs.

Setting Flags.   A related procedure, especially useful if step-by-step execution is not available, is to set flags. A flag is any device that alerts you to a situation. For example, if the lesson has been failing because it takes the square root of a negative number, you can add a routine immediately before that point to check the value of the variable. If the value is less than zero, the routine can temporarily halt execution, and display the values of relevant variables on the screen. Again, this helps trace the source of the problem.

Numbering Displays.   Another useful technique is to have each display numbered for easy reference. This becomes more useful the larger the program is. It is difficult and tedious to describe verbally each display on which there is a problem. It is far easier to note an identification number. A related technique is to identify on each display the part of the program currently being executed, such as the subroutine name. When the lesson is completely debugged the numbers or names can be removed.

On-line Comments.   If possible, it is helpful to incorporate into the lesson a means whereby the student can leave on-line comments. Thus, if the student wants to comment about some aspect of the lesson, pressing a particular key permits the comment to be typed in. These comments are stored on disk for later use by the developers.

Fixing Bugs.   Once you have found the problem with the program, it must be corrected. Although this would appear to be straightforward, it can be very tricky. A change may often cause a new error. A good policy when fixing a bug is to save the existing part of the lesson before exchanging or replacing it. In this way, should the correction not work, you can retrieve the original segment and try again.

Another good technique is to change only one thing at a time. That is, do not try to resolve all problems in a lesson at once. If you try to do this, you will create interactions between problems, making further diagnosis difficult or impossible. Work on one problem at a time, ensuring that each is fixed before proceeding to the next.

For additional techniques on locating and fixing program errors, see Bruce (1980).

STEP 9—SUPPORT MATERIAL PRODUCTION

Computer programs usually cannot stand completely alone, although many people like to maintain that they can. The general population is not sufficiently familiar with computers that people know how to operate them without a guide. Consequently the next step in our model is the production of these supporting materials.

The four kinds of auxiliary material we discuss are:

Student manuals
Instructor manuals
Technical manuals
Adjunct instructional material

The Student Manual

Although a good CBI lesson should strive for ease-of-use as much as possible, assume a manual is still necessary. Although a student manual should be short, there are a variety of kinds of information that a student should be able to obtain without even knowing how to turn on the computer. Additionally, a student manual is a resource for the instructor to learn what students will be doing and, to some extent, to determine if the program is appropriate for the students. While developers usually think of manuals as references only for the user, they should not overlook the fact that potential purchasers often make their decision based on the manuals, as manuals are easier to browse through than the programs.

Following is a summary of most of the things a student manual may have. This is not a list of *necessary* content but of possible content. What is necessary will be a function of your lesson and your students. Some of these elements are trivial and are included here simply as a reminder, a sort of checklist for manual writing. Others may be quite lengthy.

Title Page. The title page should clearly identify the program name, authors and other credits, copyright, and copyright date. As with books, the title page need not be the cover. A cover may just specify a title. The title page should include the additional information.

Table of Contents. Just about any document on paper, unless it is fewer than about five pages, should have a table of contents with page numbers.

Important Warnings. Warnings may include comments on diskette care, or actions to avoid that can disrupt the program or even damage the computer. There is the danger with some people, especially adolescents, that warning them not to do something will encourage them to do it. With some student populations, it may be better to include these warnings in the instructor's manual.

Introduction. An introductory section may include a short statement of the purpose and objectives of the lesson and what the student will be doing. These should be in the vocabulary of the student, not that of the computer scientist or the instructional designer. Objectives should not be stated behaviorally, but generally.

Equipment You Need. More detailed technical requirements should be in an instructor or technical manual. For the student, you should include those things about the computer that should be checked, such as the brand, color or monochrome monitor, and whether external attachments such as a printer are required. Do not include details such as memory requirements, model numbers, and whether special purpose internal computer options must be installed.

Startup of Program. Startup includes how to insert disks, turn on or restart the computer and attached equipment, and if necessary any operating system commands required. Preferably there will be none of the last category. Lessons should be designed to be easy to start.

Trial Run. Everyone likes to get started on a computer program as fast as possible, often without reading the manual. Sometimes the best way to learn how a program works is to get into it, rather than reading about it. This is especially true for simulations and games. A "trial run" allows the student to quickly see what the lesson is like and what it does, usually without any scoring or data recording. Such an option is worth considering. If included, the manual should have directions for accessing and ending such a sample program.

Normal Running of the Program. There are a variety of kinds of useful information regarding the main program. Procedures for user control, answering questions, making choices at menus, getting help, and ending a session are generally very important. It is useful to give the student some idea of lesson length and organization in order to plan for enough time to finish the program or a section of it.

Content Summary or Supplementary Information. Although this should be included with caution in student manuals, it is sometimes useful to have a summary of the material the lesson covers. This is more useful for older students or for the instructor in those cases where there is no separate instructor manual. It is also useful as an advance organizer to prepare the student, and as a review after studying the lesson. The danger is that some students may consider it a replacement for the lesson. Supplementary information is information on the topic not included in the lesson. A science lesson on plants may include readings for the advanced student on plants not covered by the program, or on how to start a greenhouse or garden. This information may also be put in a separate manual or adjunct instructional materials.

Forms or Worksheets Used during the Program. Although forms and worksheets may be a separate set of materials, they are sometimes included in a student manual, especially if few in number. Logs for students to record their use of the program, data recording sheets for laboratory simulations, or musical staffs for music composition following a music lesson are examples.

Technical Information. This should be kept to a minimum in a student manual and should generally be put in a technical manual for programmers or instructors who are very familiar with computer operation. This may include information on connecting and using a printer, a mouse, a videodisc player, or other input and output devices. It may also include troubleshooting suggestions for when something goes wrong. The best thing to include here is advice as to when the student should ask the instructor for assistance or report a problem.

Suggestions for Further Study.   This may include references and a bibliography, resources such as free government information, suggestions for research, experiments, or interesting activities.

Index.   If a manual is more than a few pages, an alphabetic index with page numbers should be included to facilitate finding specific information.

Quick Reference Guide.   When the student manual is long it is wise to include a quick reference guide. This is a one-page summary of the most important information, such as the important keys, how to sign on, and how to exit or get help. This is especially important for complex lessons such as simulations and games that rely on many keypresses being available at all times. We have listed and discussed the quick reference guide *after* the index because a good place for a quick reference guide is on the back cover of the student manual.

The Instructor Manual

All the items in a student manual need also to be known by the instructor. If a student manual exists, information need not be repeated in an instructor manual—the instructor can always consult the student manual. Basic things like the title page with date and credits and a table of contents should be included even if redundant. We only list and discuss those things which should be in an instructor's manual that are not already included in the student manual, or which are different than in the student manual.

Title Page.   Although this is basically the same as for students, the instructor version should emphasize what permission is given to the instructor concerning production of backups, putting the program on networks, and reproduction in general. It should also include a telephone number or other means of obtaining assistance. Although this is likely to be contained in the technical information section, it should also be at the front of the manual so it can be found easily.

Important Warnings.   In addition to those things in the student manual, the instructor manual should explain what to emphasize to students. It may include those things that you do not wish to tell students but which the instructor should know to look out for, such as those key sequences which will stop a program immediately or restart the computer.

Introduction.   This section is very different from the one in the student manual. It should include more detailed purpose and objectives and should describe the student population for which the lesson is designed, the students' grade or age, prerequisite knowledge required, and prerequisite skills (such as typing). It may describe the methodology and instructional strategies used. Most important, it should include suggestions for integrating the material into the curriculum. This includes describing what prior class topics would be helpful, vocabulary used in the lesson, how to introduce and use the lesson in class, how to show the lesson's relevance and motivate students, possible assignments which use the lesson, and follow-up activities both for in class and as homework.

Equipment Needed. This section may be more technical than for students. It may refer not only to the computer brand, monitor type, and attachments required, but also the computer model number, memory and diskette requirements, network requirements or capabilities, and other software required such as the computer's operating system.

How to Make Backups. A warning to make backups and directions on doing so should be in the instructor manual unless there is also a technical manual. This section should describe write-protecting diskettes, making the copies, and explain that only copies should be used with students.

Setup of Equipment. This section may also be more relevant for a technical manual if one is produced. If in the instructor manual, it should include whether to write-protect diskettes, which is possible if no data are to be written on them, how to connect monitors and printers, and how to set up a network if appropriate.

Starting the Program. This is the place for any special instructions for procedures that are done only once, such as creating student records files or copying the program to a hard disk drive. It may also include some of the things also in the student manual: proper insertion of diskettes, turning on the computer and restarting it, making sure all equipment is turned on, and startup commands if they are necessary.

Trial Run. If the program has the capability for testing the program, there should be a section explaining it. Instructors often need to try out a program and quickly review its features to be prepared for dealing with student questions and problems. This section should describe how to access a trial run and how to end it.

Normal Running of the Program. In addition to those things included for the students, the instructor manual may include a map or flowchart describing how students will go through the program.

Summary of Content. While optional for a student manual, this is almost mandatory for an instructor manual. Remember that instructors are likely to buy a lesson or choose to use it based on the manual, not by going through the lesson.

Also, instructors should be able to refresh themselves on the topic and be prepared for student questions without going through the program. The instructor manual should include a complete description of the content and instructional approach along with sample displays of menus, presentations, questions, feedback, and results or report pages.

Forms or Worksheets Used during the Program. In addition to those included in the student manual, the teacher manual may include forms for photocopying and distributing to students, for grading, or for using in conjunction with instructor options available within the lesson such as reporting student performance in the lesson.

Test Item Bank. The instructor manuals accompanying many ordinary textbooks include author-prepared test items for classroom tests. Recently, some textbook manufacturers have begun providing such test item banks on computer diskettes for input into word processing programs. If an item bank is included, it is most useful in both forms. The diskette form should *not* be on the same diskettes the students use, for obvious security reasons.

Transparency Masters. Also common in regular textbooks, transparency masters for computer courseware may help the instructor introduce the software to students, give assignments, or give a preview of content. As with test item banks, it would be even more useful if transparency masters were also on computer diskettes in the format of a popular computer graphics program for the intended computer. This would allow more experienced instructors to modify the transparencies while maintaining a very professional appearance.

How to Access and Use Instructor Options. This section will include a description of options for accessing stored data, analyzing them, printing them, and clearing out old student information or signons. Another useful instructor option is a review mode. This is similar to a trial run. In a review mode the instructor is able to go through all the lesson's presentations without having to answer questions correctly, without storing data, and with greater user control than students have. It is also useful for demonstrations, such as when the instructor wants to demonstrate the lesson's main features to a group of students. Instructor options may also include override features. With these the instructor can allow a student to skip a section or take a final quiz even though the lesson would not at that time permit it. We should always assume that instructors know much more about their students than a computer program does and that instructors can use such overrides wisely.

Technical Information. If not included in a separate technical manual, specific computer requirements and program detail should be made available to the instructor. This may include memory and disk storage needs, hard disk requirements, files and program structure for each disk, names of data files which are created or changed, how to get printer output, using special input devices like the mouse, game paddles, touch panels, and using other output devices like videodisc players and audio. It may include a description of changes you can make to the program and how to make them, such as adding your own words to a vocabulary game. It may discuss the relative advantages of color versus monochrome monitors. It should definitely explain what to do when something goes wrong, including a telephone number or other means to obtain technical assistance.

Suggestions for Further Study. Though similar to the information in the student manual, these suggestions may also include resources for the instructor to learn more about the topic. A bibliography may include original source material or other classroom materials that may be purchased.

Index. Because an instructor manual will be longer, an alphabetic index with page numbers is more important than in a student manual. Instructors have a greater need to use the manual as a reference, for example, to find essential information quickly when a student has trouble and asks a question.

Quick Reference Guide. This is more likely to be needed for instructors than for students. It should include access to instructor options, overrides, trial run options, and possibly frequently required procedures such as for startup and producing backups. A good place for the quick reference guide is the back cover.

The Technical Manual

A technical manual is only necessary if there is technical information beyond what is reasonable for an instructor manual. Examples of things that indicate a technical manual is necessary are extensive directions for using the program on a microcomputer network, for using graphics plotters or laser printers, or when a program has extensive authoring capabilities which allow instructors to enter information and questions of their own. As an appendix, a technical manual may include printouts of the program, flowcharts, or block diagrams showing program files and functions.

A list of diagnostic procedures is especially useful here or in an instructor manual. Diagnostic hints will identify common "things that go wrong" and solutions that may solve the problems. Common problems are diskette damage, which backup diskettes should remedy; and data files filling up, which instructor options should remedy.

Adjunct Instructional Material

Sometimes a lesson requires extensive adjunct material, such as practice sheets, maps and other large diagrams, videotapes or photographic slides, or scoring sheets for games. These may be included in a student manual if they are short and do not require reproduction. They should be kept separate if the instructor should reproduce them, or if students should not access them until after completing the program, as with quizzes.

Computer Tools for Production of Support Material

Computer desktop publishing programs such as PageMaker (Aldus, 1989) greatly facilitate production of student manuals, instructor manuals, technical manuals, and adjunct instructional materials on paper. With desktop publishing software it is possible to capture displays from a lesson and incorporate them directly into a manual. This is not only easier, but it guarantees that the manual is accurate. Reproducing a display from a lesson by hand is likely to introduce small errors. Desktop publishing software allows for high quality output on laser printers and very high quality output at professional print shops on phototypesetters, the equipment used by professional printers for books. Some of the latest word processing software can do much of what desktop publishing software does.

CONCLUSION

The two steps that we have described in this chapter result in your first useful products. You will have a program that can be used, together with a variety of supporting materials. There is always a sense of great accomplishment when these are completed. However, there is still more to do, namely final evaluation and revision. These are described in the next chapter.

REFERENCES AND BIBLIOGRAPHY

AIMTECH CORP. (1988). *IconAuthor.* [Computer Program]. Nashua, NH: AIMTech Corp.

ALDUS. (1989). *PageMaker.* [Computer Program]. Seattle, WA: Aldus Corp.

ALLEN COMMUNICATION. (1985). *Quest.* [Computer Program]. Salt Lake City, UT: Allen Communication, Inc.

APPLE COMPUTER. (1980). *Apple SuperPILOT.* [Computer Program]. Cupertino, CA: Apple Computer, Inc.

APPLETON, W.C. (1987). *Course Builder.* [Computer Program]. Knoxville, TN: TeleRobotics International.

ASYS COMPUTER SYSTEMS. (1989). *ProPi.* [Computer Program]. Bellingham, WA: ASYS Computer Systems.

AUTHORWARE. (1989). *Authorware Professional.* [Computer Program]. Minneapolis, MN: Authorware, Inc.

AVNER, A., SMITH, S., & TENCZAR, P. (1984). CBI authoring tools: Effects on productivity and quality. *Journal of Computer-Based Instruction, 11*(3), 85–89.

BARKER, P. (1987). *Author Languages for CAL.* London: Macmillan Education Ltd.

BRUCE, R.C. (1980). *Software Debugging for Microcomputers.* Reston, VA: Reston.

BURGER, M.L. (1986). Authoring languages/systems comparisons. *AEDS Journal, 19,* 190–209.

CLARIS. (1988). *MacDraw.* [Computer Program]. Mountain View, CA: Claris Corporation.

COMPUTER TEACHING CORPORATION. (1985). *TenCORE.* [Computer Program]. Savoy, IL: Computer Teaching Corp.

CONTROL DATA CORPORATION. (1988). *PCD-3.* [Computer Program]. Minneapolis, MN: Control Data Corporation.

COURSEWARE APPLICATIONS. (1988). *Unison.* [Computer Program]. Champaign, IL: Courseware Applications, Inc.

CRANDALL, J.A. (1987). *How to Write Tutorial Documentation.* Englewood Cliffs, NJ: Prentice-Hall.

CROWELL, P. (1988). *Authoring Systems.* Westport, CT: Meckler Publishing.

CROWELL, P. (1989). Authoring systems: Genesis through revelations. *Instructional Delivery Systems, 3*(2), 19–21.

FAIRWEATHER, P.G., & O'NEAL, A.F. (1984). The impact of advanced authoring systems on CAI productivity. *Journal of Computer-Based Instruction, 11*(3), 90–94.

GROGONO, P., & NELSON, S.H. (1982). *Problem Solving and Computer Programming.* Reading, MA: Addison-Wesley.

HANNUM, W. (1986). Techniques for creating computer-based instructional text: Programming languages, authoring languages, and authoring systems. *Educational Psychologist, 21*(4), 293–314.

HUNTLEY, J.S., & ALESSI, S.M. (1987). Videodisc authoring tools: Evaluating products and a process. *Optical Information Systems, 7*(4), 259–281.

IMSATT. (1988). *IMSATT-2000.* [Computer Program]. Falls Church, VA: IMSATT Inc.

INTERNATIONAL BUSINESS MACHINES. (1988). *OS/2 Version 1.1.* [Computer Program]. Armonk, NY: International Business Machines Corp.

KEARSLEY, G. (1984a). Authoring tools: An overview. Journal of Computer-Based Instruction, 11(3), 67.

KEARSLEY, G. (1984b). Instructional design and authoring software. *Journal of Instructional Development,* 7(3), 11–16.

KEARSLEY, G. (1988). Authoring systems for intelligent tutoring systems on personal computers. In D.H. Jonassen (Ed.), *Instructional Designs for Microcomputer Courseware.* Hillsdale, NJ: Lawrence Erlbaum.

KERNIGHAN, B., & PLAUGER, P. (1976). *Software Tools.* Reading, MA: Addison-Wesley.

KERNIGHAN, B., & PLAUGER, P. (1978). *The Elements of Programming Style.* New York: McGraw-Hill.

KHERIATY, L. (1984). *PC/Pilot.* [Computer Program]. Bellingham, WA: Washington Computer Services.

LEARNCOM. (1986). *SAM.* [Computer Program]. Cambridge, MA: Learncom.

LEDIN, G., & LEDIN, V. (1979). *The Programmer's Book of Rules.* Belmont, CA: Lifetime Learning Publications.

LOCATIS, C.N., & CARR, V.H. (1985). Selecting authoring systems. *Journal of Computer-Based Instruction,* 12(2), 28–33.

LOMMEL, J. (1986, July). What matters in an authoring system: The results of a Delphi study. *Data Training,* pp. 39, 42–46.

MACK, B., & HEATH, P. (Eds.). (1980). *Guide to Good Programming.* New York: Halsted Press.

MERRILL, M.D. (1985). Where is the authoring in authoring systems? *Journal of Computer-Based Instruction, 12,* 90–96.

MERRILL, M.D. (1987). Prescriptions for an authoring system. *Journal of Computer-Based Instruction, 14*(1), 1–10.

MICROSOFT. (1985). *Microsoft Windows.* [Computer Program]. Redmond, WA: Microsoft Corp.

PRESSMAN, R.S. (1982). *Software Engineering: A Practitioner's Approach.* New York: McGraw-Hill.

RIDDLE, W., & WILEDON, J. (1980). *Tutorial on Software Design; Description and Analysis.* IEEE Computer Society Press.

SCHAEFGES, T.M., EISENBERG, J.D., & STOCK, R.A. (1982). *Beginning Tutor.* Savoy, IL: Courseware Applications, Inc.

SHNEIDERMAN, B. (1980). *Software Psychology.* Cambridge, MA: Winthrop Publishers.

T.H.E. JOURNAL. (1988). Directory of authoring software. *T.H.E. Journal, 16*(1), 19, 22–24.

TROLLIP, S.R., & BROWN, G. (1987). Designing software for easy translation into other languages. *Journal of Computer-Based Instruction, 14*(3), 119–123.

SUMMARY OF PROGRAMMING

BEFORE YOU START

Research and evaluate available authoring software (programming languages and authoring systems) and choose that which best meets your needs.

ERROR PREVENTION

Refer to a flowchart while programming.
Program subroutines first.

IMPLEMENTATION ON THE COMPUTER

Plan off-line.
Use routines that you have developed before.
Amend existing routines rather than creating new ones.
Modularize the lesson for efficiency.
Use tracing paper for graphics, sticking it over the screen or graphics tablet when creating pictures.
Take advantage of computer tools such as graphics software.
Document your lesson thoroughly. Make changes to the documentation whenever you change the program.
Make sure your lesson works before making it efficient.

ERROR DETECTION

Find and eliminate known bugs first.

Use a systematic approach to error detection.

Debug with data whose consequences are easily determined.

Use a set of responses that will give predicted results.

On each display press all the keys. Only expected ones should have any effect.

Whenever a response is expected of a student, type in unexpected answers, nonsense, and nothing at all. See how the program responds.

Use debugging tools provided for the computer.

Print identifying numbers on displays to facilitate reference.

Eliminate one bug at a time.

Save existing parts of a lesson until certain they are unneeded.

Incorporate, if possible, a mechanism whereby students can make on-line comments.

SUMMARY OF SUPPORT MATERIALS

STUDENT MANUAL—POSSIBLE CONTENTS

Title page	Starting the program	Technical information
Table of contents	Trial run	Further study ideas
Warnings	Normal running	Quick reference guide
Introduction	Content summary	Index
Equipment	Forms or worksheets	

INSTRUCTOR MANUAL—POSSIBLE CONTENTS

Title page	Starting the program	Instructor options
Table of contents	Trial run	Technical information
Warnings	Normal running	Further study ideas
Introduction	Summary of content	Index
Equipment	Forms or worksheets	Quick reference guide
Backups	Test item bank	
Equipment setup	Transparency masters	

TECHNICAL MANUAL—POSSIBLE CONTENTS

Title page	Authoring options
Table of contents	Program printouts
Networking	Flowcharts
Peripheral devices	Block diagrams
Diagnostic hints	Index

ADJUNCT INSTRUCTIONAL MATERIAL—POSSIBLE CONTENTS

Practice sheets	Photographic slides
Diagrams	Audiotapes
Maps	Videotapes
Game scoring sheets	Videodiscs

12

EVALUATION

You have now reached the final step in the development model, evaluation. At this point the lesson has been implemented on the computer and all auxiliary material produced. As we have emphasized repeatedly, the key to a successful lesson is to test it and revise it many times. In Step 5 you should evaluate the design. Based on that evaluation some of Steps 1 through 5 may have to be redone and re-evaluated. In Step 7 you should evaluate the flowcharts and storyboards. Based on that evaluation the flowcharts and storyboards may be revised and evaluated again. Now it is time to evaluate the completed computer lesson and its auxiliary materials.

This is the most comprehensive evaluation and includes three sub-steps. In the first, the materials are reviewed by subject-matter experts and other instructional designers to assess the content, appearance, and attention to good instructional practices. In the second, representative students use the lesson under your supervision to provide detailed feedback on its quality. Finally, in the third part, the instructional effectiveness of the lesson is validated with students working in normal instructional circumstances.

In the programming step, the lesson was implemented on the computer and then debugged to ensure it functioned correctly no matter what the user did, no matter how strange or unexpected the responses. We assume that the program has reached this stage before this evaluation step is begun. If the lesson has been implemented on the computer by someone else, you should proceed with the evaluation only when satisfied with the lesson's operation.

Lessons *always* need revision. Unfortunately, for a variety of reasons they do not always receive the attention they need before being used. Sometimes the effort required to reach this point has been so great that the designer decides to forego the evaluation step. Sometimes the pressures of time constraints are such that only a cursory review is undertaken. *This is a mistake.* The extra effort required to complete a thorough evaluation is always well spent and you will be helping yourself and your students by doing it. The lesson is yours, and major flaws in the content or functioning of the lesson will reflect on you. Furthermore, allowing a program to be used that has not been evaluated has potential for damaging the whole field of computer-based instruction. Whether valid or not, poor examples of computer-based instruction tend to support the idea that all computer-based instruction is poor. The medium as a whole is judged by selected examples from it. This situation is very different from that of books, where a bad book is regarded only as a bad book, and not as evidence that books as a medium are undesirable.

The designer should not have an attitude of whether to do evaluation, but rather how much to do. Sufficient time must be allocated to evaluate and revise repeatedly, until the lesson both functions properly and teaches well. As with most stages in the development process, this always takes longer than anticipated.

This final review is facilitated greatly if previous review and revision in the earlier steps are done properly. Changes to the program at this late stage can be costly.

QUALITY REVIEW PHASE

The first phase is called the quality review phase because it is here that the lesson is subjected to quality control procedures. To assist in this process we have provided a Quality Review Checklist (Appendix B) that can be used to remind you of the most important considerations. It is organized into seven parts:

> Language and grammar
> Surface features of the displays
> Question and menus
> Other issues of pedagogy
> Invisible functions of the lesson
> The subject matter
> Off-line materials

The process of checking the lesson is slow and sometimes tedious, but it is essential that it be done thoroughly. It is wasteful to have a potentially good lesson fail because of the existence of easily correctable problems. We advocate going through the lesson six times, once for each of the first six parts of the checklist, and through the supplementary materials once. These should be done in the above order, paying attention each time only to the considerations of that part of the checklist. If you try to pay attention to everything at once, you will miss many problems.

You can speed up the process by temporarily numbering each display on the screen. This makes it much easier to reference a particular display and facilitates finding it when you make the necessary changes to the program. The checklist has space both for display numbers and for your comments. If you make your own checklist, you should leave plenty of room for comments, particularly if your lesson is long.

The checklist should be used purely as a device to remind you of the many aspects to check. It is not intended to tell you what to do, but rather to ensure that you make deliberate decisions about every attribute or feature of the lesson. Nothing should be in the lesson or left out of it due to oversight or lack of thought, but only as the result of a decision you have made.

Part 1—Language and Grammar

The first part of the checklist deals with the language and grammar used in the lesson. These should be of the highest standard, setting an example for everyone using the lesson. You should be consistent in your use of conventions, words, and punctuation, and should take great care that the level and style of language is appropriate for your intended audience.

Completion of this part may be facilitated by going through a printed version of the lesson. This makes cross checking from one section of the lesson to another easier. It also allows you to annotate the corrections directly over the original text, which makes changing the program quicker because of the ready reference to where each change has to be made.

1.1 Reading Level. Before going through the lesson for the first time, you should familiarize yourself with the nature of the target population so that you will be able to judge whether the reading level of the lesson is appropriate. A common error is for the instructional text to be at the appropriate level, but have directions or the student manual at too high a level.

1.2 Cultural Bias. Two types of cultural bias can be found in lessons: language and references. The former refers to language that is understandable by only a particular cultural or ethnic group, while the latter refers to information or contexts that are directly related to or linked with a particular cultural heritage. The word *trunk* (of a car) would not be meaningful in Great Britain even though English is spoken. In the United States we would not know what the *boot* of a car is, which is the word they use in Great Britain. Similarly, giving arithmetic word problems with examples from baseball would be as meaningless to students in most other countries as an example from cricket would be to Americans. If your lesson contains such material, you should give consideration to eliminating it, keeping in mind that your intended users may not be the only ones to use it.

Sometimes culturally biased material is unavoidable. In the United States, for instance, it would be unrealistic to teach algebra and geometry without referring to miles, gallons, or pounds. Such lessons would have to be rewritten for export, because other countries use metric measurements. Similarly, the comma (,) is used instead of the decimal point (.) in many countries. This is true both of the written and spoken form. So what in the United States is "one point five" becomes "one comma five" elsewhere. Unfortunately, some programming languages do not even take this into account.

Dealing with culturally oriented materials is a matter of compromises. On the one hand, the instructional materials need to be understood by the students, while on the other, complete elimination of ethnic or cultural references is both impossible and undesirable, because the instruction would become bland and uninteresting. Developers need to become sensitive to the issue and make balanced, intelligent decisions.

1.3 Technical Terms and Jargon. Every field has terms associated with it that are often not understood by newcomers. If such terms are included in a lesson, they should be relevant to what is being learned. Furthermore, they should never be used without first being defined and explained. If the technical term has a common abbreviation, it too should be introduced in the context of its expanded form. For example, CRT is used more frequently than cathode-ray tube, and CPU more often than central processing unit.

Jargon is language whose meaning is known only by people related to a particular field or profession. A common occurrence in computer-based instruction is the use of computer-related jargon, particularly when giving instructions to the student. Sometimes the jargon occurs in the lesson itself or on accompanying printed instructions.

We have often seen instructions given to users, such as "Insert your diskette in Drive 1, and boot up your computer." To some users this may be comprehensible, but to many others it is not only meaningless, but intimidating as well. Another common use of computer jargon occurs when a lesson encounters a programming error. Rather than providing an easily understood message, many programs display the message provided by the computer's operating system. This may take a form like:

*** 〉255 ERR

or

*** STR OVFL ERR.

Such messages are typical of feedback written by people insensitive to the needs of users. Messages like this can be found in many computer applications, particularly in those not instructionally oriented. What should be provided is a clear message in plain English telling the user what to do.

Unexplained abbreviations or acronyms are another form of jargon. Sometimes, even if an explanation has been given, their use can be intimidating. For example, the following abbreviations are frequently used: CPU (central processing unit), I/O (input/output), ROM (read-only memory), RAM (random-access memory), CRT (cathode-ray tube), and DOS (disk operating system). To many users, a sentence using these abbreviations can be difficult to understand. An example of such a sentence would be: "Your CRT will tell you when RAM has been loaded by DOS."

Be cautious when writing or reviewing computer-based materials. It is very easy to unwittingly incorporate jargon or unexplained abbreviations. Because they use the jargon every day, people assume that everyone else does so.

1.4 Spelling, Grammar, and Punctuation. It is usually a good idea for these to be checked by someone other than the author. We tend to miss our own errors in spelling, grammar, and punctuation. If there are important content words with difficult or ambiguous spelling, determine the desired spelling at the beginning of the process. During the evaluation phase, check that these conventions have been maintained.

1.5 Spacing. Before starting the production of a lesson, decide on conventions for paragraphing, spacing between sentences, and hyphenation. Also assess whether page breaks are at appropriate points. For example, unlike books, a computer-based instruction presentation should not change pages in the middle of a sentence. There are several acceptable conventions for paragraphing: leave a blank line between paragraphs without indenting the first word; leave a blank line and indent the first word; or continue a paragraph directly after the previous one, with the first word indented. Between sentences one generally leaves two spaces, with a single space after commas. If you are unsure of normally accepted practice, the names of some popular writing style handbooks are included in this chapter's bibliography.

Part 2—Surface Features

In this part you should assess what we call the surface features of the lesson. By this we mean what is seen on the display other than the spelling and grammar dealt with on the first part. This includes the aesthetics of display presentations, quality of student input, and related topics. Although questions and menus are treated separately in the next part, everything discussed here also applies to them.

2.1 Displays. Pay attention to the aesthetic quality of each display. Displays should be uncluttered, without too much information being shown at once, and should be relevant to the goals of the lesson. It is often difficult to avoid clutter on many microcomputers, where the typical display size is forty or so characters wide by twenty-four lines deep. On higher resolution screens, the lesson developer has more control over what appears. Displays often become cluttered as new information is added, such as when different storyboards are overlaid. Overlaid sections should not overlap or be too close together. In addition to displays being aesthetically pleasing, they should attract attention to the important information.

2.2 Presentation Modes. Information may be displayed as text, graphics, with color, and as sound. Each of these should be used appropriately.

2.3 Text Quality. Assuming text is used appropriately, its quality should also be assessed. Avoid scrolling, which is when text is put onto the screen line by line with the previous line being pushed up to make way for the new one. The result is that the entire text moves on the screen. Scrolling text is impossible to read until the scrolling stops. Reading is easier and more natural when text starts at the top of the screen and writes downward. Also consider whether text is unnecessarily wordy and whether the text styles are easy to read.

2.4 Input. Are the input devices used (keyboard, mouse, touch panel, and so on) the best for each type of user input? Input should also be designed so as to keep user typing or other physical action efficient, and to prevent or detect user errors. If the lesson uses a touch-sensitive screen or light pen it is usually a good idea for the program to provide keypress equivalents. These devices are often un-reliable and may be unavailable, preventing the user from progressing unless a keypress alternative is available.

Fortunately, the most common type of tactile input or "pointing device" today is the mouse. Computer mice are much more reliable than touch panels and light pens. They tend not to require keypress equivalents. In fact, the mouse is fast becoming accepted as a better form of input for selection of screen locations than the keyset.

2.5 On Completion.   At the end of a lesson the student should be clearly informed that the lesson has ended. The student should be taken to a reasonable place after completing the lesson. If the lesson is independent and not connected to any others, nor to any curriculum, then it is usually not important what hap-pens at the end of the lesson. Normally, it is advisable to have a final display in which you tell the student what to do. For example, you could say to remove the disks and return them to the instructor, or to press some special combination of keys to indicate termination.

If the lesson is part of some larger curriculum, it is important to check that the student is returned to the correct point in that curriculum. This usually entails passing information from the lesson to a controlling program. These data may include performance scores, time on-line, and the fact that the student has com-pleted the lesson successfully, unsuccessfully, or not at all.

Part 3—Questions and Menus

One of the most important aspects of any instructional lesson is the qual-ity of questions and feedback and how they are deployed in the instruction. They take on added significance if they are used for evaluating what the student knows, either on a quiz or test. Because of their importance, it is essential that the student be able to concentrate on the content of the answer and not its format. This part of the review deals specifically with questions, how they are presented, and how the lesson evaluates answers. Because menus are closely related we deal with these at the same time.

3.1 Menus.   A menu is a common way of providing the student with con-trol over accessing different parts of a lesson. Its operation is very simple: the stu-dent types a letter corresponding to the chosen option or clicks it with a mouse. Several aspects of menus should be checked. The menu should be well labeled, especially if there is more than one menu in the lesson, so the student knows where he or she is in the lesson. The directions for making the choice must be clear, and the feedback must be informative should an inappropriate choice be made. It should be easy to correct an incorrect choice. If, after typing a letter, the student has to press ⟨return⟩ to activate the choice, a correction can usually be made by using the erase or arrow key before ⟨return⟩ is pressed. If a choice, such as clicking with a mouse, immediately causes branching, an option to return to where you came from is advisable. Although not a necessary feature, many lessons mark menu items as the student completes them. Not only does the menu thus serve as a progress report, but the student is guided as to which item is the logical next choice.

3.2 Questions. Almost all computer-based instruction lessons contain some questions. These were discussed extensively in Chapter 2. There are several aspects of questions that should be scrutinized carefully in this part of the evaluation phase. Assess whether questions are relevant to the objectives and are about important information, whether they occur throughout the lesson (in contrast to all being at the end), if they are designed so responses are not laborious and yet force the student to think and process the information at a deep level. There should be a variety of types of questions that require not only recognition and pressing a single key, but remembering, understanding, applying, evaluating, typing, constructing, drawing, and so on. Also consider if the placement of each question, before or after the information that answers it, is appropriate.

3.3 Answering Questions. First, it should be obvious to the student how to respond to each question. There must be no doubt or ambiguity as to the procedure. For example, if there were a question like "How many humps does a camel have?" you should indicate whether there is a restriction on how the answer should be entered ("2" versus "two"). Whenever possible, of course, all correct and likely responses should be allowed. There should also always be an indicator or cursor on the screen to show where the answer will appear when entered.

It should be easy and obvious how to correct erroneous input before it is acted upon by the program. With the exception of test programs, most lessons should provide the option of requesting the answer. It is appropriate in most lessons to have options for help and for trying again after incorrect answers.

→A student should never be forced to answer a question correctly to proceed. It is very frustrating for a student to encounter a question, not know the answer, and be forced to continue answering (frequently with desperation) until the correct answer is chanced upon. It is better to provide the correct answer or appropriate remediation after a specified number of attempts. A practice that we like is to provide increasingly informative feedback after each successive wrong answer, with the correct answer being given after three attempts.

There are a few common causes for questions like this. Frequently, the lesson designer makes assumptions about how answers will be entered and then caters only to that type of input. For example, if the question were "Who was the first president of the United States?" anticipated correct answers would be "Washington," "George Washington," "Geo. Washington," and "President Washington." There may even be a few others. The problem arises, not with these alternatives, but with the possibility of someone making an error with respect to the capitalization of the first letters. On some microcomputers, upper and lower case are treated identically, but on those that are not, failing to capitalize the first letters could lead to the answer "washington" being judged incorrect, rather than being regarded as being a grammatical error. In a case like this, the student would be certain that the answer was correct, but would be constantly told that it was not. If no way out of this question were provided, the student would become frustrated.

3.4 Format of Feedback. The example above raises another important consideration when designing the feedback to answers. It is important that the feedback differentiates between answers that are wrong and those that are of inappropriate format. In the example, "Jefferson" would be an incorrect response. However, if the given answer were "washington" in lower case, grading it as wrong would be both misleading and unfair. Far more appropriate would be the response, "You have the right person, but you should capitalize the first letter."

Another situation in which inappropriate feedback is frequently given is at a menu. If the options are numbered 1 through 5, and the student types either "a" or "6," an appropriate response would be, "That is not one of the options. Press ⟨return⟩ to try again." An inappropriate response would be "No!" or "That's wrong."

You should also assess whether feedback is sufficiently noticeable to attract the student's attention. Very short messages such as "yes" or "no" are sometimes not even seen, leaving the student wondering what is happening. Lastly, consider whether the type of feedback, such as whether it is text or graphic, visual or auditory, is the best choice.

3.5 Quality of Feedback. The final aspect of questions that should be checked is the *quality* of feedback provided. We have already differentiated between appropriate and inappropriate feedback. However, even feedback that is appropriate may not be acceptable. Feedback should always be constructive. It should be supportive rather than demeaning, it should avoid slang, and it should increase the student's capability of performing better in the future. It is better to indicate a wrong response with information as to the correct one, than to inform the student that he or she is "stupid" or "a dummy." It is more appropriate, especially for adult audiences, to avoid feedback such as "Right on!" Humorous feedback in any form tends to pall after a while.

Feedback should also not be misleading or ambiguous. One student project we observed used a cartoon figure of an icicle man to lead the learner through a lesson on glaciers. On several occasions, after answering a question, we received the feedback "Freeze your fingers." At first we thought we had answered incorrectly, but gradually realized that it was actually positive feedback, if you happen to be an icicle!

Feedback should be related to the student response. Common expected errors, which typically identify student misconceptions, should receive different feedback than unexpected ones. Discrimination errors (confusing similar but different things) should help clarify the subtle distinctions. Lastly, feedback should be based on intelligent judging of the student's response, in contrast to simple-minded judging such as checking for one particular word or phrase with perfect spelling.

Part 4—Other Issues of Pedagogy

In this part you should assess other instructional factors such as user control, interactions other than questions, and the extent to which the lesson maintains student motivation.

4.1 General. There are a number of general pedagogical issues you should assess. Although you obviously considered the computer to be a good medium for the objectives, a lesson often evolves into something different than initially envisioned and it is useful to once again assess whether the computer is the appropriate medium. Can the lesson, as it now appears, be done as well or better with a book, videotape, or hands-on learning? The computer is more likely to be an appropriate choice if the lesson adapts to student performance, or if the content taught is very difficult, expensive, unsafe, or uninteresting when taught in another way. Related to the question of computer suitability is whether the methodology employed is the appropriate one.

The amount of information you can present without having the student actively do something varies according to the student's level. It is far easier for an educated adult to read page after page of uninterrupted text than it is for a child. Presentation of information should be broken up by student activities, such as questions relating to the information just presented. Too much uninterrupted text probably means you are using the computer as a page turner, which is usually not exploiting the medium very well. Related to the information chunk size are the lesson's overall length and encouraging spaced practice. A lesson should be designed to make short learning sessions convenient, between fifteen minutes to an hour depending on the methodology and content difficulty, and to encourage students to study for short periods of time on several occasions.

Lastly is the question of mastery level. Some methodologies tend to introduce new information, such as tutorials, while others are intended to foster mastery, such as drills and some simulations. Assessing the appropriate level of mastery means asking yourself if the lesson activities are in keeping with the desired mastery levels. If a high level of mastery is desired, students may need to repeat interactions until they consistently do things right. Instructional games, although motivating and good for integrating a variety of skills and knowledge, are generally not good when a high level of mastery is desired.

4.2 Student Control. There are basic controls that the student should almost always be able to perform, such as moving forward to the next display, reviewing, exiting and returning to complete the lesson at a later time, and asking for help or directions. It should be obvious to the student how to do these things. There should be adequate protection that the student does not do irreversible actions by accident, such as terminating and grading a test or deleting the results of simulation runs. You should also ensure that inappropriate types of control are avoided. Menus with many choices are inappropriate for very young children, as are permanent termination or determining item sequence in drills.

Of the above issues, control of forward progression is the most vital. Forward progress in a lesson should be at the control of the student and not accomplished through use of timing commands. Whenever the progress of displays is controlled by the computer someone is going to have difficulties. This is particularly true if the display automatically erases information on the screen. One can be almost certain that there will be some interruption just as a timed sequence appears, causing the student to miss some vital information. It is better to let the student control the pace at which progress is made. A ten-second display, for example, will always be too long for some people, too short for others, and just right for virtually nobody.

When evaluating a lesson's student control features, you should press each advertised key to ensure it operates properly. You should also press a representative sample of other keys, such as one of the numbers, a letter, and the remaining function keys, such as ⟨return⟩ and ⟨esc⟩, to make sure that they do not cause malfunctions, such as overwriting of displays or execution errors.

4.3 Motivation.   Motivation was discussed in the chapters on tutorials, drills, and games. Although many CBI proponents tout the computer for its motivational advantage, you should not assume that students will be motivated just because instruction is on a computer. In fact, students with computer anxiety may experience decreased motivation with CBI. When assessing motivation, check that such anxiety is minimized through ease-of-use and appropriate safety nets.

Lesson characteristics that relate to motivation include maintaining an appropriate level of challenge, for example by increasing difficulty as the student progresses, arousing curiosity, such as by surprising or apparently discordant information, maintaining confidence, which can be done with appropriate objectives and instruction which makes accomplishing them possible, and maintaining satisfaction, as is done with supportive feedback, encouragement, and procedures which the student perceives as fair.

Be suspicious about competition between individuals as a motivational device. Competition between an individual and the computer is likely to be safer and competition between teams is often best because it fosters cooperation and peer teaching between team members.

Assess whether motivational techniques emphasize intrinsic or extrinsic motivation, and aim for the former. Also, do not go too far with motivational techniques to the detriment of other instructional factors. Students will generally be satisfied with a very easy lesson, but they will not learn much. Students also like a lot of control, but too much has been proven detrimental. Seek a good balance between fostering attitudes and achievement.

4.4 Interactions.   You should have already assessed the frequency and quality of questions. But in lessons that have significant interactions other than questions, especially simulations and games, the frequency of those interactions should be assessed. Other interactions include making choices and decisions, composing, taking notes, making evaluations and judgments, constructing, and drawing. A variety of interaction types should be sought. Think about every interaction and whether it is important, whether it is relevant to the objectives, and whether it enhances comprehension, memory, or transfer of what is learned to real-world activities.

4.5 Animation and Graphics. As with student actions, the primary thing you should ask about animation and graphics is whether they reinforce the lesson's objectives. Assess as well whether they should be more or less detailed and whether they are professional looking. Animations should not be so slow as to bore the student, nor so fast that students miss whatever is being illustrated. User controlled speed and repeatability are generally good. Very complex graphics may take a long time to display, which is as bad as a slow animation.

Part 5—Invisible Functions

Invisible functions are those features that are not seen when running the lesson. They include acquisition and presentation of data, and what happens when students enter and leave the lesson.

To adequately and thoroughly test invisible features you must usually run the lesson in the form it will be used by a student, in contrast to running it as an instructor or programmer. If you are using a programming language that allows development in interpreted mode and delivery to students in compiled mode, the lesson should be tested in compiled mode. Authoring systems typically provide a "student mode" for testing lessons during development, which is different than the final lesson for real students. While the developer is provided assistance in writing lessons, the student is automatically taken care of by a software bureaucracy that keeps records and scores. If you are using a system like this, do the evaluation in the real "student" mode.

5.1 Records and Data. For most educational applications, instructors need to keep a record of how students are performing. If this is the case, data accuracy must be assessed. One way of doing this is to go through the lesson, keeping track on paper of how you respond to each question. At the end, the lesson's data should match yours. If other data are required, such as item analysis data, time to completion, or number of attempts at each question, these should be recorded too. You should check that the data are stored permanently, if this is necessary. If data are stored for individual students, check that identification links are correct and that data for different students does not get mixed up. Data for evaluation of the instructional materials, in contrast to that for evaluation of students, does not require student identification. Lastly, consider whether instructors should have control over whether and what data is collected. In some cases, instructors may consider data collection unnecessary and even annoying because it will fill up disks and require management. Also, whether programs are run from a single diskette, individual students' diskettes, hard disks, or networks may affect where data is stored and whether it can be stored.

5.2 Security and Accessibility.   All data collected should be accessible to those who are authorized to see it. This may be visually on the computer screen or printed out for a permanent record. Data collection and access should conform to the legal requirements of where the lesson is to be used. In the United States, the Privacy Act of 1974 and its amendments generally preclude access to personal information, such as test or academic scores, by anyone who has no legal need to it. Thus, it is inappropriate and illegal to post scores or grades by name or any other publicly identifying means (such as Social Security Number) unless authorized to do so by each student. Furthermore, one student should not see another's data, nor should an instructor see the records of students in another instructor's class.

In a computer-based lesson, therefore, the lesson designer must ensure that an unauthorized person cannot access another individual's data. This can be accomplished with passwords, careful management of the disks on which data are stored, and encryption of data.

Security not only means preventing unauthorized access to data, but preventing data tampering, such as changing grades, and preventing vandalism, such as deleting program files. The best protection against these are encryption of data and good backup procedures.

5.3 Too Much Data.   Many types of program errors do not appear until a lesson is used many times. Developers frequently run a program a few times and fail to find such errors. Such errors are common when lessons store data on student performance. If the lesson is designed to keep records of all students, you should test what happens if the planned capacity is exceeded. For example, if the lesson is designed to keep records of thirty students, see what happens if you create thirty-five or forty. There are two common ways that programs handle situations like this. The first is to ignore excessive records. The second is for the newest record to replace the oldest, which means the oldest is lost. This is sometimes referred to as the first-in–first-out method, because the first record stored is the first to be deleted. Both methods result in records being lost. You should ensure that the method used is suitable for your needs. It is always advisable for the program to display a message asking students to inform the instructor *before* the record capacity has been reached.

If a lot of data may be stored for individuals, you should also check that an error does not occur when a lot of data is stored. This is more likely to occur on a system with limited mass storage such as floppy diskettes.

Lastly, consider whether appropriate options are given to the instructor to deal with too much data. There should be provisions for deleting all or part of the data, for making backups of data files, and for printing data files.

5.4 Restarting.   An important invisible feature is how a lesson handles the situation when the lesson terminates accidently. This may occur in a number of ways: The user may inadvertently press 〈reset〉 or another key that ends the program; the computer may fail, because of a power failure, for example; or a program execution error may occur. Whatever happens, unless the lesson is short, important data should be retrievable. If possible, the student should have the option of restarting at or near the point where termination occurred. This means that the necessary data should be stored permanently *as they are generated* and not just at the end of the session.

A similar situation is when you allow the student to terminate the lesson voluntarily with the intention of returning to it later. Almost any lesson longer than about ten minutes should have such an option. However, when building in restarting options, developers sometimes neglect to consider their impact on first time students. We have seen lessons assume when there is any stored restart data, that the next use of the lesson is by the same student wishing to restart. A lesson must be able to distinguish first time students from returning students and treat them accordingly.

Part 6—Subject Matter

In this part you should review the lesson with emphasis on content. If you are not an expert on the subject yourself, you should enlist one to do this for or with you. If you do ask someone else to assist you, however, ensure that the program is free of all functional errors first. The existence of glaring errors and program malfunctions will divert your reviewer's attention from the content to the functioning of the lesson, which would not be of much help to you.

Even if you are knowledgeable about the subject and have reviewed the lesson yourself, it is advisable to have someone else look at it too. It is easy to become so close to your lesson that it is difficult to view it objectively.

6.1 Goals and Objectives. During this phase of the content review, you should pay attention to two major points. The objectives or goals should be explicitly stated. This is usually done at the beginning of the lesson, so that the student knows what the lesson covers. An exception is with very young students or those who would have trouble understanding the objectives. The objectives should be stated in the vocabulary of the students. One should not have to already know the content to comprehend the objectives. They should be stated in a way that students perceive them as useful and relevant to their own needs. Lastly, these objectives should be considered useful by experts in the content area, or by the teachers that will use the lesson. It is not very helpful to have a lesson meet its objectives, if the objectives are trivial or irrelevant.

6.2 Information. The information provided in a lesson must be relevant to its objectives and must be accurate and complete. Ensuring content accuracy includes checking that facts are correct, that correct answers are judged to be correct, that the use of terminology is correct, contemporary, and consistent, and that all graphic material is accurate. Some subjects are very easy to review, such as basic arithmetic, and some difficult, such as history or many scientific topics. You should also check that the subject is covered with sufficient depth for your objectives. The level of detail, complexity, and realism should be appropriate for the objectives. Too little will result in a trivial lesson and too much will result in a lesson that frustrates rather than teaches.

6.3 Content Emphasis. A common error by beginning developers, especially when unfamiliar with the lesson's subject matter, is to teach those things that are easy and familiar rather than the really difficult things. The lesson should emphasize those things most relevant to the objectives and most likely to be difficult for the student. For example, if a chemistry lesson's objective is to teach about the common properties of different groups of elements, it would be a misplaced emphasis to ask questions only about when the elements were discovered or what their chemical symbols are. A better emphasis would be to ask about the structure of the nuclei or the number of free electrons.

6.4 Organization. Some subjects have an inherent or well-established conceptual sequence, such as math. Others have less (or less obvious) organization. You should assess whether the lesson organization conforms to and therefore reinforces the subject matter's organization. Consider also the organization from the student's point of view. If the subject-matter organization is very complicated, it may need simplification before presentation to students. Additionally, students always come to a lesson with some prior knowledge so you should consider the relationship of the student's knowledge to the subject matter, building upon what the student already knows when possible.

Developers often assume that students will perceive the organization inherent in the content. A useful technique is to explain, perhaps with a diagram, the organization to students. Consider whether this should be done in the lesson.

This and all aspects of reviewing subject matter should be done by or with a real subject-matter expert.

Part 7—Off-line Materials

Success of a program may depend as much upon the off-line support materials as on the computer programs. These may require review by both the instructional designer and the subject matter expert.

7.1 Manual—General. Several general aspects of manual content should be assessed. Unless it is very short, any manual should have a table of contents and index to assist in locating information. A quick reference guide for lesson operation is usually recommended. At the very beginning of a manual there should be clear statements of equipment required, warnings about essential safeguards like backing up the program, and where to go or call for technical assistance.

7.2 Manual—Lesson Operation. Most manuals accompanying computer-based lessons contain directions for making the lesson operational. These include how to turn on the computer, how to load the program and make it run, how to enter information, how to save data, and how to turn everything off. You should test that they are correct by doing what they tell you, rather than by just reading them. They should be easy to follow and should not contain jargon. These directions should be different, both in reading level and content, for students and instructors. Instructors should be given additional information such as procedures for first time use of the lesson and for making backups.

7.3 Manual—Lesson Content. If the manual includes a summary of prerequisite material, an outline of what the lesson covers, its relevance, and how it fits into the overall curriculum, you should check that the information is both accurate and complete. These should be reviewed by the subject-matter expert as well as the designer.

7.4 Auxiliary Materials. In addition to a manual, some lessons require special forms or scoresheets for the student to use. In the game *Snooper Troops,* for instance, there is so much information that can be collected from interviews or clues about so many different suspects, that the manual contains blank pages on which to write it. If the lesson is to be used by many students, each should have his or her own manual or these materials should be in a form easily reproducible. You should assess these materials for readability and ease of use. Additionally, you should question whether any useful materials have been omitted. For example, many textbooks include transparency masters and a test item bank for instructors. These may be useful for instructors using CBI as well.

7.5 Other Resources. If the lesson refers to materials the student may use, check whether they are provided in the off-line materials. If they are not, as in the case of other lessons or books, check whether they are available at all. It is frustrating to be referred to resources, only to find that they are not available.

Conclusion to the Review Phase

The Quality Review Phase is a most important one, particularly if the lesson under review has not been written or implemented by you. Although it takes a considerable amount of time to go through a long lesson six times in addition to its off-line materials, it is essential to take this time before the lesson is used by students. Once you are satisfied with the lesson's functioning and content and have made the necessary revisions to your satisfaction, you are ready for the second stage in the evaluation process, pilot testing.

PILOT TESTING

Pilot testing is the process of testing your lesson by having representatives of your target population use it while you monitor their progress and performance. Although other people may have already provided you with feedback on the lesson, there is no substitute for having real students do the same. It is an essential step which should never be omitted.

Pilot testing is a seven-step process. The steps are:

Select the helpers.
Explain the procedure to them.
Find out how much of the subject matter they know already.
Observe them go through the lesson.
Interview them afterwards.
Assess their learning.
Revise the lesson.

Each of these steps is important if you want to obtain useful information from the process.

Select the Helpers

The best helpers are students much like those for whom the lesson is designed. Find at least three: one should be representative of the best of the potential students; one an average student; and one similar to the slowest of the students that will use the lesson. This spread of capabilities will enable you to test informally whether the lesson meets the needs of your entire target population. Of course, because of the small numbers involved, one can only use the information gathered in the pilot test as helpful guidance rather than as a definitive statement of fact. What this means is that if the three students all report favorably about the lesson, it is likely to be successful in wider use, but not definitely. We have found it most useful to observe one student at a time. In this way, you can devote all your attention to one and will not miss anything important.

Explanation

Before the pilot students start the lesson, you should explain the purpose of what you are doing. You should say that the lesson is in the process of being developed and that it is essential to test it before releasing it for general use. Ask the students to proceed through the lesson as though taking it for credit and not to ask you for any assistance. Encourage them to make notes about the lesson whenever they have a comment to make. This note-taking is facilitated if you can provide some easy means for the student to identify each display they want to comment on. This can be done either by having a display number appearing on the screen (in the top right corner, perhaps), or by having a paper version of each display available on which notes may be written. If the students are proficient typists, having an on-line comment facility is very convenient.

You should also explain that you will observe them at all times and will ask for a variety of information about the content and operation of the lesson at the end of the session. Encourage the students to be very critical.

Determine Prior Knowledge

Before the students begin the lesson, ensure that you know what previous exposure they have had to the subject matter and how much they know of it. You must then relate this to whether each is a good, average, or poor student. This information is important when interpreting the data you collect during the rest of the session. The best pilot students will have the necessary prerequisites but will not be familiar with the lesson content itself.

Observation

Throughout the session, you should unobtrusively observe the student interacting with the lesson. It is surprising how much information you can glean from just watching body language. You can tell immediately when a student is having difficulty understanding the material or is confused by the directions on the screen. You can tell when a student is unsure of what to do, or of what options to choose. You can also tell when the person is enjoying the experience and when they are bored.

As the student progresses, take notes about the behavior exhibited, noting particularly the type of behavior and where in the lesson it occurred. It is very important not to interrupt the student. If you have a question, such as why they answered a particular question as they did, write it down and ask it after they complete the lesson.

Final Interview

As students complete the lesson, you should interview them. Discuss any comments either of you have written down. The difficult aspect of the interview is that if you are the lesson's designer or programmer, you may well be told many things that bruise your ego. It is very difficult, for example, to have spent hundreds of hours producing what you regard as a masterpiece, only to have someone tell you that it is not very good.

When a situation like this occurs, when a student is very negative about one of your lessons, you should resist the temptation to explain why a display was designed in a particular way, or why you had structured the content the way you did. It is easy to become defensive about your lesson, but doing so will only reduce the effectiveness of the entire process by inhibiting the student from making further comments. If you keep in mind that any criticism you receive during the pilot-testing phase will ultimately benefit your lesson, it will be easier for you to handle. Remember also that anything your pilot students do not like, other students may not like, and you will not be around to explain your reasons to them.

The type of information you should seek in this interview relates both to the content of the lesson and to its operation. Ask whether the structure and logical flow of the subject matter seemed appropriate to the student or whether another structure would have been easier to understand. Find out whether the amount of control the student had for moving within the lesson was sufficient or whether greater freedom or constraint should be incorporated.

In addition to obtaining the students' reactions to the content and operation of the lesson, ask them how they felt about it. Was it enjoyable? Boring? Interesting? Useful? Would they have finished it if you were not there watching them?

Would they recommend it to their peers? These affective responses often provide useful insights into how the lesson is really perceived.

Assess Their Learning

Although student opinions and observations of their activity in the lesson are valuable, how much they learned is also important. Assessment of their achievement should follow their use of the lesson. This may be a written test or an oral examination probing and examining all aspects of the content to see what they do or do not remember and understand.

Revise the Lesson

Once you have accumulated the data from each student, you should decide whether the lesson needs further revision. Sometimes this is a very difficult decision to make, particularly if the reviews were contradictory. A good strategy to follow if this happens is to have a few more students take the lesson and solicit their views. If you decide to make major revisions to the lesson, you should always *repeat* the pilot-testing process with the new version.

Pilot testing is crucial for the production of quality lessons and should not be overlooked. Your decision should concern the *amount* of such testing and revision to undertake, not whether it should be done. There is a word of encouragement and caution, however. Good developers always regard their lessons as being *imperfect* and are constantly eager to improve them. It is important to realize, however, that at some point the extra effort you will expend to make an improvement may not be time- or cost-effective. You should terminate the development process when the lesson accomplishes its purpose, not when you regard it as being perfect.

VALIDATION

The final stage in the evaluation process is validation of the lesson—the process of checking how well the lesson works in the real instructional setting. This is sometimes known as field testing. No matter how positively the students in the pilot-testing phase reviewed the lesson, it is important to put the lesson through this final scrutiny.

There are two main reasons for the importance of this phase. First, the real setting in which the lesson is to be used invariably is quite different from where it was pilot tested. The computer may be in the middle of a busy classroom, causing a steady flow of diversions to the student taking the lesson. All the prerequisite skills may not be present to the degree you had expected. Supplementary materials may not be available. Second, although every attempt is made in the pilot test to use helpers who span the range of abilities of the target population, you will typically find students in the middle of the range and not the ends. Furthermore, data collected from only three or four students can never generalize completely to the entire population. The true test of a lesson occurs when it is exposed to a large number of students in their natural instructional setting.

The procedures we recommend are those commonly called summative evaluation. However, summative evaluation implies evaluation done *after* all development and revision is done. Although we recommend the same procedures, we encourage their use as a part of the revision process. Summative evaluation has received more thorough a treatment in other texts than we can provide here. We recommend you read one or more of the books listed at the end of the chapter to acquaint yourself more fully with this process.

Assessment of Achievement

The primary goal of validation is to ensure that students learn what is intended. There are several ways of doing this. The first is to measure the amount students know of the subject matter before taking the lesson, and again afterwards. Any gain in the amount known can be attributed to your lesson, assuming there have been no other instructional episodes covering the same topic. A second and common method is to use the results of how the students performed on the lesson itself as an indicator of how well it taught. For example, if the students performed well on a final test in the lesson, that is evidence they have learned the subject matter. Yet another way is to give the students a test on the subject matter some time after they had taken the lesson to determine whether they retain the information taught.

Each one of these methods has advantages and drawbacks, which are well discussed in the literature. Our position is that the best validation is the one that measures whether the students can use the information in the setting for which the instruction was designed. For example, if the students were given an instructional simulation which was designed to teach them problem-solving skills, the best test is to give them a variety of problems related to but not the same as the ones in the instructional lesson. In this way you assess whether what was taught has transferred to the situations for which the skill was needed.

A negative example will help illustrate the point further. Assume that students learn how to operate some complex equipment by means of a computer simulation. At the end of the program, which has both introduced the equipment and provided practice in operating it, all students pass the final test on the simulation. Despite the fact that all students performed well on this final test, that is not sufficient validation, because there has been no test of whether these students could operate the real equipment. It is quite possible for the lesson to have done an excellent job at teaching students how to operate the simulated equipment, but a very poor job of teaching them how to operate the real equipment.

Assessment of Attitude

In addition to ensuring that a lesson teaches what it was intended to do, you should assess how well the students liked the lesson. Although you should interpret attitudinal data cautiously, it often provides valuable information. One thing is certain: if the students all report they did not like the lesson, then there is little doubt that it needs revision. If they provide positive reports, this must be treated with a little more skepticism.

The importance of gathering affective information can be illustrated by the following anecdote. In the early years of the PLATO system at the University of Illinois, there was apparently a statistics instructor who wanted to test the value of computer-based instruction. To do this he divided his class into two groups; one received the traditional series of lectures and laboratory sessions, while the other spent most of its time using lessons on the computer. At the end of semester, both groups were given the same final examination, and the group using the computer performed better. Based on the evaluation, it would appear that the computer version of the class was the better of the two because it resulted in better achievement. However, it transpired that in the following semester, not a single student that had been in the computer section took a follow-up course, whereas a number of students from the traditional section did.

In this example, the lesson achieved part of its goal, namely to teach certain elements of statistics. However, it failed in another, perhaps more important goal, namely to foster an interest in statistics.

It is also advisable to assess the attitude of instructors toward the lesson. This is in part a practical consideration. It will be instructors, not students, who decide to use the lesson in a course. If instructors do not like it, the lesson will never get much use.

COMPUTER TOOLS FOR EVALUATION

The computer tools most overlooked for evaluation is the CBI program itself. A lesson may have built-in collection of data that will assist in its own evaluation. The data collected may be very detailed. Some developers collect all keypresses (or other actions) the student makes. This allows the developer to recreate the student's path through the lesson, responses to questions, requests for help, and so on. At the other extreme, the lesson may collect summary information such as the percentage of correct and incorrect responses and the number of student initiated requests such as for help, the glossary, or the main menu.

Collecting information automatically allows you to run some pilot students without supervision. Under supervision a student tends to work more diligently. Alone, the student may more frequently request answers, ask for help, or go back to the menu and skip around in the lesson.

A useful evaluation tool for complex lessons with a large degree and variety of student control is a student simulation routine. This is a program which sends keypresses and other simulated student actions to your program, giving the appearance that a student is running the lesson. A simulator may be run over and over, testing all the pathways through a lesson, all the strange combinations of student actions, what happens when a lot of data is stored in disk files, and so on. It allows thorough testing without real students. Of course, student simulation does not allow as realistic evaluation as do real students and is not a substitute for real students. It is not very good for assessing the quality of answer judging and cannot assess at all how well the lesson teaches. It is a good technique to use in addition to real students for testing program robustness and data collection. Lastly, student simulation is not always possible. It depends on the capabilities of the computer operating system and authoring software.

Evaluation generates data which must be analyzed in some way. Useful computer tools for data analysis are computer spreadsheet programs and statistical analysis programs, for example *SYSTAT* (Wilkinson, 1984). Statistical programs can perform descriptive or experimental analysis of student lesson performance and test scores. Most evaluation data stored in diskette files can be accessed by statistical software for analysis. Today, all but the most trivial statistical procedures are done with computer programs.

REVISION AND SUBSEQUENT EVALUATION

We cannot stress enough that lesson development does not end here. The preceding evaluation was intended to identify deficiencies in the draft lesson. These must be corrected. Sometimes major problems are identified which require major changes. However, if earlier evaluations (such as after Steps 5 and 7) were done well, it is rare for major problems to surface at this point.

If the changes needed are very minor, such as grammar and spelling correction, it may not be necessary to do subsequent evaluation. However, most evaluations uncover some problems at a deeper level. The lesson is too dull. The answer judging is not very intelligent. There are bugs in user control or data collection. After revision you should do more evaluation, primarily pilot testing and validation.

CONCLUSION

Evaluation is essential to the production of a lesson of high quality. You need only review some commercially produced software to realize how frequently evaluation is neglected. Much commercial software has functional problems, aesthetic problems, and often content weaknesses. We hope that you will not be satisfied with such lack of quality and will take the time to evaluate your lessons thoroughly before making them generally available. As we have already said, the effects of distributing poor-quality lessons is far greater than that of poor-quality books. Unfortunately, the attitude prevails that any bad computer-based lesson means that all computer-based instruction is bad.

All the earlier procedures we described, such as needs analysis, collecting resources, brainstorming, flowcharting and storyboarding, and attention to instructional factors, only increase the *probability* of a good lesson. Assuming those things have been done well, thorough evaluation and revision *guarantee* a good lesson.

REFERENCES AND BIBLIOGRAPHY

ANDERSON, R.C. (1972). How to construct achievement tests to assess comprehension. *Review of Educational Research, 43,* 145–170.

BERK, R.A. (Ed.). (1981). *Criterion-Referenced Measurement: The State of the Art.* Baltimore, MD: Johns Hopkins University Press.

BERK, R.A. (Ed.). (1981). *Educational Evaluation Methodology: The State of the Art.* Baltimore, MD: Johns Hopkins University Press.

BLOOM, B.S., HASTINGS, J.T., & MADAUS, G.F. (1971). *Handbook on Formative and Summative Evaluation of Student Learning.* New York: McGraw-Hill.

BRIGGS, L.J. (Ed.). (1977). *Instructional Design: Principles and Applications.* Englewood Cliffs, NJ: Educational Technology Publications.

COOLEY, W.W., & LOHNES, P.R. (1977). *Evaluation Research in Education.* New York: Irvington Publishers, Inc.

DUDLEY-MARLING, C., & OWSTON, R.D. (1987). The state of educational software: A criterion-based evaluation. *Educational Technology, 27*(3), 25–29.

FOWLER, H.W. (1977). *A Dictionary of Modern English Usage.* New York: Oxford University Press.

GRONLUND, N.E. (1981). *Measurement and Evaluation in Teaching.* New York: Macmillan.

HODGES, J.C., & WHITTEN, M. (1977). *Harbrace College Handbook.* New York: Harcourt Brace Jovanovich.

JACKSON, D.N., & MESSICK, S. (Eds.). (1967). *Problems in Human Assessment.* New York: McGraw-Hill.

JONES, N.B., & VAUGHAN, L. (1983). *Evaluation of Educational Software: A Guide to Guides.* Austin, TX: Southwest Educational Development Laboratory and Northeast Regional Exchange, Inc.

LEGGETT, G., MEAD, C.D., & CHARVAT, W. (1978). *Prentice-Hall Handbook for Writers.* Englewood Cliffs, NJ: Prentice-Hall.

MEHRENS, W.A., & LEHMANN, I.J. (1973). *Measurement and Evaluation in Education and Psychology.* New York: Holt, Rinehart and Winston.

MicroSIFT. (1982). *Evaluator's Guide for Microcomputer-based Instructional Packages.* Eugene, OR: University of Oregon, International Council for Computers in Education.

OWSTON, R. D. (1987). *Software Evaluation: A Criterion-based Approach.* Scarborough, Ontario: Prentice-Hall Canada.

SAROYAN, A., & GEIS, G.L. (1988). An analysis of guidelines for expert reviewers. *Instructional Science, 17,* 101–128.

STRUNK, W., & WHITE, E.B. (1979). *The Elements of Style.* New York: Macmillan.

TUCKMANN, B.W. (1978). *Conducting Educational Research.* New York: Harcourt Brace Jovanovich.

WALKER, D.F., & HESS, R.D. (Eds.) (1984). *Instructional Software: Principles and Perspectives for Design and Use.* Belmont, CA: Wadsworth Publishing.

WILKINSON, L. (1984). *SYSTAT.* [Computer Program]. Evanston, IL: SYSTAT, Inc.

SUMMARY OF EVALUATION

QUALITY REVIEW

Use the checklist.
Check the language and grammar.
Check the surface features.
Check questions and menus.
Check all invisible functions.
Check the subject-matter content.
Check the off-line material.
Revise the lesson.
Apply the same quality review procedure to the revised lesson.

PILOT TESTING

Enlist about three helpers.
Explain pilot-testing procedures.
Find out how much they know about the subject matter.

Observe them go through the lesson.
Interview them afterwards.
Assess their learning.
Revise the lesson.
Pilot test the revised lesson.

VALIDATION

Use the lesson in the setting for which it was designed.
Use the lesson with students for which it was designed.
Evaluate how the students perform in the setting for which you are teaching them.
Obtain as much performance data as you can from different sources.
Obtain data on student achievement due to the lesson.
Obtain data on student attitudes towards the lesson.

13

COMPUTER-MANAGED INSTRUCTION

INTRODUCTION

This chapter describes computer-managed instruction (CMI) systems. These systems provide administrative support to instructors for managing instructional materials and activities. We begin with a review of the history and theory of computer-managed instruction. We then give our own description of the "state of the art" of this technology. Lastly, we show and describe a prototype CMI system for microcomputers.

Computer-managed instruction (CMI) was among the first successful uses of the computer in instruction. In the early days of mainframe computing, before facilities were available for students to work individually at computer terminals, several university and military projects developed programs to aid in the management of classroom instruction, and to keep track of student progress on tests and instructional modules. These programs were developed to deal with the data processing needs of individualized instruction and mastery learning programs. Such programs (Bloom, 1976; Keller, 1968) arose as alternatives to traditional group-based instruction.

Individualized instruction and mastery learning require more frequent testing of students, keeping records on the educational progress and activities of individual students, and reporting of information. Instructors involved in such programs find themselves overburdened with scoring tests, filling out performance and activity sheets for each student, and analyzing student information to produce class reports. Little instructor time is left for working with individual students on things for which they need help—the whole idea of individualized instruction programs.

In answer to these problems, computer programs were developed that included a database of course structure and objectives, and test items and instructional activities linked to each objective. After a student takes a test covering relevant objectives, the computer scores the test and provides a prescription of activities that teach the objectives not yet mastered. Additionally, the computer stores the information about the student's past progress and current activities.

The instructor periodically receives reports showing individual student and total class progress.

EARLY CMI SYSTEMS

Among the first CMI systems was the Program for Learning in Accordance with Needs (PLAN), begun in about 1966 (Flanagan, 1969, 1970; Flanagan, Shanner, Brudner, & Marker, 1975). This CMI system was oriented towards elementary and secondary school curriculum management. Developed by the American Institutes for Research and later marketed commercially by Westinghouse Learning Corporation, PLAN provided service to many school districts across the country. In its early implementations, information on student achievement tests was entered into a computer terminal via punch cards and processed at a central mainframe computer. The computer scored the achievement tests and on a daily basis provided printouts showing individual student achievement by curricular objectives, instructional materials recommended for each student, and various summary reports across time and across students.

Soon, several school districts, universities, and businesses began developing CMI systems. Early systems typically required students to take progress tests on optical scanning sheets (the same kind of computer-scoreable sheets that are used for most national exams). These were either mailed to a center having the necessary computer hardware or were entered into a local scoring machine and transmitted to a remote computer. The remote computer scored the tests, stored information from the new student data, and produced reports that were either mailed back or transmitted electronically to the school. Reports of different types were available: such as for individual students at any point in time (showing progress on objectives and current activities), summary information for a student over a period of time, and summary information for groups of students.

As telecommunication networks became more widely available, CMI activities became easier and more interactive. The U.S. Navy CMI system (Hansen, Ross, Bowman, & Thurmond, 1975; Mayo, 1974), begun in 1973, allowed students to take a test using an optical sense answer form, feed the form themselves into an optical form reader, and get a printout almost immediately showing their results, progress, and next assignment. The analysis and data storage was still on a remote computer connected by telephone to the scoring machine and printer.

The Computer-Assisted Instruction Study Management System (CAISMS) begun in 1974 (Anderson et al., 1974) permitted students to take a test interactively on a computer terminal and receive immediate results and study assignments on the same terminal. Little instructor intervention was needed for day-to-day student activity. This management system also provided instructors with programs to facilitate course grading, report generation for individuals or groups of students, communications with students, and scheduling of discussion sections and other resources.

In November 1974 a conference on CMI projects (Mitzel, 1974) reported twenty-four operational CMI systems. Most systems were operating on mainframe computers, but a few existed on minicomputers. Microcomputers did not yet exist. Great progress was predicted for the future of CMI, and many experts felt that it would prove more successful and cost-effective than computer delivery of instruction (CBI). Research evaluating the effectiveness of instructional computer programs (reviewed in Bangert-Drowns, Kulik, & Kulik, 1985) provided evidence that CMI was more effective than CBI for older students. Baker (1978) provided the first comprehensive discussion, both theoretical and practical, on the design and implementation of CMI systems. Although Baker deals with mainframe CMI systems, his discussion of theoretical, social, and management issues is still pertinent to microcomputer-based systems.

FUNCTIONS OF CMI SYSTEMS

As Baker described CMI at the time, the typical functions of a system were the following: input and storage of student data (primarily test scores and activities completed), input and storage of curricular data (generally objectives, test items linked to objectives, and instructional materials or activities linked to objectives), retrieval and analysis of the data relating student scores and activity to the curriculum data, and generation of various reports showing individual or group progress and current status. The primary purpose of the analysis and reporting was to provide diagnosis and prescription of student learning problems or needs and appropriate instructional activities to remedy them.

Baker categorized CMI systems into small-scale (managing a single course at a single institution), medium-scale (managing multiple courses at a single institution), and large-scale (managing multiple courses at multiple institutions).

Specific CMI systems added features beyond the basic ones Baker discussed. On mainframe systems that could provide computer-based instruction as well as CMI (for example, PLATO), the CMI system provided *routing* of students directly to the appropriate computer programs and back to the management program after their completion.

Some added generalized roster or gradebook features, allowing instructors to enter and use information they had always kept about students, such as names, addresses, grades on classroom tests and homework, attendance, and so on.

Some added an "attention needed" feature, allowing the instructor to query the computer as to which students most needed attention and why. The computer would analyze the status of all students and produce a display or printout. One student might be identified as not having taken any quizzes in three weeks. Another as having received a very low score on the most recent test. Another as having completed all instructional units for the current semester and having nothing to do.

Systems with many terminals provided administration of exams on-line. This has advantages and disadvantages. On-line exams may be scored immediately and the test data accurately transferred to the CMI database. This reduces the time the instructor spends scoring tests and entering data, as well as reducing data entry errors. However, on-line examinations, if they are to be scored automatically, limit tests to objective items.

CMI systems integrated with CBI also provided a common base for the CBI component. That is, the CMI system takes care of asking and storing names, teaching about use of the keyboard, and providing instruction about general lesson procedures, and so on. This not only is efficient, eliminating redundant directions and activities at the start of every CBI lesson, but it also encourages standardization of procedures across lessons, making them easier for students.

Similarly, some CMI systems provided information for students, which was in contrast to Baker's point of view, that the CMI system's primary purpose was providing information to instructors. This typically is a subset of that information available to the instructor, providing the students with their own scores, status, and assigned activities.

Some CMI systems provided scheduling of scarce resources. Scarce resources are anything less numerous than the students. Textbooks, desks, paper, and pencils are generally *not* scarce resources. There are enough to go around and do not require scheduling. In contrast, reference books, computers, instructors, laboratory equipment, films, seminar rooms, and instructor office hours are all scarce resources. A CMI system can provide a calendar and scheduling program for such resources, allowing students to sign up and reserve in advance the use of a computer, an appointment with an instructor, or use of a videotape. Such scheduling enables efficient use of limited resources as well as fair access to them by all students. This feature can also alert the instructor when more of a particular scarce resource is needed.

The final CMI system feature we discuss, which was added on large-scale systems, is communications features for instructors and students. Because CMI systems are used in and partially automate individualized instruction systems, they increase the tendency for students to work alone and have less interaction with other students and instructors. There is a tendency for classes to meet less as a group with the instructor. As a result, the opportunities for instructors to make announcements to all students are restricted, and the ability of individual students to ask for help, make an appointment, and so on, are limited. Communication features allow instructors to easily leave announcements that all students will see next time they use the system, and allow students and instructors to exchange messages. If most students and the instructor use the CMI system on a daily basis, on-line communication can be more efficient and effective than mail or the telephone.

These additional features of some CMI systems are not the essential ones, according to Baker. On some large-scale CBI systems such as PLATO, many of these features are considered a part of the general system (or operating system) while the CMI component is only that part which coordinates tests, objectives, and assignments. However, since these activities are all aspects of the management of instruction, we believe they should be considered in the design and evaluation of

CMI systems. Similarly we regard any system which includes these features to be a type of CMI system.

FACTORS INHIBITING CMI IN SCHOOLS

The same year that Baker's book on CMI was published, 1978, saw the introduction of commercially available microcomputers such as the Apple II, the Radio Shack TRS-80, and the Commodore Pet. As a result, elementary and secondary schools, and to a lesser extent universities, began switching from the use of mainframe and minicomputers for educational purposes to using microcomputers. The introduction of microcomputers in schools was a great *setback* for the use of CMI for two reasons. First, the effectiveness of a CMI system assumes and requires a shared database of all students' academic data. Independent microcomputers do not share any data, so developing CMI systems for them was harder than for large computers. Early attempts to network microcomputers or to have them share a single, large mass-storage device were limited in success.

Second, with the development (for microcomputers) of many CBI programs and other software useful in classrooms, also came copy protection. Almost all software, from $30 math drills to $300 word processing programs were copy protected. Copy protection of programs prevents their management via CMI programs in several ways. It is usually impossible to use the software on a network or shared mass storage device. More importantly, copy-protected software often must be run by restarting the microcomputer. As a result, a coordinating CMI system cannot activate a CBI lesson or instructor utility, let alone return to the CMI system after that program's completion.

Separate from the issue of copy protection were several other factors preventing good CMI on microcomputers. The lack of adequate networks until fairly recently prevented maintenance of centralized databases and the incompatibility of software impeded management of microcomputer courseware. Most microcomputers allow and encourage developers to design totally different user interfaces, data storage techniques, and peripheral devices. It is very difficult, perhaps impossible, to design a good CMI system that can control many different lessons which use different methods of entry, exit, data storage, and so forth.

The result is that medium- and large-scale CMI has grown very little, and perhaps even decreased, in schools. In contrast, CMI has grown more in industry and military training, where mainframes are still used and much courseware is internally produced and does not contain copy protection. There are some large school districts throughout the country that use CMI systems, but they are few and far between.

Separate from medium- and large-scale CMI systems are small, or perhaps even mini-CMI systems. That is to say, some specific CBI lessons or curricula have CMI components designed into them. For example, in the Milliken Math Sequences (Milliken, 1980) the CMI component stores student scores by name in a centralized database. It determines what drills the student must do next based on scores, and allows the instructor to manage the database, such as producing reports and removing old data to begin new classes. However, these mini-CMI systems are unique to a particular software series and cannot deal with off-line materials. If several such software packages are used, the instructor must work separately with the different CMI options for each package.

RECENT FACTORS ENCOURAGING CMI IN SCHOOLS

Very recently, we have become more optimistic about the future of CMI. First, the technology of microcomputer networking is rapidly progressing. Second, mass storage devices have increased in capacity while decreasing in cost. The result is to enable microcomputer networks to work with a single, very large database. Third, there has been a considerable decrease in the use of copy protection and hence an ability to run software stored on a networked database. And fourth, especially on Macintosh microcomputers, there is growing agreement on interfaces, data storage formats, and data interchange techniques.

As a result of the above changes, it is possible to design a CMI system that runs on a microcomputer network and manages a database stored on a mass storage device (for example, a large hard disk drive) available to all microcomputers on the network. The database may contain many things: CBI lessons, test-item files, objective and other curricular files, assignment (both on-line and off-line) files, and student data files. When lessons are not copy protected and contain more compatible data and entry/exit formats, the CMI system may control routing of students between lessons, interpret data generated by lessons, and pass useful information to lessons (such as student and instructor names, dates and time, previous lesson progress, or pretest scores). The CMI system can easily provide all the functions discussed above, routing, data storage, analysis, reporting, on-line examinations, general information, scheduling, and communications.

CMI AS A BASIS FOR CBI IMPLEMENTATION

It is our contention that CMI can and should be the basis of any medium- or large-scale CBI implementation. In the remainder of this chapter we explain why this is so and describe the phases of implementing a CMI system. We end with an illustration of a prototype CMI system.

By medium-scale CBI implementation we mean an entire CBI curriculum, such as high-school algebra or chemistry. The CBI materials might be any combination of tutorials, drills, simulations, or other methodologies supporting the curriculum, and would certainly include noncomputer activities such as textbooks, laboratory sessions, lectures, and discussions. Large-scale CBI refers to the management of several curricula within a school or across several schools. Again, the CBI materials would be in addition to other instructional activities and media.

Small-scale CBI refers to a situation in which individual instructors choose to use or experiment with one or a few microcomputers to supplement current teaching in their own classes. We do not believe that small-scale CBI implementation requires initial implementation of CMI.

What are the reasons that CMI is a good prelude to and basis for CBI? There are several reasons:

CMI implementation can *reduce instructor work loads* by automating tedious and routine functions such as grading, scheduling, and keeping track of resources. In contrast, beginning with CBI typically *increases* an instructor's workload. Thus, prior implementation of CMI can offset the extra learning and work involved in CBI and make it smoother.

CMI can be *introduced in phases* and adapted to meet the needs and concerns of any particular instructor or group of instructors. Initial implementation might be to provide gradebook facilities. Later phases might include test scoring, test administration, and student routing. Thus, implementation can accommodate an instructor's comfort level and expertise with computer technology. Furthermore, it can begin by replacing those tasks instructors do not typically like, such as grading, *rather than* replacing those activities instructors typically do like, such as working individually with their students.

CMI can be done with *just one computer*. This is a situation that instructors typically face—having one computer in their classroom. Although there are useful teaching functions that can be accomplished with one computer, they are few in number. In contrast, the initial phases of CMI are easily accomplished on a single computer used by the instructor. As one progresses to more sophisticated phases of CMI, additional computers are added.

CMI provides an excellent way to organize and *integrate* both CBI and traditional (off-line) instructional materials. The system permits sequencing, avoiding redundancy, and communicating with students as to when each resource should be utilized. It also helps instructors keep track of what work students have done both on and off the computer.

CMI helps instructors and curriculum planners *determine curriculum needs*. By collecting achievement data from progress tests and CBI lessons and by cross-referencing those data with the intended objectives, it becomes apparent which objectives are being met and which are not. Thus, rather than developing redundant materials or changing parts of the curriculum that are already working well, energy may be channeled into producing materials for those objectives that require attention. New development may be on a computer or any other medium. Subsequently, the CMI system's data collection and analysis can assess the success of newly created or changed components.

CMI may be used for either *individualized* or *group instruction*. Although CMI systems were created to meet the data organization needs of individualized and mastery learning programs (Baker, 1978), we do not believe that such a distinction remains necessary. First, we endorse a broadening of the definition of CMI to include not only the individualized testing and assignment components of instructional systems, but group testing, resource scheduling, grading, and other instructional management functions, which are equally useful in group instruction, and may be even more useful for large group instruction such as college lecture-oriented courses.

Second, new technologies are blurring the distinction between individualized and group instruction. Whereas it used to be the case that a course might be all group or all individualized instruction, today we see many cases where some individualized CBI is included in a course that is otherwise largely group oriented. At all levels, from elementary school to college, instruction is becoming more eclectic with group-oriented components (such as lectures, discussions, and team projects) and individual-oriented components (such as reading textbooks, CBI, and term papers). Even if a course is largely group oriented, whenever there are individualized components, CMI can ease data management for the instructor and guide the student through the activities.

CMI provides a basis for *evaluation* of both students and instruction. Especially when achievement testing is automated, a CMI system can assist in grading and can assess (by virtue of their association with particular objectives and achievement measures) which instructional materials are teaching successfully. The former alleviates the tedious job of grading, while the latter permits more frequent course improvement.

CMI can *solve some problems posed by incompatible software and hardware*. Educators wishing to use CBI today are faced with an array of different brands and models of microcomputers and software intended for particular microcomputers. In addition, even software packages designed for the same model microcomputers are typically incompatible in terms of student access and data collection. Students and instructors must deal with the frustration of knowing a number of different access methods. One program requires restarting the computer. Another requires a special startup disk. A third requires using the computer manufacturer's special DOS disk first, and then typing in commands to run the program. Although these different techniques also present problems for good automation, a CMI system can deal with them better than students and instructors, thus easing the burden. Even if the instructional software does not allow the CMI system to route the student to and from it directly and to transfer data automatically, the CMI system may include directions to students and instructors and provide facilities for data to be transferred in a manual but guided fashion.

INCREMENTAL IMPLEMENTATION OF CMI AND CBI

In the preceding section we made the case that it often makes sense to begin with CMI rather than with CBI. However, that is not to say that one should start with a fully fledged large- or even medium-scale CMI system. Rather, CMI and subsequently CBI should be phased in. What we mean by this is as follows.

Take the example of an instructor in a school that has recently begun installation of computer facilities. The school has one or more central lab facilities as well as mobile computer carts for use in classroom. A reasonable way to proceed is to start using the computer technology in a simple way and then gradually extend its use—what we call an incremental implementation.

First, the instructor should learn to use the computer via simple class management and material preparation programs. A word processing program may be used to develop handouts, exercises, assignments, and lecture notes. A gradebook or spreadsheet program can be used to score tests and compute term grades. A database or test item banking program should be used for producing and printing copies of tests. A graphics program may be used for producing handouts and in small groups may be used as an electronic blackboard. A time-line program may be used for planning classroom schedules. The database program may also be used to inventory classroom materials, library books, and parent mailing lists. The spreadsheet program can also be used as an electronic blackboard program in teaching some subjects, such as math, science, or business.

When comfortable with basic computer usage and having used it to automate some regular teaching functions, the instructor progresses to a second phase of CMI implementation. This and subsequent phases require multiple computers, either in the classroom or in a central lab facility. The main feature of the second phase is networking the microcomputers. This is essential for good organization. Multiple, unconnected microcomputers only complicate organization of data and activities, and get in the way of automating them. Connecting the microcomputers so they share databases (such as student data and CBI programs) and resources (such as printers and telecommunication devices) enables a high degree of organization and automation. With the microcomputers networked, CMI components may be implemented for student signons, data collection, and routing to individual CBI lessons. Routing to lessons should be simple at this point, limited to students choosing from a hierarchy of menus with some capability for the instructor to turn parts of the hierarchy on or off.

In the third phase, assuming sufficient microcomputers are available, CMI components can schedule resources and provide communications and on-line progress testing. On-line testing is the most important component and ultimately facilitates the major advantages of CMI, namely, automatic assignment of appropriate instructional materials and evaluation of both students and the curriculum. Some testing systems, such as *The Examiner* (Trollip & Brown, 1989) which was described in Chapter 6, can be activated automatically by a CMI system.

The fourth phase adds more sophisticated routing to CBI lessons. Instructors may make assignments for any student or group of students. For lessons which permit it, data such as the student's name and previous activity may be passed from the CMI system and other data returned to the CMI system such as performance in the lesson.

The fifth phase adds procedures for automatic assignment and routing based on progress tests. This requires valid and reliable progress tests and good cross-referencing of test items, curricular objectives, and instructional materials.

The sixth phase, and a continuing one, is to provide features that the instructor desires. These are likely to include analysis and reporting functions that aid in day-to-day as well as semester-to-semester duties. Graphs that show a student's activity and progress might be useful for parent/instructor meetings. A summary listing of test scores and other information might be useful for final grading. A summary of lesson popularity and effectiveness might be useful for planning subsequent semesters. Lastly, the weaknesses in the curriculum pointed out by progress test scores would lead to requests for added instructional materials to complement the instructional system.

The point of a phased implementation as we have just described is to progress to each successive phase as instructors become comfortable with the activities involved in the preceding phase. Failure can easily result from trying to implement a full-fledged CMI system right from the start. For each of the phases described, instructors may require a semester or even a full academic year to become competent and comfortable with the activities. Then they are ready to move on to something more complex.

A PROTOTYPE CMI SYSTEM

We end this chapter by describing and illustrating a hypothetical CMI system. The design of CMI depends on many factors. Chief among them are the instructor and student activities to be automated, the type of instructional materials being managed, the educational level of the students and the amount of control they are given over their learning activities, and the number of courses and instructors involved.

For our example we choose a somewhat complex case, namely the management of instruction across several courses and departments at the university level. We begin by assuming that the fictitious North Woods University has several microcomputer instructional classrooms on campus that are interconnected by a network and share a single large database of student data and courseware. From any microcomputer all faculty members can retrieve information on their advisees or students enrolled in their classes. Similarly, from any microcomputer, students can sign on to the network and access instructional materials and advice for all university courses in which they are enrolled. Access to personal records is restricted by virtue of both a person's signon (whether student or faculty member) and passwords. A design decision of the North Woods University (NWU) instructional system is that every student and every instructor has only *one* signon, from which all appropriate programs and data can be accessed. This provides for good integration of all relevant data across the system. For example, by unifying the instructional system with the university's academic data processing database, advisors can see not only a student's current course activity, but grade history and any other information an advisor requires. It is even possible, given this level of integration, that the system could be used for course registration.

The Student Perspective

Figure 13–1 shows the initial signon page for the network. In Figure 13–2 a student, William Long, has typed in his name and is now prompted to enter his

```
┌─────────────────────────────────────────────────────┐
│                                                       │
│   NORTH  WOODS  UNIVERSITY  INSTRUCTIONAL  SYSTEM     │
│                                                       │
│        Please type your name and press return .       │
│                                                       │
│               ▶                                       │
│                                                       │
│                                                       │
│                                                       │
│                                                       │
│                                                       │
└─────────────────────────────────────────────────────┘
```

Figure 13-1   Signon to the CMI system.

```
┌─────────────────────────────────────────────────────┐
│                                                       │
│   NORTH  WOODS  UNIVERSITY  INSTRUCTIONAL  SYSTEM     │
│                                                       │
│                                                       │
│        Name        ▶  William Long                    │
│                                                       │
│        Please type your identification number and press return . │
│                                                       │
│               ▶                                       │
│                                                       │
│                                                       │
│                                                       │
└─────────────────────────────────────────────────────┘
```

Figure 13-2   Hypothetical student signing on the system.

identification (Social Security) number. A name is insufficient to distinguish students reliably, for students may have identical names and should not be forced to use a modified name just to suit the system.

In Figure 13–3 William has entered his ID number as well. This, and not his name, uniquely identifies him on the system. He is now prompted for a password, which prevents other persons from using the computer system under his name. This is essential, because the system includes personal data, tests, grades, and other sensitive information.

In Figure 13–4 the system has informed William that he entered his password incorrectly and must try again. A well-designed system must allow the student to change the password at will to maintain privacy.

When William successfully signs on (Figure 13–5), he sees a page which consists of his personal instructional activities (the options listed vertically) and

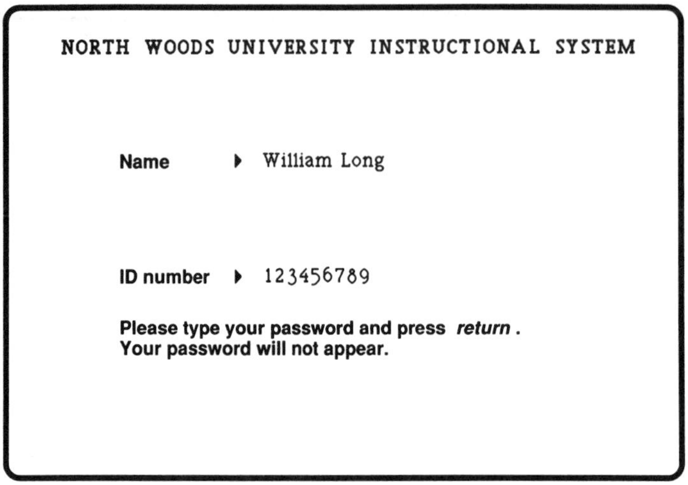

NORTH WOODS UNIVERSITY INSTRUCTIONAL SYSTEM

Name   ▶ William Long

ID number   ▶ 123456789

Please type your password and press *return* **.**
Your password will not appear.

Figure 13-3 Having entered a unique identifying number the student must now enter a secret password.

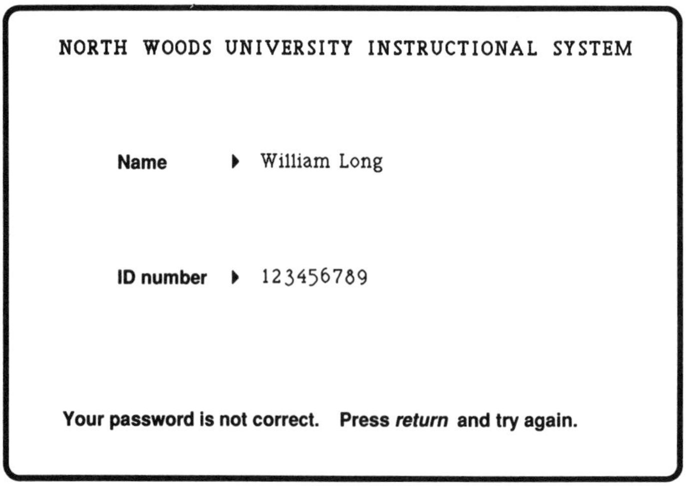

NORTH WOODS UNIVERSITY INSTRUCTIONAL SYSTEM

Name   ▶ William Long

ID number   ▶ 123456789

Your password is not correct.   Press *return* **and try again.**

Figure 13-4 The student is prompted to correct his password.

those management activities to which all students have access (the options listed horizontally at the bottom of the screen). Using a mouse or other pointing device, William can point to and choose individual CBI lessons (the first two options on the vertical list), courses (Calculus II through Intermediate German I), or the general options to read or write electronic mail, see schedules, see information about his academic status, get help on using the system, or exit and sign off.

Figure 13-6 shows a sample schedule. Having chosen the schedule option on Figure 13-5 and then choosing the Math Computer Lab schedule, William can obtain information about computer availability and, by pointing, choose a day and time to reserve a computer. Because all computers are networked, the appropriate computer can prevent any other student from signing on at the time William has reserved it. Again there are options along the bottom of the screen which

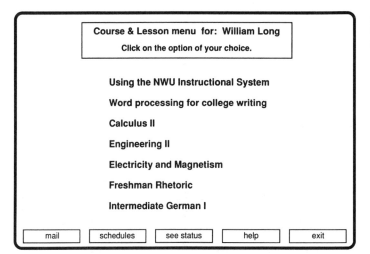

Figure 13-5 The student has signed on and sees personal assignments and other system options.

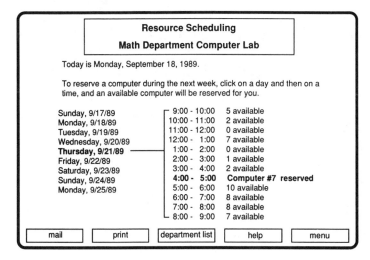

Figure 13-6 Using a scheduling option to reserve a computer in the Math Department computer laboratory.

can be pointed at for other actions. For example, if the microcomputer has an attached printer, William can obtain a printout of his reservation.

The most important options listed on Figure 13–5 are the courses, Calculus II, Engineering II, Electricity and Magnetism, Freshman Rhetoric, and Intermediate German I. These names are identical to the university courses in which William is enrolled. Through the use of a networked university-wide CMI system, students have access from any computer to instructional materials and guidance for all their courses. A course option, as we will see next, provides the student with on-line instruction (CBI), progress tests for instructional decision making, and advice and assignments for activities not on the computer such as reading the textbook, discussion and review classes, or films.

In Figure 13–7 William picks the Calculus II course and receives the information shown. Based on the work he has done on the computer, he is ready to take

```
┌─────────────────────────────────────────────────────────────┐
│                                                               │
│  Calculus II Curriculum      William Long - ID# 123456789     9/18/89  │
│                                                               │
│                                                               │
│   You have completed the first 5 lessons.                     │
│                                                               │
│   If you have done the required off-line assignments, send your  │
│   instructor a message requesting the Unit 1 exam.            │
│                                                               │
│   You may review previous lessons if you wish.               │
│                                                               │
│   Click on one of the options below.                         │
│                                                               │
│                                                               │
│                                                               │
│                                                               │
│                                                               │
│  [ mail ]  [ course map ]  [ review-map ]  [ help ]  [ menu ] │
│                                                               │
└─────────────────────────────────────────────────────────────┘
```

Figure 13-7 Having chosen calculus, the student receives status and choices of what to do in that course.

a unit posttest (similar to the typical university hourly exam) *assuming* he has also completed his off-line work. The computer, of course, cannot tell whether he has done noncomputer work. While it is possible to allow the student to take a test based just on CBI progress, here it is deemed better to allow instructors some control. To take the test, William must use the *mail* option to send an electronic letter to the course instructor, in which he indicates he has completed all the off-line work. The instructor, as we will see later, may choose to permit the test, sending a response back to William to that effect.

A little later, in Figure 13-8, we see that the instructor has enabled William's test. When William chooses the Calculus II option on his main menu again, he sees this page. He has several options (along the bottom) such as reviewing CBI lessons before taking the exam.

Later (Figure 13-9) William signs on in a proctored lab to take the test.

```
┌─────────────────────────────────────────────────────────────┐
│                                                               │
│  Calculus II Curriculum      William Long - ID# 123456789     9/18/89  │
│                                                               │
│                                                               │
│                                                               │
│   You have completed the first 5 lessons and your instructor has  │
│   indicated you are ready for the Unit 1 exam.               │
│                                                               │
│   You may review previous lessons first, if you wish.        │
│                                                               │
│   Exams must be taken in proctored rooms.  See your instructor  │
│   if you do not know where and when you may take an exam.    │
│                                                               │
│   Click on one of the options below.                         │
│                                                               │
│                                                               │
│                                                               │
│  [ mail ]  [ take exam ]  [ review-map ]  [ help ]  [ menu ]  │
│                                                               │
└─────────────────────────────────────────────────────────────┘
```

Figure 13-8 The student is ready to take a computerized calculus test and is given directions about where to do so.

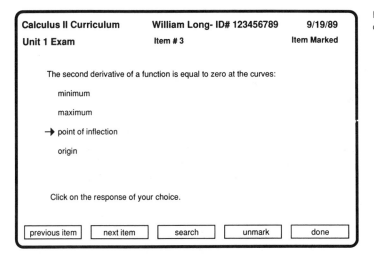

Figure 13-9 Taking the computerized calculus test.

Tests must be taken in a proctored lab for security because even though students sign on with a name and secret password, there is no way for a computer to know that the person working is really the person whose name is typed. Nor can the computer tell if the student has a friend sitting next to him or her to help on the exam, or if the student has a textbook or notes handy. In a proctored room, a proctor may check photo identification to be sure the correct person takes the exam and ensure that no cheating occurs. The proctor may also be of assistance to students concerning exam procedures or provide help in the event of a computer malfunction. In Figure 13-9 William is on the third item of his test. In keeping with the principles of Chapter 6, he can move around freely among items, mark items for later review, and change answers.

When he eventually clicks on the *done* option he will receive test feedback (not shown) followed by his next Calculus II assignment (Figure 13-10). This dis-

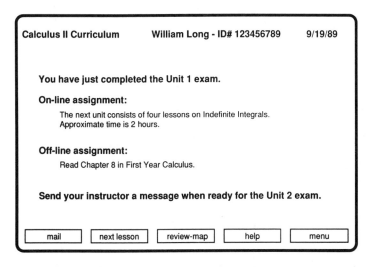

Figure 13-10 Based on performance in the test just taken, the student is given both on-line and off-line assignments.

play tells William that he has successfully passed Unit 1 and is ready for the next unit. He is informed about the CBI lessons and the off-line assignments for the next unit. Along the bottom of the display are the usual options.

The next day William signs on and, from his main menu (Figure 13–5), chooses the *see status* option. He sees the display in Figure 13–11 which summarizes all his current on-line and off-line assignments and his status within the on-line assignments.

Returning to the menu, William chooses the Calculus II option and receives the display shown in Figure 13–12. It should be obvious by now that every time a course option is picked, such as Calculus II, the student may receive a different activity. Depending on the course and its structure, the student may have a choice of lessons or may be directed, as in the case of Calculus II, to a specific

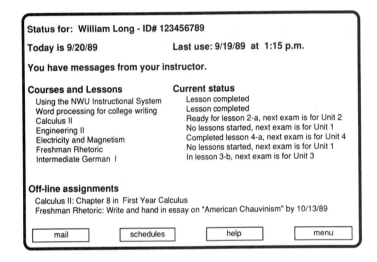

Status for: William Long - ID# 123456789

Today is 9/20/89   **Last use: 9/19/89 at 1:15 p.m.**

You have messages from your instructor.

Courses and Lessons   **Current status**
Using the NWU Instructional System   Lesson completed
Word processing for college writing   Lesson completed
Calculus II   Ready for lesson 2-a, next exam is for Unit 2
Engineering II   No lessons started, next exam is for Unit 1
Electricity and Magnetism   Completed lesson 4-a, next exam is for Unit 4
Freshman Rhetoric   No lessons started, next exam is for Unit 1
Intermediate German I   In lesson 3-b, next exam is for Unit 3

Off-line assignments
Calculus II: Chapter 8 in First Year Calculus
Freshman Rhetoric: Write and hand in essay on "American Chauvinism" by 10/13/89

| mail | schedules | help | menu |

Figure 13–11 A display showing the student's status in all assignments.

Calculus II Curriculum   **William Long - ID# 123456789**   **9/20/89**

You have chosen the next lesson in this curriculum:
"Using the Integral Tables."

Click on one of the options below.

| mail | do lesson | review-map | help | menu |

Figure 13–12 Preparing to study a CBI lesson in the calculus curriculum.

lesson. William is now told he is ready for a particular lesson. Even so, the options along the bottom of the screen include ones that allow him to review previously studied CBI lessons for this course (by pointing at the *review-map* option).

Two days later, having done some of his calculus lesson, William chooses the *review-map* option and sees the display in Figure 13–13. This is an abbreviated map showing the layout of the entire on-line portion of the Calculus II curriculum. The map shows that the course begins with a pretest (which William took at some time in the past) to assess whether the student is ready for the course, or which may direct the student to study some or all of the course's units. There are six units in Calculus II, each ending with a posttest that determines if the student is ready for the next unit. Posttests may also be used for grading, if the instructor so desires. At this time William has completed all the lessons in Unit 1 and has just begun Unit 2. The completed lessons are shown in dimmed (non-bold) type and William can point at any completed lesson to review it. A lesson in review mode is frequently abbreviated and does not take as long as the original lesson.

Summarizing the activities and options for our imaginary student William Long, the CMI system administers diagnostic tests based on which he is given study assignments, both on and off the computer. The computer automatically routes him to on-line assignments and keeps track of his progress, but an instructor must intervene to tell the system when off-line assignments are considered done. The system accommodates all of William's courses, each of which has its own unique structure. Not all have on-line tests or CBI lessons. Some may be strictly sequenced like Calculus II, while others may provide a menu of options for the student to choose in any order desired. Even when a course is sequenced in a strict fashion, the system may provide the student with the option to review. At almost any time, students may see their status and assignments for all courses, may see the map for a course to ascertain their progress in the course, may write and read electronic mail to communicate with instructors, and may see schedules and make reservations for scarce resources.

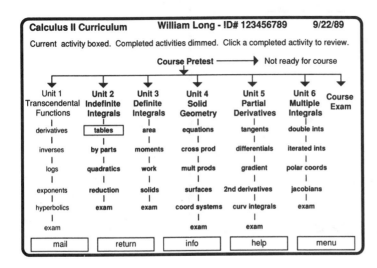

Figure 13-13 Viewing the curriculum map of the calculus course, also showing what parts the student has completed or is currently studying.

The Instructor Perspective

We now look at how the CMI system is used by Janet Brown, the professor who teaches the Calculus II course. She signs on the network in the same way as any student (as in Figures 13–1 through 13–4). However, the system recognizes that she is an instructor and displays a menu of instructor options, Figure 13–14. Janet may do many things. She may see a roster of students in any course she teaches (or to which she has authorized access) or a roster of students whom she advises. She may see the catalog of all NWU courses and CBI lessons or may inspect and try out CBI lessons or tests. She may read and reply to electronic mail from students or other faculty. Like a student she may see schedules and make reservations, but as an instructor she may also be able to set reservation schedules, determining, for example, the number of students that may enroll in an exam review session, the time and location where computerized exams may be taken, or the hours that the Math Department Computer Lab is open.

In Figure 13–15 we see that Janet Brown has chosen to see the course roster for Calculus II. Since this is a large enrollment course (taken by all freshmen science and engineering students), there are multiple sections to facilitate instructor management. Sections might also correspond to teaching assistant assignments, so that Janet can assign each of her teaching assistants a different section for student help and grading. She is now looking at Section C, in which William Long is enrolled. Student names are shown with their unique ID numbers, as is necessary in the case of the two John Smiths. Janet does not need to type long ID numbers however, or even names to access student records. She may pick a student by pointing and clicking with the mouse. Along the bottom of the screen are many management options for a course roster. They include adding and deleting students from the roster, seeing the progress data for any individual, printing the roster, reading or writing electronic mail, and so on.

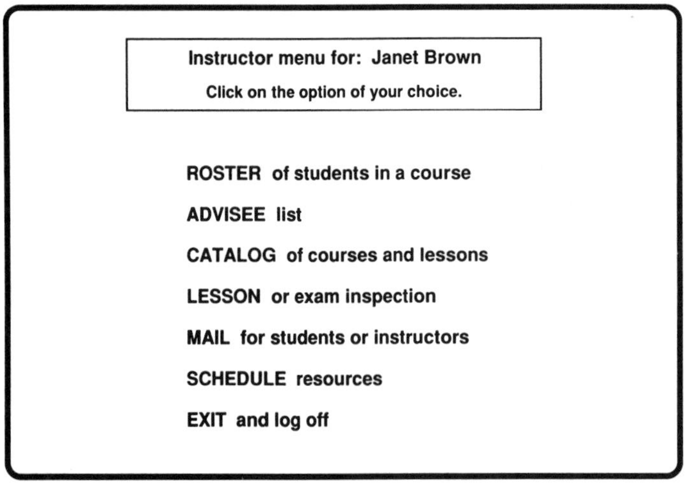

Instructor menu for: Janet Brown

Click on the option of your choice.

ROSTER of students in a course

ADVISEE list

CATALOG of courses and lessons

LESSON or exam inspection

MAIL for students or instructors

SCHEDULE resources

EXIT and log off

Figure 13-14 The main instructor options in the CMI system.

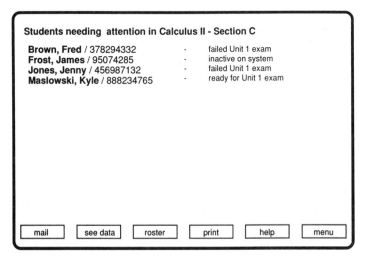

Roster for: Calculus II - Section C   Instructor: Janet Brown

Aronson, Susan / 987654321	**North, Harry** / 478294814
Brown, Fred / 378294332	**Ostowisk, Susan** / 194827482
Dillinger, Alice / 834765935	**Prentice, Alfred** / 938571647
Frost, James / 95074285	**Quinn, Colleen** / 817382946
Harlow, William / 013265478	**Rich, Debby** / 039482749
Jones, Jenny / 456987132	**Smith, John** / 183965827
Long, William / 123456789	**Smith, John** / 118827562
Maslowski, Kyle / 888234765	**Smith, Lester** / 020393874
Nelson, Terry / 828461008	**Vance, Karen** / 773472109

add	delete	see data	attention	print
mail	options	new section	help	menu

Figure 13-15 The calculus instructor's roster of students and activity options.

One of the very powerful options a good CMI system may provide is the *attention* option. In Figure 13–16 we see that Janet Brown has chosen this option. The computer scans all records and displays the names of those students who need attention soon. From this section four students are listed together with reasons they need attention. This feature allows the instructor to check who needs help quickly, which encourages doing so often. The instructor needs not look through each student's records, test scores, or file folders, nor wait for students to come asking for help.

In Figure 13–17 we see that Janet Brown has chosen to *see data* for William Long (choosing that option from Figure 13–15 or from 13–16 if William had been on the attention needed list). She can see a summary for all of William's on-line

Students needing attention in Calculus II - Section C

Brown, Fred / 378294332	-	failed Unit 1 exam
Frost, James / 95074285	-	inactive on system
Jones, Jenny / 456987132	-	failed Unit 1 exam
Maslowski, Kyle / 888234765	-	ready for Unit 1 exam

mail	see data	roster	print	help	menu

Figure 13-16 The list of calculus students needing immediate attention.

Data for: William Long - ID# 123456789
Last use of system: 9/18/89 at 1:15 p.m.

Courses and Lessons	Status	Score	Time
Using the NWU Instructional System	completed	95%	1:25
Word processing for college writing	completed	83%	2:10
Calculus II	ready for Unit 1 exam	90%	2:25
Engineering II	not started	-----	0:00
Electricity and Magnetism	completed 4-a	87%	4:53
Freshman Rhetoric	not started	-----	0:00
Intermediate German I	in 3-b	91%	3:35

assign	delete	reorder	password	rename
next person	prev person	save	abort	print
mail	see course	roster	help	menu

Figure 13-17   Detailed data about a student and the available instructor options.

assignments. Among the many available options, she can choose to see detailed data for her own course (Calculus II), including the map (Figure 13–13) that visually shows William's location within the course activities.

As seen in Figure 13–18, she can also choose to modify William Long's on-line assignment. In this display she is inspecting the catalog of Math Department courses and can add or drop William from them. She could also add or delete individual CBI lessons which are not associated with particular university courses.

In Figures 13–19 and 13–20 Janet Brown uses the system's electronic mail facilities. In Figure 13–19 she reads William Long's letter requesting permission for the next test. In Figure 13–20 she replies to him, indicating that permission has been granted.

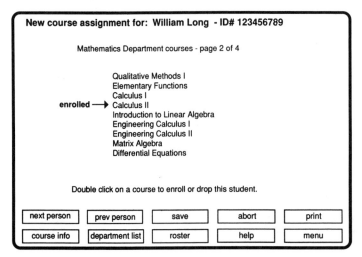

New course assignment for: William Long - ID# 123456789

Mathematics Department courses - page 2 of 4

Qualitative Methods I
Elementary Functions
Calculus I
enrolled ⟶ Calculus II
Introduction to Linear Algebra
Engineering Calculus I
Engineering Calculus II
Matrix Algebra
Differential Equations

Double click on a course to enroll or drop this student.

next person	prev person	save	abort	print
course info	department list	roster	help	menu

Figure 13-18   Modifying a student's CBI assignments.

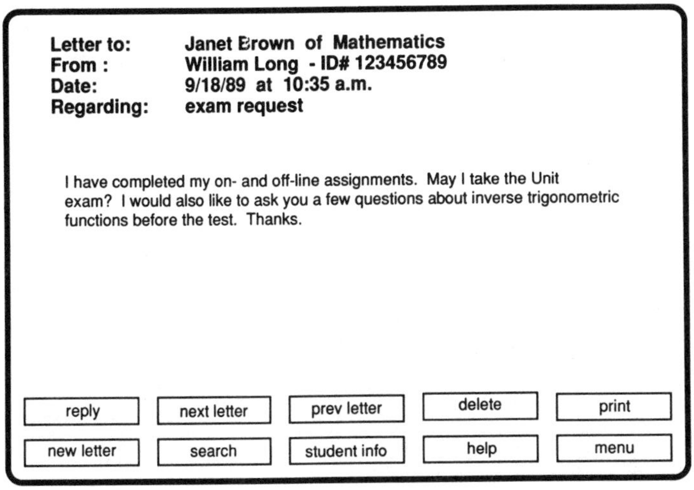

Letter to: **Janet Brown of Mathematics**
From :   **William Long - ID# 123456789**
Date: **9/18/89 at 10:35 a.m.**
Regarding: **exam request**

I have completed my on- and off-line assignments. May I take the Unit
exam? I would also like to ask you a few questions about inverse trigonometric
functions before the test. Thanks.

reply	next letter	prev letter	delete	print
new letter	search	student info	help	menu

Figure 13-19 The instructor reading a student's request for a test.

Finally, in Figure 13–21, another faculty member, Dennis Harrison, has signed on the system and chosen to see information about one of his advisees, William Long. The advisor sees a summary of current assignments very similar to that shown to students (Figure 13–11) and course instructors (Figure 13–17). The advisor cannot access details of courses unless he actually teaches them, but can access other information about the student such as grades and academic history. If Dennis Harrison were to note a problem in a course, such as Calculus II, he could send electronic mail to Janet Brown to discuss the problem. Although not shown, the faculty advisor may access a roster of all advisees (similar to the course roster in Figure 13–15) and a list of advisees needing attention (similar to Figure 13–16).

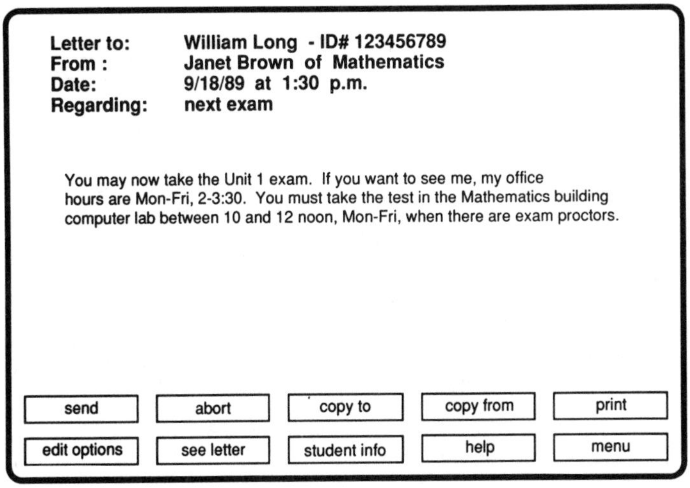

Letter to: **William Long - ID# 123456789**
From :   **Janet Brown of Mathematics**
Date: **9/18/89 at 1:30 p.m.**
Regarding: **next exam**

You may now take the Unit 1 exam. If you want to see me, my office
hours are Mon-Fri, 2-3:30. You must take the test in the Mathematics building
computer lab between 10 and 12 noon, Mon-Fri, when there are exam proctors.

send	abort	copy to	copy from	print
edit options	see letter	student info	help	menu

Figure 13-20 The instructor answering the student message.

```
┌──────────────────────────────────────────────────────────────┐
│  Advisor Report                    Advisor: Dennis Harrison    │
│  Student: William Long - ID# 123456789   Date:   9/19/89       │
│     Status:        Second semester Freshman                    │
│     GPA:           3.2 with 15 credit hours                    │
│     Declared major: none                                       │
│     Expected major: Engineering                                │
│                                                                │
│  Courses and Lessons        Status          Score     Time     │
│                                                                │
│    Using the NWU Instructional System  completed   95%   1:25  │
│    Word processing for college writing completed   83%   2:10  │
│    Calculus II            ready for Unit 1 exam    90%   2:25  │
│    Engineering II         not started             -----  0:00  │
│    Electricity and Magnetism  completed 4-a        87%   4:53  │
│    Freshman Rhetoric      not started             -----  0:00  │
│    Intermediate German I  in 3-b                   91%   3:35  │
│                                                                │
│  Off-line assignments                                          │
│    Calculus II: Chapter 8 in First Year Calculus               │
│    Freshman Rhetoric: Write and hand in essay on "American     │
│    Chauvinism" by 10/13/89                                     │
│                                                                │
│   [ mail ]  [ grades ]  [ roster ]  [ print ]  [ help ]  [ menu ] │
└──────────────────────────────────────────────────────────────┘
```

Figure 13-21 An advisor viewing information about a student advisee.

CONCLUSION

Computer-managed instruction was among the first uses of the computer in education but faded almost into obscurity due to the shift from mainframe computers to microcomputers. It now has the potential for a comeback due to advances in mass-storage technology and availability of networking. We believe instructors will benefit by using computers to assist in instructional management before using them for delivery of instruction. Even small CMI systems provide the basis for course improvement by reducing the instructor's time spent with management functions and freeing them for teaching and helping functions. A large-scale, integrated CMI system, such as that illustrated in this chapter, should be the long-term aim of any educational institution wishing to utilize computer technology fully to improve instruction. Such a system can integrate all teaching, learning, and administrative functions in a way that enables all members of the educational community to teach and learn more efficiently.

REFERENCES AND BIBLIOGRAPHY

ANDERSON, D.O., & GLOWINSKI, D.J. (1982). Effective use of a computer-managed instruction program. *Journal of Learning Disabilities, 15*(9), 555–556.

ANDERSON, T.H., ANDERSON, R.C., ALESSI, S.M., DALGAARD, B.R., PADEN, D.W., BIDDLE, W.B., SURBER, J.R., & SMOCK, H.R. (1975). A multifaceted computer based course management system. In O. Lecarme & R. Lewis (Eds.), *Proceedings of the Second World Conference on Computers in Education.* Amsterdam: North Holland Publishing Co.

ANDERSON, T.H., ANDERSON, R.C., DALGAARD, B.R., PADEN, D.W., BIDDLE, W.B., SURBER, J.R., & ALESSI, S.M. (1975). An experimental evaluation of a computer based study management system. *Educational Psychologist, 11*, 184–190.

ANDERSON, T.H., ANDERSON, R.C., DALGAARD, B.R., WIETECHA, E.J., BIDDLE, W.B., PADEN, D.W., SMOCK, H.R., ALESSI, S.M., SURBER, J.R., & KLEMT, L.L. (1974). A computer based study management system. *Educational Psychologist, 11*, 36–45.

BAKER, F.B. (1971). Computer-based instructional management systems: A first look. *Review of Educational Research, 41*(1), 51–70.

BAKER, F.B. (1978). *Computer-Managed Instruction: The*

ory and Practice. Englewood Cliffs, NJ: Educational Technology Publications.

BAKER, F.B. (1981). Computer-managed instruction: A context for computer-based instruction. In H.F. O'Neil, (Ed.), *Computer-Based Instruction: A State-of-the-Art Assessment*. New York: Academic Press.

BANGERT-DROWNS, R.L., KULIK, J.A., & KULIK, C-L.C. (1985). Effectiveness of computer-based education in secondary schools. *Journal of Computer-Based Instruction, 12*(3), 59–68.

BLOOM, B.S. (1976). *Human Characteristics and School Learning*. New York: McGraw-Hill.

BLUHM, H.P. (1987). Computer-managed instruction: A useful tool for educators? *Educational Technology, 27*(1), 7–13.

BORTON, W.M. (1988). The effects of computer-managed mastery learning on mathematics test scores in the elementary school. *Journal of Computer-Based Instruction, 15*(3), 95–98.

BROWN, N.P. (1982). CAMEO: Computer-assisted management of educational objectives. *Exceptional Children, 49*(2), 151–153.

BRUNO, J.E. (1987). Admissible probability measures in instructional management. *Journal of Computer-Based Instruction, 14*(1), 23–30.

FEDERICO, P-A. (1982). Individual differences in cognitive characteristics and computer-managed mastery learning. *Journal of Computer-Based Instruction, 9*(1), 10–18.

FEDERICO, P-A. (1983). Changes in the cognitive components of achievement as students proceed through computer-managed instruction. *Journal of Computer-Based Instruction, 9*(4), 156–168.

FLANAGAN, J.C. (1969). Program for learning in accordance with needs. *Psychology in the Schools, 6*(2), 133–136.

FLANAGAN, J.C. (1970). The role of the computer in PLAN. *Journal of Educational Data Processing, 7*(1), 7–17.

FLANAGAN, J.C., SHANNER, W.M., BRUDNER, H.J., & MARKER, R.W. (1975). An individualized instructional system: PLAN. In H. Talmadge, (Ed.), *Systems of Individualized Education*. Berkeley: McCutchan.

GOODSON, B. (1984). Software report: Are computer-managed instruction programs worth the trouble? *Electronic Learning, 4*(1), 8.

HANSEN, D.N., ROSS, S.M., BOWMAN, H.L., & THURMOND, P. (1975). *Navy Computer-Managed Instruction: Past, Present, and Future*. Memphis, TN: Memphis State University, Tennessee Bureau of Educational Research and Services. (ERIC Document Reproduction Service No. ED 114 051)

HOUGHTON MIFFLIN. (1986). *Houghton Mifflin Computer Management System*. [Computer Program]. Boston: Houghton Mifflin.

KELLER, F.S. (1968). "Good-bye, teacher . . . ". *Journal of Applied Behavior Analysis, 1*, 79–89.

LECHOWICZ, J.S., & WISE, F.H. (1976). Tagging course objectives for the computer. *Educational Technology, 16*(4), 40–41.

LEIBLUM, M.D. (1982). Computer-managed instruction: An explanation and overview. *AEDS Journal, 15*(3), 126–142.

LILLIE, D.K., HANNUM, W.H., & STUCK, G.B. (1989). *Computers and Effective Instruction: Using Computers and Software in the Classroom*. White Plains, NY: Longman.

LOCKARD, J., ABRAMS, P.D., & MANY, W.A. (1987). *Microcomputers for Educators*. Boston: Little, Brown and Company.

MAYO, G.D. (1974). Computer based instructional systems. *Journal of Educational Technology Systems, 2*(3), 191–200.

MIDDLETON, M.G., PAPETTI, C.J., & MICHELI, G.S. (1974). *Computer-Managed Instruction in Navy Training*. (TAEG Tech. Rep. No. 14). Orlando, FL: Training Analysis and Evaluation Group.

MILLIKEN PUBLISHING CO. (1980). *Milliken Math Sequences*. [Computer Program]. St. Louis: Milliken Publishing Co.

MITZEL, H.E. (Ed.). (1974). *An Examination of the Short-Range Potential of Computer-Managed Instruction*. (Conference proceedings for Grant No. NIE-C-74-0091). National Institute of Education.

ROBINSON, C.A., TOMBLIN, E.A., & HOUSTON, A. (1981). *Computer-Managed Instruction in Navy Technical Training: An Attitudinal Survey*. (Tech. Rep. No. NPRDC-TR-82-19). San Diego: Navy Personnel Research and Development Center. (ERIC Document Reproduction Service No. ED 212 290)

SWOPE, W.M., COREY, J.M., EVANS, R.M., & MORRIS, C.L. (1982). *Analysis of Factors Affecting the Performance of the Navy's Computer-Managed Instructional System*. (Tech. Rep. No. TAEG-TR-119). Orlando, FL: Naval Training Analysis and Evaluation Group. (ERIC Document Reproduction Service No. ED 223 240)

TELEM, M. (1982). CMI and the MIS—An integration needed. *AEDS Journal, 16*(1), 48–55.

TROLLIP, S.R., & BROWN, G.B. (1989). *Examiner, V 2.1*. [Computer Program]. Mendota Heights, MN: Media Computer Enterprises.

VAN MATRE, N. (1980). *Computer-Managed Instruction in the Navy: I. Research Background and Status*. (Tech. Rep. No. NPRDC-SR-80-33). San Diego: Navy Personnel Research and Development Center. (ERIC Document Reproduction Service No. ED 196 411)

WAGER, W. (1985). Computer-managed instruction—How teachers and principals can improve learning. *NASSP Bulletin, 69*(478), 22–27.

14

INTERACTIVE VIDEO

WHAT IS INTERACTIVE VIDEO?

Interactive video in the context of computer-based instruction occurs when a student interacts with a computer that uses video as one of its output devices. Our position is that interactive video is an extension of computer-based instruction, giving the designer capabilities not available if the computer were used by itself. The following example illustrates one use of interactive video in instruction.

A medical student in pediatrics must learn to diagnose rare childhood diseases. But because they are rare, the student does not have much opportunity to encounter them. The medical student sits at a computer system with both a computer display and a television connected to a videodisc[1] player, a device which presents prerecorded video, as does a VCR. The student sees "live" motion video presentations of health professionals examining babies. Text and audio explain what is being done in each examination. The student must periodically answer questions that require careful observation of the examination and the children. After the instruction the student goes through a simulated case study. The computer asks the student how to proceed with the examination. The student requests a test of the infant's reflexes. A doctor or nurse on-screen performs the test and the student observes the reflex responses of the child. The student can then make a diagnosis or continue with the examination. The student continues, having the baby crawl, checking the medical history, and so on. Eventually, the student makes a clinical diagnosis that the child is either normal or exhibits some disfunction. The computer then gives feedback about the examination and the diagnosis.

The scenario above, based upon the instructional program *Assessment of Neuromotor Dysfunction in Infants* (Blackman, Lough, & Huntley, 1984; Blackman, Albanese, Huntley, & Lough, 1985), illustrates the use of interactive video, which combines the technologies of video (television) and computers to provide the advantages of both.

The primary advantages of video are lifelike images and sound. However,

---

[1]By convention, references to an optical disc are spelled with the letter *c*, while references to a magnetic disk are spelled with the letter *k*.

video is usually linear and not under the user's control. A standard video program progresses from start to finish—we cannot do much to change the pace or order of events.

The advantages of computer technology have been discussed extensively: interactivity, data storage and processing, and so on. However, the visual and auditory quality of most computers is still below that of ordinary video.

It is the position of some authors (for example, Iuppa, 1984) that interactive video is primarily video instruction with the computer as a control device. Our position is quite different. We believe that interactive video is computer-based instruction augmented by a video peripheral for high quality visual and aural presentations. The most common video peripheral used today is the analog videodisc player, although more powerful *digital* video devices such as compact disc interactive (CDI) and digital video interactive (DVI) are becoming available.

BACKGROUND

Until very recently, the visual and auditory quality of computer-based instruction was far below most other media, including books, live instruction, film, and video. CBI developers longed for higher quality output. The connection to the computer of video devices, first videotape and then videodiscs, was a great leap that has made CBI a medium suitable for content that is very visual or aural in nature.

The first interactive video applications, in the 1970's, used videotape players. The computer and videotape player could provide "live" video instruction such as a narrator demonstrating and explaining how to operate some equipment, with questions that the student would answer or simulations to practice the procedure. High quality motion video and audio were combined with student interaction.

Videotape machines, however, are hard to control by a computer. They are very slow at searching and displaying particular video information, are not good at displaying still images such as photographic slides, and are prone to tape wear and breakdown. In the 1980's the *videodisc* player came into fairly widespread use.

A videodisc stores the same information as a videotape but in a format more like a phonograph record. Looking like a smooth silver record, the videodisc contains prerecorded information recorded in a spiral beginning at the center and ending at the outer edge. It usually contains thirty minutes of video and stereo sound. The diagram in Figure 14-1 illustrates a videodisc and where the information is stored on it. A magnified view (Figure 14-2) shows how information is recorded along the spiral path. Microscopic indentations in the metal surface, varying in length, store video and other information in the same way bumps on a phonograph record store sound. The holes are detected by a laser beam reflected off a thin metal surface as the disc spins. The metal surface is protected by layers of transparent plastic on both sides.

The videodisc and videodisc player have several advantages over videotape and videotape recorders:

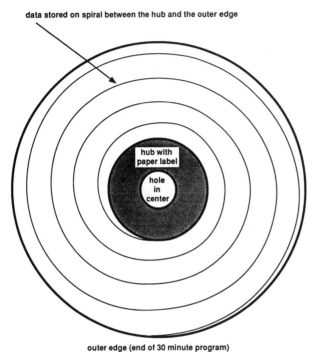

data stored on spiral between the hub and the outer edge

hub with paper label

hole in center

outer edge (end of 30 minute program)

Figure 14-1 Diagram of a videodisc showing one side. Videodiscs may have information recorded on one side or on two sides, like phonograph records. The scale of the spiral is greatly exaggerated. The spiral on a real videodisc circles the center 54,000 times.

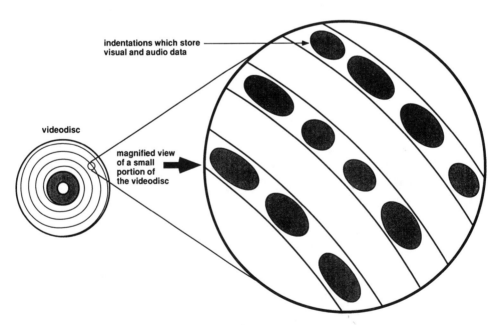

indentations which store visual and audio data

videodisc

magnified view of a small portion of the videodisc

Figure 14-2 Magnified view of a small section of the videodisc. Tiny indentations, called pits, which vary in length, store video, sound, and other information.

Discs are more durable, lasting years without wear or breakage.

Discs store and display many still images with high quality.

Produced in large quantities, discs are cheaper than videotapes.

Images are quickly retrieved, usually in about two seconds.

Videodisc players are easily controlled by computer.

Currently they have some disadvantages as well, although these are gradually being eliminated:

Videodisc players cannot record; they only play videodiscs.

Interactive videodiscs are limited to thirty minutes (sixty minutes with a special and more expensive player), whereas videotapes contain up to six hours of video.

Today, the most common form of interactive video consists of a microcomputer (usually an IBM-PC or compatible) connected to a videodisc player utilizing 12-inch analog videodiscs. Currently under development are various kinds of *digital* compact videodiscs, which we will describe later.

The 12-inch analog videodisc, stores video, stereo sound, and auxiliary control information. It is played on a videodisc player which has the components diagrammed in Figure 14–3. The *laser pickup* is a laser beam that reads information off the videodisc as it spins, analogous to a diamond needle reading music from a phonograph record. However, the laser is just a beam of light, so there is virtually no wear of the videodisc. The *inputs* allow for direct control by an operator (via buttons on the player or a remote control button device) or from an external computer. The *outputs* send information to a connected video monitor and to an external computer.

The microprocessor inside the videodisc player controls everything, receiving and interpreting inputs, controlling the videodisc and laser pickup, and sending data to the appropriate outputs. The internal microprocessor has an associated *memory* for storage of information. Although videodisc players vary in many ways, almost all those used for interactive applications have these parts.

LEVELS OF INTERACTIVE VIDEODISCS

There is a tendency to equate *videodisc* with *interactive video*. A videodisc is only a medium for storage of video information, just like a floppy disk is a medium for storing computer data. The information on a videodisc is not inherently interactive—that depends on how it is used. As a result, the following *levels* of interactivity have become widely accepted to distinguish different amounts or kinds of interactivity.

Level-0

Many videodiscs (and videotapes) contain movies or educational presentations that are watched from start to finish. The user does not interact in any way.

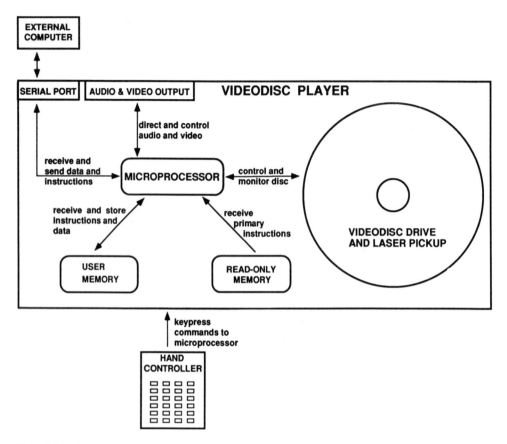

Figure 14-3   Components of a videodisc player.

These are referred to as Level-0 interactive video programs. The zero signifies that they are not interactive at all.

Level-1

In this level the user controls a videodisc manually with a hand controller. Searching, stopping, slow motion, fast motion, and other user controls are all possible. The user must have information, usually in a printed catalog, of what information is located where on the disc. A popular videodisc typically used as a Level-1 program is *The First National Kidisc* (Green, 1981). This thirty-minute videodisc contains a variety of educational activities for children: tying rope knots, making paper airplanes, dancing, jokes and riddles, sign language, identifying flags, music, and the like. The various activities make use of the videodisc's capabilities for fast and slow motion, stereo sound, and so on. To use any activity, the operator must type in a number that indicates where that activity begins. On some videodisc players you can type in a chapter number. The box the videodisc is stored in contains a table of contents with chapter numbers. On other videodisc players you must use the scan (fast forward) feature or type in a frame number. A thirty-minute videodisc consists of 54,000 frames, or still images, which look like regular motion video when played at 30 frames per second.

Level-2

In this level the microprocessor inside the videodisc player is utilized, automatically loading and running a program which is stored on the videodisc as part of the audio track. The user still interacts via the hand controller, but because of the internal computer control program the user does not have to know the location of information. The videodisc can display menu options from which the student can choose, or questions for the user to answer, just like in CBI programs. Level-2 programs are dependent on the type of videodisc player used. For example, *Let Your Fingers Do the Talking: Deaf Awareness* (Alberta Vocational Centre, 1987), is a Level-2 videodisc program designed for Sony videodisc players, while *Producing Interactive Videodiscs* (Minnesota Mining & Manufacturing, 1982) is designed for Pioneer videodisc players.

Level-3

In this level an external computer is connected via an input/output port on the videodisc player. The user can interact via the computer keyboard, with a mouse or touch panel, or with any other input devices attached to the computer. Furthermore, the system can display computer text and graphics as well as the full-motion video. The program can be stored on any computer storage medium, such as floppy disks or a network, and can be very large and sophisticated. *Assessment of Neuromotor Dysfunction in Infants* (Blackman, Lough, & Huntley, 1984) is a Level-3 videodisc program.

Level-3 programs are generally considered the most flexible and powerful form of interactive video, but also the most expensive and difficult to produce. Recently, designers have begun to talk about *Level-4* and *Level-5* programs, although usually such labels are just an attempt to claim they are better than competitive products.

We wish to stress that the interactivity level should usually be applied to a particular program or application. *The First National Kidisc* is usually used as a Level-1 program, but anyone can design a Level-3 application using it in conjunction with an attached computer. The videodisc may be designed with a particular level of interactivity in mind, but it can generally be used in a program with a higher or lower level of interactivity.

We have already stated our perspective, that instructional interactive video means computer-based instruction with video as an associated output. With that in mind, we will focus the rest of our attention on Level-3 applications, which combine all the capabilities of CBI with those of video.

VISUAL PRESENTATION MODES OF INTERACTIVE VIDEO

In Level-3 interactive video there are two sources of visual output, namely computer and video, and three typical ways of combining them, what we call the visual presentation modes: two screen, one screen switched, and one screen overlaid.

Two Screen

In this mode the computer is connected to one display and the videodisc player is connected to another. They can display visual information simultaneously. The advantage of this mode is increased information capacity. For example, in an art appreciation lesson, a full screen of computer text can describe a painting shown on the video display. There are some important instructional design issues regarding two-screen presentations, such as whether the student is attending to the appropriate display at any time, and whether the student may be overwhelmed by the amount of information.

One Screen Switched

In this mode the computer and video share a single display and just one or the other may display information at a particular time. Its advantage is having the lowest cost of the three modes. However, its information capacity is lowest and it can be disrupting to the viewer to be switched back and forth between computer and video images.

One Screen Overlaid

In this mode the computer and video share a single display and both may display information simultaneously. The computer may display text on top of moving video images, or computer-generated arrows or boxes may highlight important video information. The information capacity of overlaid programs is higher than one screen switched but lower than two screens. The major advantage of overlaid programs is stimulus control and cueing. Computer generated text, boxes, or arrows can draw attention to or describe important aspects of the video image. But overlaying is expensive because a special device is needed to combine the video information, which is analog, with the computer information, which is digital. This device is usually an interface card which plugs into a slot of the computer and connects by cables to the videodisc player and video monitor.

Other presentation modes are possible, though infrequently used. It is possible to attach two displays where one has overlaying and one is just a computer display. It is also possible to have multiple overlaid displays, such as for "multi-image" presentations.

Although the overlaid mode is often considered to be the best, we believe each has its own advantages and that research is needed to determine under what circumstances each is best. In cost, overlaying is most expensive and one-screen switching usually the cheapest. In information capacity, two-screen mode is usually the greatest and one-screen switched mode the lowest. Research is needed to resolve issues of attention, stimulus control, and suitability of the different modes for particular instructional strategies, such as tutorial or simulation. Lacking research evidence, the instructional designer must make intelligent choices and assess their effectiveness with pilot testing before finalization of a program.

ADVANTAGES OF INTERACTIVE VIDEO AND VIDEODISCS

The primary advantage of interactive video is the ability to present information that the computer cannot. In medical education, interactive video permits the student to see a surgeon operating, a pediatrician examining a child, or a nurse helping deliver a baby. In law education, interactive video permits the student to observe a courtroom in action and play the role of the defense attorney. In Chapter 4 (Simulations), we pointed out that the most difficult thing to simulate is human behavior. Interactive video helps make such simulations more realistic.

Although interactive video is also possible with videotape material, videodiscs provide several advantages for interactive video programs:

Fast Random Access

The primary weakness of a videotape player for interaction is that it can take a long time to get to the part of a videotape that you wish to play. Even on a short videotape it can take a minute or more to locate a particular video or audio segment. In a tutorial or drill this is annoying. In a simulation or instructional game it is entirely impractical. But with a videodisc you can jump to any segment in a few seconds or less. This makes the videodisc good for fast and constant interaction.

One well-known videodisc is a driving tour of the city of Aspen, Colorado (see Massachusetts Institute of Technology, 1983). The producers drove down every street in the city with a video camera on top of their car, recording everything they saw. Using the videodisc, you can see what they saw. At any street corner, you can choose to continue straight, turn left or right. However, the video information for a cross street is often recorded on a different part of the disc. *1st Avenue* may be recorded near the beginning of the disc (the first few minutes) while *Elm Street* might be near the end. If you choose to turn onto *Elm Street,* the videodisc must search for that program segment. On a videotape player, that search might take a minute, which would completely destroy the illusion of real driving. On a videodisc player the search, and thus the *turn,* might take a second—well within the limit of turning onto a new street, so the illusion of driving is retained.

Fast access time makes instruction more realistic, enjoyable, and more efficient.

Freeze and Still Frames

When you look at motion video you see people walking and talking. But the motion you see is an illusion, created by a fast succession of many still pictures. In the United States, motion video is produced by 30 still "frames" every second. A thirty-minute videodisc program is actually a collection of 54,000 still video frames.

The same is true for a videotape. On most videotape players you can pause and see a single still image. However, when you pause a videotape, the still image *degrades* significantly. If you pause for very long on a single videotape frame, the tape wears down and the still image is eventually destroyed. Furthermore, it is difficult on videotape players to find and display the exact frame you want.

With a videodisc, all three of these problems are eliminated. The video image does not degrade when you pause. The video image never wears out, even if you look at if for a year. And knowing an image's frame number (1 through 54,000) you can quickly and accurately access it whenever you like.

As a result of these improvements over videotape, the videodisc is excellent for both *freezing* and for *still frame* display. Freezing is when the student pauses a motion image. Perhaps a gymnastics student is watching a videodisc teaching particular gymnastics moves and sees a particularly complicated technique. The student can press a "stop" button and the motion freezes, showing the particular positions of the hands and feet. The student can also press a "step" button to move ahead to the next image in the sequence, showing what the gymnast is doing just one thirtieth of a second later. This cannot be done well with videotape.

In contrast to freezing, a still frame is a single stationary picture that is *not* part of a motion sequence. It may be a photograph of a person, a page of text, or a graphic diagram such as in a book. If a videodisc were filled with such still images, rather than with motion video, it could contain 54,000 of them. Thus, a single side of one videodisc can contain all the pictures stored in 675 photographic slide trays. A videodisc may make use of only a few still images, such as diagrams accompanying a narration or text menus permitting user choice. Or a videodisc may make extensive use of still images, such as the well-known videodiscs that contain photographic collections of the art of Vincent Van Gogh (North American Philips Corporation, 1982) or the Smithsonian Institution's archives of airplane photographs (Smithsonian Institution, 1983).

The large visual capacity of a videodisc for still images can also be a disadvantage. Imagine trying to find the photograph you want out of 54,000 if you don't know where it is. Looking at each photo for just one second, it could take you up to fifteen hours to find what you want! A printed catalog would help, but even if you used just one line to describe each image the catalog would be about a thousand pages long. Finding what you want could still take a while. This potential problem is solved by the third advantage of the videodisc player, its capacity for computer control.

Computer Control

Videodisc players come in many varieties. Some are meant for home use, called *consumer* players. These are inexpensive and intended primarily for watching movies. Unfortunately, they do not usually have a connection for an external computer. *Industrial* videodisc players, meant for business, industry, and schools, almost all have industry standard connections for computers. Most new videodisc players have a standard *serial* connection, the same type of connection used for modems and sometimes for printers. Almost all computers have serial ports on them, so can easily be connected to and control newer model industrial videodisc players.

The external computer controls the videodisc player by communicating with its small internal microprocessor. That microprocessor is programmed to understand a variety of commands from external sources, commands requesting the player to start, stop, search, play, speed up or slow down, and so on.

Let us return to our example of a videodisc containing 54,000 art photographs. Searching through these by browsing with a hand controller can take hours. But information about the location and nature of every photograph can be stored in a computer database. You could then ask to see "all pictures by Picasso" or "all twentieth-century oils from Italy" or "Van Gogh's pictures of sunflowers" and the computer could control the videodisc player to retrieve and show you those pictures. Thus, while computers alone are excellent for the storage and retrieval of textual and numeric information, combined with a videodisc player, they are also excellent for the storage and retrieval of visual information.

Capacity

The previous discussion about still frames and computer control gave some indication of the capacity of the videodisc. Yet we have already pointed out that a videotape can hold up to twelve times as much video as a videodisc. Although that would appear to be greater capacity, it must be remembered that the videotape is primarily useful for regular motion video; it cannot be used effectively for individual still frames. The videodisc has great capacity for individually accessible still frames.

Additionally, the videodisc can be used to store digitized sound information (although in analog form) and computer programs or data. Again, a videotape cannot effectively store such information because it must be accurately located and accessible. A videodisc cannot only store many voice segments and computer data files, but can locate and retrieve any one of them in a few seconds, just like a still frame.

Quality

The great capacity of the videodisc for still frames, sound segments, and computer data, and its value for rapidly accessible motion segments as well, is only worthwhile if the quality of that information is high. The quality of motion video on a videodisc is as good as the best television studio videotape machines and better than most home video cassette recorders. The quality of still images, as previously stated, is far better than most videotape machines. Furthermore, computer data, programs, and digitized voice are stored in a form on videodisc that preserves them almost perfectly.

Durability

The aforementioned quality of images and other videodisc data would not be very important if the quality did not last. Videotape is well known to lose its quality each time it is used. When you play a videotape, the tape is actually dragged across a spinning metal "head" which reads the magnetic information stored on the tape. The tape wears away a little bit each time it is used. The recorded surface of a videodisc, in contrast, has nothing touch it. The recorded surface is a thin metal film with tiny indentations on it. The videodisc player aims a laser beam at the surface which reflects off it and back into a sensing device in the videodisc player. The laser beam causes absolutely no wear on the videodisc. Thus, videodisc images look the same after a thousand uses as after one use. Additionally, the thin metal film is sandwiched between two hard transparent plastic sheets for protection. It is impervious to dust and general handling. Videodisc manufacturers claim that a disc should last a hundred years without degradation of the information stored on it. Of course, it will be about eighty years before we know if they are right.

CONSTRAINTS OF INTERACTIVE VIDEO

Cost

The field of interactive video is not without difficulties. Some of these problems are likely to be alleviated in the future as computer and video technology both improve and eventually merge. At this time, the technologies are rather different, computers being digital and most video being analog. That makes exchanging and combining computer and video information difficult. But new forms of "digital" video are under development which promise to bring the two together.

Above all, the primary impediment to the use of interactive video is cost. Producing a videodisc is expensive. Producing any kind of quality video is expensive, but then putting your video on a disc rather than a tape is even more expensive. Like records, current videodiscs are stamped out in a large manufacturing plant. The cost of producing a single standard videodisc is between $2,000 and $3,000. Subsequent copies are inexpensive ($10 to $20 each), so videodiscs possess economy of scale. If you plan to make and distribute thousands of them, they are more economical than videotapes. If you are distributing a few dozen, they are much more expensive. In any case, design and production of videodiscs is considerably more expensive than design and production of computer programs.

Lastly, distribution of interactive video depends upon educators who not only have the necessary computer equipment, but also the equally expensive videodisc players and interfaces. The constraint of equipment required is compounded by the problem of equipment compatibility.

Compatibility

Just as in the world of computers, where there are Apple II's, Macintoshes, IBM's, Amigas, and various others, there are many types of videodiscs, videodisc players, and computer-videodisc combinations.

Videodiscs themselves vary in size, capacity, and format of the stored information. While most common videodiscs are 12 inches, 8-inch and 5-inch videodiscs also exist. Some players can play all three, some only one or two. Among the more common 12-inch videodiscs, there are two formats which affect video capacity and interactivity, constant angular velocity (CAV) and constant linear velocity (CLV).

CAV videodiscs are those which always turn at the same number of rotations per second (thirty) and store thirty minutes of video. The information format on a CAV videodisc is shown in Figure 14–4. The scale of the information is greatly distorted, since a real videodisc has 54,000 tracks and the diagram shows only a few. CAV discs are limited in capacity because by allocating an entire turn to each track, most of the tracks spread the information out more than necessary and thus waste space. But CAV discs can search for a frame very fast because each video frame (one thirtieth of a second of video) is a single concentric circle on the videodisc. Locating the beginning and end of any frame is easy. Additionally, the CAV format makes freezing or showing a still frame easy because if the laser beam just stays in one place, the same frame will be picked up for each rotation. Fast search, freezing, and still frames allow for easily programmed interactivity.

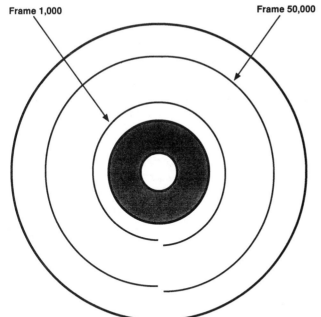

Frame 1,000

Frame 50,000

Figure 14-4 How information is stored on a CAV videodisc. Each frame is one complete rotation of the disc. Locating a frame and showing it as a still is easy.

CLV videodiscs are those which turn at a varying number of rotations per second in order to store up to sixty minutes of video. The information format on a CLV videodisc is shown in Figure 14–5. The scale of the information is again greatly distorted. CLV discs may store sixty minutes of video, twice the capacity of a CAV disc. The greater capacity is achieved through more efficient use of space on the recording surface. Near the center of the disc, each frame occupies a single

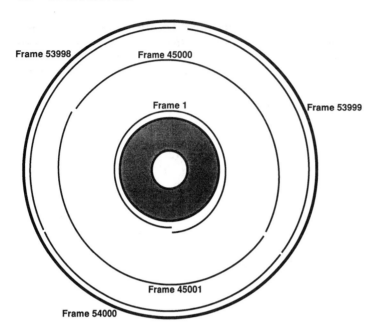

Frame 53998

Frame 45000

Frame 1

Frame 53999

Frame 45001

Frame 54000

Figure 14-5 How information is stored on a CLV videodisc. Each frame occupies the same length segment and except near the center, a frame is always less than one complete rotation. Locating a frame and showing it as a still are difficult.

rotation but towards the outer edge, each turn can fit progressively more frames. This space efficiency comes at the expense of interactivity, for one loses the capability of quick searches and sometimes of freezes or still frames. Searches are slow because frames can begin and end anywhere. Freezing or displaying a single still frame is difficult because with each turn of the disc, several frames are picked up by the laser. On most videodisc players, if you pause with a CLV disc, the image goes black. Some very new videodisc players can freeze or show a still frame by storing the information from one frame in a video memory and refreshing the video display thirty times per second from that memory rather than from the disc itself.

CLV discs are best for movies and other linear video programs. Even on the newest players which permit freezing on CLV discs, searching for a frame is much slower than on a CAV disc.

The greatest compatibility problem occurs when you connect a computer to a videodisc player and wish to combine computer and video information on an overlaid display. Two difficulties arise. Different computers require different types of software, and different computers produce displays in different ways. As a result, each model computer (for example, IBM versus Macintosh) requires a different interface to combine computer and video information. Different computers also require different programs and languages to control the videodisc player and deliver an interactive video program. The developer of an interactive video program may choose from any of a number of computer models, any of a number of types of software, any of a number of videodisc players, any of a number of interfaces for combining computer and video information, and any of a number of monitors for displaying video and computer visuals. Given all the choices, there are many possible combinations. A program written for one combination of equipment is unlikely to work on another, even if only one element, such as the interface, is different. Because of this equipment variety, it is impossible for any school or business to have all the combinations necessary to run even a small number of commercially available interactive video programs.

At this time, the most popular interactive video configuration is the IBM *InfoWindow* system, which utilizes IBM or compatible computers, Pioneer videodisc players, the *InfoWindow* display and interface, and a variety of development software. Because it is becoming popular, more developers are producing programs that use it, and it may become the standard configuration for IBM-compatible microcomputers. No such standard exists for other model computers, such as for the Macintosh.

The problem of hardware and software compatibility is by far the greatest impediment to the advancement of this new field. Potential users who are already wary of the investment in expensive video equipment cannot rely on the equipment they do purchase being able to run future programs of interest to them.

TYPES OF INSTRUCTIONAL INTERACTIVE VIDEO PROGRAMS

Interactive video programs may use any of the instructional methodologies we have already discussed, plus other methodologies not very common among computer-based instruction. We will discuss, with examples: tutorial, drill, simulation, educational game, instructional databases, help systems, and generic videodiscs.

Tutorial Programs

An example of a pure tutorial program is a Level-3 program called *Introduction to Computer Literacy* (J.A.M., 1984). It comprises four videodisc sides (a total of two hours of video information), several associated computer diskettes, and manuals. The program runs under either two-display mode *or* the one switched display mode. The majority of presentation is video, with a narrator teaching and demonstrating the various concepts of computers (hardware, software, telecommunications, and new technologies such as robotics). Directions and menus for user control are video still frames. Still frames are also used for a lot of the content, some being text frames defining concepts, and some being pictures with text labels or descriptions. The computer periodically asks multiple-choice questions for the student to answer, and provides an index and glossary of terms. The program is generally under the student's control. Using the menus and index the student can study sections in any order, can freeze motion at any point, back up and review a section, and exit. When a question is answered incorrectly, the student has the option, with a single keypress, of repeating the video segment that covers the information tested by that question. Data are stored about student performance, and instructor options allow inspection of student progress.

If a student watches and reads everything and answers all questions, the program requires about sixteen hours, although only two hours of actual video is recorded. This is in part because a text still frame is only one thirtieth of a second of video, but can take several minutes to read and understand. It is also because there is substantial text presented by the computer in the form of questions and the glossary, which a student may consult as frequently as desired.

While *Introduction to Computer Literacy* is a standard tutorial program, most interactive video programs combine some tutorial with other methodologies, such as simulation. Although *The Puzzle of the Tacoma Narrows Bridge Collapse* (Fuller, Zollman, & Campbell, 1982) is a program teaching the physics of wave motion, it begins with the filmed presentation of a famous bridge collapse. This dramatic and startling presentation is intended to motivate the student by gaining attention, as in the Keller & Suzuki (1988) ARCS model, and raising curiosity, as in the Malone (1981) model. This is followed by a simulation in which the student experiments with the effect of wind on a model bridge. The student can choose different wind speeds and wind speed fluctuation rates and can investigate their effect on wave motion (bending) of the bridge. Following the simulation, the program uses the tutorial methodology to teach the mathematics involved in wave motion and to analyze in more detail how wave motion can actually cause a large bridge to collapse.

Drill Programs

Drills are not as common among interactive video programs as they are among standard CBI programs. However, there are cases were students must learn visual information, in contrast to verbal information. *Let Your Fingers Do the Talking: Deaf Awareness* (Alberta Vocational Centre, 1987), teaches English sign language. Sign language is visual in nature and learning the skill is much more effective if one watches a person going through the motions, rather than looking at pictures. It is also a skill which requires many hours of practice. The videodisc permits the student to practice as much as necessary, receiving feedback and guidance. The emphasis is on watching and understanding sign language, since the videodisc cannot observe and give feedback on the student's own sign language performance.

Simulation Programs

Interactive video simulations are particularly popular in medical training. *Assessment of Neuromotor Dysfunction in Infants* (Blackman, Lough, & Huntley, 1984), discussed in the opening of this chapter, is an example. In *Cardiopulmonary Resuscitation* (Hon, 1982a,b) the computer is connected not only to a videodisc player but also to a mannequin with internal sensing devices. The video demonstrates proper CPR technique. The student then performs the technique on the mannequin. The computer uses the sensing devices to assess how well the student has performed and provides feedback via videodisc presentation. Videodisc simulations are also used in science education, such as *Chemical Reactions* (Smith & Jones, 1988). This simulation allows the student to perform chemistry experiments by manipulating chemicals, flasks, and other apparatus on the video display. The program uses a touch screen so the student need only touch a flask to pick it up and pour its contents.

Educational Game Programs

Educational games are surprisingly few in number among Level-3 videodisc programs. This may be because interactive videodisc is at this time used primarily for adult instruction and designers think of instructional games as being for children. One example is *The Name Game* (MindBank, 1987). The instructional objective of this program is to improve the cognitive skills needed to be a good salesperson, such as listening, concentration, motivation, and memory. The objectives are taught in the context of a cocktail party. For example, you meet and talk to various people and must remember the names of those you meet despite the distractions around you. The program provides instruction on the skills as well as practice during the party.

Database Programs

The great visual capacity and quality of its images make a videodisc ideal for storing, cataloging, and retrieving large amounts of visual information. Database programs permit the student to learn by exploring or doing research. *University of Iowa Visual Databases* (Huntley, 1985) include over 40,000 still images of art, including paintings, sculpture, and architecture. The computer permits the student to search and inspect art of different types, of different periods, by different artists, or using different materials. This large collection of art slides was previously only available to researchers in the university museum's art-history archives. Now it is available to any student in the university library. Instructors can give students specific art criticism or analysis assignments which may be accomplished as well with the videodisc program as with the slides. Students can use the visual database programs in conjunction with standard textbooks and reference works. Such databases have application wherever large quantities of visual information are used: art, travel, architecture, zoology, anatomy, space science, and many more.

Help System Programs

Iuppa and Anderson (1988) have suggested how interactive video might provide an excellent means of help and instruction on the operation of computer programs as the user begins working with them. An accountant using a new business forecasting program, for example, must spend much time with manuals, experimenting with the program, and asking other people for help when it is not clear what to do. With a videodisc player attached to a separate video display, the computer can run the forecasting program on its display, while the video display can give textual or narrated help as to what the program does and how to operate it. If the accountant presses a "help" button at any time, the computer can detect where in the program the user is and present context-sensitive help and directions in video format. The interactive video component would only be necessary when the accountant first learns the program, but could be available at any time. When a person has learned enough to no longer need it, the video component could be moved to the computer of another person learning the software.

Generic Videodiscs

A number of developers have produced videodiscs containing a large amount of instructional video but *without* any particular lessons or computer programs in mind. For example, the *Bio Sci Video Disc* (Clark, 1983) contains a wide variety of video information of use to biology teachers. It contains thousands of photographs of animals, plants, ecology, microorganisms, and human anatomy. The disc contains action video segments with time-lapse photography of cells growing and dividing, and animations of protein synthesis and DNA replication. It provides the biology teacher, on one disc, the equivalent of a hundred slide trays, dozens of film strips, and several short motion picture films on various topics in biology. The developers did not provide lessons using specific methodologies, although third-party developers, and teachers, have developed drills on identifying birds, tutorials on ecology, and other lessons using the wealth of video material on the disc. Other discs, free of specific lesson methodology but containing valuable video material usable in many ways by teachers, have been created in the sciences, art, music, language, and history.

FACTORS IN THE DESIGN OF INTERACTIVE VIDEO PROGRAMS

Many of the decisions made in the design and development of an interactive video lesson are the same as those for the standard methodologies discussed in Part 1. Here we discuss factors unique to interactive video or that take on new significance in the interactive video domain.

Level of Interactivity

We have discussed the three levels of interactivity in programs (four, if you include Level-0). Although there are educational uses of Level-1 and 2 videodisc programs, our interest here is computer-based instruction, which implies Level-3 or higher programs. The instructional methodologies we have discussed require the processing and interactive power of the computer as well as the visual realism of video. The lower levels of interactivity may be chosen when low cost and portability are essential and very simple methodologies are suitable.

Mode of Display

The three common display modes are one overlaid screen, one switching screen, and two screens. Switching is usually the cheapest, but provides the least powerful control of visual stimuli and the least information capacity. It may have the disadvantage of disorienting the user when switching occurs. It may be the best choice for a program where the computer is used very little or not at all for display, but rather for user control, branching, storage, and judging.

Two screen programs are sometimes cheapest (depending primarily on the cost of the monitors needed) and provide the greatest information capacity. They do not provide the stimulus control of overlaying. This configuration may have the disadvantage of confusing users about what to look at first when there is information on both displays. It is preferred for certain kinds of applications, such as visual databases, where descriptions or associated textual material must appear simultaneously with the visual information, yet where you do not wish to detract from the visual stimuli by covering it up.

Overlaying is generally the most expensive, provides best control of stimuli, and has moderate information capacity. It is the most difficult to design and develop for, but is most beneficial where there is substantial visual material from both the computer and video, and the computer visuals are used to point out, describe, or elaborate upon aspects of the video.

Input Devices

Level-2 programs, not having an attached computer, are limited to the videodisc player's own remote control keypad for user input. The remote control keypad contains numbers and various control functions (play, stop, search, etc.) but *not* the full alphabet. It is generally used only for player control and user choice at menus or multiple-choice questions.

With a videodisc player attached to a computer, the keyboard opens up the possibility of much more varied and appropriate interactions. The keyboard is the most common input device for Level-3 interactive video, but there are several problems. One is that many people cannot type and do not understand the location and meaning of various function keys. For the first-time (or one-time) user of an interactive video program, such as at an information kiosk, lack of familiarity with the keyboard may prevent the user from using the program properly. Second, the keyboard is not ideal for some kinds of interactions, such as selecting points or drawing on the screen. Third, in public settings like malls and airports, keysets may be broken or stolen and, at best, are hard to mount for easy use.

Some of the above problems are solved with the touch panel and the mouse. The touch panel is a device covering the display, which senses the user touching a part of the display. Touch panels work by various methods, by electrically sensing pressure, by the finger interrupting beams of infrared light, or by the finger interrupting sound waves. The touch panel is excellent for selecting options on the screen by pointing, such as choosing from menus, answering multiple-choice questions, or touching user control options like "menu," "repeat," or "end." The touch panel is the input device of choice in stores, malls, and airports where interaction is simple (choosing), because it is very natural (pointing) and requires no training. It requires no horizontal surface as does a keyboard or mouse. The touch panel's disadvantage is that it is only good for choosing. It is sometimes used for drawing, but its resolution (and in particular the resolution of the human finger) is not precise enough for drawing details. Touch panels also have a tendency to get out of alignment, causing user input errors, and to become dirty with fingerprints. Lastly, the use of a touch panel is very tiring with repeated use.

The mouse is both a pointing and drawing device. It has variable resolution. In other words, moving the mouse an inch on a desk may be scaled to either draw a line on the screen 1 inch long, 1 foot long, or 1 pixel long. Thus, it has the potential for very high resolution. The mouse is a little harder and less natural to use than a touch panel, but is easier for pointing and drawing than a keyboard. It is a less expensive device than either the keyboard or touch panel. Currently all computers come standard with keyboards, so a mouse is usually an extra cost. However, more and more personal computers are also coming with a mouse as standard equipment. The mouse is still not a suitable device in public areas such as malls. It requires a horizontal surface for operation and is best used in conjunction with a keyboard, where the keyboard is used for typing (entering alphanumeric information) and the mouse for selecting and drawing.

Interaction Strategy and Instructional Methodology

Choosing an instructional methodology and associated interaction strategies is, of course, a part of overall instructional design. Given that interactive video is being used, certain methodologies may be more appropriate. The selection or availability of input devices may constrain or determine the interaction strategies to some extent. Although interactive video may be appropriate for any methodology, some methodologies are considered more appropriate by developers, primarily simulations and instructional databases. The use of a touch panel as the sole input is satisfactory only for database programs, such as selecting merchandise from a store catalog. A keyboard, or keyboard plus either touch panel or mouse, is usually necessary for other methodologies.

Computer Presentation versus Video Presentation

A difficult decision in the design of interactive video programs is which information should be presented by the computer and which by the videodisc player. This factor is complex for several reasons. It depends on what the visual presentation is: text, graphic, lifelike still, live action, or a combination of above. It depends on the level of realism required. It depends on whether the visual information is likely to be modified frequently. It depends on the level of user control over the stimulus you desire (for example, the ability to zoom in on details). It depends on the use of color. Lastly, it depends on the outcome of on-going research which is attempting to determine how type of presentation (computer or video) affects human learning, and under what circumstances. Let us look at each of these.

Although just one or two years ago, computer text was of lower quality than video text, and thus harder to read, that situation has now changed. Computer text on current IBM and Macintosh computers is very flexible in size, style, orientation, and color, and can be of quality comparable to printed text. Computer-generated text has the advantage of being easily altered or replaced, while videodisc-based text may require disc re-mastering for changes.

Similarly, the quality of computer graphics has improved radically in the last year or two, while that of video graphics (like video text) is essentially unchanged, being based on the NTSC (National Television Standards Committee) standard for video images. For graphics such as diagrams, schematics, simple pictures, maps, text-related graphics such as boxes and arrows, and for simple animation, computer graphics are easy to develop and modify and are of equal quality to video graphics. The videodisc is still the medium of choice when lifelike images, such as photographs or live motion, are required. The more realistic your images must be, the more likely video should be used.

Information put on a standard videodisc is not easily altered. It may be overlaid and may be faded, but is not easily changed in terms of color, size, or location on the display. All visual images must be created and stored as such on the videodisc. Displays that change under user control are more appropriate as computer-generated visuals. Things that change over time (for example, alphanumeric information like addresses and phone numbers, or the name of the president of the United States) are better presented by the computer. Of course, the need to change visual information *and* the need to have lifelike motion may both be present. If that is the case, newer forms of interactive video such as *Digital Video Interactive* (DVI) may be more appropriate than analog videodiscs.

The quality and variety of color in computer graphics is currently changing very rapidly. Only recently, computers have progressed from being able to provide a few colors to millions, thus equaling or surpassing the realism of video. But in video, the realism of motion causes our mind to "enhance" color features and make things look more realistic than they are. The choice of whether to use the computer or video for color effects depends most on your computer's own color capabilities.

The decision to use computer or video for any particular visual component of a lesson is a critical one. Currently, we have only rules of thumb and intelligent guessing to guide us, as little research has been done to investigate these parameters for interactive video. Acker & Klein (1986) demonstrated differential learning with video versus computer displayed information, but their research did not use computers with the graphics, text, and color capability available today.

Type of Visual Presentation

In combination with the above considerations, the type of information presentation for any program segment can vary more widely in interactive video than in standard CBI. The designer may choose among textual presentation, speech, graphics, still video (photo), or motion video. An entire program is likely to make use of all these types. But the choice of which to use for any segment will vary. As always, our emphasis is that the choice should be a deliberate one based on learning theory (such as attention, memory, and motivation) and logistics (space, cost, and nature of the content).

Types of Audio Presentation

Although still in need of considerable research, the choice between text and speech can be assisted by existing instructional research. Speech may be better for poor or beginning readers, tends to be advantageous when accompanying and describing pictorial information, is better for getting the user's attention, and is more appropriate for temporal information such as poetry or music. Text can be read at the student's own rate, will tend to take less instructional time, is more easily rehearsed, is easier to take notes from, and is more appropriate for spatial information such as geography and many math and science topics. Interactive video provides an excellent facility for "dual channel" presentation, meaning simultaneous use of sound and visuals. While research indicates that some combinations, such as narration with pictorial information, increase learning, other combinations such as narration with displayed text impede learning and should be avoided.

When information is more pictorial rather than verbal in nature, the choice is between graphics, photos, and motion video. There is a tendency in interactive video to overuse motion video, often poorly such as with the talking head. Motion is usually necessary when a process is being learned, such as how to operate a machine, or when lifelike realism is required. In other cases, stills may be suitable and take up far less space on the videodisc. Among still images, the choice between graphics or photos depends on the amount of realism and detail needed. Drawings and diagrams simplify and can emphasize essential features of the presentation. Photos may contain more overall detail and are more realistic, but may be more difficult for the student to learn from.

Realism and Detail

The above decisions, text versus speech and graphics, photos, or motion video, relate in large part to the issue of detail and realism. We have discussed this extensively with regard to computer simulations and the same considerations apply here. When transfer of learning is a primary goal, and when students are at an appropriate learning level, the detail and realism of speech, photos, and perhaps motion video may be advantageous. For the beginning student, text and simplified graphics may be better. These are *overall* considerations which may be overridden because of particular circumstances, such as when the content is more appropriate for text or a process is being taught that is more amenable to motion video.

Global User Control

In addition to the usual kind of global user controls, such as reviewing, returning to menu or directions, and temporary exit from a program, an interactive video program may contain global user control of the video information. For action video or speech this may include the ability to pause and continue play. For some applications, the ability to search or browse the video information or to play in fast or slow motion is useful. These capabilities, all of which are fairly easy on a videodisc player, give the user much of the same control they have when reading a book, rather than being constrained to receive information only in the manner foreseen by the developer.

Local User Control

While *global* user controls are those available anywhere in a program, *local* user controls are those only available at appropriate times. Skipping sections and asking for the answer to a question or for a hint are common types of local control. Some of the above mentioned capabilities, such as searching and browsing, may also be local controls. The advantage of global control over local control is that the student does not have to be told whenever they are available (they are always available) and the screen need not be cluttered with options. If many such options are possible, they may be combined into a pull-down menu or a menu obtained via a single keypress.

Video Safe Area for Video, Photographs, and Computer Graphics

The design and production of video material for interactive video programs requires considerable care. Not all of the surface of a display monitor is usable, and not all of the view seen through a television camera's viewfinder will appear on the screen. The *safe area* (Figure 14–6) is that part of the video display which is usable.

If photographic slides or 35 mm film are used for producing still images or motion, be aware that the dimensions of slides and film (which are the same, a ratio of 2 units high by 3 units wide) are not the same as video (3 high by 4 wide).

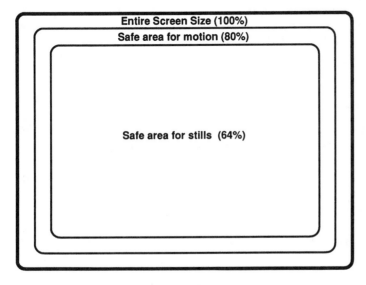

Entire Screen Size (100%)
Safe area for motion (80%)
Safe area for stills (64%)

Figure 14-6 The safe area of a video monitor.

Unlike motion film and video, slides are often oriented vertically (3 high by 2 wide) in which case the dimensions are even more disparate from those of the video display. Slides may be reduced to within the safe area and then bordered with a graphic image, but visual detail will be lost. Alternatively, slides may be cropped to within the safe area, in which case some visual material is lost but detail is preserved for the remainder.

The video display area on a monitor is sometimes greater than the computer display area on the same monitor. That is, when overlaying computer graphics on video information you are unable to overlay video at the edges. The developer must see to it that information to be overlaid be within the computer display area. This varies from one model computer to another.

Color

Color hues, brightness, and saturation are all important in interactive video programs. Most producers avoid highly saturated colors. It is also essential to match or keep these parameters constant throughout a videodisc program, which means doing so when producing field footage and editing.

Video Transitions

Edits, or the transition from one video sequence to another, have constraints not present for regular linear video. In linear video, fancy transitions such as fades and dissolves are often used. These are avoided in interactive video in favor of regular cuts with black between scenes. There are several reasons for this. First, fancy transitions waste video space, which is smaller on a thirty-minute videodisc than on videotape. Secondly, any videodisc segment may be programmed to branch to almost any other on a disc, so different types of transitions (a fade after one and a dissolve before another) may conflict. Thirdly, fast interaction such as in simulations requires quick entry into and out of video segments, which transition effects detract from. Some newer interactive video overlay equipment provides the capability to do transitions under computer control, but in most cases these transitions must be recorded on the videodisc itself, which is unchangeable.

Digitized Video

Some newer computer-video interfaces provide the capability to *digitize* video images. That means the video image is converted into digital data and can be stored, retrieved, and manipulated by the computer. A digitized video image may not look as realistic as the original video image and can occupy a lot of computer memory and storage space, but it is much more flexible. It may be changed in size, color, orientation, and location.

Using Film for Videodisc Production

When recording live material for a videodisc, motion segments may be recorded either on videotape or motion picture film. Video is easier and cheaper to record and edit, but film produces action which when frozen produces a sharper, more stationary image. Film images are sharper because film permits fast shutter speeds, freezing the action. Most video cameras have an effective shutter speed of a thirtieth of a second, causing motion to blur. The reason film produces more stationary images is explained in the next section.

Video Interlacing and Frame Flicker

Standard (NTSC) video is displayed using a technique called *interlacing*. Of the 525 screen lines presented in every one thirtieth of a second (a frame), about half, the odd lines, are shown in the first one sixtieth of a second (called the first *field*), and then the even ones are shown in the second one sixtieth of a second (the second *field*). By flipping between odd and even lines, smoother motion is seen. Figure 14–7 shows how interlacing works, with each frame composed of two fields.

A video camera thus captures one sixtieth of a second of motion for each *field*. A moving image will not only change a little during the one sixtieth of a second, but will be different from one field to the next. When a videodisc freezes on a frame, it is switching back and forth between its two fields sixty times a second. When a videodisc freezes on a frame with motion, the fields are slightly different images. Switching rapidly back and forth between them you appear to see one image which jitters. This effect is called *frame flicker*.

Film, as explained above, can use fast shutter speeds to freeze action, producing a very sharp still image. If a single film frame is transferred to both fields of a video frame, very steady freezes will result, eliminating frame flicker. But direct transfer of film frames to video frames is difficult because standard motion picture film contains twenty-four frames per second while video contains thirty frames per second. A technique called three-two pulldown (Figure 14–8) is used to transfer each second of film motion to a corresponding second of video motion. As illustrated, the first film frame is copied to three video *fields*. The next film frame is copied to *two* video fields. Alternating back and forth in this way, twenty-four frames are copied to sixty fields.

On the resulting videodisc, three out of five frames will have fields which are identical. If the videodisc freezes on any of those frames there will be no flicker. On the other two out of five frames there will be flicker. To prevent freezing on frames which contain flicker, special signals or *cues* called *white flags* are encoded on the videodisc. The white flags indicate what frames are good to freeze on and which are not. If a videodisc player attempts to freeze on one of the two frames that may contain flicker, the player will automatically jump to the adjacent frame without flicker.

Another way to avoid frame flicker is to use motion picture film in a special camera which shoots thirty frames per second. Then each film frame may be copied to each of the two video fields corresponding to a video frame, as illustrated in Figure 14–9.

A third way to avoid frame flicker is to use a special video process which takes the two video fields composing a frame, creates a single "average" field, and copies that average field to both fields on the videotape. Although the resulting

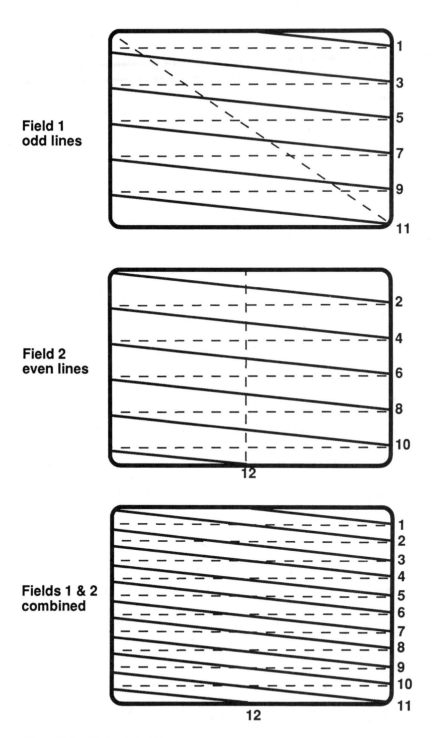

Figure 14-7 Video interlacing. The odd lines of field 1 (top) plus the even lines of field 2 (middle) occur so rapidly that the human eye sees them as a single frame (bottom). The diagram is simplified, showing only a few of the 525 lines in a real video image.

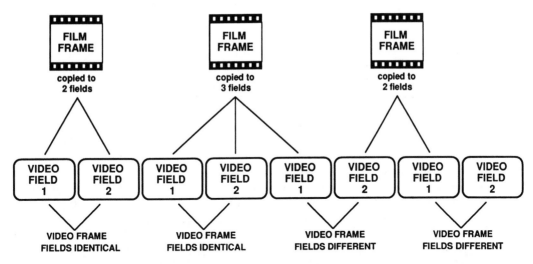

Figure 14-8   Three-two pulldown, in which the twenty-four frames corresponding to one second of motion picture film are transferred to the thirty frames corresponding to one second of videotape.

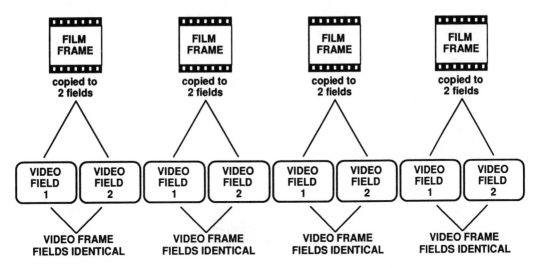

Figure 14-9   Thirty frame-per-second film transferred to thirty frame-per-second videotape. Each film frame is copied to both fields of a video frame.

frame is slightly different than the original, both of its fields are identical and there will be no frame flicker if the frame is frozen.

Text Size and Interlacing

NTSC video uses a technique called *interlacing*. However, when text is displayed on an NTSC video screen, the horizontal top and bottom edges of the letters appear to jitter as a result of interlacing. The effect is magnified for smaller letters. Two ways to deal with this is to use larger letters or to turn off interlacing. Some interfaces allow switching between interlacing and non-interlacing. Interlacing looks better for motion video and realistic still images, while non-interlacing looks better for still text images and simplified drawings.

Sound

There may be more than one source of sound in an interactive video program. The videodisc itself contains high fidelity sound, with the capability of stereo and CX noise reduction. The computer may also present sound in one of two ways, synthetic or digitized. Synthetic sound, usually speech or music, is created directly by the computer under program control. The program contains information about pitch, volume, and duration of sounds which special software interprets and converts to sound. Digitized sound is real sound which is processed by the computer to turn it into digital data. Digital data can be stored, retrieved, and processed by the computer. It sounds much more realistic than synthetic sound, but generally not as lifelike as regular analog sound. The advantage of computer-delivered sound is that it can be changed without re-mastering a videodisc. Also, a videodisc can only deliver analog sound when in "play" mode, not on a still or freeze frame, so analog sound cannot be associated with still frames, such as a narrator describing a picture. Computer-generated sound is limited by the computer's data storage capacity, not the videodisc's thirty-minute capacity, and can be played during still images or along with computer graphic or text images. Another form of digitized sound, called *still-frame audio,* makes use of digitized sound which is stored on the videodisc instead of on the computer. It provides greater audio capacity and is playable while looking at a still video frame.

All videodiscs provide at least two audio tracks for stereo sound. However, the two tracks can be used to store completely different messages. On some videodiscs, one track is in English and the other is in Spanish or another language. On some videodiscs, one track explains content at a simple level and the other track explains it at a more advanced level. On others, one track contains speech and the other music, allowing the user a choice of voice, music, or both.

Auxiliary Videodisc Data

Videodiscs contain information other than video and audio. Auxiliary information includes picture stops, chapter divisions, and program dumps. A picture stop is a signal that automatically stops the videodisc when it reaches that point and displays a still frame. This provides, for example, the capability to stop precisely at a particular still frame at the end of a section, allowing the student to decide what to do next. Chapter divisions divide the disc content up into major sections that are typically described on the videodisc jacket. Both picture stops and chapter divisions are useful for ease of user control in Level-1 and Level-2 programs. The same effects can be accomplished independently by the external computer in a Level-3 program.

A program dump is generally the code for a Level-2 program. It is automatically loaded when the videodisc is started and executed by the microprocessor inside the videodisc player. It is stored on the audio portion of the videodisc and usually occupies just a few seconds of audio space. If a program dump is to be stored on a videodisc, it is usually necessary to first produce a *check disc,* which contains all the video and audio, so that exact frame numbers of stills and program segments may be obtained and inserted into the final program. Check discs are also obtained by videodisc producers to make sure the video and audio are correct and of high quality before duplicating many copies of a disc.

Although program dumps are generally used for Level-2 programs, it is possible for a Level-3 program to load and call program dumps as subroutines. This can speed up and reduce the size of a Level-3 program. However, it may constrain your selection of videodisc players, as the format of program dumps has not been standardized across all players.

Disc Geography

The layout of video and audio segments on the videodisc, meaning their relative locations, is called disc geography. In Level-0 and to some extent in Level-1 videodisc programs, disc geography is determined by the order in which the user will see and hear the information. But for Level-2 and especially for Level-3 programs, the videodisc player will frequently branch from place to place. It is not necessary, indeed it is impossible, for the video to be placed in the order it will be seen. Different users will see the contents in different orders. Rather, placement of information on the disc is chosen to optimize speed of access to program segments.

Although a videodisc player can search and find information quickly, usually in under three seconds, even those pauses can be a problem in simulations or other fast moving programs. Frequently accessed information, such as a program main menu or directions, must be accessible as fast as possible. Feedback after answering a question should occur without a long pause. Suppose that in a chemistry experiment, combining two chemicals would cause a color change on contact. In a simulation of that experiment you would want the color change to occur instantly, not in two or three seconds. The closer video frames are on the disc, the faster the player may change from one to the other. On newer videodisc players, if images are within 100 frames of each other, the search time is almost imperceptible and there is no "video blanking" between the two segments. Video blanking is a brief display of black when switching from one image to another. In general, speed of switching from one program segment to another is enhanced by a few easy rules.

First, place frequently used general information, such as menus and directions, closer to the middle of the disc, for example, fifteen minutes into a thirty-minute program.

Second, if space is available, put frequently used information in more than one place, typically at the beginning, middle, and end. The program may then branch to whichever copy of the information is at the closest location.

Finally, put related segments, such as a question and its feedback, close together on the disc. The more likely a segment is to follow another segment, the closer it should be. For example, feedback for a correct response should be closer than feedback for possible but unlikely incorrect responses.

Following are some other rules-of-thumb for disc geography which do not relate to access time:

Avoid putting still frames in the first hundred or so frames. Because information is packed more densely in the center of the disc, there tends to be more distortion there.

Put orienting information, such as the title and credits, on the beginning frames of a disk. Although a Level-3 program will often not begin at the first frame, people will often try playing the disc as if it were a Level-1 program, so you want them to see something sensible at the beginning.

Put color bars and audio test signals someplace on the disc to allow for monitor and other equipment adjustment when people use the program.

If space allows, put still frames in more than one place, just in case some frames are lost or damaged during mastering and duplication.

If you have a small number of still frames and if space allows, put three adjacent copies of each still frame on the disc. You may then branch to the middle copy, and even if a one-frame search error occurs, the correct image will be seen.

If program dumps are included on the disc, put them on a portion where the video is black. This prevents seeing any extraneous video when loading a program dump. Additionally, program dumps which are to be loaded automatically by the player must be located at the very beginning of the right audio track.

DEVELOPMENT OF INTERACTIVE VIDEO PROGRAMS

In Part 2 we described and illustrated a model for developing computer-based instruction materials. Although that model requires modification to be applied to interactive video development, many of its activities and considerations are the same. We therefore provide the following checklist as a guide for interactive video development which can be used in conjunction with the development model in Part 2. Differences between Part 2 and the model implicit in this checklist arise in part because interactive video programs include both computer and video material. More importantly, because an optical videodisc is very expensive to produce, development does not permit the same cycle of draft-review-revise as we encourage for the easily changed magnetic medium of computers. The developer must determine that the program design and materials are good in the steps *before* mastering the videodisc. This may be done with check discs, but not as many times as with magnetic computer diskettes. Thus, detailed formative evaluation is evident early in the process. Not all the activities or evaluation elements in this checklist will be necessary for all projects. Like our lists of factors in Part 1, this checklist is intended to remind the developer of typical steps, decisions, and potential problems.

Although most of the activities in the checklist should be familiar from Part 2, the following new terms are introduced.

Client refers to the person for whom the program is being developed and who probably is paying for it. Although developers often produce CBI as a personal project of their own choosing, videodisc programs are almost always produced as a team effort for a paying client. Satisfaction of the client is essential, so evaluation should include *client check-off* at key points. That means the client has thoroughly reviewed the products up to that point and has given approval to go ahead with the next step.

Editing is the process of putting together a final videotape from a number of different sources (*original source material*) including videotapes produced in a studio, videotapes produced in the field, photographs, motion picture films, computer graphics, and so on. An *off-line edit* means planning the sequence of the final videotape on paper, much like storyboarding or scripting for a computer program. An *on-line* edit refers to the process of actually doing the editing in a video studio. Most editing today is done with computer-controlled equipment, so an on-line edit means entering into the computer a number of editing steps and then having the computer perform the functions.

Edits on the final master tape refers to points where video or audio material from different sources were joined together. The joining of video and audio must be very precise. Although the material may look and sound good, an improperly done edit may prevent mastering of a videodisc.

Dub or *dubbing* are video terms meaning to copy. Dubbing a videotape means making a copy of it onto another tape. Dubbing audio means copying audio from one source, such as an audio tape, to the audio track of a videotape without affecting any other information on the videotape.

Time code refers to magnetic signals on a videotape which measure the time, accurate to one thirtieth of a second, from the beginning of a video program. Time code allows very accurate location of specific content. When making a videotape, precise use of time code allows the designer to determine what frame numbers will contain specific video images.

Lead in and *lead out* are the signals at the beginning and end of a videotape before and after the program material. Lead in and lead out are usually pure black with no audio.

Synchronization refers to coordination of different program components, video, audio, and computer-generated visuals or audio. To overlay computer graphics with a videodisc motion sequence requires displaying and erasing the computer graphic at just the correct time while the videodisc is playing.

The *mastering company* is a company which produces videodisc masters from videotapes or other source material. A videodisc master is used to produce many copies of a videodisc.

CHECKLIST FOR DEVELOPING INTERACTIVE VIDEO PROGRAMS

Planning

- [ ] Determine the client's needs and constraints.
- [ ] Determine the budget, including:
- [ ]   personnel for content, video production, and programming
- [ ]   talent (actors) for audio and video

☐   video production and editing facilities
☐   video sets and props
☐   computer programming facilities
☐   audio production and editing facilities
☐   photographic processing
☐   travel
☐   check discs
☐   videodisc mastering
☐   replication (making copies) of videodiscs
☐   program evaluation
☐   production of manuals
☐   maintenance of the final program
☐   license fees for authoring software
☐ Draft a plan for project management.
☐ Create a project timeline or PERT chart.
☐ Have personnel begin logs of all project activity.
☐ Determine what existing resources can be used.
☐   instructional design resources
☐   video and computer production resources
☐   authoring software
☐   content area resources
☐ Meet with the Client and discuss:
☐   costs and timelines
☐   program options and the relative benefits or trade-offs of each
☐ Form project teams and assign responsibilities, including:
☐   director
☐   instructional designers
☐   writers
☐   video and audio crews
☐   subject matter experts
☐   graphic artists
☐   computer programmers
☐ Hire (or schedule for future work) auxiliary personnel, including:
☐   talent
☐   external evaluators
☐   consults for content, design, video, or computer

Analysis

☐ Analyze student characteristics and needs.
☐ Analyze task, environment, and economic needs and constraints.
☐ Learn the content thoroughly.
☐   Do a search for all relevant information.
☐   Read all manuals, texts, and other materials.
☐   Interview experts, including the Client or Client's staff.

☐ Interview people who currently do the activities to be taught.
☐ Have an expert "test" you to assess your understanding of the content.
☐ Create a complete content outline.
☐ Check the accuracy and completeness of the content outline with experts.
☐ Determine the most appropriate combination of media.
☐ Determine the most appropriate video and computer equipment.
☐ Determine the most appropriate development and delivery software to use.
☐ Determine the cost of facilities for production and for delivery.
☐ Create an initial project plan including a revised budget, media, equipment, and content.
☐ Present initial project plan to clients for client check-off.
☐ Begin acquiring or leasing facilities for the project.
☐ Meet with the Client and discuss:
☐ revised costs and timelines
☐ revised program options and the relative benefits or trade-offs of each

Design

☐ Refine goals in conjunction with Client and subject-matter experts.
☐ Hold brainstorming sessions to generate creative ideas.
☐ Consider Gagne's nine events of instruction and conditions of learning:
☐ attract and maintain the learner's attention
☐ inform the learner of the lesson objectives
☐ stimulate the learner's recall of relevant prior knowledge
☐ present relevant stimulus materials
☐ guide the learner's acquisition of the content
☐ require the learner to use and apply new knowledge
☐ provide corrective feedback concerning the learner's performance
☐ provide cumulative assessment of the learner's progress
☐ enhance learner's retention of the content and transfer of learning
☐ Consider Bloom's cognitive taxonomy of educational objectives:
☐ knowledge
☐ comprehension
☐ application
☐ analysis
☐ synthesis
☐ evaluation
☐ Experiment a lot, trying out various prototypes, objectives, strategies, and interaction methods.
☐ Write instructional objectives.
☐ Meet with Client and review instructional objectives.
☐ Choose instructional strategies.
☐ Choose lesson methodology.
☐ Design main lesson sequence and structure.
☐ Design learning events and activities.
☐ Create a draft flowchart (Level-1).

- [ ] Meet with Client to approve the Level-1 flowchart.
- [ ] Create a complete (Level-3) program flowchart.
- [ ] Design the software components underlying the lesson, including:
  - [ ] program files
  - [ ] content and student progress databases
  - [ ] the structure and interrelationships of those files
  - [ ] conventions for coding, documentation, and data storage formats.
- [ ] Write a draft script with all text, whether audio, video, or computer text.
- [ ] Have instructional designers and content experts review the draft script.
- [ ] Meet with Client to approve the draft script.
- [ ] Carefully script all text paying attention to the following considerations.
  - [ ] Use upper and lower case properly.
  - [ ] Avoid flashing, inverse, and poor colors for cues.
  - [ ] Use boxes, arrows, proper colors, and large text for cues.
  - [ ] Avoid overuse of emphasis techniques.
  - [ ] Avoid crowded screens.
  - [ ] Use good indentation, functional areas, and other organizational cues.
  - [ ] Assess all text in terms of relevance to the instructional objectives.
  - [ ] Avoid fancy fonts.
  - [ ] Assess overall text aesthetics.
- [ ] While scripting, produce associated print materials.
- [ ] Do a "dress rehearsal" of the scripts, reading them out loud and timing them.
- [ ] Check available videodisc time based on scripts, still frames, and other information on the disc.
- [ ] Revise the scripts based on the dress rehearsal and timing.
- [ ] Design graphics paying attention to the following considerations.
  - [ ] All graphics should support important information.
  - [ ] Keep graphics simple.
  - [ ] There should be only one primary idea per graphic.
  - [ ] Use compatible and meaningful colors.
  - [ ] Limit the number of colors.
  - [ ] Use headings and labels to explain and clarify graphic information.
  - [ ] Use graphics as visual analogies.
  - [ ] Pay attention to graphic placement in terms of functional areas.
  - [ ] Assess overall aesthetics of graphics.
- [ ] Create primary storyboards from scripts and graphics.
- [ ] Create secondary storyboards from scripts and graphics.
- [ ] Create a CBI prototype—a computer program simulating the lesson's video and audio portions

Internal Review of Scripts, Storyboards, and CBI Prototype

- [ ] Is the design interactive?
- [ ] Is interaction frequent?
- [ ] Is interaction varied?
- [ ] Is the most important and more difficult content emphasized?

☐ Are examples varied?
☐ Are both examples and non-examples included?
☐ Are cues faded?
☐ Are definitions of important terms provided?
☐ Does lesson structure correspond to content structure?
☐ Does the student apply knowledge or skills to new problems?
☐ Does the program show or simulate rather than tell?
☐ Is practice distributed throughout the program?
☐ Is program organization shown through menus, maps, diagrams, and organizers?
☐ Is student attention maintained throughout the program?
☐ Is humor used appropriately?
☐ Is the student given reinforcement and encouragement?
☐ Is remediation provided when needed?
☐ Is good user control allowed where possible?
☐ Are different paths provided for different types of students?
☐ Are typical student questions anticipated and addressed?
☐ Are there advance organizers?
☐ Are there section objectives, overviews, and summaries?
☐ Is there a glossary?
☐ Is color used appropriately?
☐ Is motion used appropriately?
☐   Remember that stills with audio can be as effective.
☐   Motion is good for procedural learning.
☐   Motion is good in simulation.
☐ Are motion segments well designed?
☐   Plan for the safe-area of the monitor.
☐   Avoid sequence clues.
☐ Are still-frames well designed and used appropriately?
☐   Put stills in several places on a disk (start, middle, end).
☐   Put down three identical frames if space permits.
☐   Put stills close to related video material.
☐   Don't put stills just at the beginning or just at the end.
☐   Limit still frames to one idea.
☐   Use blank space liberally in stills.
☐   Use blank lines between text segments.
☐   Use consistent functional areas on still frames.
☐   Don't hyphenate.
☐   Use bulleted lists.
☐   Include the following special stills on the videodisc.
☐   title page
☐   credits page
☐   thank you messages
☐   copyright message
☐   color bars
☐   test pattern for adjusting monitor focus

- [ ] photos of key project people
- [ ] touch panel alignment pattern
- [ ] glossary of key terms
- [ ] project and lesson objectives
- [ ] information about instructor options
- [ ] directions to the learner
- [ ] Is audio used appropriately and is the audio quality adequate?
- [ ] Are the two audio tracks taken advantage of?
- [ ] Consider bilingual messages.
- [ ] Consider use of music.
- [ ] Avoid sequence clues in the audio.
- [ ] Include an audio test tone in the videodisc.
- [ ] Is the level of realism appropriate for the learner's experience?
- [ ] Is the level of realism appropriate for the method of presentation?
- [ ] Simple line drawings may often be just as good.
- [ ] Consider increased realism as the lesson progresses.
- [ ] Are user control options appropriate, sufficient, and well designed?
- [ ] Are navigational aids provided for the user?
- [ ] Avoid too many choices on menus.
- [ ] Use a maximum of three levels of menus.
- [ ] Put frequently chosen menu options first on the menus.
- [ ] Are menu choices clear?
- [ ] Allow the user control of pace.
- [ ] Consider control of program parameters (e.g., sound effects).
- [ ] Allow global access to menu, introductions, objectives, and lesson map.
- [ ] Provide help on lesson operation.
- [ ] Consider providing help on content.
- [ ] Provide access to a glossary.
- [ ] Allow temporary termination at any time.
- [ ] Consider video control: reverse, repeat, pause, slow, step, and scan.
- [ ] Provide access to summaries.
- [ ] Allow the student to exit from a section.
- [ ] Consider providing an index to videodisc and other lesson content.
- [ ] Is an instructor mode present for easy use of lesson?
- [ ] Is video and each audio track exactly thirty minutes or less?
- [ ] Arrange all segments to minimize search and access time.
- [ ] Avoid stills and audio at the beginning of disc where distortion occurs.
- [ ] Include some video black before and after motion sequences.
- [ ] A Level-2 program dump must be at the beginning of the disc.
- [ ] Avoid video on Level-2 program dump frames, or soon after.
- [ ] All audio, video, and computer content should be relevant to objectives.
- [ ] Review the materials using the *Quality Review Checklist* in the appendix.
- [ ] Revise scripts, flowcharts, storyboards, and CBI prototype until satisfactory.
- [ ] Have appropriate level students pilot the prototype, and revise until satisfactory.

Client Review of Scripts, Storyboards, and CBI Prototype

☐ Meet with Client to review the CBI prototype, timeline, and budget.
☐ Revise scripts, flowcharts, storyboards, and CBI prototype until Client approves.
☐ Reassess project cost and adherence to the budget and schedule.
☐ Final pre-production meeting with client.
☐   Go through the entire program making sure Client understands and approves everything.
☐   Be certain everyone understands that once production begins, any changes are expensive.

Initial Production of Video and Computer Components

☐ Make decisions concerning medium of visual and aural source material.
☐   Use videotape for footage with little motion.
☐   Use film to avoid frame flicker in motion segments that may be frozen.
☐   Use thirty frame-per-second film if equipment available and sound will be dubbed separately.
☐ Create a standard video script or video "shot list" with talent lines and notes to the director.
☐ Have the director review and approve the video script.
☐ Create video sets and props.
☐ Hire talent.
☐ Rehearse the script with talent and video staff.
☐ Final meeting with video director before video production.
☐ Shoot field segments (film or video).
☐ Shoot studio segments (film or video).
☐ Record associated audio information.
☐ Produce digital audio.
☐ When creating still frames (photography, videotape, or computer graphics):
☐   Avoid saturated colors.
☐   Avoid text with serifs.
☐   Assure that the text size is readable. Use larger text if group reading is intended.
☐   Consider television aspect ratio for photos in portrait mode.
☐   Consider television aspect ratio for photos in landscape mode.
☐   Consider cropping or shrinking photos for appropriate fit.
☐   Consider television safe area with respect to your monitor.
☐   Consider television safe area with respect to computer overlay.
☐   Assure that still frames are always placed on both fields of a video frame.
☐   For photos, use high shutter speed, good light, fast film, and wide aperture.
☐ Shoot still frame photography.
☐ Produce associated graphics information (such as menus, title frames, or directions).
☐ Produce the computer program in parallel with video and film production.
☐   Follow your flowchart when programming.
☐   Test and debug the computer program using an existing videodisc.

Pre-Mastering

☐ Review master tape production guidelines from the mastering company.

☐ Communicate with mastering company on schedule for check disc and mastering.

☐ Create an off-line edit list before doing on-line editing.

☐ Do on-line editing.

☐ With twenty-four frame-per-second film, use three-two pulldown and white flags.

☐ Check for correct field dominance of the videotape.

☐ Dub audio.

☐ Insert chapter stops if used.

☐ Insert picture stops if used.

☐ Insert white flags if three-two pulldown is used.

☐ Insert still-frame audio if used.

☐ Produce the master tape, including:

    ☐ time code if not dubbing to 1 inch videotape

    ☐ lead in

    ☐ color bars

    ☐ audio test tone

    ☐ program exactly thirty minutes long

    ☐ lead out

☐ Dub master tape to 1 inch videotape.

☐ Create a copy of the master tape.

☐ Add time code to 1 inch videotape.

☐ Evaluate the copy of the master tape.

    ☐ Check for good video and audio edits.

    ☐ Check for consistent color levels and brightness.

    ☐ Check that each audio component is on the correct track.

    ☐ Check that audio levels are consistent.

    ☐ Check that audio is synchronized well with video start and stop points.

    ☐ Check that audio is appropriate for the students' age and education.

    ☐ Check that opening is appropriate for Level-1 play.

    ☐ Evaluate based on *internal review of scripts, storyboards, and CBI prototype.*

☐ Evaluate the computer program.

    ☐ Synchronization of computer and video based on reading frames and status.

    ☐ Information that will soon change should be on the computer, not the video.

    ☐ Avoid using computer text mode.

    ☐ Include a touch panel alignment routine if touch panels are used.

    ☐ Check for good error handling, such as for missing files or incorrect hookup.

    ☐ Evaluate based on *internal review of scripts, storyboards, and CBI prototype.*

Formative Evaluation Using a Check Disc

☐ Create a complete log of the audio and video contents of the check disc.

☐ Check all audio and video content for quality and accuracy.

- ☐ Check for accuracy of frame numbers.
- ☐ Check correct execution of any Level-2 program dumps.
- ☐ Check accuracy of other cues such as chapter stops, picture stops, white flags.
- ☐ Insert frame numbers based on the check disc into the Level-3 computer program.
- ☐ Check operation of the Level-3 program.
- ☐ Evaluate entire program based on *internal review of scripts, storyboards, and CBI prototype*.
- ☐ Have Client review complete program.
- ☐ Revise all program components until Client check-off.

Mastering and Duplication

- ☐ Double-check format of the master tape.
- ☐ Fill out any required forms by the mastering company.
- ☐ Prepare accompanying material: videodisc cues, Level-2 dumps, still-frame audio.
- ☐ With the materials sent, include the name and phone number of a contact person.

Creation or Revision of Auxiliary Materials

- ☐ Create or revise the student manual.
- ☐ Create or revise the instructor manual.
- ☐ Create or revise the technical manual for programmers.
- ☐ Include quick reference guides in student and instructor manuals.
- ☐ Revise all auxiliary instructional materials (which were drafted during the design phase).
- ☐ Design packaging for the program (such as disc labels, jackets, and diskette boxes).

Evaluation of the Final Videodiscs

- ☐ Check a sample of discs for frame number accuracy.
- ☐ Check a sample of discs for audio and video quality and accuracy.
- ☐ Check a sample of discs for correct execution of the Level-2 program, if any.
- ☐ Check a sample of discs for accuracy of cues and white flags.
- ☐ Check operation of the Level-3 program.
- ☐ Evaluate based on *internal review of scripts, storyboards, and CBI prototype*.
- ☐ Do formative evaluation to determine if the needs of the client have been met.
- ☐ Do formative evaluation to determine revisions needed to manuals.
- ☐ Do revision based on the formative evaluation.

Final Production of Manuals and Project Documentation

- ☐ Create screen images from the actual displays using display capture software.
- ☐ Finalize the student manual.
- ☐ Finalize the instructor manual.

☐ Finalize the technical manual.

☐ Finalize any auxiliary instructional materials.

☐ Finalize packaging for the program.

☐ Finalize documentation inside the computer programs.

☐ Assure safe storage of all original source material.

☐ Produce a final log of all audio and video material on the videodisc.

☐ Organize and store all documentation for later use and program revision.

Summative Evaluation

☐ Field test all materials for improvement of future videodiscs or auxiliary materials.

☐ Perform cost-effectiveness evaluation for clients and final reports.

☐ Write final reports.

For further readings on the design and development of interactive video programs, see Daynes & Butler (1984), DeBloois (1982), Floyd & Floyd (1982), Iuppa (1984), Merrill & Bunderson, (1979), Minnesota Mining & Manufacturing (1982), Parsloe (1984), and Wright (1984). For discussion of two graduate courses on interactive video design, see Alessi (1988) and Allen & Erickson (1986). Our checklist is a synthesis and simplification of the content of these and other sources.

It should be obvious that developing interactive video programs requires a lot of work and great attention to detail. The University of Nebraska at Lincoln holds workshops several times a year on design and development of interactive videodiscs. Participation in such a workshop is an excellent precursor to directing or even working on a videodisc development team.

THE FUTURE OF INTERACTIVE VIDEO

The availability in the near future of digital video devices is expected to significantly increase the power of interactive video instruction. Two new technologies, digital video interactive (DVI) and compact disc interactive (CDI), use compact disc technology.

Compact discs, such as the popular music compact discs, store information in digital form, the same as data is stored on a computer diskette. The music compact disc player converts the digital information back to analog for playing through conventional amplifiers and speakers. The quality of sound is very high because digital storage does not add any noise to the music, as do analog devices such as phonographs or cassette tapes. The quality remains high because, like a videodisc, the information is read by a laser beam which does not cause wear to the recorded surface.

In a similar fashion, digital video interactive takes analog video signals from a videotape and converts them into digital information. The information is stored on the same kind of compact disc as is music. A computer with a DVI player and interface can display the video information on a computer monitor. Additionally, since the information is in digital form, a computer program can easily combine it with computer text, graphics, and sound. The computer program can also manipulate digital video images. They can be shrunk to fit in a corner of the display monitor, enabling computer text to be displayed elsewhere without covering any part of the video. A portion of the video can be magnified to fill the entire monitor, showing more detail. A video still image, such as of a painting by Picasso, can be displayed on the right while a narrator can be seen describing the picture on the left. A still video image, such as an airplane photograph, may be animated, colorized, changed in size, or similarly modified in many ways. DVI provides these and other capabilities which are difficult or impossible with analog videodiscs. However, the image quality of DVI is currently not as good as that of analog videodiscs.

Compact disc interactive (CDI) is an attempt to design and market a standard compact disc which can contain music, video, text, computer programs, or any combination. The amount of audio and video can vary, depending on the quality desired. Information is also in digital form, which provides the same flexibility as described for DVI. Again, image quality is not currently as good as that of analog videodiscs. The potential advantage of CDI is to provide standardization in the field of interactive video, so that purchasers and producers would be able to buy one set of equipment that works with all programs.

CONCLUSION

The video devices we have been discussing use optical technology, where a laser beam retrieves the information from a quickly spinning metal disc imbedded in a protective plastic covering. Optical storage devices provide the very large information capacity required for video, as well as durability and fast access. Until recently, *storing* information on the disc, which is also done with a laser, required very expensive equipment. This is because there is so much information in a video picture, and there are so many video pictures in a program, that the data must be stored in a very dense format. Although analog videodiscs are still fairly expensive to create, the cost is decreasing. Digital compact discs, which have a bigger market, are more quickly becoming inexpensive to produce. Thus, just as microcomputers opened up the door to personal computing and desktop publishing, in conjunction with optical video storage they are now creating what is termed *desktop video*. Information from a television camera can be digitized, stored, and edited so as to create a complete instructional video program. What once required a large and costly television studio is becoming possible with increasingly less expensive computer and video equipment.

The future of interactive video, from a *hardware* standpoint, lies in recordable digital storage which is increasing in capacity while decreasing in cost. This will eventually result in the merging of computer technology and television technology. From a *software* and *instructional* standpoint, the future depends on tools enabling us to use the technologies easily, and on our knowledge of how to use them to facilitate learning.

REFERENCES AND BIBLIOGRAPHY

ACKER, S., & KLEIN, E. (1985). Visualizing spatial tasks: A comparison of computer graphic and full-band video displays. *American Educational Research Association.*

ALBERTA VOCATIONAL CENTRE. (1987). *Let Your Fingers Do the Talking: Deaf Awareness.* [Videodisc]. Calgary, CANADA: Alberta Vocational Centre.

ALESSI, S.M. (1988). Learning interactive videodisc development: A case study. *Journal of Instructional Development, 11*(2), 2–7.

ALLEN, B.S. (1986). A theoretical framework for inter-activating linear video. *Journal of Computer-Based Instruction, 13*(4), 107–112.

ALLEN, B.S., & CARTER, C.D. (1988). Expert systems and interactive video tutorials: Separating strategies from subject matter. *Journal of Computer-Based Instruction, 15*(4), 123–130.

ALLEN, B.S., & ERICKSON, D.M. (1986). Training interactive videodisc designers. *Journal of Instructional Development, 9*(2), 19–28.

BALSON, P.M., EBNER, D.G., MAHONEY, J.V., LIPPERT, H.J., & MANNING, D.T. (1986). Videodisc instructional strategies: Simple may be superior to complex. *Journal of Educational Technology Systems, 14*(4), 273–281.

BLACKMAN, J.A., ALBANESE, M.A., HUNTLEY, J.S., & LOUGH, L.K. (1985). Use of computer-videodisc system to train medical students in developmental disabilities. *Medical Teacher, 7*(1), 89–97.

BLACKMAN, J.A., LOUGH, L.K., & HUNTLEY, J.S. (1984). *Assessment of Neuromotor Dysfunction in Infants.* [Videodisc and computer program]. Coralville, IA: Cognitive Design Technologies, Limited.

BOSCO, J. (1986). An analysis of evaluations of interactive video. *Educational Technology, 26*(5), 7–17.

BRODY, P. (1984). *Research on and Research with Interactive Video.* Paper presented at the Annual Meeting of the American Educational Research Association, New Orleans, LA. (ERIC Document Reproduction Service No. ED 246 885)

CLARK, D.J. (1983). *Bio Sci Video Disc.* [Videodisc]. Seattle, WA: Videodiscovery, Inc.

DALTON, D.W. (1986). The efficacy of computer-assisted video instruction on rule learning and attitudes. *Journal of Computer-Based Instruction, 13*(4), 122–125.

DALTON, D.W., & HANNAFIN, M.J. (1986). *The Effects of Video-Only, CAI Only, and Interactive Video Instructional Systems on Learner Performance and Attitude.* Paper presented at the Annual Convention of the Association for Educational Communications and Technology, Las Vegas, NV. (ERIC Document Reproduction Service No. ED 267 762)

DAYNES, R., & BUTLER, B. (1984). *The Videodisc Book: A Guide and Directory—1984 Edition.* New York: John Wiley and Sons.

DEBLOOIS, M. (1982). *Videodisc/Microcomputer Courseware Design.* Englewood Cliffs, NJ: Educational Technology Publications.

DEBLOOIS, M. (1984). *Effectiveness of Interactive Videodisc Training: A Comprehensive Review.* Falls Church, VA: Future Systems, Inc.

DESHLER, D., & GAY, G. (1986, December). Educational strategies for interactive videodisc design. *Educational Technology, 26*(12), 12–17.

ELECTRONIC VISION. (1987). *IVD Toolkit.* [Computer Program]. Athens, OH: Electronic Vision.

FLOYD, S., & FLOYD, B. (Eds.). (1982). *Handbook of Interactive Video.* White Plains, NY: Knowledge Industry Publications.

FULLER, R.G., ZOLLMAN, D.A., & CAMPBELL, T.C. (1982). *The Puzzle of the Tacoma Narrows Bridge Collapse.* [Videodisc]. New York: John Wiley and Sons.

GAY, G. (1985). *Interaction of Learner Control and Prior Conceptual Understanding in Computer-Assisted Video Instruction.* Paper presented at the Annual Meeting of the American Educational Research Association, Chicago. (ERIC Document Reproduction Service No. ED 265 845)

GREEN, B.S. (1981). *The First National Kidisc.* [Videodisc]. New York: Optical Programming Associates.

HANNAFIN, M.J. (1984). Options for authoring instructional interactive video. *Journal of Computer-Based Instruction, 11*(3), 98–100.

HANNAFIN, M.J., & HUGHES, C. (1986). A framework for incorporating orienting activities in computer-based interactive video. *Instructional Science, 15,* 239–255.

HANNAFIN, M.J., & PHILLIPS, T.L. (1987). Perspectives in the design of interactive video: Beyond tape versus disc. *Journal of Research and Development in Education, 21*(1), 44–60.

HANNAFIN, M.J., PHILLIPS, T.L., & TRIPP, S.D. (1986). The effects of orienting, processing, and practicing activities on learning from interactive video. *Journal of Computer-Based Instruction, 13*(4), 134–139.

HON, D. (1982a). *Cardiopulmonary Resuscitation.* [Videodisc and computer program]. Oklahoma City, OK: Interact, Inc.

HON, D. (1982b). Interactive training in cardiopulmonary resuscitation. *Byte, 7*(6), 108–138.

HUNTLEY, J.S. (1985). *University of Iowa Visual Databases.* [Videodisc]. Iowa City, IA: University of Iowa, Weeg Computing Center, CAI Lab.

HUNTLEY, J.S., & ALESSI, S.M. (1987). Videodisc authoring tools: Evaluating products and a process. *Optical Information Systems, 7*(4), 259–281.

HUNTLEY, J.S., & LOW, N. (1986). *Scripter.* [Computer Program]. Coralville, IA: Cognitive Design Technologies, Limited.

ISBOUTS, J. (1983, September). Making a videodisc on Vincent Van Gogh. *E&ITV,* 73–77.

IUPPA, N.V. (1984). *A Practical Guide to Interactive Video Design.* White Plains, NY: Knowledge Industry Publications.

IUPPA, N.V., & ANDERSON, K. (1988). *Advanced Interactive Video Design: New Techniques and Applications.* White Plains, NY: Knowledge Industry Publications.

J.A.M. (1984). *Introduction to Computer Literacy.* [Videodisc and computer program]. Rochester, NY: J.A.M. Inc.

KEARSLEY, G.P., & FROST, J. (1985). Design factors for successful videodisc-based instruction. *Educational Technology, 25*(3), 7–13.

KELLER, J.M., & SUZUKI, K. (1988). Use of the ARCS motivation model in courseware design. In D.H. Jonassen (Ed.), *Instructional Designs for Microcomputer Courseware.* Hillsdale, NJ: Lawrence Erlbaum.

LAMBERT, S., & SALLIS, J. (1987). *CD-I and Interactive Videodisc Technology.* Indianapolis: Howard W. Sam & Co.

MALONE, T.W. (1981). Towards a theory of intrinsically motivating instruction. *Cognitive Science, 5,* 333–369.

MASSACHUSETTS INSTITUTE OF TECHNOLOGY. (1983). *Discursions: Architecture Machine Group.* [Videodisc]. Cambridge, MA: Massachusetts Institute of Technology.

MERRILL, P.F., & BUNDERSON, C.V. (1979). *Guidelines for Employing Graphics in a Videodisc Training Delivery System. ISD for Videodisc Training Systems. First Annual Report. Vol. III.* (ERIC Document Reproduction Service No. ED 196 413)

MILHEIM, W.D., & EVANS, A.D. (1987). Using interactive video for group instruction. *Educational Technology, 27*(6), 35–37.

MINDBANK, INC. (1987). *The Name Game.* [Videodisc and computer program]. Ingomar, PA: MindBank, Inc.

MINNESOTA MINING & MANUFACTURING. (1982). *Producing Interactive Videodiscs.* [Videodisc]. St. Paul, MN: Minnesota Mining & Manufacturing.

NORTH AMERICAN PHILIPS CORPORATION. (1982). *Vincent Van Gogh: A Portrait in Two Parts.* [Videodisc]. North American Philips Corporation.

PARSLOE, E. (1984). *Interactive Video.* Cheshire, UK: Sigma Technical Press.

REEVES, T.C. (1986). Research and evaluation models for the study of interactive video. *Journal of Computer-Based Instruction, 13*(4), 102–106.

REEVES, T.C. (1989). The role, methods, and worth of evaluation in instructional design. In K.A. Johnson & L.J. Foa (Eds.). *Instructional Design: New Alternatives for Effective Education and Training.* New York: Macmillan.

SCHNEIDER, E.W., & BENNION, J. L. (1981). *Videodiscs.* Englewood Cliffs, NJ: Educational Technology Publications.

SCHWARTZ, E. (1985). *The Educators' Handbook to Interactive Videodisc.* Washington, D.C.: Association for Educational Communications & Technology.

SEAL-WANNER, C. (1988). Interactive video systems: Their promise and educational potential. *Teachers College Record, 89*(3), 373–383.

SIGEL, E., SCHUBIN, M., & MERRILL, P.F. (1980). *Video Discs: The Technology, the Applications, and the Future.* New York: Van Nostrand Reinhold.

SMITH, S.G., & JONES, LL. (1988). *Chemical Reactions.* [Videodisc and computer program]. Armonk, NY: International Business Machines Corp.

SMITH, S.G., JONES, L.L., & WAUGH, M.L. (1986). Production and evaluation of interactive videodisc lessons in laboratory instruction. *Journal of Computer-Based Instruction, 13*(4), 117–121.

SMITHSONIAN INSTITUTION. (1983). *National Air and Space Museum Archival Videodisc 1.* [Videodisc]. Washington, D.C.: Smithsonian Institution.

WRIGHT, E.E. (1984). *Level III Videodisc Project Task Analysis.* Atlanta, GA: Comsell, Inc.

15

ARTIFICIAL INTELLIGENCE AND INSTRUCTION

"Artificial intelligence" is a phrase that has recently become very popular. Both the research literature and marketing materials contain frequent references to applications that are described as intelligent. Our response to this trend is complex because there are so many issues involved.

On the positive side, the research into intelligent systems has already produced and will continue to provide valuable insights into the problems of learning and instruction, and hence should be actively pursued. Furthermore, there are useful spinoffs from research into artificial intelligence that can be used immediately in the classroom. On the other hand, the development of even a single intelligent, instructional program currently requires an enormous amount of effort and a diversity of talents, and hence is unlikely to be undertaken by most people. Additionally, much of the material that is currently labeled as being intelligent is no more than courseware with sophisticated branching, and so the consumer is often being misled as to what an intelligent program can and should do. Software is often labeled "intelligent" as an advertising ploy, much like software being labeled "user friendly" when it is not.

Overall, while we believe that research and development on artificial intelligence techniques are important, we doubt such techniques will be widely used in the *near* future because to be effective they require careful preparation and substantial effort by already overburdened teachers. Work by several researchers on authoring tools for intelligent computing (Begg & Hogg, 1987; Kearsley, 1988) has the potential, if successful, to make intelligent systems development easier in the shorter term.

WHAT IS ARTIFICIAL INTELLIGENCE?

It is hard to define artificial intelligence because it is changing rapidly. Programs that were claimed to exhibit intelligence a few years ago, such as chess-playing games and grammar checkers, are no longer thought of as intelligent. Programs considered intelligent today will not be so in a few years. Once an application becomes commonplace on a computer, we tend not to consider it intelligent. While many say that programs that exhibit human-like behavior are intelligent, there is disagreement as to which human-like behaviors qualify. Certainly motor activities are not considered intelligent, however, language activities such as speech and understanding speech are. Most agreement revolves around the notion that truly intelligent systems should be able to monitor their own strategies and to improve them as circumstances dictate. That is, they should be able to learn.

In this chapter we discuss three categories of work in artificial intelligence that impact instruction: expert systems, instructional modeling, and natural language comprehension. Expert systems are programs that contain a representation of an expert's knowledge in a form that can be used by other people. Instructional modeling refers to student, content, and pedagogical models, all of which are components embedded in any type of CBI program (tutorial, simulation, game, etc.) to permit more flexible and effective delivery of instruction. This area is often called Intelligent CAI, but we refrain from using that phrase because it can be applied equally well to the use of any AI techniques in computer-based instruction. Finally, natural language comprehension is the ability of a computer to recognize language as it is spoken or written by people and to act on it in an appropriate way.

There are other areas of artificial intelligence which have not yet had much impact on instruction, such as machine vision and robotics. These are not our concern at this time. Also we do not discuss what some educators call *intelligent microworlds*. Many so-called applications are nothing more than sophisticated simulations, with the phrase *intelligent* added to mean "new and improved."

EXPERT SYSTEMS

Expert systems are programs designed to mimic expert human performance in a narrow domain. Although it was not long ago that one could enumerate virtually all the existing major expert system projects, today it is impossible to keep track of all the systems that have been built, or to know all the fields that are using expert-systems technology.

The most frequently cited expert system is MYCIN (Shortliffe, 1976; Buchanan & Shortliffe, 1984), an expert system to aid physicians in the diagnosis and treatment of infectious blood diseases.

A typical expert system like MYCIN works by interacting with the user, asking questions that it needs to make decisions or give advice. Its knowledge may comprise hundreds of "IF . . . THEN" rules. If, during questioning, the conditional part of a rule is satisfied, then the consequence is given to the user, sometimes with an indication of confidence as to its likelihood. In most expert systems, the user may ask *why* a consequence follows, in which case the system will give a reason.

A typical expert system has two major components, namely a knowledge base and an inference engine (sometimes called a production system). The knowledge base contains the content and the relationships between elements of the content. The inference engine is the program that takes the rules, decides which questions to ask, and works out the decisions. An expert system shell is an inference engine with an interface that allows a user to enter a knowledge base creating an expert system.

Although the inference engine can greatly influence how an expert system functions, it is the knowledge base that is of greatest interest to us. A typical knowledge base has three parts: decisions to be made on the basis of data gathered, questions to gather the required data, and rules that operate upon the data. We illustrate a very simple knowledge base below. (Note, knowledge bases can exist in text form as well as in a form to be used by a computer.)

Example of a Knowledge Base

As researchers in the computer-based instruction field, we are sometimes asked by teachers whether computer-based instruction should be used in a particular course that they teach. Instead of having the discussion we would ordinarily have with the teacher on this topic, we could incorporate its details into an expert system. Any teacher could then use the expert system to help answer this ubiquitous question. The boxed text of Figure 15–1 exemplifies this expert system.

As you can see, even a simple knowledge base becomes complicated rather rapidly. However, once the work has been done to build it, it can be a very useful tool.

Capturing an expert's knowledge in this form has already yielded dividends in terms of usefulness. Many businesses routinely use expert systems to help them conduct everyday tasks. Banks use expert systems to process loan applications; universities use expert advisors to help students decide which courses to study; computer companies use expert systems to help them design computer configurations. And so on.

Scale of Expert Systems

Existing expert systems vary considerably in size and sophistication. Many demonstration or *small-scale* expert systems exist which can do a reasonably good job of providing the same level of expert advice as a single expert. A few *large-scale* expert systems exist, like MYCIN. These are based on a thorough compilation of almost all available knowledge on a particular topic, obtained from several experts, textbooks, reference works, research reports, and other sources. Such expert systems can give useful advice even to real experts in the field. However, such large-scale systems are few in number and very expensive to develop.

Uses and Advantages of Expert Systems

Most expert systems are designed to help solve problems. They do so by capturing the essence of expertise in the form of a computer program. Essentially they model an expert's knowledge and how the expert uses it. However, it requires a great stretch of the imagination to think of these programs as being real experts. We think of an expert as being someone whose real skills lie in an ability to deal with the unexpected—to be able to analyze new information and to combine it with existing knowledge to produce valid proposals or solutions. Current expert systems do not do this: what they do is to mimic one or more expert's knowledge and advice in a well-defined domain. They cannot deal with the unexpected, nor can they generate new solutions. Furthermore, if an expert on which the system was based provides incorrect advice, so will the system.

You may ask, then, why expert systems are receiving so much attention. Their utility lies in the fact that they are able to *replicate* an expert's opinion in a certain domain. That is, using an expert system it is possible to have your expert in many places at the same time. A bank, for example, may only have one or two people authorized to process loan applications. They may spend most of their time dealing with relatively routine applications, which may not take advantage of their skills. By preparing an expert system that mimics how the loan officers deal with these routine applications, most applications can be handled automatically via computer. The officers can then spend time processing unusual or complicated applications.

Expert Systems and Instruction

From an instructional perspective, most existing expert systems have little direct utility because they are not designed to teach or instruct (although an enterprising student can use one in a type of discovery mode). Their lack of teaching ability arises from the absence of any instructional strategies, the inability to compare what a student knows with what the expert knows, and the inability to determine what to do when the student's knowledge differs from expert knowledge.

The structure of expert systems, however, lends itself to be adapted for tutoring. GUIDON, for example, is an expert tutor for teaching diagnosis of infectious diseases (Clancey, 1979). It supplements MYCIN's knowledge base in medicine with its own expertise in tutoring to form an instructional program for students. GUIDON has been quite successful in its own right, and has yielded very useful information about the problems of transforming systems like MYCIN into teaching programs (Clancey, 1983).

The problem with systems like GUIDON is that they take enormous amounts of time to produce. The knowledge base underlying MYCIN itself took many person years of effort. To this must be added the great effort required to establish the tutoring rules that underlie GUIDON. Of course there is the hope that once the tutoring rules have been established they will not have to be redone for other applications. There have been attempts to develop generalized tutoring systems (Woolf & Cunningham, 1987), but so far they have been limited to several lessons sharing a common subject or instructional strategy. We continue this discussion later in the chapter.

If expert systems are so time consuming to produce, it is reasonable for you to ask where their benefit lies for education. Someday authoring software may make expert-system development easier, but it will be some time before such authoring systems are commercially available. However, there is an observation made in virtually every expert-system project that has caught our attention. It is that the researchers involved in the development of knowledge bases underlying

SHOULD I USE COMPUTER-BASED INSTRUCTION IN MY CLASSROOM?

DECISIONS THAT MAY BE MADE:
The possible decisions to be made based on the original question are:

D1. Yes. You should use computer-based instruction in the course.
D2. No. You should NOT use computer-based instruction in the course.

QUESTIONS:
In order to reach one of these decisions, we must gather all relevant information. This is done through questions.

Q1. Are the computer-based materials to be used by the teacher or by the students?
    a) The teacher
    b) The students
Reason for asking this question: The resource requirements are different for these two users. That is, many more computers will be needed if students will be using them.

Q2. Is there a computer available with a large enough screen for all the students to read what is on it?
    a) Yes
    b) No
Reason: If the students cannot read the material, there is no sense in spending the time or money in acquiring the software.

Q3. Can such a system be bought?
    a) Yes
    b) No
    c) Do not know
Reason: If the students cannot read the material, there is no sense in spending the time or money in acquiring the software.

Q4. How many students would have to share each computer in the class?
    a) Two or fewer
    b) Three or four
    c) Five or more
Reason: For computer-based instruction to be viable, there have to be enough computers to handle the student load.

Q5. Where will the software come from?
    a) It will have to be designed and created.
    b) It will be acquired.
Reason: If the software has to be created, someone has to do it. If it has to be acquired, money may have to be available and it must meet the instructional needs.

Q6. Are there people available with the skills to design and create the software?
    a) Yes
    b) No
Reason: Creating instructional software is a difficult process that is rarely successful unless carried out by experienced people.

Q7. Do these skilled people have the time to create your software?
    a) Yes
    b) No
Reason: If they do not have the time, they will not do what you want.

Q8. Do they have a copy of *Computer-Based Instruction: Methods and Development* or a similar CBI design textbook available?
    a) Yes
    b) No
Reason: Developers should always have the necessary resources available.

. . . And so on.

RULES:

Rules are also necessary. They combine the information from the questions to make decisions.

R1. IF Q1(a) AND Q2(a) AND Q3(b) THEN D2.
(This reads as follows: If Question 1 is answered with alternative a, and Question 2 with a, and Question 3 with b, then Decision 2 is taken.)
Reason: IF the materials are to be used by the teacher AND IF the equipment is not available to enable all students to read the screen AND IF such equipment cannot be bought, then do NOT use computer-based instruction in the course.

R2. IF Q1(a) AND Q2(a) AND Q3(a) THEN D3.
Note: There is no D3 in the list of Decisions. We call this an intermediate decision. It is used to make the Rules following more manageable (see Rule 5).
Reason: IF the materials are to be used by the teacher AND IF the equipment is not available so that all students can read the screen AND IF such equipment can be bought, THEN proceed with the questioning.

R3. IF Q1(a) AND Q2(a) THEN D4.
Reason: IF the materials are to be used by the teacher AND IF the equipment is available so that all students can read the screen, THEN proceed with the questioning.

R4. IF (D3 or D4) AND Q5(a) THEN D5.
Reason: IF either D3 or D4 is true (the material will be used by the teacher and the equipment exists or can be bought) AND the software will have to be created, THEN proceed with the questioning.

R5. IF Q1(b) AND Q4(a) THEN D5.
Reason: IF the material is to be used by students AND no more than two students will have to use a computer, THEN proceed with the questioning.

R6. IF D5 AND Q6(a) AND Q7(a) AND Q8(a) THEN D1.
Reason: IF D5 is true AND IF there are skilled people available to create the software AND IF they have the time AND IF they own a copy of this essential resource THEN you should go ahead and use computer-based instruction in the course.

R7. IF D5 AND Q6(a) AND Q7(a) AND Q8(b) THEN D2.
Reason: IF D5 is true AND IF there are people available with the skills to create the software AND IF they have the time AND IF they do NOT own a copy of this essential resource THEN you should NOT use computer-based instruction in the course (obviously the quality would not be good enough!).

R8. IF D5 AND Q6(a) AND Q7(b) THEN D2.
Reason: IF D5 is true AND IF there are skilled people available to create the software AND IF they do NOT have the time THEN you should NOT use computer-based instruction in the course.

. . . And so on.

Figure 15-1 An expert system for deciding when to use computer-based instruction.

expert systems have themselves become para-experts in the subject matter. It seems impossible to be involved extensively in the structuring of expert knowledge without oneself acquiring a substantial amount of expertness (Johnson, 1986). We think that this is a variation of the old saying: *"The best way to learn something is to teach it."*

Building Expert Systems as a Tool for Learning

This suggests a more immediate use of expert systems for instructional purposes which is both natural and promising (Starfield & Bleloch, 1983; Trollip & Lippert, 1987). We believe that it is possible to encourage learning by creating a constrained environment in which students construct expert systems in the content areas that they are attempting to learn. Since a working expert system can take tens of thousands of hours to build, we envisage a mini or prototype version that can be constructed in a matter of hours rather than years, and which avoids most of the time-consuming detail of a real-world counterpart.

This approach turns the student into a *knowledge engineer*—a person whose job it is to extract expertise from an expert and turn it into a form (the knowledge base) usable by a computer program that underlies an expert system (the shell). Instead of being tutored by a traditional or intelligent computer program, the students themselves create small knowledge bases for incorporation into a simple, existing program that is based on IF · THEN structures. Many commercial expert system shells are available for microcomputers such as the IBM-PC and the Macintosh. With an expert system shell, students need only enter questions, rules, and decisions into the program as text (like in our example earlier in the chapter) and the shell generates an operational expert system.

The resulting product may be thought of as a prototype expert system, whose expertise is very unrefined. In fact, the resulting system may exhibit no expertise whatsoever. It might have far less knowledge than the average expert, and may well have incorrect knowledge. But it is the process of *constructing* the knowledge base that is critical. Incorporating the knowledge base into an expert system shell, rather than just leaving it on paper, has additional benefits: It motivates the student to pay close attention to the fundamental relationships of the content domain; it permits easy testing of the internal validity of the knowledge base (such as that all questions are used or all rules reference questions that exist); and it allows easy refinement of all parts of the knowledge base. Our experience suggests that maximum benefit is obtained when students work on these prototype systems in teams (Trollip & Lippert, 1989).

An Example of Students Constructing an Expert System

Trollip and Lippert (1989) report a study conducted by Trollip in a class he taught on *Intelligent CAI*. Most students in the class were graduate students in the College of Education at the University of Minnesota who had a particular interest in instructional uses of computers. An assignment was given to create a prototype expert system to aid developers of CAI courseware in designing the layout of their title screen displays. The pedagogical purpose was to help the students develop an understanding of the major factors underlying screen design. It was not expected that any useful product would result that could actually be used by software developers.

Students in the class worked in groups of two or three and used the expert system shell described by Starfield and Bleloch (1983). Each group had to identify its own experts and resources, create its own knowledge base, and implement it using the shell. Before the projects were handed in, each "expert system" was demonstrated to the class. Finally, all students had to complete a questionnaire summarizing their attitudes and observations about the technique as an instructional tool.

There were six projects handed in. There was reasonable consistency across projects with respect to the expertise incorporated, although there was variability as to how well the knowledge base was implemented. Groups interviewed different numbers of experts, with most spending time with three or four. From these interviews and from reading the literature and testing various designs on subjects, about ten to fourteen variables appeared that affect the design of title pages.

Several characteristics surfaced about the process that appeared to be common to all projects. First, the projects generated a tremendous amount of peer interaction, not only in terms of dividing the work, but more so in debating how the gathered information could be summarized into useful rules. This intellectual interaction is a very positive attribute of this learning environment. Second, the assignment forced the students to evolve ways of extracting information from the experts. An expert may express preference for one design over another, but unless the reasons why can be elicited, it is almost impossible to incorporate this into a knowledge base.

A third characteristic became apparent while reviewing the assignments in class. Even though each team had spent many hours preparing its system, obvious discrepancies arose during the demonstration. This public airing of a system provides an opportunity for a group discussion and cross-fertilization of ideas not readily available through other means.

Everyone thought that constructing knowledge bases and implementing them is a viable instructional tool, although there was some disagreement as to whether it has universal applicability. The majority thought that it could definitely be used in high school, while there was uncertainty whether students below sixth grade would benefit from the approach. Questions were also raised as to whether weak students would have the diligence to complete such a task, even though everyone agreed that it is highly motivating (although sometimes frustrating when trying to condense the gathered information into well-formulated and sensible rules).

Advantages of Students Building Expert Systems

Among the aspects noted as being advantageous were that the process is highly motivating; that it forces interactions with an expert—in itself a valuable experience; it requires the formulation of good questions to ask of the expert, which means that careful thinking and planning is necessary; and it makes one distinguish between relevant and irrelevant information.

Among the disadvantages noted were that the process is initially so open-ended that it is frustrating not to know in which direction to go at first. In our opinion, this may be an advantage because the frustration lies in deciding how to approach the task and how to organize the information—both valuable pursuits. Other potential disadvantages are that it is easy to become side-tracked (a disadvantage from a time perspective, but interesting from a learning point of view); and that constraints in using the shell may detract from the content.

Everyone agreed that for the approach to be effective with school children, the teacher would have to provide initial instruction in how to use the shell, initial direction as to how to approach the project, and would have to be available to resolve difficulties or frustrations. Everyone also commented on the redundancy of information collected, but most felt that this is an advantage because it builds confidence in the knowledge being synthesized in the knowledge base and provides reinforcement in the direction being followed. Finally, all groups reported that they used pictorial representations of the information, such as decision tables and decision trees, to help them check their knowledge base, particularly when they were using the shell for verification.

Overall, all the students who participated in the class found the project to be very interesting and were optimistic about its potential use as a normal instructional activity. To quote one student:

> I really improved my reasoning skills with this project. It taught me how to think more clearly and logically, how to precisely lay out my thoughts in detail. In my team, we both noticed a change in our ways of thinking about halfway through working on the decision tree. Something just "clicked" that enabled us to really focus our attention.

Cautions for Students Building Expert Systems

Overall the project met expectations. From an instructor's perspective, it gave some insights into the strengths and benefits of the approach. The strengths are reflected above in the comments of the students, but it seems some caution needs to be observed. First, it is time consuming to construct even a prototype expert system of twelve to fifteen rules (groups report spending between twenty-five and forty hours total on the project). This means that the technique must be used sparingly. Second, the instructor must provide direction and be available to give support and advice. And third, the shell itself must be easy to use.

You may want to try this idea out by *completing* the knowledge base we started in Figure 15–1, on advising whether computer-based instruction should be used in a classroom. You will find the exercise highly instructive. If you can incorporate it into an expert system shell, you will be able to observe the entire process. That knowledge base was printed as a figure on facing pages for you to easily copy as a starting point for the exercise.

Expert Systems for Instructional Design

One other application of expert systems is worth mentioning. This is the development of an expert system to aid in instructional design. Although such an expert system is not currently available commercially, work is underway in several places that may soon result in benefits to the areas of instructional design and computer-based instruction. In Merrill's system (Merrill & Li, 1989), questions would be put to an instructional designer or content expert about the subject content, its organization, the characteristics of the students, the media available, the level of mastery required, and so on. Based on the answers to the questions and on the system's rules, advice would be given about instructional strategy, sequence, media, and so on. When complete, such systems should provide teachers with the same help that a program like *MYCIN* provides physicians.

Summary

Although it will be some time before large-scale expert systems become widespread in education, we believe that having students construct limited ones is an effective instructional technique. For the student, it affords the concrete opportunity not only to solve a problem in an interesting and relevant way, but simultaneously to witness and modify the process of solving the problem. The student can no longer operate by memory alone, plugging variables into memorized formula, basically solving problems by applying a recipe without critical analysis of the constraints and conditions of the problem. Students are actually forced into a critical appraisal of the features of the problem and their own cognitive resources that have bearing on the problem. The result is not only a refinement of stored knowledge, but a refinement of cognitive skills and the conscious awareness of their extent and limitations.

For the instructor, the construction of knowledge bases acts as a tool to explore the acquisition, organization, and utilization of knowledge by individual students. This diagnosis implies that the instructor is better able to assist and remedy learning where necessary. Moreover, overall pedagogy will also benefit because instructors will be better equipped to address the issues and processes students employ and will be aware of the inevitable discrepancies that become apparent and which need interpretation.

INSTRUCTIONAL MODELING

Traditional CBI

Traditional CBI programs (mostly of the tutorial, drill, simulation, or game varieties) embed their pedagogy within the content of the lesson. That is, very specific instructional techniques are selected and tailored to the particular content of the lesson. The most immediate result of this is that such lessons provide limited adaptation to student needs. If a foreign language vocabulary lesson uses a drill technique and a particular student is having trouble with that technique, the lesson is not likely to search for a different instructional approach. A live teacher, in contrast, seeing that a student is having trouble, might do any number of things to adapt: using analogies, switching to reading in context, or perhaps just taking a break. It is this human adaptability that some artificial intelligence techniques attempt to emulate in the traditional CBI methodologies discussed in Part 1 of this book. We agree with researchers who maintain that a primary goal of artificial intelligence techniques is to produce computer-based instruction that is more adaptive (Park, Perez, & Seidel, 1987).

Another result of the traditional CBI approach is that the instructional components (asking questions, permitting student control, giving hints) must be programmed anew for each lesson and changed considerably for each different subject area. In contrast, a live teacher does not need to relearn how to teach for each day's lesson. General techniques such as demonstrating, asking questions, answering student questions, giving hints, and making suggestions, are used by a teacher over and over for different content.

Artificial intelligence techniques aimed at making the computer act more like a live teacher should not only enhance lesson adaptability, but should enable good pedagogy, once programmed, to be reused in many different lessons.

Pedagogical Models

Pedagogical models are the first component needed to accomplish this. A pedagogical model is a computer program component that embodies rules for teaching in a more general fashion than does traditional CBI. This implies that the instructional strategies should not be bound to the content.

Examples of such general pedagogical rules are:

If the student makes an error, check the prerequisite knowledge.

If the student is not responding, ask if he or she is confused.

If the student is making lots of errors and has been working for more than thirty minutes, suggest taking a break.

If the student is doing very well, switch to more challenging material.

These are very general teaching rules. Much more specific ones are possible which are still not tied to specific content. For example:

If the student replies incorrectly to a foreign language question, ask to hear the original question restated to be sure it was understood.

If the student calculates an addition problem incorrectly, ask to see the solution one step at a time.

If the student solves a science problem incorrectly, ask for an identification of the known and unknown quantities.

A teacher, of course, embodies thousands of such general and specific rules. Programming them into a computer is very difficult, yet this is the goal of many intelligent CBI programs.

Although we say that such a pedagogical model should be independent of content, we know that this is an exaggeration. A teacher's own "rules of teaching" incorporate many exceptions that are tied to specific content and that do not work well with other content. For example, the use of analogies may work well for certain science concepts but not for foreign languages nor even for related math concepts. Rote learning may work well for addition facts, while an algorithmic approach works better for learning multiplication. Certain science principles may be best understood when learned by a discovery technique—a technique not likely to work well for English grammar. Still, a human teacher typically figures out these exceptions, using past knowledge from other teaching experiences, rather than being told them by someone else. Similarly, a pedagogical model should be able to "figure out" what to do when the existing rules don't work well.

So a teacher's behavior is not just a function of fixed rules. It is the result of adapting those rules to the current situation, which includes the specific content to be taught and the particular students learning it.

Student Models

The next necessary component of an intelligent instructional system is a *student model*, which represents the student's current understanding of the content. A traditional CBI program has a simple representation of student understanding, typically a record of questions answered correctly and incorrectly. A student model, rather than focusing just on the observable student performance, *infers* what aspects of the content the student understands (definitions, concepts, rules, principles, relationships), and perhaps how well they are understood. The model needs to be constantly updated based on new information because initial inferences may be wrong, and because as the student progresses his or her understanding will change.

The student model is a primary basis for decisions made by the rules embodied in the pedagogical model. Elements of the student model representing incomplete or incorrect understanding will cause rules for helping, clarifying, or repeating to be activated. Elements of the student model representing complete or correct understanding will activate rules for increasing complexity, switching to a new topic, ending the lesson, and so on.

Content Models

You may well ask how does the program assess the completeness and correctness of the student model? It requires something with which to compare the student model, namely, the *content model*. The content model is a third program component and represents an optimal representation of the content. It is usually a database of the facts, relationships, and overall organization of the content.

Content Structure

Different subject matter areas have different structures (Hannum, 1988). Two common types are the hierarchical and the network. A hierarchical organization is the common tree structure with multiple prerequisites for each higher level. In other words it is a structure of superordinate and subordinate relationships, as illustrated in Figure 15–2 for a topic in science, namely the classification

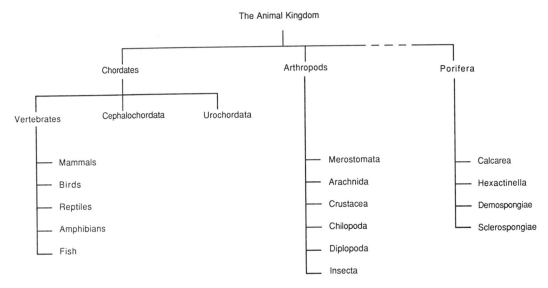

Figure 15-2 Hierarchical organization: Partial hierarchy in a science topic—classification of animals.

of living organisms. Only a small part of the hierarchy is shown. The complete hierarchy would consume several pages.

A network structure is shown in Figure 15–3 for a topic in art, the paintings of Vincent Van Gogh. Again, only a small portion of the content is shown, including only fourteen of Van Gogh's several hundred works. A complete network representing all of Van Gogh's work and related aspects of his life would consume many pages. Rather than a neat structure where each piece of information connects to a few superordinate and subordinate areas, any piece of information in the semantic network (typically called a *node*) may connect to many others with lines representing their *relationships*. In Figure 15–3, the periods of the artist's life and work (the Dutch Period, the Paris Period, and so on) are connected by lines indicating temporal relationships. Any particular picture, such as *Peasant Cottages,* is connected to a period with the relationship that it was a picture completed during that period. A picture may be related to many other things. In this network, *Peasant Cottages* is related to the node *scenes,* indicating it is one of many Van Gogh pictures depicting a scene, such as landscapes. There are many other nodes to which *Peasant Cottages* might be connected, indicating the date it was completed, the art materials used, what Van Gogh said about it in his letters, and so on.

Depicting Content and Its Structure in the Computer

Subject-matter content may be stored in a computer in many ways. The hierarchically organized content may be stored as a database with the common outline format, as in Figure 15–4. The network may be stored as a partial matrix

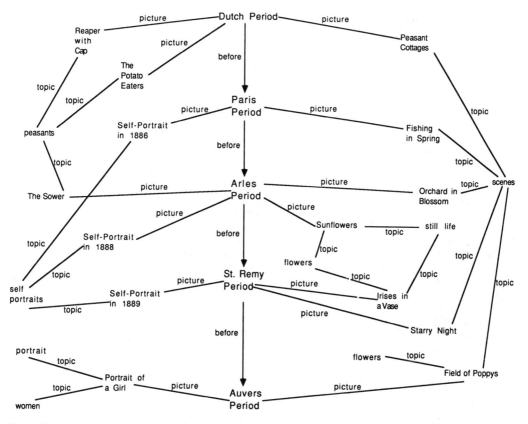

Figure 15-3 Semantic network organization: Partial network on the art of Vincent Van Gogh.

with the rows and columns describing the information and the cells describing the relationships between any two pieces of information, as shown in Figure 15-5 for a small portion of the Van Gogh network.

You should not necessarily equate these content models with the expert systems discussed in the previous section. Although some researchers have used expert systems as the content model in a lesson, typically the content model is greatly simplified. It usually represents the content as we can reasonably expect the novice student to understand it, rather than as we expect the expert to understand it.

Depicting Student Knowledge in the Computer

Given some such database representing the optimal form of the knowledge, the student model contains a database of similar form but different contents. That is, for the art network represented in Figures 15-3 and 15-5, the data in a corresponding student model, for a student who has just begun studying the lesson, might look like Figure 15-6. Note that some relationships in the content

The Animal Kingdom - Classification by Phylums

Chordates
  Subphylums
    Urochordata
    Cephalochordata
    Vertebrates
  Classes
    Agnatha
    Chondrichthyes
    Osteichthyes
    Amphibians
    Reptiles
    Birds
    Mammals
Arthropods
  Description
    segmented bodies and
    exoskeletons
  Classes
    Merostomata
    Arachnida
    Crustacea
    Chilopoda
    Diplopoda
    Insecta
Porifera
  Description
    sponges and similar aquatic
    species
  Classes
    Calcarea
    Hexactinella
    Demospongiae
    Sclerospongiae
Coelenterates
  Description
    aquatic, radially symmetric
  Classes
    Hydrozoa
    Scyphozoa
    Anthozoa
    Ctenophora
Platyhelminthes
  Description
    flatworms, bilateral symmetry
  Classes
    Turbellaria
    Trematoda
    Cestoda

Nematoda
  Description
    roundworms
Nematomorpha
  Description
    horsehair worms, parasitic
Acanthocephala
  Description
    spiny-headed worms, parasitic
Rotifers
  Description
    animals shaped like wheels
Bryozoa
  Description
    microscopic aquatic animals in
    colonies
Brachiopoda
  Description
    lamp-shells, two-shelled
    animals
Mollusks
  Description
    soft bodied, aquatic, shells
  Classes
    Pelecypoda
    Gastropoda
    Cephalopoda
    Scaphopoda
    Polyplacophora
Annelida
  Description
    segmented worms
  Classes
    Oligochaeta
    Hirudinea
    Polychaeta
Echinoderms
  Description
    symmetric marine animals with
    endoskeleton
  Classes
    Crinoidea
    Asteroidea
    Ophiuroidea
    Echinoidea
    Holothuroidea
Hemicordata
  Description
    acorn worms

Figure 15-4 Outline representing the content model for the science topic in Figure 15–2.

	Dutch	Paris	Cottages	Sunflowers	Landscape
Dutch					
Paris	followed				
Cottages	during	before			
Sunflowers	followed	followed	not related		
Landscape	common during	common during	theme of	not related	
Still Life	not common during	not common during	not related	theme of	some theme overlap

Figure 15-5   A partial matrix representing the *content model* from Figure 15-3.

	Dutch	Paris	Cottages	Sunflowers	Landscape
Dutch					
Paris	?				
Cottages	during	?			
Sunflowers	not covered	not covered	?		
Landscape	common in	?	theme of	?	
Still Life	?	common in	?	not covered	?

Figure 15-6   The *student model* corresponding to the content of Figure 15-3.

model (shown by question marks) are missing in the student model, meaning that the student is unaware of them. Some of the relationships in the student model are different, indicating misunderstanding or partial understanding of the information. In many cases the program has indicated that a particular relationship has not yet been covered.

The student model is more than just this database. It includes the program that operates on the database, modifying it based on student performance to reflect (by inference) what the student does and does not understand. If, for example, the student is asked a question in the art lesson about *Sunflowers* and answers with, "It was painted during the Paris Period," the program might insert "during" into the cell connecting Paris and Sunflowers. This is wrong, of course, so some mark might also be included in that cell to represent a misunderstanding.

The Task of a Pedagogical Model

With the content model and the student model having very similar formats (in fact, the student model may simply be additional numbers or pointers added to or overlaid on the content model), the task of the pedagogical model becomes much clearer. It constantly compares the content and student models and where it finds differences, chooses among its tool-kit of instructional techniques to remedy the deficiency. Such a process is not trivial for there will typically be many points of difference between the two models, and the pedagogical model must decide, at any time, what difference to attend to and how to deal with it.

Structure of an Intelligent CBI Program

Putting this all together, the flowchart in Figure 15–7 represents the general structure of an intelligent CBI program. Our example (not every such program will follow the same structure) is composed of four basic modules which are performed in a repeating cycle with input and output from several databases.

The *executive* module oversees the other programs and calls each when needed. Typically it will call them in a repeating cycle. It begins and ends student sessions and arranges data storage and retrieval. It may permit special functions for teachers, such as being able to go through the lesson in review mode (so the teacher can familiarize him or herself with the lesson). It may also be responsible for refining any of the databases and their structure (Park et. al., 1987, pp. 37).

The *analysis* module compares the student and content databases, looking for and analyzing differences. Differences may reflect partial student

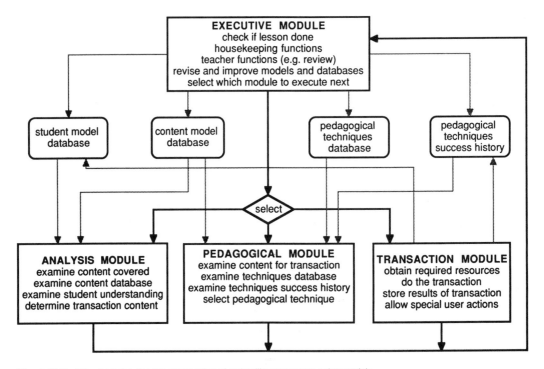

Figure 15-7 Flowchart showing the organization of an intelligent program using models.

knowledge, incorrect knowledge, or student knowledge better than that of the content model.

The *pedagogical* module selects a course of action based on the results of the preceding analysis. To do this it may examine a database of available subject matter content (such as text, questions, and pictures), a database of available pedagogical techniques (for example: give the student some information, ask the student a question, or let the student make a choice), and a database showing the history of success of the various techniques for this student.

The *transaction* module engages in some input or output function based on the results of the analysis and pedagogical modules. It may present new information, review information, require student interaction, ask if the student is confused, give advice to the student, or change topics. The transaction module may also store information about the transaction, update the student model, and permit special student actions such as requests to temporarily end or return to the lesson menu.

Research in Intelligent CBI

Having looked briefly at how intelligent CBI (more often called ICAI, for Intelligent Computer-Assisted Instruction) works, we turn now to some of the work of major researchers in this area.

Burton and Brown (1982) propose that there are two broad types of intelligent computer-based instruction programs: the "black-box" method, and the "glass-box" or "articulate" method. In the former, the program evaluates what the student produces rather than how the outcome was reached. In the latter, the program is as concerned with how the student reaches a conclusion as with the conclusion itself.

SOPHIE—*Black-box Technique*

A typical "black-box" program is *SOPHIE-I* (Brown, Burton, & DeKleer, 1982). In this program the student is given a simulated piece of electronic equipment that is malfunctioning. The student must diagnose the problem by taking appropriate measures or by asking specific questions. The system is designed to answer hypothetical questions about the system such as "What would be the output voltage if the beta of Q3 were 8?" In this case, the system has to set the value of Q3 to the hypothetical one and calculate the appropriate output. For this to be meaningful, the program must have a built-in "expert" that evaluates the system under the given conditions and ensures that the generated output is realistic (that is, it would not have blown up some component).

The system is also designed to evaluate hypotheses. To do this, the system has to keep track of all the measurements made by the student so that it can evaluate whether a hypothesis is rational given these measurements or merely a wild guess. Furthermore it can generate its own hypotheses about potential faults. The student using *SOPHIE-I* is given feedback about the system, but no information about how it was determined. This is because the computer model of the circuit is unlike the one a human would build.

WEST—Glass-box Technique

The "glass-box" approach maintains that it is more powerful not only to provide the student information about hypotheses and answers to queries, but also to give insights into why particular problems are arising. An example of this approach is the work of Burton and Brown (1982) on the program *How the West Was Won* described in Chapter 5. They called their program *WEST*.

A drawback of the original program, *How the West Was Won,* is that it gives the student no direct feedback as to the usefulness of strategies and no instruction on how to play the game better. Burton and Brown put it this way:

> One of the prerequisites for a productive informal learning environment is that it be made enticing to the student by enabling him to control it. The student must have the freedom to make decisions (incorrect as well as correct ones) and observe their results. While a student's incorrect decisions sometimes lead to erroneous results that he can immediately detect, they often produce symptoms that are beyond his ability to recognize. For an informal environment to be fully effective as a learning activity, it often must be augmented by tutorial guidance that recognizes and explains weaknesses in the student's decisions or suggests ideas when the student appears to have none (p. 79).

What Burton and Brown wanted the program to achieve is a balance between saying too much, thus diminishing the student's processing of the knowledge or information, and letting the student pursue an erroneous line of reasoning too far. Furthermore, the coaching should not detract from the enjoyment of the game. To accomplish all of this requires the program to determine what the student knows, when to interrupt, and what to say. They called the part of the program which does this the *Coach,* because it acts like a sports coach, observing the players and giving occasional advice on how to improve.

The Coach developed for *WEST* was based on the idea of *Issues* and *Examples.* Issues are concepts used by the Coach to determine what is relevant at the current stage of the game. Examples are specific instances of these concepts. The underlying belief is that the best chance of improving a student's skill is to illustrate instructional advice with concrete examples. There are three levels of Issues: mathematical skills, rules and strategies particular to *WEST,* and skills relevant to game playing, such as learning from one's opponent. Most of the data on which the Coach bases its decisions come from a comparison of what the player does with what an expert would do in the same circumstances. Thus *WEST* contains not only a representation of expert knowledge, but also the tutorial expertise to use the information productively.

When *WEST* was evaluated against *How the West Was Won,* its traditional progenitor, it was found that students using *WEST* displayed a greater variety of patterns in their mathematical expressions, and, moreover, enjoyed the game more.

The type of tutoring accomplished by *WEST* can be seen in a growing number of other programs as well. Among the best known are *ACE* (Sleeman & Hendley, 1982), which analyzes student explanations of solutions; *SPADE,* a program for debugging programs (Miller, 1982); *WHY,* which teaches the causes of rainfall (Stevens, Collins, & Goldin, 1982); and *BUGGY,* a program that diagnoses students' misconceptions of arithmetic skills (Brown & Burton, 1978).

SCHOLAR

Carbonell's *SCHOLAR* program (Carbonell, 1970) was an early attempt to include modeling of the content. The program incorporates a semantic network of the geography of South America. This network comprises an array of elements linked by clearly specified relationships. So Argentina would be a sub-concept of country, be located in South America, have latitude limits of 22 and 55 degrees south, and so on. Similarly, country would be a sub-concept of states, be part of a continent, and so on.

The program is written in such a way that if the student asks "What is the latitude of Argentina?" the program will locate the element *Argentina,* find the relationship *latitude,* and present the value of the element linked with that relationship: in this case 22 to 55 degrees south. As long as the appropriate relationships between elements exist, the program is capable of responding to unanticipated inputs from the student. Modern programs that provide the student this level of interaction, much like a traditional Socratic Dialog, are called *mixed initiative tutors* (Kearsley, 1987). Mixed initiative tutors usually depend on the student being able to interact easily with natural language. This brings us to the last area of artificial intelligence we will discuss.

Summary

Research into *intelligent* systems has produced valuable insights into the problems of learning and instruction, and hence should be actively pursued. However, the development of even a single intelligent instructional program currently requires an enormous amount of effort and a diversity of talents, and hence is unlikely to be undertaken by most people. While we believe that research and development on artificial intelligence techniques is important, we doubt such techniques will be widely used in the *near* future because of the efforts required to produce them and to integrate them into normal instruction.

NATURAL LANGUAGE UNDERSTANDING

The oldest and perhaps most controversial area of artificial intelligence is natural language comprehension. Through most of the history of computers, researchers have tried to program them to understand what we say or write and be able to respond in intelligible language, either written or spoken. We say the area is controversial for several reasons. Despite the promises and predictions of computer scientists, progress on natural language comprehension has been slow. Some have argued that it may never be done well at all. Others question whether success will be good for or detrimental to society and human-kind.

Although there are four general areas of natural language computing (speech input, text input, speech output, and text output), we are concerned here with only the first two, which constitute computer understanding of language. The latter two are far easier and although progress is still needed, language output even on microcomputers is rapidly improving.

Computer Comprehension of Text

Computer comprehension of text is the easier of the two input modes. It is easy for a computer to process text, that is, to parse text into words and phrases. But recognition and simple processing of text is very different from understanding it. As an example, consider a computer processing the sentence, "He was ill because he ate to much at dinner." The reader may immediately notice a spelling error, the use of *to* instead of *too*. This is easy because the reader understands the meaning, namely, that the amount eaten was *more than appropriate*. A computer is easily programmed to recognize all the words and even to check that they are all valid English words, by looking them up in a dictionary database. But to detect the to/too error, the computer must understand the meaning, not just the surface form. Even though natural text input is easy at the level of word recognition and look-up, programming understanding remains very difficult. The programmer must include understanding of *context* in a natural language program, as well as *general knowledge of the world,* recognition of a very large number of words and phrases, relationships of words such as synonyms, antonyms, and so on.

Computer Comprehension of Speech

Computer comprehension of spoken language is far more difficult. In addition to the programming difficulties discussed above, it is hard just to program the computer to detect and parse spoken words and phrases. The speech patterns (accents, pronunciation, speech rate) of individuals vary considerably. At an even more basic level, the pauses between words are so short that it is often difficult to differentiate individual words. Lastly, while text is more permanent and a computer may process it as much as necessary, speech is transitory, and the computer must detect and process it at the rate it is spoken.

Despite these difficulties, much research has occurred and still is occurring in the area of natural language understanding. This is because it is an area of interest to almost all users of computers. Business, industry, and government all have considerable interest in natural language capabilities for computers. They have the funds to spend on research in this area, and education will benefit from the results.

Benefits

How will natural language benefit computer-based instruction? It would seem obvious, initially, that all CBI methodologies would benefit from natural language input. First, the quality of computer-directed interactions could be greatly improved. Methodologies using questions posed to the student would be able to ask questions requiring entire sentences as answers, and would be able to make adequate judgments as to the adequacy of the answers. True Socratic tutoring would be possible, in which the student is not *told* information but *discusses* it with the tutor. Secondly, student-directed interactions would become feasible. Perhaps most important in this regard, the student would be able to ask questions of the computer, just as a student may do of a live teacher.

Problems

These advantages may not be the only result of natural language capabilities in CBI. With natural language comes ambiguity. People often misunderstand one another. Forsaking the constrained language of computers for natural language may result in more occasions where the computer misjudges a student response or misunderstands the nature of a student's question. Just as some people have a tendency to be unnecessarily wordy when talking, natural language with computers may encourage students (and someday computers) to start "rattling on" (Dear, 1987). At a more pragmatic level, encouraging the development and use of natural language in CBI will force educational institutions to purchase more expensive computer equipment that has the power needed to deliver such instruction. In the short term, this may be more detrimental to the use of computers in schools than more traditional CBI.

Authoring Tools

It is not the place of this, an introductory book on computer-based instruction, to discuss the techniques of natural language understanding in a computer program. Indeed, the methods are extremely complex. They will only become widely used when programming tools, especially authoring systems, come with the capability built-in. It will be some time before this is the case. The reader should not confuse the "answer-judging" capabilities of authoring languages and systems with natural language understanding. Although sometimes advertised as such, the answer judging of current authoring tools is not true language understanding.

Authoring tools may permit the developer to specify lists of synonymous words, may ignore word order or capitalization, and may ignore minor spelling errors. But in general, all require that the author do a fairly complete job of predicting and entering the responses a student may make. Some use tricks that allow the author to make it look like the program understands what the student has typed. But the flexibility of responding appropriately to a wide variety of reasonable answers is almost always missing. Current authoring tools essentially do pattern matching with a few rules for substitution, ignoring of specified character strings, and modification of the strings to be compared. Programs which understand language not only do pattern matching, but also syntactic analysis (categorizing parts of speech, tense, mode, and so on) and semantic analysis (identifying the meaning of the words).

Summary

Despite these doubts, we are confident that in the future researchers will be successful, and that *someday* it will be easy to develop CBI with natural language capability, both textual and spoken. Recognizing that the day will someday come, we feel compelled to end this chapter by posing a philosophical question. Are artificial intelligence techniques, natural language understanding in particular, really in the best interest of human development?

On the negative side of this argument is the contention that computers are intellectual crutches. If computers can speak to us, they can read to us, and people may no longer have a reason to learn to read. If we can speak to computers, we can dictate to them while they type, and people will no longer need to learn how to write. This argument can be extended to mathematics and the sciences without much difficulty. If computers do our thinking for us, will we become weaker intellectually, just as a person who continues using a crutch too long finds that the leg muscles atrophy through disuse?

On the positive side is the counter-argument that there are always greater intellectual challenges before us, and that as computers free us from each successive intellectual task, we have the time to tackle new and greater tasks. We leave it to the reader to ponder these issues, the answer to which may represent a great intellectual challenge, one which will affect the future of humanity.

CONCLUSION

We have ended this book with chapters on *Computer-Managed Instruction, Interactive Video,* and *Artificial Intelligence and Instruction.* These represent three aspects of computer-based instruction that will become increasingly prevalent in the future. We purposefully placed them after the basic methodologies and the instructional design model because we believe it is essential to have a good grasp of the fundamentals of the field before venturing into these more difficult areas.

We have written this book based on the assumption that successful computer-based instruction requires both a knowledge of the methodologies available and a methodical approach to the instructional design process. We also believe that the path to success is a developmental one of building on prior knowledge and experience. Tutorials, drills, simulations, instructional games, and tests are the foundations of computer-based instruction, and novice instructional designers should gain experience by designing and implementing several of these before attempting projects that are more ambitious. In fact, producing tutorial instruction first will provide a solid basis for designing all other methodologies, such as simulations or games.

In addition to having a firm grasp of all the methodologies, you should use a methodical approach to design the instruction. The model we propose in Part 2 of the book offers one such model. It has been tested and has worked successfully for many people. It is a simple model that provides all the essential elements for designing effective instruction. We do not regard it as being rigid, but rather a good set of guidelines that can be molded to suit each designer's environment. If you are a novice, use the model as it is for a few projects and then amend it as appropriate. If you are an experienced designer, we hope that it provides insights and enhances the model you are currently using.

Computer-based instruction is an exciting and volatile approach to education. On the one hand, it has the potential of providing poor instruction at great cost. We hope that our model's systematic approach to design and implementation will prevent this from happening. On the other hand, computer-based instruction also has great potential for improving instruction. We hope that the ideas and issues we have raised in this book will help you realize this potential.

REFERENCES AND BIBLIOGRAPHY

BEGG, I.M., & HOGG, I. (1987). Authoring systems for ICAI. In G. Kearsley, (Ed.), *Artificial Intelligence and Instruction: Applications and Methods.* Reading, MA: Addison-Wesley.

BROWN, J.S., & BURTON, R.R. (1978). Diagnostic models for procedural bugs in basic mathematical skills. *Cognitive Science, 2,* 155–192.

BROWN, J.S., BURTON, R.R., & DEKLEER, J. (1982). Pedagogical, natural language and knowledge engineering techniques in SOPHIE I, II, and III. In D. Sleeman and J.S. Brown (Eds.), *Intelligent Tutoring Systems.* New York: Academic Press.

BUCHANAN, B.G., & SHORTLIFFE, E.H. (1984). *Rule-based Expert Systems: The MYCIN Experiments of the Stanford Heuristic Programming Project.* Reading, MA: Addison-Wesley.

BURTON, R.R., & BROWN, J.S. (1982). An investigation of computer coaching for informal learning activities. In D. Sleeman and J.S. Brown (Eds.), *Intelligent Tutoring Systems.* New York: Academic Press.

CARBONNEL, J.R. (1970). AI in CAI: An artificial intelligence approach to computer assisted instruction. *IEEE Transactions on Man-Machine Systems, 11,* 190–202.

CLANCY, W.J. (1979). Tutoring rules for guiding a case method dialogue. *International Journal of Man-Machine Studies, 11,* 25–49.

CLANCY, W.J. (1983). The epistemology of a rule-based expert system: A framework for explanation. *Artificial Intelligence, 20,* 215–251.

DEAR, B.L. (1987). AI and the authoring process. *IEEE Expert, 2*(2), 17–24.

DEDE, C., & SWIGGER, K. (1988). The evolution of instructional design principles for intelligent computer-assisted instruction. *Journal of Instructional Development, 11*(1), 15–22.

HANNUM, W. (1988). Designing courseware to fit subject matter structure. In D.H. Jonassen (Ed.), *Instructional Designs for Microcomputer Courseware.* Hillsdale, NJ: Lawrence Erlbaum.

HAYES-ROTH, B., & THORNDYKE, P.W. (1985). Paradigms for intelligent systems. *Educational Psychologist, 20*(4), 231–241.

Building Expert Systems. Reading, MA: Addison-Wesley.

JOHNSON, P.E. (1986, February). Cognitive models of expertise (Technical Report). *Symposium on Expert Systems and Auditor Judgment,* University of Southern California.

KEARSLEY, G. (1987). *Artificial Intelligence and Instruction: Applications and Methods.* Reading, MA: Addison-Wesley.

KEARSLEY, G. (1988). Authoring systems for intelligent tutoring systems on personal computers. In D.H. Jonassen (Ed.), *Instructional Designs for Microcomputer Courseware.* Hillsdale, NJ: Lawrence Erlbaum.

HAYES-ROTH, F., WATERMAN, D.A., & LENAT, D.B. (Eds.). (1983). *Building Expert Systems.* Reading, MA: Addison-Wesley.

JOHNSON, P.E. (1986, February). Cognitive models of expertise (Technical Report). *Symposium on Expert Systems and Auditor Judgment,* University of Southern California.

KEARSLEY, G. (Ed.). (1987). *Artificial Intelligence and Instruction: Applications and Methods.* Reading, MA: Addison-Wesley.

KEARSLEY, G. (1988). Authoring systems for intelligent tutoring systems on personal computers. In D.H. Jonassen (Ed.), *Instructional Designs for Microcomputer Courseware.* Hillsdale, NJ: Lawrence Erlbaum.

LAWLER, R.W., & YAZDANI, M. (1987). *Artificial Intelligence and Education, Volume 1.* Norwood, NJ: Ablex Publishing.

MERRILL, M.D., & LI, Z. (1989). An instructional design expert system. *Journal of Computer-Based Instruction, 16*(3), 95–101.

MILLER, M.L. (1982). A structured planning and debugging environment for elementary programming. In D. Sleeman and J.S. Brown (Eds.), *Intelligent Tutoring Systems.* New York: Academic Press.

PARK, O-C., PEREZ, R.S., & SEIDEL, R.J. (1987). Intelligent CAI: Old wine in new bottles, or a new vintage? In G. Kearsley, (Ed.), *Artificial Intelligence and Instruction: Applications and Methods.* Reading, MA: Addison-Wesley.

QUILLIAN, M.R. (1969). The teachable language comprehender. *Communications of the ACM, 12,* 459–476.

SCHANK, R.C., & CHILDERS, P.G. (1984). *The Cognitive Computer.* Reading, MA: Addison-Wesley.

SELF, J. (Ed.). (1988). *Artificial Intelligence and Human Learning: Intelligent Computer-Aided Instruction.* London: Chapman and Hall.

SHORTLIFFE, E.H. (1976). *Computer-Based Medical Consultations: MYCIN.* New York: American Elsevier.

SLEEMAN, D., & BROWN, J.S. (Eds.). (1982). *Intelligent Tutoring Systems.* New York: Academic Press.

SLEEMAN, D., & HENDLEY, R.J. (1982). ACE: A system which analyses complex explanations. In D. Sleeman and J.S. Brown (Eds.), *Intelligent Tutoring Systems.* New York: Academic Press.

STARFIELD, A.M., & BLELOCH, A.L. (1983). Expert systems: An approach to problems in ecological management that are difficult to quantify. *International Journal of Environmental Management,* pp. 261–268.

STARFIELD, A.M., SMITH, K.A., & BLELOCH, A.L. (1990). *How to Model It: Problem Solving for the Computer Age.* New York: McGraw-Hill.

STEVENS, A., COLLINS, A., & GOLDIN, S.E. (1979). Misconceptions in students' understanding. *International Journal of Man-Machine Studies, 11,* 145–156.

TROLLIP, S.R., & LIPPERT, R.C. (1987). Constructing knowledge bases: A promising instructional tool. *Journal of Computer-Based Instruction, 14,* 44–48.

TROLLIP, S.R., & LIPPERT, R.C. (1989). Constructing knowledge bases: A process for instruction. In P.A. Hancock & M.H. Chignell (Eds.), *Intelligent Interfaces.* Amsterdam: North Holland.

WENGER, E. (1987). *Artificial Intelligence and Tutoring Systems: Computational and Cognitive Approaches to the Communication of Knowledge.* Los Altos, CA: Morgan Kaufman.

WOOLF, B., & CUNNINGHAM, P.A. (1987). Multiple knowledge sources in intelligent teaching systems. *IEEE Expert, 2*(2), 41–54.

APPENDIX A

SUMMARY OF INSTRUCTIONAL FACTORS

FACTORS IN TUTORIALS

INTRODUCTION:
Title page
Presenting objectives
Directions
Stimulating prior knowledge
Pretesting

STUDENT CONTROL:
More control for adults
Global controls
Menus and termination
Mouse control

MOTIVATION:
Intrinsic vs. extrinsic
Challenge
Curiosity
Imagery and fantasy
Control
Attention
Relevance
Confidence
Success and satisfaction
Motivation in moderation

PRESENTATION OF INFORMATION:
Mode of presentation
Length of presentation
Text layout
Graphics and animation

Color
Focusing attention
Text quality
Text organization
Instructional prompts
Providing help

QUESTIONS AND RESPONSES:
Frequency of questions
Type of questions
Quality of questions
Graphics in questions
Relevance of questions
Placement of questions
Mode of response
Response economy
Response prompt

JUDGING RESPONSES:
Intelligent judging
Type of answer
Length
Time limits
Help and escape options

PROVIDING FEEDBACK:
Positive and corrective
Timing of feedback
Text feedback
Graphic feedback

477

Error-contingent feedback
Subsequent attempts

RREMEDIATION TECHNIQUES:
Repetition
Restatement
New information
Increased detail
More practice
Assignment to other media

SEQUENCING LESSON SEGMENTS:
Linear lessons
Branching lessons

Assessing student level
Restarting
Student control of sequence

CLOSING OF A TUTORIAL:
Temporary termination
Permanent termination
The final message
Exiting the program

FACTORS IN DRILLS

INTRODUCTION:
Title page
Objectives
Directions
Initial student control

ITEM CHARACTERISTICS:
Item type
Graphics in items
Item difficulty
Pacing
Item quality
Color
Item list selection
Item generation by an algorithm

ITEM-SELECTION PROCEDURE:
Random selection
Flashcard queuing
Variable interval performance queuing
Retirement criteria
Termination criteria
Resurrection
Restarting

RESPONSE CHARACTERISTICS:
Response type
Response prompt

Response economy
Provision for help requests
Provision for termination

JUDGING RESPONSES:
Intelligent judging
Type of answer
Length
Time limits
Help and escape options

FEEDBACK:
Positive and corrective
Text feedback
Graphic feedback
Timing of feedback
Error-contingent feedback

ITEM-GROUPING PROCEDURES:
Grouping into subdrills
Group selection in a session
Review from past subdrills
Endless continuum technique

MOTIVATING THE STUDENT:
Competition
Color, pictures, and sound
Setting goals and scoring

Adjunct reinforcement
Session length

DATA STORAGE:
For item selection
For item retirement
For drill termination
For restarting
For reporting student progress

FACTORS IN SIMULATIONS

TYPES OF SIMULATIONS:
Physical
Process
Procedural
Situational

INTRODUCTION TO THE SIMULATION:
Title page
Objectives
Directions
Opening

THE UNDERLYING MODEL:
Fidelity
Objects
Precision
Sequence
Number of solutions
Time frame
Location of the user
Primary actor/reactor

PRESENTATIONS:
Mode
Type
Fidelity

STUDENT ACTIONS:
Fidelity
Visual or conceptual
Frequency
Choices

For class comparisons
For drill evaluation

LESSON CLOSING:
Temporary termination
Permanent termination
Data storage
Final message
Exiting the program

Objects to manipulate
Events to react to
Systems to investigate

FEEDBACK:
Natural or artificial
Immediate or delayed

SEQUENCE:
Linear
Cyclic
Complex

STUDENT CONTROL:
Initial choices
Returning to choices
Seeing directions
Internal restarts
Termination
Restarts after termination

COMPLETION OF THE SIMULATION:
Different for different simulation types
Success or failure
Student choice to rerun

TERMINATION OF THE SIMULATION:
Temporary termination
Permanent termination
Data storage
Final message
Exiting the program

FACTORS IN GAMES

MAJOR CHARACTERISTICS:
Goals
Rules
Competition
Challenge
Fantasy
Safety
Entertainment

TYPES OF GAMES:
Adventure
Arcade
Board
Card or gambling
Combat
Logic
Psychomotor
Role-playing
TV quiz
Word

INTRODUCTION OF THE GAME:
Goal
Rules
Players
Equipment
Procedures
Constraints

Penalties
Directions
Choices

THE BODY OF THE GAME:
Scenario
Level of reality
Cast
Roles of players
Uncertainty
Curiosity
Competition
Relationship of learning to goals
Skill vs. chance
Wins and losses
Choices
Information flow
Turns
Action types
Modes of interaction
Graphics

CONCLUSION:
Recognizing the winner
Rewards
Providing information
Final message
Exiting the program

FACTORS IN TESTS

BEFORE THE TEST: STUDENT
Easy access to information
   directions on computer use
   directions for the test
   restrictions
   content of the test
Maximizing user control
   chance to practice
   control of progress
   test initiation
Safety nets and barriers
   errors difficult to make
   recovery after errors

DURING THE TEST: STUDENT
Easy access to information
   directions
   items
   unanswered items
   items to be reviewed
   time remaining
   freedom to respond or not
   marking items to review
   changing responses
   leaving comments
Maximizing user control
   examinee controls progress

terminating the test
recovery from termination
Safety nets and barriers
errors difficult to make
recovery after errors

AFTER THE TEST: STUDENT

Easy access to information
results
feedback on results
how to leave the system
returning to see results
printed results
further information

BEFORE THE TEST: INSTRUCTOR

Easy access to information
access to test
number of questions
passing score
time limit
order of items
Maximizing user control
changes should be easy
Safety nets and barriers
errors difficult to make
recovery after errors

DURING THE TEST: INSTRUCTOR

Easy access to information
monitoring capability
examinee cheating
termination recovery
Maximizing user control
changes should be easy
Safety nets and barriers
errors difficult to make
recovery after errors

AFTER THE TEST: INSTRUCTOR

Easy access to information
results
test data
student comments
printouts
security of results
privacy of results
data manipulation
data deletion
data display format
Maximizing user control
changes should be easy
Safety nets and barriers
errors difficult to make
recovery after errors

APPENDIX B

QUALITY REVIEW CHECKLIST

PART 1: LANGUAGE AND GRAMMAR

Feature	Display Number	Comments
1.1 Reading level Is it appropriate for the students? Is it appropriate for the content? Is it consistent throughout?		
1.2 Cultural bias Is culturally biased language avoided? Are culturally biased references or examples avoided?		
1.3 Technical terms and jargon Are they relevant? Are they explained? Are abbreviations used appropriately?		
1.4 Spelling, grammar, punctuation Are they correct? Are they consistent?		
1.5 Spacing Are page breaks at good points? Are sentence and paragraph styles consistent? Is hyphenation appropriate? Are margins appropriate and consistent?		

PART 2:   SURFACE FEATURES

Feature	Display Number	Comments
2.1 Displays Are they uncluttered? Is overwriting avoided? Are they aesthetic? Do they maintain attention to important information?		
2.2 Presentation modes Is text used appropriately? Are graphics used appropri- ately? Is color used appropriately? Is sound used appropriately?		
2.3 Text quality Does text scroll? Is text lean? Is text layout attractive? Are type styles always easy to read?		

2.4 Input
Are input devices appropriate?
Are there keyboard equiva-
    lents for touch input?
Is input efficient?
Do input methods prevent or
    detect errors?		

2.5 On completion
Is the lesson end indicated?
Is student taken to correct
    place?
Is student given appropri-
    ate credit?		

PART 3: QUESTIONS AND MENUS

Feature	Display Number	Comments
3.1 Menus Is orienting information included? Is it clear how to make a choice? It is clear how to fix an incorrect choice? Are completed sections indicated?		
3.2 Questions Are they relevant? Are they well spaced? Is response economy promoted? Is comprehension emphasized? Are there a variety of types? Is placement before or after content appropriate?		
3.3 Answering questions Is is clear how to respond? Can input be corrected? Can the answer be requested? Can help be requested? Is more than one try allowed? Is there a way to leave the question without answering?		
3.4 Format of feedback Is feedback given? Does it attract attention? Is it erased when no longer relevant? Is it the appropriate type (text, graphic, markup, or sound)?		
3.5 Quality of feedback Is it supportive? Is it corrective? Is it clear? Is it answer contingent? Does it identify discrimination errors? Is response judging intelligent?		

PART 4: OTHER ISSUES OF PEDAGOGY

Feature	Display Number	Comments
4.1 General Is the computer appropriate? Is the methodology appropriate? Are directions available and clear? Is information in appropriate size chunks? Is spaced practice encouraged? Is lesson length appropriate? Is mastery level appropriate? Does lesson adapt to the learner?		
4.2 Student control Does student determine pace? Can the student review? Are temporary termination and bookmarks available? Are there safety nets and barriers? Are directions available? Is help available? Can student leave comments? Is inappropriate control avoided?		

4.3 Motivation
Is motivation intrinsic?
Is computer anxiety minimized?
Is challenge appropriate?
Are curiosity, confidence, and
    satisfaction maintained?
Is competition appropriate?
Is motivation balanced with
    other instructional factors?		

4.4 Interactions Is interaction frequent? Is comprehension enhanced? Is memory enhanced? Is transfer enhanced? Is there a variety of types of interaction?		
4.5 Animation and graphics Are they relevant? Are they for important information? Is the level of detail appropriate? Are they aesthetic? Is the speed of display and motion appropriate?		

PART 5: INVISIBLE FUNCTIONS

Feature	Display Number	Comments
5.1 Records and data Are appropriate student records collected? Are records linked to the correct students? Is data for lesson evaluation collected? Is data valid for the lesson and evaluation objectives? Can the instructor control what data is collected?		
5.2 Security and accessibility Are records accessible to the instructor? Can data be analyzed and printed? Does access meet legal requirements? Can students access their own records? Is data safe from tampering? Are lesson files and content secure?		
5.3 Too much data What happens if too many student records are saved? What happens when too much data is saved for one student? Is newest or oldest data lost? Is instructor given a warning about data overflow? Is it easy for the instructor to manage data overflow? Can data be backed up?		
5.4 Restarting Is accidental termination avoided? Can a student leave the lesson at any time and start where he or she left off? Should a student be able to do this? Does restarting interfere with first-time students?		

PART 6: SUBJECT MATTER

Feature	Display Number	Comments

6.1 Goals and objectives
Are they useful?
Are they stated?
Are they worded in the student's
    vocabulary and reading level?
Will students perceive them as
    relevant?		

6.2 Information Is it relevant to the objectives? Is it accurate? Is it complete? Is the level of detail appropriate? Is the level of realism appropriate?		

6.3 Content emphasis
Is the emphasis on that content
    most related to the objectives?
Is the emphasis on the more
    difficult topics?		

6.4 Organization
Is the sequence of presentation
    appropriate?
Does lesson organization
    conform to subject-matter
    organization?
Does organization use student's
    prior knowledge?
Is the organization made clear to
    the student?		

PART 7: OFF-LINE MATERIALS

Feature	Display Number	Comments
7.1 Manual: general Is there a table of contents? Is there an index? Is there a quick reference guide? Are equipment needs clear? Are warnings clear? Are there addresses and telephone numbers for help?		
7.2 Manual: lesson operation Does it explain lesson startup? Are directions correct and clear? Do directions avoid jargon? Are there backup directions? Are there directions for the instructor's options?		
7.3 Manual: lesson content Is there appropriate introductory information? Is it accurate? Is there a content summary? Are there suggestions for curriculum integration? Are there recommendations for further study?		
7.4 Auxiliary materials Are all necessary materials provided? Are they easy to use? Are forms and score sheets provided and easy to use? Are transparency masters provided for the instructor? Is a test item bank provided?		
7.5 Other resources Is there a technical manual? If the lesson references other materials (books, pictures, etc.), are they provided? Are all materials referenced in the manuals available? Are all materials referenced in the manuals appropriate?		

APPENDIX C

STORYBOARD FORMS

The next seven pages contain storyboard forms that you may photocopy for use in lesson design. There are several forms to accommodate some of the more popular computers and display modes available today. All forms except those for the Macintosh (which uses proportional spacing) have text lines and rows indicated along the left side and top. All forms have graphics coordinates indicated along the right side and bottom.

      The first form is for Apple II computers. The character grid is for the forty character-per-line mode. The graphics coordinates are for high-resolution graphics.

      There are many display modes available for IBM microcomputers. The next four forms are for: forty characters-per-line and CGA graphics; eighty characters-per-line and CGA graphics; eighty character-per-line and EGA graphics; and eighty characters-per-line and VGA graphics.

      The last two forms are for Macintosh microcomputers with built-in screens. One form has guide lines and is more useful when using a programming language. The other form has no guide lines and is more appropriate when using an authoring system.

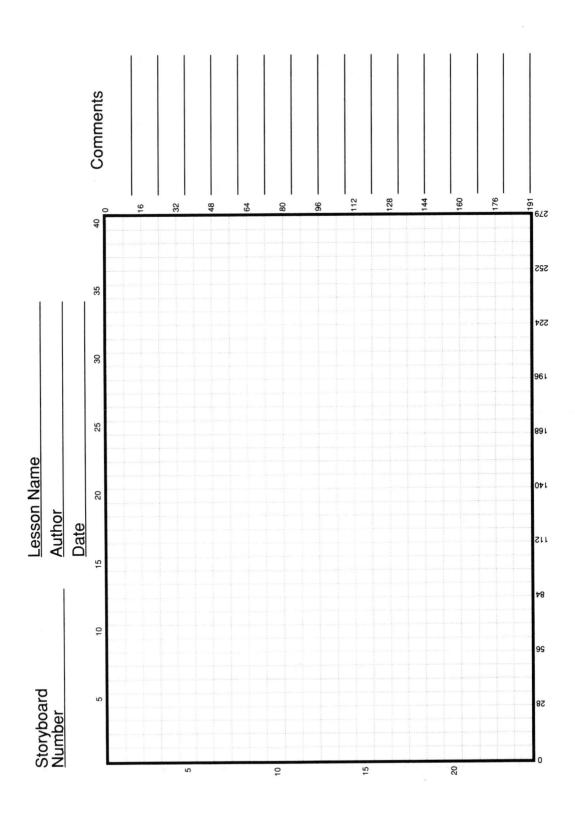

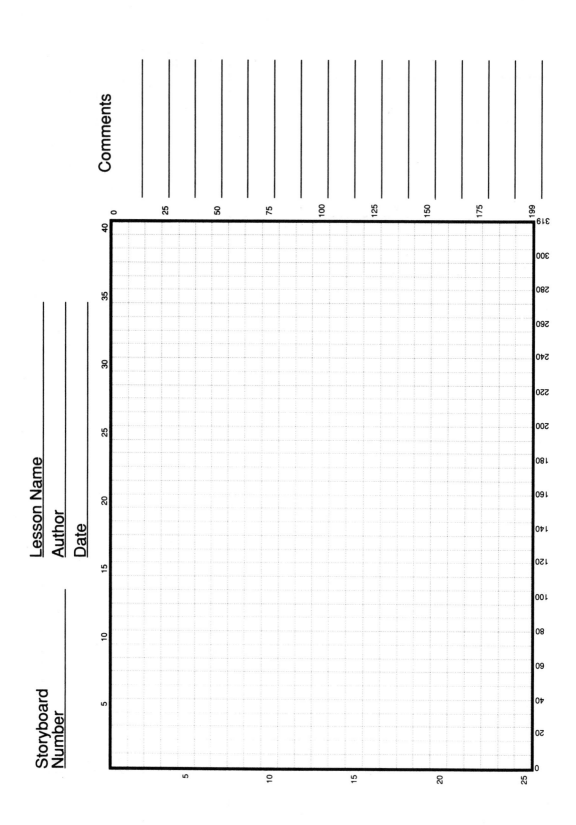

Lesson Name

Author

Date

Storyboard
Number

Comments

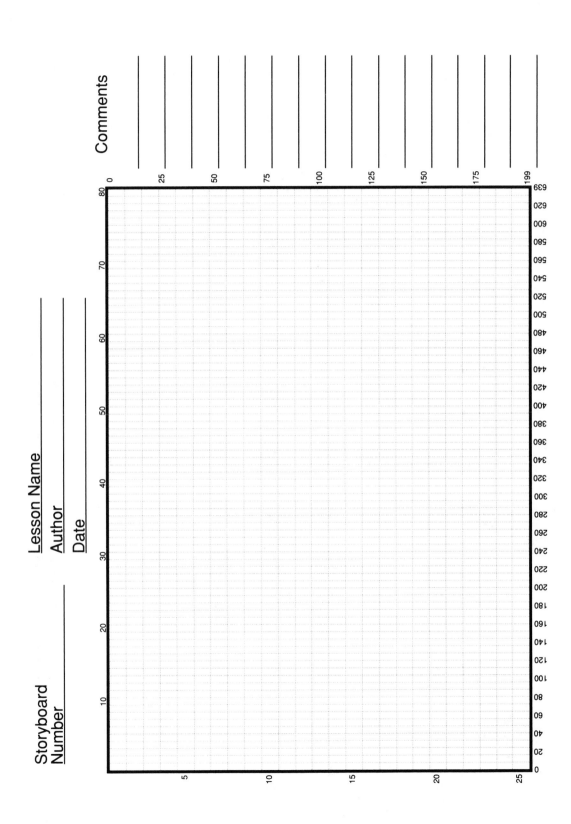

Storyboard
Number _____

Lesson Name
Author
Date

Comments

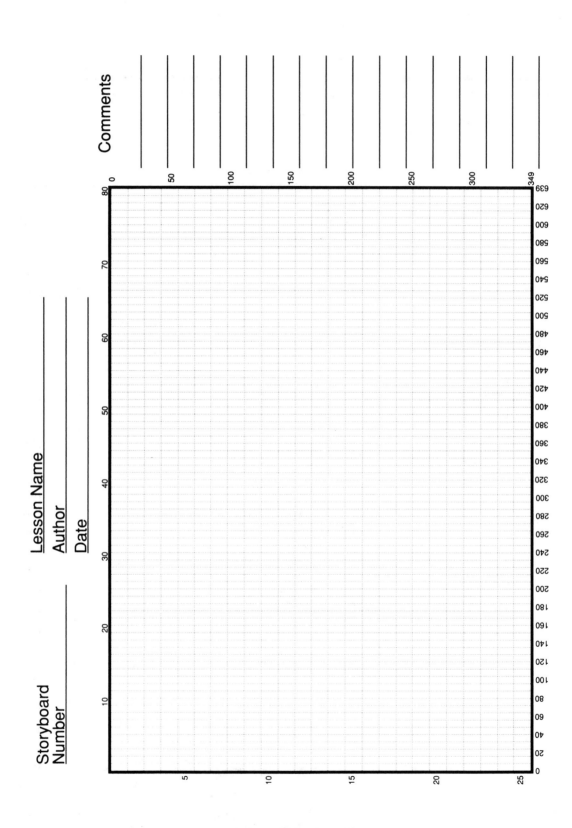

Comments

Lesson Name

Author

Date

Storyboard
Number

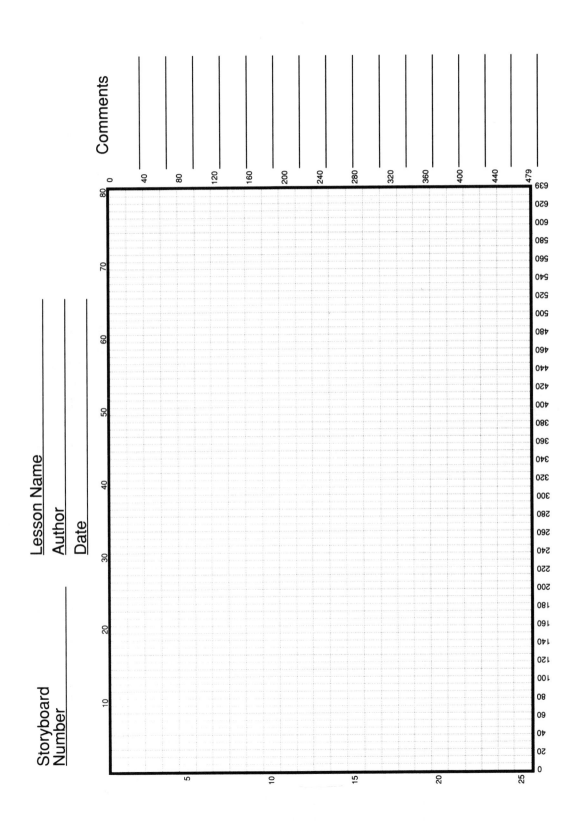

Storyboard
Number _____

Lesson Name _____
Author _____
Date _____

Comments

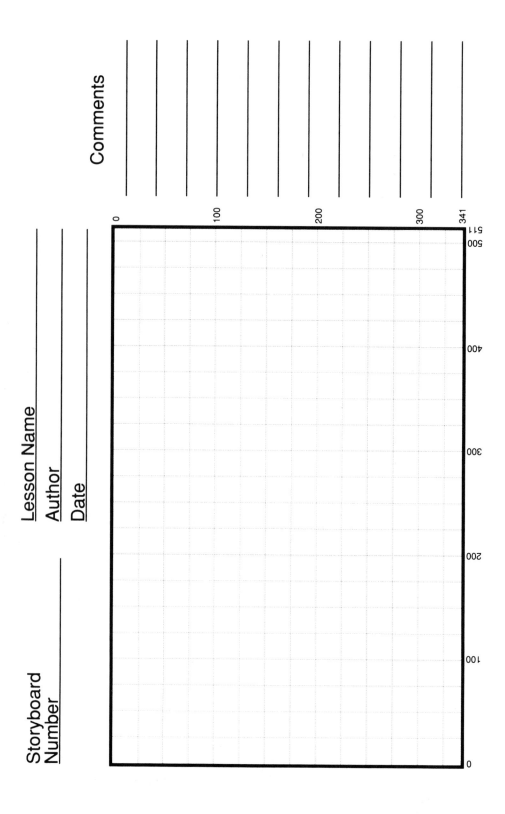

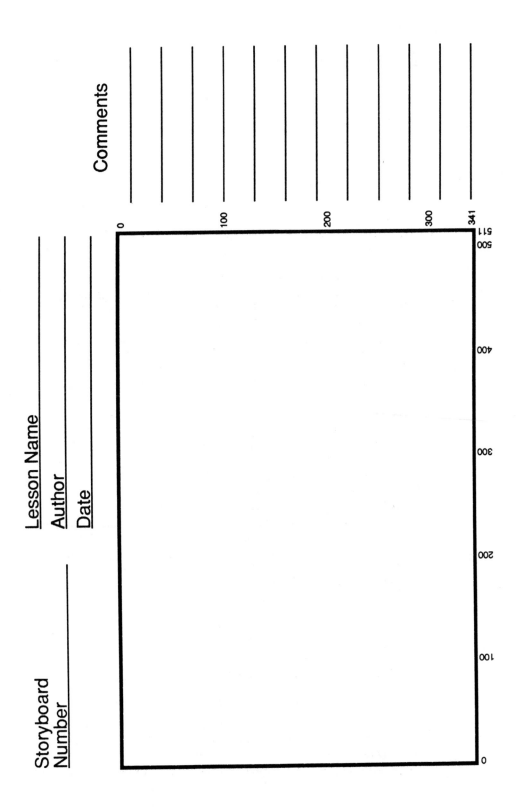

Comments

Lesson Name

Author

Date

Storyboard
Number

0   100   200   300   400   500 511

0   100   200   300   341

TRADEMARK NOTIFICATION

1·2·3 is a trademark of Lotus Development Corp.

Apple, Apple II, Apple II +, Apple IIe, Apple IIgs, SuperPILOT, Hypercard, Apple Super-PILOT, and *Macintosh* are trademarks of Apple Computer Corp.

Archeology Search is a product of McGraw-Hill.

Assessment of Neuromotor Dysfunction in Infants is a product of Cognitive Design Technologies, Limited.

Authorware Professional is a trademark of Authorware, Inc.

Balance: A Simulation of Predator/Prey Relationship is a product of Diversified Educational Enterprises.

Bio Sci Video Disc is a product of Videodiscovery, Inc.

Canvas is a trademark of Deneba Software.

Cardiopulmonary Resuscitation is a product of Interact, Inc.

Chemical Reactions is a product of International Business Machines Corp.

Chem Lab Simulation is a trademark of High Technology Software and *Ideal Gas Law* is copyrighted by High Technology Software.

Course Builder is a product of TeleRobotics International.

Decimal Darts and *Decimal Practice* are products of Control Data Corporation.

Design is a product of Meta Software.

Discursions: Architecture Machine Group is a product of Massachusetts Institute of Technology.

Dungeons and Dragons is a trademark of TSR Hobbies.

DVI is a trademark of Intel Corporation.

Easyflow is a product of Haventree Software.

EnBASIC is a trademark of Computer Teaching Corporation and is marketed for the Apple II by COMPress.

Evidence Objection is a product of University of Nebraska.

Examiner, V 2.1 is a product of Media Computer Enterprises.

Excel and *Microsoft Word* are products of Microsoft Corp.

Extend is a trademark of Imagine That, Inc.

Flight Simulator II is a product of subLOGIC Corporation.

General Chemistry is a product of COMPress.

Harvard Project Manager is a trademark of Software Publishing.

Houghton Mifflin Computer Management System is a product of Houghton Mifflin.

IBM-PC, PS/2, OS/2, and *InfoWindow* are trademarks of International Business Machines Corp.

IconAuthor is a trademark of AIMTech Corp.

IMPART is a product of CMC Limited.

IMSATT-2000 is a trademark of IMSATT Inc.

Interpreting Graphs, Dasher, DrillShell, DrillMaker, Catlab, Catgen, Standing Waves, School Transactions, Biznes, Green Globs, Graphing Equations Diffusion Game, Four-Letter Words, and *Baffles* are products of CONDUIT, The University of Iowa.

Introduction to Computer Literacy is a product of J.A.M. Inc.

IVD Toolkit is a product of Electronic Vision.

Learning tool is a product of Arborworks, Inc.

Let Your Fingers do the Talking: Deaf Awareness is a product of Alberta Vocational Centre.

MacProject, MacPaint, and *MacDraw* are trademarks of Claris Corp.

Mechanics: Physics Simulations I is a product of Stanford University.

Meet the Presidents is a product of Scholastic Inc.

Microcat is a trademark of Assessment Systems Corporation.

Micro-DYNAMO is a product of Addison-Wesley.

Micrometer, Triangles, Electron Charge, Hurkle, and *Oregon* are products of Minnesota Educational Computing Consortium.

Microsoft and *Microsoft Windows* are trademarks of Microsoft Corp.

Microtest II is a product of Chariot Software Group.

Milliken Math Sequences is a product of Milliken Publishing Co.

Monopoly is a trademark of Parker Brothers.

Mystery Disc: Murder Anyone? is a product of Vidmax, Inc.

National Air and Space Museum Archival Videodisc 1 is a product of Smithsonian Institution.

National Gallery of Art is a product of Videodisc Publishing, Inc.

NeXT is a trademark of NeXT, Inc.

PageMaker is a trademark of Aldus Corp.

PC Paintbrush is a trademark of ZSoft Corporation.

PC/Pilot is a product of Washington Computer Services.

PET is a trademark of Commodore Business Machines Corp.

PLATO and *PCD-3* are trademarks of Control Data Corporation.

President Elect is a trademark of Strategic Simulations, Inc.

Problem Analysis is a product of Park Row Software.

Producing Interactive Videodiscs is a product of Minnesota Mining & Manufacturing.

ProPi is a product of ASYS Computer Systems.

Quest is a trademark of Allen Communication, Inc.

Rocky's Boots is a trademark of The Learning Company.

SAM is a product of Sandy Corporation.

Scrabble is a trademark of Selchow and Righter.

Scripter is a trademark of Cognitive Design Technologies, Limited.

Snooper Troops is a trademark of Spinnaker Software.

Space Invaders is a trademark of Taito America Corporation.

Spectrum Job Task Analysis Database is a product of University of North Dakota Aerospace Foundation.

Stella and *Stella Stack* are trademarks of High Performance Systems.

SuperPILOT and *Apple SuperPILOT* are products of Apple Computer Corp.

SYSTAT is a trademark of SYSTAT, Inc.

TenCORE is a trademark of Computer Teaching Corp.

The First National Kidisc is a product of Optical Programming Associates.

The Name Game is a product of MindBank, Inc.

The Puzzle of the Tacoma Narrows Bridge Collapse is a product of John Wiley and Sons.

Thinktank and *More* are trademarks of Living Videotext.

TICCIT is a trademark of the Hazeltine Corporation.

Trouble Shooting Fuel Systems, Drosophila Genetics, Population Projections, Fractional Distillation Experiment, Moonwar, Pinball, Beehive, Ordeal of the Hangman, Phizquiz, How the West Was One + Three × Four, Casino Reading, and *Exambase* are products of University of Illinois.

TRS-80 is a trademark of Tandy Corporation.

Type Attack is a trademark of Sirius Software.

Unison is a trademark of Courseware Applications, Inc.

University of Iowa Visual Databases is a product of The University of Iowa.

Vincent Van Gogh: A Portrait in Two Parts is a product of North American Philips Corporation.

Visual Interactive Programming and *MacFlow* are trademarks of Mainstay.

Where in the World Is Carmen Sandiego? is a trademark of Broderbund Software.

INDEX

AUTHOR

Abrams, P.D., *15, 409*
Abt, C.C., 172, 187, *202*
Acker, S., 429, *450*
Adams, M., 22, *85*
Adinall, E., 172, *202*
Albanese, M.A., 410, *450*
Albright, R., 263, *271*, 289, *294*
Alessi, S.M., 3, 4, 5, *14, 16*, 109, *116*, 116, 136, 154, *159*, 346, *360*, 388, *408*, 448, *450*
Ali, A.M., 46, *85*
Allen, B.S., 448, *450*
Alpert, D., 1, *14*
Anderson, D., 43, 72, 158, *160, 408*
Anderson, J.R., 11, 13, *14*, 46, 72, *85*
Anderson, K., 425, *451*
Anderson, R.C., 11, 12, *14*, 50, 57, 61, 65, 72, *85, 86*, 278, *294*, 385, 388, *408*
Anderson, R.I., 208, 213–14, 223, 238, *241, 242*
Anderson, T.H., 388, *408*
Andre, T., 50, *85*
Anzai, Y., 133, *159*
Appleton, W.C., 297, 310, *318*, 345, *360*
Artwick, B.A., 156, *159*
Atkin, J.M., 20, *85*
Atkinson, R.C., *116*
Avner, A., 73, *360*

Baek, Y.K., 42, *85*
Baker, E.L., 4, *14*
Baker, F.B., 389, 393, *408, 409*
Balajthy, E., *14*
Balson, P.M., *450*
Bangert-Drowns, R.L., 2, 4, *14, 15*, 389, *409*
Banks, W.P., 11, 13, *14*
Barker, P., 346, *360*
Baron, D., 263, *272*
Becker, H.J., 2, *14*
Begg, I.M., 452, *475*
Bennett, R.E., 4, *14*
Bennion, J.L., *451*
Berger, D.E., 11, 13, *14*

Berger, M., 164, 165, 166, *203*
Berk, R.A., *385*
Berlyne, D.E., 191, *202*
Bertrand, P.A., 263, *271*, 289, *294*, 296, 307, *318*
Biddle, W.B., 50, 61, 65, *85*, 388, *408*
Bierman, R., 263, *272*
Bigham, D., 180, *202*
Bitter, G.G., *14*
Bitzer, D.L., 1, *14*
Black, J.B., 39, *85*
Blackman, J.A., 131, *159*, 410, 415, 424, *450*
Bleloch, A.L., 458, 459, *475*
Bloom, B.S., *385*, 387, *409*, 441
Bloomfield, D., 177, *202*
Bluhm, H.P., 3, *14, 409*
Boettcher, L.L., *242*
Boocock, S.S., *202*
Borg, W.R., *85, 159*
Bork, A., *14*
Borton, W.M., *409*
Bosco, J., *450*
Bower, G.H., 11, 13, *14*
Bowman, H.L., 388, *409*
Briggs, L.J., 19, 83, *86, 271*, 278, *294*, *385*
Brinko, K.T., *116*
Brody, P., *450*
Bronstein, R.H., 182–83, *202*
Brook, D., *203*
Brown, D., *242*
Brown, G.B., *361*, 395, *409*
Brown, G.C., 223, 224, 225, 226, 228, 229, 230, 231, 232, 233, 234, *242*
Brown, J.S., 469, 470, 471, *475*
Brown, N.P., *409*
Bruce, B., 22, *85*
Bruce, R.C., 353, *360*
Bruder, I., 2, *14*
Brudner, H.J., 388, *409*
Bruner, J.S., 23, *85*, 133, 137, *159*
Bruno, J., 238, 239, 240, 241, *242, 409*
Buchanan, B.G., 453, *475*
Bunderson, C.V., 42, *86*, 448, *451*

Burger, M.L., 346, *360*
Burke, R.L., 43, *85*
Burrett, H.J., *85*
Burton, J.K., 11, *16*
Burton, R.R., 469, 470, 471, *475*
Butler, B., 448, *450*

Cabrera, B., 120, 121, *159*
Calfee, R.C., *116*
Campbell, T.C., 424, *450*
Camuse, R.A., *14*
Carbonnel, J.R., 471, *475*
Carlisle, K.E., *294*
Carnine, D., *294*
Carr, V.H., 346, *361*
Carroll, J.M., *202*
Carter, C.D., *450*
Carter, C.J., *14*
Carter, G., 134, 137, *160*
Chabay, R.W., 12, *15*, 31, 60, *86*
Chaiklin, S., 5, *14*
Charvat, W., *385*
Childers, P.G., *475*
Clancy, W.J., 455, *475*
Claris, *271*
Clark, D.J., 426, *450*
Clark, R.E., 5, 13, *14*, 133, *160*
Clements, D.H., *14*
Cline, H.F., 4, *14*
Collins, A., 471, *475*
Cooley, W.W., *385*
Corey, J.M., *409*
Cormier, S.M., 13, *14, 160*
Crandall, J.A., *360*
Crawford, C., *202*
Criswell, E.L., *271*
Crothers, E.J., *116*
Crowell, P., 346, *360*
Crowley, M.E., *160*
Cunningham, P.A., 455, *475*

Daiute, C., *14*
Dalgaard, B.R., 388, *408*
Dalton, D.W., 5, *14, 450*
Darc, F.C., 126, *160*
Daynes, R., 448, *450*

Deal, R., 158, *160*
Dear, B.L., 63, *85*, 473, *475*
DeBloois, M., 448, *450*
Dede, C., *475*
DeKleer, J., 469, *475*
Denault, J.M., 147, *160*
Dennis, D., 164, 165, 166, *203*
Dennis, J.R., 139, *160*
Deshler, D., *450*
Diamond, B., 141, 157, *160*
DiVesta, F.J., 24, *85*
Doerner, D., *160*
Dudley-Marling, C., *385*
Dufault, G., 285, *294*
Dugdale, S., *85*, 174, 175, 187, 201, *202*
Duke, R., *160*, *202*
Durrett, H.J., 42, 43, *85*
Dwyer, F.M., 38, 40, 42, *85*, *339*

Eades, D., 147, *160*
Eastman, L.A., *242*
Ebersberger, W.S., 249, 272, 285, *294*
Ebner, D.G., *450*
Eifferman, R.R., 190, *202*
Eisenberg, J.D., 341, *361*
Ellington, H., 172, *202*
Elliott, L., 180, *202*
Engelmann, A., 46, *85*, 284, *294*
Entwistle, W., 223, *242*
Erickson, D.M., 448, *450*
Evans, A.D., *451*
Evans, R.M., *409*

Fairweather, P.G., 343, *360*
Fakhro, S.Q., 4, *14*
Farnell, C., 263, *271*, 289, *294*, 296, 307, *318*
Faust, G.W., 278, *294*
Federico, P.-A., *409*
Feeley, J.T., *16*
Feldman, K.V., 8, *15*, 46, *86*
Flanagan, J.C., 388, *409*
Fleming, M., 11, 13, *14*, 34, 38, 46, *86*, 278, *294*, *339*
Fletcher, K.A., 1, *15*, 23, *86*
Floyd, B., 448, *450*
Floyd, S., 448, *450*
Foshay, W.R., *294*
Foster, H., *160*
Fowler, H.W., *385*
Frayer, D.A., 46, *86*
Friel, S., *15*, *160*
Frost, J., *451*
Fryeberg, P., 8, *15*
Fuller, R.G., 424, *450*
Fuson, K.C., *116*

Gagne, E.D., 11, 13, *14*
Gagne, R.M., 13, *14*, 17, 19, 22, 83, *86*, *160*, 234, *242*, 262, *271*, 278, 287, *294*, 441
Garet, M., 158, *160*
Gay, G., *450*
Gayeski, D.M., 264, *271*
Gaynor, P., 72, *86*
Gebhardt-Seele, P.G., *14*
Geis, G.L., *385*

Ghatala, E.S., 46, *86*
Gibbs, G.I., *202*
Glowinski, D.J., *408*
Goldenberg, E.P., *14*
Goldin, S.E., 471, *475*
Goodson, B., *409*
Goodwin, 36
Gravander, J.W., 91, *116*
Green, B.S., 414, *450*
Greenblat, C.S., *202*
Greeno, J.G., 110, *117*
Grogono, P., *360*
Gronlund, N.E., *242*, *385*

Hagman, J.D., 13, *14*, *160*
Haladyna, T.M., *242*
Hall, K.A., 50, *86*
Hannafin, M.J., 5, 13, *14*, 24, 26, *86*, 271, *450*
Hannum, W., 47, *86*, 262, *271*, *294*, 346, *360*, *409*, 463, *475*
Hansen, D.N., 388, *409*
Hastings, J.T., *385*
Hawisher, G.E., *14*
Hawkins, J., *14*
Hayes-Roth, B., *475*
Hayes-Roth, F., *475*
Heath, P., *361*
Heines, J.M., 30, *86*, *339*
Heller, P., 295, *318*
Hendley, R.J., 471, *475*
Hernandez, N., 196, *202*
Hess, R.D., *16*, *340*, *385*
Hilgard, E.R., 11, 13, *14*
Hodges, J.C., *385*
Hoffman, C.K., 287–88, 289, 291, *294*
Hogg, I., 452, *475*
Holland, J., 239, *242*
Hon, D., 424, *450*
Hooper, S.R., 5, *14*
Horowitz, P., 10, *16*
Houston, A., *409*
Hughes, C., *450*
Hunter, B., 3, *14*
Huntley, J.S., 131, *159*, 296, *318*, 322, *339*, 346, *360*, 410, 415, 424, 425, *450*
Hyatt, G., 147, *160*

Isbouts, J., *450*
Iuppa, N.V., 411, 425, 448, *450*, *451*

Jackson, D.N., *385*
Johnson, D.W., 3, *15*
Johnson, P.E., 458, *475*
Johnson, R.T., 3, *15*
Jonassen, D.H., 3, *15*, 50, 65, *86*, 91, 117, *294*
Jones, D., 164, 165, 166, *203*
Jones, L.L., 424, *451*
Jones, N.B., *385*

Kagan, J., 190, *202*
Kahn, E.H., 4, *14*
Kane, D., 167, 168, 169, *203*
Kearsley, G., *271*, *294*, 346, *361*, *451*, 452, 471, *475*

Keller, F.S., 387, *409*
Keller, J.M., 12, *15*, 20, 32–33, *86*, 138, *160*, 424, *451*
Kelman, P., *14*
Kemp, J.E., *271*
Keppel, G., *117*
Kernighan, B., *361*
Kerr, S.T., 4, *15*
Kershaw, R.C., 4, *14*
Kheriaty, L., 342, *361*
Kibbey, D., *85*, 174, 175, 187, 201, *202*
Kinnear, J.F., 123, 132, 134, 153, 155, 156, *160*
Kirkpatrick, M., *117*
Kitabchi, G., 4, *15*
Klausmeier, H.J., 8, *15*, 46, *86*
Klein, E., 429, *450*
Klein, J.D., *117*
Klemt, L.L., 388, *408*
Koran, M.L., 8, *15*, 46, *86*
Kosslyn, S., *85*
Kozma, R.B., 11, *15*, 263, *271*, 289, *294*
Kramlinger, T., 272, 285, *294*
Kulhavy, R.W., 72, *86*
Kulik, C-L.C., 2, 4, 5, *14*, *15*, 72, *86*, 389, *409*
Kulik, J.A., 2, 4, 5, *14*, *15*, 72, *86*, 389, *409*

Ladenburg, T., *160*
Lahey, G.F., 46, *86*
Lambert, S., *451*
Lane, E.T., 121, *160*
Laudenburg, T., *15*
Laurillard, D., 13, *15*
Lawler, R.W., *475*
Layne, B.H., 42, *85*
Lechowicz, J.S., *409*
Lederman, L.C., 136, *160*
Ledin, G., *361*
Ledin, V., *361*
Leggett, G., *385*
Lehmann, I.J., *385*
Leiblum, M.D., *409*
Lenat, D.B., *475*
Lepper, M.R., 12, *15*, 31–32, *86*, *117*, *202*
Leung, H., 174, 175, 187, *202*
Levie, W.H., 11, 13, *14*, 34, 38, 46, *86*, 278, *294*, *339*
Lewis, M.W., 5, *14*
Li, Z., 461, *475*
Lienart, D., 310, *318*
Lillie, D.K., *409*
Lippert, H.J., *450*
Lippert, R.C., 458, *475*
Lippey, G., 207, *242*
Liu, A., 175, 176, *203*
Locatis, C.N., 346, *361*
Lockard, J., *15*, *409*
Lohnes, P.R., *385*
Lommel, J., 346, *361*
Lord, F., 238, *242*
Lough, L.K., 131, *159*, 410, 415, 424, *450*
Lovelock, C.H., 179, 180, *202*
Low, N., 296, *318*, 322, *339*, *450*

body of, factors in, 186–200
   cast, 189
   choices in, 186, 194–97
   competition, nature of, 171, 192–93
   curiosity, presence of, 191–92
   information flow, 197–99
   learning-objectives relationship, 193
   level of reality, 189
   modes of interaction, 200
   role of players, 189–90
   scenario, 187–89
   skill vs. chance in, 193
   turns, 199
   types of action in, 199
   uncertainty, presence of, 190–91
   wins and losses, 193–94
   conclusion of, factors in, 200–201
   definition of, 162–70
   descriptions of, 162–70
   factors in, 479–80
   flowcharting for, 296
   interactive video, 425
   introduction of, factors in, 183–86
   major characteristics of, 170–72
   preliminary sequence for, 288
   purpose of using, 182–83
   retention promoted by, 83–84
   structure of, 183
   types of, 172–82, 189
   See also Situational simulations
General Chemistry, 19, 60
Generic videodiscs, 426
Glass-box technique, 470–71
Global user control in interactive video, 430–31
Goals
   assessing, 376
   defining, 251–52
   determination of, 245, 251–58, 272
   of game, 170, 184, 190–91
   motivation in drills from setting, 113
   terminal, 253, 255–58
Graduate Record Examination (GRE), 209, 212
Grammar, evaluation of, 366–68
Graphic analogy, 38, 39
Graphic feedback, 72–73
Graphic presentation, 33–34
Graphics
   assessing, 374
   as cue, 39, 40
   in drills, 94–95, 116
   producing, 349–50
   in storyboarding, 325–27, 333, 336–37
   in tutorial questions, 59–61
   in tutorials, 38–42
   video vs. computer, 429
Graphics programs, 249
Graphics scanners, 349
Green Globs, 201
Grids, storyboarding, 322, 325
Grouping procedures, drill item, 108–12

Group instruction, CMI for, 393–94
Guidance of student, 7–8
GUIDON, 455

Harvard Project Manager, 255
Haventree Software, 309
Help, providing, 49, 69, 313–14, 425–26
Hidden information in game, 191
Hierarchical sequence in linear lesson, 77
Hierarchical structure, 47, 463–64
Hierarchy, semantic network as, 262
High Performance Systems, 141, 157, 158, 159, *160*
High Technology Software, 120, 121, 134, *160*
Hint, providing a, 72
Houghton Mifflin, *409*
How the West Was One + Three X Four, 163–64, 165, 174, 177, 184, 185, 187, 194, 199, 470
Humor, use of, 71, 320
Hurkle, 174, 177
Hybrid authoring systems, 343
Hypercard, 30–31, 158, 264

IBM-compatible microcomputers, 250
IBM InfoWindow, 26
IBM microcomputers, 2, 157, 307, 342, 344
IBM Secondary School Computer Education Program, 3
ICAI (Intelligent Computer-Assisted Instruction), 469
IconAuthor, 297, 310, 345
Icon-oriented authoring systems, 297, 343–46
Idea generation, 246, 265–70, 273
Ideas, elimination of, 274–77
IMPART, 116
IMSATT, 342, *361*
IMSATT–2000, 342
Incidental learning, 182, 193
Incremental implementation of CMI and CBI, 394–96
Indexes to manuals, 356, 359
Indirect pointing devices, 62
Individual differences, CBI and, 13
Individualized instruction, 387, 393–94
Industrial videodisc players, 418
Inference engine of expert system, 453–54
Information
   assessing, 376–77
   source of, in game, 198
   types of, 44–46, 197–98
Informational choices, 194–95
Informational help, 49
Information capacity of display, color graphics and, 42
Information chunk size, 372
Information domain of learning, 262–63
Information flow in games, 197–99

Information Referenced Testing (IRT), 238–41
InfoWindow system, 423
Input devices
   assessing, 368–69
   for interactive video, 427–28
   for simulation, 148
   See also specific devices
Instances of concept, 45–46, 284
Instruction
   process of, 6–9, 46
   using computer for, 5–6
Instructional analysis, 287
Instructional design resources, 259, 261
Instructional modeling, 453, 461–71
Instructional Systems Design (ISD) approach, 244
Instructor(s)
   CMI from perspective of, 404–8
   role in tests. *See* Test(s), computerized
   simulated, 132
Instructor manual, 356–59, 362
Instructor options, accessing and using, 358
Intellectual skills domain of learning, 263
Intelligent CAI. *See* Instructional modeling
Intelligent CBI, 468–71. *See also* Artificial intelligence
Intelligent environments, 10
Intended learning, 193
Interaction
   assessing, 373–74
   in games, modes of, 200
   in tutorial. *See* Questions; Responses in tutorials
Interaction strategy, 428
Interactive video, 410–51
   advantages of, 416–20
   background, 411–13
   constraints of, 420–23
   defining, 410–11
   design of program, factors in, 426–38, 441–42
   future of, 448–49
   program development, 438–48
   types of instructional programs, 423–26
   videodiscs, levels of, 413–15, 423, 436–37
   visual presentation modes of, 415–16, 429
Interactivity, level of, 426
Interlacing, 433, 434, 435–36
Intermediate objectives, 252
Internal documentation, 350
International Business Machines (IBM), 344, *361*, 423
Interpreting Graphs, 59
Interrupt in flowchart, 312–14
Interview after pilot testing, 380–81
Intrinsic motivation, 31
Intrinsic scenario, 188

Introduction to Computer Literacy, 423–24
Invisible functions, evaluation of, 374–76
Involvement of student in simulation, 144–45
Issues, 470
Item banks, test, 205, 206, 207, 211, 358
Item characteristic theory, 235, 236
Item generation, 211
Item response theory, 235
Items, drill
  characteristics, 94–97
  grouping procedures, 108–12
  selection procedures, 97–106, 114
  types of, 94
Item selection process for test, 226–27, 228
IVD Toolkit, 296, 322

J.A.M., 423, *451*
Jargon, 367
Joystick, 200
Judging routines, 349
Judgment of tutorial responses, 65–69, 89

Keyboard, use of, 26, 148, 200, 427
Knowledge
  prior, 22, 379–80
  procedural, 46
  propositional, 46
  student, depicted on computer, 465–67
Knowledge base of expert system, 453, 454, 456–57
Knowledge engineer, 458

Laboratory simulations, 134
Language(s)
  authoring, 341, 342
  evaluation of, 366–68
  natural language comprehension, 453, 471–74
  object-oriented, 348
  programming, 296–97, 341, 342
  simulation, 157–59
Laser beam, 420
Laser pickup, 413
Laser printer, 207
Latent trait theory, 235
Layout of text in tutorials, 35–38
Lead in and lead out, 439
Leanness of tutorial, 43
Learncom, 343
Learner-controlled instruction, concept of, 1
Learning
  active, 12
  assessing student, 9
  building expert systems as tool for, 458–60
  designing procedural, 46
  discovery, 6, 7–8
  five domains of, 262–63
  identifying types of, 287

incidental, 182, 193
instructional objectives of games and, 193
intended, 193
mastery, 387
after pilot testing, assessing, 381
transfer of, 13, 83–84, 133, 135–37
Learning Company, The, 196
Learning map, 287, 288–89, 291
Learning-objectives relationship in games, 193
Learning Tool, 263, 289
Leaving a game, 196–97
Length
  of drill session, 114
  of student response, 69
  of test, 210–11
  of text in tutorial, 34–35
Lessons. *See* Tutorials
Letter menu, 27
Let Your Fingers Do the Talking: Deaf Awareness, 415, 424
Level-0 interactive video program, 413–14, 437
Level-1 flowchart, 295, 297–98, 300, 311
Level-1 interactive video program, 414–15, 437
Level-2 flowchart, 295, 297, 298–99, 301, 312–14, 347
Level-2 interactive videodisc program, 415, 436–37
Level-3 flowchart, 295, 297, 299–302, 303, 304, 315–17, 347
Level-3 interactive video program, 415, 423, 436, 437
Libraries of often-used routines, 348
License fees, 346
Linear lessons in tutorial, 77–78
Lists, item, 95–96
Locus of control, 12–13, 24
Logical error in flowchart, 305–7
Logical simulations, 141–42
Logic games, 177–78
Logo programming, 3, 10
Long-term memory, 97
Lotus Development, 255

MacDraw, 349
MacFlow, 263, 264, 289, 296, 307, 309
Macintosh computer, 2, 29, 30, 157, 158, 250, 307, 333, 344, 345, 349
MacProject, 255
Mainstay, 289, 309, 310
Management of classroom instruction. *See* Computer-managed instruction (CMI)
Manipulations in simulation, 149
Manuals
  assessing, 377–78
  instructor, 356–59, 362
  for interactive video program, 447–48
  student, 199, 354–56, 362
  technical, 359, 362
Mapping software, 249

Marking questions, 53, 54
Markup, answer, 73–74
Massachusetts Institute of Technology, 417, *451*
Mass storage devices, 392
Mastering company, 439
Mastery learning, 387
Mastery level, 372
Matching questions, 50
Mechanics of tutorial text quality, 44
Mechanics—Physics Simulations I, 120, 121
Media resources, 259
Meet the Presidents, 180, 181
Memory, 11–12, 97
Menus, 24–29, 30, 369–70
Methodologies, instructional, 9–10, 287–88, 428
Microcomputers, 1, 250, 391
  networks, 391, 392, 395
  See also specific microcomputers
MicroDynamo, 141, 157, 158
Micrometer, 60
MicroSIFT, *385*
Microsoft, 255, 344
Microsoft Windows, 344
Microsoft Word, 263
Microsoft Word Version 4, 255
Milliken Math Sequences, 391–92
Milliken Publishing Co., 391, *409*
MindBank, Inc., 425, *451*
Minnesota Educational Computing Consortium (MECC), 36–38, 39, 40, 41, 60, 63, 172, 174, *203*
Minnesota Mining & Manufacturing, 415, *451*
Mitre Corporation, 1
Mnemonics, 48
Modeling, instructional, 453, 461–71
Modularization, 348, 351
Monopoly, 170, 185, 189, 190, 198
Moonwar, 177, 179, 194, 199
More, 263
Motivation, 12
  assessing devices for, 373
  curiosity and, 191–92
  in drills, 111, 112–14
  games and, 182–83, 191–92, 197
  intrinsic vs. extrinsic, 31
  in moderation, 33
  objectives and, 20
  simulation and enhancement of, 133
  theories of, 31–33, 424
  in tutorials, 31–33, 88
Motor skills domain of learning, 263
Mouse, use of, 2, 26, 61–63, 68, 69, 148, 200, 369, 428
Mouse-oriented menu, 27, 28
Multiple-choice questions, 50–53, 63
Multiple-choice tests, 238
Multiple-selection answers, 66–67
Multiple-string answer, 68
MYCIN, 453, 454, 455

Name Game, The, 425
Natural feedback, 151, 152

Natural language comprehension, 453, 471–74
Needs assessment, 252
Negative words in questions, 58
Networks, microcomputer, 391, 392, 395
Network structure, 262, 464, 465
Neutral responses, feedback following, 71
New-application questions, 57
NeXT computer, 2
Node, 464
Non-instances of concept, 45–46, 284
Norm-referenced testing, 209
North American Philips Corporation, 418, *451*
NTSC (National Television Standards Committee) standards, 429, 433
Number menu, 27
Numeric answers, 67
Numeric-plus-string answer, 68

Objectives
  assessing, 376
  behavioral, 19–20
  of games, learning and, 193
  instructional, 210
  intermediate (enabling), 252
  motivation and, 20
  simulation, 138
  specification of learning, 251–52
  terminal, 252, 279, 280
  of test, 210
  in tutorial, presentation of, 19–21
Object oriented graphics programs, 349
Object-oriented languages, 348
Objects of simulation, 142
Observation of pilot testing, 380
Off-line edit, 439
Off-line materials, evaluation of, 377–78
Off-line organization of program, 347–48
One screen overlaid mode in interactive video, 416, 426
One screen switched mode in interactive video, 416, 426–27
1–2–3, 255
On-line comments, 353
On-line edit, 439
On-line exams, 389–90
On-line storyboarding, 251
On-line testing, 395
"Opening scene" in simulations, 139–40
Operating system software, 250
Optical scanners, 207
Ordeal of the Hangman, 164–66, 182, 185, 186, 188, 189, 192, 194
Oregon, 172, 173, 177, 179, 193, 194
Organization
  assessing, 377
  hierarchical, 47, 463–64
  off-line, of program, 347–48
  principle of, 11

tutorial text, 44–47
Organized queuing, 97–102, 114
OS/2 operating system, 344
Out-of-list error, 107
Overlaid screen mode in interactive video, 416, 426–27
Overlay, graphic, 40, 41
Overlaying displays in storyboarding, 324–25, 333, 334–35
Overview display, 230

Pacing of drills, 95
PageMaker, 360
Paging, 35
Paired-associated drills, 94, 107
Paragraphs, layout of, 35
Paraphrase questions, 57
Parker Brothers, 170
Pascal, 296
Passing score, 212
Passwords, 223, 224
Pause and erase subroutine in flowchart, 302, 304
PCD–3, 345
PC Paintbrush, 322
PC/PILOT, 342
Pedagogical models, 462–63, 467–68
Peer review of design, 292
Penalties of game, 185
Perception, 11
Permanent termination
  of drill, 104–5
  of tutorial, 83–84
Phizquiz: A Problem-Solving Test in Elementary Mechanics, 167–69, 175, 192, 193, 194, 195, 199
Physical simulations, 119, 120–23, 153, 155
PILOT, 341
Pilot testing, 378–81, 385–86
Pinball, 174, 175, 193
Pioneer videodisc players, 423
Planning, interactive video program development and, 439–40
PLATO, 1, 26, 383, 389, 390
Pointing devices, 62–63. *See also* Mouse, use of
Pools of questions, 205, 206, 207, 211
Population Dynamics Group, 125, *160*
Population Projections, 125
Positive feedback, 71
Posttests, 403
Power rule of student control, 32
Practice, 8–9, 217–18
Precision of simulation, 142–43
Preliminary lesson description, 286–91
Pre-mastering, 446
Premature termination of drill, 105–6
Preparation phase of CBI development, 251–70
  content, learning the, 246, 262–65, 272
  idea generation, 246, 265–70, 273
  needs and goals of lesson, determination of, 245, 251–58, 272

resource materials, collection of, 246, 258–61, 272
Presentation of information, 6–7
  assessing modes of, 368
  computer vs. video, 428–29
  in simulations, 145–48, 154–57
  of test results, 213
  in tutorials, 33–49, 88–89
President Elect, 196
Pretesting in tutorial, 22–23
Primary text display, 319–21, 329–30
Principles, 46
Printout of test results, 222
Prior knowledge, 22, 379–80
Privacy Act of 1974, 221, 375
Problem Analysis, 249, 285
Problem solving, 10, 287
Procedural help, 49
Procedural knowledge, 46
Procedural simulations, 119, 120, 126–27, 150, 153, 156
Procedures, identifying, 288
Process simulations, 119, 123–25, 150, 153, 155–56
Producing Interactive Videodiscs, 415
Profile of test, 223, 226, 227
Program control, 24
Program dump, 436–37
Program for Learning in Accordance with Needs (PLAN), 388
Programming, 247, 341–53, 361–62
  choosing authoring software, 346–47
  error detection and correction, 351–53
  rules for good, 347–50
Programming languages, 296–97, 341, 342
Programming tools, 249
Project management software, 249
Prompting editor, 342
Prompts, 47–49, 59–61, 63–64
ProPi, 345
Propositional knowledge, 46
Psychomotor games, 178–79
Pugh-Roberts Associates, 141, 157, *160*
Pull-down menu, 29, 30
Punctuation, checking, 367
Puzzle of the Tacoma Narrows Bridge Collapse, The, 424

Quality of tutorial questions, factors affecting, 57–59
Quality Review Checklist, 365, 482–89
Quality review phase, 365–78, 385
Quest, 343
Questions
  answering, 370–71
  computerized construction of test, 206
  evaluation of, 370–71
  pools of, 205, 206, 207, 211
  test, 211–12
  in tutorials, 49–65, 89
  writing, 320

Queuing, organized, 97–102, 114
Queuing parameters, 103–4, 105

Radio Shack TRS–80, 391
Random access on videodisc, fast, 417
Randomness in game, 191
Random selection, 97
Reactions in simulation, 149
Reading level, 44, 58, 366
Realism
  in graphics, 39–40
  in interactive video, 430
  of simulation, 143, 147–48
  of student actions, 150
Reality
  advantages of simulation over, 130–33
  level of, in game, 189
Recall, drill item selection to enhance, 97
Records, assessing accuracy of, 374
Re-education, 241
Reference guide in manuals, quick, 356, 359
Reinforcement, adjunct, 113–14
Related scenario, 188
Relevance in ARCS motivation theory, 33
Relevant features, 45, 283
Remediation, 77, 90
Repetition, principle of, 11–12, 97
Research in intelligent CBI, 469–71
Resource materials, collection of, 246, 258–61, 272
Resources
  assessing off-line, 377–78
  providing student with helpful, 222
  scheduling of scarce, in CMI, 390
Responses in tutorials, 59–65
  feedback about, 69–77, 89
  judgment of, 65–69, 89
  mode of, 61–63
  response economy, 63
  response prompt, 63–64
  subsequent attempts, 74–77
Responses on test, flexibility of, 219–20
Response variety, motivation from, 113
Restarting
  assessing process of, 375–76
  of drill, 114
  of simulations, 150
  of tutorials, 80–83
Results, test, 221–22, 231–32, 233, 234
Resurrection, 105
Retention, 8, 83–84
Retirement criteria in drills, 102–3
Review and reviewing
  of drill items, 110
  of flowchart, 327–29
  internal, of interactive video program, 442–44
  quality review phase, 365–78, 385
  of storyboards, 327–29, 337–39
Revision
  design, 292–93

evaluation and, 384
  after pilot testing, 381
  of storyboards, 329
Reward for winning game, 201
Rocky's Boots, 166, 167, 177, 179, 191, 192, 193, 196, 199
Role of players in game, 189–90
Role-playing games, 179–80
Role-playing simulations, 127–30
Routing, 231, 389, 395
Rule-Example method, 46
Rule learning, 287
Rules of game, 171, 184

Safe area, video, 431–32
Safety, 131, 171
Safety barriers, 214, 218, 221, 230
Safety nets, 215, 217, 221, 231
Salience of prompts, 48–49
SAM (System for Authoring Micro-training), 343, 344
Satisfaction in ARCS motivation theory, 33
Scenario, game, 187–89
Scheduling of scarce resources in CMI, 390
Scheduling programs, 255
SCHOLAR, 471
Scholastic Achievement Test (SAT), 209
School Transactions, 127–29, 134, 145, 153, 156
Scoring, 113, 207, 212, 230, 231
Scrabble, 185
Scripter, 296, 322
Scrolling, 35, 59
Secondary text displays, 320, 321, 330–32
Security, assessing, 375
Selection procedures
  drill item, 97–106, 114
  test item, 226–27, 228
Semantic network, 262, 464, 465
Semantic similarity, drill item grouping by, 109
Sensory curiosity, 192
Sensory modalities, 34
Sentences, layout of, 35
Sequence
  of simulation, 143–44, 153, 288
  of tutorial lesson segments, 77–83, 90
Sequence description of lesson, 288–89
Short-answer questions, 56–57
Short-term memory, 97
Simulations, 10, 119–62, 287, 288, 417
  advantages of, 130–35
  vs. other methodologies, 133–34
  phases of instruction, 134–35
  vs. reality, 130–33
  automated assessment of performance in, 233–34
  body of, 140–53
    presentations, 145–48, 154–57
    sequence of simulation, 143–44, 153, 288

student actions, 148–50, 154–57
    student control, 150–51
    system reaction or feedback, 151–57
    underlying model, 140–45, 154–57
  classification of, 119–20
  completion of, 153
  factors in, 137–38, 479
  fidelity in, 135–37, 147, 154–57, 234
  flowcharting for, 296
  interactive video, 424–25
  introduction to, 138–40
  languages and systems, 157–59
  physical, 119, 120–23, 153, 155
  procedural, 119, 120, 126–27, 150, 153, 156
  process, 119, 123–25, 150, 153, 155–56
  retention promoted by, 83–84
  situational, 119, 120, 127–30, 145, 150, 153, 156–57
  student simulation routine, 383–84
  as tests, 135, 232–35
Single-selection answer, 66
Single-string answer, 67–68
Sirius Software, 203
Situational simulations, 119, 120, 127–30, 145, 150, 153, 156–57. *See also* Games, instructional
Skill(s), 46
  chance vs., in games, 193
  concept analysis of, 280–86
  identifying required, 288
  task analysis and breakdown of, 278–80
Smithsonian Institution, 418
Snooper Troops, 172, 173, 176, 179, 191, 192, 195, 196, 197, 378
Software
  to aid in development of CBI, 249
  compatibility of hardware and, 394, 420–23
  controversy over use in classroom, 5
  storyboarding, 322–24, 325
  See also Tools, computer
Software Publishing, 255
Solutions to simulation, number of, 144
SOPHIE-I, 469–70
Sound
  digitization of, 34, 436
  in interactive video, 430, 436
  as presentation mode in tutorial, 34
  storyboarding for, 325, 326, 333, 336
Spacing, 35, 368
SPADE, 471
Spectrum Job Task Analysis Database, 285, 286
Speech
  computer comprehension of, 472
  as mode of response, 63
Spelling, checking, 367
Spinnaker Software, 173, 174
Spreadsheets, 249

Standard (NTSC) video, 429, 433
Standing Waves, 121–22
Startup of program, in manuals, 355, 357
Statistical software, 249
Stella, 141, 157–59
Stella Stack, 158
Still-frame audio, 436
Still frame display, 418
Storage, data. *See* Data storage
Storyboard forms, 490–97
Storyboarding, 247, 250, 295, 319–40
  computer tools for, 296
  graphics displays, 325–27, 333, 336–37
  overlaying displays, checking fit of, 324–25, 333, 334–35
  primary text, writing and revising, 319–21, 329–30
  producing, 321–24, 332–33
    grids, 322, 325
    software, 322–24, 325
  reviewing, 327–29, 337–39
  secondary text, writing and revising, 320, 321, 330–32
  for sound, 325, 326, 333, 336
  in telephone example, 329–39
Strategic choices, 195
Student(s)
  chart of characteristics of, 252–57, 274
  CMI from perspective of, 396–403
  comments on test, 220
  construction of expert system by, 458–60
  pilot testing by, 378–81
  review of storyboards by, 328–29
  role and involvement in simulation, 144–45
  role in tests. *See* Test(s), computerized
Student action
  in games, types of, 199, 354–56, 362
  in simulations, 148–50, 154–57
Student manual, 199, 354–56, 362
Student models, 463, 465
Student simulation routine, 383–84
Subdrill grouping, 108–10, 111, 112
Subject matter, evaluation of, 376–77
Subject-relevant materials, primary uses of, 260
Subject resources, 258–59, 261
Subroutines, 300, 348
Subroutine symbols, 299, 300
Subskills, 46
Summary of contents in instructor manual, 357–58
Summative evaluation, 382, 448
Supplementary information in student manual, 355
Support material production, 247, 353–60
  adjunct instructional material, 359, 363
  computer tools for, 360
  instructor manual, 356–59, 362
  off-line, assessing, 377–78

student manual, 199, 354–56, 362
  technical manual, 359, 362
Surface features, assessing, 368–69
Synchronization, 439
Syntax error, 351
Synthetic sound, 436
SYSTAT, 384
System reactions. *See* Feedback
Systems, simulation, 157–59

T.H.E. *Journal*, *361*
Table of contents in student manual, 354
Taito America, *203*
Task analysis, 278–80, 281, 282, 285–86
Teachers, problems facing, 4–5
Technical information and requirements in manuals, 354–59
Technical manual, 359, 362
Technical terms, 366–67
Telephone example, 248. *See also specific steps in development of CBI*
Templates or template games, 182
Temporary termination of drill, 104
Temporary tutorial ending, 83
TenCORE, 342
Terminal goals, 253, 255–58
Terminal objective, 252, 279, 280
Termination
  closing of tutorial, 83–84, 90
  of drill, 104–6
  of test, 218–21
Test(s), computerized, 10, 205–43, 287
  adaptive testing, 235–38
  administered in prototype CMI system, 400–402
  administration, 208
  Admissible Probability Measures testing (APM), 238–41
  characteristics of test, 208–13
  computerized construction of, 205–7
  example of testing program, 223–32
  factors in, 480–81
  flowcharting for, 296
  implementation, 213–15
  instructor's role in
    before test, 215–17, 223–27
    during test, 218–19, 229
    after test, 221–22, 231
  preliminary sequence for, 288
  results, 221–22, 231–32, 233, 234
  retention promoted by, 83–84
  simulations as, 135, 232–35
  student's roles in
    before test, 217–18, 227–29
    during test, 219–21, 229–31
    after test, 222, 231–32
  termination of, 218–21
  testing of, 216
  types of, 209
Testing
  on-line, 395
  pilot, 378–81, 385–86
Test item bank, 205, 206, 207, 211, 358

Test parameters, 216, 223–25, 226
Text, computer comprehension of, 472
Text, tutorial
  organization of, 44–47
  as presentation mode, 33
  layout, 35–38
  length of, 34–35
  quality, 43–44
Text displays
  graphic displays fitted simultaneously with, 326–27
  primary, 319–21, 329–30
  secondary, 320, 321, 330–32
  video vs. computer quality, 428–29
Text feedback, 72
Text quality, assessing, 368
Text size, interlacing and, 435–36
Thematic prompts, 48
Thinktank, 263
TICCIT project, 1, 23
Time code, 439
Time frame of simulation, 144
Time limit
  on answering questions in tutorials, 69
  on test, 212–13
Timing of feedback in tutorials, 72
Title page
  in manuals, 354, 356
  of tutorial, 19
Tools, computer, 249–51
  for collecting resources, 260–61
  for determining needs and goals, 253–55
  for evaluation, 383–84
  for flowcharting, 263–64, 307–10
  for idea generation, 267
  individual vs. integrated, 249, 250
  for learning content, 263–64
  for preliminary lesson description, 289
  for revision of design, 292
  software and hardware compatibility, 394, 420–23
  for storyboarding, 296
  for support material production, 360
  for task and concept analysis, 285
Top-down approach to programming, 348
Touch panels, 26, 148, 200, 427–28
Traditional CBI programs, 461–62. *See also* Drills; Games, instructional; Simulations; Tutorials
Transfer of learning, 13, 83–84, 133, 135–37
Transitions, 43, 432
Transparency masters, 358
Trial run in manuals, 355, 357
Trouble Shooting Fuel Systems, 126, 127
TSR Hobbies, 189, *203*
Turns in games, 199
TUTOR, 341
Tutorials, 10, 17–90, 287, 288
  closing of, 83–84, 90
  factors in, 477–78

Tutorials (*cont.*)
  feedback about responses, 69–77, 89
  flowcharting for, 296
  interactive video programs, 423–24
  introduction of, 18–23, 88
  judgment of responses in, 65–69, 89
  motivation in, 31–33, 88
  preliminary sequence for, 288
  presentation of information in, 33–49, 88–89
    color and its use, 42–43
    graphics and animation, 38–42
    instructional prompts, 47–49
    layout of text, 35–38
    length of text, 34–35
    mode of, 33–34
    providing help, 49
    text quality, 43–44
    type of information and text organization, 44–47
  questions and responses, 49–65, 89
    factors affecting quality, 57–59
    frequency of, 50
    functions of, 49–50
    graphics in, 59–61
    placement of, 61
    relevance of, 61
    types of, 50–57, 63
  remediation, 77, 90
  restarting, 80–83
  sequencing lesson segments in, 77–83, 90
  student control of lesson in, 23–31, 88

TV quiz games, 180–81
Two-screen presentations of interactive video, 416, 426–27
Type Attack, 193
Typing errors, 61, 302

Uncertainty in game, presence of, 190–91
Unison, 343
U.S. Navy CMI System, 388
University of Illinois Aviation Research Laboratory, 238
University of Iowa Visual Databases, 425
Unknown errors, 351–52

Validation, 381–83, 386
Validity of simulation test, 234
Variable interval performance (VIP) queuing, 99–102, 114
Verbal information, 44
Verbal learning, 287
Verbatim questions, 57
Versa Computing, Inc., 180, 181, *203*
Video, interactive. *See* Interactive video
Video blanking, 437
Video digitizers, 349, 432
Videodisc, 410, 411–13
  capacity of, 419
  components of, 413, 414
  constant angular velocity (CAV), 421, 422
  constant linear velocity (CLV), 421–22

  durability of, 419–20
  generic, 426
  levels of interactive, 413–15
  quality of information on, 419
Video safe area, 431–32
Videotape recorders, 411
Video transitions, 432
Visual Interactive Programming, 310
Visual modalities, 34
Visual presentation modes of interactive video, 415–16, 429
Visual subject, presentation in simulation of, 145

Warnings in manuals, 354, 356
Web structure, 47, 262
WEST, 470–71
Westinghouse Learning Corporation, 388
Where in the World Is Carmen Diego?, 180
White flags on videodisc, 433
WHY, 471
Winner of game, recognizing, 200–201
Wins and losses in game, 193–94
Within-list error, 107
Word games, 182
Word processing, 249, 263
Workbooks, 116
Worksheets in manuals, 355, 358
WYSIWYG editors, 343

ZSoft, 322

3149424 2

Contents

Introduction in English   7

日本語序文   8

中文简介   9

한국어 소개   10

Einleitung auf Deutsch   11

Introduzione in italiano   12

Introducción en español   13

Introdução em português   14

Introduction en français   15

Wstęp po polsku   16

Введение на русском   17

Websites   19–352

Index of Designers   353–362

Index of URLs   363–368

Free CD-ROM   inside back cover

Layout by Günter Beer & Sigurd Buchberger
www.webdesignindex.org
Cover and book design by Pepin van Roojen
CD Master by Sigurd Buchberger

Introduction by Pepin van Roojen and Kevin Haworth

With special thanks to Justyna Wrzodak, Reese Lee,
Scriptware and LocTeam for translations

Web Design Index 8

ISBN 978 90 5768 122 6
The Pepin Press | Agile Rabbit Editions
Amsterdam & Singapore

Cover Image

Illustrations on front cover (Reawaking) and page 6 (Dream) are
taken from images by Maciej Mizer – www.mosk.pl (see page 295).

The Pepin Press BV

P.O. Box 10349
1001 EH Amsterdam
The Netherlands

Tel +31 20 4202021
Fax +31 20 4201152
mail@pepinpress.com
www.pepinpress.com

10 9 8 7 6 5 4 3 2 1
2012 2011 2010 2009 2008

Manufactured in Singapore